Why Do You Need This New Edition?

4 reasons to buy this new edition of *Thinking about Women*

1 The new **History Speaks: Yesterday's Feminists Talk about Today's Issues** box appears in each chapter and features a historic feminist "brought back to life" to discuss a contemporary issue.

2 **Thinking Further,** a new section inserted into many graphs and feature boxes, probes students with critical thinking questions.

3 **New content on contemporary topics** has been added:

- gender and the economic recession
- immigration
- virginity pledges and the abstinence only movement

- sexual assault and the military
- the sexualization of popular culture
- gender, retirement, and Social Security
- gender and the 2008 elections, among others!

4 **Updated examples, data, and new research** have been included throughout.

PEARSON

NINTH EDITION

Thinking about Women
SOCIOLOGICAL PERSPECTIVES ON SEX AND GENDER

MARGARET L. ANDERSEN
University of Delaware

with
DANA HYSOCK WITHAM
Indiana University of Pennsylvania

Allyn & Bacon

Boston   Columbus   Indianapolis   New York   San Francisco   Upper Saddle River
Amsterdam   Cape Town   Dubai   London   Madrid   Milan   Munich   Paris   Montreal   Toronto
Delhi   Mexico City   Sao Paulo   Sydney   Hong Kong   Seoul   Singapore   Taipei   Tokyo

Publisher: Karen Hanson
Associate Editor: Mayda Bosco
Editorial Assistant: Alyssa Levy
Executive Marketing Manager: Kelly May
Marketing Assistant: Janeli Bitor
Production Editor: Claudine Bellanton
Manufacturing Buyer: Debbie Rossi
Cover Designer/Administrator: Kristina Mose-Libon
Editorial Production and Composition Service: Laserwords

Credits appear on page 451, which constitutes an extension of the copyright page.

Library of Congress Cataloging-in-Publication Data
Andersen, Margaret L.
   Thinking about women : sociological perspectives on sex and gender / Margaret L. Andersen with Dana Hysock Witham. — 9th ed.
      p.   cm.
   Includes bibliographical references and index.
   ISBN-13: 978-0-205-84095-3
   ISBN-10: 0-205-84095-7
      1. Women--United States—Social conditions.   2. Feminism—United States.
3. Social institutions—United States.   4. Social change.   5. Feminist theory.
I. Witham, Dana Hysock.   II. Title.

   HQ1426.A6825 2011
   305.420973--dc22

2010033245

10 9 8 7 6 5 4 3 2 1   RRD-VA   14 13 12 11 10

Allyn & Bacon
is an imprint of

www.pearsonhighered.com

ISBN 10:   0-205-84095-7
ISBN 13:   978-0-205-84095-3

For my grandmother,
Sybil R. Wangberg
(1895–1995)

A woman who always said she was just ordinary
but who was very special to those of us who loved her

MLA

For my mother,
Cheryl M. Hysock

Her sacrifices have made my dreams possible.

DHW

Brief Contents

Contents

3 ⌁ Gender, Culture, and the Media   55

4 ⌁ Sexuality and Intimate Relationships   81

PART IV   GENDER AND SOCIAL CHANGE: FRAMEWORKS OF FEMINISM

Preface

The ninth edition of *Thinking about Women*, like its earlier editions, introduces readers to how gender operates in society and how gender inequalities are found through studying women's lives, thus also allowing to really see how gender shapes men's lives, too. The presence of gender in society is ubiquitous—seen virtually everywhere, including the influence on women's and men's self-concepts as well as their relationships, attitudes, beliefs and values, life opportunities, and other social behaviors. The long life of *Thinking about Women* (first published in 1983) indicates the strong interest in this subject, but also the vitality of feminist scholarship over this period of time. It is an honor—and, frankly, a lot of fun—to continue revising the book to reflect the new ideas and new discoveries that emerge from research and theory about gender and women's lives.

Each new edition of *Thinking about Women* also provides an opportunity to think about how new generations of students might be thinking about gender. Students in my classes now have come of age at a time when it appears to them that women have it made, that barriers to women's achievements are a thing of the past—a past that they actually know very little about. This provides an opportunity not only to try to connect to different generations but also to observe and analyze the changes that have taken place—and those that have not—in both women's and men's lives.

For young students reading this book, feminism may seem a thing of the past. The new visibility of women in prominent positions in society, the opening of new fields of work and study to women, changes in women's and men's roles in the family, and, in general, more liberal attitudes among much of the public on matters relating to gender make it seem that feminism is no longer needed. Indeed, much progress has been made in transforming women's lives. But, as you will learn in this book, women and men continue to be unequal in many ways, and despite the progress that has been made, gender and the differences it makes still permeate women's and men's lives.

In this book, you will see how gender is socially constructed—that is, formed through early learning patterns that are continuously reinforced throughout all social institutions. You will also see how gender intersects with other social factors, especially race and class, but also sexual orientation, age, religion, and nationality, among others. A large part of the book focuses on gender in major social institutions, including the economy and work, families, health care, religion, criminal justice, education, and government. The book also reviews the development of feminist thought and its relationship to the women's movement over time.

Although the title of the book suggests that the text is only about women, that is not the case. Gender influences everyone in society. The new scholarship on gender first emerged from taking women's lives seriously. Thus, much, but not all, of the focus of *Thinking about Women* is on women, but not to the exclusion of men. Men's lives are influenced by gender, too, but in different ways than women's lives. How gender organizes relations between and among women and men is an important part of this book.

Furthermore, understanding gender means not treating women as a single category—as if all women's experiences were the same. Gender is also tangled with systems of race, class, and sexual inequality. From the early years when the feminist movement was largely centered on the lives and experiences of White women, feminist scholars now anchor their work in recognizing the interrelationship among gender, race, and class—and increasingly, sexuality.

Thinking about Women develops from the empirical research and feminist theory that has taught us how much gender matters in society. It presents the most current scholarship on gender, but in a style that is accessible to those who have never thought much about it before, as well as to those who have been introduced to studying women in other undergraduate courses or life activities. *Thinking about Women* is grounded in a sociological perspective, although it can be used in interdisciplinary courses.

ORGANIZATION OF THE BOOK

Thinking about Women is organized in four parts. Part I, Introduction, acquaints students to the study of gender as it is rooted in feminist analysis. This section presents the sociological framework that underlies this book and shows how research on women and women's studies has developed from the feminist movement. Part I, also includes discussion of men's studies and its connection to feminist scholarship.

Part II, Gender, Culture, and Sexuality, focuses on the social construction of gender and the representation of gender in culture, particularly in the media. Chapter 2, The Social Construction of Gender, reviews the influence of gender socialization and the role of gender in shaping women's and men's identities. Chapter 3, Gender, Culture, and the Media, analyzes the increasing significance of the media and popular culture on the social construction of gender. Chapter 4, Sexuality and Intimate Relationships, examines the relationship between gender and sexuality as social constructions. This chapter shows how gender and sexuality reinforce each other.

Part III, Gender and Social Institutions, examines the institutional structures of work, family, health, religion, criminal justice, education, and politics. Chapter 5, Gender, Work, and the Economy, details research on women's work and economic status. The chapter includes a discussion of poverty and welfare reform, as well as the ongoing struggle of balancing work and family—a theme also picked up in Chapter 6. Chapter 6, Gender and Families, focuses on the historic evolution of contemporary family forms and emphasizes the diversity of women's experiences in families. It also includes discussion of various problems for families, including family violence, teen pregnancy, and child care. Chapter 7, Women, Health, and Reproduction, looks at the consequences of gender inequality for women's health compared to men's and also includes an extensive discussion of reproductive politics. Chapter 8, Women and Religion, conceptualizes religion as both a source of women's oppression, but ironically, also a source for women's liberation. Chapter 9, Women, Crime, and Deviance, studies crime and women—both as victims and perpetrators. It also examines women's victimization by violence and discusses how men's violence is related to gender roles. Chapter 10, Gender, Education, and Science, looks at schooling, but it also shows how the construction of scientific knowledge is influenced by the exclusion of women from positions of scientific leadership. Finally, Chapter 11, Women, Power, and Politics, provides a transition to the last section on social change and looks at engagement of women in political institutions. This chapter also includes an overview of the women's movement and other forms of women's political activism.

The final part of the book, Part IV, Gender and Social Change: Frameworks of Feminism, introduces students to feminist theory and its link to the women's movement historically and now. Chapter 12, Women and Social Reform: Liberal Feminism, reviews the evolution of liberal feminism, showing students how the term *liberal*—though widely stigmatized in conservative discourse—is a specific feminist philosophy with important implications for social change. By detailing the historical evolution of liberal feminism, students can examine their own assumptions about the dominant strategy of "equal rights" that has characterized much feminist transformation of society. Chapter 13, Contemporary Frameworks in Feminist Theory, reviews more radical perspectives and updates the discussion of theory to include multiracial feminism, postmodernism, and queer theory. Throughout, the presentation of theory emphasizes the need to examine one's underlying assumptions—theoretical or common sense—and to understand the different strategies needed to improve women's lives.

NEW TO THE NINTH EDITION

Each new edition of *Thinking about Women* benefits greatly from the comments of faculty and students who have read earlier versions of the book. One such comment in this round of reviews was that today's students do not understand the significance of past feminist thinkers and how they relate to today. Thus, the book includes a **new feature in every chapter:** *History Speaks: Yesterday's Feminists Talk about Today.* This boxed feature provides a brief biographical sketch of a historic feminist and briefly discusses some of her key ideas. The box then asks students to reflect on what this person might be thinking and saying about a contemporary issue that stems from the chapter content. So, for example, students are introduced to Margaret Sanger in Chapter 7 on women and reproduction and are then asked to think about what she might be saying about a topic like abstinence-only sex education. Or, in Chapter 4, students are introduced to Audre Lorde and asked to reflect on what she would be saying about same-sex marriage. This feature not only provides some introduction to historic feminists but it also includes a critical thinking exercise that encourages students to relate historic feminist ideas to contemporary social issues.

Another **new feature has been added,** *Thinking Further,* which appears in some boxes and/or graphs. This feature asks students a critical-thinking question that helps them interpret what they see in the box or figure and encourages them to ask new questions and think about additional insights that stem from the material presented. This feature appears throughout the text.

The ninth edition has a pleasing visual format with new photos and graphic features throughout that makes the text more visually appealing to today's generation of visual learners. This edition also maintains the box features on media, research, and men that were introduced in the prior edition, including *A Focus on Research; Media Matters;* and the retitled *A Closer Look at Men*. Thus, each chapter (except Chapter 1) has four boxes on the following themes:

- **History Speaks: Yesterday's Feminists Talk about Today**
  Example (Chapter 5): A biographical sketch of Emma Goldman is presented and a question is posed about her likely analysis of today's high poverty rate among women and the role of the federal government in providing social support programs.

- **Focus on Research**
  Example (Chapter 6): A discussion of "opting out" frames an interesting question: Are well-educated, middle-class women dropping out of the labor market to raise children? The media claim this is a strong trend, but is it? This box feature examines new sociological research on this topic.

- **Media Matters**
  Example (Chapter 11): This box features new research on media coverage of First Ladies and poses a critical-thinking question about media coverage of Michelle Obama as the first African American First Lady.

- **A Closer Look at Men**
  Example (Chapter 4): The theme of this box is about the peer socialization of young boys in which homophobic insults reinforce social norms of masculinity.

Throughout this new edition, current research has been incorporated and examples have been updated to appeal to contemporary students. Also, figures and empirical data reflect the most current information.

Pedagogical Features

In addition to the boxed features, students and instructors will find useful pedagogical elements that enable learning and discussion. *Chapter Summaries and Themes* conclude every chapter. These are intended to highlight the major points of each chapter, thus enhancing student learning.

Each chapter also includes *Discussion Questions/Projects for Thought*, which can be used for in-class projects or research assignments and papers.

All *key terms* at the end of each chapter are also defined in a glossary at the end of the book. *Chapter outlines* open each chapter so that students will know what key ideas to look for. *Graphics* are found throughout the book, developed by the author, to help students learn to interpret data; these have been updated to the most recent available.

SUPPLEMENT

Instructor's Manual and Test Bank (ISBN 0-205-00103-3)

For each chapter in the text, this valuable resource provides Essay Questions, Classroom Activities & Student Assignments, and Suggested Readings. The Instructor's Manual and Test Bank is available to adopters at www.pearsonhighered.com.

CHAPTER-BY-CHAPTER CHANGES

In addition to the updating and incorporation of new research, here are some of the *highlights* of individual chapters:

Chapter 1   Studying Women: Feminist Perspectives
- new material on race, class, and gender intersectionality
- new graph of a 2009 survey on American men's and women's attitudes

Chapter 2   The Social Construction of Gender
- revised definition and discussion of intersexed persons

Chapter 3   Gender, Culture, and the Media
- new material on gender and the body, including representations of body size in the media
- new material on aging and gender
- updated content analyses of depictions of gender in the media
- new section on media, gender, and human agency
- new material and discussion of controlling images
- added discussion of new forms of media, like feminist blogs
- more on sexualization in the media
- reorganized theory section
- more on gays/lesbians
- new study on violence against women on TV

Chapter 4   Sexuality and Intimate Relationships
- added discussion of heteronormativity
- added transgender discussion and research
- update on same-sex marriage policies
- new section on sex work and sex trafficking
- revised discussion of menopause and menstruation

Chapter 5   Gender, Work, and the Economy
- new data on recent increases in poverty
- discussion of the recession's impact on women
- updated data throughout
- revision of section on impact of economic restructuring

- new section on immigrant women and work
- trimmed and reorganized section on work environments
- new section on retirement and Social Security

Chapter 6   Gender and Families
- more on "opting out"
- new data on intimate partner violence and marital rape
- new research on abstinence pledgers
- new research on single mothers
- new research on cohabitation
- inclusion of new research on children of the gender revolution

Chapter 7   Women, Health, and Reproduction
- new research on breast cancer, including women and care work survival
- updated health statistics throughout
- current work on HIV/AIDS
- more on binge drinking and environmental risks on college campuses
- updates on abortion
- revision of reproductive technology section to include infertility and the public stereotypes of "Octomom"
- more on black Muslim women and body image

Chapter 8   Women and Religion
- more material on Muslim women and immigrants
- new box on the ex-gay movement, gender, and religion
- focus on diversity in religion and tension between oppression and liberation

Chapter 9   Women, Crime, and Deviance
- new research on how gender shapes African American girls' use of inner-city violence
- data from task force reports regarding sexual misconduct allegations at U.S. military academies
- inclusion of research on "hogging"

Chapter 10   Gender, Education, and Science
- new research on gender and science
- updated data on education gaps by gender and race

Chapter 11   Women, Power, and Politics
- new introduction to put 2008 election into context
- discussion of Palin and Clinton in the 2008 election
- new data on women in elected office
- new data on opinions about women in politics
- new research on sexual harassment/rape in the U.S. military

Chapter 12   Women and Social Reform: Liberal Feminism
- new box on feminism and romance

Chapter 13   Contemporary Frameworks in Feminist Theory
- new box on Latino working-class feminist men

PowerPoints (ISBN 0-205-06637-2)

The Lecture PowerPoint slides follow the chapter outline and feature images from the textbook integrated with the text. This supplement is available to adopters at www.pearsonhighered.com.

ACKNOWLEDGMENTS

Both of us are grateful to our friends, colleagues, and family who support our work. It is collective work that produces what we know about women—and the new perspectives on men that feminism has inspired. Thus, there are many people to thank for sharing ideas, providing resources, and encouraging both of us. We thank Maxine Baca Zinn, Ronet Bachman, Kathyrn Bonach, Anne Bowler, Arlene Hanerfeld, Valerie Hans, Alex Heckert, Elizabeth Higginbotham, Melanie Hilde-brandt, Beth Mabry, Shana Maier, Elizabeth Mansley, Meghan Rich, and Howard Taylor for the many conversations and other forms of support that sustain this work. Our undergraduate and graduate students have also strengthened this book through their questions and ideas. We have written this book with them in mind.

Special thanks also go to the many people who provided assistance that made finishing this book possible: Tammy Harvey, Dianna DiLorenzo, Sarah Hedrick, Linda Keen, Joan Stock, and Judy Watson all worked to make our lives a little easier. Thanks as well to Katie Grunert and Stephanie Scovill for research assistance that supported this revision. Most especially Dana gives her deepest gratitude to Scott Witham who reminds her of her strength when she is doubting her ability. Maggie thanks Richard Rosenfeld for putting up with frantic efforts to balance too many projects and for keeping us afloat!

Finally, we would like to thank the reviewers for their feedback on the manuscript:

Cassandra Carter; State University of New York at Albany
Ingrid Castro; Northeastern Illinois University
Paula Gelber Dromi; California State University, Los Angeles
Andrea Haar; University of Colorado, Denver
Johnnie Johnson; Joliet Junior College
Mary Kelly; San Diego State University
Florence Maatita; Southern Illinois University, Edwardsville
Anna Ryan; State University of New York at Albany
Sarah Winslow-Bowe; Clemson University

About the Authors

Photo by Ambre Alexander

Margaret L. Andersen is the Edward F. and Elizabeth Goodman Rosenberg Professor of Sociology at the University of Delaware. She is the author of several books, including *On Land and On Sea: Women in the Rosenfeld Collection; Living Art: The Life of Paul R. Jones, African American Art Collector;* and *Sociology: The Essentials* (coauthor, Howard F. Taylor). She has also written three bestselling anthologies: *Race, Class, and Gender* (coedited with Patricia Hill Collins); *Race and Ethnicity in U.S. Society: The Changing Landscape* (coedited with Elizabeth Higginbotham); and *Understanding Society: Readings in Sociology* (coedited with Kim Logio and Howard F. Taylor). She is the former vice president of the American Sociological Association and past-president of the Eastern Sociological Society.

She is a recipient of the Jessie Bernard Award given annually by the American Sociological Association for scholarship widening the horizons of sociology to include women, as well as the Robin M. Williams Lecture Award from the Eastern Sociological Society. She has also received the 2004 Sociologists for Women (SWS) Feminist Lecturer Award, given annually to someone in the nation whose work benefits women. She currently serves as the chair of the National Advisory Board of Stanford University's Center for Comparative Studies in Race and Ethnicity.

Dana Hysock Witham is Assistant Professor of Sociology at Indiana University of Pennsylvania (IUP). She received her Ph.D. from the University of Delaware where she did her dissertation research on peer sexual harassment in high schools. She is an active member of the Eastern Sociological Society (including serving as cochair for the Committee on the Status of Women), Sociologists for Women in Society, and the American Sociological Association. She is well regarded by her students and recently received special recognition by the IUP African American Cultural Center for her continued support of graduating students of color.

1

Studying Women: Feminist Perspectives

Have you ever asked yourself:

- Why do so many women spend so much time and money on beauty and diet products—even when some of these products are detrimental to their health?
- Why is violence so much more likely to be committed by men—either against other men or against women and girls?
- Why are there not more women in fields such as science and math, even though, when girls are young, they do at least as well, if not better, in these subjects at school?
- When you look at news images of demonstrations in the streets of Afghanistan—and other countries—why are most of the people men?
- Why is there no national sport where all the athletes are women that routinely draws stadium-filling crowds?
- What would happen if every woman in the United States stayed home from a job for just one week?
- How would your life change if you woke up tomorrow morning and were a different gender?

You could ask yourself many questions like these—and you will find that such questions guide much of the content of this book. If you find them intriguing—or you want to know the answers—then you already have the kernel of imagination that can sprout the study of gender in society.

Gender refers to the cultural expectations and societal arrangements by which men and women have different experiences in society. As you will learn throughout this book, gender relations are complex, variable, and deeply entrenched in society. Gender shapes all facets of our experiences—what we think, how we interact with others, what opportunities are likely to be available to us, even how we walk and talk! There is no simple or single way to think about gender, but how gender affects women and men in society is a fascinating subject—and one that is important to making social changes that will improve people's lives.

WHY STUDY WOMEN?

Maybe you think that studying women is no longer as important as it once was because women seem to have it made—at least compared to the past. Formal barriers to discrimination have been removed. Women have moved into many of the top professional positions, are now the majority of college graduates, and are more visible in positions of power than at any other time in the nation's history. The position of women in U.S. society has changed dramatically. The majority of women are employed, and they now number close to half of those in the workplace.

Attitudes have changed, too. When asked if they want to work outside the home or stay at home, *both women and men* are more likely than in the past to say they would prefer to work outside the home rather to stay at home. But in another interesting change, a substantial number of men (29 percent) say they would actually prefer to stay at home (Saad 2007b). Among women, actually choosing just one—home or work—is unusual because balancing the two is more common. Studies of college women indeed find that most want to include careers, marriage, and motherhood in their futures (Hoffnung 2004).

These changes have led many to conclude that women now have it made and that no further change is needed. Consider the following facts, however:

- Today, women college graduates who work full time earn, on average, 77 percent of what men college graduates earn working full time (DeNavas-Walt et al. 2009).
- Despite three decades of policy change to address gender inequality at work, women and minorities are still substantially blocked from senior management positions in most U.S. companies (Glass Ceiling Commission 1995; U.S. Department of Labor 2009).
- Twenty-nine percent of all households headed by women are poor; the rates are higher for African American women, Latinas, and Native American women, and the rate has been increasing (DeNavas-Walt et al. 2009).
- Each year, one-quarter million women are raped or sexually assaulted; two-thirds of these violent acts are committed by friends, acquaintances, or intimate partners (Bureau of Justice Statistics 2008).
- Despite the fact that they are the most likely to be employed, women of color are concentrated in the least-paid, lowest-status jobs in the labor market (U.S. Department of Labor 2009).

These facts indicate that although women have indeed come a long way, there is still a long way to go. Little wonder that there is a substantial gender gap in women's and men's perception of society's treatment of women: Women are much more likely than men to perceive job discrimination based on gender (see Figure 1.1 on page 4).

Look around, and you will see many signs of the status of women in society. In the grocery store, for example, women are clustered in those departments (deli and bakery) that are least likely to lead to promotion; men, on the other hand, predominate in departments such as produce and groceries, where the majority of store managers begin (Padavic and Reskin 2002). In schools, women constitute a large majority of elementary school teachers, but through the higher grades and into college, women become a smaller proportion of the faculty. Despite the recent movement of more women into political office, the vast majority of those who make and enforce laws are men, particularly among those holding the most influential positions.

Differences between women and men can also be observed in interpersonal interaction. Watch the behavior of men and women around you—how they act with each other and with those of the same sex. In public places, men touch women more often than women touch men. Men also touch women in more places on the body than women touch men. Despite stereotypes to the contrary, men also talk more than women and interrupt women more than women interrupt men or men

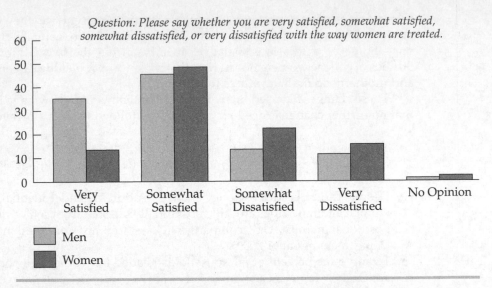

FIGURE 1.1   Perceptions of Society's Treatment of Women

Source: Data from Lydia Saad. 2001. "Women See Room for Improvement in Job Equity." Princeton, NJ: The Gallup Organization. www.gallup.com. Reprinted with permission.

interrupt each other. Women are more likely than men to smile when interacting with others (especially when with men), even when they are not necessarily happy. Men, in general, are less restricted in their demeanor than women and use more personal space. Although these patterns do not hold for all men and all women, nor necessarily for people from different cultural backgrounds, in general they reflect the different ways that women and men have learned to interact (Mast and Hall 2004; Hecht and LaFrance 1998; Hall 1998).

Many current social problems also call attention to the status of women in society. Violence against women—in the form of rape, sexual harassment, incest, and wife beating—is common. Changes in U.S. families mean that more families are headed by women. Although there is nothing inherently wrong with such arrangements, women's low wages mean that female-headed households have an increased chance of being poor. As a consequence, the rate of poverty among children in such households has increased dramatically in recent years. As a final example, the national controversy over health care also has particular implications for women. Although women live longer than men, they report more ill health than men do, spend their later years with more disabling conditions, and tend to take primary responsibility for the health of others in their families (National Center for Health Statistics 2009).

Thinking about women helps us understand why these things occur. For many years, very few people thought seriously about women. Patterns affecting the lives of women were taken for granted as natural or to be expected. Few people questioned the status of women in society, presuming instead that studying women was trivial, something done only by a radical fringe or by frivolous thinkers. Even

The modern image to the right plays off the classic poster of "Rosie the Riveter"—a poster produced during World War II as a device to recruit women into wartime production work.

now, studying women is often ridiculed or treated with contempt. For example, conservative talk-show hosts portray feminism as "leftist extremism," "out of touch with the mainstream," and "an attempt to transport unpopular liberalism into the mainstream society" (Limbaugh 1992:186–187). Attacks on new multicultural studies, of which women's studies has been a strong part, have accused such studies of only striving for "political correctness" and weakening the traditional "standards" of higher education. Despite these claims, women's studies has opened new areas for questioning, has corrected many of the omissions and distortions of the past, and has generated new knowledge—much of which has important implications for social policy. Moreover, by bringing attention to the study of gender, studying women has opened new ways to think about and study men.

Women's studies, as a field of study, is relatively new, having been established in the late 1960s and early 1970s to correct the inattention given to women in most academic fields. Because of the influence of the feminist movement, scholars in most fields have begun thinking seriously about women. Women's studies is now a thriving field of study. Studying women and men as gendered subjects has often required challenging some of the basic assumptions in existing knowledge—both in popular conceptions and in academic studies. Scholars have found that thinking about women changes how we think about human history and society, and it revises how social institutions are understood. Thinking about women also reveals deep patterns of gender relations in contemporary society. Much of the time, these patterns go unnoticed, but they influence us nonetheless. Often, we take these patterns of everyday life for granted. They are part of the social world that surrounds us and that influences who we are, what we think, and which opportunities are available to us. Women's studies scholarship is transformative; it informs our understanding of women's experiences and changes our thinking about society.

As you can see from the title of this book, women are the major focus of study here. But when you think about women, you also have to think about men. Why, then, does this book focus on women? Men have traditionally been such a primary focal point that many people seem to assume (falsely) that a primary focus on women is somehow out of balance. But focusing on women brings new questions to light and shows how gender shapes everyone's experience, including men's, as you will see especially in the boxed feature of this book, "A Closer Look at Men." Through focusing on women, we can see the influence of gender in society—and this raises new questions about men, as well. Moreover, despite the changes that have occurred in women's lives, women remain disadvantaged relative to men, although, as we will see, this depends on other factors, including race, social class, and sexual orientation, among other social factors.

The purpose of this book is to show how a sociological perspective explains women's lives and the structure of gender in society. A single book cannot discuss all of the research and theory that has been developed to understand gender in society, but it can show how thoroughly gender permeates the structure of society and women's and men's lives within it.

THE SOCIOLOGICAL IMAGINATION

Patterns in gender relations are found throughout society, although much of the time these patterns remain invisible to most people. At some point, however, you may start to notice them. Perhaps at school you see that women tend to major in different subjects than men or that men tend to be more outspoken in class. Perhaps at work you notice that women are concentrated in the lowest-level jobs and are sometimes treated as if they were not even there. It may occur to you one night as you are walking through city streets that the bright lights shining in the night skyline represent the thousands of women—many of them African American, Latina, Asian American, or immigrant women—who clean the corporate suites and offices for organizations that are dominated by White men.

Recognizing these events as indications of the status of women helps you see inequities in the experiences of men and women in society. Once you begin to recognize these patterns, you may be astounded at how pervasive they are. As the unequal status of women becomes more apparent, you might feel overwhelmed by the vast extent of a problem most people have never acknowledged. What you see might become troubling, and you may find it difficult to imagine how these long-standing inequities can be changed. But once you start to question the position of women in society, you will want to know more and will begin to ask questions such as: What is the status of women in society? How did things become this way? How can we change the inequalities that women experience?

Adrienne Rich (1976), a classic feminist thinker and poet, early suggested that simply asking "What is life like for women?" creates a new awareness of the status of women in society and history. Whether it is asking "Why is there so much violence against women?" or "Why is it that women clean the offices and men manage them?"—by virtue of asking, you are creating new questions and issues for investigation. It is this process of questioning that gives birth to a sociological and a feminist imagination.

The **sociological imagination** was first described by C. Wright Mills (1916–1962), an eminent sociologist and radical in his time. Mills's radicalism was founded, in part, on his passionate belief that the task of sociology is to understand the relationship between individuals and the society in which they live. He argued that sociological understanding must be used in the reconstruction of more just social institutions. Except for the masculine references in his language, his words still provide a compelling argument that sociology must make sense of the experiences of women and men as they exist in contemporary society. He writes:

> *Nowadays men often feel that their private lives are a series of traps. They sense that within their everyday world, they cannot overcome their troubles, and, in this feeling, they are often quite correct. What ordinary men are directly aware of and what they try to do are bounded by the private orbits in which they live. . . . The sociological imagination enables its possessor to understand the larger historical scene in terms of its meaning for the inner life and external career of a variety of individuals. . . . The first fruit of this imagination—and the first lesson of the social science that embodies it—is the idea that the individual can understand his experience and gauge his fate only by locating himself within his period, that he can know his chances in life only by becoming aware of those of all individuals in his circumstances (Mills 1959:3–5).*

Mills's ideas are strikingly parallel to the feminist argument that women can see how their private experiences are rooted in social conditions by discovering their shared experiences with other women. In fact, Mills professes that the central task of sociology is to understand personal biography and social structure and the relations between the two. His argument is best illustrated in the distinction he makes between personal troubles and social issues.

Personal troubles are part of the personal experience of an individual. They are privately felt, and they involve only those persons and events in an individual's immediate surroundings. **Public issues** are events that originate beyond one's immediate experience, even though they are still felt there. Public issues involve the structure of social institutions and their historical development. Mills's own example is that of marriage. He says, "Inside a marriage a man and a woman may experience personal troubles, but when the divorce rate during the first four years of marriage is 250 out of every 1,000 attempts, this is an indication of a structural issue having to do with the institutions of marriage and the family and other institutions that bear upon them" (1959:9). Mills's point is that events that are felt as personal troubles often have their origins in the public issues that emerge from specific historical and social conditions.

Another example is that of a woman who is beaten by her partner. She experiences deep personal trouble, and perhaps her situation appears to her as unique or as only a private problem. When others in the society have the same experience, then it becomes a public issue. Common patterns in the experiences of battered women reveal that battering is more than just a private matter. It has its origins in complex social institutions that define women as subordinate to men and men as holding power over women—in other words, in power relationships formed by gender. In this sense, battering is both a personal trouble and a public issue. As Mills would conclude, it is then a subject for sociological study. For feminists, this junction between personal experience and the social organization of gender roles is also a starting point for thinking about women.

The relationship between personal troubles and public issues reveals an essential premise of the sociological perspective—that individual life is situated in specific social and historical environments. These environments condition not only what our experience is but also how we think about it. Thinking about women from a sociological perspective asks us to look beyond taken-for-granted ways of seeing the world and, instead, to see how social structures generate the patterns of everyday life. The concept of social structure is central to sociology. **Social structure** refers to the organization of society that shapes social behavior and social attitudes (see Figure 1.2). This is a broad and abstract concept, one that emphasizes the collective and social basis for behavior, not individual motivations and actions. Of course, abstract realities like social structure ultimately have their origins in how individuals behave, but it is the collective and persistent results of

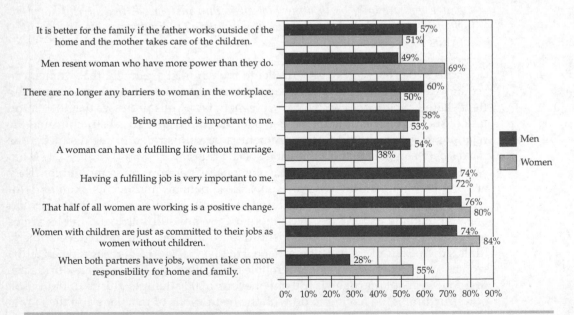

FIGURE 1.2   American Women and Men: What Do They Think?

Source: Gibbs, Nancy 2009 (October 14). "The State of the American Woman." *Time.* www.time.com

Thinking Further: The survey results above are based on a national sample of adults in the fall of 2009. What facts stand out to you about the graph above? Were you to ask these questions to people you know, how might they compare to this national sample?

that behavior that make social structures. Social structures shape individual and group choices, opportunities, and experiences. People can feel the effects of social structures in most of what they do. The observation of social structure is the basis for sociological inquiries.

The concept of social structure is aptly described in the feminist philosopher Marilyn Frye's discussion of oppression. Using the metaphor of a bird cage and supposing that you are looking at the cage from the perspective of the bird, Frye observes that if you look only at one wire, you cannot see the other wires; you miss seeing the whole, because you are focusing only on one part. Even if you look at each wire, discovering all of its properties, you will still not see the whole. Only when you step back from the cage and look at its structure as a whole—seeing all of the parts in relationship to each other—can you understand why the bird cannot escape the cage. As Frye writes, it is then

> *perfectly obvious that the bird is surrounded by a network of systematically related barriers, no one of which would be the least hindrance to its flight, but all of which, by their relations to each other, are as confining as the solid walls of a dungeon. It is now possible to see and recognize: One can study the elements of an oppressive structure with great care and some good will without seeing or being able to understand that one is looking at a cage and that there are people there who are caged, whose motion and mobility are restricted, whose lives are shaped and reduced (1983:4–5).*

Oppression and social structure are not the same thing. Some social structures are clearly beneficial to some groups. Frye's metaphor, however, helps us understand the meaning of social structure and, in studying oppressed groups, helps us see the social structural basis for group oppression.

As you will see throughout this book, gender is one element of social structure that, along with class and race, shapes the experience of all groups in society. This book uses a sociological perspective—that is, one that helps us see the structural origins of individual and group experiences in society. The study of women requires more than a sociological perspective, however. Scholarship on women is interdisciplinary. This means that the perspectives of multiple disciplines—whether history, anthropology, psychology, economics, or the humanities—contribute to understanding the position of women in society. Although the primary focus of this book is sociological, much of the research on which the book is based is also interdisciplinary.

Gender scholarship is rooted in the feminist movement. Feminist thought has stimulated and enriched our understanding of women's lives in society. Feminism shares certain premises with sociology—namely, understanding that the origins of women's experiences lie beyond individual realities, as Frye's work shows. Feminism, like sociology, points us to understanding the social basis of women's experiences. At the same time, feminism is based on a philosophy of change, particularly that we can build a more just society for women if we consciously understand and seek to transform the social behaviors and institutions that are the basis for women's experiences.

DEFINING FEMINISM

Feminism is not easy to define because it includes a variety of political perspectives and ideas. As this book will show, there is no single feminist perspective, and feminist theories and programs for social change sometimes differ quite substantially from one another. Moreover, feminism among young women has evolved compared to that of their feminist foremothers, as we will explore in the feature of this book called "History Speaks" (see page 16).

First, feminism begins with the premise that women's and men's positions in society are the result of social, not natural or biological, factors. Although different varieties of feminist thought have developed, feminists generally see social institutions and social attitudes as the basis for women's position in society. Second, because there are structured inequities between women and men, feminists believe in transforming society on behalf of women. Feminism is a way of both thinking and acting; in fact, the union of action and thought is central to feminist programs for social change. Third, feminists believe that women's experiences, concerns, and ideas are as valuable as those of men and should be treated with

In 1968, one of the first feminist demonstrations was a protest against the Miss America pageant in Atlantic City, New Jersey. Widely covered by the media, it called the public's attention to how women were routinely defined in a demeaning way as sexual objects.

equal seriousness and respect. This does not mean that women have to be like men, but that women's interests should be central in movements for social change.

Public opinion polls indicate that the majority of women in the United States support feminist issues such as equal pay for equal work; improved child care policies; reduced violence against women; and greater opportunities for women regardless of their race, class, or sexual orientation. Why, then, is the label "feminist" so controversial? The word *feminism* conjures up different images to different people. As a result, many who might even agree with feminist ideas and programs for change find it difficult to call themselves feminists (McCabe 2005). Sometimes not calling oneself a feminist reflects actual disagreement with feminist policies and perspectives, as will be seen in the discussion of antifeminist movements in Chapter 8. Often, people are reluctant to call themselves feminists because of misunderstandings about what it means. Feminism is often equated with being a lesbian, which, in turn, is equated with man-hating; thus, for many, rejection of feminism is linked to fears and stereotypes about lesbians. Others feel it is risky to become a feminist, fearing that friends and lovers might reject or tease them. These reactions show how threatened people can be by a movement that advocates change in women's lives. Some have come to think that feminism is no longer necessary, assuming that discrimination has been eliminated by recent reforms and that women and men now stand on relatively equal terms. This book will examine these assumptions, but the point is that many hesitate to call themselves feminists, even when they agree with the ideas of feminism. The negative label associated with feminism is a serious impediment to improving women's lives.

Why is being a feminist so stigmatized? For some, feminism conjures up images of aggressive fanatics, as if to be feminist means one cannot be gentle and kind, be reasonable, or have good relationships with men. This is simply not true, as any careful look at the diverse women and men who are feminists would show. Others will say, "I'm not a feminist; I'm a humanist," reflecting their belief in the betterment of life for all persons—men and women alike—but such a view does not preclude being a feminist. In fact, if one really is in favor of the betterment of all human beings, then it is logical to call oneself humanist, antiracist, *and* feminist.

The fact that the label "feminist" carries a stigma to some reflects the deep and continuing devaluation of women throughout U.S. society. Popular stereotypes of feminists as angry, radical, man-hating, "feminazis" encourage this kind of thinking. Some feminists are, indeed, angry—angry about the injustices women face in the workplace, angry about violence against women, angry about persecution of gays and lesbians, and angry about the persistent denigration of women in popular culture. Many feminists are also radical thinkers, particularly if we take *radical* to mean looking at the roots of women's status in society. Feminism includes a wide range of feeling, thought, and ways of being, none of which are so narrow and ugly as the popular stereotype of feminists suggests.

Many feminists are men, although men may find calling themselves feminists especially difficult. Adopting a pro-woman attitude puts men and women at odds with the dominant culture. Men may think that by calling themselves feminists, they will be thought of as gay, itself a stigmatized identity in the dominant culture. As you will see in Chapter 4 on sexuality, this labeling, rooted in the homophobic attitudes of our culture, is a form of social control. It is society's way of trying to force men and women into narrowly proscribed gender roles. Men who call themselves feminists—some of whom are gay, others of whom are not— are men who support women's rights, who do not believe men are superior to women, and who are willing to work for liberating social changes for women and men. This shows another point learned from feminism—that men are subjected to cultural expectations about masculinity that affect their emotions, identities, and social roles.

The fact is that feminism is threatening to those who want to protect the status quo. This has been vividly shown in a global context when, in 1994, Taslima Nasrin of Bangladesh was threatened with death by Muslim extremists in her home country. Nasrin is a novelist and poet who, in her writing, has challenged fundamentalist Islamic decrees on the role of women. When religious leaders called for her death, the Bangladesh government sought to arrest her. Islamic radicals renewed their death threat and offered a $5,000 reward to anyone who killed her. She has since been living in exile.

This case is an extreme one, but one need not witness such extremes, nor leave the United States, to see how threatening feminism is for many. Conservative women's groups have targeted women's studies programs, accusing them of being like-minded, distributing misinformation, and brainwashing women. The fact is that becoming a feminist does change the way you think, because it gives you a critical awareness of relationships and social systems that you might have previously taken for granted. And, feminist programs for change would dismantle the privileges that many (though not all) men get simply by virtue of being men.

Although not everyone who reads this book will be or become a feminist, each reader should at least be willing to examine the questions that feminism raises in order to learn what constitutes feminist thinking. Doing so will help you describe and understand women's and men's experience in contemporary social institutions and make informed judgments about social policies and actions that affect all people's lives.

WOMEN'S STUDIES AND THE INCLUSION OF WOMEN

Women's studies, with its origins in the feminist movement, rests on the premise that changing what we know about women will change women's and men's lives. Consequently, developing women's studies as an academic field is seen as part of the process of transforming women's place in society.

Since the resurgence of feminism in the 1960s, women's studies has produced a dramatic outpouring of studies and theories about women in society. These studies have questioned the assumptions and biases of existing work in almost every field, including science, the humanities, and the social sciences. Women working in different fields have discovered that much of what stood for knowledge in their disciplines is either overtly sexist or has ignored women altogether. Often, academic women have found that they have more in common with each other than they do with the men in their disciplines. Feminist scholars have forged

The rights that women have won have resulted from the mobilization of women.

new ideas that are critical of much thinking in traditional disciplines. Feminist reconstructions of academic scholarship have now touched every discipline and have resulted in major changes in the assumptions, theoretical frameworks, and research data in different fields in the arts, humanities, social sciences, and sciences.

Examples from many disciplines show that when women's experiences are taken seriously, new methods and perspectives are established. For example, in history, feminist scholars have criticized the "women worthies" approach for recognizing only women who meet the male standards for eminence in history. Although it is important to recognize the contributions of prominent women in history, such women stand out because they are exceptional. In their transformations of historical scholarship, feminist historians have shown how even the periods used to define time frameworks in history are based on men's achievements and men's activities (Lerner 1976). The Renaissance, for example, is typically depicted as a progressive age that encouraged humanism and creativity; yet, for women, the Renaissance was a time of increased domestication of bourgeois wives and intensified persecution of witches—most of whom were single peasant women. To see the Renaissance from a woman-centered perspective is to see that this was a period marked by increased restriction of the power of women (Kelly-Gadol 1976), not just the era of creativity and humanism that has been the dominant characterization of the time.

Similarly, in the area of psychological development, feminists have revised models of development that have been based on male experience. Gilligan's (1982) classic work on moral development shows how theories of moral development took men's experience as the norm and then measured the women's experience against it. In fact, as Gilligan has shown, women's moral development follows a different plan from men's, with women's orientation toward morality being more contextual than that of men. In other words, women make moral judgments based on their assessments of conflicting responsibilities in a given situation, whereas men are more likely to make moral decisions based on their judgments of competing rights and abstract principles. Gilligan's point is to show not only that men and women have different conceptions of morality but also that men's experiences were taken by psychologists to be a universal standard by which both men and women are evaluated. Deriving women's experiences from the particular experiences of some men only makes women appear incomplete, inadequate, or invisible (McIntosh 1983).

Since its inception in the late 1960s/early 1970s, women's studies has developed a more inclusive view of women. "Woman" is no longer considered a unitary category in women's studies. That is, women's studies fully recognizes the diversity of women's experiences, because of social factors such as race, sexual orientation, nationality, age, social class, and so forth. So, on the one hand, women are a definable social category, identifiable and understood simply in terms of their social status *as women*, but women are also differentiated because of their location in *multiple social statuses*. Understanding how these different experiences *intersect* within a given group's experiences and among women is one of the most important contributions of women's studies and it has spawned, as we will see, the growth of fields such as Black feminist studies (Collins 1990; Andersen and Collins 2010; Crenshaw 1991), as well as Latina studies, sexuality studies, and an increasing concern with global and cross-national studies of women.

One objective of women's studies scholarship is to see all groups in relationship to one another and to include multiple human groups in the concepts, theories, and content of human knowledge. Including women and people of color in our studies reveals hidden assumptions in what we learn from more exclusionary studies. Inclusive thinking—that in which women's and men's experiences are seen in relationship to the other and in which multiple human groups are included in the concepts, theories, and content of human knowledge—is a new way of thinking in academic studies. Revealing the assumptions embedded in ideas or knowledge helps us envision the process by which knowledge can become genuinely inclusive and take gender, race, and class together as part of the complexity of human experience.

THE GROWTH OF MEN'S STUDIES

The development of more inclusive work on women has spawned the development of another new field: **men's studies.** As scholars have revised their thinking about women, they have likewise reconsidered the lives of men (Kimmel and Messner 2007; Messner 1997). The field of men's studies is different from just studying men. Men's studies specifically challenges the patriarchal bias in traditional scholarship, which has tended to take men as the given universal standard against which others are judged.

Men's studies is also explicitly feminist. In fact, men's studies emerged from the women's movement when men, too, began to see how gender and sexism shaped their lives. Men's studies challenges existing sexist norms and, like women's studies, has an activist stance. It is not just knowing about men that is important. Men's studies encourages using that knowledge to create a more just world.

Like women's studies, men's studies takes gender as a central feature of social life, seeing how gender shapes men's ideas and opportunities; thus, men's studies is not just about men but sees men as gendered beings. Without men's studies, there is a tendency to presume that only women are gendered, as if gender affects only one group. We know, however, that gender affects the experiences of us all, although in different ways, depending on factors such as one's social class, sexual orientation, nationality, or race. Because of this, men's studies also sees diversity among men as important to understanding men's lives. Not all men are sexist in their attitudes and beliefs, although as a group, men benefit from gender privilege; again, however, this varies by social class and race.

Men's studies, like women's studies, also recognizes the importance of sexuality within the matrix of gender, race, and class domination. Heterosexuality is a privileged form of sexual identity; consequently, gays and lesbians suffer oppression because of their sexual orientation. Together, men's studies and women's studies have analyzed the social structures that generate heterosexual privilege, now leading to new areas of inquiry within gay and lesbian studies.

THE SIGNIFICANCE OF GENDER, RACE, AND CLASS

The transformation of knowledge through women's studies has shown the inadequacy of generalizing from studies of men to thinking about women. **Faulty generalization** takes knowledge from one experience and incorrectly extends that knowledge to another (Minnich 1990). Women's studies has shown how not to generalize from the experience of men to the experience of women. Similarly, studies by and about women of color have shown the importance of not generalizing from the experiences of White, middle-class women to all women. Doing so only replaces one false universal (White men) with another (White women).

Developing inclusive thinking reminds us that women's experiences vary by race, class, age, and other social factors. Although women as a group share many common experiences, recognizing and understanding the diversity of those experiences are equally important in the construction of descriptions and theories about women's lives.

For example, much is now known about the "second shift" women experience whenever they are employed and also do most of the housework in their own homes. But this is not a new development for African American women, who, since slavery, have worked in the homes and raised the children of White women while also caring for their own families. Analyses of domestic work that ignore the

HISTORY SPEAKS: YESTERDAY'S FEMINISTS TALK ABOUT TODAY

Anna Julia Cooper and the Value of Black Women's Studies

"If you object to imaginary lines, don't draw them."
—Anna Julia Cooper (1892 [1988]: 300; cited in May 2007:79)

Born in slavery in 1858, Anna Julia Cooper (1858–1964) overcame extraordinary odds, becoming one of the earliest feminists and an advocate for education for Black women. Cooper's mother was a slave; her father (in name only) was the mother's master, a fact about which the mother would not speak. Following the abolition of slavery (1865), Anna Julia Cooper attended a school (starting at age 9) founded by a religious group whose purpose was to educate former slaves and their families. Shining as a pupil, Cooper was admitted to Oberlin College—one of the first colleges in the United States to admit women. She received her B.A. and M.A. degrees (in mathematics) from Oberlin and at age 67 (in 1925) received a Ph.D. from the Sorbonne in Paris—only the fourth African American woman to receive a Ph.D.[1]

After beginning a teaching career, Cooper had to give it up when she married because married women were routinely barred from teaching—a practice that continued well into the twentieth century. When Cooper's husband died only two years after their marriage, she returned to teaching and had a long career as an educator and advocate for educating Black women and men. In fact, she became quite controversial when she insisted that the "colored only" high school in Washington, DC provide the same college-prep curriculum that sent students from all-white high schools to Harvard, Yale, and other Ivy League colleges.

Cooper is now understood to be one of the first Black feminist thinkers in the United States. She wrote multiple books, insisting over the course of her life on educational rights for Black women and men. Although she was writing long before the development of Black feminist scholarship, Cooper's work foretells the ideas that are now the basis of Black women's studies. In the words of her biographer, Cooper "insisted upon an inclusive model of liberation and human rights" (May 2007: 1). She argued for the right of marginalized people to define and speak for

---

[1]The first three were Georgiana Simpson (in German, University of Chicago). Sadie Tanner Mossell Alexander (in Economics, University of Pennsylvania) and Eva Beatrice Dykes (in English Phililogy, Radcliffe).

themselves, and also saw people's experiences and identities as linked. She articulated the concept that Black women's knowledge was grounded in their particular social location in society.

Thinking Further: If Anna Julia Cooper were here today, she would no doubt be a strong advocate for not just educating Black women and men, but also including in that education the particular experiences of Black American women and men. In addition, she would challenge White students to negate the racial divisions that still shape group experiences. If she were on your campus, what curricular changes might she want to make?

For further information, see: May, Vivian M. 2007. *Anna Julia Cooper, Visionary Black Feminist*. New York: Routledge; Johnson, Karen A. 2000. *Uplifting the Women and the Race: The Educational Philosophies and Social Activism of Anna Julia Cooper and Nannie Helen Burroughs*. New York: Garland Publishing; Cooper, Anna Julia. 1892. *A Voice from the South by a Black Woman from the South*, reprinted by New York: Oxford University Press, 1988.

domestic labor of women of color, including the relations with White women such a labor system creates, are faulty and incomplete. One of the major challenges for feminist studies is to create knowledge that penetrates the complex dynamics of race, class, and gender relations in shaping the experience of all persons.

Gender, race, and class are overlapping categories of experience that shape the experiences of all people in the United States. This means that race relations shape the experiences of White people *and* shape the experiences of people of color but in different ways. In the same vein, gender shapes the experiences of women and shapes the experiences of men; furthermore, class relations affect not just the poor and working class but also the experiences of elites and the middle class.

Each of these categories also overlaps with others. This results in distinct experiences for members of different race, gender, and class groups. Individuals may feel the salience of one or another category at a given time, but their life experiences are shaped by the confluence of all three. As an example, an Asian American woman who hears a derogatory remark about Asian Americans experiences racism, but she may also be stereotyped as a woman. That stereotype, however, is likely to be unique to Asian American women (e.g., that they are submissive and passive), whereas a gender stereotype about another racial group of women may manifest itself differently (e.g., that all blondes are dumb). An Asian American woman's experience will depend not only on her gender and race but also on her class. Her identity at any given time may be centered in any one or more of these experiences, but the point is that her position in society (including the opportunities available to her and what people think of her) is conditioned by her race, class, *and* gender position.

This perspective on the simultaneity of gender, race, and class is different from the additive model that has characterized some thinking about women of color. The term *double jeopardy,* for example, has been used to describe the disadvantage that women of color experience because of their race and their gender. This phrase, however, conjures up images of race and gender as separate experiences, whereas they are integrally related in the experiences of different groups. Race, class, and gender form a **matrix of domination**, meaning the particular configuration of race, class, and gender relations in society that together establishes an interlocking system of domination; no one of them can really be understood without understanding the others, as well (Collins 1990; Andersen and Collins 2010).

Consider the following: White women may be privileged by their race but disadvantaged by their gender and class. Likewise, African American men may be privileged by their gender, but in the context of race and class oppression, this means something different from saying that White men are privileged by their gender. In fact, thinking about race and class oppression in the lives of African American, Native American, and Latino men makes a term such as *male privilege* even seem out of place. Analyses that are inclusive of race, class, and gender also do not see White men as a monolithic group. Although White men have historically benefited from their gender and race position, class differences among them, not to mention differences in White men's behavior and beliefs, make universal statements about men inaccurate, just as it is incorrect to generalize to all women based on the experiences of some. As you will see throughout this book, studying women requires an understanding of race and class, too. Scholarship about women of color is newly emerging and is an important dimension of women's studies.

A SOCIOLOGICAL FRAMEWORK FOR THINKING ABOUT WOMEN

The framework for this book is distinctly sociological. Although much of the research within it comes from other fields or from interdisciplinary work, a sociological perspective forms the core of the book. As you have already seen, the social structural analysis provided by sociological thought is essential to comprehending the situation for women in society. In addition, sociology is an **empirical** discipline, meaning that its method of study is the observation of events in the social world through research. Sociologists observe social events, discover their patterns, and formulate concepts and theories that interpret relationships among them. An important point about empirical studies is that when the theories that explain observed events no longer make sense of what is observed or when one's observations change, then revisions are necessary.

Sociology is also a discipline that claims social improvement as part of its goal. Most sociologists believe that sociology should contribute to the improvement of social life. They differ in how to produce this change—some emphasizing gradual improvement through existing governmental and political channels and others believing that only radical social change can solve contemporary social problems. Regardless of their differences, sociologists believe that the purpose of sociological investigation is to generate improved social policies and consequently to generate social change. Sociologists share with feminists the idea that knowledge should provide the basis for improving the lives of women in society.

▉ Chapter Summary and Themes

Gender refers to the cultural expectations and societal arrangements by which women and men have different experiences in society.

Gender influences all aspects of our lives—our thinking, our interaction, and our life chances. Moreover, it can be seen in the experiences of men, as well as women.

Despite the changes that have been made, women have hardly achieved equality with men.

On numerous indicators, women are disadvantaged relative to men, whether in earnings, the likelihood of poverty, the risk of violence, and opportunities for advancement. Furthermore, these patterns are exacerbated for women of color.

Evidence of women's status in society can be found by looking critically at everyday life.

Gender is so pervasive that it can be seen. Once you become attuned to it, you are likely to be surprised by how pervasive gender is in social relations. Thinking critically about gender—and observing its influence in society—is the basis for women's studies.

The sociological imagination links the experiences of individuals in society to the more abstract social structures of which they are a part.

This insight, fundamental to feminist thought, has also been developed by sociologist C. Wright Mills, especially in his distinction between *personal troubles* and *social issues*. Troubles affect a given individual (or individuals), but social issues are found in the structure of society. Seeing this connection requires understanding the concept of *social structure*.

There is no single definition of feminism, but it is premised on the belief in social justice for women.

Although the majority of people support feminist values, there is a stigma that many attach to the label *feminist*. Despite the misunderstandings associated with feminism, it is premised on belief and actions that promote respect, equality, and the value of women's lives.

The scholarship produced by women's studies has transformed knowledge.

Women's studies is a field originating in the feminist movement and committed to the growth of knowledge about and for women. As women's studies has developed, it has also spawned new work in men's studies—scholarship that takes a feminist perspective to interpret how gender influences men.

Because feminism is about the lives of all women, it is important to understand the interrelationships among gender, race, and class.

Generalizing from the experiences of any one group of women leads to false and incomplete conclusions. Developing an inclusive perspective on race, class, and gender helps you see both commonalities and differences among women—and corrects misleading claims that all women are oppressed relative to men.

A sociological framework for thinking about women is marked by a focus on empirical observation, as well as an understanding of the significance of social structures.

Sociology is an empirical discipline, meaning it is based on careful and systematic observation. A sociological perspective helps you see gender as a socially structured phenomenon.

■ Key Terms

empirical	matrix of domination	social structure
faulty generalization	men's studies	sociological imagination
feminism	personal troubles	women's studies
gender	public issues	

■ Discussion Questions/Projects for Thought

1. Think about one of the other courses you are currently taking. How are women depicted in this course? If you were to use the phases of curriculum change discussed in this chapter to analyze the presentation of women in this other course, what would you say?

2. Interview your friends and/or family about what feminism means to them. What assumptions do they make about those who call themselves feminists? What does this reveal to you about how feminism is popularly defined? Having done this, go to the website for one of the national feminist organizations—such as the Feminist Majority (www.feminist.org) or the National Organization for Women (www.now.org)—and compare what people think to the actual agenda of these feminist organizations. Does this change your understanding of "feminist"?

3. Put yourself in a familiar situation—perhaps at a party or in a classroom or an office. Ask yourself the question similar to what Adrienne Rich has posed: What is life like for women in this situation? What new questions might you ask that would reveal more about women's experiences in this setting than what might be immediately apparent? The rights that women have won have only come from the mobilization of women.

2

The Social Construction of Gender

To understand what sociologists mean by the phrase *the social construction of gender,* watch people when they are with young children. "She's so sweet," someone might say while watching a little girl play with her toys. Or, watch children play with each other. Boys are more likely to brag and insult other boys (often in joking ways); girls are not likely to play this way with other girls. When playing, girls are more likely than boys to engage in "pretend" play; boys are more likely to engage in physical play (Lindsey and Mize 2001).

You can also see the social construction of gender in another way: Try to buy a gender-neutral gift for a child—that is, one not specifically designed with either boys or girls in mind. You may be surprised how hard this is. The aisles in toy stores are highly stereotyped by concepts of what boys and girls do and like. Even products such as diapers and kids' shampoos are gender stereotyped. Diapers for boys are packaged in blue boxes; girls' diapers are in pink. Boys might wear diapers with little animals on them; pink borders with flowers might adorn girls' diapers. You can continue your observations by thinking about how we describe children's toys. Girls play with dolls; boys play with action figures!

When sociologists refer to the **social construction of gender,** they are referring to the many different processes by which the expectations associated with being a boy (and later a man) or being a girl (later a woman) are passed on through society. This process pervades society, and it begins the minute a child is born. The exclamation "It's a boy!" or "It's a girl!" in the delivery room sets a course that from that moment on influences multiple facets of a person's life. Indeed, with the modern technologies now used during pregnancy, the social construction of gender can begin even before birth. Parents or grandparents may buy gifts that reflect differently gendered images, depending on whether the child will be a boy or a girl. Expectant parents may decorate babies' rooms in different colors or with different images depending on the child's gender. Parents may even prefer to have a child that is a particular sex—and, in some countries, may be more likely to give the child away if she is a girl. All of these expectations and behaviors—communicated through parents, peers, the media, schools, religious organizations, and numerous other facets of society—create a concept of what gender means in society. These ideas deeply influence who we become, what others think of us, and the opportunities and choices available to us. *The idea of the social construction of gender is that society, not biological sex differences, is the basis for gender identity.* To understand this fully, we begin with a discussion of biological sex differences.

BIOLOGY, CULTURE, AND SOCIETY

What significance does biology have in shaping the different experiences of women and men in society? Biological explanations of differences between women and men are commonplace and widely held. It used to be said that women's status in society was somehow "natural," stemming from the fact that women bear children. Although this is believed less now than in the past, how often have you heard people, perhaps even feminists, say, "Oh, he's just behaving that way because of too much testosterone (the so-called male hormone)?" Or, have you heard some referring to an observed difference between women and men say, "That's just the way women are"? Biological explanations of gender in society have deep roots in people's thinking, but, as you will see, there is not a fixed relationship between biological features of human beings and the social beings we become. The link between biology and human life is highly mediated by social and cultural influences.

The Biological Basis of Sex Identity

The biological sex of a person is established at the moment of conception and is elaborated during the period of fetal development in the womb. During conception, each parent contributes 23 chromosomes to the fertilized egg, for a total of 46 (or 23 chromosomal pairs). One of these pairs determines the sex of the offspring; they are called the **sex chromosomes.** Under normal conditions, the sex chromosomes consist of an X from the mother's egg and an X or a Y from the father's sperm. The 23 paternal chromosomes (including the X or Y sex chromosome) are selected randomly when the sperm is formed. Genetically normal girls have a pair of X chromosomes (designated 46, XX), and normal boys have the chromosomal pair XY (designated 46, XY). Because the sex chromosome from the ovum is always an X, the chromosome carried by the father's sperm (either an X or a Y) determines the sex of the child. Despite popular belief, there is no evidence that Y chromosomes are stronger than Xs. In fact, the XY male chromosome pair forms a

Years ago, it would have been unimaginable to think of women playing professional football. In 2010, the first ever woman football coach was appointed in a Washington, DC high school.

link that is less viable in genetic coding than is the XX female pair. This fact accounts, in part, for the greater vulnerability of male fetuses in the womb and may contribute to higher prenatal and early childhood mortality rates for males (Harrison 1978).

Following fertilization of the egg, a complex process of *fetal sex differentiation* begins. Before the sixth week of development, the XX and XY embryos are identical; the external genitalia of the embryo remain identical until the eighth week of development. During the sixth week of fetal development, the Y chromosome stimulates the production of proteins that assist in the development of fetal gonads. Sexual differentiation also involves complex genetic messages encoded on the Y chromosome, the X chromosome, and the non-sex chromosomes.

Ambiguous Sexual Identities

Under normal circumstances, the process of fetal sex differentiation results in unambiguous sex characteristics; however, cases of chromosomal abnormalities sometimes occur, resulting in biologically mixed or incomplete sex characteristics. Studies of such cases reveal the complex relationship between biological sex and the social construction of gender.

Intersexed persons are those born with mixed sex characteristics. This can result from a variety of conditions, such as chromosomal patterns where some cells carry the XX chromosomal pattern and others XY. Or, there may be other physical conditions where a person carries physical characteristics associated with both females and males. *Intersex* is the term now used to refer to the different kinds of anatomical conditions that do not fit the usual way of identifying females and males. Sometimes they do not show up at birth, only appearing upon puberty—and sometimes they are never fully apparent.

Because in our culture, sex is typically assigned at birth and according to the appearance of the external genitalia, cases of intersexed persons allow us to look carefully at the role of biology and culture in the development of gender identity. Studies of intersexed people reveal the complex interaction of genetic, biological, and cultural factors in the development of a social gender identity. In one case, a genetic male was born with a tiny penis (1 centimeter long) and no urinary canal. At age 17 months, the child was reclassified as a girl. She was given a new name, hairdo, and clothing. Shortly after the sex reassignment, the parents noticed a change in the older brother's treatment of her. Before the sex reassignment, he had treated his "brother" roughly; now he was very protective and gentle toward his new "sister." By age 3, the daughter had developed clearly "feminine" interests. "For Christmas, she wanted glass slippers, so that she could go to the ball like Cinderella, and a doll. The parents were delighted. The girl continued to receive typically girlish toys from her parents. She continued more and more to show feminine interests, as in helping her mother" (Money and Ehrhardt 1972:125).

In another well-known case of sex reassignment, the reassignment resulted from accidental mutilation when a biological male, age 7 months, had his penis burned off during a routine circumcision. The boy was recreated as a girl, using surgical and hormonal treatment. This child had difficulty adjusting to her identity and at age 14 chose to live as a man, undergoing extensive surgery to partially restore his penis and have a mastectomy. At age 25, he married a woman and adopted her children. Some have concluded that his case reveals that one's sense of sex identity is innate, but there is another side to this argument. When the child was growing up as a girl, her peers teased her mercilessly and refused to play with her; she also spent much time having her genitals scrutinized by doctors. By the time the child was a teenager, she was miserable, contemplated suicide, and was then told of what had happened earlier in life (Diamond and Sigmundson 1997). Although biological identity may have played some role in the child's difficulties, it is also clear that social factors (such as peer ridicule) strongly contributed to the child's difficult adjustment. Thus, the case is evidence for the strong interplay of culture and biology.

These cases demonstrate that biological sex alone does not determine gender identity. In fact, one's gender identity can be different from one's genetic sex. Research shows that rearing is the key factor in determining gender identity, even though prenatal hormones can have some effect on behavior (Money and Ehrhardt 1972; Preves 2003; Fausto-Sterling 2000). In other words, gender identity cannot be reduced to biological categories alone.

You can also see the strong influence of culture when you think about transgendered people. **Transgender** refers to those people who diverge from the binary (male or female—one or the other) system of gender. Whereas the binary system of gender tells us we have to be either male or female, transgendered people fall outside of these social norms. Yet, they report that they experience enormous pressure to fit within gender norms. They may try to hide their gender identity in many situations. Similarly, those who undergo a sex change report enormous social pressure, particularly during their transition period. This is because people generally are expected to be one sex or the other. Whatever their biological sex, many transgendered people have to actively manage and negotiate a gender identity that does not fall into just one category (Gagne and Tewksbury 1998).

Nature/Nurture and Sexually Dimorphic Traits

Controversies about the relative effects of nature versus nurture on human social behavior have been plentiful in the popular mind and scientific literature for years. Although the nature/nurture debate is often posed as an either/or question, human characteristics emerge from the complex interdependence of biological factors and social systems. Indeed, even traits that would seem to be primarily biological, such as body size and strength, hormone levels, and brain development, are affected considerably through environmental influences. Body size provides a good example. Although men are, on average, larger than women, body size is known to be influenced by diet and physical activity, which, in turn, are influenced by class, race, and gender inequality. Explanations of sex differences that ignore such sociological factors are incomplete and misleading.

Genetic research itself shows the strong effect of culture on the expression of genetic traits. Geneticists use the term *genotype* to refer to inherited genetic characteristics; the *phenotype* is the observed expression of the genes as they interact with each other and with the environment in which they appear. This is no simple process, although popular conceptions of genes imagine them as mechanical things that exert a direct influence on human behavior. The expression of genetic codes is, in fact, a complex process, involving the molecular structure of DNA and protein synthesis (Fausto-Sterling 1992). Even the most simple traits involve complex processes of genetic expression. Explaining these traits requires an elaborate and multidimensional analysis. Simple assertions claiming a direct association between genetic structure and social behavior do not match the intricacy of this process.

Sex differences that appear between males and females are known as **sexually dimorphic traits.** These include physical as well as social and cultural differences; they are traits that occur in different frequencies among male and female populations. For example, color blindness is a sexually dimorphic trait that is found more often in men than in women. Although rare, color blindness can be found in women. Most sexually dimorphic traits are distributed in both male and female populations. They are dimorphic usually because there is a significant difference in their distribution between the two populations, not usually because a sexually dimorphic trait appears only in one sex.

Statistical measures of the variation of a trait within a given population represent the degree to which the population deviates from the typical case. Most sex differences are distributed widely throughout the population, leaving a broad range of variation on any given trait appearing among men or among women. Body weight provides a good example. On the average, men weigh more than women, but weight differences among women and among men far exceed the average weight difference between men and women as populations. A sex difference may be found when comparing male and female populations as a whole, but it may not be found when comparing any given male–female pair.

The point is that the *variability within gender is usually larger than the mean difference between genders.* Sexually dimorphic traits are so labeled because they are found in different frequencies in men and women. For any given trait, there may be a substantial degree of overlap between the two populations. Usually, sexually dimorphic traits represent quantitative, not qualitative, differences between the sexes.

Discussions of male–female traits almost always emphasize traits that are different instead of similar in men and women. But the vast majority of human traits are shared by both men and women. Because knowing a person's biological sex does not provide a very accurate prediction of his or her physical characteristics, you have to wonder why biological differences are so often claimed as explaining inequality between the sexes.

Biological Determinism

An argument that reduces a complex event or process (such as social identity) to a single monolithic cause (such as the form of one's genitals) is called **biological reductionism.** A related form of argument is known as **biological determinism.** Determinist arguments are those that assume that a given condition (such as the presence of a penis) inevitably determines a particular event (such as male aggression). Explaining observed social differences between men and women as the result of biology is a biologically determinist argument. Determinist and reductionist arguments are closely related and can be made in any number of forms, including psychological, economic, and cultural contexts. Biological determinism and reductionism have been especially rampant in the discussion of gender and race differences, and they typically oversimplify the known scientific research from contemporary scientific studies that shows a very complex relationship even between genetic structures, the brain, and the social environment.

Take, for example, the idea that hormonal differences explain presumed differences in men's and women's aggressive behavior. To begin with, both males and females have measurable quantities of the three major sex hormones—estrogen, progestin, and testosterone. Hormonal sex differences are caused by differences in the levels of production and concentration of each, not in their presence or absence per se. The greater production of testosterone in males is because of stimulation by the testes, whereas in females the ovaries secrete additional estrogens and progestins. Before puberty, however, there are few or no sex differences in the quantity of sex hormones in each sex; at this time, all of the sex hormones are at very low levels. If high levels of testosterone were needed to produce aggression, then we would expect to see little difference in aggressive behavior between prepubescent boys and girls. Much research, however, shows that boys are more aggressive at an early age, thereby contradicting the implications of biologically determinist arguments.

Similarly, following menopause, women actually have lower levels of estradol (the major estrogen) and progesterone (the major progestin) than do men of the same age (Hawkins and Oakey 1974; Hoyenga and Hoyenga 1979; Tea et al. 1975). Because there is no empirical evidence that older men are more feminine than older women, this calls into question the idea that hormonal differences explain differences in the behavior of the sexes. Moreover, changes in testosterone levels do not consistently predict changes in aggressive behavior. Studies of "chemical castration" show that the procedure is not very effective in reducing violent or aggressive behavior in men. Similarly, studies of castrated rhesus monkeys show no straightforward relationship between castration and the lessening of aggression (Fausto-Sterling 1992). Much of the research on hormones and aggression shows that experiential factors (such as stress, fatigue, or fear) may have a greater effect on hormonal production than hormones have on behavior (Fausto-Sterling 1992).

In sum, reductionist arguments do not account for the complexities of patterns of human aggression or for the wide variation in patterns of aggression among and between men and women. No single hormonal state is a good predictor of any form of social behavior. Studies of the relationship between hormones and aggression typically confuse biological and social facts anyhow, because measuring and defining aggression is itself a matter of interpretation.

Biologically reductionist arguments rest on the assumption that differences between the sexes are "natural." Yet, it is quite difficult, if not impossible, to distinguish so-called natural and social events. Cultural attitudes influence what we think of as natural, since what is deemed natural is typically only that which we believe is unchangeable. Biology itself is neither fixed nor immutable, because biological processes themselves can be modified through cultural conditions. The fact is, human biology sets extremely broad limits for behavior. Most of us vastly underuse our biological capacities, including both motor skills and cognitive ability.

The Difference Culture Makes

If differences between women and men were determined by biological factors alone, we would not find the vast diversity that exists in gender relations from society to society, nor would what it means to be a man or a woman vary from one culture to another. Culture clearly matters, and it matters a lot.

Sociologists and anthropologists define **culture** as "the set of definitions of reality held in common by people who share a distinctive way of life" (Kluckhohn 1962:52). Culture is, in essence, a pattern of expectations about what are appropriate behaviors and beliefs for the members of the society; thus, culture provides prescriptions for social behavior. Culture includes the *norms* that shape everyday life—that is, the expectations about how to act in any given situation. Culture also establishes the *values* and *beliefs* of a society—those commonly held ideas that members of a society broadly share. Culture tells us what we ought to do, what we ought to think, who we ought to be, and what we ought to expect of others.

The concept of culture explains a great deal to us about variation in human lifestyles and human societies. One feature of a culture is that its members come to take cultural patterns for granted. Thus, culture provides its members with tacit knowledge, and much of what members believe as true or what they perceive as real is learned to the point where it is no longer questioned. Culture provides assumptions that often go unexamined but that, nonetheless, fundamentally guide our behavior and our beliefs. Cultural norms vary tremendously from one society to another and, within any given society, from one historical setting to another and among different groups in the society.

You can see the influence of gender norms in everyday life, all around you. Just imagine, for example, that tomorrow you woke up and were no longer a woman but a man, or no longer a man, but a woman. What would change? First, your appearance would undergo a great transformation, not just because of physical differences, but also because of the norms we associate with being a man and being a woman (your hair, what you wear, the adornments you put on your body, even the color of the lotions and creams that you likely use). You would likely talk differently, sit differently, even think differently, given what we know about men's and women's differing attitudes about a large array of subjects (see Figure 2.1).

The specific cultural expectations for women and for men vary from society to society, but in every known culture, gender is a major category for the organization of cultural and social relations. In most Western cultures, people think of man and woman as dichotomous categories—that is, separate and opposite, with no overlap between the two. Looking at gender from different cultural viewpoints challenges this assumption, however. Many cultures consider there to be three genders, or even more. Consider the Navajo Indians. In traditional Navajo society, the *berdaches* were those who were anatomically normal men but who were

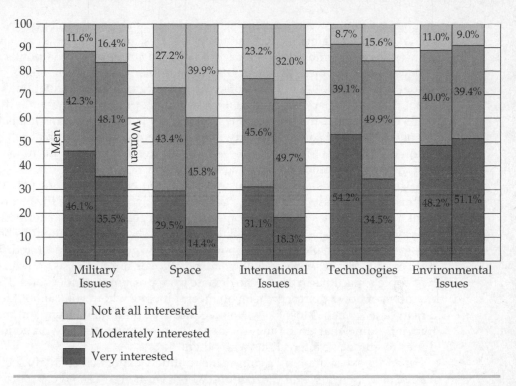

FIGURE 2.1   Gender, Socialization, and Public Concerns

Source: General Social Survey, 2008. Chicago: National Opinion Research Center. Reprinted with permission.

defined as a third gender and were considered to be intersexed. Berdaches married other men. The men they married were not themselves considered to be berdaches; they were defined as ordinary men. Nor were the berdaches or the men they married considered to be homosexuals, as they would be judged by contemporary Western culture. Similarly, in some African and American Indian societies, there are those who are biological females living as men, known as manly hearted women. They are considered "female men," but they do not have to dress or act like men; they only have to have enough money to buy wives (Lorber 1994; Nanda 1998; Amadiume 1987; Blackwood 1984).

Another good example for understanding the cultural basis of gender are the *hijras* of India. Hijras are a religious community of men in India who are born as males, but they come to think of themselves as neither men nor women. Like berdaches, they are considered a third gender. Hijras dress as women and may marry other men; typically, they live within a communal subculture. An important thing to note is that hijras are not born so; they choose this way of life. As male adolescents, they have their penises and testicles cut off in an elaborate and prolonged cultural ritual—a rite of passage marking the transition to becoming a hijra.

Hijras occupy a special place within Indian culture and society, a situation stemming from Hindu religion, which, different from Western culture, values the ambiguity of in-between sexual categories. Hinduism holds that all persons contain both male and female principles within themselves, and Hindu gods are commonly seen as sexually ambiguous. Hijras are believed to represent the power of man and woman combined, although they are impotent themselves. Hijras perceive sexual desire to result in the loss of spiritual energy; their emasculation is seen as proof that they experience no sexual desire. Their special place within Indian society is evidenced at Indian weddings, where hijras often perform rituals to bless the newly married couple's fertility. They also commonly perform at celebrations following the birth of a male child—an event much cherished in Indian society and the cause for much celebration (Nanda 1998).

These examples are good illustrations of the cultural basis of gender. Even within contemporary U.S. society, "gender bending" shows how the dichotomous thinking that defines men and women as "either/or" can be transformed. Cross-dressers, transvestites, and transsexuals illustrate how fluid gender can be and, if one is willing to challenge social convention, how gender can be altered. The cultural expectations associated with gender, however, are strong, as you can witness by people's reactions to those who deviate from presumed gender roles. Think, for example, of how you react when you meet someone whom you cannot identify as a man or a woman. Most likely, you feel unsure about how to act. You may even find this somewhat unsettling—evidence of how much we rely on gender categories to guide our interactions with others.

Gender expectations in a culture are routinely expressed subtly in social interaction, as, for example, in U.S. culture, where women smile and cry more than do men, and where women have more frequent eye contact with others (Basow 2003; Robinson and Smith-Lovin 2001; LaFrance 2002; Lombardo et al. 2001; Anderson and Leaper 1998). At other times, gender expectations are not so subtle, as in the cultural practices of Chinese foot binding, Indian suttee, European witch hunts, and the genital mutilation of women documented in some African countries. Within U.S. culture, extreme physical practices are also evidenced in the sadistic treatment of women in pornography and in the common surgical practices of facelifts and silicone implants.

Sociologists use the term *gender* to refer specifically to the social and cultural patterns that we associate with women and men in society. **Sex** refers to the biological identity and is meant to signify the fact that one is either male or female. One's biological sex usually establishes a pattern of gendered expectations, although, as we have seen, biological sex identity is not always the same as gender identity, nor is biological identity always as clear as this definition implies. *Gender* is a social, not a biological, concept. Simply put, being "female" and "male" are biological facts; being a woman or a man is a social and cultural process—one that is constructed through the whole array of social, political, economic, and cultural experiences in a given society. Even the distinction between sex and gender is not as clear cut as one might think.

Gender can construct our concepts of biological sex identity. Although this probably sounds odd, why do doctors feel compelled to force those born with mixed sex characteristics to be one sex or the other through medical intervention (Fausto-Sterling 2000)? Physicians advise parents of those who are given a sex reassignment and genital reconstruction to give the child a new name, a different hairstyle, and new clothes—all intended to provide the child with the social signals judged appropriate to the new gender identity. Human beings make up the system by which we classify bodies; the meaning attached to this is not inherent in the body itself, but in the social meaning our bodies acquire because of culture.

Cultural expectations associated with gender can also change how we experience what would otherwise be thought of as purely bodily events. Menopause provides a good example. Menopause is a biological event—the cessation of the menstrual cycle. But how menopause is experienced, indeed whether it is even named, is a cultural phenomenon. In the United States, menopausal women are culturally depicted as cranky, uncontrollably emotional, and irritable. Indeed, as the population bulge known as Baby Boomers has reached middle age, menopause has become a major industry, replete with advice books, products, and a cultural movement. In North America, menopause is viewed in pathological and medical terms, and menopausal women are stereotyped as depressed (even though many women experience this as a happy time of life). Comparatively, in Japan, women rarely express menopausal discomfort—a fact explained by anthropologists as resulting from the positive role given Japanese women as they age and the fact that menopause is culturally defined as a social, not a biological, change in life. In other words, how women experience menopause depends not just on physiological changes per se, but on the cultural attitudes that surround this phenomenon (Lock 1993, 1998).

In sum, gender is a social construct that establishes our definitions of self, our relations with others, and our life chances. As a concept, gender emphasizes the social and cultural experience within society. Moreover, gender is not just an individual attribute. Instead, it is part of the social structure of society and thus has an institutional component—to which we now turn.

The Institutional Basis of Gender

Social institutions are established patterns of behavior with a particular and recognized purpose; institutions include specific participants who share expectations and act in specific roles, with rights and duties attached to them. Institutions define reality for us insofar as they exist as objective entities in our experience. They are "experienced as existing over and beyond the individuals who 'happen' to embody them at the moment. In other words, institutions are experienced as a reality of their own, a reality that confronts the individual as an external and coercive fact" (Berger and Luckmann 1966:58). Institutions arise within particular and historic environments and constitute the social structure of society. Although the idea of institutions is an abstract one, the various institutional forms within society form the social structure that guides our collective lives.

Understanding gender in an institutional context means that *gender is not just an attribute of individuals; instead, gender is systematically structured in social institutions*, meaning that it is deeply embedded in the social structure of society. Gender is created, not just within families or interpersonal relationships (although these are important arenas of gender relations), but also within the structure of all major social institutions, including schools, religion, the economy, and the state (i.e., government and other organized systems of authority such as the police and the military). These institutions shape and mold the experiences of us all.

Think again about the things you thought you would change about yourself were you suddenly to become a member of the other gender. Most likely the things you would list stem from institutional arrangements in society. If you thought of products that you use as a man or a woman, such as body products, those products are produced, bought, and sold in economic institutions that are organized around gender, class, race, and other social factors (such as age). If you imagined that your attitudes might change, think of how those attitudes are promoted through media institutions or established within families—both of which are institutions organized by gender. Or, perhaps you imagined different religious proscriptions for how women and men are to act and be—again, reflecting the institutional structure of religion. All of these examples show how the institutional structure is the backdrop for gender relations in society.

Furthermore, institutions are themselves gendered, just as you might think of individual people and social groups being gendered. To say that an institution is gendered means that the whole institution is patterned on specific gendered relationships. That is, gender is "present in the processes, practices, images and ideologies, and distribution of power in the various sectors of social life" (Acker 1992: 567). The concept of a *gendered institution* was introduced by Joan Acker, a feminist

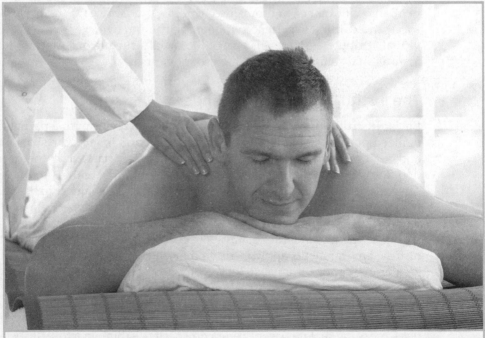

As gender roles have changed, so has men's use of spas and beauty products. But ask yourself if there are still gendered practices involving such behaviors.

sociologist. Acker uses this concept to explain not just that gender expectations are passed to men and women within institutions, but that the institutions themselves are structured along gendered lines. **Gendered institutions** are the total pattern of gender relations—stereotypical expectations, interpersonal relationships, and men's and women's different placements in social, economic, and political hierarchies. This is what interests sociologists, and it is what they mean by the social structure of gender relations in society.

Conceptualizing gender in this way is somewhat different from the related concept of gender roles. **Social roles** are the culturally prescribed expectations, duties, and rights that define the relationship between a person in a particular position and the other people with whom she or he interacts. For example, to be a mother is a specific social role with a definable set of expectations, rights, and duties. Persons occupy multiple roles in society; we can think of social roles as linking individuals to social structures. It is through social roles that cultural norms are patterned and learned. **Gender roles** are the expectations for behavior and attitudes that the culture defines as appropriate for women and men.

The concept of gender is broader than the concept of gender roles. **Gender** refers to the complex social, political, economic, and psychological relations between women and men in society. Gender is part of the social structure—in other words, it is institutionalized in society (Acker 2005; Martin 2004; Risman 2004). *Gender roles* are the patterns through which gender relations are expressed, but our understanding of gender in society cannot be reduced to roles and learned expectations alone.

The distinction between gender, as institutionalized, and gender roles is made most clear perhaps by thinking about analogous cases—specifically, race and class. Race relations in society are seldom, if ever, thought of in terms of "race roles." Likewise, class inequality is not discussed in terms of "class roles." Doing so would make race and class inequality seem like matters of interpersonal interaction. Although race, class, and gender inequalities are experienced within interpersonal interactions, limiting the analysis of race, class, or gender relations to this level of social interaction individualizes more complex systems of inequality. Moreover, restricting the analysis of race, class, or gender to social roles hides the power relations that are embedded in race, class, and gender inequality (Lopata and Thorne 1978).

Understanding the institutional basis of gender also underscores the interrelationships of gender, race, and class, because all three are part of the institutional framework of society. As a social category, gender intersects with class and race; thus, gender is manifested in different ways, depending on one's location in the race and class system. For example, given the fact that African American women have historically been more likely to work in paid employment than White women, they have tended to reject gender stereotypes for women (Dugger 1988; Kane 2000). Research also finds that Black women and Black men strongly support various Black feminist attitudes—especially in recognizing the dual influence of race and gender on Black women's experience (Simien and Clawson 2004).

Institutional analyses of gender emphasize that gender, like race and class, is a part of the social experience of us all, not just of women. Gender is just as important in the formation of men's experiences as it is in women's (Messner 1998). From a sociological perspective, class, race, and gender relations are systemically structured in social institutions, meaning that class, race, and gender relations shape the experiences of all. Sociologists do not see gender simply as a psychological attribute, although that is one dimension of gender relations in society. In addition to the psychological significance of gender, gender relations are part of the institutionalized patterns in society. Understanding gender, as well as class and race, is central to the study of any social institution or situation. Understanding gender in terms of social structure indicates that social change is not just a matter of individual will—that if we changed our minds, gender would disappear. Transformation of gender inequality requires change both in consciousness and in social institutions.

SOCIALIZATION AND THE FORMATION OF GENDER IDENTITY

The fact that gender is a social, not a natural, phenomenon means that it is learned. Although rooted in institutions, gender is passed on through social learning and is enacted through what sociologists call gender roles. Gender roles are the patterns of behavior in which women and men engage, based on the cultural expectations associated with their gender. Gender roles are learned through the process of socialization. It is through the socialization process that individuals acquire an identity based on gender. **Gender identity** is an individual's specific definition of self, based on that person's understanding of what it means to be a man or a woman. In other words, it is through the socialization process that gender is socially constructed.

Young girls and boys learn gender-based skills in many contexts, including within the family.

Sanctions and Expectations

Through gender socialization, different behaviors and attitudes are encouraged and discouraged in men and women. That is, social expectations about what is properly masculine and feminine are communicated to us through the **socialization** process. Families, peers, teachers, the media, sports teams, and religious groups all act as agents of socialization. Although probably none of us becomes exactly what the cultural ideal prescribes, our roles in social institutions are conditioned by the gender relations we learn.

Some persons become more perfectly socialized than others, and sociologists have warned against the idea of seeing humans as totally passive, overly socialized creatures (Wrong 1961). To some extent, we probably all resist the expectations society has of us. Our uniqueness as individuals stems in part from this resistance, as well as from variations in the social experiences we have. Studying patterns of gender socialization does not deny individual differences, but it does point to the common experiences shared by girls as they become women and boys as they become men. However much we may believe that we were raised in a gender-neutral environment, research and careful observation show how pervasive and generally effective the process of gender role socialization is. Although some of us conform more than others, socialization acts as a powerful system of social control.

Peter Berger (1963) describes social control as something like a series of concentric circles. At the center is the individual, who is surrounded by different levels of control, ranging from the subtle (such as learned roles, peer pressure, and ridicule) to the overt (such as violence, physical threat, and imprisonment). According to Berger, it is usually not necessary for powerful agents in the society to resort to extreme sanctions, because what we think and believe about ourselves usually keeps us in line. In this sense, socialization acts as a powerful system of social control.

The conflicts we encounter when we try to cross or deny the boundaries between the sexes are good evidence of the strength of gendered expectations in our culture. Although most of us resist the idea that we are controlled, because we like to think we are individuals, the effects of social expectations are easily apparent. What happens, for example, if you deviate from your expected gender role? Men who do so will likely be presumed to be gay, indicative of the link between gender socialization and expectations about sexual identity, something we will discuss later. Women who deviate from expected roles will be labeled "tomboys" or will be judged as "unladylike."

The pressure to adopt gender-appropriate behavior is evidence that the socialization process controls us in several ways: (1) it gives us a definition of ourselves, (2) it defines the external world and our place within it, (3) it provides our definition of others and our relationships with them, and (4) the socialization process encourages and discourages the acquisition of certain skills by gender.

Gender socialization is a powerful process involving our individualism, as well as the multiple forms that gender roles can take. Gender expectations confront us everywhere and shape our identities and relationships with others, perhaps even at times when we might wish they did not. Some argue that the pressures of gender socialization are even more restrictive of boys, at least at the early ages, than of girls. Men's roles are more rigidly defined, as witnessed in the more severe social sanctions brought against boys labeled as sissies, compared with girls who are thought of as tomboys. For girls, being a tomboy may be a source of mild ridicule, but it appears to be more acceptable (at least until puberty) than being a sissy is for boys.

Some researchers explain this finding as the result of **homophobia,** defined as the fear and hatred of homosexuals (Pharr 1999). Homophobia acts as a system of social control because it encourages boys and men to act more masculine, as a way of indicating that they are not gay. Homophobia further separates the cultural roles of masculinity and femininity by discouraging men from showing so-called feminine traits such as caring, nurturing, emotional expression, and gentleness.

HISTORY SPEAKS: YESTERDAY'S FEMINISTS TALK ABOUT TODAY

Simone de Beauvoir and Gender Socialization

"One is not born, but rather becomes, a woman."
—Simone de Beauvoir (1953: 267)

Simone de Beauvoir (1908–1986) was born in Paris and became one of the earliest and influential feminists when the second wave of the women's movement emerged in the late 1960s. She was a French intellectual and writer who wrote numerous novels, short stories, as well as plays and intellectual essays. But it was her book, *The Second Sex* (published in 1949 in two volumes) that captured the attention of feminists worldwide and made her one of the intellectual founders of modern feminism. In it, she argues that women have been considered to be "others," subordinate to men who, in this way of thinking, are constructed as full subjects, while women are perceived as only incidental.

de Beauvoir was progressive not only in her ideas but also in her own lifestyle. The daughter of a strict, religious mother and an aristocratic, deeply conservative father, de Beauvoir was educated in Catholic schools as a young girl, but came to question religion and the institution of marriage, especially following the death of her dear friend and schoolmate, Elizabeth Mabille (known as Zaza). De Beauvoir thought her young friend died of heartbreak as the result of her conflicts with her family over an arranged marriage. From then forward, de Beauvoir eschewed marriage, even though she had the famous French existential philosopher, Jean Paul Sartre, as her lifelong lover. She and Sartre held what we would now call an "open" arrangement as romantic partners,

wherein each had other periodic affairs, in de Beauvoir's case with both women and men as lovers. During the 1940s, she was dismissed from her teaching post in Paris by the Nazi government. She was later dismissed from a different teaching job because of complaints from a parent that she was corrupting the minds of young women.

Feminist writing was almost unheard of during de Beauvoir's life, but her book, *The Second Sex*, is still seen as an important feminist text. The book comprehensively examines biological, psychological, philosophical, historical, anthropological, and literary studies of women and develops an argument that the social arrangements by which women become seen as appendages of men are damaging to human minds.

Thinking Further: Suppose that Simone de Beauvoir were to return to life and observed an elementary school in your community. What might she see? How would her observations illustrate her comment about how one becomes a woman? How would she see young boys "becoming men"?

For further infomation, see Musset, Shannon. 2005. "Simone de Beavoir (1908–1986)." *Internet Encyclopedia of Philosophy*, http://www.iep.utm. edu/beauvoir/; and de Beauvoir, Simone. 1953. *The Second Sex.*, Translated By H. M. Parshley. Volume II (New York: Knopf): 267.

Conformity to traditional roles takes its toll on both men and women, and research shows that those who conform most fully to gender-role expectations experience a range of negative consequences. For example, higher male mortality rates can be attributed to the stress in masculine roles. The cultural association between masculinity and aggression can also help explain the high rates of violence that encourage behaviors in men that put them at risk in a variety of ways.

For women too much conformity to gender expectations also produces many negative consequences. Women who score as "very feminine" on personality tests tend to exhibit more feelings of depression and say they do not feel in control of their lives (Sayers et al. 1993; Sprock and Yoder 1997). The cultural expectations associated with gender and beauty are known to produce a whole range of negative health consequences. The dominant culture promotes a narrow image of beauty for women. Women and young girls who internalize this ideal—one that is generally impossible to achieve—often end up being disturbed about their body image, feeling they are never adequate. Millions then engage in constant dieting, even when they are well within healthy weight standards. Purging themselves of food via eating disorders or cycling through fad diets can all have serious health consequences. Many young women develop a distorted image of themselves, thinking they are "overweight" when they may actually be dangerously thin. And, despite the known risks of smoking, increasing numbers of young women smoke and do so not only because they think it "looks cool" but also because they think it will keep them from gaining weight (Logio 1998; Zucker and Landry 2007).

Race and Gender Identity

Gender socialization does not occur apart from the other features of our lives. Gender identity is also mediated by our racial identities. For example, many of the characteristics associated with feminine stereotypes, such as that women are dependent on men or that women are weak and more helpless than men, are not typical of many women of color. African American women, for example, like White women, are socialized to place primary emphasis on nurturing their loved ones, but they are also socialized to be self-sufficient, to aspire to an education, to regard employment as part of the role of women, and to be more independent than White women (Collins 1987).

This does not mean that women and men of color are unaffected by gender socialization. It is only to say that gender is manifested differently among different groups. In other words, gender identities intersect with racial identities. African American, Asian, and Latino men, for example, construct concepts of masculinity in the context of negative stereotypes about them that are both race and gender based (Chen 1999). Women of color likewise develop their gender consciousness in the context of their racial and class status in society. Together, gender, race, and class influence how all people—including White people—learn and develop their gender identity.

Research regarding Black and White families illustrates this point, showing both similarities and differences in the long-term goals, parenting practices, parental roles, and disciplinary strategies of Black and White parents of boys and

A CLOSER LOOK AT MEN

Guyland

Sociologist Michael Kimmel, long known as a scholar in men's studies, has found a new phase in the socialization of young men into adulthood. He calls it "Guyland." Guyland is a space in time where Kimmel argues young men, roughly aged 16 to the late-20s, are poised between adoleseence and adulthood—"stuck," if you will, in a social space that is neither childhood nor adulthood. Young men in "Guyland" party a lot, drift from job to job, play video games a lot, watch sports, and generally "hang around" other guys. But, based on over 400 interviews and many observations of and conversations with young men around the country, Kimmel argues that this is a unique social space—one that has become a stage in life with its own rules and limitations.

Although not all "guys" are the same in Guyland, Kimmel observes that in Guyland, men hang out with other men. Women may be present, but they are peripheral to the main action. Indeed, Kimmel notes, there is a great deal of misogyny in Guyland (that is, woman-hating), even though it is subtly expressed. Guyland is also deeply homophobic, even though it is a homosocial (largely all male) space. Women allowed into Guyland have to play by the men's rules. It is a space where men play out masculinity —engaging in behaviors that Kimmel says are "ill-conceived and irresponsibly carried out"

(p. 19). Men drink too much, engage in locker room talk about women, disparage being a good student, and talk about sports.

The men Kimmel observed and interviewed are largely White, middle class, and college educated (or in college). They seem caught in a world where masculinity is ambiguous—old norms defined manhood as emerging through certain and sequential stages of adult development—school, work, then family. But these sequences no longer hold, as women have emerged as independent, capable of forging their own futures with or without men. As a result, men seem anxious—not sure of their place in the world. This anxiety (not consciously known) produces the behaviors and attitudes of Guyland. On the one hand, men are supposed to be special, but at the same time, social changes have made men vulnerable. Guyland and its associated behaviors and attitudes is a way to express manhood in a world when being a man is no longer a certain thing.

Thinking Further: Observe the elements of Guyland on your campus or in your community. What does it look like? How would an analyst of gender interpret what you see?

Source: Based on Kimmel, Michael. 2008. *Guyland: The Perilous World Where Boys Become Men.* New York: HarperCollins.

girls. But these patterns are influenced both by the gender of the child and the race and class of the family. Thus, both Black and White parents value their child getting a good job and a good education and having a strong and loving family as priorities. But education and a job are more of a priority for Black parents than for Whites; both Black and White parents emphasize this less if they are of higher-class status. Thus, among upper middle-class White parents, family is the most important priority, whereas for Black parents, education and jobs are ranked as most important. Furthermore, these priorities do not change according to the gender of the child. White parents, in general, are also more likely to emphasize happiness for their children. White parents also stress the importance of obedience for boys; Black parents are more likely to emphasize discipline by the withdrawal of certain privileges. The researchers use their conclusions to argue that gender is not a monolithic influence since gender patterns in socialization are so strongly shaped by race and class as well (Hill and Sprague 1999). Such conclusions show the importance of using a multidimensional understanding of socialization—one that examines race and class along with gender, not just gender alone.

New experiences that families face can also change gender expectations within the family. This is especially evident in studies of immigrant groups, a phenomenon of increasing importance in U.S. society. Studying Mexican immigrants in the United States, Hondagneu-Sotelo has found that men's expectations about their roles change as the result of the migration experience. Because families are often separated during the early phases of migration, men may live in bachelor communities when they first migrate. They learn to cook and clean for themselves. Once the family is reunited, the men do not necessarily discard these newly learned roles (Hondagneu-Sotelo 1992, 1994). Clearly, generalizations about gender-role socialization need to be carefully examined in the context of the experiences of different groups. As you read the results of studies, including those related here, you should ask yourself if the same conclusions would be reached depending on the race *and* gender of the research subjects.

SOCIALIZATION ACROSS THE LIFE COURSE

Socialization begins at birth, and it continues throughout adulthood, even though gender roles are established very early. When we encounter new social experiences, we are socialized to adopt new roles through the expectations others have of us. This section examines the processes and consequences of gender socialization as it occurs throughout the life course.

Infancy

Beginning in infancy, boys and girls are treated differently. Research on infant socialization shows, in fact, how quickly gender expectations become part of our experience. Studies find that as early as age 18 months, toddlers have learned to play mostly with toys judged to be appropriate for their gender (Caldera and Sciaraffa 1998). Parents describe their babies differently, depending on their gender—including descriptions rating their male children as more intelligent than female children (Furnham and Gasson 1998). In one telling study, researchers observed mothers playing with their infants (in a laboratory setting). Although the infants' behaviors did not differ for boys and girls, mothers engaged in more conversation with their infant daughters, but were more likely to give instructions to their sons. Generally, the mothers also interacted more with daughters than sons (Clearfield and Nelson 2006). This and countless other studies show how differently parents treat infants, depending on the infant's sex. This may be unintentional or subtle, but it has an effect on later life, nonetheless.

You can even observe this yourself. Watch parents and children in some public setting and determine if you see what one set of researchers has systematically observed: Fathers and mothers are more likely to let boy toddlers walk alone than they allow girls to do. Who pushes strollers? These same observers found that even when children are out of strollers, mothers are more likely to push the empty stroller than are fathers (Mitchell et al. 1992). Do you see the same patterns?

Parents are not the only agents of gender socialization, however. Other children have just as important an impact on learning gender roles. Children of all ages notice the sex of infants and use it as a basis for responding to the child. Preschool girls also show more interest in interacting with babies than do preschool boys, a pattern that is most pronounced among children whose parents hold gender-stereotyped attitudes (Blakemore 1998). Peers develop expectations and definitions of gender-appropriate behaviors and use those expectations as the basis for their interaction with others.

Childhood Play and Games

Research in child development emphasizes the importance of play and games in the maturation of children. Through play, children learn the skills of social interaction, develop cognitive and analytical abilities, and are taught the values and attitudes of their culture. The games that children play have great significance for the children's intellectual, moral, personal, and social development and for their gender identity.

George Herbert Mead, a social psychologist and major sociological theorist in the early twentieth century, described three stages in which socialization occurs: imitation, play, and game. In the *imitation stage,* an infant simply copies the behavior of significant persons in his or her environment. In the play stage, the child begins "taking the role of the other"—seeing himself or herself from the perspective of another person. Mead argues that taking the role of the other is a cognitive process that permits the child to develop a self-concept. Self-concepts emerge through interacting with other people and from learning to perceive how others see us. The other people most emotionally important to the child (e.g., parents, siblings, or other primary caregivers) are, in Mead's term, significant others. In the *play stage,* children learn to take the role of significant others, primarily by practicing others' social roles—for example, "playing Mommy" or "playing Daddy."

In the *game stage,* children are able to do more. Rather than seeing themselves from the perspective of only one significant other at a time, they can play games requiring them to understand how several other people (including more than just significant others) view them simultaneously. Playing baseball, to use Mead's example, involves the roles and expectations of many more people than does "playing Mommy." Eventually, children in the game stage learn to orient themselves not just to *significant others* but to a generalized other, as well. The generalized other represents the cultural expectations of the whole social community. Mead's analysis of the emergence of the self emphasizes the importance of interpretative behavior in the way the child relates to others in the social environment. Early activity, especially through play, places children's experiences in a social environment; therefore, meanings communicated through play help the child organize personal experience into an emerging self. Children's play, then, is a very significant part of the socialization process.

MEDIA MATTERS

The (Un)Popularity of Gender-Neutral Child Rearing

Many parents use advice books to guide them in the rearing of their children. Have such books been influenced by feminism, such that they help parents raise their sons and daughters in more gender-neutral ways?

In her analysis of 34 parenting books and 42 articles posted on parenting websites, Karin Martin found that virtually all of these sources acknowledge that gender is a social construction (not fixed by biology) and that socialization plays a major role in gender development. A significant number of self-help sources encourage parents to permit children to move beyond gender stereotypes; 25 of the sources do so directly and 16 others do so at least to some extent. Although the various sources support gender-neutral child rearing to differing degrees, advice sources portray such child rearing as good for children's well-being and the well-being of society.

But there are also clear limits to how far advice sources suggest parents go with gender-neutral child rearing. Much of the advice available to parents offers some acceptance of gender nonconformity (i.e., boys doing "girl" things and girls doing "boy" things) and advises parents "not too worry." But at the same time, these sources emphasize that gender nonconformity can be problematic, especially with regard to possible homosexuality. Some sources told parents not to worry because gender nonconformity "does not lead to homosexuality." Others told parents not to worry too much because doing so might make nonconformity worse, implying that homosexuality would be a problematic outcome.

Martin concludes that although feminist values have been incorporated into child-rearing advice, experts do not fully advocate for gender-neutral child rearing because of the prospect of encouraging homosexuality. Her research shows how deeply gender socialization is tied to social attitudes about sexuality.

Thinking Further: Peruse a local bookstore in the children's section and note which books are featured. What gender images are found within? Do any of them portray images that challenge existing gender norms?

Source: Based on Martin, Karin A. 2005. "William Wants a Doll: Can He Have One? Feminists, Child Care Advisors, and Gender-Neutral Child Rearing." *Gender & Society* 19 (August): 456–479.

Research reveals the pervasiveness of gender stereotyping as it is learned in early childhood play. The toys and play activities that parents select for children are a significant source of gender socialization. Studies of parents find that they gender stereotype toys for boys and girls of all ages, although toys for infants and toddlers are somewhat less stereotyped (Campenni 1999). Children also quickly pick this up. Given a choice between playing with a tool set or a dish set, preschool boys will pick the tool set, saying that their fathers think playing with the dishes would be "bad" (Raag 1999; Raag and Rackliff 1998). Clearly, parents' values influence the gender play of children. Fathers are more likely to be involved in physical play with boys than with girls; not surprisingly, then, boys are more likely to play physically than girls, whereas girls engage in more fantasy or "pretense" play (Lindsey et al. 1997). Fathers, especially, discourage actions (particularly in boys) that violate gender norms (Martin 2005).

Gender patterns are not fixed. Young girls now express a greater number of occupational aspirations than they did in the past—more so, in fact, than young boys. In general, gender beliefs are shaped by a number of changes that people experience over the life course, such as marriage and employment (Vespa 2009), but the foundation for one's gender beliefs is laid down during childhood. Even with change, however, the world children encounter is laden with gender-stereotypic expectations. Children themselves impart gender expectations to each other. For example, researchers observing children's activities have found that when girls disregard the ordinary gender "codes" and transgress into other activities, boys try to regulate girls' transgressions (McGuffey and Rich 1999). Young people are also bombarded with gendered images from books, video games, television, and, increasingly, computer networks. Again, you can see this for yourself by looking at Facebook pages. Compare the ads sent to men and women on Facebook and chances are that you are going to see highly gendered images directed at you based on the simple fact of your gender identification!

Even with a greater awareness in society of gender stereotypes and with publishers and advertisers recognizing the influence they have on young children, studies of children's literature show that males are still overwhelmingly shown as aggressive, argumentative, and competitive. This is happening even though publishers have published guidelines for nonsexist portrayals (Evans and Davies 2000). Female characters are more likely to be depicted using household objects, whereas male characters use nondomestic objects (Crabb and Bielawski 1994). Girls and women are still depicted as less adventurous and more domestic than boys. Fathers are generally less visible in children's books. Books written by African Americans are more likely to show girls and women as less dependent and more competitive, but they also show them as more nurturing than do books written by White authors. And, while there have been times when African Americans have become more visible in children's books, they have actually become *less* visible in children's award-winning books in the beginning of the twenty-first century (Clark 2007; Clark et al. 1993).

In video games—one of the major outlets for children's play—traditional gender roles and violence are central themes. Using a sample of Nintendo and Sega Genesis games, researchers found that 41 percent of the games had no female characters at all, 28 percent portrayed women as sex objects, and 80 percent included aggression or violence as the strategy. Half of the games included violence directed at others; the other half depicted violence toward women (Dietz 1998). All told, these sources of socialization send powerful messages to young boys and girls. The numerous examples that can be found in children's play, literature, and other cultural systems demonstrate how gender is socially constructed.

Even among college students, studies find that women students have less free time than men do (because they have more obligations, such as family and work activities) and thus are less likely to play computer games. When they do, they play in smaller chunks of time (Winn and Heeter 2009). Game players will see highly stereotyped images of men and women. Women are usually minor characters, depicted in highly sexualized ways, are more often victims than heroines, and generally are casted in seemingly innocent roles. Men, on the other hand, are seen as aggressive, muscular, highly capable, and frequently carrying weapons (Dickerman et al. 2008; Dill and Thill 2007; Miller and Summers 2007; Burgess et al. 2007). Does it matter? Absolutely. Researchers find that men exposed to such games are much more likely to define women as sexually provocative and help-less. Young men are even more likely to say that game-playing reduces the time they spend studying and even sleeping (Ogletree and Drake 2007). In sum, although most people would say that these images in young people's play and game are just for fun, research finds that they have a significant effect on the gen-der values and identities that young women and men form.

Socialization and the Schools

Although we tend to think of the family as the primary source of social values and identity, peers, teachers, the media, and additional significant others are impor-tant agents of the socialization process. Schools, in particular, exercise much influ-ence on the creation of gendered attitudes and behavior, so much so that some researchers call learning gender the "hidden curriculum" in the schools.

Within schools, curriculum materials, teacher's expectations, educational tracking, and peer relations encourage girls and boys to learn gender-related skills and self-conceps. Teachers and older children display expectations that encourage children to behave and think in particular ways; moreover, these expectations are strongly influenced by gender. Teachers, for example, respond more often to boys in the classroom. Even when they do so in response to boys' misbehaving, they are calling more attention to the boys (Sadker and Sadker 1994). Differences between boys and girls become exaggerated through practices that divide them into two distinct human groups (Thorne 1993). For example, children are often seated in separate gender groups or sorted into play groups based on gender; these practices heighten gender differences, making them even more significant in the children's interactions. Boys tend to be the center of attention in school, even when they are getting attention for disruptive behav-ior; girls are, in general, less visible and more typically praised for passive and acquiescent behavior (Sadker and Sadker 1994; American Association of University Women 1998).

These gender-typical behaviors have consequences for what children learn in school. Although boys and girls enter schools with roughly equal abilities, and although overall gender differences in such important areas as math and science are no longer pronounced, girls report liking these subjects less than boys do and they express little confidence in their math and science abilities. Those who report liking math and science have higher self-esteem and have higher career aspira-tions than other girls. Moreover, gender expectations influence other course-taking patterns, so that girls are far more likely than boys to take courses in social sciences, foreign languages, and the arts and humanities—suggesting how pat-terns of thinking become arrayed along gender lines (American Association of University Women 1998; Mead 2006; Phillips 1998). These patterns also have pro-found effects on the extent of gender segregation in the labor market as young men and women become adults.

Families and schools are not the only sources of gender socialization. One of the reasons that gender is so extensive in its influence on our lives is that it is so pervasive throughout all social institutions. Gender expectations are also visible at work, in voluntary organizations, in health care organizations, and in athletics. Religion, as you will see in Chapter 8, also has a significant effect on our concepts of who we are and our consciousness of gender. Families and schools are primary sources for some of the earliest influences of gender socialization, but the process of learning and enacting gender goes on throughout people's lifetimes.

Adult Socialization and the Aging Process

As we encounter new experiences throughout our lives, we learn the role expectations associated with our new statuses. Although our gender identities are established relatively early in life, changes in our status in society—for example, graduation, marriage, or a new job—bring new expectations for our behavior and beliefs.

Aging is perhaps the one thing about our lives that is inevitable; yet, as a social experience, it has different consequences for men and women. Cross-cultural evidence shows that aging is less stressful for women in societies where there is a strong tie to family and kin, not just to a husband; where there are extended, not nuclear, family systems; where there is a positive role for mothers-in-law (rather than the degrading status attached to it in our society); and where there are strong mother–child relationships throughout life. Even within our own society, racial and ethnic groups attach more value to older persons, thereby easing the transition to later life. Although the elderly in African American and Latino communities experience even greater difficulties with poverty and health than do the White elderly, their valued role in the extended family seems to alleviate some of the stress associated with growing old (Atchley 2000).

Gender differences in the social process of aging can be attributed in large part to the emphasis on youth found in this culture and, in particular, to the association of youth and sexuality in women. Cultural stereotypes portray older men as distinguished, older women as less desirable. As a woman ages, unlike a man, she will generally experience a loss of prestige; men gain prestige as they become more established in their careers.

The effects of aging for women and men are, however, strongly influenced by factors such as one's class, race, and other social factors. The cumulated inequities that women experience because of gender, race, and class continue into their older years—both in the social and economic value placed on them. And, as we will see further in Chapter 7 on health, these inequities have consequences for the physical and mental health that different groups experience. Research consistently demonstrates that poor women are less likely to receive good-quality health care. In fact, financial resources are one of the best predictors of health for both women and men. Being in a subordinated race, class, or gender group makes some groups more vulnerable to problems of physical and mental health at all stages in the life course, but these can become more acute in old age.

For women, the caregiving responsibilities that mark younger years continue as they grow older. Even during so-called retirement, women most often do the unpaid labor associated with caring for others (Richardson 1999). Researchers have found that there can actually be increased differentiation in the gender roles of men and women in their older years because of women's ongoing caregiving responsibilities (Dentinger and Clarkberg 2002). And one's well-being as an older person depends a great deal on one's level of education and the resources one has—such as during retirement. Because they have generally had lower levels of earnings during their younger adult years, women typically have less retirement pension and receive less in Social Security than men do—even though women are also more likely to be dependent on Social Security and other forms of government assistance during retirement than are men (Moen et al. 2001; Warren et al. 2001; Morgan 2000; O'Rand and Henretta 1999; Gregoire et al. 2002).

Despite these problems for older women, aging also relaxes some of the social pressure experienced by younger people. How positively one experiences the aging process depends to a large extent on the economic and cultural resources one has available, as well as the social supports received from family and friends. One study of retired African American professional women has documented, for example, the satisfaction that these women experience from their achievements, especially in regard to the social supports they both create and rely on over a lifetime of confronting racism (Slevin and Wingrove 1998).

There is little doubt that women experience significant disadvantage during the aging process (Calasanti and Slevin 2001). At the same time, however, the capacities and strengths that women acquire over their lifetimes also give them certain advantages as they grow old. Older women report higher levels of emotional support than do older men, and they tend to have more extensive social contacts and friendships. In general, the fact that women work throughout their lives to nurture social and emotional networks helps them maintain this connection in their older years, whereas men may experience greater social isolation. Better social support also has a known positive effect on people's ability to withstand stressful life events; thus, this learned ability among women helps them face the difficult problems of death, loss, and, perhaps, poor health in their elder years (Gibson 1996; Stoller and Gibson 2000).

THEORETICAL PERSPECTIVES ON THE FORMATION OF GENDER

Social scientists use different theoretical perspectives to explain gender socialization and the formation of gender. Each carries different assumptions, but all contribute to our understanding of the social construction of gender identity.

Identification Theory

According to **identification theory,** children learn gender-appropriate behaviors by identifying with their same-sex parent. This explanation is based on a Freudian psychoanalytic perspective that assumes that children unconsciously model their identities on the behavior of their parents. Identification theory posits that children learn behaviors, feelings, and attitudes unconsciously; through unconscious learning, children develop motivational systems. The child's identification with the same-sex parent, coupled with the powerful emotion associated with the parent–child relationship, results in an unconscious psychosexual bond that shapes the child's sex-role identity.

Empirical evidence to support the perspective of identification theory is, at best, shaky. Because the focus of this theory is on unconscious states of mind, it is impossible to measure directly the internal motivation of the child. Instead, researchers study motives indirectly by examining characteristics of the parents and associating those characteristics with behaviors and attitudes of the child. Such associations do not show a causal relationship between the parents' characteristics and the personality tendencies of their child. Because there is no direct way to observe the process of identification, this theory remains largely speculative; moreover, evidence that children are oriented to same-sex models is inconclusive, casting further doubt on the validity of identification theory.

Chodorow's (1978) theory of gender identity is related to the perspective of identification theory. Chodorow argues that modern nuclear families are characterized by an "asymmetrical structure of parenting," meaning that parenting is characterized by a division of labor in which women "mother" and men do not and in which women's work is devalued. This creates a dynamic of identification in which only girls adopt the personality characteristics associated with mothering. In Chodorow's theory, called **object relations theory,** as boys and girls develop their own identities, they must become psychologically separate from their parents. Boys, who gender-identify with their fathers, form personalities that are more detached from others because family structures in this society are based largely on the father's absence. Girls, who gender-identify with their mothers, become less detached because the mother's role in the family is one of close attachment to others. Girls' personalities, then, are more focused on attachment behaviors and on orientation to others. Boys, on the other hand, have personalities characterized by repression of their emotional needs and their commitments to others. Chodorow's work maintains some of the orientation of identification theory in its emphasis on unconscious psychic processes. It is distinguished, though, from traditional psychoanalytic theory by its placing of gender identity clearly in the context of the division of labor by gender in work and in the family.

Because the family form Chodorow analyzes is not universal, critics have questioned whether it holds only for White, middle-class nuclear families. Would this theory, for example, hold in families marked by different cultural traditions and a different family structure? This has been examined in the context of Chicano families (Segura and Pierce 1993). Chicano families are characterized by *familism*—a concept describing the generally large size of Chicano families, the existence of multigenerational households, the value placed on family unity, and the high level of interaction between family and kin (Baca Zinn and Eitzen 2010). Segura and Pierce found that Chodorow's analysis is useful in describing the experiences of Chicana mothers and their daughters. Chicana mothers' identities tend to revolve around family and home, and they tend to identify more with their daughters than with their sons; however, Chicanas do not practice exclusive mothering. Mothering figures include other women, such as grandmothers, aunts, or godmothers, just as African American communities often involve the extensive engagement of "othermothers" (Collins 1990) in the care of children and kin. As a result, young Chicanas identify not only with the mother but also with other women in the family system. Considering the cultural representation of women within Chicano culture as sacred and self-sacrificing, Segura and Pierce conclude that Chodorow's point about gender identification and attachment is particularly salient for Chicanas.

Chodorow's analysis of families sees them in relationship to particular cultural ideals and social forms. The importance of her work lies in the connection it makes between gender identity and family structure. Her theory also suggests that transformation in family structures is a necessary prerequisite toward creating more gender-balanced personalities.

Social Learning Theory

A second theoretical perspective is **social learning theory.** Whereas identification theory rests on the idea of unconscious learning, social learning theory emphasizes the significance of the environment in explaining gender socialization. Social learning theory is a behaviorist orientation, meaning that it sees social behavior as explained in terms of human responses to the environment. According to behaviorists, appropriate social responses are positively rewarded, whereas inappropriate responses are punished. Social learning, then, occurs through an ongoing process of reinforcement from other people. Like identification theorists, many social learning theorists believe that children model themselves on the behaviors and attitudes of same-sex parents. From a social learning perspective, behavior is not fixed according to early established patterns; rather, behavior and attitudes change as the situations and expectations in the environment change. Learning gender roles, although very significant in childhood, continues throughout life. As a consequence, one's gender identity is not fixed or permanent except when the social environment continues to reinforce it.

Again, similar to identification theory, social learning theory rests on the assumption that children model their behavior according to the roles of same-sex significant others, but social learning theorists point out that parents are not the only significant role models. A wide array of images and expectations in the culture serve as reinforcement for gender identity. Empirical evidence to support social learning theory comes from the vast amount of research on variations in parental expectations for children of different sexes, stereotypic responses from teachers and peers, and the influence of institutional practices that reinforce gender stereotypes. One implication of social learning theory is the view expressed by some feminists that women need women as role models in positions of leadership and authority to compensate for the learned sense of self that they acquire through traditional socialization practices.

FOCUS ON RESEARCH

College Majors and the Value of Gender

You may not think of your college major as a reflection of your gender identity, but the choices people make frequently reflect how gender is constructed in society. Moreover, the value associated with different social roles is strongly related to gender—with those roles associated with women often the more devalued roles in society.

Take college majors. Although you may not consciously think about gender when selecting a major, gender is nonetheless a likely factor in this decision. And, we see the outcome of this gendered decision by looking at the gender composition of different college majors.

Prior to the 1970s, the vast majority of college women majored in either nursing or education. Since the 1970s, women have increased their representation in various fields, but college majors remain highly segregated by gender.

Sociologists Paula England and Su Li examined this pattern by studying trends in women's and men's choices of major over a 30-year period (from 1971 to 2002). They used data published annually by the National Center for Education Statistics—data that report the number of women and men receiving bachelor's degrees and in what fields of study. England and Li found that there was a marked decline in the segregation of women and men in different majors in the first decade they studied (1971 to 1981), as women moved into fields such as business, the sciences, and the social sciences. However, this decline slowed in the later years that they investigated.

England and Li asked the further question of what influences these patterns in college majors by gender. Keep in mind that for fields to be gender balanced, not only do women have to move into fields typically occupied by men, but men must also move into fields predominantly occupied by women. It is here where England and Li's results are most interesting.

Through clever ways of analyzing these national data, England and Li found that not only have women's choices to move into nontraditional majors slowed, but as majors "feminized" (that is, as more women entered them), men avoided those majors. The limited extent to which desegregation of college majors has occurred is therefore the result of women making new choices, but desegregation is stalled by the choices men are making.

England and Li interpret these results as reflecting the cultural devaluation of fields associated with women. Until social roles associated with women are as valued as those associated with men, gender inequality in various realms of life, including college majors, is likely to continue.

Source: Based on England, Paula, and Su Li. 2006. "Desegregation Stalled: The Changing Composition of College Majors, 1971–2002." *Gender & Society* 20 (October): 657–677.

Cognitive-Developmental Theory

The third theoretical framework used to explain gender-role learning is **cognitive-developmental theory**. This theory is based largely on the work of Swiss psychologist Jean Piaget and, more recently, psychologist Lawrence Kohlberg (1966). Piaget suggested that children create schemata—mental categories that emerge through interactions with the social world. These schemata, in turn, are used in the child's subsequent encounters with his or her environment; thus, the child accommodates and assimilates new information into this existing stock of knowledge. According to Piaget, all children experience distinct stages of cognitive development, thus the developmental process is marked by alternate states of equilibrium and disequilibrium. In other words, as the developing child discovers new information or experiences in the world, he or she must adjust previously existing schemata to fit these new observations. At various points in cognitive development, the child reaches equilibrium because the child's reasoning ability is limited. Most importantly, cognitive-developmental theory emphasizes that the process of social development is one in which the child interacts with the social world through the mediation and active involvement of his or her cognitive abilities.

Kohlberg uses Piaget's perspective to explain the emergence of children's gender identities. According to Kohlberg, children discover early that people are divided into two sexes. They come to know their own sex, and they categorize others as either male or female. As their own gender identity stabilizes, they also begin to categorize behaviors and objects in the social world as appropriate for one sex or the other. At this point, gender has become an organizing scheme for the developing child, and the child attributes value to the traits and attitudes associated with his or her own sex. Children also begin to believe that gender is an unchanging category. As a result, they model their own behavior on the behaviors of those of the same sex, and they develop a strong emotional attachment to the same-sex parent.

Symbolic Interaction and "Doing Gender"

The previous three theoretical perspectives have been developed primarily by psychologists. Both the cognitive-developmental perspective and social learning theory are related to a perspective in sociology called *symbolic interaction*. According to **symbolic interaction theory,** people act toward things (including objects, abstract ideas, and other people) based on the meaning those things have for them. That meaning evolves from culture. From this perspective, the socialization process develops as people (initially, young children) take on the roles of others around them. In this sense, the concept of *role models,* as in social learning theory, is an important one. Critical to the symbolic interactionist perspective, however, is the idea that people reflect on how others see them and through this reflection form their self-concepts. From this point of view, the self is established as one becomes an object to oneself—something on which people reflect. Symbolic interaction also emphasizes the ability of humans to form and understand symbols; it is through symbolic interpretation that consciousness and, therefore, the self are formed.

Evolving from symbolic interaction is a new way of conceptualizing how gender is formed. This is called the **"doing gender"** perspective. This perspective sees gender as an accomplished activity—accomplished through the interactions one has with others (West and Zimmerman 1987; West and Fenstermaker 1995; Jurik and Siemsen 2009). Stated another way, this perspective analyzes gender not as something essential to men and women nor fixed in biological status or social roles. Instead, it sees people as constantly re-creating gender meanings and gendered social structures whenever they act in gender-typical ways. From this point of view, gender is routinely reproduced in everyday interaction. It is not an individual trait; rather, it is created through social interaction.

From the perspective of "doing gender," whenever someone interacts with another in a way that displays a particular configuration of gender, gender is "done." This perspective conceptualizes social structure as existing only insofar as actors continue to act in ways that reproduce gender relations. Gender is thus constituted through routine social interaction, as individuals (consciously and unconsciously) engage in behaviors identified with specific gender meanings. The woman who smiles at a man (even though she may not like him), the man who opens doors routinely for women (regardless of who is more conveniently able to do so), the woman who dresses in feminine clothes, or the man who takes the lead in dancing are all "doing gender." Harmless though their behavior may seem, it contributes to the social reproduction of gender relations in society.

"Doing gender" emphasizes the fluid character of gender identity. Rather than seeing gender as a fixed or learned set of roles, this framework interprets gender as an ongoing and fluctuating series of behaviors that is created through social interaction. A good way to illustrate this is the case of Billy Tipton, a famous jazz musician who died in 1989 at age 74. Tipton married five times and had three adopted sons. Not until the day he died did many learn that the man whom everyone thought was such a fabulous musician and loving husband and father was really a woman! Few knew of how he had "done gender." Tipton began his identity as a woman in the 1930s, when he was relatively young—a time when an unwritten code in the jazz world kept women from being hired. One cannot help but marvel at the effort it took to maintain this social identity and to imagine how his life would have been different, including what his career would have been, had it been known that "he" was a woman (D. Smith 1998; Middlebrook 1998).

This is a highly unusual example of doing gender, but understanding gender as an accomplished act helps one see how people create the gender categories that constitute being a man and being a woman. Whether putting on makeup (Dellinger and Williams 1997), asserting oneself in a group, or exercising power in an organization, one may be doing gender in a way that continually re-creates, but also can change, the social definition of gender. The doing gender perspective also suggests that people enact gender to varying degrees and that socialization into gender roles is not just a passive process whereby people simply internalize others' expectations (Messner 2000).

As an example, think about the experience of being a tomboy. We have already seen that sanctions against tomboys steer young girls into behaviors judged appropriate for their gender. But research on tomboys also shows that young girls actively resist conforming to gender-appropriate roles. Thus, girls who are tomboys are not just trying to "be boys," but are actively constructing a concept of themselves as embodying traits of both genders (Carr 1999).

The doing gender perspective sees people as also engaged in **gender displays**—that is, demonstrations of behavior that communicate gender identities. Gender displays may be subtle, perhaps hardly conscious, but they may also be hypermasculine or hyperfeminine. *Hypermasculinity,* for example, can be defined as gender displays that strongly portray one's presentation of self as aggressive, domineering, and controlling. Hypermasculinity is also associated with militaristic aggression and some forms of sport—showing as well how "doing gender" is promoted by institutional structures.

Comparing Theoretical Perspectives

There are important differences between these four perspectives. Identification theorists assume that imitation of same-sex persons is motivated by fear—the fear of separation from a psychosexual love object. Cognitive-developmental theorists assume a more positive motivational basis for learning—namely, mastery. In the cognitive-developmental framework, children are actively involved in the construction of the social world. In contrast, both social learning and identification theories assume a somewhat more passive view of the child's development.

Both the social learning and cognitive-developmental perspectives emphasize the role of culture in shaping gender identity. Social learning theorists have a more deterministic view, however, in that they see culture as a model and reinforcer for what the child becomes. In the cognitive-developmental framework, the child does more than simply react to the culture. He or she searches for patterns in the culture and actively seeks to structure and organize the concepts of the world that the culture provides.

The perspective of doing gender takes a completely interactionist point of view—that is, seeing gender as real only insofar as people continue to do it. This perspective has been criticized for understating the significance of institutional arrangements in shaping gender relations. It tends to make power differences between men and women less visible and understates the significant economic and political advantages that existing social arrangements give to men. Like the other perspectives, however, it helps us see how gender is constantly reproduced through the behaviors of women and men. Each of these theories shows us how central gender is to the formation of our gender identity. From the day we are born to the day we die, social expectations about our gender confront us in the everyday world. These external social expectations become internalized in our self-concepts, and they become identities through which we experience the social world.

Limitations of the Socialization Perspective

Questions about gender identity and socialization as an origin for gender differences are more than academic matters. Whether women hold the status they do because they choose their positions or whether there are structural obstacles to their well-being lies at the heart of many public policy discussions about the status of women. Of course, socialization and structure are highly interrelated; as this chapter has shown, gender socialization originates in gendered institutions. If men and women become different from each other as the result of socialization and social structures, should social policies treat them differently or the same? This question is the focus of many current debates, affirmative action being one example. The framework of U.S. law, based on the principle of equality, theoretically means that all groups should be treated the same. If men and women are different as the result of their social experiences, should we expect that treating women like men will result in fairness and justice for them? If we develop gender-blind policies, will they assist only women who make choices as men would make them? In a world where policy values sameness, not difference, how do we recognize, value, and support the lives of women and men, regardless of the gender roles they take on? Should women have to become like men to be accorded the privileges men hold?

These questions are well illustrated by the desegregation of two formerly all-male military academics: Virginia Military Institute (VMI) and The Citadel. The U.S. Supreme Court ruled in 1996 that women could not be excluded from state-supported military academies such as The Citadel and VMI. This case followed the public spectacle when Shannon Faulkner had earlier fought for two and a half years to gain admission to The Citadel. Once admitted, she was subjected to extreme humiliation, both by the other cadets and by instructors. After this debacle, which ultimately caused her to leave, two other women left The Citadel after a serious hazing incident in which they were sprinkled with nail polish remover and their clothes set on fire. In the court case that ultimately gave women the constitutional right to attend such academies, attorneys defending VMI argued that women were "not capable of ferocity, are more emotional, and cannot take stress." This was countered by the expert testimony of sociologist Michael Kimmel who argued that the exclusion of women from military academies was based on gender stereotypes that supported their culture of masculinity (Kimmel 2000).

At issue in this case was whether women were so different from men that they could not succeed in rigorous military training or whether there were structural obstacles to their success. In its ruling, the Supreme Court clearly indicated that excluding women was a violation of the equal protection clause of the Fourteenth Amendment to the U.S. Constitution. Although the number of women who might choose to attend a military academy may now be small, such cases make us think about how women's capabilities are shaped by the opportunities they have.

This case also shows that matters of gender socialization have serious implications for social policy. Socialization does not occur in a vacuum. It is a process by which human beings adapt to their environment, and in this society that environment is one structured on gender inequality. Socialization does not explain the origins of inequality by itself, but it is a very effective way of explaining how that inequality is reproduced. If we limit ourselves, however, to thinking of gender differences as only a matter of learned choice, we overlook the patterns of institutionalized gender inequity that pervade society. Stated differently, the socialization process shows how individuals become gendered persons, but it does not explain the social-structural origins of gender inequality.

Another caution about seeing gender solely in terms of socialization is that people are not mere receptacles for social life; rather, they actively participate in and create social change. Role-centered perspectives may exaggerate the extent to which we become socialized, leading to an oversocialized view of human life. Focusing on gender roles also tends to exaggerate the differences between the sexes because, by definition, its emphasis tends to be on differences, not similarities. In gender-role research, gender differences typically are built into research designs. The items on questionnaires, for example, or the factors selected for manipulation in experimental studies necessarily reflect the differences that a researcher wants to test. The end result may be that the research literature on gender roles exaggerates and polarizes masculine and feminine differences.

Not all girls and boys grow up in the gender-stereotyped way that the research literature sometimes suggests; nevertheless, research on childhood learning underscores the point that gender socialization is situated within social institutions that tend to value masculine, not feminine, traits. Were values associated with women— such as flexibility, orientation toward others, and cooperation—to be incorporated into dominant social institutions, then we might well produce more gender-balanced boys and girls. As it is, the process of socialization throughout life separates men and women and creates gender differences among children and adults.

■ Chapter Summary and Themes

Although biological causes of gender differences are commonly believed, culture is more significant in shaping who we become as women and men.

Biology sets very broad limits for human behavior and is a poor predictor of what people become. Cases of those born as biologically intersexed can be used to show the significance of social factors in shaping gender identity. Carefully observing gender differences can also reveal that there are usually greater differences among people within gender categories than across such categories, even though men and women are culturally described as "opposite sexes."

Gender is a social construction, meaning that gender is created through social learning and the structure of social institutions.

Many social scientists distinguish the concepts of sex and gender, *sex* being used to refer to one's biological identity as male/female and *gender* being used to refer to the social and cultural patterns associated with being men and women. Social institutions also guide how gender is constructed in society, with significant variation across diverse cultures.

Gender is embedded in social institutions; social institutions can also take on the characteristics associated with gender.

Gender is not just an individual attribute, but is deeply embedded in social structures. Thus, while gender is a social role—in the sense that people enact the social expectations passed on to them—gender is also a social structure— that is, part of the whole structure of society, not just located "within" individuals. Put differently, gender is in society and a gendered society is within us.

The process of gender socialization shapes various aspects of our lives, including gender identity, attitudes, and self-concepts.

Gender is a learned phenomenon, acquired through diverse influences of family, peers, schools, the media, and other socialization agents. Studies of childhood socialization reveal how early gender expectations are passed on to young children. The influences of socialization persist, however, over the life course, resulting in different experiences for women and men as adults, including into one's older years.

Gender does not exist in isolation from other social factors; as a result, one's identity is shaped by the interactive influence of race and gender, along with other social factors.

Gender identity is manifested differently depending on one's race, ethnicity, and other factors. Even when recognizing the influence of gender as a social category, one must be careful not to overly generalize from the experience of any one group.

Different theoretical perspectives on the social construction of gender emphasize different dimensions to this process.

Theories can be used to understand the social processes by which people "become gendered." Some theoretical perspectives emphasize psychodynamic processes, such as same-sex identification. Others, such as social learning theory, emphasize environmental influences. The perspective of "doing gender" interprets gender as activity that is accomplished through everyday interaction. All contribute unique ways of viewing how gender is created and maintained in society.

■ Key Terms

biological determinism	gender roles	sexually dimorphic traits
biological reductionism	gendered institution	social construction of gender
cognitive-developmental theory	homophobia	social institutions
culture	identification theory	social learning theory
"doing gender"	intersexed persons	social roles
gender	object relations theory	socialization
gender display	sex	symbolic interaction theory
gender identity	sex chromosomes	transgender

■ Discussion Questions/Projects for Thought

1. Describe the playing you remember from your childhood. Who did you play with? What did these games communicate about gender? How have they affected your current interests, skills, and aspirations? It would be interesting to discuss this question in mixed-gender groups.

2. Identify some of the research studies described in this chapter, and develop some experimental observations that let you replicate these studies. You could do this in the same setting as the original research or introduce new conditions or research subjects that let you develop further questions raised by the subject. For example, take a walk some place where you are likely to see men and women with baby strollers. Who pushes the stroller when the baby is in it and when the stroller is empty? Observe places where you are likely to see toddlers and their mothers and/or fathers. Is there a difference in whether boy toddlers and girl toddlers are allowed to walk on their own? How much distance do the parents let each girl and boy roam before going to get them? Does this vary depending on the sex of the parent?

3. Interview a racially diverse group of men and women, asking them to define what womanhood and manhood means to them. What do their answers tell you about the interplay of race and gender in the construction of people's identities?

CHAPTER

3

Gender, Culture, and the Media

It is said beauty is in the eyes of the beholder. A team of scientists has even concluded that beauty can be scientifically determined—or so the headlines promise. According to their claims, women who have been wondering whether they are sexually attractive can now determine how they measure up against a scientific standard that purports to be the perfect measurement for a woman's body: weight in pounds, divided by 2.205 (to convert to kilograms), multiplied by height in inches times 0.0254 (to get meters), then that number times itself and divided into the weight.

Does this sound like a hoax? Not if you think that a sound source of information is one of the world's leading medical journals, *Lancet*. In 1998, a group of scientists from England conducted a study in which they asked a group of 40 male undergraduates to observe pictures from magazines such as *Playboy* and rate the sexiness of 50 naked women of various shapes and sizes, but without faces. The results—that the men's judgments matched the body-mass index described above—were published in *Lancet* and reported throughout the world (Tovée et al. 1997, 1998; Browne 1998).

Cultural images of women's beauty—and implicit ratings of their bodies—are rampant throughout the culture. One only has to glance at a magazine stand or skim through advertisements to see that we are bombarded with ideals for women's appearance—ideals that rarely match what real women actually look like. Perhaps you think that such images do not really affect you. But advertisers know you are wrong—why else would they spend the vast sums of money to produce such images if they had no effect? Surveys find that Americans spend about 68 hours per week exposed to various forms of media, including television, radio, film, music, the Internet, newspapers, books, and magazines (U.S. Census Bureau 2009).

There is a strong "celebrity culture" that pervades national life and shapes the ideals that women and men develop, especially with regard to gender.

Many of the images you see admonish women to be afraid—afraid of aging, afraid of food, afraid of being alone, afraid of having too small a bust or too big a bust. Advertisers promise that with the right products, a woman can be beguiling and seductive, *so long as she changes how she looks*. Smooth your skin, wear the right scent, change your hair color, buy the right clothes, color your lips, and, above all, be thin! Why? To attract men. And, if the ads don't work, the articles tell you month after month how to please men: "Touch him this way," "The one word he's dying to hear during sex," "How to make scent your secret weapon" (taken from an article on so-called "man-entrancing elixirs" at the workplace—as if all women needed at work was the sexual attention of men!).

These are powerful messages, and although you might think no one takes them seriously, consider the impact that images of thinness have on women's eating disorders—a phenomenon especially common among younger women who literally starve themselves trying to attain the cultural ideal of thinness. These messages are so pervasive that a recent report has concluded that "throughout U.S. culture, and particularly in mainstream media, women and girls are depicted in a sexualizing manner. These representations can be seen in virtually every medium" (American Psychological Association 2007).

Advertisements are only one source for the ideas generated about women. The mass media and popular culture in various forms all contribute to the social construction of gender. Popular music, advice columns, television shows, and other cultural materials all carry explicit and implicit suggestions about gender. Cultural icons such as "Barbie" and "Ken" teach girls and boys from a young age about gender ideals. Although children may play with such dolls as a fantasy world, they nonetheless communicate strong messages about our gender identities and our relationships.

Consider this: Each of us sees thousands of advertisements per day. Advertisements not only sell the products we use but they also convey images of how we are to define ourselves, our relationships, and our needs. If men were shown in advertisements in the way women are routinely shown, people would probably find it laughable. How often are women displayed in ads in their underwear or lying on beds? Do you see men in such poses? Yes, the use of men as sex objects in advertisements has increased, but not nearly as often as for women. The demeanor of women in advertising—in the background, on the ground, or looking dreamily into space—makes them appear subordinate and available to men.

Advertisements also portray stereotyped racial images of men and women. Just walk through your local grocery store and look at products carefully. What do you see? Indian chiefs on corn meal, Native American princesses on butter, Black mammies on pancake mix, Mexican banditos on salsa, and "hot" Latinas on margarita mix. Even the popular website ratemyprofessors.com uses an icon of a chile pepper to designate faculty that students think of as "sexy"—an implicit use of a racialized icon to designate sexual attractiveness.

These images merge racial and gender stereotypes, as if Latin men are all rogues, African American women are docile and servile, and Native American women are beguiling. Whites do not escape such stereotyping either. Stereotypes about blonde women as being sexy, but dumb, are common in the culture, often in the form of jokes.

You can also observe the pervasiveness of gender images in popular culture by analyzing the content of films, magazines, videos, or music lyrics. Indeed, every object of popular culture seems to deeply embed gendered images. (See the following "Focus on Research" box on gender and the media.) These depictions cannot be taken lightly; research on college students shows that exposure to sexualized imagery of women has an effect on students' attitudes about the adversarial character of sexual relationships and on students' willingness to accept interpersonal violence and to believe in myths about rape (Kalof 1999).

Magazine covers also focus on how women should make themselves appealing to men. Even buying a Father's Day card can be a challenge should your father not like to golf or fish. Most Father's Day cards narrowly cast fathers into those two leisure roles. You might even think of how gender images are apparent in things people name: their pets, their e-mail addresses, or their nicknames.

The ideas and images presented to us, whether through advertisements, cyberspace, or the products we choose, exert a powerful influence over our lives

FOCUS ON RESEARCH

Gender in the Media

Numerous studies have reported how gender is depicted in the media. Although you cannot judge the effect of such images simply by observing them, research finds them to be so pervasive that they are bound to have profound effects. Indeed, much research links the presence of such images to issues such as weakened self-esteem, poor physical and mental health, academic achievement, and body dissatisfaction (American Psychological Association 2007). Although it is impossible to summarize the many research articles that analyze the content of the media, here are some of the current observations:

- On prime-time television, 23 percent of all sexual behaviors involved leering, ogling, staring, or catcalling at female characters; most of these comments were made by men (Lampman et al. 2002).
- Eighty-four percent of prime-time television shows involve at least one incident of sexual harassment, with an average of 3.4 incidents per program (Grauerholz and King 1997).
- Sexually objectified images of women are a large proportion of the content of music videos; a recent study of the most popular

videos on Black Entertainment Television found that 84 percent of the music videos placed women in sexually provocative positions, compared to 35 percent of the male characters in these videos (Ward and Rivadeneyra 2002).
- Between 1990 and 2004, of the 4,000 characters in G-rated films, 75 percent of all characters were men; 83 percent of the narrators were men, and 72 percent of speaking characters were men; there was no change over this time period (Kelly and Smith 2006).
- Forty-six percent of teen-rated computer video games show female characters in sexual themes, including pronounced cleavage, large breasts, or provocative clothing; such depictions were far less common for male characters (Haninger and Thompson 2004).
- Sexualized self-presentations by women on Internet network sites such as MySpace and Facebook are common (Kornblum 2005).
- The distinction between women and girls is blurred in advertising, with young girls (often very young girls) being made up to look like adults and adult women being portrayed as little girls (Cook and Kaiser 2004; Merskin 2004).

and greatly influence how we think about gender. Popular culture conveys an impression about the proper roles of women and men, their sexual and gender identities, and their self-concepts. The ideas we hold about women and men, whether overtly sexist or more subtle in their expression, create social definitions that we use to understand ourselves and the society in which we live. The ideas that people have of one another guide their behavior, even though there is little correlation between what people believe and say and what they actually do. What is known or believed about women and gender relations, even when it is based on distortions of social realities, influence our mental experiences. Unless challenged, these experiences reproduce the social structure of gender in society.

Ideas, although based in the interpretive realm of thought, direct our behavior and constrain how we see each other and how others see us. Ideas also affect how society works, who gets rewarded, and how things should and should not be. For example, if we believe that women's proper place is in the home, we are not likely to object to the sexist practices of employer discrimination. If we believe that women are as capable as men, however, we are likely to support policies and changes that would make more opportunities available to them.

This chapter studies how, where, and why gender is constructed through culture. Culture, including language, the media, and the messages and narratives that we experience in everyday life, exert a powerful influence on how we define gender—and how we re-create gender through our own presentation of cultural realities. Let's begin with an examination of language.

GENDER AND LANGUAGE

One of the first ways we see the influence of culture in the construction of gender is in how we speak. As the system by which we generally communicate with each other, language both reflects and reinforces the cultural systems in which it is used. Note that this is a two-way process: Language reflects the values of the dominant culture and therefore is one way that stereotypes are communicated and reproduced. But language can also produce changes in society, because by changing how we speak, we can communicate new meaning systems to others.

Although it may seem trivial to insist on nonsexist language (e.g., calling women *women* instead of *girls*), changes in what we say can influence how we think. Language can also be used to break social stereotypes. For example, it is now commonplace to address women as *Ms.*, but not that many years ago all women were referred to as either *Miss* or *Mrs.*—as if the single-most important feature of a woman's identity were her marital status. The practice of women's changing to their husbands' names when married also reflects the old idea that women are the property of men. Although women do not think about it that way today, the unquestioning act of changing one's name does reflect the idea that a woman's identity is less important than a man's. To show this, can you think of people you know where the man changed his name when married? Similarly, a seemingly innocent practice such as using the word *guys* to refer to all people makes women invisible; research has found that when people hear the word *man* used, even in a generic way, they nonetheless visualize men (Hamilton 1988).

The fitness culture that has developed in recent years promotes good health, but at the same time, promotes a focus on the body that can develop in unhealthy ways.

These are not trivial issues. Language reflects the social value that is placed on different groups in society. Language also reflects the power dynamics that are found in society. Racial epithets provide a good example; the numerous negative terms that have been used to label racial–ethnic groups hold very negative connotations. Likewise, feminists have pointed out that terms such as *chicks, gals, foxes, hotties,* and *babes* demean women by associating them with animals, little girls, or lustful creatures.

However, language is contextual—that is, what something means varies depending on the situation in which it is expressed. Thus, women who are good friends might refer to each other as "girl" or "girlfriend" and this can be affirming, not demeaning. On the other hand, a man who refers to his secretary as his "girl," given the power differences in that relationship, is trivializing her status and reaffirming the power relationship that exists between them. Similarly, lesbian women may affectionately refer to each other as "dykes"—as a way of reclaiming a stigmatized status—but this approbation has a highly negative and hateful meaning when used by homophobic persons who use it to demean or insult. The important thing to notice here is that language is used in a context, and, when that context is marked by power differences between people or groups, the meaning of language reflects those power relationships.

The gendered nature of language is not only a matter of content but also of *how* people communicate. Much research has been done on this subject, and there is no simple way to summarize it, but one of the basic questions has been whether women and men use language in different ways and what this means in terms of power relationships between them (Cameron 1998). Studies have shown, for example, that despite the stereotype of women as talkative, in a variety of settings (including classrooms, meetings, and other social interactions), men take more than their "share" of talk time. In addition, men are more likely to interrupt women in conversation, whereas women are more likely to use hesitancy in speaking—perhaps deferring to others, speaking more softly, laughing, or just being silent in group discussion. Again, context matters, since scholars have also shown that, even though women talk less than men, men also use silence as a way to assert their power. Silence can control interaction by expressing little interest in the other or withholding information.

Someone who does not respond may dominate interaction by controlling topic development in conversation or refusing to recognize others' contributions (Anderson and Leaper 1998; Mast and Hall 2001; Crawford and MacLeod 1990; Tannen 1993). Studies of gender and language have generally focused on questions of differences between women and men, leading to debate about how significant such differences are. Popular stereotypes suggest that the differences are large and real, such as in the bestseller, *Men Are from Mars, Women Are from Venus* (Gray 1994)—an advice book for improving relationships, premised on the idea that women and men communicate differently. So popular is the idea that men and women are fundamentally different that this book has sold over 30 million copies and spawned a huge industry of related products, talk shows, workshops, and on-line advice about relationships.

The focus on differences between men and women, not just in studies of language but in studies of all forms of social behavior, has been so strong that at times it seems the only alternative way of thinking is to deny the significance of gender differences altogether (Crawford 1995). Certainly gender differences do exist, and they are reported throughout this book; but it is important to understand that gender is a changing social construct and one that reflects complex patterns of social behavior and social change. At the same time, even in recognizing differences between men and women as a whole, we should also be careful not to overgeneralize about women. On all matters of social behavior, language included, there is significant variation *within* gender and by race, class, ethnicity, as well as social context.

GENDER, POPULAR CULTURE, AND THE MEDIA

Language is but one dimension of what can broadly be referred to as **popular culture**—the beliefs, practices, and objects that are part of everyday traditions. Popular culture includes popular music, film, magazines, television, and some forms of the arts that are widely accessible to the public. Popular culture has an enormous influence on the cultural values of a society and is one of the dimensions of life that has been widely examined by feminists because of its significance in the social construction of gender. Take, for example, romance novels—a subject carefully studied by feminist scholars because of its influence on the fantasy lives of millions of women. Such novels portray women as needing men, although feminist critics also point out that women read such novels as an escape from the domestic demands of others (Radway 1984; Salmon and Symons 2003). At the same time, popular culture can provide for millions of women (and men) alternative images—such as in the growing popularity of feminist murder mysteries where independent, savvy, strong, and sometimes armed women work as private investigators, prosecutors, or sleuths of other kinds.

Images from popular culture reveal numerous contradictions with regard to gender. On the one hand, much of popular culture is deeply stereotyped by gender. A quick perusal of a greeting card rack will show you this. Women are ridiculed for aging (as are men, but in different ways), whereas cards presumably for men commonly promise them voluptuous, full-breasted women to make their day! Simultaneously, popular culture can be transformative, as exemplified by some contemporary performance art involving the portrayal of transgendered selves. As you begin to examine one of the most influential sites of popular culture—the media—you should keep in mind that culture is an ever-changing and dynamic process that is not an abstract thing, devoid of people's ability to interpret, resist, and change.

Analyzing the Media

What do you see in the media? Even a cursory look at advertising, television, film, or other media forms reveals gendered images of women and men that permeate everyday life. Those who systematically study the media look at what images are projected and how they influence people. To accurately assess what is depicted in the media, social scientists use careful methods of observation, most often what is called *content analysis*.

Content analysis is a research method whereby one systematically analyzes the actual content of documents, images, or other cultural artifacts. By counting and describing in detail particular images or textual parts within a particular media form, researchers can systematize their observations of the media's content. Of course, describing the content does not show how people respond, but it does give a report of what is there. Other research methods can then examine people's responses—both conscious and unintended—to media content.

When you examine the media carefully, you might be surprised at how pervasive gender-based images are. In television ads, for example, where are you more likely to see women: in service roles or professional roles? Men are less likely to be shown cooking, cleaning, shopping, or washing dishes. When men are shown in the context of family life, they are usually engaged in activities stereotypically associated with men—in cars or mowing the lawn. Moreover, men are usually seen with boys, not girls, and rarely with infants. And, although nurturing images of men are now more frequent in the media, in magazines, they most often appear in those read by women, not men (Vigorito and Curry 1998; Kaufman 1999).

Television, music videos, magazines, and film all convey powerful messages about gender. Even a cursory look at the covers of women's magazines shows a cultural obsession with gender, especially regarding women's appearance. Stand in the line at the grocery store and what do you see? Covers promising quick and easy diets—of course, right next to mouth-watering, rich desserts that women can cook. Next to these promises are admonitions to women to please men—if not through food, through sex. From *Cosmopolitan* to *Ladies' Home Journal*, magazines promise all kinds of sex tips intended for men's satisfaction. And young women's magazines similarly present limited possibilities to young girls. A study of *Seventeen* magazine, for example—one widely read by young women—finds that the overarching message about work to young women is that women work primarily to meet and assist more powerful men (Massoni 2004).

Media and the Body Culture

Throughout the media, gendered images of bodies tell both women and men that they should be a particular form, a look, even a size. Of course, few, if any, women and men actually attain the ideals promoted in the media, but a huge amount of effort (and money!) is spent both creating and pursuing media ideals. Whatever the media form, women are constantly told to cut body fat. Men, on the other hand, are encouraged to get bigger. Such presentations construct social definitions of gender that link masculinity with power, strength, and dominance, while women are "cut down to size." These presentations have become even more present in the media and popular culture over time, especially given a widespread cultural emphasis on fitness. Certainly, emphasizing fitness can be a good thing—promoting good health and well-being. But portrayals of what it means to be fit are deeply gendered. If you analyze the images shown in fitness magazines, as researchers have done, you will see that for women, fitness tends to mean toning, slimming down, and attracting men. For men, it means taking control, performing, and being powerful (Dworkin and Wachs 2009; Barriga et al. 2009).

These gendered admonishments about fitness have produced a culture wherein both women and men constantly scrutinize and survey their bodies. This phenomenon can be understood only in a cultural context where bodies—not our minds, beliefs, and values—become the main signal of who we are. It is little wonder, then, that so many young girls and women report being very dissatisfied with how they look—a fact that is linked to lower self-esteem, lowered academic performance, and depression—to say nothing of the money spent on various body products (American Psychological Association 2007).

Portrayals of Aging

Within such a culture, aging bodies are particularly reviled, especially the aging bodies of women. Studies find that older women are vastly underrepresented in the media, even compared to other nations. Older women tend to play incidental roles in television ads, appearing primarily in stereotypical roles. They are mostly shown in advertisements for food and medical products, rarely for products involving fun, travel, or even electronics. Older people are seldom portrayed as spokespersons or experts (Lee et al. 2006). Older women, in particular, are stereotyped in the media as perfect grandparents or happy "golden agers." Although these may seem like positive portrayals, they also minimize the actual experiences of women as they age (Hatch 2005). The prevalence of anti-aging ads also suggest that older women are worthwhile only if they continue to look young (Calasanti 2007).

What about men? The most prevalent images of men and aging in the media seem to focus on Viagra! Does this suggest that to age well, men must maintain sexual virility? Viagra ads tell men that they should remain sexually potent to be "real men" (Brubaker and Johnson 2008; Irvine 2006). Moreover, if you look at Viagra ads carefully, you will also see that successful aging for men includes being financially very well off.

All of these images portray rather narrow constructions of gender and aging. For women, the message is: If you have to age (an inevitable fact!), you should do all you can to maintain a youthful appearance. It is as if the ideal woman is still a child—young, unblemished, sexy, and fit. For men, the message is: Maintain your power, your dominance, and be always ready for sex.

MEDIA MATTERS

Where Are Older Women in Popular Films?

Although women generally live longer than men, men enjoy longer screen lives than women do. Culturally speaking, older men are also valued more than older women—a phenomenon that results from many factors, but certainly images produced in popular culture are important. How do popular films portray older women?

Martha Lauzen and David Dozier analyzed 88 of the 100 top-grossing films of 2002. They found women accounted for 28 percent and men for 72 percent of the 3,142 characters in the films analyzed. In comparing the age and gender characteristics of the actual U.S. population and the film population (age 13 years and older), Lauzen and Dozier found that men in their 30s and 40s were overrepresented in films. Men in their 30s made up 19 percent of the population. However, this age group comprised 29 percent of the characters in popular films. Similarly, men in their 40s made up 19 percent of the U.S. population but comprised 26 percent of the film population. Boys in their teens and men in their 20s and 50s were slightly underrepresented in popular films. Men age 60 and older were underrepresented: Only 8 percent of male characters were age 60 or older, although this group made up 18 percent of the U.S. population.

As expected, women in their 20s and 30s were overrepresented in the films analyzed. Women in their 20s made up 16 percent of the U.S. population but represented 23 percent of the film population. There was a 14-point difference between the U.S. population and the film population for women in their 30s (18 percent and 32 percent, respectively). Adolescent girls were slightly underrepresented, as well as women in their 50s and 60s. Interestingly, female characters in their 40s matched the U.S. population distribution. These findings indicate that female characters in film continue to be younger than their male counterparts.

Lauzen and Dozier's research also found that older men continue to have a "purpose" as they age: Male characters in their 40s, 50s, and 60s were more likely than same-aged female characters to play leadership roles on film. Similarly, male characters in their 30s, 40s, and 50s were more likely to have occupational power than were female characters. The implication of these portrayals is that men are perceived as serving a purpose throughout their lives, whereas women are perceived as less purposeful as they age.

Lauzen and Dozier's research illustrates how popular films perpetuate negative cultural views of gender and aging, thus contributing to the double standard in our culture for older women and older men.

Thinking Further: Replicate this study for the most current year, and see if you get the same results. (Try doing this using the 10 top-grossing films for last year; see www.ibd.com for this information). Or select the films from one of the categories for last year's Academy Awards and see if you get the same results by observing how gender and aging are depicted in these films.

Source: Lauzen, Martha M., and David M. Dozier. 2005. "Maintaining the Double Standard: Portrayals of Age and Gender in Popular Films." *Sex Roles* 52 (April): 437–446.

Presenting Women's Sports

One positive change in the media is the increased coverage of women's sports. How are women athletes depicted? Researchers have analyzed the representation of women athletes in *Sports Illustrated* and *Sports Illustrated for Women*, finding that women were presented as powerful, strong, fit, and "pro-woman." Indeed, feminist themes were often used in such portrayals, such as by asking, "What if women ruled?" in the ad copy. But, at the same time, the tendency was to show only the most attractive athletes, and the coverage of women athletes emphasized their nurturing character (Gordy 2002).

Researchers have also analyzed the cover photographs in media guides for the NCAA (National Collegiate Athletic Association), finding that women are less likely to be portrayed as active participants in sport and more likely to be shown in passive and traditionally feminine poses (Buysse and Embser-Herbert 2004). Even a casual perusal of the morning paper shows that women's sports are relegated to the back page, if they are covered at all.

Gender, Children, and the Media

Children's television may be one of the most stereotypical sources of gendered images. Considering the number of hours that children spend watching television, this means that such images are a powerful source of gender socialization. Ninety-eight percent of U.S. homes are equipped with at least one television, and these are turned on an average of five hours a day. By the time a child is 15 years old, she or he will have spent more hours watching television than attending school. Moreover, analysts estimate that in nearly half of U.S. households (42 percent) televisions are on most of the time; Black children are even more likely than White or Hispanic children to live in these "constant television households" (Gitlin 2001).

Does this matter in terms of what children learn about gender? Numerous studies find that children's attitudes about gender are influenced by the amount of television they watch. Children report that they want to be like certain television characters when they grow up. And, children who watch the most television are those who hold the most stereotypical, gender-typed values (Signorielli 1989). In television, children see more male characters than they do female characters. Although there is some change in the gender stereotypes that children see on television, they are still pervasive in this and other media forms. Children's programming is still more likely to show male characters in more active and individualistic activity and in occupational roles (Davis 2003; Powell and Abels 2002; Kelly and Smith 2006).

Violence in children's media is also associated with gender. Over one-third of children's commercials include acts of aggression. You might expect that this would be associated with commercials that include only boys, but aggression is found more often in commercials that include boys and girls. However, aggression is much more frequently associated with White boys than with children of color (Larson 2003). Other research also finds that boys become more desensitized than girls to violent content in the media (Klinger et al. 2001).

Diverse, but Controlling, Images

On various forms of diversity in society, the mass media and popular culture promote narrow definitions of who people are and what they can be. As we have seen, although aging is inevitable, women and, increasingly, men are warned to fight the signs of aging. Youth, not age, for women is defined as beautiful. For all groups, light skin is promoted as more beautiful than dark skin, regardless of race,

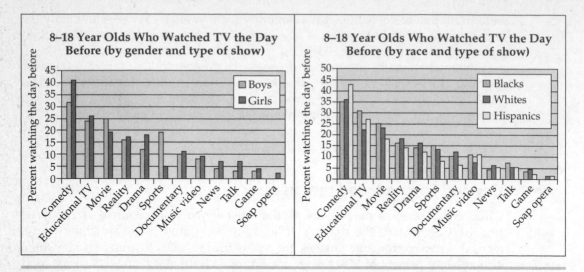

FIGURE 3.1 Media Use by Young People (by gender and by race)

Source: From "Generation M: Media in the Lives of 8–18-Year-Olds—Report" (#7251), The Henry J. Kaiser Family Foundation, March 2005. This information was reprinted with permission from the Henry J. Kaiser Family Foundation. The Kaiser Family Foundation, based in Menlo Park, California, is a nonprofit, private operating foundation based in Menlo Park, California, dedicated to producing and communicating the best possible analysis and information on health issues.

although being tan is seen as more beautiful than being pale. Even in magazines targeted for Black women, the models typified as most beautiful are generally those with the lightest skin and straight or wavy hair, resulting in color stratification even within the African American population (Glenn 2009; Herring et al. 2003; Craig 2002). European facial features are also pervasive in the images of Asian and Latino women.

Taken together, these images reinforce gender stereotypes and limit the possibilities that people see for themselves. In this way, the images in the media can be defined as controlling images (Collins 1990). The concept of **controlling images** refers to the power of the media and popular culture to direct our concepts of ourselves and others. It is meant to highlight the power of those running the media to shape our consciousness and self-concept. The images we see in the media are not just neutral, appearing without effect. The media are a source of authority in society, producing what you might think of as *cultural narratives*—frameworks by which people come to understand themselves and their world.

Controlling images of gender are compounded when you look at race, social class, sexuality, and age. Although Latinos and African Americans tend to watch more television than White people, they are underrepresented in the media and, when shown, are usually in subordinate and stereotypical roles. Black men are most often portrayed as athletes, criminals, or entertainers. Only occasionally are Black and Hispanic people shown as complex, loving, and intelligent people (Dines and Humez 2002). Asian American and Native Americans are virtually invisible on television and often play "disappearing" roles—in the background or catering to the needs of more dominant groups. If you look at magazines targeted toward young, White women, chances are that most images of African American men will show them with bare chests and gold chains around their neck—an image based on racist images that sexualize Black men.

Women of color are stereotyped in television programs as humorous but dominating characters. And much research has been done analyzing the image of

HISTORY SPEAKS: YESTERDAY'S FEMINISTS TALK ABOUT TODAY

Alice Walker: In Search of Women's Culture

"Womanist is to feminist as purple is to lavender."
—Alice Walker (1983: xii)

Although not of "yesterday," as she is still very much active and alive, Alice Walker (1944–present) is already a "classic" feminist. She is the author of numerous books, including the best- selling novel, *The Color Purple* (1982), which won both the National Book Award and the Pulitzer Prize, later becoming a movie. Born one of eight children of a Georgia sharecropper, Walker was able to attend Spelman College in Atlanta and, later, Sarah Lawrence College in New York. She published her first novel in 1970 and has since prolifically published poetry, novels, and short stories.

Walker introduced the term *womanist* to the feminist movement, positing it as the opposite of "girlish" and intended to reference the courage and strength of women of color and the capacity of women to love other women. She is intent on finding and loving the writing of Black women—a process she described as "saving the life that is your own." In her classic essay, "In Search of Our Mothers' Gardens," she asks what it meant for Black women to be writers—long before the

renaissance of Black women's writing and culture that emerged in the late twentieth century. She poignantly asks how many Black women were creative geniuses whose art and culture has been buried by the history of racism and sexism. And, in discovering the cultural creations of women in the past, Walker says she finds her own creative self.

Thinking Further: Ask yourself these questions: Who are the women of the past and present that you think of as creative geniuses? What were/are the conditions in which their creativity emerged? How has it been supported and/or suppressed? What does this tell you about how different forms of social inequality influence the production of culture?

Sources: Walker, Alice. 2009. "Alice Walker's Garden." www.alicewalkersgarden.com; Johnson, Jane. 2007. "Biography of Alice Walker." womenshistory.about.com; Walker, Alice. 1983. *In Search of Our Mother's Gardens: Womanist Prose by Alice Walker.* New York: Harcourt Brace Jovanovich.

women of color found in popular music. Hip-hop and rap refer to women as "bitches" and "ho's." In most music videos, women of color are turned into commodities—appearing as property, or something to be had. Other images in music videos show women of color as vacuous and empty—looking into space with dreamy eyes averted from the camera. Analysts argue that such depictions teach women (and men) a narrow definition of being sexy and beautiful (Perry 2003).

Concepts of social class and its relationship to gender are also taught through these media narratives. Working-class people are largely invisible on television except when presented as spectacles on talk shows or in comedies, suggesting that there is something funny about their life situations. Working-class women are most often objects of laughter, and rarely do we see realistic portrayals in the media of women in working-class jobs. Working-class men are most likely seen in beer commercials or police shows (Bettie 1995; Grindstaff 2002; Leistyna 2005). Instead, the media promote a belief that everyone can be middle class and that the accoutrements of social class are available to anyone who works hard enough. Thus, poor mothers are depicted as dependent—an image that has increased over time and is most commonly associated in the media with African American women (Misra et al. 2003).

In recent years, gays and lesbians have become more visible in the media. Popular TV shows forthrightly give visibility to gay and lesbian life and produce positive images of lesbian and gay people. Advertisers have sought to expand their commercial markets, so there are now more lesbian and gay characters being shown on television. But many argue that lesbians and gay men are still cast in stereotypical ways, with little realistic portrayal of real gay and lesbian lives and homophobic jokes are still routine in many popular TV comedies. Analyses of TV situation comedies finds that gay/lesbian characters are a tiny proportion (2 percent) of those shown and the characters are almost all young, well-to-do men (Fouts and Inch 2005; Avila-Saavedra 2009). Still, the increased visibility of lesbians and gays in the media can influence public acceptance of gays and lesbians and generate support for equal rights protection (Gamson 1998).

Even the news, something to be taken seriously and as objective truth, is loaded with controlling images associated with gender, race, class, and sexuality. Women, and especially women of color, usually report the "soft" news or human-interest stories; men's voices carry the authority of world events, although change is afoot with the appearance of women anchors such as Katie Couric, Rachel Maddow, and Diane Sawyer on major news networks. Yet, women of color are still more likely appear on the news as reporters in late-night hours, weekends, and holidays when the "senior" staff has time off. And, men remain the vast majority of political pundits and are far more likely to be interviewed, heard, and seen in news reports. Even in reports of rape, women's experiences are often filtered through men's voices; and, in celebrity rape cases, male voices are much more "championed"—that is, the men, not the women, become the story's focus (Moorti 2002). And, if you want a feminist perspective on the news, you have to search for alternative media, which at least is now more accessible given the growth of blogs, text messaging, "tweets," and other new forms of electronic communication that allow for a more open form of exchange (Beins 2009; see, for example, feministing.com).

Violence, Sexualization, and the Media

Many have targeted the controlling images of women that appear in the media as contributing to the high rates of violence against women in society. There is a long-standing debate about the effects of exposure to pornography on attitudes and behaviors about violence. Do the violent images found in the media matter? A classic, early study found that exposure to violent pornography was related to a greater likelihood of men engaging in sexual aggression and being less sympathetic to rape victims (Donnerstein and Linz 1986). Subsequent studies have found such things as that seeing stereotypical sexual imagery in music videos affects college students' attitudes, encouraging them to see sexual relationships as adversarial (Kalof 1999). Even observing "virtual" scantily clad characters on the Internet has been shown to be related to more sexist attitudes and the acceptance of rape myths, such as "women asked for it" (Fox and Bailenson 2009). But others caution against seeing a direct relationship between exposure to violent images in the media and the actual commission of violence (Sternheimer 2007).

The debate rages on about the effects of violent and demeaning images and the conclusions are complex—mainly because the effects of violent imagery (whether in video games, television, or others sources) cannot be separated from the violence that actually occurs in society. Even if there is not a direct causal relationship between viewing violence against women and then engaging in it, there is little doubt that the images found in popular culture are pervasive and demeaning. Thus, young girls, even if they are critical of media ideals, think boys will judge them by how well they match the ideal (Milkie and Peltola 1999). People do not just passively internalize media images and distinguish between fantasy and reality (Currie 1997), but media images form cultural ideals that have a huge impact on people's behavior, values, and self-image.

Still, violence against women in the media seems to be increasing. A recent study has found that violence against women and teen girls on television has increased substantially in recent years (over the period from 2004 to 2009)—and at rates higher than overall increases in violence on TV. The most frequent form of violence against women is beating, followed by threats, shootings, rape, stabbing, and torture, in that order. Furthermore, violence against women on TV is increasingly graphic (Parents Television Council 2009). Whether such violent images *directly* affect behavior toward women remains in question, but the effect cannot be trivial. If nothing else, it desensitizes people to violence.

In addition to violence, the sexualization of women in popular culture seems to be increasing (Levy 2005). Popular shows like *Girls Gone Wild* represent what some call the "pornification" of mainstream culture—a culture eager to sell soft porn imagery to a young, male audience (Mayer 2005). Also, the sexualized imagery of women in popular culture is also strongly racialized.

Asian women are vastly overrepresented on Internet pornography sites, reproducing stereotypes of them as sex objects (Gossett and Byrne 2002). And the pornification of culture reaches into younger and younger girls. Think of the T-shirts you may have seen for girls as young as 5 years old that say "Sexy" or "Flirt."

A CLOSER LOOK AT MEN

Men's Beliefs about Women's Breasts

Research on media representations of women has consistently documented that women's bodies are sexually objectified in all types of media outlets. In advertising, women's bodies, particularly their breasts, are used to sell just about anything from hair care products to fishing line. Hypersexualized female characters are commonplace in music videos and video games. Research finds that women's views of their bodies are negatively affected by this sexual objectification. However, little is known about how these representations affect men's views of women's bodies.

Using a sample of 656 predominantly White, heterosexual undergraduate men, Monique Ward, Ann Merriwether, and Allison Caruthers examined the relationship between men's use of media and their beliefs about women's bodies, particularly their breasts. Participants were given surveys that measured their level of exposure to the three media formats popular among young men: prime-time comedies and dramas, music videos, and popular men's magazines, including *GQ*, *Maxim*, *Men's Health*, and *Playboy*. Additionally, two measures were used to examine participants' endorsement of traditional gender ideology. Finally, participants were asked to complete surveys that assessed their attitudes toward breastfeeding and childbirth.

Ward and colleagues found that frequent and involved media use contributed to men's greater acceptance of traditional gender ideology that constructs women as sexual objects. Specifically, men who (1) read men's magazines frequently, (2) viewed television programs with the goal of learning about the world, and (3) agreed with the notion that "television presents things as they are" (i.e., realistically) were more likely to accept traditional gender ideology. Additionally, the researchers found that men's endorsement of traditional gender ideology was significantly related to their expressing more negative views toward childbirth (i.e., "I think seeing childbirth would be disgusting"), less support for public breastfeeding, and more concern that breastfeeding would interfere with marital relations.

The authors conclude that media representations of women overemphasize the sexual aspect of women's breasts (and bodies), and when men endorse this ideology, it is more difficult for them to embrace the reproductive functioning of women's bodies in general and women's breasts in particular.

Source: Ward, L. Monique, Ann Merriwether, and Allison Caruthers. 2006. "Breasts Are for Men: Media, Masculinity Ideologies, and Men's Beliefs about Women's Bodies." *Sex Roles* 55: 703–714.

All told, images in the media and in other forms of popular culture construct a vision of gender that contributes to the denigration of women in society. Although you cannot tell what effect media images have simply by reporting on the content of the media, there is little question that media images influence how we define ourselves and others. The media create narratives—that is, frames by which people come to understand the world around them. Although people seldom just passively internalize these narratives, the narratives do shape the understanding that people have of the social world, even though people interpret what they see in creative and diverse ways. But these media narratives are a powerful influence on our social understandings and they construct images of women and men that can shape our social relationships and our social values. People are not, however, without the power to change these images, but being aware of them and their potential influence is a first step toward change.

Theorizing the Media's Influence

The media provide a common basis for social interaction in society. People talk about the latest episodes of their favorite programs, sing the lyrics of various songs, dress like the models in music videos, desire the bodies they see in magazines, and so on. The very nature of the media makes the images seen less fluid and emergent than they would be in reality. In the media, ideas and characters seem fixed, giving a singular and narrow definition of reality. Rarely does the public get a glimpse of how these images are actually produced. Instead, they appear as objective truths.

Several approaches have been developed to explain the depiction of women by the media. These include the reflection hypotheses, role-learning theory, organizational theories of gender inequality, the capitalist organization of the media, and social constructionist/postmodernist theories.

The Reflection Hypothesis

The first and theoretically the simplest explanation of the depiction of women by the media is called the **reflection hypothesis** (Tuchman 1979; Tuchman et al. 1978). This hypothesis assumes that the mass media reflect the values of the general population. Images in the media are seen as representing dominant ideals within the population, particularly because the capitalistic structure of the media is dependent on appealing to the largest consumer audience. According to Gerbner (1978), the ideals of the population are incorporated into symbolic representations in the media. The reflection hypothesis asserts that, although media images are make-believe, they do symbolize dominant social beliefs and images.

The volumes of data produced by marketing researchers and ratings scales indicate that popular appeal is significant in decisions about programming content. Observations of shows such as soap operas also reveal that television attempts to incorporate into its programming social issues that reflect, even if in an overblown way, the experiences (or, at least, the wishes) of its viewers. Although viewers may escape into soap operas as a relief from daily life, the fact that they can do so rests on some form of identification (even if fanciful) with the characters and the situations portrayed (Modleski 1980).

The reflection hypothesis leaves several questions unanswered. To begin with, as content analysis studies have shown, much if not most of what the media depict is not synchronized with real conditions in people's lives. In part, this phenomenon is explainable by a time lag between cultural changes and changes in the media (Tuchman et al. 1978). It is also explainable by the fact that the media portray ideals, not truths; furthermore, people may not actually believe what they see in the media, and, if they do, it may be because the media create, not reflect, viewers' beliefs. A causal question is asked in theoretical explanations of media images: Do the media reflect—or create—popular values? The reflection hypothesis makes the first assumption; other explanations begin with the second.

Role-Learning Theory

The values and images of women and men in the media represent some of the most conservative views of women and men. **Role-learning theory** hypothesizes that sexist and racist images in the media (and the absence thereof) encourage role modeling. That is to say, "the media's deleterious role models, when internalized, prevent and impede female accomplishments. They also encourage both women and men to define women in terms of men (as sex objects) or in the context of the family" (Tuchman 1979). The assumption that the media encourage role modeling is the basis for feminist criticisms of the media's depiction of women.

The role-modeling argument assumes that the media should truthfully reproduce social life and that there is some causal connection between the content of the media and its social effects (Tuchman 1979). In other words, the role-modeling argument assumes that media images produce stimuli that have predictable responses from the public. This is an argument that sees human beings as passive receptacles for whatever media inputs are poured into them. People may, in fact, view media images much more critically or even with cynicism, making it unlikely that they would modify their behavior in accordance with the images. This possibility does not deny the fact that people, especially children, do learn from the media; rather, a criticism of role-modeling theory suggests that it is an oversimplified perspective. As you will see in examining postmodernism, many recent feminist theorists see role-learning theory as too one-dimensional and simplistic in assuming that images in the media are internalized by viewers.

Organizational Theories of Gender Inequality

Although both the reflection hypothesis and the role-modeling argument alert us to the fit between images and reality, neither adequately explains the reasons for sexism in the media. Other scholars have attempted to explain sexism in media content by studying gender inequality within media organizations. This perspective assumes that the subordinate position of women and people of color in the media influences the ideas produced about them. If women and people of color are absent from the power positions where ideas and images are produced, then their worldviews and experiences will not be reflected in the images those organizations produce. In addition, because those who occupy power positions come to share a common worldview, the ideas they produce tend to reflect the values of the ruling elite.

White women and people of color have made many inroads into media careers, but behind the scenes these appearances are deceiving. Almost half (43 percent) of women in radio news and 48 percent of women in television news have said that discrimination has hurt their careers. At the same time, however, much progress has been made. White women have made substantial progress in the news workforce, and the pay gap that continues for women is mostly the result of differences in the years of experience. Minority women and men have made some progress, but remain underrepresented in media employment and have, of late, actually been losing ground (Papper 2007).

Do the numbers of women and minorities in the media matter, as far as explaining the images of women and racial–ethnic groups that appear? The argument that increasing the number of women and minorities employed by the media will transform the images portrayed of them presumes that men and women and Whites and people of color hold different values; this belief has not been consistently demonstrated in research. People who work in an organization become

Women have begin appearing as news anchors in the media, but are often placed in subordinate positions to men. Does the man in this photograph appear in any way more dominant? How do things like body posture influence our concepts of gender relationships?

socialized to accept the organization's values. Those who do not conform are less likely to build successful careers; hence, organizational workers more often than not adopt the values of the organizations in which they are employed. Within the media, professional attitudes discourage workers from offending the networks. Professionalism encourages workers to conform to the bureaucratic and capitalist values of their organization (Tuchman 1979). This influence affects how all workers portray gender and racial issues in the media because the organizational culture discourages controversy. That men and women working in the media adopt similar values to each other tells us not so much that men and women think alike, but that all workers' behaviors and attitudes are shaped by the organizations in which they are employed.

Capitalism and the Media

A fourth perspective used to explain sexism in the media attributes sexism to the capitalist structure of media organizations. According to this approach, it is in the interests of sponsors to foster images that are consistent with the products they sell. Many of these products encourage particular values; for example, promoting obsessive cleanliness is necessary to sell the numerous household cleaning products placed on the market.

This perspective also claims that it is in the interests of the capitalist power elite to discourage images of reality that would foster discontent. Not only will sponsors promote any values that will sell but they will also encourage traditional views that uphold the status quo, while discouraging and stereotyping those that challenge it. When the media respond to social criticism, they do so within the limits of existing institutions. For example, following the civil rights movement, when pressure was generated to increase the number of Black Americans in the media, more Black Americans appeared in advertisements and on television programs, but they were and continue to be primarily depicted in middle-class settings where they hold middle-class value systems and are not critical of U.S. society. Likewise, as noted previously, the feminist movement was depicted by the media as radical, trivial, and extremist. As the women's movement gained public support, the media selected its more moderate programs and leaders for public display.

An economic perspective of the media reminds us that the media are owned and controlled by the major corporations of U.S. society (see Figure 3.2). From this perspective, Marx's idea is true that those who control economic production also control the manufacture and dissemination of ideas. The economic structure

Viacom owns:

- MTV
- BET (Black Entertainment Television)
- Nickelodeon
- VH1
- Comedy Central
- Paramount Pictures
- Dreamworks
- Simon and Schuster Publishers
- 39 television stations
- 185 local radio stations
- Outdoor Systems billboards
- TV Land
- Nick at Nite
- Spike TV
- CBS News
- 33 television stations
- And more....

Disney owns:

- Disney Pictures
- Miramax Films
- Touchstone Pictures
- Hollywood Pictures
- Pixar
- ABC Television Network
- 10 local television stations
- ESPN network
- ABC Family Television
- Disney Channel
- 15 other cable networks
- 50 local radio stations
- 16 magazines
- Hyperion Publishing
- 5 Disneylands
- Disney stores
- Disney Cruise Line
- Disney Shopping Inc.
- Muppets Holding Company
- And more......

FIGURE 3.2 Media Monopolies: Who Owns What?

Source: Based on data from *Columbia Journalism Review.* 2010. *Who Owns What?* www.cjr.org.

of the media explains much about why women continue to be shown as sex objects and household caretakers. These images are consistent with capitalist needs to maintain women's services in the home and to make commercial objects out of everything, including sexuality.

In itself, this explanation encourages a somewhat conspiratorial view of media owners and management who, although they are motivated by economic profit, may not have the specific intent of exploiting women. This perspective, along with the gender-inequality approach, gives us, however, a more complete understanding of sexism in the media. Observing the economic and social organization of the media causes us to ask who produces media images and how these images define legitimate forms of social reality.

Depictions in the media can also be seen as social myths by which the meaning of gender in society is established. Anthropologists study social myths to gain an insight into the culture and social organization of a people. Myths provide an interpretation of social truths, beliefs, and relationships that guide a society in its vision of the past, present, and future. They establish a "universe of discourse" that integrates and controls its members, gives them a common reality, and creates structures for what is said, done, and believed (Tuchman 1979). By creating a universe of discourse among their audience, the media act as powerful agents of social control. They engage people in passive fantasies, encourage dreams and visions that are consistent with the social structure, and establish a common basis for social interaction. In a fundamental way, the depiction of women, as well as men, in the media infiltrates our social consciousness and embeds itself in our imagination.

Social Construction Theory and Postmodernism

Each of the preceding perspectives implicity assumes that the influence of the media is unidirectional—that is, there is little indication of how viewers (or readers) actually respond to these images. Also, these perspectives assume that, whatever the source of media images, they have a deleterious effect on those who watch or read them. This assumption is challenged by the arguments of *social construction theory* and *postmodernism*—perspectives that assume a more active perspective on the response of viewers to images perceived in various media outlets.

Social construction theory sees people as constructing gender through their ongoing interaction with others. In this framework, gender is a system of meanings that people enact; moreover, even when "doing gender," people may not internalize what they do. This does not mean that stereotypes and patterns of behavior associated with one gender or the other do not exist—only that *gender is a fluid category, one constantly changing and evolving through human interaction*. The social constructionist approach, as you saw in the previous chapter, is a less simplistic approach to the study of gender in society than the essentialist framework, which sees gender as more fixed. More than seeing gender as a matter of differences, social constructionists see people as having **human agency**—that is, as actively creating their lives, even if within the context of social structures that supersede them. From this point of view, even when people conform to social stereotypes, they may do so without internalizing a belief in them. Furthermore, enacting gender may even be a form of resistance to traditional gender roles, as when people act "superstereotypically" as a way of mocking dominant expectations.

Postmodernism also views society as constructed through social meaning systems, emphasizing that such systems of meaning are highly fluid and changeable (see Chapter 13). From this perspective, symbols and representations are especially important to study because they reveal the meaning systems that shape society at any point in time. Postmodernist theory has generated renewed interest in cultural studies, since it is through culture that one sees the various representations that define modern life. From a postmodernist perspective, social structures do not just determine gender identity nor other forms of identity. Rather, identity is constructed through the subjective understandings that people bring to their reading of "social texts" (i.e., cultural images) (Currie 1997; Walters 1995).

Postmodernist theory tends to be highly abstract and has been criticized by some feminists for being so, since it is difficult for anyone but those highly trained in elite academic programs to understand it. But, an important point derived from postmodernist theory is that social actors are creative in constructing their identity, or, specifically, in the case of gender, what it means to be a woman or man.

In a concrete example of the study of cultural images from a postmodernist perspective, Dawn Currie (1997) has examined teen magazines and asked how young girls read feel about the images of femininity such magazines convey. Currie designed a study using small *focus groups* (i.e., discussion groups whose conversation is observed and recorded by the researcher). The focus groups of teen girls observed images taken from *Seventeen* magazine and discussed what they had seen. Currie found that the girls did not just passively accept the images as ideals; instead, they selectively chose ads that they enjoyed and rejected the images conveyed in others. She argues that these young readers distinguished between fantasy and reality and were often quite critical of ads that they saw as making no sense or posing unrealistic images. Indeed, the girls were quick to reject images that they saw as inconsistent with their own identity.

This does not mean that the images in the magazines were completely without influence. In fact, when asked whom they most wanted to be like, many of the girls chose celebrities who had just been featured in *Seventeen*. Currie suggests that the formation of gender identity, as influenced by the media, is not a one-way process. Young women actively mediate what they see and what they think, thus emphasizing the role of human creativity in the formation of self, instead of seeing people as passive objects into whom cultural images are inserted.

We can see that social construction theory and postmodernism go beyond theories of learned gender roles and gender differences by insisting on seeing agency (i.e., human creativity) in human behavior. This does not mean that domination by highly influential media industries is insignificant, nor does it mean that we should view the sexist images of gender in the media uncritically. Rather, these theoretical perspectives suggest that women and men view these images with an ability to shape the meanings of what they see, without necessarily completely internalizing such cultural ideals. Social construction theory and postmodernism add a strong social constructionist dimension to understanding how knowledge is created in society—a subject long studied in a field known as the *sociology of knowledge*.

THE SOCIOLOGY OF KNOWLEDGE

The preceding discussion underscores three essential sociological points: that knowledge in society is socially constructed, that knowledge emerges from the conditions of people's lives, and that knowledge is embedded in ideological systems. Knowledge is not just simple truth statements. Rather, knowledge is often generated from and tends to reinforce institutions that support existing social arrangements (i.e., the status quo). Whether reflected in language, the media, popular culture, or the arts, knowledge of gender is a powerful social construction.

In sociology, the study of the social construction of ideas is called the **sociology of knowledge**. The sociology of knowledge begins with the premise that ideas emerge from particular social and historical settings and that this social structural context shapes, but does not determine, human consciousness and interpretations of reality. Studies in the sociology of knowledge relate ideas and consciousness to social structure and human culture. Intellectually, this perspective originates primarily in the works of Karl Marx and Karl Mannheim, both of whom, in distinct ways, grappled with the relationship between human knowledge and human existence. It was Mannheim who, in the early twentieth century, labeled the study of the sociology of knowledge and delineated its core ideas, but Marx's study of ideology and consciousness is the intellectual precursor of Mannheim's endeavor.

Marx and the Social Construction of Knowledge

Karl Marx (1818–1883) based his study of human ideas on the premise that the existence of living human beings—that is, their actual activities and material conditions—forms the basis for human history and the ideas generated in this history. Although Marx recognized that human beings live within particular physical settings (including climatic, geographical, and geological conditions), it is the social relationships formed in these settings that make up human society. In other words, human beings transform their environmental conditions through the activities in which they engage. Human society and history emerge as people use their labor to create their social environment. Marx argued that human beings are distinguished from animals by the fact of their consciousness. Although we now know that other animal species have linguistic ability and rudimentary systems of social organization, no other species has the capacity of humans for the elaboration of culture.

Marx's argument is that ideas follow from human behavior. In other words, thinking is derived from the actual activity in which human beings engage. Within Marx's framework, it is not the consciousness of persons that forms the bonds (and chains) of human society; rather, specific relationships among people shape human society and therefore people's ideas.

Marx is not denying that social relations involve an interpretive dimension. He is arguing, however, that ideas emerge from our material reality. This theory suggests that changes in consciousness alone do not generate social changes. Instead, the material conditions of society must be changed if we are to liberate people from oppression.

Marx goes one step further by arguing that within society, the dominant ideas of any period are the ideas of the ruling class. It is they who have the power to influence the intellectual production and distribution of ideas. You can see what he means by thinking about the vast power of media monopolies. Where do you get your news? The Internet? Television? Newspapers? Books? Radio? Magazines? Whatever the source, the chances are that this outlet is owned by the same large corporation that owns several of the other media outlets. Moreover, given the concentration of media monopolies, there are only a few major corporations that own the various media outlets that provide you with information (see Figure 3.2).

The power of media monopolies over the images and ideas available to people is hard to overestimate. Marx thought that in capitalist societies, those who own the means of production also determine the ruling ideas of the period. As Marx writes,

> *The ideas of the ruling class are in every epoch the ruling ideas: i.e., the class which is the ruling material force of society, is at the same time its ruling intellectual force. The class which has the means of material production at its disposal, has control at the same time over the means of mental production, so that thereby, generally speaking, the ideas of those who lack the means of mental production are subject to it.* (The German Ideology, in Tucker 1972:136).

From a Marxist perspective, under capitalism, what people think is shaped by the class system because, under capitalism, the ruling class controls the production of ideas. The ideas that are disseminated through communications systems, including the media, language, and other cultural institutions, authorize a reality that the ruling class would like us to believe. According to Marx, when subordinate groups accept the worldview of dominant groups, they are engaged in **false consciousness**

Feminists add to Marx's perspective on the social construction of ideas, arguing that men, in general, own the means of production (that is, capitalist industries) and therefore determine the ruling ideas of any given time. Sexist ideas justify the power of men over women and sanction male domination, just as racist ideas attempt to justify White supremacy. From a feminist perspective, ideas serve not only capitalist interests but also men's interests.

According to Canadian scholar Dorothy Smith (1990), in patriarchal societies men's ideas are also shaped by the gender-based division of labor. Men typically do not do the work that meets the physical and emotional needs of society's members. As a result, men's ideas (especially of those who engage primarily in intellectual work) assume a split, or bifurcation, between mind and body, and rational thought is accorded the highest value. This belief in the bifurcation of mind and body is made possible only because the labor of women provides for men's physical needs, mediates their social relations, and allows them to ignore bodily and emotional experience as an integral dimension of life.

Likewise, in racially stratified societies, the gender-based division of labor intersects with the racial division of labor. The ideas of White people, particularly those having the most privilege, are likely to take the labor of racial groups for granted, making it appear invisible or unimportant. Oddly enough, the ideology that supports racial inequality tends to define racial groups as "lazy" and "unwilling to work." This ideological belief does not reflect reality, but rather distorts the experiences of racial groups whose actual work affords certain Whites the privilege of not having to do menial labor. In addition, in societies structured by both race and gender privilege, the ideologies of sexism and racism intersect. Think, for example, of dominant cultural images of women on welfare (usually presumed to be women of color). The idea that they do not want to work pervades popular thinking, as if raising children on a meager income is not work.

Sexism as Ideology

Karl Mannheim (1893–1947) further developed the sociology of knowledge. Mannheim's sociology of knowledge relates ideas to the conditions under which they are produced. His work also provides a foundation for feminist scholarship because he develops the thought that ideas grow out of the relationship of knowledge to social structure.

Mannheim saw the task of the sociology of knowledge as discovering the relational character of thought. How are ideas embedded in the social experience of their producers and the social-historical milieu within which ideas are formed? All ideas must be evaluated within the context of their social making. This view is true not only for the grand ideas of intellectual history but also for the consciousness of human beings in their ordinary experience (Berger and Luckmann 1966).

New ideas are most likely generated during periods of rapid social change, according to Mannheim. He explains this belief by suggesting that as long as group traditions remain stable, then traditional worldviews remain intact. New ideas appear when old traditions are breaking up, although the persistence of customary ways of thinking is also likely to make new ideas appear to be "curiosities, errors, ambiguities, or heresies" (1936:7).

Mannheim is best known for his study of ideology. **Ideology** refers to a system of beliefs about the world that involves distortions of reality at the same time it provides justification for the status quo. Following from Marx, Mannheim sees ideology as serving the interests of groups in the society who justify their position by distorting social definitions of reality. Ideologies serve the powerful by presenting us with a definition of reality that is false and yet orders our comprehension of the surrounding world. When ideas emerge from ideology, they operate as a form of social control by defining the status quo to be the proper state of affairs.

From Mannheim's work, we can understand **sexism** as an ideology that defends the traditional status of women and men in society. Although, as Mannheim says, no single idea constitutes an ideological belief system, the collective totality of an ideology (such as sexism) permeates our consciousness and our comprehension of the world in which we live. It is here that the sociology of knowledge merges with the political goals of feminism because in debunking sexist ideology, the social-historical origins of sexist thought are found and new definitions of reality can be forged. Although Mannheim is careful to distinguish political argument from academic thought, he recognizes that the unmasking of ideological systems is a function of sociological theory.

The sociology of knowledge helps us understand how ideas reproduce our definitions of social reality; who produces ideas; under what conditions ideas are made; and the consequences of ideas and beliefs that, in the case of sexism, systematically define women and men in stereotypical and distorted terms. It gives you a context for understanding the ideas and images of gender that this chapter has documented.

Chapter Summary and Themes

The gendered images that we can observe throughout society generate cultural scripts that produce stereotypes about women and men.

The images of women and men that we see around us are pervasive and often taken for granted, despite their enormous influence. Although they change over time, they bombard us with images of women as thin, as sex objects, and as tied to home. Such images create a concept of the proper roles for women and men, significantly influencing our self-esteem and our definition of others.

Language shapes our definition of reality, but it can also transform how we think about gender.

Many people think that feminist criticisms of sexist language are trivial, but language shapes our definition of reality. When language embeds sexist assumptions, it can shape how and what people think. Thus, changes in language both reflect and generate changes in people's consciousness.

Empirical observations of the media reveal numerous ways that gendered images define men and women in narrow and stereotypical ways.

Content analyses of various forms of culture document how different groups are depicted. Whether in television, magazines, the Internet, films, or other forms of popular culture, images of women in the media tend to restrict women to narrow roles. Images of men are similarly restricting. Furthermore, gendered images are compounded by race, class, sexual orientation, and age, among others. All of these images have a profound impact on our identities, our images of others, and our sense of social possibilities.

Theories about gender and the media analyze the relationship between images in the media and the social realities that they both reflect and create.

Images in the media to some extent reflect the values of a culture, but they also operate to create those values. Moreover, the images do not appear in a vacuum. Audiences are not just passive vessels, but actively respond to what they see—sometimes internalizing these ideals, other times critically responding to them. The capitalist structure of media industries influences how the media are organized and why the media promote the images and ideas that we observe.

The sociology of knowledge theorizes that all ideas are generated within a social context.

Understanding the social context in which ideas are generated—and believed—is a critical component of sociological thinking. What we think and the ideas made available to us are shaped by the social and historical context, including the influence of powerful organizations that produce the ideas of the time.

■ Key Terms

content analysis
controlling images
false consciousness
human agency

ideology
popular culture
postmodernism
reflection hypothesis

role-learning theory
sexism
social construction theory
sociology of knowledge

■ Discussion Questions/Projects for Thought

1. Identify some aspect of popular culture (such as MTV videos, current children's films, television sitcoms) and develop a systematic way to observe the gender images portrayed. What do these images convey to the audience? Using the theoretical frameworks used to explain the depiction of women in the mass media, how would you explain the presence of these images? What do you suppose their effect is?

2. Compare the images of men to those of women in any of the following forms of popular culture: sports or hobby magazines, women's magazines versus men's magazines, television news programs and crime dramas, popular music from different time periods, or similar areas. What do your observations tell you about the portrayal of men where there are different intended audiences? How does the historical time period affect these images? Whose interests are best served by these interests, and how does this illustrate the theoretical perspectives discussed in this chapter?

3. Ask a group of women to observe advertisements in a women's magazine and talk about what they see in the images. Based on what they say, would you say that these women have internalized the ideal that these images suggest, do they resist it, or something in between? What does this tell you about social construction theory and postmodernism?

4

Sexuality and Intimate Relationships

THE SOCIAL CONSTRUCTION OF SEXUALITY

Sexuality is an essential part of your identity and your relationship to others. It involves deep emotional feeling and intimacy as well as issues of power and vulnerability in relationships. Human sexual expression takes a variety of forms, although the expression of sexual behavior is influenced and constrained more by cultural definitions and prohibitions than by the physical possibilities for sexual arousal. In fact, what distinguishes human sexuality from sexual behavior among animals is that "human sexuality [is] uniquely characterized by its overwhelmingly symbolic, culturally constructed, non-procreative plasticity" (Caulfield 1985:344). Much of what we assume about sexuality, however, is distorted by assuming that sexuality is a "natural drive" or an internal state that is acted out or released in sexually exciting situations. But anthropologists and others have pointed out that what is seemingly natural about human sexuality is that it is shaped by culture. How sexuality is expressed and felt varies according to the cultural context.

Across cultures and within our own, human sexual expression includes a wide range of behaviors and attitudes. Although we tend to think of our sexuality as internally situated, it involves a learned relationship to the world. The feminist movement and the gay/lesbian movement have inspired a new openness about sexuality and have helped free sexual behavior from its traditional constraints; yet, the persistent belief that heterosexuality is the only natural way of expressing sexual feeling continues to blind many people to other possibilities for human sexuality.

Even though people like to think of sexuality as a private matter, social institutions direct and control sexuality. Thus, some forms of sexual expression are seen and treated as more legitimate than others. Heterosexuality is a more privileged status in society than is homosexuality. Because of this, heterosexuals (or at least those presumed to be so) have more institutional privileges than gay, lesbian, and bisexual people. Although many states now allow same-sex marriage, in most states only heterosexual couples may legally marry. Married heterosexual couples get employee health care benefits, but large numbers of employers deny this benefit to same-sex couples. Federal policies do not allow same-sex couples to file joint tax returns. In these and other ways, gays and lesbians are more directly controlled by institutional policies than are heterosexuals.

That heterosexuality is institutional can be seen by the many laws, religious doctrines, and family and employment policies that explicitly and implicitly promote **heteronormativity**—meaning the norms and institutional structures that presume and enforce heterosexuality as the only acceptable form of sexual expression and identity (also referred to as **heterosexism**). Heteronormativity also presumes that people fall into only one of two sexual identities—straight or gay—whereas people now recognize that there is a wide range of sexual identities possible.

One of the major social factors influencing sexual relationships is gender. We have already seen that beliefs about sexuality influence gender socialization. But gender also influences sexuality. The two (gender and sexuality) exist in a *dialectical* relationship—that is, each influences the other. Current scholarship on sexuality shows that gender is itself constructed through the regulation of sexual behaviors. That is, "cultural and institutional [systems] . . . sustain sexual norms" (Ward and Schneider 2009:435). By enforcing norms of heterosexuality, institutionalized patterns enforce a binary system of gender relations—that is, one wherein women and men are forced into "either/or" categories of "woman" and "man." Enforcing adherence to these categories is sustained through heterosexual norms—that is, *heteronormativity.*

For now, if you suspend the idea that there is a single and unchanging way of expressing sexual feelings, you are much more likely to understand human sexuality and intimacy in all their variety and forms. This is difficult for many people because of the strictures to think only in terms of "natural heterosexuality," but you will understand the connection between gender and sexuality better if you debunk the idea that only one form of sexuality is somehow natural. Looking historically and cross-culturally will help you do so.

THE HISTORY OF SEXUALITY IN THE UNITED STATES

It is commonly thought that over time sexual behavior and attitudes have become less restrained and more uninhibited. Most people believe that sexuality was largely repressed in the past and that only recently have sexual ideas and practices become more liberated. Such a reading disregards the variability and change in sexual attitudes and behaviors and the differing historical ways in which sexuality has or has not been regulated. The history of sexuality is not a simple story of movement from repression to liberation or ignorance to wisdom (Freedman and D'Emilio 1988). Sexuality is constantly reshaped through cultural, economic, familial, and political relations, all of which are also conditioned through the prevailing social organization of gender, race, and class relationships at given times.

Historians of sexuality have argued that the dominant meaning and practice of sexuality have changed from their primary association with reproduction within families in the colonial period to their current association with relationships of emotional intimacy and physical pleasure for individuals (Freedman and D'Emilio 1988). The separation of sexuality from reproduction, because of the widespread availability of birth control, means that sex can be loosened from its traditional association with family. Additionally, sexuality has become more commercialized, and the tie between sexuality and reproduction has been loosened. Groups within society experience these broad-scale transformations in sexuality in different ways, however. For example, sexuality for women is still more closely linked to reproduction than it is for men; working-class and poor women are more likely to have to "sell" their sexuality than are middle-class or elite women. Gay and lesbian sexuality is more directly controlled by the state and more subjected to continuing repressive attitudes.

You have to take care not to overgeneralize about sexual experience only from the experience of dominant groups. To say that sexuality in the colonial period and early nineteenth century was a family-centered, reproductive sexual system grossly distorts the sexual experiences of enslaved African American men and women.

For them, family systems were neither recognized by the state nor respected by the dominant culture; sexual reproduction was often forced, not for purposes of a family-centered life, but for purposes of economic exploitation. Sexual exploitation was an integral part of the system of slavery. The images of African American men and women that emerged during that period to justify sexual exploitation continue to influence contemporary sexual stereotypes of African American women and men (Collins 2004).

Three patterns recur in the history of sexuality (Freedman and D'Emilio 1988). First, political movements that attempt to change sexual ideas and practices thrive at times when an older system is undergoing rapid change and disintegration. For example, the movements of sexual liberation that emerged in the 1960s occurred while there were great transformations taking place in women's and men's roles, the definition and shape of family relationships, and the social behavior of young people. Even technological change played a part as the easy availability of birth control made possible the separation of sexuality and reproduction. Further transformations in broad-based gender relations (including women's increased labor force activity and their later marriage and increased likelihood of divorce) created a context in which movements for increased sexual tolerance and diverse forms of expression have flourished.

The second recurring pattern is the fact that sexual politics are integrally tied to the politics of race, class, and gender. Class and race hierarchies are often supported through claims that working-class people and people of color are sexually promiscuous and uncontrolled. These false images are then used to justify systems of social control; furthermore, gender inequality is maintained through controlling sexual images of women and men. The idea in the early twentieth century that professional women were "sexually inverted" (a veiled way of calling them lesbians) is a good illustration of how gender inequality is supported through manipulation of sexual ideas. Likewise, the contemporary belief that women who are raped must have "asked for it" maintains a fundamental injustice in the balance of power between men and women in the eyes of the state.

The third historical pattern is that the politics of sexuality are often linked to other social concerns, especially social movements and moral campaigns in which images of impurities and vice are used to stir public concern. For example, in the early twentieth century, fears of immigration were fueled by claims that immigrant women were wanton prostitutes. Rather than examining the economic needs of women immigrants, opponents incited moral outrage to further restrict immigration. In contemporary politics, those who have resisted programs on sex education in the public schools have based their position on the claim that distributing condoms will encourage promiscuous behavior (Irvine 2002).

The history of sexual attitudes and behaviors reveals strong interconnections between sexual politics and other dimensions of race, class, and gender relations. Historically, systems of sexual regulation are highly correlated with other forms of social regulation. At the same time, historical analysis reveals the ever-changing nature of sexual meaning systems and sexual mores. Thus, reflection on the history of sexuality is a good way to see how sexuality is socially constructed and how it intersects with other features of the social structure.

CONTEMPORARY SEXUAL ATTITUDES AND BEHAVIOR

Changes in sexual attitudes and behaviors in the latter half of the twentieth century have been so extensive that they have been called a *sexual revolution*. This term is used to describe the greater freedom now found in sexual behavior, as well as the more liberal attitudes that many hold about sexuality. Surveys of sexual behavior and attitudes show that sex is more likely than in the past to take place outside of marriage, young people initiate sexual behavior at a younger age, people are more tolerant of diverse sexual practices, and more people—men and women—have sex with more than one partner in a lifetime. All of these and other changes associate the sexual revolution with greater sexual freedom.

The sexual revolution, however, has not necessarily separated the fusion between gender and sexuality. Some say that the sexual revolution has simply made women's sexual behavior more like men's—at least as indicated by the frequency of sex, number of sexual partners, and other measures of sexual behavior (Ehrenreich 1987; Laumann et al. 1994). Others say that traditional gender expectations still permeate sexual relationships, with women expected to be more passive and men expected to initiate and control sex. Although there have been changes in women's sexual behavior, there are many ways that gender continues to influence sexuality—and vice versa.

The sexualization of women—even young girls—is increasingly tied to the marketing of products, thus linking the objectification of women to this consumption-based culture. Bratz dolls, introduced in 2003, have created a more sexualized image for young girls' play. Although more ethnically and racially diverse than Barbies, they project a sexualized, gendered image that can negatively affect girls' self-image.

Women's sexuality has traditionally been associated with passivity and men's with power. Although these definitions are loosening, they continue to influence how sexuality is understood. Men's sexuality is still associated with performance and achievement; in fact, the very term describing the absence of sexual arousal in power is a term that associates sex with power: *impotence*. Women's sexuality, on the other hand, is seen as something to be contained and controlled or as something dangerous and enticing. You can see this in the dichotomous labeling of women as either good girls or whores. Research, in fact, finds that women who are virgins in their young adult years perceive that they are rewarded for virginity; men of the same age, on the other hand, think they are stigmatized for virginity (Burgess et al. 2001).

In general, men are much more likely to be praised for being perceived as sexually very active. Of course, men have to negotiate the boundaries that gender and sexuality construct: Being a "stud" is a positive social identity for men (with no equivalent identity for a woman), but a man who is too casual in his sexual behavior may get labeled as a "player." It is hard to even imagine what a woman "player" would look like because women are not generally perceived as having the power in relationships that allows them to "play" men. What do you think a woman engaging in this behavior would be called, and what does this label suggest about gender, power, and sexuality? Although it has changed over time, the *double standard* that has differentiated women's and men's sexual behavior for years still casts them in different sex-gender roles. You can clearly see this connection by thinking about what produces stigma and praise for men and women in their sexual behavior.

The connection between gender and sexuality can also be seen in how women's sexuality has been defined as male centered. We saw in the previous chapter how much sexual advice is given to women about how to please men sexually. Even the definition of sexual intercourse that most people think of as "having sex" is based on the centrality of the penis. Most people think that sexual intercourse specifically means penile-vaginal intercourse. This was also apparent during the scandal involving President Clinton's affair with Monica Lewinsky, when he argued that, despite their sexual conduct, they had not had "sexual relations."

Phallocentric thinking is that which assumes that women need men for sexual arousal and satisfaction. Phallocentric thinking is historically revealed by Sigmund Freud's theory of the double orgasm—a sexual myth that long distorted the understanding of female sexuality. Freud's argument, and one that was widely believed, was that women have two kinds of orgasms: clitoral and vaginal. Clitoral orgasm, in Freud's view, was less "mature." He maintained that adult women should transfer their center of orgasm to the vagina, where male penetration made their sexual response complete. Freud's theory of the double orgasm has no basis in fact. The center of female sexuality is the clitoris; female orgasm is achieved through stimulation of the clitoris, whether or not accompanied by vaginal penetration (Masters and Johnson 1966). For nearly a century, the myth of the double orgasm led women to believe that they were frigid—unable to produce a supposedly mature sexual response.

Phallocentric thinking continues to appear in the assumption that women's primary sexual orientation is naturally directed toward men. **Compulsory heterosexuality** refers to the institutionalized practices that presume that women are innately sexually oriented toward men (Rich 1980). In a social system structured on compulsory heterosexuality, women's sexual relationships with other women are seen as deviating from acceptable social norms—unless, as in pornography, women's sexual relationships with each other are performed for men's pleasure. The social sanctions brought against women who are not identified as attached to men show how heterosexuality is maintained through social control. The concept of compulsory heterosexuality indicates the degree to which sexual choices, relationships, and privileges are structured by social institutions.

Contemporary sexual attitudes represent some loosening of rigid judgments about sexual behavior, but, predictably, these attitudes, too, are shaped by gender. For example, men are three times more likely than women to think that extramarital sex is morally acceptable, and 81 percent of men, compared to 55 percent of women, think that premarital sex is acceptable (Gallup 2003). Such differences can lead to significant conflict between men and women.

Some argue that changes in sexual attitudes have moved so far as to now being harmful to women—especially young women and girls. The fashion industry markets sexually provocative clothing to young women, including very young girls. (Think of shirts that say, "Hot," "Sexy," or "Slut"—or the thongs being marketed to girls as young as 8 years old). On college campuses it is not unusual for women to display highly sexualized behavior (making out with other women in bars, for example) as a way of pleasing and entertaining men. Pole dances have become a popular form of exercise. These and other examples have led to the sexualization of our culture and the sexual objectification of women (see "Focus on Research").

FOCUS ON RESEARCH

The Sexualization of Young Girls

The American Psychological Association (APA), the national organization of professional psychologists (clinicians and faculty), became concerned about the increasing sexualization of young girls in U.S. culture. An appointed task force of experts on gender and adolescence reviewed the existing research appropriate to this topic and produced a major report detailing the causes and consequences of the sexualization of young girls in contemporary culture.

The APA report defines sexualization as occurring when any one of the following characteristics applies:

- a person's value comes only from his or her sexual appeal or behavior, to the exclusion of other characteristics;
- a person is held to a standard that equates physical attractiveness (narrowly defined) with being sexy;
- a person is sexually objectified—that is, made into a thing for others' sexual use, rather than seen as a person with a capacity for independent action and decision making; and,
- sexuality is inappropriately imposed upon a person (APA 2007:2).

This extensive research report notes the many places where sexualization occurs, particularly in the media, in popular culture, and in commercial products. The report concludes that sexualization is harmful to young girls on a number of counts. Some of the conclusions include:

- Girls' "chronic attention to attractiveness" impedes other forms of mental and physical development.
- Sexualization undermines girls' self-confidence and leads to various forms of dissatisfaction with their appearance.
- Sexualization is related to high rates of depression and eating disorders, as well as lowered self-esteem.
- Sexual objectification leads to diminished sexual health, including less likelihood of using birth control and practicing safe sex.
- Exposure to sexualized images is related to greater acceptance of sexist beliefs, including myths about sexual violence.

The APA report, which can be viewed in its entirety on the APA website (www.apa.org), concludes with numerous recommendations for girls, parents, and professionals about how to address this problem.

Source: American Psychological Association. 2007. *Report of the APA Task Force on the Sexualization of Girls.* Washington, DC: American Psychological Association.

Ariel Levy, a young, feminist journalist, calls this the development of "raunch culture." She argues that in the 1970s, the feminist movement and the sexual liberation movement were fused—each pursuing goals of loosening former restrictions on women's sexuality and social freedoms. As time has progressed, young women have come to see themselves as sexually liberated, but the feminist analysis of power that linked feminism and sexual liberation is now absent in the social context of young women's lives. As a result, Levy argues, young women mistake sexual freedom for the actual liberation of women, thus further objectifying women as sexual beings whose primary purpose is the pleasure of men (A. Levy 2005). One consequence, according to Levy, is that "bimbos enjoy a higher standing in our culture than Olympians right now" (p. 20).

Also signaling the sexualization of the culture is a relatively new form of sexual interaction, known among students as "hooking up," where sex is more casual and more frequent than was true in the past. *Hooking up* refers to sexual behavior that includes no ongoing commitment to the other person. For some, hooking up means kissing; for others, it means sexual-genital play but not intercourse; and for still others, it means sexual intercourse. Although hooking up is associated with sexual freedom, studies find that students perceive others to be more comfortable with it than they are themselves. Men also express more comfort with these casual, noncommitted sexual relationships than women do, and it seems that men still maintain the power in such relationships.

Hooking up is also not as casual or risk-free as its cultural acceptance suggests. Women who are perceived as hooking up too frequently risk being considered overly promiscuous (although men are not). Women who "hook up" are far more likely than those who do not to experience sexual violence; one survey found that one-quarter of those who hook up experience unwanted sexual intercourse, with three-quarters of the incidents of unwanted sexual intercourse on campus occurring while hooking up and under the influence of alcohol (Armstrong, Hamilton, and Sweeney 2006; Bogle 2008; Flack et al. 2007).

Changes in sexual attitudes are also found in the fact that the public has become more liberal about topics such as homosexuality, with 55 percent of the public now saying that homosexual relations should be legal—more saying so than at any time in the past (see Figure 4.1; Saad 2008). Women are more likely to agree with legalization of homosexual unions than are men; Whites are more likely to agree than are Blacks and Latinos, although Black women and Latinas are less homophobic than Black and Latino men (Lewis 2003; Battle and Lemelle 2002; Herek and Gonzalez-Rivera 2006). Studies find that those with more traditional gender role attitudes are most inclined toward homophobia (Whitley 2001; Alden 2001). Not surprisingly, conservative Christians are also more homophobic than those with other religious beliefs (Finlay and Walther 2003). But it has also been found that knowing someone who is gay leads to greater acceptance (Morales 2009).

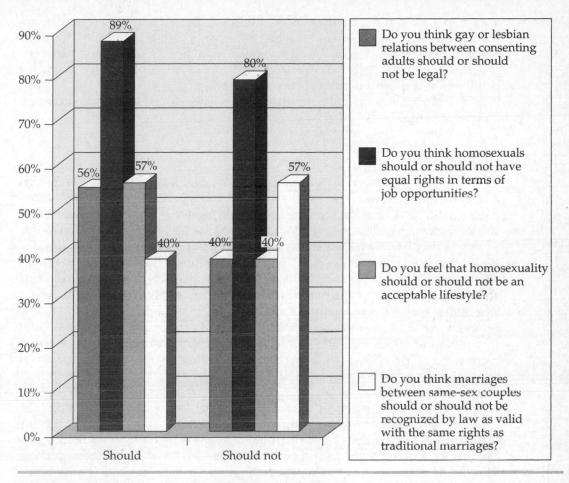

FIGURE 4.1   Public Support for Gays and Lesbians

Source: "Gay and Lesbian Rights." 2009. *The Gallup Poll*. Princeton, NJ: Gallup Organization.

SEXUAL DEVELOPMENT OVER THE LIFE CYCLE

Once you understand that sexuality is not a fixed, biological phenomenon, you can better understand how sexual identity emerges—both over historical time and within individual life courses. Even the biological processes that are associated with sexual development for women—menstruation and menopause—can only be fully understood as social, as well as physiological, processes.

Both menstruation and menopause are socially understood as key to women's sexual identities. Menstruation marks the time when a girl "becomes a woman"—as if the capacity to bear children is the sole definition of woman-hood. And, menopause—the time when a woman's biological capacity for bearing children ends—is also socially defined as a time when women become "old" and asexual. Both ideas are rooted in sexist assumptions that women's childbearing capacity defines their sexual and gender identities. You see this best by examining some of the myths that have developed about menstruation and menopause.

Menstruation

Menstruation is a universal phenomenon, yet, like menopause, it is one that takes on different meanings in various cultures. Historically in western cultures, menstruation has been depicted as disabling women, making them "unfit" for work that was, in reality, reserved for men. In many cultures, menstruation is seen as symbolic of women's strength, and elaborate rituals and rites of passage symbolize that power (Powers 1980). In other cultures, menstruation is seen as symbolic of defilement, and elaborate practices may be developed to isolate and restrict menstruating women. In the nineteenth century, for example, Southeast Asian women could not be employed in the opium industry, for it was believed that if a menstruating woman was nearby, the opium would turn bitter (Delaney et al. 1988). In contemporary U.S. culture, menstruation is depicted as secretive and invisible, as best seen in the advertising industry, which advises menstruating women to keep their "secret" protected, yet to feel confident, secure, and free.

As with menopause, most studies of menstruation associate it with disease. Exaggeration and alarm run throughout discussions of menstruation, probably showing more our culture's fear of women's reproductive processes than a genuine understanding of the menstrual cycle. Consider, for example, the apprehension generated by the so-called dangers of premenstrual syndrome (PMS). If you believed news tabloids, PMS would be understood as responsible for a wide range of deviant behaviors, including insanity, murder, and other criminal acts. When scientists declare that 25 to 100 percent of women experience PMS, what does that mean? It may simply mean that most women recognize bodily signs of oncoming menstruation, although it is possible that a small proportion of women do find the physical changes associated with menstruation to be incapacitating (Fausto-Sterling 1992).

Most certainly, many women do experience premenstrual tension, but the definition of PMS as a medical problem gives the medical profession, not women themselves, the authority to interpret and "treat" PMS (Markens 1996). The social construction of PMS as a disease or syndrome also means that any positive feelings and experiences associated with premenstrual cycles—such as enhanced feelings of sensuality, high-energy states, or feelings of general well-being—are also ignored, since PMS becomes defined by medical authorities as a problem to be treated by them. Public attention to PMS also presumes that only women, not men, are regulated by bodily phenomena—reminiscent of traditional arguments of biological determinism.

These cultural attitudes can shape how young women experience menstruation. Studies show that most premenstrual girls (and boys of the same age) believe that menstruation is a physically and emotionally disruptive event. Associating menstruation with fear and repulsion encourages feelings of shame and can discourage young girls from discussing menstruation with each other, which would potentially provide them more information and support. Menstruation symbolizes the reproductive and sexual potential of women, and its onset occurs at the same time that young girls are developing their sexual identities. The meanings given to this experience are contextualized by a society that both devalues and trivializes women, by defining them as sexual objects. This is bound to affect women's experiences with menstruation and, in particular, to affect how young girls see their developing sexual selves (J. Lee 1996).

From a sociological point of view, menstruation is not just a physical process; it is laden with social and cultural meaning. Physiological conditions such as menstruation cannot be understood entirely without a consideration of the social context in which they occur. This is also seen with regard to the process of menopause.

Menopause

The biological process of aging is clearly one that is universal and inevitable. Although aging is a physiological process, the physiological changes associated with aging are greatly affected by the social context in which aging occurs. Nutrition, for example, affects the biological health of aging persons, but social factors such as living alone or in an institution are known to affect dietary habits, as are factors such as income, cultural preferences for food, and exercise. Aging is also aggravated by stress—a condition generated by a variety of social and psychological difficulties.

For women, the aging process has its own strains. In a society in which women are valued for their youth and beauty, aging can be a difficult social and psychological experience. Birthday cards that joke about women deteriorating after age 29 and commercials for creams that "hide your age spots" tell women that they should be ashamed of growing old. It should be no surprise, then, that a biological process such as menopause can become a difficult psychological experience.

Cultural beliefs about biological events imbue such events with significance different from what is produced by the physiology alone. As an example, popular literature is full of images defining menopause as a disease—a fact that has severely biased both the scientific and popular understanding of menopause. The social context in which middle-aged women live, including their life histories and family relationships, is a more important predictor of emotional response to menopause than are the actual hormonal changes associated with menopause. Most women do not report menopause as a time of crisis, and there is no research to support the usually assumed association between menopause and serious depression (Fausto-Sterling 1992). Depression and mental illness among menopausal women are a function of other factors in their experience, not menopause per se.

Cross-cultural studies also show the extent to which menopause is shaped by cultural beliefs. Studies find, though, that the experience of menopause varies significantly across cultures, with women in some cultures experiencing far fewer symptoms of menopause than women in cultures where aging for women is devalued. Moreover, despite widespread stereotypes of menopausal women, many women report their menopausal years as a time of increased freedom accompanied by feelings of competence and empowerment. Such attitudes frequently outweigh the physiological effects of aging (Wray 2007; Hvas 2006). In cultures where menopause is considered as a time of social—not just biological—changes, women subjectively experience menopause differently. In some cultures, postmenopausal years are defined as a time of women's greater power and prestige (Lock 1998; Dickerson-Putnam 1996). Even within the United States, women's views of their sexuality are shaped by whether they emphasize the cultural and social basis of menopause, rather than just accepting the medical model of menopause (Winterich 2003).

Still, social myths portray the menopausal woman as prone to depression and anxiety, lacking sexual interest, and emotionally volatile; however, research indicates that when these problems exist, they stem just as much from the social devaluation of aging women, as from the physiological process of aging itself (Defey et al. 1996). If society valued all women, not just those who are young, White, and middle class, the aging process would likely not be filled with the emotional and social difficulties some women experience (Stoller and Gibson 2000).

RACE, SEXUALITY, AND POWER

Although most people think of sexuality only in personal or individualistic terms, feminist perspectives examine sexuality within the context of power relationships. The term **sexual politics** refers to the link between sexuality and power (Collins 2004, 1990). The particular forms of sexual oppression experienced by different groups depend on the group's location in the race, class, and gender system.

Race and Sexual Politics

Sexuality and power are linked through the intersections of race, class, and gender oppression. Indeed, race and class oppression are supported and maintained through sexual politics, meaning that sexuality is one of the mechanisms by which systems of oppression are expressed and maintained.

You can see this if you think about controlling images that define subordinated groups, as well as the degree of protection afforded dominant groups who engage in sexual deviance. For example, historically, Black men have been defined as sexually threatening, and Black women have been regarded as "loose." Controlling images

HISTORY SPEAKS: YESTERDAY'S FEMINISTS TALK ABOUT TODAY

Audre Lorde and Same-Sex Marriage

"We must recognize differences among women who are our equals, neither inferior nor superior, and devise ways to use each others' difference to enrich our visions and our joint struggles."

—Audre Lorde (1984: 123)

Audre Lorde (1934–1992), African American feminist poet and essayist, was one of the first contemporary feminists to identify the connection between sexuality, race, gender, and power. Her 1984 essay, "Age, Race, Class, and Sex: Women Redefining Difference" remains a powerful analysis of how different systems of inequality work together to define people as "other" and "different." Identifying herself as a Black lesbian feminist socialist mother, she was one of the first to challenge binary ways of conceptualizing sexuality—and its interrelationship with race, gender, age, and class. She passionately articulated a vision for feminist thought and practice that still resonates today.

Lorde started her career as a librarian and held a bachelor's degree from Hunter College and a master's degree in library science from Columbia University. Her extraordinary book of essays, *The Cancer Journals* (1980), chronicled her own struggle with breast cancer and has since been a source of inspiration and support for many. Lorde refused to see herself as a victim, either from cancer or from her social status. She wrote with power, a deep spirit of spirituality, and a commitment to social justice. Near the end of her life, when she was living in St. Croix, she changed her name to Gamba Adisa, meaning "she who makes

her meaning clear." This nomenclature shows how powerful her work has been.

Lorde was a courageous writer. She read her first lesbian love poem in public in 1971—a poem that was rejected by her editor in a collection of her poetry. The poem was instead published in *Ms.* magazine. One of her frequently cited statements is: "The master's tools will never dismantle the master's house" (Lorde 1984: 112), referring to the importance she placed on Black women's self-definition and self-empowerment (Collins 2000:117).

Thinking Further: Suppose that you had the chance to talk with Audre Lorde. (You can experience this vicariously by reading her work!) How do you see sexual orientation as connecting to age, race, class, and gender? What do you think Lorde would say about today's public debate about same-sex marriage? Do you think you can use "the master's tools" (such as existing legal frameworks) to promote social justice?

Sources: Lorde, Audre. 1984. *Sister/Outsider*. Trumansburg, NY: Crossing Press; Collins, Patricia Hill. 2000. *Black Feminist Thought: Knowledge, Consciousness, and the Politics of Empowerment*, 2nd ed. New York: Routledge; www.biography.com; www.famouspoetsandpoems.com.

of Latinas describe them in dichotomous terms—either "hot" or "virginal"—and Latinos are stereotyped "macho." Asian American women are stereotyped as sexually beguiling but passive; Asian American men are thought of as asexual.

Controlling images also apply to working-class and poor people, who are portrayed as promiscuous and "slutty." To see how these controlling images operate, think about what it would mean to see a poor or working-class woman dressed in very high heels, tight jeans, and a very low-cut shirt. These same "styles" are marketed to well-to-do women with designer labels: Jimmy Choo, Juicy Couture, or "True Religion" jeans—which cost over $200 per pair! This can only be explained through an analysis of sexual politics and their relationship to race, class, and gender inequality.

The sexual politics of race, class, and gender oppression are also apparent in the perpetration of sexual violence against women of color. Sexual violence has been a means of controlling and exploiting African American women (Collins 2004, 1990). During slavery, for example, African American women were used as sexual objects for the pleasure and economic benefit of White men. Marriage between African American women and men was not recognized. The rape of African American women by White slaveowners both made African American women sexual objects for White men and added to the population of slave labor.

Both African American women and African American men are subjected to sexual violence, although the forms of sexual violence they have experienced are gender specific. Rape, pornography, and prostitution have been forms of sexual violence used to dominate and control Black women. Historically, lynching was a form of sexual violence used to control Black men. As Angela Davis (1981) argues, the myth of the Black rapist is one that was conjured up to justify the violence Whites directed against African American communities. Defining Black men and women as uncontrollably lustful and sexually uninhibited is a way of claiming the moral superiority of Whites and ideologically justifying social control and sexual violence (Collins 2004).

Controlling images that were historically developed by ruling classes to justify slavery and other forms of oppression can still be seen today. Dominant images of Black men still depict them as sexually threatening and uncontrolled. Pornography is replete with images of Black, Asian, and Hispanic women as sexual objects, frequently in bondage, wrapped in chains and ropes—reminding us of slavery (Collins 1990; Tuan 1984). Frequently, images of Black women (both in pornography and in advertisements) sexualize them in the context of nature, as if to say that Black women are wild, uncontrolled, and animalistic. Depicting human beings as animals encourages their exploitation by implying that they can be bought and sold and need taming; even if seen with affection, they are treated condescendingly as pets. Either way, the image of Black women as associated with nature constrains and exploits their sexuality.

Asian American women, for example, are still stereotyped as passive and subservient, willing to please and serve White men. The extensive use of exotic-looking Asian women in travel advertisements are evidence of this stereotype. (Leong 1996; Espiritu 1997). Cultural myths also portray Native American women as sexually free and as using their charms to negotiate treaties between White men and Native populations (Tuan 1984). Native American men appear on the cover of romance novels as savage and lustful, with swooning blonde women in their arms (Nagel 2003).

Men are not excused from these racialized sexual images. Men, in general, are seen as unable to control their sexual urges and as needing sex all the time. But, as with women, this stereotype is mediated by racial images. White men are seen as overly interested in sex, but they are not demonized to the extent that men of color are. Thus, Asian American men are stereotyped as asexual; Latinos are seen as driven by machismo and as sexually "hot"; Native American men are stereotyped as exotic but fierce; Black men are regarded as dangerous; and Arab men are stereotyped as mysterious and dangerous.

All of these images distort the actuality of women's and men's sexual experiences and mask the extent to which power relationships shape the intersections of race, class, gender, and sexuality. Although sexuality is thought to be purely personal and private, examining it in the context of race, class, and gender relationships reveals the extent to which structural power relationships influence the experience of all groups of women and men.

Sex Work and Sex Trafficking

Sexual politics is not just about imagery and stereotyping, however. The link between sexuality and power has important consequences for how people are treated. You see this especially in the phenomena of sex work and sex trafficking.

Sex work is defined as employment within the sex industry and can include work done by either women or men, although women are a far larger percentage of sex workers. Sex work includes prostitutes as well as anyone who provides commercial sexual services, including phone sex, erotic dancers and strippers, pornography models, and Internet sex services. Because sex work is unofficial labor (that is, "under the table"), it is impossible to know its extent.

You can think about sex work in two ways: one, as another form of the oppression of women or, two, as a form of commerce that can be studied just as you would any other form of work (Weitzer 2009; Barton 2006). Each perspective reveals different truths about sex work. The oppression model uncovers the victimization of women (and some men) that occurs within the vast sex industry. High rates of violence, subjugation by controlling men, and the exploitation of women's bodies are clearly part of the sex industry. And the sex industry is connected to criminal behavior, leaving women vulnerable to arrest and imprisonment, in addition to the risk of disease, including HIV/AIDS. Moreover, although there is an economic hierarchy in sex work, poor and working-class women, immigrant women, and women of color are among the most vulnerable sex workers.

But studying sex work as another form of commercial labor also reveals that sex work is organized like many other occupations. There is a gender division of labor, with men more likely to be managers and owners, and women as workers. Studies in this vein investigate topics such as mobility within sex occupations, job satisfaction, and the social organization of the work. Some suggest that sex work can be empowering for women, given that some sex workers report that they have more control over their work as sex workers than do women in legitimate forms of work. Research also finds that the risk sex workers experience depends in part on the kind of sex work one does, with street walkers running the highest risks of violence and disease (Sanders 2005).

Sex trafficking refers to the transporting (often involuntary) of women and girls for purposes of commercial sex. Sex trafficking is a well-organized, global system that generates billions of dollars for those who control it. Estimates of the number of women and girls (often young children) are difficult to establish, but some claim that as many as 1.5 million adults and children involved in this practice (U.S. Department of State 2009), more than half of whom are women and young girls. Sex trafficking is linked to other forms of forced labor (also referred to as *human slavery*).

Human trafficking occurs sometimes by fraud, other times by force or coercion. Victims may be actively recruited and then told that they have "debts" they have to pay through sex work. Sex trafficking is also linked to international tourism, where people travel to other nations with the explicit purpose of purchasing sexual services. Sex trafficking particularly preys on women who are vulnerable to economic exploitation—often women from poor nations, women who are immigrants, and other women (and men) desperate for economic support.

Sex work and sex trafficking show the extent to which sexuality—its use and misuse—is part of the social-institutional structure of society. Sexuality is both part of the political economy (that is, political and economic relationships in society) at the same time that it is part of our most intimate relationships.

LOVE AND INTIMATE RELATIONSHIPS

Intimate relationships are an important context in which gender identity is created, re-created, and understood. Such relationships are an important source of love and caring; they provide many forms of social support and are critical to our social identity. Within intimate relationships, gender identity is continually reproduced. Gender is constantly reenacted and reinterpreted in the context of interpersonal relationships.

People tend to think of love and intimacy as individual choices, but intimate relationships, like other social relationships, are conditioned by the cultural context, historical period, and institutional structures in which they occur. Even something as abstract as the concept of love illustrates the significance of historical context in shaping intimacy. Popular images of love see it as unpredictable, uncontrollable, and never ending; yet, the specific meaning of love is one that has evolved over time. In ancient Greek society, for example, social norms defined love for elite Greek men as occurring between them and boys. With the ascendance of the Catholic Church in medieval Europe, love was defined as occurring only within marriage; sex was defined as sinful if it occurred outside the marital relationship. In the nineteenth century, during the Victorian period, strict moral codes regulating sexual behavior were established. Many have linked those strict moral codes to the evolving manufacturing system. The industrial revolution moved work from the home to the factory, requiring new forms of social control to encourage discipline among workers. Strict control of the emotions and sexuality was one way to enforce such discipline. At the same time, the move to a capitalist society in the West created new concepts of love.

The transition to a capitalist society polarized men's and women's roles and created new concepts of individualism. The separation of family from economic production (see Chapter 6) created separate spheres of activity in the home and in the factory. Relationships at work became more impersonal, while the family was increasingly defined as the place for intimacy and caring. The ideal woman was then one who devoted her life to her husband and children; men, on the other hand, were to be independent, disciplined, and emotionally restrained (Cancian 1987). These transformations continue to influence our concepts of love and intimacy. Contemporary society emphasizes the significance of intimate bonds, even while human relationships are easily broken through workings of the economy. Intimacy is defined differently for men and for women; women are still defined as more "other oriented" and responsible for emotional ties, and men are defined as more isolated and individualistic.

Intimate relationships take many forms, each revealing different sociological dynamics. Intimate relationships may include a sexual relationship or may be based only on emotional intimacy, such as in close friendships. The sexual orientation of partners in an intimate relationship is important, however, because it locates the relationship in an institutional system that differently values and rewards intimacy based on heterosexual versus homosexual bonds. Understanding this helps us see how society structures and creates sexuality and intimacy.

Most people believe that relationships are formed simply because people like or are attracted to each other. But there is another sociological dimension to all relationships, including friendships, heterosexual love, and gay, lesbian, and bisexual relationships. All forms of these relationships are situated within relationships of power, social institutional structures, and systems of inequality based on the intersections of gender, race, and class. Although intimate relationships—whether sexual or not—are formed, in part, by the individual attitudes and attributes of those within them, they are significantly shaped by the institutional and historical context in which they develop, including the race, class, gender, and sexual politics of society.

First consider the dimension of power. **Power** is defined by sociologists as an individual's or a group's ability to influence another person or group. The exercise of power can take many forms, ranging from persuasion to physical force. Power is institutionalized in society—meaning that social institutions are structured in ways that give more power to some than to others. Under **patriarchy,** men as a group have more power than do women. This institutionalized power, structured at the societal level, also influences the interpersonal and intimate relationships between women and men. Some research has shown that men's greater control of resources influences their power in relationships with women and that the greater a woman's contribution to household income is, the more power she exercises in family decision making. Even when wives earn more than their husbands, studies find that gender dynamics within the marriage reinforce the husband's power (Tichenor 2005, 1999; Pyke 1994).

Power relationships thus permeate both individual relationships and institutional structures. At the individual level, you can see this in the high rates of intimate partner violence (see also Chapter 9). But even in the absence of violence, people have to negotiate power within relationships—whether they are heterosexual, gay, lesbian, or bisexual relationships. Institutionally, power is reflected in the different treatment of groups, depending on their sexual status. But, it is important to understand that these power structures—at whatever level they are experienced—are built into society.

Power in institutions is seen in how heterosexual institutions structure intimate relationships. **Heterosexism** is the institutionalized set of behaviors and beliefs that presume heterosexuality to be the only acceptable form of sexual expression; a heterosexist system negatively sanctions those who act or are presumed to act otherwise. This context provides structural privileges for those in heterosexual relationships, while denying privileges and rights to those who do not assume a heterosexual identity. For example, although they may be in long-term, loving, and committed relationships, gays and lesbians do not receive the same insurance benefits that married couples might. Because gay partners are not considered a part of the immediate family, they might also be denied visiting rights if a partner is hospitalized and under critical care.

Heterosexism can also discourage the formation of relationships, particularly as heterosexism is manifested in homophobia. **Homophobia** is defined as the fear and hatred of homosexuality. Homophobia can discourage intimacy between same-sex friends if it makes them fear being labeled as gay or lesbian. This is especially, but not exclusively, apparent in relationships among men, where homophobia establishes boundaries of intimacy between them. Despite cultural strictures that discourage gay relationships between men, much of men's interaction is in homosocial settings (i.e., segregated settings that include only men). Studies of interaction between men in such settings find that their interaction is based on emotional detachment, competitiveness, and the sexual objectification of women (see the box, "A Closer Look at Men"). Through these forms of interaction, social concepts of masculinity are re-created and reinforced, with boundaries created between men that keep them from being identified as gay (Pascoe 2008). Men also interact in ways that disassociate them from qualities associated with women. Thus, homophobia not only limits the character of intimacy among men but it also reinforces sexist attitudes toward women.

This argument shows how damaging homophobia is to all kinds of relationships. By ridiculing and punishing affection between members of the same sex, homophobia shapes the expectations and expression of intimacy. Thus, heterosexual friends of gays and lesbians may find themselves "suspect" in the eyes of others, or heterosexual women who display intimacy in public may be ridiculed and accused of being lesbians. In these and other ways, homophobia

A CLOSER LOOK AT MEN

"Dude, You're a Fag"

Research on sexual harassment has consistently found that young men experience being called "gay" more than young women in school. Many scholars of masculinity have documented that homophobic insults and jokes are a common way for young men to express verbal aggression toward one another. But homophobic insults and jokes are not directed exclusively toward gay men. In fact, young heterosexual men are often victimized by homophobia when they fail to conform to traditional masculine gender-role expectations. What does it mean when young men call each other "fag"?

To answer this question, C. J. Pascoe conducted fieldwork at a moderately diverse suburban high school in north-central California. She spent a year and a half observing interactions among students and formally interviewed 49 students (36 boys and 13 girls) at the school. Pascoe found that being called a "fag" was the worst insult one young man could direct at another and literally reduced the target to "nothing." The young men in her study felt that homophobia was just part of what it meant to be a guy; however, Pascoe recognizes that this homophobic insult goes beyond simple homophobia. Being called a "fag" is *gendered homophobia* since, according to her interviewees, this insult applies only to boys and not girls.

Many of the young men whom Pascoe interviewed expressed that "fag" has nothing to do with sexuality or sexual preference; indeed, several young men acknowledged that they would not direct the term at a gay peer. According to these young men, a boy can be gay but still be identified as masculine. Being a "fag" by their definition is the opposite of masculine. Because homophobic insults and jokes are such an integral part of boys' peer culture, the frequent usage of the term *fag* reminds young men that they can be called "fags" at any time if they do not engage in sufficient and appropriate masculine behavior. Pascoe found that the threat of being called a "fag" was an effective strategy for controlling young men's behavior.

Finally, Pascoe found that the term *fag* is also racialized and is not applied to all young men in the same way. Caring about the way they dress and/or their appearance would certainly create the opportunity for young White men to be called a "fag." However, for young Black men who participate in the "hip-hop" culture, concern about clothing and appearance does not indicate a "fag" position, but rather identifies them as members of a certain cultural and racial group.

Pascoe's research illustrates the powerful gendered and racialized meanings attached to young men's use of the "fag" insult. Young men employ this term to police not only their own but also other young men's behavior.

Source: Pascoe, C. J. 2008. "Dude, You're a Fag": *Masculinity and Sexuality in High School.* Berkeley, CA: University of California Press.

and heterosexist institutions frame and shape the intimate relationships of many (see Table 4.1).

It is useful to think of heterosexism and homophobia in terms of the system of social control developed in Chapter 2. There is a continuum of social control mechanisms, ranging from peer pressure (such as ridicule and joking) through institutional mechanisms (manifested in law and social policy) to terrorism and violence (as in hate crimes) that punish homosexual behavior and distribute societal privileges based on the presumption of heterosexuality.

TABLE 4.1   Debunking Myths about Gays and Lesbians

Myth	Reality
There is a gay gene that causes homsexuality.	There is no scientific proof to this claim, even though the media typically use a medical model to frame news stories about research on gays and lesbians. Furthermore, scientists working on the human genome project have not identified a so-called "gay gene" (Horton 1995; Conrad 1998).
Homosexuality is biologically caused.	Although increasing numbers of people believe this (including gays and lesbians), there is no conclusive evidence that it is true. Sexual identity is socially constructed over the course of one's lifetime and emerges in the context of social relationships and social institutions (Simon and Gagnon 1998; Schwartz and Rutter 1998; Rust 2000).
Gays and lesbians are sexual deviants.	Most sexual deviance, such as child abuse, rape, incest, and other forms of sexual deviance, is committed by heterosexual men. Although gay men are less likely than heterosexual men to be child molesters, gay men who are found guilty of this crime are seven times more likely to be imprisoned, even controlling for prior record, admission of responsibility, and the seriousness of the crime (Walsh 1994; Freund and Watson 1992).
Children growing up in gay and lesbian families are psychologically harmed and are likely to become gay themselves.	Children growing up in gay and lesbian households are no more likely to become gay than are children raised in heterosexual households. The major harm that comes to such children is the stigma that they experience from the homophobic reactions of others (Stacey and Biblarz 2001).
Racial minorities are more tolerant of gays and lesbians than are Whites because of their greater sympathy with oppressed minorities.	The reverse is true—that is, African Americans hold more homophobic attitudes than do Whites. At the same time, however, African Americans are more supportive than Whites of gay civil liberties and antidiscrimination policies (Lewis 2003).
Most gay men are rich.	It is difficult to compare the earnings of gay couples with heterosexual couples, since sexual orientation is not included as a variable in national census data; however, there is significant class variation among gay men, as there is among lesbians. Perceiving gays as all rich White men also ignores those who are people of color and those who are poor, working class, and/or disabled (Gluckman and Reed 1997; Smith 1983).

Interracial Relationships

Intimate relationships are also formed in the context of class and race inequality. Thus, research on friendship finds that working-class friendships have a high degree of reciprocity and interdependence with regard to material goods and services; middle-class friendships, on the other hand, tend to emphasize shared leisure, focus on networks of interesting friends, and place a high value on individualism (Walker 1995). Class and race also shape such basic facts as what relationships are formed, as data on the small number of racial intermarriages clearly show. Historically, racial intermarriage was prohibited by law. For example, California state law in 1880 prohibited Chinese Americans and White Americans from marrying. Later, California

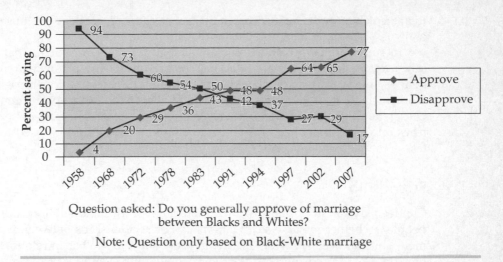

Question asked: Do you generally approve of marriage
between Blacks and Whites?

Note: Question only based on Black-White marriage

FIGURE 4.2   Public Support for Interracial Marriage

Source: Carroll, Joseph. 2007. "Most Americans Approve of Interracial Marriages." *Gallup Poll*,
April 16. www.gallup.com.

laws were written to prohibit marriage between Whites and Filipinos, Japanese,
Hindus, American Indians, and Malaysians (Takaki 1989). Not until 1967 were such
state laws, including those in the South prohibiting marriage between Whites and
those defined as "Blacks," declared unconstitutional by the U.S. Supreme Court.

The vast majority of Americans (77 percent; Carroll 2007) say they approve of
marriage between Blacks and Whites (see Figure 4.2). Still, interracial marriage is
rare, with only 4 percent of all marriages being interracial (U.S. Census Bureau
2009). Interracial dating is more common, but the likelihood of doing so is
strongly influenced by social context. Whether or not one's parents have a circle of
diverse friends and whether young people have a diverse circle of friends are the
two strongest predictors of interracial dating (Clark-Ibanez 1999). Patterns of
racial segregation in society also shape the likelihood of interracial dating. When
high schools have greater racial diversity, cross-race friendships increase. In those
schools with small numbers of racial minorities, students more likely have friends
only in their own group (Quillian and Campbell 2003). But persistent racial segregation in schools and neighborhoods thwarts these possibilities.

Within interracial relationships, people have to negotiate the boundaries that
frame people's attitudes about such relationships—attitudes that are held by White,
Black, Latino, and Asian groups (Childs 2005). Most people also encounter significant resistance from their families for dating interracially—a pattern found among
both Black and White families. Most families are not extremely hostile, but express
strong enough feelings about this to put stress on the interracial couple (Majete
1999). And, although most Blacks and Whites express a color-blind stance toward
interracial marriages, when pressed, they raise numerous qualifications and concerns about such pairings (Bonilla-Silva and Hovespan 2000). Generally speaking,
among college students, racial minorities are more accepting of interracial dating

than are White students; students in the Greek system on college campuses are generally less accepting than non-Greeks (Khanna et al. 1999).

In sum, intimate relationships are shaped by the same forces that structure other relationships. Intimate relationships are one of the primary arenas where gender relationships are played out. Within intimate relationships, men and women create their identities and develop beliefs about appropriate gender roles. Understanding gender and intimacy requires the same analysis of social structures and institutionalized beliefs and behaviors that would be used to examine less personal social behavior.

Friendship

Gender plays an important role in structuring the intimate relationships between people—whether in same-sex relationships or relationships between women and men. This has been shown to be true in friendships as well as in relationships that include a sexual partnership. Research shows, for example, that men are more likely to be intimate with women than they are with other men, even though they report more same-sex friendships than do women. Within friendships, men tend to focus on shared activities, whereas women are more likely to emphasize talking and emotional sharing as the basis for friendship (McNelles and Connolly 1999).

However differently expressed, friendship is clearly important to both men and women. Despite long-held assumptions that women's primary identity is attached to men, research now shows the important role that friendships between women have, including women who live within stable heterosexual relationships. Studies of friendship indicate that friendships do not happen automatically. Making and keeping friends is a complex process, not just a matching of people with similar

Researchers find that friendship among men is more common when men resist narrow ideas about their gender roles. Women's friendships tend to be more intimate.

attitudes and social backgrounds. How one makes and keeps friends is intricately connected to the gender, race, and class relationships in which one lives. For example, professional women put great financial resources (in the form of travel, phone bills, dinners, and the like) into the making and keeping of good friends. Less research has been done about friendships among working-class and poor women and among women of color; however, research does indicate the extent to which support from other women is a necessary part of women's ability to cope with the stress generated from class and race oppression (Moremen 2008).

Research finds that men and women place the same value on intimacy, but they have different ways of assessing it. Women are more likely than men to speak of the importance of being able to reveal themselves and be intimate in friendships. Women also engage in more diverse activities with their friends than men do. Men report their friendships with women as more satisfying and more intimate than their friendships with other men; women, on the other hand, find their friendships with other women and with men to be equally satisfying (Baldwin and Keelan 1999; Yaughn and Nowicki 1999; Siwatu 2003).

Intimacy between men is strongly influenced by the restrictive sanctions generated by homophobia. The fear of being called gay may makes men distance themselves from one another. Men who rate themselves as more "masculine" actually have fewer cross-sex friendships than men who identify with some "feminine" personality traits (Reeder 2003). Studies also find that men who resist the dominant social constructions of masculinity are more likely to form friendships, whereas those who most conform to masculine norms have "comrades," but are less likely to form intimate friendships (D. Levy 2005). Friendships between men are also influenced by the social settings in which the men work. Competition in the workplace, as well as time spent with family commitments, may discourage closer interaction with other men. One consequence is that men, different from women, have fewer close friends in older age and have less intimate interaction with people beyond the family as they grow older (Field 1999).

In sum, research on friendship shows the significance of sociological factors in what friendships are formed, what they mean, and how they are experienced. Although friendship is idealized as what happens when two people "click," in actuality, friendship, like love, is culturally mediated.

LESBIAN, GAY, BISEXUAL, AND TRANSGENDER EXPERIENCES

Sociological and popular understanding of gay, lesbian, bisexual, and transgender relationships has been greatly distorted by the false presumption that only heterosexual relationships are normal ways of expressing sexual intimacy and love. We live in a culture that tends to categorize people into polar opposites: men and women, Black and White, gay and straight. On the subject of sexual desire, however, researchers conclude that such bipolar categories of sexual desire do not exist for most people (Schwartz and Rutter 1998). Culture creates understandings about how people are sexual; people adapt definitions of their own sexual identities depending on their experiences over the course of a lifetime.

It is not surprising that a majority of people assume the sexual identity prescribed by the dominant culture, but this fact should not be taken as evidence of a so-called normal or biological drive. Heterosexual identity emerges from the many scripts that boys and girls learn early in life, including the belief that men have an overpowering sex drive and that women link love, sex, and attachment. (See, as an example, "Media Matters.")

There is a long-standing assumption that sexual orientation is an "either/or" identity—that is, a person is either gay or straight. Recent scholarship on sexual

---

MEDIA MATTERS

Heterosexuality in Children's Films

You probably do not think of children's films as depicting sexuality. The movie rating system is intended to guide parents, thus shielding children from content judged as inappropriate for their age. G-rated films are classified as "appropriate for all ages," presumably containing no sexual images or scenes that would offend parents. But sociologists Karin Martin and Emily Kayzak have systematically studied children's G-rated films and found that even for very young children, these films are filled with images of sexuality—heterosexuality, in particular.

The researchers systematically reviewed all G-rated films released between 1990 and 2005 and that grossed over $100 million dollars—in other words, films that are widely known and seen, perhaps repeatedly, by children throughout the country. Innocent as they may seem, films such as *The Lion King, The Little Mermaid, Chicken Run, Aladdin*, and others teach children specific images of heterosexual, romantic love, which are strongly linked to heterosexuality.

Martin and Kayzak found that heterosexual love is typically a major plot line in these films; only two of the films they included in their sample had no such theme. Children's films typically conclude with a heterosexual happy ending and heterosexuality is also depicted as something really special—amplified by film effects that surround heterosexual lovers with sparkles, fireworks, flowers, and other magical images. Heterosexual love is seen as a place of freedom, where people truly find themselves and live happily ever after.

Moreover, these movies also script images of racial inequality. Thus, sexualized characters are often darker-skinned, buxom, and suggestively dressed, such as Esmerelda in *The Hunchback of Notre Dame*. Partial nudity for all women characters is common. Women are often portrayed as being noticed, commented on, or "caught" by men's gazes. Men's bodies, on the other hand, are portrayed as comical: their crotches, genitals, and backsides are the frequent "butt" of jokes.

These researchers conclude that children's media "depict a rich and pervasive heterosexual landscape" (p. 332). They argue that heterosexual love and relationships are glorified in popular culture, giving even the youngest children clear signals about what is normal and desirable.

Thinking Further: View three of your favorite films from your childhood. Look at them as a researcher would, noting and carefully documenting the images you see that in any way depict love, friendship, and men's and women's bodies. Do your findings match those of the study above? What effect do you think these films had on your ideas about love, sex, and romance?

Source: Martin, Karin A., and Emily Kayzak. 2009. "Hetero-romantic Love and Heterosexiness in Children's G-Rated Films." *Gender & Society* 23 (June): 315-336.

identity, however, challenges this dichotomy. **Transgender** people are those who "live their lives in a gender that is not the gender they were assigned at birth" (Schilt and Westbrook 2009: 441). Transgender people challenge the either/or construction of gender and sexuality that is part of the dominant culture. **Bisexual** people are those who have sexual relationships with people of both sexes. You might notice that this very definition assumes an either/or construction of gender, showing how complicated it is to describe the diversity of sexual and gender identities in a society that defines people as only one or the other.

Throughout life, cultural proscriptions try to direct and channel people into socially proscribed sexual identities, even though human beings are capable of a variety of sexual attractions. But the sexual scripts we learn early in life make it not surprising that most people become heterosexual, whatever their biological inclinations.

Studying the history of sexuality reveals that the categories of "homosexual," "gay," and "lesbian" have been created at specific historical points in time. As much as some people revile homosexuality and think of it as biologically based, the term was not invented until the nineteenth century by Havelock Ellis, an early sexologist, who saw it as sexual inversion. Not until the early twentieth century, however, were the terms *homosexuality* and *heterosexuality* widely publicized—as the public became increasingly fascinated with the scientific study of sex. The contemporary meaning of the term *gay* is even more recent. Used in the first half of the twentieth century primarily as a self-satirizing and flippant adjective, *gay* came to be used in the 1960s in a positive light to celebrate a community with a shared lifestyle. Specifically, gay was meant to shed the stigma that had come from the medicalization and criminalization of gay people (Money 1988). Associated with gay liberation, the term *gay*

Some states now legally recognize same-sex marriage—the result of mobilization by the gay, lesbian, bisexual movement and its allies.

took on a positive and self-affirming meaning—the result of political activism (Fetner 2001; D'Emilio 1998).

Recent scholarship on transgender identities and bisexuality challenges the binary (i.e., "one way or the other") or dualistic thinking that is represented by the assumption that a person is either heterosexual or homosexual. The emergence of **queer theory** has underscored the idea that all sexual identities are socially constructed and that the categories of sexuality that we presume to be fixed can be disrupted and changed (Gamson 1995). Queer theory posits that institutional practices create sexual identities and that the boundaries that distinguish legitimate and illegitimate sex are politically constructed. Without questioning how sexual categories are constructed, theorists perpetuate the idea that only one form of sexuality is normal and all others are deviant, immoral, and wrong (Seidman 2003, 1994). Queer theory emerged from a criticism of gay and lesbian studies that these terms are not inclusive enough (Stein and Plummer 1994). That is, such studies do not incorporate the multiple sexual identities that people can assume, and in so doing, new light has been shed on studies of bisexuality, transgendered people, and gay and lesbian politics (Rust 1995; Firestein 1996; Califia 1997).

From a social constructionist view, all forms of sexuality are socially constructed. Even if there is a biological basis to sexual orientation, what people become in their sexual identity and how they express it is as much the result of social experiences as it is a fixed biological fact. Cultural proscriptions, stigmas, and practices influence the construction of all people's sexual identities; moreover, sexual orientation is an ongoing process that occurs over the development of the life course. Gay, lesbian, and bisexual identities, like heterosexual identities, are constructed through an ongoing series of events and meaning systems (Rust 2000). For example, the *coming out* process rarely involves a single incident. Instead, someone in the process of coming out begins to see himself or herself in new ways and may develop new social contacts and reinterpret earlier experiences in a way that enables a new definition of self to emerge. Likewise, those who develop heterosexual identities are likely to support that identity through a system of consistent social supports and meaning systems that may even include denial or reinterpretation of experiences of being attracted to members of the same sex.

Current research shows that the development of sexual identity is not a linear or unidirectional process, with persons moving through a defined sequence of steps or phases. People do not move predictably through certain sequences in developing a sexual identity. While they may experience certain "milestones" in their identity development, many people move back and forth over a period of time between lesbian or gay identities and heterosexual identities. Some experience periods of ambivalence about their identities and may switch back and forth between a lesbian, heterosexual, and bisexual identity over a period of time. Studies of lesbian and bisexual women also find that some continue alternative identities even after defining themselves as lesbians; thus, some people defining themselves as gay may not necessarily keep that identity (Rust 1995). Some people may engage in lesbian or gay behavior but not adopt a formal definition of themselves as such. Certainly many gays and lesbians never adopt a public definition of themselves as gay or lesbian, instead remaining "closeted" for long periods of time, if not entire lifetimes.

This research shows the socially constructed basis of sexual identity and how sensitive sexual identity is to its societal context. Changing social contexts (including dominant group attitudes, laws, and systems of social control), relationships with others, and even changes in the language used to describe different sexual identities all affect people's self-definitions. As an example, political movements can encourage people to adopt a sexual identity that they previously had no context to understand, but there can be negative consequences to assuming a publicly gay identity. In just one example, a study of gay and lesbian-activist academics found that there were negative consequences for them in terms of discrimination in hiring, bias in promotion decisions, exclusion from professional networks, harassment, and devaluation of their work on gay and lesbian subjects (Taylor and Raeburn 1995). This context, where the stigma attached to gay identities is played out in power relations between dominant and subordinate groups, affects people's willingness to publicly claim a gay or lesbian identity.

Although sexual identity is socially constructed, individuals usually experience their sexual identities as stable. They perceive changes in their identities as part of the process of discovering their sexuality, often reinterpreting earlier life events as indications of some preexisting identity. From a sociological point of view, changing one's sexual identity is not a sign of immaturity, as if someone has missed a so-called normal phase of development; change is a normal outcome of the process of identity formation (Rust 1995).

Understanding the socially constructed basis of sexual identity is in stark contrast to ideas that sexual orientation is biologically determined. Such ideas are popular, not only among those who promote heterosexual orientation as "normal" but also among many lesbians and gays. Is there a biological basis for homosexuality? Periodic reports appear in the media claiming to have found a "gay gene" or other scientific evidence for the biological basis of homosexuality. On close examination, however, such studies are typically based on very small research samples, without the scientific controls needed to prove a genetic or biological basis to homosexuality (Gagnon 1995; Hamer et al. 1993; Rist 1992). Although there may be some basis to such claims, a biological basis for sexual orientation has not been soundly established. There is far more evidence of social and cultural influences on sexual identity—studies that are rarely reported in the media. Even if there is some biological influence on sexual identity, we know that environmental influences interact with biological predisposition; therefore, trying to explain sexual orientation as a matter of biology alone is poor reasoning. The fact is that public belief in the biological basis of gay and lesbian identity, including among lesbians and gays, is stronger than the scientific evidence supports.

Various social myths permeate our understanding of gay, lesbian, bisexual, and transgender experience. First among them is the idea that these identities are sexually perverted, reflected in the erroneous belief that gays and lesbians might make sexual advances toward strangers. This is a distortion of fact. Research consistently finds that it is heterosexual men who are the most frequent perpetrators of sexual abuse and other sexual crimes. Fears that gay and lesbian parents will have deleterious effects on their children are also unsupported by research. Research finds that there is little difference in outcomes for children raised in gay/lesbian households and those raised in heterosexual households. What differences exist are the result of other factors—not the sexual orientation of parents per se. The most significant difference found comparing children in these two groups is the homophobia and discrimination that is directed against children in lesbian and gay families, who are then more likely to be stigmatized by others. Children raised in gay and lesbian households are also less likely to develop stereotypical gender roles, and they are more tolerant and open-minded about sexual matters. They are no more likely to become gay themselves than are children who are raised in heterosexual households (Stacey and Bibliarz 2001).

Another social myth, one especially associated with gay men, is that they are all rich and leading expensive lifestyles. Yet, studies find that workplace discrimination against lesbians, gay men, and bisexuals is extensive (Gluckman and Reed 1997). Data from national surveys report that gay and bisexual men earn actually 11 to 27 percent less than heterosexual men with the same experience, education, occupation, and region of residence. There is some evidence that lesbian and bisexual workers earn less than heterosexual women, but the difference is not so strong, probably because of the general depression of all women's wages (Badgett 1995). Many gays and lesbians remain closeted in the workplace to avoid the discrimination that comes from being "out" (Croteau 1996). There are well-documented risks to being "out" in the workplace, including discrimination in hiring, exclusion from social and professional networks, harassment and intimidation, and, for those doing research on gay and lesbian issues, a devaluation of their work (Taylor and Raeburn 1995; Schilt and Westbrook 2009).

The greatest difficulty that lesbians, gay men, bisexuals, and transgender people face stems from homophobia within society. Insensitive, homophobic comments that are routine in public, and the feeling of being excluded mar the everyday experience of those who differ from heterosexual norms. Just seemingly appearing to look different than heterosexual norms require can result in teasing or homophobic comments. At the other extreme are hate crimes, including violence or even murder—crimes that target those who are gay, lesbian, bisexual, or transgendered. If as much time and energy invested in providing supportive social environments for all people as is spent telling homophobic jokes, bashing gays, and engaging in hate crimes, we would likely build a more caring society that embraced and sustained a diversity of loving relationships.

In recent years, political activism has resulted in greater visibility and acceptance of gays and lesbians, but homophobia and hate crimes are still rampant, as cruelly exemplified by the murder of Matthew Shepard, a young student in Wyoming who was beaten by two young men in 1998 and left to die in a remote field. After beating him and leaving him to die, the young men who killed him also beat up two Hispanic young men, yelling racial epithets at them as they did. This horrid incident shows how homophobia is linked to hatred stemming from racial prejudice and violence. It should teach us about the connections between forms of sexual, racial, and gender oppression (Jenness and Broad 1997; Ferber 2000; Jenness and Grattet 2001).

Now, the vast majority of people (89 percent) support equal rights for gays and lesbians, though fewer think if it morally right (48 percent) (Saad 2008; see also Figure 4.1). And, a growing number of corporations are developing nondiscriminatory policies, adding sexual orientation to diversity training and extending employee benefits to domestic partners. Gays and lesbians are also protected to some extent by constitutional law. A 1996 decision by the U.S. Supreme Court (*Romer* v. *Evans*) ruled that one cannot be denied equal protection of the law based on sexual orientation. Change is slow, however, and sometimes contradictory, as evidenced by the public resistance to same-sex marriage. Although an increasing number of states have legalized same-sex marriage, it is difficult to predict whether additional states will allow or restrict this right for same-sex partners. Gay marriage is discussed further in Chapter 6.

■ Chapter Summary and Themes

Human sexuality is a socially constructed experience.

Although people think of sexual relationships as private and between two individuals, there are numerous social influences on how people create and experience sexual relationships. Gender is one of the most significant of such influences, resulting in different sexual experiences and identities for men and women.

The formation of sexual identity comes from social and cultural influences, not simply biology.

Social attitudes about heterosexuality and homosexuality shape how different sexual identities are judged and valued in society. Lesbian women, gay men, and bisexuals have fewer sexual rights and privileges because of the social structure of heterosexism and homophobia in society.

The history of sexuality reveals how it is shaped through cultural, economic, and political relations, including those of class, race, and gender.

Sexual ideas and practices tend to change the most when there are other transformations taking place in women's and men's roles. These changes have historically been generated by sexual and feminist social movements. Sexual politics are also significantly intertwined with the character of racial and class inequality in society.

Contemporary sexual attitudes and behaviors show greater tolerance for diverse sexual practices, although sexual attitudes and behaviors are also influenced by gender and other social factors, such as race, religion, age, and so forth.

Although there is evidence of greater tolerance for diverse sexual lifestyles, gender stereotypes and traditional attitudes still influence the degree of acceptance of sexual freedom. Homophobia is also common in society and is part of the mechanism of social control by which gender and sexual conformity is sought.

Sexual politics intersect with race and class politics.

Sexual stereotypes socially construct our images of different racial and class groups, with women and men of color being particularly stereotyped in sexual terms. These sexual politics are part of the system by which race, class, and gender inequalities are supported and sustained.

Human sexual development, although a physiological process, is also imbued with social and cultural meaning.

Life cycle events, such as menstruation and menopause, take on different social meanings in different cultural contexts. The meanings that are associated with these processes can shape how people actually experience them.

Gender identity is also constructed through the social character of intimate relationships.

Power shapes intimate relationships in ways that can be identified as gender based, as well as class and race based. Homophobia both directs hostility toward gays and lesbians and discourages intimacy among men. It is one of the mechanisms for reproducing gender inequality. Intimate relationships such as friendships are also shaped by the social context of race, gender, and class relations.

Gay and lesbian experience has been misunderstood by ideas that posit heterosexuality as the only socially legitimate way to express love and sexual desire.

New scholarship shows that gay, lesbian, and bisexual identity is socially constructed. Although gays and lesbians lack the social and institutional support given to heterosexual relationships, social attitudes about gays and lesbians are becoming more tolerant.

■ Key Terms

bisexual	homophobia	sex trafficking
compulsory heterosexuality	patriarchy	sex work
heteronormativity	power	sexual politics
heterosexism	queer theory	transgender

■ Discussion Questions/Projects for Thought

1. How would you describe the *sexual norms* on your campus? How are people's sexual attitudes and behaviors linked to gender in this setting?

2. Over a period of one week, keep a written log of the homophobic comments and incidents that you observe. At the end of the week, review what you have seen and discuss what it means to say that *heteronormativity* is enforced through the social norms of everyday life. As you do this exercise, be aware that what you hear will be hurtful to many. You should keep this sensitivity in mind when discussing this project. How would you feel if such comments were directed toward someone you love?

3. Pick an area of popular culture (a TV series, greeting cards, popular songs, children's cartoons, etc.) and do a content analysis of the images of love depicted therein. Pay attention in your observations to how these images are linked to gender. How do your observations support the idea that the dominant culture promotes *compulsory heterosexuality*?

5

Gender, Work, and the Economy

Women have it made, don't they? Formal barriers to gender discrimination in the workplace have been removed. Women pursue jobs in fields that, not that long ago, were closed to them. Women are visible as major CEOs, fabulously wealthy talk-show hosts, physicians, lawyers, and even sports analysts at professional football games. It would seem that women's equity in the workplace has been achieved.

But look again. Where do you see the majority of women workers? Most likely as fast-food servers, hotel cleaners, cashiers and sales clerks, and other jobs not nearly so prestigious as those above. And, although all fields of professional employment are open to women, women remain heavily concentrated in work traditionally defined as "women's work" (secretaries, nurses, and teachers). Yes, progress has been made, but how much and for whom?

Too often, there is an absence of public discussion around the actual status of women. The recession that the nation experienced beginning in 2009 is a case in point. Most of the public was well aware of the high rate of unemployment, the large number of housing foreclosures, and the losses people experienced in their savings and retirement funds because of large declines in the stock market. But during all the public discussion and analysis by news pundits, how much did you hear about the impact of the recession on women? Probably not much, despite the fact that, as we will see in this chapter, women, as well as men, have been hard hit by this crisis. Without an analysis of gender—and its connection to race and class—you miss the full impact of the recession on men *and* women. Throughout this chapter, you will learn to analyze how gender, race, and class work together in shaping the economic status of women.

We begin by simply noting the persistent wage gap between women and men. In 2008, women who were employed year-round and full time earned $35,745; men $46,367. Women still earn only 77 percent of what men earn—progress since the early 1970s when women earned 63 percent of men's wages, but it's a large and persistent wage gap nonetheless. Furthermore, even with the same levels of education, women earn less than men (again, comparing those working full time, year-round). In 2008, women with a college degree earned $47,018; men earned $65,800—a 71 percent gap (U.S. Census Bureau 2010).Why? This is a question examined throughout this chapter.

The subject of women and work is not, however, just about money. Where you work, what you do, how you are valued at work, and whether you advance in your job are all matters entangled with gender. Women's work is obscured by various social myths, many of which have persisted over time. These myths include that women, particularly women of color, are taking jobs away from men because of affirmative action; that women are now equal to men at work; that women's work is less valuable than men's; and that women who are at home with children are not working—the last myth being central in dominant group stereotypes of poor women. We examine these myths throughout this chapter.

HISTORICAL PERSPECTIVES ON WOMEN'S WORK

One of the first things to know about gender and work is that you cannot understand gender without also understanding class and race. Gender shapes the experiences of all women at work, but exactly how this happens differs for women, depending on other factors such as class, race, ethnicity, age, and sexual orientation. How gender shapes the experience of a top woman executive, for example, will be drastically different from how it shapes the experience of her housekeeper. For both women, gender matters, but so do class and race. You see this clearly in examining the history of women's work.

A brief history of women's labor cannot possibly capture the diverse experiences of different groups of women, but it can reveal the broad patterns in the evolution of women's work. Any single group, however, has a unique historical experience, one that is distorted by lumping different groups together under single labels, such as Hispanic or Asian American. Asian American women's history of work varies considerably, for example, among Chinese Americans, Japanese Americans, Korean Americans, and Southeast Asian Americans. Moreover, the work experiences of contemporary Asian American immigrants are substantially different from those of Asian groups migrating to the United States in the last century. Similarly, Puerto Rican women have a more recent historical experience than Chicanas, whose families may predate many White settlers in the southwestern United States. Luckily, scholars are now documenting the work experiences of these different groups (Amott and Matthaei 1996; Takaki 1989, 1993; Espiritu 1997).

At the broadest level, however, the historical transformation of women's work can best be described as falling in three basic periods: the family-based economy, the family-wage economy, and the family-consumer economy (Tilly and Scott 1978). These periods have been derived from studies of White European women's history, but they help organize the complex social structural changes that mark the development of the work system in the United States and the place of different groups of women within it.

The Family-Based Economy

The first period, the **family-based economy,** dates roughly from the seventeenth century to the early eighteenth century. The family-based form of economic production was one where the household was the basic unit of the economy, since economic production was largely based on households, including small farms, large plantations, and haciendas. Although the specific form of different households would vary under this economic system, and different racial–ethnic groups were involved in different dimensions of this economy, the defining characteristic of this economic period was the household as the basic unit of production.

There would be little distinction during this period between economic and domestic life, since all household members (including non-blood kin, children, slaves, and other laborers) were all responsible for production. The typical household unit would largely have been agricultural, although, as cities developed, so did retailing; artisans' wives would also engage in household labor. In both rural and urban settings, the work of women and men was interdependent. Although the specific tasks done by each might vary, both women and men would be seen as contributing to the productivity of the whole.

White women's labor during this period was highly dependent on their class position and their marital status. Single women (unwed and widowed) might work in others' households doing traditional tasks such as spinning, weaving, and sewing (Kessler-Harris 1982). Women in these households would supervise much of the household work, especially the labor of children. White women might also supervise the labor of slaves. White women were also engaged in agricultural labor and the production of cloth and food, although elite women would not likely engage in such labor.

African American women in the family-based economy labored as slaves, although in many states, African American men and women worked as free laborers, doing a variety of jobs as skilled craft workers, farm laborers, and domestics. African Americans were forcibly brought to the United States by the slave trade, beginning in the early seventeenth century and persisting at least until 1807, when England and the United States agreed, at least in law, to prohibit the trade. It is estimated that over 9.5 million Africans were transported to the United States, the Caribbean, and Brazil during this time, not counting the probably 20 million who died in passage (Genovese 1972).

Black women in slavery did most of the same jobs as men, although in addition, they worked in the masters' homes and on behalf of their own families (Jones 1985). The plantation economy functioned somewhat like the domestic economy because the plantation, like a household, functioned as the major unit of production. In the U.S. South, one-quarter of White families held slaves, although half of the slaves lived on farms with fewer than 20 slaves and three-quarters lived on farms with fewer than 50 slaves (Genovese 1972).

Under slavery, slaves provided most, if not all, of the productive labor, while White slaveowners had total control and ownership of slave labor and the profits it generated. The plantation economy represented a transition between an agriculturally based society and an industrialized one because the population of slaves worked as a cheap and fully controlled labor force. After the abolition of slavery, African American women and men entered the labor market as free laborers, but even then, they could not compete equally for the same jobs available to White women and men.

The early history of Chicana labor was also influenced by a family-based economy. The United States annexed Mexican territory in the Southwest following the Mexican-American War in 1848. Before the U.S. conquest, Mexican families in the Southwest worked primarily as agricultural units. A strong gender division of labor was maintained, with women's work located primarily in the home but contributing directly to the family-based production. As you will see in the following section, the transition to a wage-based economy upset existing patterns of Chicana labor and family life (Baca Zinn and Eitzen 2010; Dill 1988).

Similarly, labor patterns for Native American women were disrupted by the U.S. conquest of Native American lands. Although particular forms of labor, its meaning, and its relationship to other social systems varied across Native American societies, in general Native American societies accorded great respect to women, even when there was a marked division of labor between women and men. Colonization by Whites radically disrupted this way of life, while also imposing external institutions onto Native American societies (Amott and Matthaei 1996).

The Family-Wage Economy

In the second period of the transformation to advanced capitalism, called the **family-wage economy,** the center of labor moved out of the household and into the factory system. This shift was the result of industrialization that began in England in the mid-eighteenth century, followed in France and the United States somewhat later. In the family-wage economy, workers earned their living outside the home and the household became dependent on wages that the workers brought home. The shift to wage labor and the production of commodities outside the home had several consequences for women's work, notably leading to the development of dual roles for women as paid laborers and as unpaid housewives.

With industrialization, the household was no longer the primary center of production, although women's work in the home was still socially and economically necessary. As the focus of work moved beyond the home, the worth of all persons became measured in terms of their earned wage; therefore, the work of women in the home was devalued. In addition, with for-profit goods (not just for exchange or subsistence) being produced largely outside the home, international mercantilism developed, further eroding the position of women (Dobash and Dobash 1979).

In a wage system, producing, distributing, and purchasing goods requires cash. Although women and children worked for wages in the factory system, they received less pay than men did and, in fact, were chosen as workers because they were a cheap supply of labor. Male control of the wage-labor system, along with the capitalist pursuit of greater profits, weakened women's earning power (Hartmann 1976). Because cash resources were needed to survive in the new economy, women became more financially dependent on men (Tilly and Scott 1978).

African American women in the United States during this period worked primarily as domestic workers. Until 1940, as many as 60 percent of African American women labored as private domestic workers (Rollins 1985). African American men worked primarily in agriculture and as service workers, where seasonal unemployment and low wages prevented them from assuming the role of family breadwinner—the mark of masculinity and achievement in White, patriarchal societies.

The history of work for other groups in the United States shows similar patterns of the intersection of race, class, and gender oppression during industrialization and the move to a wage-based economy. In the Southwest, Chicanas were employed in the expanding agricultural market, which often forced whole families to migrate to find seasonal labor. The newly industrializing agricultural economy placed men in mining, railroad work, and agricultural field work as pickers; women were employed in canning and packing houses and in the textile industry; and Chicanas also continued to work as domestics—mainly as servants, laundresses, cooks, and dishwashers (Baca Zinn and Eitzen 2010).

The experience of Asian women in the United States has been one of exclusion. The Chinese Exclusion Act of 1882 prevented male Chinese laborers from bringing their wives to the United States. Other legislation restricted the entry of Asian immigrants and prohibited marriage between Asians and Whites. Those Chinese, Japanese, Filipino, and Korean women who were in the United States were stereotyped as cheap sex objects and worked in restricted occupations primarily as merchants' wives, domestics, laborers, or prostitutes (Chow 1987; Amott and Matthaei 1996).

In the Northeast, White immigrant women filled factory jobs in the textile and garment industries, where wages were low and working conditions hazardous. Other immigrant women worked as domestic workers. In fact, in 1870, one-half of all women wage earners in the United States were domestic workers. By 1920, the percentage of women working as paid domestics declined to 18.5 percent, reflecting employment changes for women as they moved into new fields as clerical workers, teachers, and nurses. Still, domestic work remained a major source of employment for Japanese and Chinese women immigrating to the United States in the first half of the twentieth century (Glenn 1986). Domestic work continues to be a major means of employment for contemporary immigrant women, particularly Latinas (Romero 1992; Hondagneu-Sotelo 2001) and new immigrants.

As production and commerce grew, management became more complex, which led to vast increases in clerical and administrative occupations. The invention of the typewriter created a new concentration of women in the clerical labor force. The typewriter was introduced to the public in 1873 and, because there was a shortage of labor for the new jobs it created, women were recruited for typing jobs based on the ideological appeal that they were naturally more dexterous than men (Benet 1972). In other fields, too, women were recruited when labor shortages necessitated a new workforce. As public education was expanded in the late nineteenth century, women were said to be naturally suited for a profession that required patience, nurturing, and the education of children. Similarly, when the middle class organized the public health movement of the early twentieth century to ward off the "contagions" of the poor, female nurses were recruited to serve doctors and to bring "feminine compassion" to the sick (Ehrenreich and English 1973).

The Family-Consumer Economy

The third period of economic change is called the **family-consumer economy.** This period, also characteristic of the present, is really an extension of the family-wage system, as it developed through the twentieth century. In this period, technological change has increased productivity; the mass production of goods has created households centered on consumption and reproduction (Tilly and Scott 1978). In the family-consumer economy, paid economic production occurs outside the home, but the household labor of family members does contribute to their economic standing.

During this period, women's work as housewives is often coupled with their participation in paid labor; thus, women's economic productivity is even higher than it was in the past (Tilly and Scott 1978). Public institutions (such as schools, welfare systems, and the fast-food industry) also take over activities that were once located in the household. Women consequently become defined primarily as consumers, even though, in most cases, their wages are still necessary for household support.

Over the twentieth century and into the twenty-first, women's labor force participation has continued to rise. During World War II, women entered the labor force in unprecedented numbers. The usual image of women's work during this time is one of women entering the paid labor force during the war, only to return home at the war's end. In fact, three-quarters of those who were employed during the war had worked for wages before. Historians estimate that a sizable group of new women workers would have entered the labor force anyhow; thus, the influx of women to paid work during the war is not as dramatic as usually assumed. Women saw the emergency as an opportunity to get ahead; women of color, professional women, and older women took advantage of the reduction in discrimination to enter well-paying jobs (Kessler-Harris 1982). During the war, women were employed not so much in unprecedented numbers but in unprecedented jobs—jobs that were well paid, were industrialized, and gave a new legitimacy and value to the work that women did (Sacks 1984). At the conclusion of the war, many women did not leave the paid labor force but took jobs in other areas—jobs that did not pay as well as those they had left. Women were laid off after the war at a rate double that of men and were shunted into jobs in the clerical and service sectors. Older women, married women, and racial–ethnic women had a hard time finding jobs after the war.

Since World War II, White women have dramatically increased their employment rates, resulting in convergence of the measures of labor force participation between White women and women of color. Women continue, however, to work in occupations highly segregated by race and gender (see Table 5.1).

In sum, the history of women's labor shows that women's work has been essential to economic productivity. Indeed, women's work, and particularly that of women of color, has been the foundation for the development of economic institutions in the United States. Women of color have always worked outside the home and thus have had to combine work and family in ways new to some White women. White women, at the same time, have been used as a reserve supply of labor, being kept out of the labor force unless there was a labor shortage or a particular demand for cheap workers. As you will see, transitions in the role of women in the paid labor force have also been buttressed by belief systems that make women's labor patterns seem natural and to be expected.

Ideology and the History of Women's Work

In Chapter 3, *ideology* was defined as a belief system that seeks to explain and justify the status quo. The economic and technological changes that marked the transitions from the domestic economy to the consumer economy were historically accompanied by changes in the ideological definition of womanhood. The *cult of true womanhood* (Cott 1977), popularized in the nineteenth century, glorified women's ideal place as the home, where women were seen as having a moral calling to serve their families. The aristocratic lady of leisure became a model to be emulated and set the ideal, although not the reality, for women of the bourgeois class. At the same time, the Protestant ethic, which stressed individualism, success, and competition in the workplace, also encouraged White women to submerge their wills to piety, purity, and submissiveness (Kessler-Harris 1982). At least in White bourgeois families, women's destiny became defined as a separate sphere in which home, duty to the family, and religion would prevail.

Despite these ideals, working-class women and women of color continued to work both in the public labor force and in the home. The reality of their working lives in the early industrial period stands in contradiction to the myth of true womanhood. Only the most affluent families could maintain an idle woman; most women worked long hours in factories and then at home. While the cult of true womanhood was at its peak, African American women were working as slaves, and no ideal of femininity was bestowed on them. The myth of the ideal woman could be created only at the expense of other women because African American, immigrant, Latina, Asian, and poor women still performed the necessary household and factory tasks.

For example, around the turn of the twentieth century in the United States, the woman who stayed at home to do her own housework became a symbol of middle-class prosperity (Davis 1981). Consequently, women of color and immigrant women who had found employment as domestics were expelled from White middle-class homes and replaced by new technological devices that promised to make women's work easy. In fact, some of the advertising campaigns for new products in this period (such as irons) presented explicit images of these new products purging middle-class homes of the alleged germs and social diseases of Black and Chinese women (Cowan 1976). Homes became depicted during this period as bulwarks of defense against the rapid social changes occurring in the industrial workplace.

The new ideology of domesticity portrayed women's place in the home as a moral alternative to the effects of the bustling, nervous organization of public labor. Because many of the industrial changes taking place involved the migration of African Americans, Asians, Chicanos, and immigrants to the cities, it can be said that the cult of domesticity was intertwined with the dynamics of racism. White, middle-class women were not only seen as pious and pure but they were also perceived as the moral antithesis of allegedly inferior women of color and poor women.

At the same time, by the early twentieth century, middle-class women were expected to apply the skills of rational professional men to the maintenance of their homes. Inspired by modern models of rational management, housework (under the guise of the domestic science movement) was to be efficient, sanitary, and technologically streamlined. Order, system, and efficiency were the goals of domestic science, and the housewife was to become an engineer who would keep accurate records, color-code her appliances, maintain an efficient schedule, and, in the modern sense of the word, manage her home (Andrews and Andrews 1974). Once again, clean houses and efficient management were seen as the antithesis of immigrant lives. Racism in this period depicted racial–ethnic groups as slovenly, diseased, and ridden with contagious germs (Higham 1965; Palmer 1989). Racist fears about the underclass propelled the middle classes to a new sense of themselves as both the moral agents of society and the social engineers of the future.

It is from this period that we have acquired many of our common household practices today. During the 1920s, many of the household designs that are now commonplace were introduced. Kitchens and bathrooms were to be pretty, as indicated in the following editorial:

> *Time was when kitchens were gloomy and dark, for keeping house was a gloomy business. . . . But now! gay colors are the order of the day. Red pots and pans! Blue gas stoves! . . . It is a rainbow, in* which the cook sings at *her work and never thinks of household tasks as drudgery.* (Ladies' Home Journal, *March 1928, cited in Cowan 1976:150–151)*

Old wooden furniture was painted pastel colors, new brides were advised to keep the gray out of their husbands' shirts, and protecting the family from germs became evidence of good maternal instincts (Cowan 1976). The ideology of domesticity added an emotional dimension to what had previously been the work of servants.

Women's roles in the home were further elaborated by the new importance placed on child care and the psychological life of infants and children. In the early twentieth century, the child became the leading figure in the family, and child psychology experts admonished mothers to turn their attention to their babies' emotional development and security (Ehrenreich and English 1978). In the end, the concepts of both housewife and motherhood emphasized new standards for women's services in the home. Although technological change created the potential for a reduction in household labor, ideological shifts in the concept of women's roles increased the social requirements for women's work. Whereas housework before had been necessary labor, it now carried ideological significance, as well. As contemporary ads imply, keeping a clean house is not just labor; it is also supposed to be an expression of love. These new standards of housework effectively raise the level of consumption by individual households, leading to the conclusion shared by many social scientists that consumption, not production, is one of the major functions of contemporary household units today.

The preceding discussion shows that an analysis of women's roles in economic production cannot be separated from their roles in family life. Although the family and the economy are usually perceived as separate institutions, historically and in the present, work and family are intertwined.

WHAT IS WORK?

There are different ways to think about the concept of work. Individual levels questions include asking, What kind of work can I find? How can I earn a good income to support myself and those who depend on me? Will I be in a job that recognizes my abilities and promotes my accomplishments? Will I be treated fairly? How can

I balance work and the other dimensions of my life—school, family commitments, personal life? All of these are important questions, but sociological questions have a different focus.

Sociologists are concerned about the opportunities people have to find meaningful work, but they look beyond the individual level to analyze the *social structure of work*. This means asking how the societal patterns of gender, class, and race shape work experiences. From a sociological point of view, even the individual questions people ask about their jobs reflect gender, race, and class relations. To explain, any employed women might be concerned about balancing work and family, but exactly how these strains are felt and the resources women have to address the problem differ across social classes. A professional middle-class woman might solve part of this problem by paying someone else (most likely, a woman) to clean her house, but the woman who cleans it is not likely to have this option. For her, balancing work and family may mean holding down two or more jobs, finding friends or relatives to care for children, and worrying about having enough money to support her family. The point is that a sociological perspective on work has to analyze the gender, race, and class relations that shape the work experiences of different groups in society.

One consequence of feminist studies has been to question the traditional concept of work and its ability to include the full range of women's and men's productive activities. For example, is housework work? It does not fit the usual understanding of work—first of all, it is not typically paid, at least not when done by a member of the household. Second, unlike public forms of labor, it also tends to be invisible. And third, except when it involves outside services, it is generally not supervised. Nonetheless, housework is work—it involves repetitive actions, can be hard physical labor, and there are social standards by which it is judged. Housework involves not just the physical work of doing tasks, but also the more invisible mental efforts that are involved, such as of noticing and remembering the chores that need doing, mentally arranging the tasks that need doing, and keeping track of the work to be done (DeVault 1991). None of this mental work can be actually measured or observed; as a result, it is difficult to share, although it is an essential aspect of the work. We will examine housework further in a later section of this chapter.

ECONOMIC RESTRUCTURING, CLASS, AND GENDER STRATIFICATION

From the history that has been given, you can see that gender organizes the social and economic relations between women and men. Most societies are also organized in a system of gender stratification, although in differing ways and to differing degrees. **Gender stratification** refers to the hierarchical distribution of economic and social resources along lines of gender. Gender stratification is a form of *social stratification*, the process by which groups or individuals in a society are arrayed in a hierarchy based on their differential access to the social and economic resources of a given society. There is nothing inherent in human nature or inevitable in social organization that requires unequal access to social and economic resources, although all societies are organized around a system for the production and distribution of goods and most are marked by some degree of stratification. If inequality were an inevitable result of human nature, stratification patterns would not vary in societies to the extent that they do; moreover, we would not find egalitarian societies in the record of human history.

Socioeconomic inequality tends to emerge when there is a surplus of goods available in the society (Marx and Engels 1970). A surplus of goods creates the possibility that one group of people can appropriate the surplus for themselves. This action forms the initial basis for class systems in which one class controls the resources of other groups in the society.

In virtually all societies, women's work sustains the economy, although in many societies (such as the United States), women's work is either invisible or devalued. Women's access to societal resources is also influenced by the degree to which they control the means and forms of social and economic production. Cross-cultural research shows that women tend to have the most egalitarian status in societies in which they directly contribute to the production of goods (Leacock 1978). In hunting-and-gathering societies, for example, women produce most of the food supply. Their status in these societies is relatively equal to that of men, even though a gender division of labor still exists. In agricultural societies, although women continue to be primary producers, their status deteriorates because land, economic surplus, and, subsequently, political power are concentrated in the hands of male rulers (O'Kelly and Carney 1986).

In preindustrialized societies, women's labor in the home is a vital part of the productive system because it is in the home that goods are produced; moreover, in these societies, women also have visible roles outside the home, as they distribute their goods in markets or even operate small businesses. As industrialization advances, though, economic production is shifted from the home to the factory, and although working-class and immigrant women hold factory jobs, women's domestic labor becomes both invisible and devalued. In U.S. history, the devaluation of household labor has not only resulted in a loss of status for middle-class women who work at home but has also created a class of the most severely underpaid and socially devalued laborers—child care and domestic workers, many of whom are immigrant workers (Hondagneu-Sotelo 2001).

Class is one of the most important dimensions of women's and men's lives because it influences the access different groups have to economic, social, and political resources. Sociologists define and analyze class in different ways, but, simply put, **class** refers to the social structural position groups hold relative to the economic, social, political, and cultural resources of society. Members of a given class have relatively similar resources and tend to share a common way of life. Class matters, not just because of the different opportunities class privilege or disadvantage create for different people but because society is structured in terms of class relationships. Class is not just a matter of individual resources; it involves the relationship between class groups and whole social systems. The class system is a structured (or institutionalized) system of privilege and inequality, not simply the sum of individual opportunities.

HISTORY SPEAKS: YESTERDAY'S FEMINISTS TALK ABOUT TODAY

Emma Goldman and Social Welfare Programs

"The most vital right is the right to love and be loved."

—Emma Goldman

Emma Goldman (1869–1940) was a radical feminist, controversial in her lifetime and controversial today. Not only was she outspoken but she was also an activist, frequently arrested for her activism. Among her jail terms, she served a two-year term in prison for opposing the draft during World War I.

Goldman was born in the Russian empire and lived in a Jewish ghetto. In 1889, she moved to the United States, where she worked in the textile mills in Rochester, New York. Observing the horrid working conditions in the mills shaped her radical consciousness, especially as she observed the contrast in workers' lives and the wealth of business owners. She ardently believed in the right to free speech, women's equality, birth control, and the right of people to organize unions. She advocated that, if the nation would not assist the poor and homeless, they should steal to get food. Accused of being a communist (she was called "Red Emma'), her rights to citizenship were revoked and she was deported to the Soviet Union in 1918. Even though she died in Toronto, Canada many years later, she is buried in Chicago.

Since her death, Emma Goldman's life has been interpreted in the context of American hostilities toward the political left and toward the labor movement. No doubt, she was a radical—an anarchist who thought the government was simply a tool for big business. She had an enormous influence on many intellectuals and activists whose work has been essential in the labor movement and the women's movement.

Thinking Further: Should Emma Goldman returned today and hear of the level of poverty affecting women and their children, how might she react? How would her political views be seen by contemporary people? What debates are going on today about the role of government in social support programs and what might Emma Goldman say about them?

Sources: Goldman, Emma. 1970. *Living My Life: Emma Goldman*. New York: Dover Publications; Drinnon, Richard. 1961. *Rebel in Paradise: A Biography of Emma Goldman*. Chicago: University of Chicago Press; www.womenshistory.about.com.

Class is indicated by who controls money, who controls the labor process, and who controls the production and distribution of goods and services. Those who have such control are dominant in the class system; those who do not are dominated. Class is more than an economic relationship; it involves power relationships as well as differential access to resources and control, domination, and power. Therefore, classes vary not only in terms of their access to economic resources but also in the degree of control they have over how things are produced, who produces them, and how work is organized and managed. The working class has little control over these things; the middle class, on the other hand, exercises greater control, and the elites have the most control of all. In sum, class is part of a structured system involving control, power, and differential access to resources (Weber 2010; Vanneman and Cannon 1987; Wright 1979).

Also, class can be seen in terms of levels in a hierarchical system, typically using several common indicators to measure class standing: income, education, occupation, and place of residence. Although these indicators do not define class per se, they can be used to indicate a person's or group's class standing; these indicators also tend to be interrelated.

Class does not stand alone in shaping women's or men's experiences. As this book emphasizes throughout, class intersects both with gender and race in determining group standing in society. Systems of privilege and disadvantage cannot be described by class, gender, or race alone. The next section reviews contemporary data about women's position in the labor market, with an eye toward understanding how the class system shapes women's economic standing.

The current system of gender, class, and racial stratification is being fundamentally changed by what has come to be called economic restructuring. **Economic restructuring** is the term used to describe a multidimensional process of change in the nation's economy. This includes (1) the transition from a manufacturing-based economy to a service-based economy, (2) increasing globalization, (3) technological change, and (4) the increasing concentration of capital (i.e., economic resources) in the hands of a few. Economic restructuring is fundamentally altering the work people do, including who does it, how it is done, and what it is worth. Understanding economic restructuring is critical to understanding the position of women and men of all groups in the labor force.

Class differences among women challenge the idea that women are all doing well.

The move from a manufacturing to a service-based economy has resulted in a massive decline of jobs within the United States in the manufacturing sector, a decline that was underway even before the 2009–2010 recession. Manufacturing jobs are those that produce goods; historically, these were jobs that were often unionized, had relatively good wages, and one could get with a high school diploma—or, sometimes, less education than that. But these jobs provided relatively stable lifetime employment, usually with the same company (such as an automaker or a steel mill).

Although this sector of the economy was largely populated by White men, it has been a route for upward mobility for women and minority workers. But with economic restructuring, such jobs have drastically declined, even though goods continue to be produced. But, goods-producing jobs have been relocated overseas in what is called a *global assembly line*—or the international division of labor. Furthermore, within the United States, many such jobs are now the work of recent immigrant groups.

At the same time, job growth is in the service sector—where jobs involve the provision of services (such as food preparation and delivery, cleaning, or child care) or the processing of information (such as data-entry jobs, banking, computer work, and clerical jobs). The majority of workers are now employed in the service sector and manufacturing jobs continue to decline in number. The service-delivery segment consists of many low-wage, semi- and unskilled forms of labor and employs high numbers of women, people of color, and immigrants. What this means is that the largest share of job growth in the United States is in some of the lowest segments of the labor market where there is much less opportunity for advancement and little job stability.

Today, jobs in both the manufacturing and service sectors of the economy are located in countries where labor is cheaper. Technological advances allow work to be done, independent of national borders. Jobs may be done in one country when the profit center for the industry is located in another. The person who provides technical support for your computer, your Ipod, or your car insurance might work in India. Or, the seams of your shoes may be sewn by someone, probably a woman or young child, in a poorer nation, but sold at a huge profit margin to consumers in more affluent nations. Or, women in a poor nation may key in the data for insurance claims being processed by a giant health care corporation whose profits are held by a few in a different part of the world. In this way, economic restructuring exacerbates the growing inequality both within the United States and between Western and some Asian societies and parts of the world where natural resources and human labor are exploited for the benefit of others.

Economic restructuring is having a major impact on women and men workers within the United States. Many men who assumed they would be in the labor force until they retired are being pushed out of work. Young workers are finding it harder to find employment; those without a rather high level of education face massive unemployment. Furthermore, since economic restructuring is occurring at a time when the work force is becoming more diverse (i.e., more workers are women and members of racial minority groups), the process of economic restructuring is particularly deleterious for women and people of color. But white men are affected, too. Indeed, analysts show that one of the major reasons for the gap between women's and men's wages declining is an overall decline in men's wages, not just an increase in women's.

FOCUS ON RESEARCH

Women and the Economic Recession

During 2009, the nation entered a major recession—the worst economic crisis faced since the Great Depression of the 1930s. The unemployment rate soared as millions lost their jobs; many lost their homes as banks foreclosed on mortgages that people could no longer pay. Programs to support people in need, such as food stamps, were strained beyond capacity. New entrants to the labor market found it harder than ever to find jobs.

From the tone of the public commentary during the crisis, you would have thought that things like "recession," "economic downturn," and "foreclosure rates" are intangible economic processes that are shaped mostly by impartial market forces—or, in this case, the result of the corrupt actions of a few on Wall Street who mismanaged corporate funds. But who, in particular, did this economic crisis affect and how and did social factors, like gender and race, have anything to do with it?

Early in the crisis, Senator Edward Kennedy reported that "despite their critical role in the workforce and in raising families, women and their vulnerability in economic downturns have received too little focus. [There is a] severe and disproportionate impact of this recession on women and their families" (2008). Generally (and during the recession), men are more likely to be unemployed than women, but during the recession, the unemployment rate among women heading families was *higher* than the national unemployment rate and twice as high as that for either married men or married women. In addition:

- Women in every racial–ethnic category saw a lower percentage of wage increase compared to men in their same racial–ethnic category.
- The downturn in women's wages was significantly greater than that of men.
- The number of women among the *working poor* continued to exceed that of men. Although men were the hardest hit by job loss, remember that holding jobs does not necessarily lift women out of poverty.

- Women were disproportionately at risk of mortgage foreclosure crisis. Women are 32% more likely than men to hold subprime mortgages—that is, mortgages whose interest rates far exceed the prime rate. Moreover, this is true even when controlling for income bracket. In the highest income brackets, the disparity between women and men holding subprime mortgages actually *increases!* Black women earning twice the national median income were nearly five times more likely to receive subprime home mortgages than white men with similar incomes. This is despite the fact that women overall have slightly *higher* credit scores than men.

Despite these facts, few public policies to respond to the crisis took gender into account. Most of the job creation developed from the public stimulus package focused on jobs in fields where women have made the least progress—that is, the skilled trades like construction, highway maintenance, and so forth. Although some public funds helped support new child-care programs and housing support for home buyers, in general the focus was on "shovel ready" projects—an image that even invokes male-dominated trades.

This is not meant to say that men were not harmed by the recession. They were, but it does show that economic processes are not gender and race neutral. Quite the contrary—the workings of economic capitalism are fundamentally about processes of gender, race, and class (Acker 2005). Without public policies that address that fact, we are not likely to meet the needs of specific groups of people.

Sources: Bureau of Labor Statistics, March 2009; Fishbein, Allan J., and Patrick Woodall. 2006. "Women are More Likely to Receive Subprime Home Loans: Disparity Highest for Women with Highest Incomes" (Washington, DC: Consumer Federation of America, December 2006); Jones-DeWeever, Avis. 2008. "Losing Ground: Women and the Foreclosure Crisis." *Journal of the National Council of Jewish Women*. www.ncjw.org.

Economic restructuring means that for many groups, especially women and men in racial–ethnic minority groups and minority teens, there is not enough work; for others, it means there is too much work—long overtime hours, holding more than one job, and piecing together part-time and temporary work. The movement of labor out of the United States leaves many workers at home unemployed since jobs they formerly held are now being done mostly by women workers in other parts of the world (e.g., Asia and the Caribbean, for example) where labor is cheaper, nonunionized, and without the job benefits U.S. workers would likely receive. At home, this has made many workers "disposable" (Sklar 1994).

Economic restructuring has also resulted in the growth of low-income jobs. And, at the upper end of the class spectrum, economic restructuring has also affected the jobs of those traditionally thought of as relatively protected from economic instability. Thus, companies have eliminated layers of management, *downsizing* (shrinking the labor force) and *outsourcing* (that is, contracting with other companies to provide workers) their labor force to reduce costs and maintain business profits.

Downsizing and outsourcing eliminate the career ladders that have provided women and racial–ethnic groups (who are often clustered in middle-management positions) some opportunity for advancement. But, along with white women and people of color, older White men have also been hurt by downsizing, sometimes laid off after many years of service to a particular company. Re-entering the labor market as an older worker can be extremely difficult, as one competes with entry-level workers who can be hired at lower wages. Displaced workers, when they find new jobs, typically earn lower wages than before and, if rehired, tend to be hired into less-skilled work.

These changes in the labor market have also resulted in a growth of contingent workers. **Contingent workers** are those who are temporary employees, contract workers, and part-time workers; they are now one-third of the U.S. labor force. Although contingent work can be appealing to those who want more flexibility (or in some cases, the ability to work at home), contingent workers are less likely to receive job benefits (vacations, health insurance, unemployment insurance, retirement funds, and so forth). They also have little job security and are the group most likely to hold more than one job. Contingent workers also have to spend a great portion of their time looking for the next job or contract. Not surprisingly, women are more likely than men to be contingent workers (Hipple 2001) and the gap in pay between contingent and noncontingent workers is greater for women than men.

What does the future hold? It is hard to know for sure, but some trends are clear. The transition from a predominantly goods-producing economy to one based on the provision of services means that service-based industries, such as banking and finance, retail sales, or personal services, will predominate in the economy. Women and racial–ethnic minorities are also expected to comprise five-sixths of all new workers. And, the U.S. population is becoming more diverse. Thus, diversity in the labor force is predicted to increase in the years ahead. Many, however, will not have the education and training necessary to compete in a technologically driven labor force, unless there are massive reforms in the educational system. The best new job opportunities are likely to be in technological fields where education and technological/scientific training are required. If patterns of gender and racial inequality in scientific/technological education persist, this means that women and people of color will be disadvantaged by these structural transformations in the economy.

THE CONTEMPORARY STATUS OF WOMEN

What is women's economic status and how has it changed? More women are working than ever before, and many women now enter occupations that were previously held only by men. Women's earnings as a percentage of men's have improved, although a significant pay gap remains. At a glance, many might conclude that women's struggle for equality is over, yet on many measures women still lag behind. Women remain highly segregated in certain jobs, their earnings are low, and they experience what has popularly been labeled the *glass ceiling*, referring to subtle but nonetheless present obstacles on their ability to move up at work. How can these realities be explained?

Labor Force Participation

By 2008, 56 percent of all women were in the labor force, compared with 69 percent of men (see Figure 5.1); moreover, since 1960, married women with children have nearly tripled their labor force participation. Hispanic women are somewhat less likely than African American, Asian American, and White women to be employed, but these data are distorted by the clustering of different groups into one category as "Hispanic." Puerto Rican–origin women have the highest employment rates among Hispanic women. Cuban and Mexican American women are equally likely to be employed (U.S. Department of Labor 2009). Asian American women are even more likely than other women to be in the labor force, but, like Latinas, Asian American women's work experiences vary significantly across different groups. Recent Asian

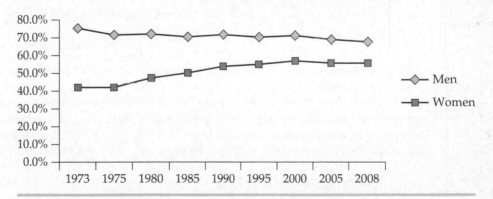

FIGURE 5.1   Labor Force Participation: 1970–2008

Source: Data from U.S. Department of Labor, Bureau of Labor Statistics. 2009 (January). *Employment and Earnings. www.bls.gov,* p. 195.

TABLE 5.1   Earnings in Selected Occupations: 2008

Occupation	Percent Women	Women's Median Weekly Income	Men's Median Weekly Income	Gender Wage Gap
CEOs	23%	$1,603	$1,999	80%
Chemical engineers	13%	$1,546	$1,562	99%
Lawyers	34%	$1,509	$1,875	80%
Physicians	31%	$1,230	$1,911	64%
College teachers	46%	$1,056	$1,245	85%
RNs	92%	$1,011	$1,168	87%
Dental hygienists	98%	$ 988	n/a	n/a
Elementary teachers	81%	$ 871	$ 994	88%
Librarians	84%	$ 811	n/a[1]	n/a
Social workers	68%	$ 779	$ 812	96%
Secretaries	96%	$ 614	n/a	n/a
Bartenders	58%	$ 457	$ 596	77%
Electrical assembly	56%	$ 453	$ 600	76%
Retail sales	52%	$ 440	$ 623	71%
Child care workers	96%	$ 393	n/a	n/a
Maids	90%	$ 371	$ 436	85%
Waiters and waitresses	73%	$ 367	$ 436	84%
Food preparation workers	61%	$ 338	$ 368	92%

Thinking Further: In which occupations do women more closely approximate men's earnings? In which is there is the largest gap? Why do you think this is true? Note that these are selected occupations. If you want to see the full list, go to the website for the Bureau of Labor Statistics (bls.gov) and in the January edition of *Employment and Earnings* under Annual Averages.

[1]n/a means there are fewer than 50,000 workers in this category—too few to be included.

Source: Data from U.S. Department of Labor. Bureau of Labor Statistics. 2009 (January). *Employment and Earnings* pp. 209–215, 251–257.

American immigrant women from nations such as Laos, Vietnam, and Cambodia experience particularly high rates of poverty as the result of low wages.

In the future, the labor force is likely to include more women and minority groups. While women's labor force participation rate has been increasing, men's has been decreasing (as shown in Figure 5.1). In 1951, 87 percent of men were in the labor force, but by 2008, this had dropped to 69 percent (www.bls.gov).

Gender Segregation

One of the most significant factors influencing women's class position is gender segregation in the labor market. **Gender segregation** refers to the pattern whereby women and men are situated in different jobs throughout the labor force. Gender

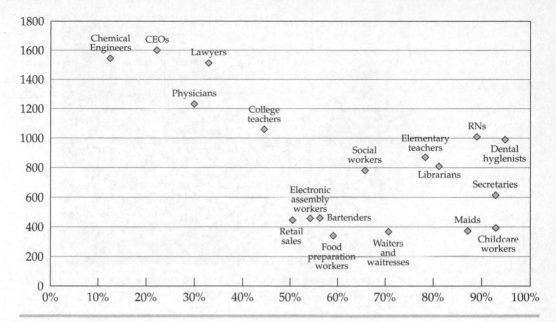

FIGURE 5.2   Income and Gender Segregation (2008)

Note: There is a downward "slope" in this chart, indicating that, in general, the higher the proportion of women in a given occupation, the lower the wages. This is what is known as a *scattergram*. A scattergram plots points along a horizontal (percent women in selected occupations) and vertical axis (women's median weekly earnings in the particular occupation plotted).

Source: Data from U.S. Department of Labor, Bureau of Labor Statistics. 2009 (January). *Employment and Earnings* pp. 209–215, 251–257.

segregation is a particular form of *occupational distribution*—a term sociologists use to refer to the placement of workers in different occupations.

Most women work in gender-segregated jobs. That is to say, women work in jobs where most of the other workers are women, and women constitute a numerical minority of workers in most jobs that have historically been identified as men's work.

Within occupational categories, women are concentrated in gender-segregated jobs. This is referred to as *internal gender segregation*. Take the example of teachers. Women are 98 percent of preschool and kindergarten teachers but 46 percent of college and university teachers (U.S. Department of Labor 2009). Similarly, among college professors, women are most concentrated within the lowest ranks. You can find evidence of internal gender segregation in virtually every occupation.

Gender segregation is further complicated by race. Chicanas, for example, are most heavily concentrated in secretarial, cashier, and janitorial jobs; Central American women primarily hold jobs as household cleaners, janitors, and textile machine operators; Filipinas mostly serve as nurses, nurses' aides, and cashiers; and Black women are most concentrated in the field of nurses' aides, cashiers, and

Although women are more numerous in business and corporate life, they often encounter a "glass ceiling" that blocks their mobility and advantages men.

secretaries (Reskin 1999). As a result, the income of women of color is less than that of any other group. Women of color are also most likely to work in jobs where most of the other workers are women and, in particular, women of color (Tomaskovic-Devey et al. 2006).

These numerical facts affect social relations at work, but they also affect women's income, since occupations with high concentrations of women of color are the worst paid of all jobs. In general, the larger the proportion of women in an occupation, the lower the pay (as shown in Figure 5.2)—a point we return to later in discussing reasons for the gender wage gap.

The data on gender and race segregation exposes the myth that women of color are entering the labor market and taking jobs away from White men. Although some individuals see this happen on occasion, the facts reveal that this can be true only in a small number of cases. The general pattern is that women and people of color work in different occupations than do White men. Why, then, has this been such a big public issue? Critics of affirmative action hiring programs make it seem that women and minorities are flooding the labor market. The data show the contrary. Even with affirmative action policy and equal employment opportunity laws, White women, African American women and men, Hispanics, Asian Americans, and Native Americans are employed in a labor market very much divided by race and by gender (Charles and Grusky 2004; Browne 1999).

To understand fully women's experiences in these different positions of work requires a closer view of women's experiences in various work settings. This gives us a picture drawn not just from government statistics but also drawn from the many studies of women and work that closely examine women's experiences in different parts of the labor market.

Women in the Professions

Women who work in professional jobs hold some of the most prestigious and better paid jobs in the labor market. And, it is in the professions where women have made some of the most visible gains. As examples, women are now one-third of all physicians, one-third of lawyers, and 23 percent of CEOs. Yet, even with these gains in professional work, women still tend to be concentrated in gender-segregated occupations (such as nursing, social work, and elementary school teaching).

Moreover, within specific professional fields, women are concentrated in the lower ranks and in less prestigious specialties. In medicine, for example, women are still more likely to specialize in pediatrics than are men (American Medical Association 2004). Also, women physicians are more likely to work in university or hospital staff positions rather than in independent practices. Similarly, in law, although women are now more widely distributed across different specialties within law, they are still more likely to be found in certain areas (such as domestic law, real estate, trust, and general practice), and they are twice as likely as men to work in public service law (Epstein 1993). Studies of lawyers also find that women are significantly less satisfied than men with the level of responsibility they are given, their chances for advancement and salary, and the recognition they get for their work (Garcia-López 2008; Hull 1999; Higginbotham 2009).

Within the professions, patterns of sponsorship and mentoring are critical to upward mobility. Studies consistently find that men are more likely to get such sponsorship than are women. Professions are socially organized like communities and, as such, involve informal roles and practices and tend toward homogeneity and exclusionary relations. Social control in professional life, as well as access to rewards, typically operates through a sponsorship system that feminists have labeled the "old boy network." Within the network, social relations with one's peers and mentors can bring access to jobs, promotions, opportunities, and status. For women and men of color, the lack of support and absence of mentoring can be especially burdensome and impede mobility in careers (Higginbotham 2001). Women and people of color excluded from the protégé system are likely to find themselves at a disadvantage when it comes to professional opportunities. The information and collegiality shared by those in the network are likely to give professional advantage to those who are "in the know." Whether by exclusion or personal choice, women and people of color who are not part of the "old boy network" are likely to find their careers detrimentally affected.

The climate in graduate and professional schools also influences women's subsequent career patterns. Studies show that the climate in these settings often reflects a male-dominated culture, which women encounter once they enter these professions. The clockwork of professional careers has also been historically developed around the presumed life course of a professional man—that is, that work comes before family. This male-centered model creates gendered institutions at the workplace; thus, one is expected to put in long hours at work—often at times in the life course when people are establishing families; professional work demands that workers be available whenever the profession calls, regardless of family or personal commitments. One may even be expected to uproot one's family, moving for a promotion or the relocation of one's job.

In some progressive firms, there is now more flexibility—for both women and men in the professions, in programs such as spousal/partner hiring efforts, flexible time, parental leave, and so forth. But many workers report that actually taking advantage of such policies can lead to the perception that one is not seriously committed to work (Stone 2007).

Because of these issues, women in most professional fields have established alternative networks of support, both for professional advancement and for personal support. Groups such as the Association for Women in Science, the Society of Women Engineers, Sociologists for Women in Society, and the American Medical Women's Association, to name only a few, have flourished. As both professional networks and local support groups for women professionals, these organizations encourage networking, information sharing, and personal support as a way of promoting the status and well-being of professional women.

Women as Clerical Workers

Women make up 75 percent of all administrative support workers, a category of the U.S. Department of Labor that includes an array of different occupations, such as bank tellers, bookkeepers, court clerks, data entry workers, general office clerks, secretaries, and others. Women are a large majority of most of these different occupations. As late as 2008, secretarial/administrative work was still the most common occupation for women (U.S. Department of Labor Women's Bureau 2010). Women are still 96 percent of all secretaries.

Over the course of the twentieth century, the number of clerical workers drastically increased, but their prestige declined and remains one of the most undervalued (and underpaid) occupations, even as the technological skills required to do the work have increased. Before the invention of the typewriter in the late nineteenth century, skills such as shorthand and accounting were men's trades, and relatively prestigious trades at that. An 1888 book titled *How to Succeed as a Stenographer or Typewriter*—a book addressed to men—states, "There are comparatively few verbatim reporters, and the young shorthand writer who has reached that distinction should consider that it gives him the rank of a scholar and a gentleman" (Baker 1888, cited in Benet 1972:39). With the introduction of mechanized switchboards and typewriters, a need for more workers developed, bringing the rapid introduction of women workers to these jobs. Business owners saved money by tapping the cheap, large, female labor market. Soon, as women predominated, the wages associated with office work declined, as did the prestige bestowed on office work.

To this day, the median weekly earnings for women in administrative support work are low, especially compared with those of men. In 2008, full-time male administrative support workers earned $651 per week, compared to $590 per week for women (U.S. Department of Labor 2009). A huge supply of women clerical workers is also provided by temporary clerical services, where workers have low wages, little control of their work, minimal social relationships with co-workers, and highly alienated attitudes toward their jobs. Opportunities for advancement are greater for secretaries than for other clerical workers, but mobility for secretaries is often dependent on the promotion of their supervisor, not just their own performance.

Full-time secretaries, except those who work in large pools where work is heavily routinized, are also tied to individualized relationships with their bosses. A secretary's status is likely dependent on that of her boss. Bosses wield enormous power over such workers and these relationships can be tricky to negotiate. Bosses may expect their secretaries to appreciate and provide non-material rewards such as emotional intimacy, praise, and affection. Yet, studies show that most secretaries resent doing personal work for their boss, but loyalty and devotion to a boss is often the basis for secretaries' rewards at work (Kanter 1977).

The increased use of computers has advantages and disadvantages for clerical workers. Computerized technology can eliminate some of the stress from routine, repetitive, and tedious aspects of one's job, but in occupations such as data entry, the work becomes more routinized. Increasingly, large numbers of women, especially women of color, work in "electronic sweatshops" entering keyboard data, with their work electronically monitored. Computer technology also brings new forms of fatigue, physical strain, and stress. Many researchers argue that the negative effects of computers are not the result of the technology per se, but of the way they are used in the workplace. Because clerical workers are seldom given any authority or responsibility for designing their workplace, it is little wonder that they suffer the consequences of poor workplace design and organization (Fox and Sugiman 1999).

Women in Blue-Collar Work

Among blue-collar workers, women have been entering the skilled trades at a rapid rate—faster, in fact, than men in recent years—but women still constitute only a small percentage of those in the more highly skilled trades—only 2 percent of construction workers and 4 percent of maintenance and repair occupations (U.S. Department of Labor 2009). Women in blue-collar work are far more likely to be employed as semiskilled machine operators than as skilled crafts workers; within the occupational categories in which they work, women earn less than men.

Women in blue-collar work also experience gender segregation on the job. Even when women are employed in the same occupational category as men, they are usually located in different industries. Thus, women are more likely to be employed in the nondurable-goods sector, whereas men are more likely employed in manufacturing, where wages and job benefits have traditionally been higher. In fact, the majority of women in blue-collar work are employed in assembly work—jobs with little autonomy and often involving repetitive tasks.

Although their numbers are small, more women are entering jobs formerly occupied solely by men.

Depending on the region of the country, women in assembly work are a disproportionate number of assembly-line workers.

Blue-collar workers in the United States, both women and men, are also increasingly affected by global restructuring of the economy. Research and management are based in developed countries (e.g., the United States), while assembly-line work is relegated to underprivileged nations (especially in Latin America and Asia). In the global assembly line, women workers are relocated from their traditional work in home-based production and are employed in factories as assembly workers. This new work gives women somewhat greater independence from traditional patriarchal arrangements but introduces them to new forms of exploitation in the form of high job turnover, little mobility, low wages, and hazardous working conditions. Their work within these settings is often justified through crude sexist and racist ideologies defining them as "fit" for this demeaning work.

The global assembly line links the experiences of women in poor nations to the consumerism in the United States that "markets gender." Barbie dolls are a good example. Barbie is the "dream girl" of the United States, each version depicting a different fantasy life of beauty, fashion, romance, and play. But most Barbie dolls are manufactured by workers not much older than those who play with her in the United States. For these workers, it would take all of their monthly pay just to buy *one* of the dolls that many U.S. girls collect by the dozens. In China, where 70 to 80 percent of all U.S. children's toys are made (Lipton and Barboza 2007), workers molding Barbie dolls earn very low wages, and human rights organizations say violations of basic rights are flagrant. Some say that it would take a worker making Barbies a full month to earn the money to buy one (Press 1996).

You do not have to look overseas to witness the conditions of women's labor in sweatshops. Within the United States, the largest number of sweatshop workers is immigrant women—many of whom work in the garment industry, although that is not the only industry that employs sweatshop labor. Sweatshops are often run by subcontractors who are selling labor to larger companies—such as the well-known brand names of men's and women's fashion. This method of subcontracting allows companies to cut labor costs, thereby increasing their profits.

The government defines a **sweatshop** as a workplace where an employer violates more than one law regarding safety and health, workers' compensation, or industry regulation. The government estimates that more than half of the laborers who work in garment production work in sweatshops where they are paid below minimum wage and work in unsafe and unhealthy workshops. Workers may also

A CLOSER LOOK AT MEN

Blue-Collar Jobs, Social Networks, and the Exclusion of Black Men

Middle- and upper-class job seekers are familiar with the phrase "It's not what you know, it's who you know." Social networks are key factors in securing employment. How important are social networks to blue-collar job seekers and to securing jobs in the blue-collar labor market?

Deirdre Royster conducted a study to examine the relationship between social networks and economic advancement of modestly educated blue-collar men. Royster interviewed 50 young men (half of whom were Black and half White) who, based on their credentials, should have similar success in the blue-collar labor market. All of the men had high levels of residential stability and sustained friendship networks; none had dropped out of school.

All of the young men in her study said that social contacts were very important in establishing blue-collar careers. However, Royster found that, although the Black and White men in her study were identical on paper (i.e., they were trained in the same school by the same instructors, they had access to the same job-listing services and work-study programs, etc.), the Black

men lagged behind their White counterparts. The Black men were employed less often in the skilled trades for which they were trained, earned less money, held lower-status positions, and received fewer promotions than their White peers.

These findings led Royster to conclude that it is not the lack of education, skill, or personal characteristics of Black men that preclude them from economic advancement. Rather, it is their racial status and the patterns of exclusion that have long existed in the blue-collar trades. For modestly educated men, social networks are pivotal in securing employment in the blue-collar sector; however, these social networks seem to benefit only White men. Royster's study demonstrates how racism continues to deny economic opportunities and social mobility to Black men because of patterns built into society, not the individual characteristics of the men.

Source: Royster, Deirdre A. 2003. Race and the Invisible Hand: How White Networks Exclude Black Men from Blue-Collar Jobs. Berkeley, CA: University of California Press.

be reluctant to file complaints for fear of losing their jobs, or, if they are undocumented workers, they may fear deportation. Despite these fears, many sweatshop workers have organized to campaign for workers' rights. A significant movement against the use of sweatshop labor to produce college logo products has also emerged on many college campuses (Bonacich and Applebaum 2000; Applebaum and Dreier 1998).

For women, as for men, being in a union has significant advantages, although union membership is declining and women are slightly less likely than men to be protected by labor unions (11 percent of employed women are represented by unions compared to 13 percent of men). African American men and women are more likely to be represented by unions than are White, Asian American, and Hispanic American men and women (U.S. Department of Labor 2009).

Union membership increases the likelihood of due process and job protection, but also the earnings of unionized workers exceed those non-union members. Despite declines in overall union membership, women and people of color are increasingly important in trade unions. Given the declines in the manufacturing industry, union members are no longer centered primarily on blue-collar labor, but include large numbers of organized service workers who, as we have seen, are more likely to be women and people of color. Women's activism within unions thus means that many unions now give greater attention to women's issues, including not only compensation and working conditions but also the development of family-friendly policies for workers. Union adoption of such issues has also been shown to depend on an increase in the membership of women in specific unions (Gerstel and Clawson 2001; Cranford 2007).

Women and Service Work

Service work is the third largest category of women's employment, accounting for 21 percent of women in the labor force. Women in service work are among the lowest paid of employed women, yet this is the most rapidly expanding area of work—one where most new jobs are predicted to be found in the future. Included in service work are fast-food workers, waitresses, and health-care assistants (e.g., nurses' aides, maids, and various personal service workers). This category of work employs large numbers of women of color, as well as older women workers returning to the labor force after years of working in the home. In 2008, the median weekly earnings for service were $537 for men and $418 for women (U.S. Department of Labor 2009); those working in private households earned even less (refer to Table 5.1 earlier in this chapter).

Service work is highly segregated by gender, even within specific occupational categories. For example, women constitute almost two-thirds of food preparation workers, but less than one-fifth of chefs. High rates of turnover and part-time employment are also common in service work, further limiting women's chances for upward mobility in those occupations.

Service work can also be one of the most degrading forms of work for women. Women service workers are often supervised by men whose attitudes can be patronizing, impatient, and overtly hostile. Sexist expectations also shape women's experiences in these occupations. Waitresses, for example, are often expected to be young and sexy, to dress in provocative clothing, and to treat even the most obnoxious customer with grace and charm. Sometimes, sexist expectations for women service workers are very explicit, as in the old requirements of some airlines that flight attendants not exceed certain weight and height standards. Even when not written into explicit employment practices, these expectations often shape women's opportunities in service occupations. For women of color in these occupations, the combination of sexist and racist attitudes and behaviors can be doubly demeaning.

For many years, employment as a domestic worker was the only choice for women who needed to work, particularly women of color. Now, although other opportunities are available, large numbers of women still work in private households where their labor is unregulated and sometimes unreported. Although it pays poorly, domestic work is often the only work available for incoming groups of immigrant women, women with little education, and women with little choice of occupation. In recent years, refugees from Latin America have entered domestic work, receiving low wages and few, if any, benefits. Domestic workers seldom face opportunities for unionization and are rarely given employee benefits such as health-care insurance, paid sick leave, retirement, or vacation. Although private-household workers sometimes have the benefit of negotiating their own work schedules and, thus, may have greater flexibility than workers in the public sector, they pay the price in terms of low wages and little job security (Repak 1994; Hondagneu-Sotelo 2001).

Women who work as domestic workers regard the independence and autonomy of the job as a positive feature of the work, but since domestic workers typically do not have co-workers, loneliness, especially for live-ins, is the most difficult part of the work. Although employers may act caring and protective, the job is still structured as a power relationship. Patterns of deferential behavior, such as referring to the domestic as "girl" and treating the domestic as if she is invisible, reveal the subordination and exploitation in this work (Rollins 1985).

Service workers, including both men and women, also engage in what sociologist Arlie Hochschild (1983) calls **emotional labor,** referring to the work people do to manage the emotions of others. Emotional labor, she argues, is work that is done for wages and that is meant to achieve a desired emotional effect in others. Technically, because housework is unpaid, it does not fit the classic definition of emotional labor. Hochschild's analysis of emotional labor involved jobs that require personal contact with the public, wherein creating a given state of mind in the client or user is part or all the product being sold. (Flight attendants were the example she used in her initial research.) Hochschild shows that as a result of the shift from a production-based to a service-based economy, and given the fact that women predominate in service-oriented jobs, emotional labor is a growing part of the work that women do. It is monitored by supervisors and is the basis for job rewards and reprimands. She concludes that doing emotional labor often requires putting on a false front; as a result, engaging in emotional labor is a source of workers' stress. Emotional labor is required in an increasing number of jobs and is therefore subject to the rules of mass production, resulting in what Hochschild calls "the commercialization of human feeling."

Earnings

Perhaps we would not care if women and men worked in racial–ethnic- and gender-segregated jobs if that fact did not have such enormous consequences for women's earnings (see Figure 5.3). Women earn only 77 percent of what men earn, at least on average (DeNavas-Walt et al. 2009). Low earnings have serious consequences for women. Those who head their own families are in an especially precarious position, since they are so likely to be poor (see Figure 5.4).

Why do these earning differentials persist? There are several explanations, beginning with overt discrimination. **Discrimination** refers to practices that systematically disadvantage one or more groups; it can be overt or covert. Overt discrimination occurs when someone treats someone differently simply because of some characteristic of the person (e.g., gender, age, sexual orientation, race, religion, or national origin, to name a few). Paying someone a different wage *because* she is a woman is discrimination, as is not hiring someone presumed to be gay or lesbian.

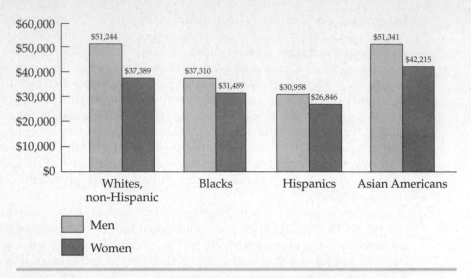

FIGURE 5.3 The Gender Wage Gap: 2008 (year-round, full-time workers)

Source: Data from U.S. Census Bureau. 2010. *Detailed Income Tables*, Table PINC-05. www.census.gov.

Overt discrimination because of someone's sex, race, or age is illegal. But discrimination is not always obvious or overt, sometimes not even to the person experiencing it. Discrimination is not just an individual action, although it can be that, but it is institutionalized, so it can occur even when individuals do not intend to discriminate. For example, in individual discrimination, an employer might think women are not qualified for certain jobs and exclude them because of this. But institutional discrimination can occur when there are structural patterns that result in women's exclusion from certain jobs—such as if women have not had the education and training needed to qualify for particular jobs. This is *institutionalized discrimination*. Institutionalized discrimination can be harder to see because it is not represented by someone making an overtly sexist comment or deliberately blocking access to a job, but this form of discrimination is realm, pervasive, and persistent.

Although overt discrimination has certainly diminished, research shows that it continues to influence work opportunities for women. Employer stereotypes about the most valuable workers influence who is hired (Neckerman and Kirschenman 1991; Moss and Tilly 2001). Studies also find that employers still imagine successful managers to be men (Willemsen 2002) and tend to rank White men as more valuable employees than either White or Black women. As a result, employers are therefore more likely to invest in white men's success (McGuire 2002). Numerous studies have also found that the stereotypes employers hold about women—and women of color in particular—continue to disadvantage women in sometimes subtle, but nonetheless, significant ways (Kennelly 1999).

Sometimes men will organize as a group to block women from entering formerly male-dominated organizations. Historically, for example, men in labor unions developed policies excluding women and minorities from union membership, thereby excluding them from better-paying union-based jobs (Padavic and Reskin 2002)). One could interpret the contemporary backlash against affirmative action policies in a similar vein—as the mobilization of dominant groups to preserve their historic privilege in the workplace.

Much of what happens to women in the labor market is not, however, caused by overt discrimination. Scholars have looked to other structural causes to explain the continuing inequality in women's and men's earnings. Two primary explanations have emerged: human capital theory and dual labor market theory.

Human Capital Theory

Human capital theory explains wage differentials as a result of different characteristics of workers. *Human capital* consists of worker characteristics, such as level of education, marital status, prior experience, training, and so forth—individual level variables. *Human capital theory* assumes that, in a competitive economic system, wage differences reflect differences in human capital. Presumably, high turnover rates, interrupted careers, and shorter participation in the labor force among women lead to lesser productivity and therefore lower wages.

Statistical studies of human capital variables (such as differences in marital status, prior work experience, and so forth) find that human capital variables explain a portion of the gender wage gap, but a significant portion of the earnings gap goes unexplained by human capital theory (Firestone et al. 1998; Avalos 1996). As human capital differences between women and men are lessened (such as providing more technical training for women and girls), the wage difference between men lessens. But human capital theory does not explain the entire wage gap. You can see this visually by looking at the gap in men's and women's wages even with comparable levels of education (see Figure 5.4). Persistent patterns of discrimination, as we have seen, and something called the *dual labor market* add to our understanding of the gender gap in wages.

Dual Labor Market Theory

Dual labor market theory analyzes the labor market as organized around both a *primary* and a *secondary market*. Jobs in the primary labor market have more stability, higher wages, better working conditions, greater chances for advancement, and due process in the administration of work roles. The primary labor market generally also provides better job benefits, such as health insurance, retirement pension plans, vacation, and other features that make these the most attractive jobs.

The secondary labor market, on the other hand, includes jobs with low pay, higher turnover and less job security, fewer employee benefits, and often irregular or arbitrary personnel practices. Working conditions in these jobs can be poor and there is usually little chance for advancement. To compare the kinds of jobs that are available in the primary and secondary market, think of a job like an entry-level job in a corporate law firm (such as a paralegal or even an attorney) or even

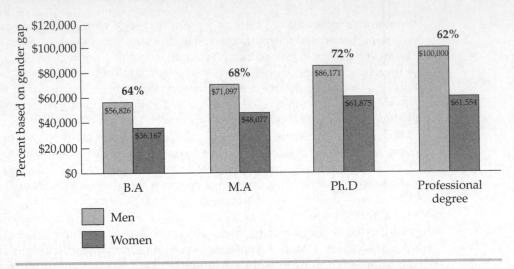

FIGURE 5.4   Median Income by Gender, Race, and Education: 2008

Source: Data from U.S. Census Bureau. 2010. *Detailed Income Tables,* Table PINC-01.
www.census.gov.

a job in a business organization where you might work as a financial analyst or
personnel manager. Jobs in the secondary labor market might include serving
food in a fast-food restaurant, sweeping floors in a school, or even "under the
table" work, such as housecleaning or babysitting (although such jobs, being
"unofficial," do not show up in labor force statistics).

Labor market data show that women and people of color (as well as younger
workers) are more likely to be employed in the secondary labor market, where
there may be numerous points of job entry, but short or nonexistent promotion
ladders, little job security, and sometimes capricious rules of job supervision. (As
a waitress, for example, you might get fired for not pleasing your supervisor.) The
dual labor market perspective causes us to look at occupational distribution by
gender as a major factor in the earnings gap between men and women and leads
us to conclude that *where* people work, not *what* their individual characteristics
are, is a better predictor of income.

Dual labor market theory points to **gender segregation** as a major cause of
wage inequality. As evidence of this, studies find that as occupations become more
populated by women, wages actually tend to decline—both for women and men.
The argument here is that when occupations become "feminized," they become
seen as less attractive careers and the work becomes less rewarded (Reskin and
Roos 1990). This has happened historically in many occupations and may be happening currently for others, such as physicians and lawyers.

Comparing human capital theory and dual labor market theory involves analyzing individual-level characteristics versus more social structural (or societal
level) features to understand the wage gap. As said earlier, both contribute to an
explanation of the gender wage gap. But societal level factors—such as the gender

composition of an occupation, the context of economic decline or prosperity, and the degree to which jobs are gender segregated—are powerful explanations of the wage gap, even though people tend to look only at individual level factors when they try to explain gender differences.

Promotions

Beyond wages, another important area of study is the analysis of gender and career advancement. The obstacles that women encounter at work have popularly come to be known as the **glass ceiling.** This phrase is meant to convey the fact that, even though most formal barriers to women's advancement have been removed, there are invisible mechanisms that prevent women from advancing. These mechanisms are "invisible" because they are built into the social structure of organizations, and they are not as obvious as formal restrictions and rules that discriminate against women.

What does the evidence tell us about women's advancement in the workplace? Most studies find that women are actually promoted more often than men—that is, if promotion means moving from one job classification to another. However, for women, promotions are most likely to be lateral (i.e., from one location in an occupational system to another of similar rank and status), whereas men's promotions are more likely to be vertical (i.e., upward in the job ranks). Even when men and women have the same qualifications, such as education and prior experience, they often do not receive similar promotions.

The gender composition of an occupation also affects the likelihood of women being hired and promoted in this occupation. Specifically, women are more likely hired and promoted into jobs with a high proportion of women. The glass ceiling is even more of a barrier for women of color. Women of color are still the most underrepresented group in senior management positions, and they are the group most frequently excluded from the most senior and powerful positions in work organizations. Institutionalized practices that identify White men as leaders and others as just workers continue to disadvantage women and people of color who then get "niched" in parts of the organization where career ladders are nonexistent. Even when White women and men and women of color are promoted, they generally have to wait longer than White men (Ridgeway 2001; Cotter et al. 2001; Maume 1999; Baxter and Wright 2000; Durbin 2002; Porter 2003).

The concept of *job ladders* reflects the fact that some jobs are more likely to be those that lead to mobility than others. Unlike men, women tend to be stuck in jobs with fewer chances for continuing upward mobility. Secretarial work provides a good example. In most organizations, there is a top limit to the "grade" of the highest secretaries in the organization. Beyond that, it is rare for secretaries to move into higher positions where there are additional career ladders. As a result, a secretary might move from being a clerk-typist to an office supervisor, but will seldom move out of this job classification to a job defined as more professional and with more chances for advancement (such as an administrative assistant or manager), even though the skills in these jobs may be the same. This has led observers to say that not only is there is a glass ceiling for women in work organizations but there is also a "sticky floor" (Berheide 1992).

Lately, scholars have also been examining the *glass escalator*—that is, the pattern whereby men in jobs traditionally predominated by women are promoted more readily than are women. There is evidence that this is true. In nursing, for example, where men are a numerical minority, studies find that men advance into leadership positions more quickly than women who are similarly located (Williams 1995). But this pattern does not hold for minority men in the same way it does for White men. Minority men in traditionally "women's jobs" typically face tense relationships with colleagues and are subjected to stereotypes by supervisors based on both their race and gender (Wingfield 2009). Patterns such as these show the extent to which gender—and its interaction with race—shape the opportunities for both women and men in the labor market.

Gender and Immigration

One of the major developments influencing women's position in the labor force is the growth in immigration that the United States has witnessed in recent years. Approximately one million legal immigrants arrive each year—a rate of immigration not matched since the 1920s, when so many European immigrants arrived. Now, the largest number of immigrants comes from Mexico, Caribbean countries, China, India, the Philippines, and Cuba (U.S. Census Bureau 2009).

Immigration has a number of consequences for women's labor force participation. Immigration is typically a family experience, as family units make decisions about who will migrate, who will work, and what impact immigration will have on family well-being. This means that women who may not have been in the labor force before will work for wages, often transforming gender roles within the family that existed prior to immigration (Hondagneu-Sotelo 1994; Foner 2005). Immigrant women can also find themselves "niched" in certain sectors of the labor market, such as domestic work or factory production, where wages are low and opportunities for advancement are poor. Still, they may find that employment brings them more independence and more opportunity to exercise influence in family decisions.

It is important, however, not to see all immigrant women as occupying low-status jobs. Immigrants arrive not only from different nations but also from different class backgrounds. Stereotypes of immigrants as poor and uneducated mask the diversity of immigrant experiences. In fact, 25 percent of foreign-born workers in the United States work as managers and professionals. Entering as scientists, physicians, business people, and other professional jobs, immigrants—both women and men—are often highly educated. Indeed, the poorest people seldom have the resources to leave their home nations, even if seeking better opportunities.

Professional women who immigrate may do so for a variety of reasons, including family reunification or better work opportunities, or seeking a more gender egalitarian society. Iranian women immigrants in the United States, for example, are largely professional workers who left Iran not only seeking better work opportunities but also to escape the patriarchal environment that emerged in Iran after the 1979 revolution (Hashemi 2007). For all immigrant women, economic opportunities in the United States, social, political, and economic conditions in their home nations, and the dynamics of family decision making all affect immigration experiences (Shih 2006).

Retirement and Social Security

The lower economic status of women in the labor force—and in the family—also makes a difference for women later in life. Compared to other western nations, older women in the United States are more likely to live in poverty (Herd 2009), in part because of the comparative lack of public pensions programs and other state-sponsored social supports.

Perhaps not surprisingly, the gap between men's and women's Social Security income is 77 percent—the same as the gender gap in wages. But the gender gap is even greater when it comes to pension income (54 percent) and earnings among those over age 65 and working (57 percent). Moreover, only 29 percent of all women over age 65 receive a pension income, including that from husbands' survivor benefits. Less than half of wage and salaried women workers even have a retirement plan, a result of women's greater likelihood of working in the secondary labor market (Hartmann and Lee 2003).

Women also hold significantly less in retirement plans ($56,320 on average for women, compared to closer to $100,000 for men, reflecting that women work fewer years and contribute less toward their retirement—in part because they have lower wages to begin with. These patterns result in lower lifetime savings for women, thus affecting their economic status in their senior years (U.S. Department of Labor 2009). And, although women's pensions have improved compared to men, there are also large race and class differences in retirement incomes based on women's race and class status (Holden and Fontes 2009; Lee 2009). Marital status affects women's economic standing later in life as well, as never-married and divorced women have half the wealth of men (Chang 2004).

Analysts have concluded that women's disadvantage during their working years spills over into retirement (Hartmann and English 2009). But, in addition, women's continuing roles in providing family care—including for older family members (see Chapter 6)—influence the economic resources they have available to them (Jefferson 2009). And, as the Baby Boomer population of the United States continues to age, these facts have serious implications for social policies in the immediate future.

Work Environments

Women's experiences at work are not just a function of earnings, promotions, and placement in the labor force. Within a work organization, one's ability to succeed, to be influential, and to be satisfied with work is shaped by the organizational climate. Whether women are seen as tokens or fully capable workers, the degree to which women are supported or harassed in the workplace, and the general climate for women—welcoming, chilly or frosty!—all impact women's opportunities in the workplace.

Sociologists have long noted that the experience of women (and racial–ethnic minority groups) in the workplace is influenced by the proportions in which they find themselves. Rosabeth Moss Kanter (1977) early showed the effects that being a token can have on one's well-being. Tokens stand out in contrast to other members of the group because their presence heightens the perceived boundaries between different groups. For instance, members of the dominant group become more self-conscious of what they have in common, and they might "test" tokens to see how they respond. The contrast between tokens and the majority also becomes exaggerated in social interaction. Tokens may receive extra attention and are easily stereotyped. Kanter argues that these perceptual tendencies—visibility, contrast, and assimilation—put more performance pressures on tokens, because they live life in the limelight. At the same time, tokens may be more closely supervised, given "silent" treatment, or not be given the training and direction required in a job (Yoder and Aniakudo 1997).

Tokens may respond by overachieving or they might try to use their uniqueness to advantage—for example, by flaunting their "only woman manager in the company" status. Or, tokens may try to become socially invisible, perhaps by acting "like a man," keeping a very low social profile, working at home, or avoiding risks—strategies of negotiating one's token status that can be psychologically damaging and may also impede advancement in the work organization. Research on tokenism shows clearly that the numerical representation of groups within various work organizations has a significant effect on women's status. For both women and people of color, having a critical mass of underrepresented groups—that is, a balanced and diverse workplace—is crucial to the advancement of all. In many workplaces, as well as in educational settings, sexual harassment persists as an obstacle to women's advancement. **Sexual harassment** is defined as the unwanted imposition of sexual requirements in the context of a relationship of unequal power. Sexual harassment was first defined as constituting illegal discrimination by Title VII of the Civil Rights Bill of 1964. A landmark Supreme Court decision in 1986, *Meritor Savings Bank* v. *Vinson*, ruled that sexual harassment violates federal laws against discrimination. This decision makes sexual harassment unconstitutional.

There are a number of social myths about sexual harassment, including the myths that it affects only a few, that women "ask for it," and that charges of sexual harassment are usually false. Because of these myths, women may find it hard to speak out against sexual harassment because the myths blame women themselves for this problem. Women who do speak out may be ignored, discredited, or accused of misunderstanding the situation. Yet, the U.S. Supreme Court has made it clear that sexual harassment is a violation of the law. Sexual harassment includes *quid pro quo harassment*—that is, a demand for sexual services in exchange for some benefit (a promotion, a grade, a raise, etc.), as well as *hostile environment* harassment—a more subtle, but also quite common, form of sexual harassment. Repeated sexual comments directed at women, references to how women look, and degrading comments about women can all constitute a hostile environment. Such environments, as well as quid pro quo harassment, are extremely damaging to women—both personally and in their work advancement.

Accurate counts of the extent of sexual harassment in the workplace are difficult to establish. Sexual harassment occurs in every kind of work setting and results in a number of problems, including stress, job turnover, depression, and physical illness (O'Connell and Korabik 2000). In traditional women's occupations, sexual harassment is usually characterized by the threat of losing a job for failing to comply with sexual demands; the harasser in those settings is typically a supervisor. On the other hand, women entering traditionally male occupations encounter sexual harassment often from other workers. In these settings, harassment expresses men's resentment of the presence of women. It can be more difficult for women workers in these jobs to bring charges of harassment, because their harassers are more likely to be co-workers (Mansfield 1991).

Sexual harassment is fundamentally a matter of the misuse of power and it is deeply linked to gender attitudes. Men are more tolerant of sexual harassment than are women. Women are more likely to see things such as sexist comments, verbal sexual advances, invitations for dates, and sexual propositions as sexual harassment than are men (McKinney and Crittenden 1992).

Gender affects work environments in many ways. And, as we saw in the previous chapter, gender and sexuality together also can influence how people experience work organization. Lesbian and gay workers may fear adverse career consequences if they "come out" at work; having to "manage" one's identity in this way is stressful (Schmidt 2003; Chrobot-Mason et al. 2001). When closeted, gays and lesbians may avoid interpersonal relationships with other workers to shield themselves from hostility and homophobia; if they then appear to be unfriendly, boring, and withdrawn, their job evaluations may suffer. When lesbian and gay workers do not fear such rejection and come out at the workplace, they find their relationships with co-workers are less stressful (Schneider 1984; Badgett and King 1997). Such studies show that objective rewards, such as earnings and promotions, are not the sole basis for gender equity in the workplace. The subjective dimensions of work—how one experiences the work environment, levels of job satisfaction, and relationships with other workers as well as with supervisors, all influence the status and well-being of women at work.

POVERTY AND WELFARE

One of the consequences of women's status in the labor market is the high rate of poverty among women and their children (see Figure 5.5). The **poverty line** is an index developed by the Social Security Administration. It is based on the lowest cost for a nutritionally adequate food plan (as developed by the Department of Agriculture). The poverty line (based also on family size) is calculated by multiplying the cost of this food plan by 3 (assuming that a family spends one-third of its budget on food), adjusted by the Consumer Price Index. In 2008, the official poverty line for a family of four (where there are three children and one parent) was $21,910.

Gender differences in poverty have increased in recent years, partially because of the fact that women now, unlike in the past, are more likely to be financially responsible for their children. This trend toward more of the poor being women

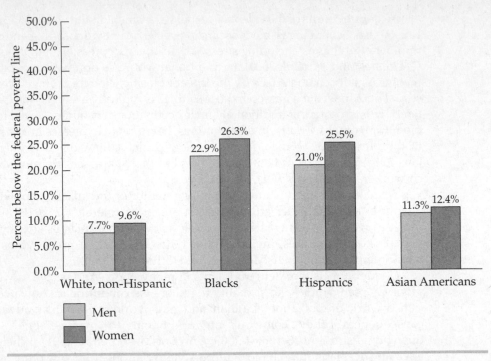

FIGURE 5.5   People in Poverty: 2008

Sources: Data from U.S. Census Bureau. 2010. *Detailed Poverty Tables.* Table POV02.
www.census.gov.

and children is called the **feminization of poverty.** In 2008, the median family income for all families was $62,621, but in family households headed by women (with no husband present), the median income was $33,073, with significant differences by race (refer to Figure 5.4). Twenty-nine percent of all female-headed households (with no husband present) lived below the official poverty line, even more when you categorize by race, too—as shown in Figure 5.5.

One consequence of the high rates of poverty among women who head their own families is the ever-growing and large number of children who are poor. Thirty-five percent of Black children, 31 percent of Hispanic children, 15 percent of Asian American children, and 11 percent of White, non-Hispanic children lived in poverty in 2008 (see Figure 5.6). Note that despite images of being the "model minority," poverty rates among Asian Americans are higher than among Whites; among Asian Americans, poverty is highest among the most recent Asian immigrants and varies dramatically across Asian Americans of different national origins (Lee 1994; DeNavas-Walt 2009).

Limited opportunities for women in the labor market are a major cause of poverty. In addition to their secondary employment status, women's continuing responsibilities for child rearing, in the absence of adequate day care and other social supports, tend to leave them poor.

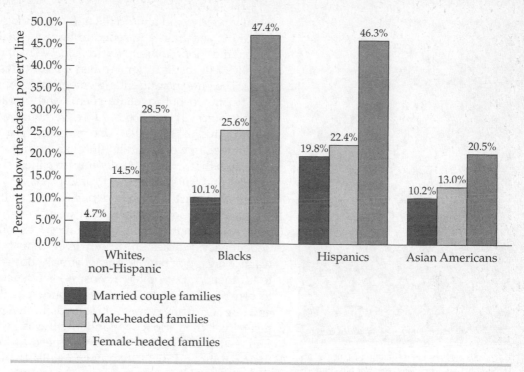

FIGURE 5.6   Poverty Status of Families with Children under Age 18: 2008

Source: Data from U.S. Census Bureau 2010. *Detailed Poverty Tables.* Table POV03 www.census.gov.

Women in poverty have been the focus of much public debate in recent years, particularly with regard to welfare. Welfare reform has been based on the assumption that welfare recipients need to work, with new welfare laws stipulating work requirements and time limits to welfare receipt. Until 1996, the major national welfare program was Aid to Families with Dependent Children (AFDC). This program was eliminated in 1996 with the passage of the **Personal Responsibility and Work Reconciliation Act,** generally known as "welfare reform." This policy places a lifetime limit of five years on receiving welfare and requires all welfare recipients to find work within two years—a policy known as *workfare.*

States now administer their own welfare programs via the program called **Temporary Assistance to Needy Families (TANF).** Under TANF, states can impose even more strict time limits and work requirements than the federal law requires. The law requires teen mothers to continue residing with their families if they are to receive welfare and also requires them to identify the father of their child. Many states have also refused to increase support payments for women who have additional children—a policy based on the erroneous assumption that women only have more children to increase the size of their support checks.

The work requirements of current welfare policy have had mixed results. Many former welfare recipients have found jobs, although the jobs they get are

Poverty rates are highest among women with children; here a homeless teen tries to comfort her infant child.

usually poorly paid and do not allow them to get the education and training needed to improve their status in the labor market (Ntiri 2000; Cancian and Meyer 2000; Institute for Women's Policy Research 2001). The bureaucratic entanglements of TANF have also frustrated both welfare clients and workers in welfare offices (Hays 2003). Moreover, with welfare reform, studies find that poor women are being encouraged to work, but discouraged from pursuing education that would actually improve their chances of economic self-sufficiency (Pearson 2007).

At the heart of public debate about welfare is the idea that poor people do not want to work and that providing public assistance encourages dependency. Studies show, however, that the low-wage work poor people find is simply not enough to lift them out of poverty. Most poor women have to combine low-wage work with public assistance and support from family and friends to make ends meet. Even then, most poor and low-income women find a wide gap between what they need to support their family and what they have available through welfare support. Contrary to public myths, poor women have aspirations to find better work, move to better neighborhoods, buy their children good clothes, and have a nest egg for emergencies. They just find it impossible to do so with the limited resources available to them. Studies of postwelfare reform also find that, as former recipients are moved into low-wage work, they often lose other benefits, such as food stamps, child-care assistance, and so forth, that helped them sustain their families (Edin and Kefalas 2005; Edin and Lein 1997; Korenman 2002; Green and Mayhew 2003; Marchevsky and Theoharis 2008).

Moreover, much of the public seems to misunderstand other facts about poor women. Most women work. Even prior to welfare reform, poor women often left welfare for work, but then found themselves in even more difficulty. The jobs poor women find tend to be low paying and unattractive, and child care is hard to come by (and to afford). Given the nature of the jobs most likely available to them, many find that they lose health insurance when they work or may experience violence from boyfriends and husbands who feel threatened by their becoming more independent by working.

The connection made in the public eye between welfare, work, and poverty also ignores the vast numbers of people (women and men) who are employed and are nonetheless poor—a group known as the *working poor.* Even among female-headed families where the householder works, 27 percent are still poor, including 13 percent where the family head works full time (U.S. Census Bureau 2009).

Many have argued that poverty among female-headed households is high because men's roles in the families have become "optional." The preceding analysis suggests something quite different: Only policies specifically designed to improve women's status, not just return men to families or women to the labor force as is, are likely to alleviate the problem of poverty among women and their children.

INTERSECTIONS OF FAMILY AND WORK

For many years, studies of work presumed that work was separate from family life—as if work and family were separate spheres of life. This assumption reflected the sexist idea that men's place was in the work world and women's place was in the family. New studies of women and work (and, now, men and work) have shown this not to be the case. Quite the contrary is true: Work and family are strongly intertwined (Moen 2004). You will see this further in Chapter 6 on families, but this relationship is apparent in studying work, especially when considering the amount of work that people do (counting both paid, unpaid, labor force, and household work), and by reconceptualizing housework as work, not just as family activity.

History shows how housework has changed and has been affected, and transformed, by gender relations in society more broadly. The earliest information on housework was gathered in the 1920s under the guise of the new science of home economics and its emphasis on rational management (Vanek 1978). In 1900, most U.S. homes had no electricity and no running water, and in 1920, one-third of U.S. families still lived on farms. But by the 1920s, a variety of canned and processed foods had become available, reducing the time a housewife spent producing and preparing food. By the 1930s, approximately 60 percent of homes in the United States had electricity, opening the way for mechanical refrigerators and washing machines and gas and electric ranges. By 1940, 70 percent of U.S. homes had indoor plumbing; in the 1950s, automatic washers replaced wringers; and in the 1960s, women's laundry work was changed by the introduction of dryers and wash-and-wear fabrics (Cowan 1976; Vanek 1978).

In the 1970s, the fast-food industry started to blossom, radically changing not only Americans' eating habits, but also the character of housework. Although these technological and commercial developments created the potential for reducing housework, ideological changes as well as actual changes in the requirements of housework have contributed to the demands of household work. Thus, although time spent on food preparation, cleaning, sewing, and mending has decreased, the introduction of cheaper clothing and linens means that there is more clothing and linen per household and therefore more laundry. Also, the invention of the automobile and the development of suburbs have meant that people spend more time transporting family members and shopping. And managerial tasks in the household have increased as financial and medical records, grocery lists, deliveries, and repairs have become routine work (Vanek 1978).

Overall, people now spend somewhat less time doing housework than in the past, but time spent in child care and shopping has increased. At the same time, child care has become seen as the work of individuals, not extended families, so, even though people now have fewer children, there is more time spent caring for them (Bianchi 2000; Bianchi and Mattingly 2004).

The Second Shift

Altogether, changes in the work that women do—both in the home and in the public labor force—have meant an increase in women's time spent working. This is referred to as the **second shift**—that is, the work women do at home in addition to the time spent in paid employment (Hochschild 1989). Economists estimate that even middle-class women are working longer hours—an estimated increase of 12 weeks per year since 1979 (Mishel et al. 2005). Coupled with the fact that women report having to work harder in their jobs than men do (Gorman and Kmec 2007), this means that when you add together paid labor and the number of hours women spend doing housework and child care, you find substantial *speedup* in the amount of work that women are doing.

Contemporary sociologist Arlie Hochschild has studied the effect of speedup on families. Based on extensive interviews with women and men in dual-career families, she has found that women develop a variety of strategies for coping with these demands of the second shift. Some feign helplessness over certain tasks as a way to get men to do them. Others avoid conflict by taking on the work themselves. Some cut back on their expectations about what is necessary in the home or reduce their working hours. Often, women turn to women friends and family members for help or, if they have the economic ability, pay other women to work for them. Some try to be "supermoms"; those who do report feeling "numb" and out of touch with their feelings. In any case, women typically pay the greater price of this added household stress (Hochschild 1989).

Hochschild (1997) has also shown that, as more women have entered the paid labor force, life for most people has become centered more and more on work. The tensions then created at home mean that many women and men run their families like efficiency experts, having to manage time spent in child care, leisure activity, and household chores as if they were managers of their personal lives. Ironically, Hochschild's research also finds that, even in corporations with "family-friendly" policies (flex-time, child-care facilities, etc.), workers underutilize these benefits. Instead, people work more and more, often not using vacation benefits, even when they feel there is a time deficit in their lives. Why? Based on her research, Hochschild concludes that the "time bind" and stress that people feel at home means that they find more satisfaction and pleasure at work than they do at home. In her words, the social worlds of work and home have been reversed, with people feeling more "at home" at work and "at work" when home.

Housework and Care Work

The second shift shows that not all women's labor is paid labor, but, because the concept of work has been tied to paid employment, housework has long gone unrecognized as work, even though it is socially and economically necessary. The work that housewives do not only takes care of people's basic needs—food, shelter, and clothing—but also socializes new members of the society. Housework benefits employers, too, because housework sustains workers, making it possible for them to return to the labor force.

Social myths about housework show us the contradictions that pervade our images of the work women do in the home. On the one hand, "staying at home" is idealized as a desirable goal for women, even while, at the same time, housework is depicted as drudgery and menial labor. In advertisements women are surrounded by happy families and a wealth of material goods. The housewives in these ads are usually cheerful, buoyant, and smiling, although pathologically obsessed with cleanliness and food. Although housework is seen as glamorous, housewives are also ridiculed as scatterbrained, lazy, and disorganized. Anyone who has seen comic strips and greeting cards that depict some bedraggled housewife has seen one facet of the contemporary myth about housework. Both the glamorized image of housework and the demeaning caricatures of housewives obscure the fact that housework is time consuming as well as physically and psychologically demanding, even though it can also be a source of satisfaction.

Who actually does housework? Changes in men's and women's beliefs and behaviors that have resulted from the women's movement mean that patterns of who does housework have changed. Men are now more involved in housework than was generally true in the past, although who does what and how much depends on a number of social factors identified by research. Studies find that men who are married to women who work full time do more housework (Stier and Lewin-Epstein 2000), but once men become coupled with a woman, they reduce the amount of time they have previously spent in housework (Gupta 1999). Women's housework, on the other hand, increases when they marry (Gager et al. 1999). Also, men tend to overestimate the amount of time they spend in housework, but women do not (Kamo 2000). And, even among children, girls do more housework than boys (Gager et al. 1999).

Care work refers to all the forms of labor (including unpaid work) that is needed to nurture, reproduce, and sustain people—in other words, work that is critical to the maintenance of social life. This includes child care and housework, but also care for older family members, those with disabilities, and the mental work required to manage a household. When you consider all these forms of work, much of it unpaid, you see how essential women's work is to the maintenance of society. Despite changes in gender attitudes and roles in recent years, women continue to do the vast majority of such work, whether they are employed or not. Care work is also organized in such a way as to reflect and reproduce the connections between race, class, and gender inequality (Duffy 2007).

Studies of care work also show that the amount of work men do is strongly influenced by the social structure of the family in which they were raised. Sociologists Naomi Gersel and Sally Gallagher studied whether men's participation in care work is influenced most by their attitudes about gender equality or the structure of their families. They found that the characteristics of the men's families were the strongest influence on their engagement in care work. Men with more sisters spent less time helping with elder parents than men with fewer sisters. Furthermore, men's employment (hours employed, job flexibility, or job stability) had no effect on their involvement in care work. Gerstel and Gallagher concluded, "It is primarily the women in men's lives who shape the amount and types of care men provide" (2001: 211).

Although the media have been reporting an increase in "stay-at-home moms," the reality is that most women simply cannot do this. Basically, families need women's incomes to make ends meet, so the idealized stay-at-home mom is a choice available only to those of certain socioeconomic classes (see more in Chapter 6). An important study of middle-class, successful professional women who have "opted out" of the labor force to stay at home also shows that they tend to do so not out of some compelling desire to be stay-at-home moms, but because of the many frustrations they have encountered in the workplace—including blocked mobility, the inflexibility of managing work and family responsibilities, and the sheer amount of gender inequality that they face at work (Stone 2007).

MEDIA MATTERS

"Opting Out": Media Images of Women Leaving the Workforce

If you believed what you saw in the media, you would think there was a massive exodus of professional women leaving the labor force to become "stay-at-home" moms. The popular media is filled with images of an exodus of women deciding to leave their jobs, despite their high levels of education and comfortable lifestyle, choosing instead to be mothers. Many have studied the media depiction of women's roles over time and concluded that traditional images of motherhood are pervasive and persistent. But, more recently, scholars Arielle Kuperberg and Pamela Stone analyzed the popular image constructed of women who have "opted out" of the labor force.

To do their study, Kuperberg and Stone conducted a content analysis using a cross-section of magazines with a general national readership, including those appearing from 1988 to 2003. They found that articles focusing on women leaving the labor force centered on three themes: "family-first/child-centric;" "mommy elite," and "making choices."

In the first theme, the researchers found that articles focused mostly on women as mothers, not wives or workers. Husbands were rarely seen, and seldom were constraints at work seen as influencing the women's decisions to stay home. Rather, children were a primary focus, as if women's roles as mothers are the sole reason they would leave work. Moreover, women's activities at home were almost exclusively focused on

the child—not the other responsibilities that are actually part of managing a household.

In the second theme, the "mommy elite," the researchers found that these national articles focused almost exclusively on very highly educated, professional women—women who had the social-class option (largely because of their husbands' status) to drop out of the labor market without consequence.

Third, the articles all treated the women's decision as if it were simply a matter of individual choice. Seldom were women shown as struggling with such a decision, involving others in their actions, with no mention of the barriers or constraints the women faced in trying to work. Women just freely chose, never facing a lack of options.

Kuperberg and Stone concluded that the media depiction of women "opting out" is monolithic—rarely showing the diversity and complexity of women's actually trying to be both workers, mothers, and wives. But they also point out how misleading these media images actually are, when seen against the actual trends of increases—not decreases—in women's labor force participation. In truth, college-educated women are working more and opting out less than educated women with lower levels of education.

Source: Kuperberg, Arielle, and Pamela Stone. 2008. "The Media Depiction of Women Who Opt Out." *Gender & Society* 22 (August): 497–515.

POLICIES FOR GENDER EQUITY

The social changes witnessed in gender relations in recent history have been the result of many groups mobilizing for change. As a result, specific policies form a framework by which some greater gender equity has been achieved, even though more needs to be done.

The **Equal Pay Act** of 1963 was the first federal legislation enacted requiring equal pay for equal work; it has been extended by various executive orders and civil rights acts to forbid discrimination on the basis of sex. Title VI of the Civil Rights Act of 1964 forbids discrimination against people on the basis of race, color, or national origin in all federally assisted programs. **Title VII of the Civil Rights Bill** of 1964, amended by the Equal Employment Opportunity Act of 1972, forbids discrimination on the basis of race, color, national origin, religion, or sex in any term, condition, or privilege of employment. This law was amended in 1972 to cover all private and public educational institutions, as well as state and local governments. Title VII was a path-breaking law for women, as it established the principle of equal rights in federal law and opened the door for women's participation in education, employment, and athletics, to name some of its major areas of impact.

Title IX of the Educational Amendments of 1972 has been especially significant in opening up athletic opportunities for women and girls. Title IX forbids gender discrimination in any educational institution receiving federal funds, thus prohibiting schools, colleges, and universities from receiving federal funds if they discriminate against women in any program, including athletics. Adoption of this legislation radically altered the opportunities available to women in sports and has transformed the face of student athletics. Indeed, this legislation laid the foundation for many of the coeducational programs that are now an ordinary part of student life.

Now, however, Title IX is under significant threat from those who see it as having taken away opportunities for men—a perception not well supported by evidence. Some college sports for men have been eliminated, although most argue that this has been the result of budget pressures on schools, not the direct result of Title IX. Proponents of maintaining strong enforcement of Title IX have argued that men still dominate in school and college sports, especially when you consider the resources provided to football—a sport that, to date, still largely excludes women.

Although federal laws do forbid discrimination in employment, because women tend to be located in different occupations than men, equal pay for equal work is inadequate for eliminating wage inequities. **Comparable worth** is the principle of paying women and men equivalent wages for jobs involving comparable levels of skill. Assessing comparable worth requires measuring the skill levels of comparable jobs and developing correlated pay scales, regardless of the sex of the job occupants (Blum 1986).

Another public policy that has proven of great importance in bringing new opportunities to women and racial minority groups in the labor market is **affirmative action.** Affirmative action has now become one of the most controversial policies for creating better opportunities for members of historically disadvantaged groups. Affirmative action developed as a policy referring to positive efforts taken to open new areas of opportunity to groups who had previously been excluded from such jobs.

Typically, an affirmative action program would identify the potential pool of eligible (i.e., qualified) workers in a given occupational category and then require employers to develop recruitment mechanisms to ensure fair opportunities to members of these groups. It includes such actions as advertising for jobs in places where women and minorities are likely to see job postings, instead of relying on word of mouth and "White men's networks" to recruit able applicants. Affirmative action policies have forced organizations to develop fair rules and uniform recruitment procedures so that some groups do not have an advantage over others.

Contrary to popular opinion, affirmative action does not set rigid quotas for jobs, although it does set goals or targets for different jobs, depending on the number of qualified women and minorities in the available pool. Affirmative action forces employers to think carefully about what the term *qualified* means; perhaps this is what has been most controversial. For example, in some jobs, performance on a written test is an important part of the application procedure, but affirmative action can mean that someone with a somewhat lower score on the test may, for other reasons, be seen as more qualified than someone whose test scores are slightly higher. If the person with the lower score is hired, it does not mean that person is not qualified (since he or she would not be hired with a significantly lower score), only that additional factors constitute the qualifications for the job. Affirmative action has also meant that diversifying the work force is itself a desirable goal.

Affirmative action has been under sharp attack from groups who perceive it as taking away opportunities from Whites and men (Steinbugler et al. 2006). The fact remains, however, that it has been critical to the success of women and people of color. The fact that it is now being so vigorously opposed by various groups shows that it has had a strong effect in opening opportunities to people who have historically have been disadvantaged because they were not White or male. Affirmative action was also upheld as constitutional by an important Supreme Court decision in 2004 involving college admissions programs (see also Chapter 11). Critics of affirmative action argue that race-blind and gender-blind policies are the only fair way to proceed, but most feminists and civil rights advocates would argue that, as the evidence in this chapter would support, as long as the society is structured (even in less visible ways) along gender-, class-, and race-stratified lines, seemingly "neutral" or color-blind policies cannot transform the institutional structures that have developed specifically out of gender and race inequities.

■ Chapter Summary and Themes

The history of women's work shows that gender is linked to transformations in the structure of labor and its relationship to household, including the social structures of race and class.

The historic move to a cash-based economy created the family wage system, based on the presumption that men were the primary breadwinners and that women worked at home. This is despite the fact that working-class women and women of color have long worked for wages. The specific histories of women of color also show that their labor has been exploited for the gain of others.

Women's status in the economy is typically buttressed by ideologies that define their work as less significant than that of men.

Historically, the cult of domesticity for White, bourgeois women defined their role as in the home. Contemporary definitions of work continue to show how women's labor is often considered a "labor of love" and thus unpaid and devalued.

Economic restructuring is producing new forms of gender stratification.

Economic restructuring includes the transition to a service-based economy, increasing globalization, enhanced use of technology, and concentration of economic resources in the hands of a few. These changes in the social organization of work have specific consequences for gender stratification, particularly in increasing the proportion of low-paying, service sector jobs—jobs that are generally filled by women and people of color.

Gender stratification is reflected in the status of women in diverse occupational categories.

Gender segregation persists throughout the labor market resulting in a concentration of women in certain occupational categories. Gender segregation is one major source for the gender gap in earnings.

Multiple factors explain the persistent gap in earnings between women and men.

The most significant explanations of the pay gap include overt discrimination, human capital theory (that is, the characteristics that workers bring to the labor market), and the presence of a dual labor market in which gender and race and class segregation persist. Gender in the workplace also affects the likelihood of promotions, as well as shaping different parts of workplace environments.

Women's status in the economy is resulting in high rates of poverty among women and their children.

Poverty has been increasing in recent years and is concentrated among women and their children. Welfare reform has attempted to reduce poverty by requiring recipients to work, but studies are showing that welfare recipients continue to be blamed for their own situation, despite the lack of social supports provided to lift people out of poverty.

Work and families are social institutions that are deeply intertwined in ways that are manifested in the second shift of work that women provide in the home.

Even with more women working in the paid labor force, a gender division of labor persists in household and other forms of care work. Women continue to provide more of this work that, even though sometimes glamorized, is generally devalued and rarely equally shared.

■ Key Terms

affirmative action
care work
class
comparable worth
contingent workers
discrimination
dual labor market theory
economic restructuring
emotional labor
Equal Pay Act

family-based economy
family-consumer economy
family-wage economy
feminization of poverty
gender segregation
gender stratification
glass ceiling
human capital theory
Personal Responsibility and
    Work Reconciliation Act

poverty line
second shift
sexual harassment
sweatshop
Temporary Assistance to
    Needy Families (TANF)
Title VII of the Civil Rights Bill
Title IX of the Educational
    Amendments

■ Discussion Questions/Projects for Thought

1. Give yourself a monthly budget of $1,825 (approximately the monthly amount that you would have if you lived at the federal poverty line). Imagine that you head your own household, with three children. Using prices from the area where you live, develop a monthly budget to account for everything you have to spend to get by. What would your life be like, and what would your children's lives be like? What does this exercise teach you about contemporary images of people from low-income families?

2. Ask several young men and women how they expect to balance work and family commitments in the future. Then interview several people who are currently employed about how they balance these commitments. What do your interviews about expectations and current realities suggest for future social policies to support families and workers?

CHAPTER

6

Gender and Families

Our boys are, in another score of years, to make the laws, heal the soul and bodies, formulate the science, and control the commerce of their generation. Fathers who, recognizing this great truth, do not prepare their sons to do their part toward accomplishing this work, are despised, and justly, by the community in which they live. Our girls are, in another score of years, to make the homes which are to make laws, heal souls and bodies, formulate science, and control the commerce of their generation (Harland 1889:202).

A woman's place is in the home—at least that's what the historical legacy tells us. In the period when the above housewives' guide was published (over 100 years ago), the glorification of the home and family was at its historical peak. The home was considered a moral sanctuary, and morality, which flourished in the home, was considered the work of women. It was women who would shape future generations. Although women's place was ideally limited to the domestic sphere, within that sphere women were charged with preserving and creating the moral fiber of society.

Today's families are one of the most rapid changing social institutions. Only 23 percent of U.S. households are married-couple families living with their own children. The vast majority of families in the United States are now either two-earner families, single-parent households, post-childbearing couples, or those who have never had children. Also, cohabitors, gay and lesbian couples, singles, and various kinds of cooperative living arrangements have to be included in any portrait of contemporary families (Krieder and Elliott 2009).

Still, the social ideal of the family persists. The family is still idealized as a private world—one in which family members are nurtured and prepared for their roles in the outside world. And, contemporary appeals to "family values" suggest that families are still believed to be the moral compass of society. The family is also a place where women still tend to provide primary care for children and manage the everyday affairs of the household, even with the increased efforts of men. The realities of contemporary households and the persistence of the family ideal create a series of contradictions, especially for women. On the one hand, the family is glorified, isolated, and assumed to be detached from public life; it is also seen as an enclave for the development of family members' personalities and for the gratification of their physical and emotional needs. At the same time, families have been undergoing rapid social changes, making it clear that families are situated within the larger context of political, economic, and social conditions—all of which are entangled with gender.

Indeed, families have been the focus of public policy debates in recent years. Should same-sex marriage be legal? Are families responsible for some of the social problems we experience—teen pregnancy, delinquency, and substance abuse, for example? What family benefits should we expect from business and government? These and other questions are part of a cultural debate about family values—a debate engaging many assumptions about gender and family life, even if such assumptions are not explicitly stated.

People experience their families in terms of personal, intimate relationships, but those relationships are conditioned by events that extend far beyond immediate family life. Families are where we first encounter social expectations, where our physical needs are met, where our primary emotional bonds are first established, and where we first encounter systems of authority, power, and social

As families have evolved in response to changing social conditions, the traditional family dinner is becoming less common. Only 28 percent of families now report eating dinner together seven nights per week—down from 37 percent in 1997. One-quarter say they eat together only three times a week or less (Kiefer 2004).

conflict. Although the family is a personal experience, many of the strains associated with family life stem from the conflicts posed by the family's relationship to other social institutions. For example, unemployment, divorce, and violence are all experienced within the family, although they are a part of broader social conditions. Also, the family is often blamed for larger social problems, even though these problems are rooted in society and not individual families. Understanding this requires some knowledge of how families have evolved.

HISTORICAL PERSPECTIVES ON MODERN FAMILIES

The history of the Western family reveals the events that have molded contemporary families. Without historical analysis, we tend to see the family as a static entity or one not influenced by social change. Knowing the history of a contemporary institution, such as the family, is like knowing the biography of a good friend—it helps you understand the present.

It is impossible to pinpoint the exact time in history when the modern family first emerged. One could trace it to the patriarchal household in the early Roman family, one of the strongest patriarchal systems known. *Patriarchal households*—defined as those where men rule over women—are found throughout Western history. One could also look to the medieval period as an era when courtly love and chivalry marked gender and class relations between men and women.

The modern household in Western society, however, is generally depicted as having its origins in the transformations of economic and political life found in the postmedieval period, roughly beginning in the fourteenth century. Historian Philip Aries (1962) locates the origins of the modern Western family in a series of gradual transformations that began in the fourteenth century and culminated in the seventeenth and eighteenth centuries. Starting in the fourteenth century, the wife's position in the household deteriorated as she lost the right to replace her husband in the management of household affairs in the event of his death, incapacitation, or insanity. By the sixteenth century, the wife was placed totally under the authority of her husband—any acts she performed without the authority of her husband or the law were considered null and void. At the end of the sixteenth century, the Church recognized the possibility of sanctification outside of the religious vocation. In other words, it became possible for institutions outside the Church to be seen as sacred at this point, and the family became an object of common piety. The marriage ceremony itself, in the seventeenth century, took on a religious form by becoming like a christening in which families gathered around the bride and groom.

Also in the sixteenth and seventeenth centuries, new importance was placed on the family, as attitudes toward children changed. Greater intimacy between parents and children established a new moral climate and, although the extension of school education made education increasingly a matter for the school, the family began to center its emotional life on that of the child. By the eighteenth century, the family began to hold society at a distance, thereby initiating the idea of the family as an enclave of private life. Even the physical character of the household changed. Homes became less open; instead of being organized around large communal spaces, they became characterized by several rooms, each specialized by function (Aries 1962). This change is explained as a result of homes becoming more organized around domestic work as commerce and production became increasingly located in the public workplace.

It is important to note that this evolution of family life was specific to the noble and middle classes and wealthy artisans and laborers. Even as late as the nineteenth century, the vast majority of the European population was still poor and lived like the medieval family, with children separated from their parents and the idea of the home and the family, as just described, nonexistent. Beginning in the nineteenth century, however, and continuing through the present, the concept of the family, as it originated in the well-to-do classes, extended through other strata of society. Still, the concept of the family as we know it today—a private and emotional sphere—has its origins in the aristocratic and bourgeois classes.

By the late eighteenth and early nineteenth centuries, these historical transformations led to what U.S. historians have labeled the **cult of domesticity** (Cott 1977). The ideology of domesticity gave women a limited and gender-specific role to play—namely, that of the person responsible for the moral and everyday affairs of the home. This ideal, coupled with economic transformations in family life, limited women's idealized experiences to the private world of the family. In actuality, of course, large numbers of women, especially women of color and working-class women, also performed wage labor. The definition of womanhood as idealized femininity, however, stemmed from the bourgeois origins of the cult of domesticity.

The cult of domesticity did provide the conditions for women's involvement in moral reform movements and, ultimately, feminism, because it encouraged women's nurturance to be turned toward social improvement (Cott 1977). In the context of the family, however, the cult of true womanhood limited women's experiences to affairs of the heart, not the mind. This ideal glorified a woman's role as homemaker at the same time that it fragmented the experience of women and men.

The idealized domestic role of women followed the transformations in women's labor (described in the preceding chapter). To review briefly, before the seventeenth century, the work role of women was not marginal to the economy or the household. In fact, as late as the seventeenth century, the household and the economy were one, the household being the basic unit of production. Domestic life in the earlier period was not splintered from public life, and households, as the basic units of economic production, consisted not only of individuals related through marriage but also of individuals with economic relationships, particularly servants and apprentices. In such a setting, women's labor, as well as that of children, was publicly visible, equally valued, and known to be economically necessary.

The emergence of capitalism, with the related rise of mercantilism, industrialization, and a cash-based economy, eroded the position of women by shifting the center of production from the domestic unit to the public workplace. This separation not only devalued women's labor in the home but it also made women more economically dependent on men (Tilly and Scott 1978). The emergence of a family-wage economy, as distinct from a family-based economy, transformed not only women's work but, equally important, the family and women's role within it (see Chapter 5).

When the workplace became separated from the home, the family, although still economically productive, became a vehicle largely for the physical and social reproduction of workers and for the consumption of goods. As more goods were produced outside the home, the value of workers became perceived in terms of their earned wages. The social value of women, especially those left unpaid as housewives, was diminished.

In addition, the status of women in the family was radically altered not only by changes in the economic organization of the household but also by political changes in the relationship of the family to the state. The displacement of large feudal households by the modern state enhanced the power of the husband over his wife. For example, in sixteenth-century England, the state assumed the powers of justice, punishment, military protection, and regulation of property originally assumed by feudal estates. At the same time, a massive propaganda campaign was initiated in support of the nuclear family. Family members were required to be loyal, subservient, and obedient to both the king and the husband (Dobash and Dobash 1979).

The patriarchal family became the cornerstone—the basic social unit—for the emergence of the modern patriarchal state (Aries 1962; Foucault 1965). As capitalism developed further, there was a shift from private patriarchy within the family to public patriarchy centered in industry and government (Brown 1981). Although individual men might still hold power in families, the male-dominated state ensures that all women are subject to a patriarchal order. Historically, the patriarchal family (and, ultimately, the state) was hierarchically structured around the power of men and morally sanctioned by the patriarchal church. With the Protestant Reformation, an ever-increasing amount of religious socialization occurred within the home. Whereas Catholicism had reluctantly sanctioned family life (and thus forbade it to the clergy), the Puritans embraced the family as an exalted, natural, and God-given order. The Protestant ethic, as it emerged, blessed the family as a unit of material labor. The ideal that one could do God's work in secular vocations encouraged a view of the family as sacred and as the place for spiritual life (Zaretsky 1976). In the end, the self-consciousness and individualism encouraged by the Protestant ethic helped ensure the subjective importance of the family. With the rise of capitalism, women's lower status in economic production was counterbalanced by their exalted status in the family as God's moral agents.

The split between work and home established by capitalism is related to a second schism—that between personal and public life. Modern capitalism depends on individual consumerism; thus, it encourages modern families to emphasize individualism, self-consciousness, and the search for personal identity. When personal identity is viewed as detached from objective material conditions, one can come to believe that personal liberation can occur without a change in the objective conditions of economic relations. The "plunge into subjectivity" (Zaretsky 1976:119) and its emphasis on lifestyle, consumerism, and personal awareness is a form of consciousness specific to, and consistent with, the ideological and economic needs of capitalist economies.

Modern families are also regulated by the patriarchal authority of the state and its various agencies. Especially in poor and working-class families, state agencies and reformers seeking to eliminate deviance regulate personal and family life through the work of professional experts. Even in the middle class, professional experts claim to know more about personal life, thereby defining individual and family needs and the character of contemporary social problems (Ehrenreich and English 1973; Illich 1977).

The development of specific family structures varies, depending on the specific historical experiences of given groups in the society. Working-class, ethnic, African American, Asian American, Latino, and Native American families did not develop in exactly the same fashion as did White, middle-class households, as you will see in a later section on racism and families. Transformations in White, middle-class households do, however, set the ideals by which other groups have been judged; the historical development of racial and ethnic families and working-class families has also been shaped by the same transformations in economic and family systems. This historical account of transformations in family life paints only a broad picture of the emergence of family life over time. Specific family histories, like other social experiences, are nested within the class, race, and gender relations of any given historical period.

The history of families shows that the family is an institution that is interconnected with economic and political institutions of society. Although we tend to think of families and personal life within them as relatively autonomous social forms, we cannot understand families without studying the interrelationships among families, the state, the economy, and gender, race, and class relations.

FEMINIST PERSPECTIVES ON FAMILIES

All societies are organized around some form of kinship system, although the definition of family changes in different cultural and historical contexts. Certain common characteristics of the family have been used to define the family. These include economic cooperation, common residence, socially approved sexual relations, reproduction, and child rearing. Anthropologists also add that, in most kinship systems, "marriage exists as a socially recognized, durable, although not necessarily life-long relationship, between individual men and women" (Gough 1975). It also appears that, in most societies, men have higher status and authority in the family than women (Gough 1975). Commonsense definitions of the family define the family to mean blood ties, although as discussed in the following section, many contemporary families do not meet this criterion. In addition, many contemporary families do not meet the criteria of common residence, socially approved sexual relations, reproduction, child rearing, or marriage, as the standard definition implies.

Feminist scholarship on families has transformed how we think about them, with family experts now using a framework of structural diversity to understand contemporary families. The **structural diversity model** is centered on several themes regarding how families form and operate (Baca Zinn and Eitzen 2010). These include the following:

- Family forms are socially constructed and historically changing.
- Family diversity is produced by the same structures that organize society as a whole.
- Families are embedded in and shaped by the intersecting hierarchies of class, race, and gender.
- Family diversity is constructed through social structure as well as the actions of family members.
- Understanding families means challenging monolithic ideas that conceive of the family in idealistic ways.

The Social Construction of Families

From a sociological point of view, the family is a social, not a natural, phenomenon. The assumption that families are natural or biological units prejudices our conceptions of the family by presuming families to be universal and detached from the influence of other social institutions. The idea that the family is "natural" is strongly held by some groups—especially conservative, religious groups. This ideal is often used to argue that women should remain in the family under the authority of men.

In fact, the meaning and character of family systems vary widely (see Figure 6.1 on page 164). Both historically and in contemporary families, persons designated as kin may extend beyond blood relations; adoption is a case in point. Blood relations may sometimes even be excluded from the social network of the family. The traditional assumption that family relations are natural also stems from the ethnocentric attitude that the ideals of our own culture are universally the most appropriate social form.

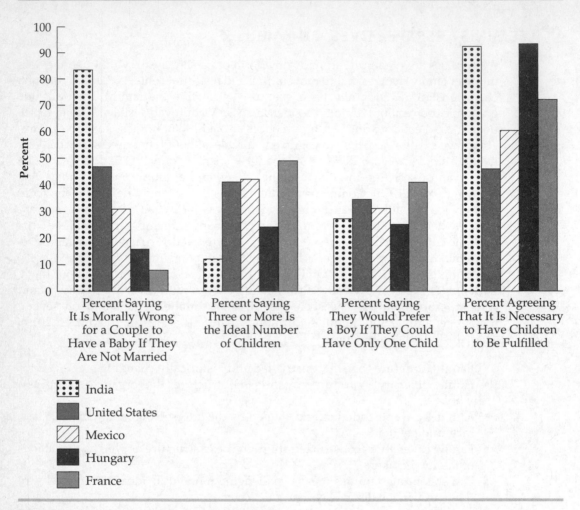

FIGURE 6.1 Family Values: A Global View

Source: Data from Gallup Organization. 2001. *The Gallup Poll.* Princeton, NJ: Gallup Organization, www.gallup.com. Reprinted with permission.

Even a cursory look at cross-cultural studies of kinship systems reveals a great variety of family forms. In India, for example, families were traditionally organized around a *joint family* system, one that was also marked by *patriarchy* (the power of men). Under this family system, the major family bond was not between married couples; rather, it was between generations, especially parents and sons, as well as among male siblings. Women were highly subordinate under this traditional system, such that, after marriage, a woman would lose all her autonomy and be highly subjected to scrutiny and monitoring by those in her husband's family—including the women in his family. Only with the birth of her sons would a woman's family status improve, and women whose husbands died were social outcasts. If not burned on their husbands' funeral pyre—a practice that was outlawed in 1829—widows were shunned and often left with no social or economic resources (Das Gupta 1995).

Family systems such as this have changed dramatically along with other transformations in Indian society. Modernization, urbanization, and globalization are all social forces that change the structure of families—in all societies. This is also evident in patterns of family life that change with immigration. For example, arranged marriages, common in many societies, are typically modified by the immigration experience. Although this traditional practice may still be valued by older generations, second-generation immigrants typically modify this practice as they are exposed to different cultural values (Zaidi and Shuraydi 2002).

Family life does not always change in a more progressive direction. For example, in Afghanistan, under the rule of the Taliban, which began in 1996, women were excluded from public life—locked within their homes where windows were painted black so that no one could see them. Women were completely under the control of men and could not appear in public without them or without the *burqa* that completely covers them, except for a small net opening for their eyes. A woman who even accidentally glanced at a man other than her husband or whose burqa might slip, revealing an ankle, would be whipped and stoned to death in public. This extreme form of **gender apartheid**—the extreme segregation and exclusion of women from public life—completely restricts women to the family and, at that, restricts domestic life to the private world of the home.

The forms families take develop in the context of broader social and economic structures. Thus, families often develop kin networks that work as systems of social and economic exchange. Kin in this context become recognized as those who share and meet socioeconomic obligations, regardless of blood ties. Among some Native American groups, traditionally, ancestry would be traced through maternal descent. Young couples would reside with the woman's parent; and, wherever they lived, the woman would assume control of the household—including the distribution of game that her husband caught (Axtell 1981). In another example, the system of *compadrazgo* among Latinos exemplifies an extended kinship network that extends beyond blood ties. *Compadrazgo* is a family system whereby those defined as kin have very strong connections to the family; in this system, kin includes not only blood relatives but also godparents (Baca Zinn and Eitzen 2010). The point is that these different family forms show that what seems natural about the Western **nuclear family**—families in which married couples live together with their children—is only that which dominant groups have defined as the ideal and that many have come to take for granted as the only family form.

Family Diversity

Class, race, and gender all influence the social structures of families. The resources that families have—or don't have—available to them have a tremendous impact on how the family operates. Families are, in fact, deeply linked to the economic and political structures found in society at large, even though popular conceptions of the family define it as a refuge from the public world. This belief, however, hides the fact that families are organized around economic purposes, as well as reproductive and emotional ones.

You can see this by looking at the importance of family networks to the economic adaptations immigrant groups make. Studies of Vietnamese immigrant families show, for example, that such families patch together a wide array of resources, based on the belief in family collectivism (i.e., the belief emphasizing collective sharing and exchange, in contrast to individualism). This collectivist attitude encourages households to share economic and social resources as a way of coping with the economic difficulties that immigrant groups face (Kibria 1994; Zhou and Bankston 1998). This example shows how intertwined the family and economy are as social institutions.

Family organization both reflects and reproduces the class system of society. The availability of work for different family members will affect the family's form, pattern relationships within the family, and shape the family's lifestyle. The economic resources available to family members will also determine much about their experience in the family, in schools, at work, and at play. Just as class arrangements influence families, so do families influence class arrangements. In the family, people learn values and personality characteristics that make them suitable as workers; families shape our understanding of class systems and the aspirations and definitions of ourselves within them.

Family diversity is seen not only across different families but also within families. Men and women, for example, experience the family in different ways. Jessie Bernard (1972), one of the foremothers of feminist scholarship in sociology, first wrote that marriage was experienced differently by women and men within the family. Research on families has since shown that not only do women and men experience the family in different ways but they also hold different expectations for marital roles, with men tending to have more traditional expectations than women do. Furthermore, single women have more expectation of egalitarian marriage roles than do married women, suggesting that people's expectations change once in a marriage (Bartling and Broussard 1999; Wilkie 1993).

You can also see the internal diversity of families by observing the power that men and women have within families. Power within marriage includes the ability to influence decisions, the degree of autonomy and independence held by each partner, and the control of expectations about family life. In most marriages, even with more women employed, men remain the sole or major earners (Raley et al. 2006); this has been found to be true in almost two-thirds of all marriages. Even when wives earn substantially more than their husbands, an increasingly common phenomenon, couples tend to negotiate marital power within the confines of traditional gender expectations (Tichenor 2005).

The Influence of Class, Race, and Gender

From the preceding information, it follows that families are shaped by the racial, class, and gender structures in society. Race and gender, along with class, organize the social structure of families and create experiences within families that are connected to the family's location in the system of race, gender, and class relations. White families, for example, benefit from some degree of racial privilege in a society that is marked by racial inequality; that privilege, however, is also influenced by the class position of the family. A working-class

White family will not have the same access to resources as an African American middle-class family; nonetheless, the African American middle-class family will likely teach family members how to deal with the racism they are likely to experience, even given their class location. Strong sociological analyses of the family thus take race, class, and gender into account in considering how families are organized, how they change, and what different members within families will experience.

In the past, studies of racial–ethnic families have been biased by the assumption that families should conform to dominant group norms (Baca Zinn and Eitzen 2010). As scholars and the public have realized that this ideal no longer reflects reality, there has been a greater willingness and ability to understand all families without judging them by some dominant ideal. Scholarship on African American, Latino, Asian American, and Native American families has also transformed many of the assumptions earlier built into family studies. New scholarship on families is also critical to understanding many current social issues—including welfare reform, teen pregnancy, and violence—since these problems are often miscast as the fault of families of color.

For example, federal policy has advocated marriage as a solution to women's poverty. No doubt, two-income households are financially better off, and female-headed households are those most likely to be poor. But suggesting that marriage will alleviate poverty among women ignores the problems that marriage itself can pose for women. Given the rates of male unemployment, incarceration, and even early death in poor communities, there is a shortage of marriageable men. In addition, as poor women themselves will say, marriage can put them at risk of violence, provides no guarantees of a stable male income, and can make women dependent on men (Butler 1996). The idea that marriage can lift women out of poverty ignores the actual conditions in which poor women live.

Promoting marriage as a solution to poverty can be traced to the cultural belief that there is something wrong with women-headed households and to beliefs that women who stay home to care for their children are not working. Rather than looking at the social structural conditions that poor women—both White and women of color—live within, such cultural beliefs instead blame families of color for their own situation.

Linking Social Structure and Human Action

It would be a mistake to think of family forms only in abstract terms, as if the behavior of people within families had no influence on family life. Sociologists use the term **human agency** to describe the intentional actions that people take in adapting to and sometimes changing the conditions they face in life. Human agency is an important part of all social life, not just families, and it reminds us that human beings—despite the social structural influences on their lives, are not merely passive creatures who simply accept whatever society expects of them.

Throughout this chapter you can see the influence of agency in families, as people make decisions about how to respond to the conditions they face. Yes, families are social structures, influenced by a wide variety of social forces that exist for any given individual, but individuals also make choices, adjust their attitudes, develop new values, and change their lives. All of these factors influence how families work and how they change.

The Family Ideal

Often, the label *the family* connotes a specific family image—that is, as a haven where people can seek refuge from an impersonal, heartless world. Yet, such an image distorts the actual character of life within families (Baca Zinn and Eitzen 2010). Although families can be a source of love, care, and support, they can also be sources of trouble, conflict, and sorrow. Likewise, the image of family as equally fulfilling to all within it can mask the work and inequities that occur within families where, despite some changes, women continue to provide the greatest share of family labor. Furthermore, the myth that families are harmonious and stable is contradicted by the rate of family divorce and the diversity of family forms in contemporary life (see Figure 6.2). The family ideal is an *ideology*—that is, a belief system suggesting that all people should live in nuclear families, that women should have husbands to support them, and that motherhood is women's major role. This ideology mystifies women's work in families and, as a result, reinforces the economic exploitation of women, as we have seen in the previous chapter (Thorne with Yalom 1992).

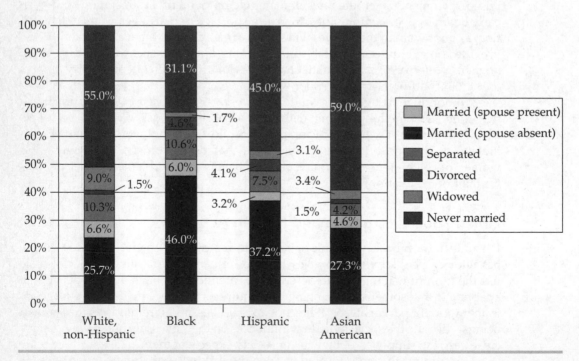

FIGURE 6.2   Diversity in U.S. Families

Source: U.S. Census Bureau. 2009. *America's Families and Living Arrangements*, Table A1. Washington, DC: www.census.gov.

MEDIA MATTERS

(Some) Mothers Are Still Missing in Action

American culture has conveyed very strong messages about what motherhood means and has promoted an idealized model of motherhood. "Ideal" mothers are presumed to be middle-class and White, to stay at home full time, and to be completely fulfilled by their role in the family. In contrast to the myths about at-home mothers, employed mothers are portrayed as being tired and feeling guilty for neglecting their children and failing to provide for their children's basic needs. Where do these mythical portrayals come from? Women's magazines are one place where cultural myths about motherhood are portrayed.

Using a content analysis of the five most popular women's and parenting magazines, Johnston and Swanson found that the magazines generally endorse several indicators of traditional motherhood ideology. One such indicator is race: Of all advertisements in the magazines analyzed, 88 percent presented White women only; 12 percent represented one or more women of color. The second indicator is employment status. Overall, employed mothers are underrepresented in women's magazines: At-home mothers were portrayed in 88 percent of all mother-related

text; employed mothers were presented in 12 percent. Interestingly, when Johnston and Swanson examined mothers' work status by race in magazine advertisements, women of color disappeared: 89 percent of working mothers and 95 percent of at-home mothers were White.

Johnston and Swanson found an interesting paradox with regard to myths about motherhood. Although the women's magazines they analyzed supported a traditional motherhood ideology, negative myths associated with traditional mothers were also sustained. At-home mothers were portrayed as unhappy, not proud, and confused. In contrast, nontraditional mothers (i.e., employed) were presented more positively. They were portrayed as happy and proud (not guilty and tired). Johnston and Swanson conclude that, through either negative portrayals or an overall lack of representation, magazines may damage the confidence of mothers whether employed or not.

Source: Based on Johnston, Deirdre D., and Debra H. Swanson. 2003. "Invisible Mothers: A Content Analysis of Motherhood Ideologies and Myths in Magazines." *Sex Roles* 49 (July): 21–33.

Because of its singular form, the word *family* implies that there is one dominant form of family life. But, as you have learned, this is not an adequate way to describe the facts of most people's family experience. At least, the plural form, *families,* is more descriptive of the diverse realities in contemporary U.S. households (Baca Zinn and Eitzen 2010).

THE DIVERSITY OF CONTEMPORARY FAMILIES

What do contemporary families in the United States look like? First, among Western industrial nations, the United States has the highest rate of marriage, despite the fact that the rate of divorce is also high. Fifty-two percent of the population (over age 15) is married. Single persons make up 30 percent of the population; 9.8 percent are divorced; 2.2 percent are separated; and 6 percent are widowed (see Figure 6.2; U.S. Census Bureau 2009). More children are now being born outside of marriage and will spend at least part of their childhood in a single-parent household. Changes are so widespread that both children and adults are likely to experience multiple changes in the composition of their families during their lifetimes (Teachman et al. 2000).

The changing character of families is especially visible in divorce statistics and the increase in single female-headed households (which includes both divorced mothers and women with children who have never been married). The United States has one of the highest divorce rates of any country in the world; annually, there are about 1 million divorces (about 3.5 for every 1,000 people), although the rate of divorce has been declining in recent years (U.S. Census Bureau 2009).

Measuring Family Status

Changes in family experiences are reflected in the complexity of U.S. Census Bureau data. Before 1980, the census routinely classified the husband as the head of the family if he and his wife were living together. Now, because of how families have changed, the Census Bureau defines **household** as a living unit containing one or more people—in other words, everyone living in a housing unit makes up a household. The person who owns or rents the household is the **householder.** The Census Bureau then goes on to distinguish family households from nonfamily households. **Family households** are those where at least two members are related by blood, marriage, or adoption. A **nonfamily household** includes those living alone and households where people live together who are not related to the house-holder (such as roommates or boarders).

Complex as these definitions may be, they reflect the diversity of household and family forms in contemporary society and they allow the Census Bureau to track and enumerate the characteristics of diverse living arrangements in society. Here are some basic facts:

- Nonfamily households are now more common and family households less common.
- Eighteen percent of all family households have female heads.
- Among Black Americans, 45 percent of family households have female heads; Hispanics, 24 percent; Whites (non-Hispanic), 13 percent; and Asian/Pacific Islanders, 13 percent (U.S. Census Bureau 2008).

These facts not only point to the variety of household forms but also show that more women now head their own households than was true in the past. This is explained by a number of factors, including later age at first marriage, high rates of divorce, less likelihood that pregnant teens will marry, and, in some communities, the high rates of incarceration of young men.

Divorce

It is well known that marriages do not endure, as the ideal implies. You will often hear it said that half of all marriages end in divorce, but this is not really true. What is true is that there are about half as many divorces in a year as there are marriages *made in one year*. Thus, the divorce rate in 2008 was 3.5 for every 1,000 persons in the population and the marriage rate was 7.3 per 1,000, but this counts only marriages and divorces *in that year* and does not include other existing marriages. Another misleading popular fact is that the average length of marriage is seven years—but this counts only marriages that end in divorce.

Thus, marriage is more stable than often assumed, even though the United States has a relatively high divorce rate. The divorce rate has also risen over time, although in recent years, it has declined somewhat. Still, even with these provisos, the idea that marriage is a lifelong commitment is not supported by the truth.

Whether or not families stay together is explained by a number of factors, including the gender roles that women and men within the family adopt. So, for example, job loss can be a source of family strain, often leading to separation and divorce. You can expect then that during periods such as the recent recession there are strains on families to stay together. In an intriguing study of a rural community that had been dependent on a single industry—a common pattern—researchers found that, when an industry closes in such a locale, men's ability to adapt to new gender roles can actually help families stay together. Men who are more flexible in their gender roles and identities, particularly with regard to their roles as fathers, are far more likely to be able to sustain marriages than are men who are more traditional in their gender roles (Sherman 2009). In other words, more flexible gender arrangements in the family can actually help people sustain relationships in the face of social structural pressures.

When people divorce, women are far more likely than men to obtain custody of children. Eighty-five percent of custodial parents are mothers. Obtaining child support is a major problem for women following a divorce, resulting not only in financial hardship but also the additional burden of coping with the legal system, including repeated visits to the courts and social services to try to receive payments. Mothers who are custodial parents are somewhat less likely to be working full time than custodial fathers, making them also more dependent on child support and/or public assistance. Close to one-quarter of custodial mothers live below the poverty line, compared with 14 percent of custodial fathers. Only 45 percent of mothers entitled to child support actually receive the full amount due; 28 percent receive partial payments, and 20 percent receive no payment at all (U.S. Census Bureau 2007).

Following divorce, both women and men have to redefine relationships with friends and families, come to terms with a changed identity, and build a new personal life. For those who are custodial mothers, this also has to happen while they carry the major burden of child rearing and parenting. Many mothers nonetheless report better relationships with their children following a divorce because they have had to redefine their relationships and their new, shared situation. Both women and men report exclusion from their married friends after divorce, but for women the exclusion is exacerbated by the change in their social-class status (Grella 1990). Women also find it difficult to have a social life outside of their family (Arendell 1992). Separated and divorced women, however, tend to be better able than men to rebuild and maintain old social bonds. Men are more likely to drop their old ties, whereas divorced women's social ties tend to reproduce their home-centered lives.

Despite the problems faced by those who divorce, for many it can be a better option than remaining in a troubled marriage. Although divorce is emotionally stressful and financially risky, many women report it as a positive option (Kurz 1995), especially if they were in abusive relationships or their husbands have left them for other women. Changes in women's roles also mean that women are less financially dependent on husbands than in the past. Even though most women are financially less well off without the benefit of a man's income, the economic interdependence that once bound women and men together in marriage is no longer as binding as it once was.

Balancing Family and Work

Changes in family structure are also reflected in the beliefs and practices of people who try to balance work and family life. Thirty-eight percent of women believe that one parent staying at home is ideal; 45 percent of men agree. These attitudes vary by age group; however, with younger people (aged 18 to 29) less likely to think it is ideal for one parent to stay at home (McComb 2001). Men are now more likely than in the past to want marriages where they share work, housekeeping, and child care. These changes in attitudes also reflect the reality faced by most couples that it is increasingly difficult to support a family based on one person's income. Indeed, now more women than ever are the primary breadwinner in their families. Twenty percent of married women now earn more than their husbands—a dramatic change from the past (Bureau of Labor Statistics 2009). Although women hold even more flexible attitudes about gender, work, and family than do men, younger men are now more skeptical about definitions of themselves that focus solely on work. What this will mean in the long run is not clear, but it surely indicates that men and women, regardless of the form of family relationship they make for themselves, have to negotiate gender options at home and at work more consciously, instead of following more rigid social roles (Gerson 2002).

Although men's and women's attitudes about sharing family work have changed over the years, actually balancing work and family demands is difficult. Integrating family and work is a balancing act for all employed women and men, but the ability to do so varies by class, gender, and marital status. In general, working-class women are more likely to give their families priority over their work, whereas professional/managerial women see work as more central to their lives. Single mothers and mothers of children who have special problems have the greatest difficulty integrating work and family (Burris 1991).

Women and men develop a number of strategies for coping with the demands of work and family. At the heart of these demands, however, are deep-seated conflicts about gender ideology—conflicts that are brought on by time pressures felt within relationships, most particularly marriage (Hochschild 1997). Women respond by trying to redefine their roles, choosing men to marry who plan to share work at home or, following marriage, trying to change the husband's understanding of his role at home. Some women force men's greater involvement in work at home by feigning helplessness over certain kinds of tasks; other women cope by trying not to impose change on their husbands, thereby avoiding conflict. Some women attempt to be "supermoms," but, as Hochschild found in her research on dual-earner families, supermoms pay the price, seeming "out of touch" with their feelings and reporting being "numb" (Hochschild 1989:196). Others respond by cutting back on work or, very often, redefining what is necessary in the home. Women also respond by seeking

FOCUS ON RESEARCH

Children of the Gender Revolution

Diversity in American families means that dual-earner, single-parent, and gay/lesbian families now outnumber the family form where there is a male breadwinner and a stay-at-home mother. Changes in the form that families take mean that family structure is less predictable for young people as they face the future than it would have been not that many years ago. How are young people understanding these changes and shaping their lives, especially when society's dominant institutions are still constructed based on the old family norms?

Sociologist Kathleen Gerson has examined this question through an extensive study of young women and men. Naming her research subjects "children of the gender revolution," Gerson studied young adults who both grew up in families where parents were living in new family forms and who are anticipating their own future in this new context. She shows that these young adults have a far more complex understanding of family life—including family ideals—than most people think.

For example, among those who grew up in homes where mothers worked, most thought this was the best option for life, even with the added stress that mothers' work created. But the young people thought that the mothers' increased sense of confidence and the financial security that mothers' work provided was worth the price. Among those whose mothers did not work, close to half wish she had. And, among those whose parents had divorced, although most wished the parents had not, they were realistic that the separation was better than living in a conflict-ridden home.

With regard to their own futures, most wanted a lifelong partner. But what exactly this means differed for various groups. Women were more likely than men to want egalitarian relationships. Three-fourths of the young adults whose parents had a dual-earner marriage also wanted such an arrangement, but perhaps surprisingly, so did the majority of women and men who grew up in traditional one-earner families. Men and women alike were also concerned about the demands on their relationship that time-consuming work would involve, especially because they also perceived that there were not strong institutional supports for child care and family leave.

Gerson concludes that young people see their future pathways as benefitting from flexible gender arrangements, but they also understand that institutions are resistant to change even though they must in order to accomodate the changes that are underway in family life.

Thinking Further: *What is your family background and how do you think it may be influencing your ideals for your family and work life? What institutional obstacles do you foresee for integrating family and work and how might institutional change make your ideals more easily attained?*

Sources: Gerson, Kathleen. 2009. *The Unfinished Revolution: How a New Generation Is Reshaping Family, Work, and Gender in America.* New York: Oxford University Press; Gerson, Kathleen. "Changing Lives, Resistant Institutions: A New Generation Negotiates Gender, Work, and Family Change." *Sociological Forum* 24 (December): 735–753.

outside help, either other female relatives or friends, or, for those with economic privilege, paying other women to do the work at home (Hochschild 1989).

Some couples try to cope with the dual demands of work and family by scaling back on some activities. This can include trading responsibilities over the life course—for example, husbands taking on greater responsibility for family and wives' carrying the major responsibility for family income. But the most common form of "scaling back" is for women to reduce their working time or limit their careers, especially following the birth of a child (Becker and Moen 1999). The ability to do so, however, depends on one's social class. Also, balancing work and family is complicated by the power differences within families. Women tend to want more change then men, especially involving housework, children, sexuality, leisure activities, and finances.

Despite the strains of balancing work and family, there are positive consequences. Men and women report more happiness when they feel they have been able to achieve some balance. It is when women perceive unfairness and when they have to make tradeoffs at work to meet family demands that unhappiness results (Milkie and Peltola 1999; Voydanoff and Donnelly 1999).

Some dual-earner couples, both married and unmarried, find it necessary, because of their job locations, to maintain separate residences. One partner may have to leave the region of residence to find work or may be relocated for an extended period of time. Some may experience an extended geographical separation from the family; others may work out a commuting relationship with partners living in separate places. Such arrangements can occur in middle-class families, probably the most common image of a commuting couple, but they are also common among working-class couples who are vulnerable to job displacement. Commuter couples also experience problems posed by their long-distance arrangements, which can include increased financial burdens and the lack of daily companionship and emotional support.

Despite potential problems, most men and women in commuter marriages report high levels of satisfaction with the relationship and report being equally committed to their partners and careers (Skirboll and Taylor 1998; Groves and Horm-Wingerd 1991). Like commuting couples, couples who reside together but do shift work find that considerable strain is put on the marriage. Studies have found that shift work has a strong effect on the likelihood of divorce. Divorce in the first five years of a marriage is three times more likely when wives have to work the night shift and six times more likely when men do (Presser 2000). These patterns show how strongly work affects family dynamics.

Cohabitation

There is a large increase in the number of single persons who are living together outside of marriage (Seltzer 2000). Since 1970, the number of unmarried persons living together has tripled, with researchers now estimating that soon a majority of persons will experience this lifestyle at some point in their lives (Sassler 2004).

Slightly more than half of couples who cohabit do marry; many live together following the dissolution of other marriages; thus, there may be children in the home. Cohabitation tends to be more common among those who are high school dropouts than among those who have attended college. And, cohabitation is slightly more common among Black and White women than among Latinas (Smock 2000).

Researchers find that there are similar patterns of interaction among partners in cohabiting relationships and those who marry, and there are similar rates of happiness within these relationships (Brown 1996). On the other hand, cohabitors have higher divorce rates when they do marry, and some studies have found higher rates of violence among cohabitors than among spouses, at least among those who have come from violent households (Jackson 1996; Nock 1995).

The likelihood of cohabitation is also related to factors such as educational status, gender-role attitudes, and political orientation, with those most likely to cohabit being more likely to have favorable attitudes toward gender equality and nontraditional gender roles. Cohabitors are also more likely to remain together when they establish an egalitarian relationship (Lye and Waldron 1997; Brines and Joyner 1999; Sanchez et al. 1998; Thornton et al. 1995; Barber and Axinn 1998).

Gay and Lesbian Families

Same-sex marriage has been the subject of much public debate in recent years, brought on both by the greater visibility of lesbian and gay relationships and the legal recognition that several states and municipalities have given to same-sex marriage. Many businesses now recognize the legitimacy of gay and lesbian relationship by extending employee benefits to domestic partners, and nearly half (49 percent) of the U.S. public believe that lesbian and gay relationships should be recognized as legally civil unions, even though a somewhat larger number (57 percent) are opposed to recognizing same-sex marriage (Gallup 2007; see Figure 6.3).

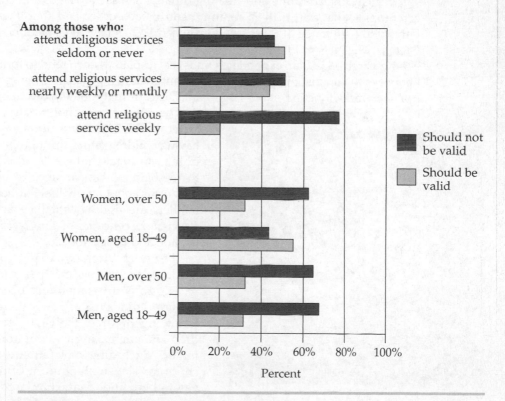

FIGURE 6.3   Acceptance of Gay Marriage

Source: Saad, Lydia. 2006. "Americans Still Oppose Gay Marriage." *The Gallup Poll.* Princeton, NJ: Gallup Organization. Reprinted with permission.

Those who are opposed to same-sex marriage argue that it threatens the institution of marriage—as if changes in the marriage institution are the fault of gays and lesbians. Clearly this is not the case, as we have seen that transformations in contemporary families come from a variety of social forces, including the greater participation of women in the labor market, smaller family size, and the growth of single and female-headed households. Attributing changes in marriage to the alleged influence of gays and lesbians assumes that gays and lesbians have the power to change social institutions, when, in fact, as a minority group in society, it seems far-fetched to blame gays and lesbians for social changes that are otherwise underway.

The resistance to same-sex marriage has also been compared to the historical resistance to interracial marriage. In both cases, people are being deprived of their civil rights. When interracial marriage was illegal, people thought interracial marriage was perverted, sexually deviant, and threatened to undermine the racial social order. By marginalizing and sexualizing relationships that differ from dominant group norms, people disempower social groups, forcing them to invent social support systems of their own (Ross 2002).

Gay and lesbian families are, in fact, creating new forms of social relationships, including adapting and creating rituals, such as marriages and commitment ceremonies, that affirm their commitment to each other and that symbolize the perceived legitimacy of these relationships (McQueeney 2003; Hequembourg and Farrell 1999; Nelson 1999).

Research on lesbian experiences finds that lesbian women tend to form extended networks of support that operate at local and national levels. In a sense, these support networks function like a large family, except that, unlike patriarchal families, they tend to be nonauthoritarian and nonhierarchical. The increasing number of lesbians having children either through in vitro fertilization, surrogate fathers, or adoption means that lesbian mothers are reconstructing existing norms about family life. Studies of lesbian mothers are finding that they actively construct new concepts of family relationships (Dalton and Bielby 2000).

Fewer children live in gay male households, both because of the association of parenting with women and because fewer fathers gain custody of their children following divorce. However, raising children is increasingly common by gay fathers, including gay fathers who adopt children. The small amount of research on gay fathers finds that, compared to heterosexual fathers, they tend to be more nurturing, less traditional in their overall parenting practices, and less accepting of

Research finds that children raised in gay or lesbian families are just as well-adjusted as children raised in heterosexual families.

the idea that being an economic provider is the main ingredient of good fathering. Research also shows that gay fathers have very positive relationships with their children, that they try to create stable home lives, and that the fathers' sexual orientation is of little importance in the overall parent–child relationship (Bigner and Bozett 1989).

Studies of lesbian households also are an interesting context for studying the division of labor in household work. Generally speaking, lesbian couples tend to have more gender equality within their households than do heterosexual couples, so long as both partners are employed. However, when one partner is the primary breadwinner and the other the primary caregiver for children, the partner staying at home becomes economically vulnerable, less able to negotiate with her partner about her needs, and more devalued as a person and a daily contributor—just like the traditional pattern where women stay home and men are the primary breadwinners (Sullivan 1996).

Many have wondered what effect being raised in a lesbian or gay household has on children. Research on this question finds that there is little difference in outcomes for children raised in gay/lesbian households and those raised in heterosexual households. Although children raised in lesbian and gay households do have some difficulties, this is mostly the result of the ridicule and stigma that they experience as the result of others' homophobic attitudes. Thus, any adjustment problems they have are the result of society's disdain for lesbians and gays, not the sexual orientation of parents per se. Children raised in gay and lesbian households are less likely to develop stereotypical gender roles; they are no more likely than children of heterosexual parents to become gay themselves, but they are more tolerant and open-minded about sexual matters (Stacey and Biblarz 2001). Overall, gay and lesbian families tend to make quite positive adjustments under stressful societal conditions (Patterson 2000). If we lived in a society more tolerant of diversity, the differences that do emerge might be viewed as strengths, not deficits.

Motherhood

The child-centeredness of modern families has tended to distract us from thinking about mothers; yet, an examination of motherhood as a social institution reveals both the objective and the subjective dimensions of this experience. Women's roles as mothers are idealized in our culture as all-loving, kind, gentle, and selfless; however, the objective conditions of motherhood in this society fill the role with contradictions, conflicts, and pleasures. Motherhood is, in fact, a social institution—one that is controlled by the systems of patriarchy and the economic relations in which it is embedded (Rich 1976). Like other institutions, motherhood involves a complex set of social relations organized around specific functions. Once established, institutions also involve a system of power relations, a division of labor, and the distribution of resources (Glenn et al. 1993).

Viewing motherhood as an institution distinguishes motherhood as something more than a caring relationship between a woman and her children (Rich 1976). Viewing mothering only in the isolated context of the family misses its connections to other social institutions. As an example, research on Latina and African American mothering finds that low-income women define their mothering as an activist activity when they are engaged in community work that they see as an extension of their mothering role. For these mothers, activism is essential to providing the safety, health care, education, and other services that they know are necessary for their children's welfare (Naples 1992). Seen in this light, mothering is work that takes place not just within the family, but throughout social institutions. It is a socially constructed practice, one wherein mothers construct an understanding of themselves and their children in relationship to the society around them.

This has been shown recently in an important research study of women who choose to become mothers, even when not with a partner. Rosanna Hertz has shown that traditional patterns of sequencing education, then marriage, and then motherhood have been disrupted by the many social changes that have affected women's lives, including the feminist movement, the gay/lesbian movement, and new technologies that enable women to bear children without men. Her research on mostly middle-class women shows how many women want to be mothers, but single mothers have redefined motherhood to include diverse patterns of constructing families (Hertz 2006). Women increasingly view work and motherhood as compatible identities, even though the dominant culture views these as competing roles (Mcquillan et al. 2008).

Because motherhood is a role exclusively reserved for women, women's identities develop in ways that reproduce mothering qualities. Nancy Chodorow has asked how the psychological structures of gender emerge from the "asymmetrical organization of parenting" (1978:49; see also Chapter 2). She notes that the role of women as mothers is one of the few seemingly universal elements of the gender division of labor. But, instead of seeing motherhood as a natural fact, Chodorow asks why the psychological characteristics of motherhood are reproduced so that women, and not men, want to be mothers and develop the capacity of nurturing others. She explains that this is the result of the gender division of labor and the psychological processes it inspires. In order to become their own person, both boys and girls must separate—psychologically—from the parent—the process of *individuation*. Because the parent most often present is a woman, individuation is complicated by gender identity. If the father is seldom present in the home, boys, who identify with the gender of the father, learn that their gender role is one of detachment and distance. Girls, on the other hand, identify with the gender of the mother; thus, their own psychological process of separation and individuation is less complete. Girls then develop more relational psychologies, whereas boys learn to be more detached.

Chodorow's argument is that gendered personalities both reflect and re-create the gender division of labor in the household. In sum, the social organization of parenting creates psychic structures that orient the person to his or her social behavior. Reversing this so that men as fathers become more nurturing requires that men be in the household on an equal basis with women. In other words, both the family and the workplace need transformation to eliminate gender inequality.

An important test of Chodorow's theory would involve studying boys and girls who are raised by men or in cultures where women are not devalued and parenthood is more equally shared. Chodorow's analysis has helped us see the importance of understanding how cultural understandings of masculinity and femininity are linked to the social organization of families and to our gendered identities. She provides an insightful explanation of the effects of family structures and the isolation of mothering from other social relationships.

Fatherhood

Fathers' roles in the family have traditionally been defined as instrumental. Fathers were presumed to be the primary breadwinners and the source of authority in the family, whereas mothers were mostly to fulfill the emotional needs of family members. Just as women have found their traditional roles to be limiting and one-sided, many men have tried to redefine their roles as fathers to include more primary care of children (Silverstein and Auerbach 1999).

A CLOSER LOOK AT MEN

Does Father Care Mean Fathers Share?

There is little disagreement among researchers that middle-class families are experiencing an economic crunch. The middle-class aspiration of buying a home, owning a car, and having money to raise and educate children now requires two incomes. With more women in the paid labor force, have men increased their share of domestic responsibilities?

Lyn Craig's research seeks to answer this question, specifically asking how mothers and fathers allocate time to children. Craig investigated what child-care tasks mothers and fathers did, whether they were doing it as "double activity" (meaning that child care is done simultaneously with other activity), and whether each was in sole charge of children at the time.

Based on an Australian sample, Craig found that mothers spend much longer than fathers in time caring for children. Physical care (i.e., feeding, bathing, dressing, soothing, etc.) accounted for more than half a mother's child-care time but a third of a father's. These care activities tend to be more structured and have to be done at certain times. Craig also found that half of father's time in interactive care (i.e., teaching, reading, playing games, talking, listening, etc.) is done as a main

activity, whereas for mothers, these activities are being done at the same time as other tasks two thirds of the time. Finally, mothers are usually in sole care of their children one-third of the time, compared to about 8 percent of the total time fathers spend with their children. This suggests that fathers in intact families are rarely alone with their children.

Craig concludes that providing child care is different in kind and quality for mothers and fathers, even when mothers work full time. Because fathers' child care tends to be the more "fun" activities, it is less like work than what mothers do. Additionally, fathers may be less constrained by their child-care duties because they spend the bulk of their child care in interactive child-care tasks, which are done on a less structured schedule than physical care. That fathers are rarely in sole charge of their children is particularly important because it suggests that fathers' child care does not relieve mothers of the responsibility for child care.

Source: Based on Craig, Lyn. 2006. "Does Father Care Mean Fathers Share? A Comparison of How Mothers and Fathers in Intact Families Spend Time with Children." *Gender & Society* 20 (April): 259–281.

Still, research shows that following the birth of a baby, most fathers tend to "help out" rather than share child care, and they continue to view caring for the baby as the mother's work. Studies also find, however, that fathers' increased involvement in child rearing is linked to greater stability in marriage, in part because wives are then happier. Still, women hold the vast share of responsibility for parenting (Wall and Arnold 2007; Walzer 1996; Belsky and Kelly 1994; Kalmijn 1999).

Families headed by single fathers have also increased, even though they are a small percentage of all families. Despite the increase in the number of single and divorced fathers, as well as the greater involvement of many men in their roles as fathers, there are few social support networks for men. Many men continue to feel pressure to put their jobs and careers first, and, although employers give lip service to increased family involvement, workers perceive that choices have to be made between family and career.

Single fathers also tend to use outside help, typically from women, and to use daughters as mother substitutes—to do child care, housework, and manage household affairs (Greif 1985). Single fathers feel competent about their skills as parents and demonstrate more mothering behaviors than do married fathers. Compared with men who are still married, single fathers spend more time with their children, report more sharing of feelings between father and child, are more likely to stay home with sick children, and take a more active interest in their children's out-of-home activities (Risman 1999).

Most single fathers are heading their own households as the result of divorce or widowhood. What about young, unwed fathers? Despite social stereotypes, many, if not most, young unwed fathers try to take some responsibility for their children, but their economic disadvantage is high. Young unwed fathers are generally less well educated than other groups, have limited employment prospects, and are more likely to engage in crime. Studies of unmarried fathers find that they are more involved with their children when their earnings are higher (Lerman and Sorenson 2000; Lerman and Ooms 1993; Marsiglio 1995). But high unemployment among young men, especially African American and Hispanic, makes it difficult for them to support their children, even though studies find that these men want to be good fathers and provide for their children (Hamer 2001). This is complicated by the high rate of imprisonment of poor, young Black and Hispanic men.

Sociological perspectives on fatherhood see fathering, like mothering, as a role, not just a biological connection to one's offspring. Neither kinship nor household membership is always necessary for a man to perform the psychological and instrumental functions associated with a father. Men who have worked to include more expressive and caretaking work in their roles as fathers report considerable rewards in creating fuller relationships with their children, although they also note that society provides little emotional, practical, or financial support for men to spend time with their children. Societal support in the form of paternity leaves, new work arrangements for parents, and transformation in our attitudes about gender and parenting are as essential for fathers' roles as for mothers' roles (see Table 6.1).

TABLE 6.1   Maternity Leave Benefits: A Comparative Perspective

Country	Length of Maternity Leave	Percentage of Wages Paid in Covered Period	Provider of Coverage
Zimbabwe	90 days	100%	Employer
Haiti	12 weeks	100% for 6 weeks	Employer
South Africa	4 months	Up to 60% depending on income level	Unemployment insurance fund
Cuba	18 weeks	100%	Social Security
Iran	90 days	67%	Social Security
China	90 days	100%	Employer
Saudi Arabia	10 weeks	50 or 100% (depending on duration of employment)	Employer
Canada	17–18 weeks (varies by province)	55% up to a ceiling	Employment insurance
Germany	14 weeks	100%	Social Security to a ceiling; then employer pays difference
France	16 weeks	100%	Social Security
Italy	5 months	80%	Social Security
Japan	14 weeks	60%	Health insurance or Social Security
Russian Federation	140 days	100%	Social Security
Sweden	14 weeks	480 days paid parental leave; 80% 390 days; 90 days, flat rate	Social Security
United Kingdom	26 weeks	90% for first 6 weeks and flat rate	Employer (refunded 92% by public funds)
United States	**12 weeks**	**0**	**n.a.**

Source: Data from United Nations. 2010. "Statistics and Indicators on Women and Men." New York: United Nations. http://unstats.un.org/unsd/demographic/products/indwm/ww2005/tab5c.htm.

RACE, GENDER, AND FAMILIES

The structural diversity model of families used here shows how significant the racial organization of society is in shaping family experiences. Examining diverse families in more detail underscores this point.

Both the historical and contemporary forms of racial–ethnic families stem from the conditions of oppression that they have experienced—conditions that, although differing from group to group, nonetheless reveal a history of structural exploitation from which women and men had to try to forge strong family ties (Dill 1988). Consider the history of African American families. Some have argued that the high rate of female-headed families among African Americans is a holdover from slavery where African American men and women could not form legally recognized marriages. Families were separated by slave sales and disrupted by the practice of slave breeding, as well as the intense racism experienced by the Black slave community (Frazier 1948).

But is slavery the basis for contemporary African American family structures? An important study of African American families in slavery and in the early twentieth century addressed this question. Historian Herbert Gutman argued that if slavery were the source of later Black family structures, we would expect the family to be less stable as we look backward in time. To test this assumption, Gutman traced five generations of kin as they adapted to the changes of postslavery society in the United States. Using 1925 census data from New York City, he found that 85 percent of kin-related Black households at that time were headed by both parents; 32 of the 13,924 families had no father present; and five in six children under age 6 lived with both parents (Gutman 1976:xix). He concluded that female-headed households are a contemporary phenomenon, not just remnants of the past.

There is little question that slaveowners used the family as a form of social control. Separation of families occurred, but slaveowners might also maintain stable families as a way of preventing slave revolts. The slave family, in other words, was subordinated to the economic interests of the owner. If it benefited him, he would break up families for sale; in fact, most slaveowners broke up families when owners were under economic pressure (Genovese 1972:453).

Such historical analyses show that slave families faced oppressive conditions, testing the adaptive capacities of men and women. Within slave communities, a subculture of resistance emerged in which family relations and women's roles fostered resistance to dominant White institutions (Davis, 1971, 1981). Furthermore, Black women in slavery provided domestic labor not only in the White households but also in their own. The labor they provided for their own family was the only labor not claimed by the ruling class; it was for the benefit of the slave community. As a result, Black women's labor in the slave community "la[id] the foundation for some degree of autonomy" (Davis 1971:5), and the Black woman became essential to the survival of the slave community. Because of her indispensable labor in the household of the oppressor, she developed a practical awareness of the oppressor's dependence on her.

The picture of the African American family emerging from historical study is one of resistance to conditions of oppression. Instead of explaining patterns in Black families as the result of slavery or individual pathology, scholars now analyze African American family life in terms of the patterns of urbanization, industrialization, and poverty in the current time, not just the past (Billingsley 1966; Frazier 1948; Staples 1971). In the early twentieth century, racial discrimination in the labor force denied African Americans employment using the skills they had acquired in slavery. Men could find only unskilled, often seasonal, and always underpaid, employment; women were more likely to find steady, although also severely underpaid, employment in private domestic labor. In 1920, 41 percent of Black women worked as servants and 20 percent as laundresses (Katzman 1978:74). Black women's labor thus made them steady providers for their family. As the twentieth century developed, continuing patterns of unemployment, the elimination of Black men through war and imprisonment, and the conditions the social welfare system established for households encouraged the formation of female-centered households.

The contemporary structure of African American households must then also be understood in terms of race relations, gender relations, and the economic context in which families are situated, not the conditions of the past. Within even the poorest of families, systems of cooperation and social exchange characterize the organization of family life (Collins 1990; Stack and Burton 1993). African American families, like an increasing number of all families, are not always organized according to dominant group ideals. Seen in this way, the role of women in the African American family can be seen for the strength it creates, not the social destruction it allegedly causes. African American middle-class families promote among their children and through their community activities a strong sense of building a just and equitable society, whereas White middle-class families are likely to encourage family members to become individually better informed and enriched (Willie and Reddick 2003; Hill and Sprague 1999).

These conclusions sensitize us to the different conditions that families face depending on their class and race location. Although certainly many African American families struggle with problems of poverty, unemployment, and violence, those problems stem from the social structural location of families in a race, class, and gender-stratified society, not from something inherently problematic in women's heading of households or in African American values.

Similar transformations of thinking have come from studies of Latino families. Like past studies of African American families, past studies of Latino families have been founded on the assumption of pathology. *Machismo* in Latino families has been assumed to encourage aggressive, violent, authoritarian behavior in men and saintly, virginal, submissive behavior in women (Staples and Mirandé 1980). Some researchers see machismo as a more benevolent feature of Latino families, encouraging honor, respect, and dignity among family members (Mirandé 1979).

Chicano families have been characterized as close-knit kinship systems, typically explained as a consequence of Chicano culture. Scholars now recognize that these family patterns represent adaptation to a hostile society that excludes Chicanos from full participation and keeps them socioeconomically marginal (Baca Zinn and Eitzen 2010; Dill 1994). Especially for women, close kinship networks provide social exchanges and support that are not available elsewhere. Studies of Latino families show considerable differences in family experiences, depending on the various social histories and contemporary status of particular groups categorized as "Latino." Thus, Chicanas (women of Mexican descent born and raised in the United States) are more likely to hold the ideal of stay-at-home motherhood than Mexicanas (Mexican women immigrants residing in the United States). Because Mexicanas are more likely to have mixed family and employment, they are less likely to dichotomize family and work in their understandings of motherhood (Segura 1998).

For all groups, family experience is bound by the broader systems of race, class, and gender inequality. So, for example, Puerto Rican families have experienced one of the most rapid rises in female-headed households, largely due to the decline of industrial employment for men in the regions where Puerto Ricans tend to be concentrated. As a result, although Puerto Rican families are traditionally headed by men, the rate of families headed by females among Puerto Ricans has nearly converged with that of African Americans. This trend is further evidence that societal conditions, not just cultural preferences, shape family structure (Baca Zinn and Eitzen 2010).

New patterns of family life in the context of widespread immigration illustrate this point well. High rates of immigration in recent years—especially from Central America, the Caribbean, and Southeast Asia—are creating a new classification of family life: **transnational families**. In these families, family members live in different countries, usually at considerable distance from one another, but with a pattern of moving back and forth across national boundaries. Thus, as in Hondagneu-Sotelo's (1997) study of transnational mothers, women may work as domestic workers in Los Angeles, while their children reside in Mexico, El Salvador, or Guatemala. The very structure of the work they do may discourage having children physically present in their new home, thus challenging strong beliefs that mothers should raise their own children. Yet, transnational mothers do not see themselves as abandoning their children; rather, they redefine motherhood to include mothers' obligations to financially support their children and to value the contributions of other caregivers (e.g., grandmothers, aunts, and friends) to the well-being of their children. Hondagneu-Sotelo concludes, "Transnational mothering radically rearranges mother-child interactions and requires a concomitant radical reshaping of the meanings and definitions of appropriate mothering" (1997:557). Other studies of transnational families show that women negotiate and sustain relationships across national borders because this is how they forge their identity and maintain a sense of security in their homeland in the face of racial oppression and class disadvantage in their new location (Das Gupta 1997; Alicea 1997).

As with African American and Latino families, family experiences among Asian Americans and Native Americans have to be understood in the context of racist policies that have discouraged strong and cohesive families. Also important is looking at the specific class locations of racial–ethnic groups (Dill 1988; Baca Zinn and Eitzen 2010). Asian Americans, for example, are typically stereotyped as the "model minority"—meaning that they have been depicted as highly successful in comparison to other immigrant groups, presumably as a result of their hard work, education, and thrift (and, by implication, the absence of these qualities among other racial–ethnic groups). This simplistic view ignores the barriers to mobility that Asian Americans have encountered and is based on the myth that hard work always reaps commensurate rewards (Woo 1992). In addition, it overlooks the diversity within Asian American groups.

U.S. policies regarding Asians have encouraged the use of Asians in specific cheap forms of labor, at the same time that they have explicitly discouraged family unity (Lai 1992). So, for example, in the nineteenth century, young Asian men were seen as desirable workers in agriculture, mining, and railroads; women were not. The Page Law, passed in 1875, intended to exclude Chinese women as prostitutes, was so strictly enforced that it functionally excluded Chinese women from coming to the United States. The Chinese Exclusion Act of 1882 prohibited the entry of Chinese laborers (men or women) and forbade wives of resident laborers from entering the United States (Takaki 1989). Later, the Immigration Act of 1924 prohibited the entry of any Chinese women to the United States, making it impossible for families of Chinese men to join them.

In addition to explicit laws restricting immigration, many Asian immigrants believed that their work in the United States would be temporary; so, in accordance with tradition, wives remained at home. As a result, the large number of men in Chinese communities in the United States made them bachelor societies. Only in Hawaii, where sugar planters thought Chinese women could control Chinese laborers through their taming influence, were women encouraged to immigrate.

Before 1868, as part of its isolationist policy, the Japanese government forbade its citizens to leave; however, with a new emperor in 1868, Japan encouraged select classes to seek education abroad. Economic depression in the 1880s encouraged many small farmers to seek opportunities in the United States, where wages were high compared with those in Japan and hard work held the promise of enabling workers to return to Japan as wealthy people—a promise that rarely came true. Japanese immigrants to the United States tended to come from middle-class backgrounds and, on the whole, were better off economically than other Asian and European immigrants to the United States. Like the Chinese, the earliest immigrants were mostly men who worked in unskilled labor in agriculture, mining, railroads, and lumber. They, too, believed their work in the United States was temporary (Glenn 1986).

Japanese women were allowed to come to the United States under the terms of the Gentlemen's Agreement of 1908. This law restricted the entry of Japanese laborers but allowed parents, wives, and children of those already in America to settle here. This law also encouraged the practice of "picture brides," particularly among Japanese and Korean immigrants. Consistent with the traditional practice of arranged marriage, Asian men in the United States would marry women who, hopeful of upward mobility, applied and were displayed in offices in many of the port cities (Takaki 1989). Until ruled unconstitutional in 1967, **antimiscegenation** laws barred marriages between Whites and "Mongolians," or laborers of Asian origins (Chow 1987). Such policies made it difficult, if not impossible, for stable Asian American families to form. This history reveals that family stability is as much a result of policies and practices that promote family life as it is of the culture and characteristics of different groups.

Among Native Americans, family lifestyles vary widely because diversity among groups is a key element of culture. The attempt to impose Western family forms on these people complicates the picture of Native American family life. Interference in these cultures by social workers, the federal government, and other outsiders might have done more to promote family and cultural disorganization than to assist these groups. Among Native American families, urbanization contributes to high rates of unemployment and dependence on public welfare (Miller 1975). Left to their own culture, Native American families tend to rely on extended family networks to fulfill family functions (Redhorse et al. 1979; Rousey and Longie 2001). The imposition of Western standards on these traditional forms creates stress for the community and the family, because adapting to both traditional and dominant societal values poses difficulties for both individuals and families.

The problems faced by diverse families underscore the point that families do not exist in a cultural and economic vacuum. Economic changes, racial and cultural conflicts, and gender relations interact to produce family systems. In sum, we can see that no single model of family life characterizes *the* American family, despite ideological beliefs to the contrary. Understanding family experiences for all groups requires an understanding of the intersections of race, class, and gender oppression in the structuring of family life.

FAMILIES AND SOCIAL PROBLEMS

Family Violence

The tensions experienced within families are evident by the extent of violence that occurs within families. These once-hidden problems now seem disturbingly common, and they have a tremendous impact on the nation's crime problem (see also Chapter 9). For example, of all those in state prisons for a violent crime, 15 percent are there for crime against a family member. And almost one-quarter of all murders (22 percent) are murders committed against a family member; the vast majority of such violence (three-fourths) is violence by men. When women are the perpetrators, their victims are most likely men. In fact, 11 percent of all violence is violence within the family (Durose et al. 2005; Catalano 2007).

Partner Violence

Studies indicate that the overwhelming amount of domestic violence is directed against women (see Table 6.2). Family violence is, in fact, the strongest predictor of female homicide. Violence against women in families is a form of social control—one that emerges directly from the patriarchal structure and ideology of the family.

TABLE 6.2   Victim–Offender Relationships in Nonfatal Violent Victimizations: Rate in a Given Year (age 12 and older)

Victim–Offender Relationship	Women (as victims)		Men (as victims)	
	Rate (per 1000 persons)	Percent	Rate (per 1000 persons)	Percent
Intimate	4.2	21.5%	0.9	3.6%
Other relative	1.7	8.9	1.2	4.6
Acquaintance	7.0	36.2	8.6	34.3
Stranger	6.5	33.4	14.4	57.4

Thinking Further: Based on the information displayed in the table above, who has the greatest likelihood of experiencing violence by a stranger? By an intimate partner? By a relative? What do you think explains this?

Source: Catalano, Shannon. 2007. *Intimate Partner Violence in the United States.* Washington, DC: U.S. Department of Justice, Bureau of Justice Statistics.

Historically, wife beating has been a legitimate way to express male authority. The transformation from the feudal patriarchal household to the nuclear family had the effect of strengthening the husband's power over his wife by placing systems of authority directly in the hands of individual men, not in the indirect rule of the state. Throughout the seventeenth, eighteenth, and nineteenth centuries, men could, within the law, beat their wives, and there was little community objection to their doing so as long as the method and extent of violence remained within certain tacit, and sometimes formally documented, limits. For example, eighteenth-century French law restricted violence against wives to "blows, thumps, kicks, or punches on the back if they leave no traces" and did not allow the use of "sharp edged or crushing instruments" (Castan 1976, cited in Dobash and Dobash 1979:56–57). One ancient code, from which we get the phrase *rule of thumb,* allowed a man to beat his wife with a stick no thicker than his thumb (Dobash and Dobash 1977).

A number of risk factors contribute to the likelihood of violence in any relationship, notably power imbalances that occur between partners, with the least powerful and most dependent partner being most at risk. Unemployment of the abuser is another risk factor for violence. Studies find that unemployment increases the risk of violence fourfold, suggesting that threats to the provider role undermine the construction of masculine identity, creating a potential for violent expressions (Campbell et al. 2003). Homicide as the result of domestic violence is linked to the presence of firearms. In general, intimate partner violence is linked to a variety of social factors. Alcohol and drugs are part of the mix, present in about 40 percent of violent

Domestic violence is the result of expressions of men's power.

incidents. Physical disability is linked to violence; partners who are disabled are more likely to be victims of violence. In addition, patterns such as a prior history of violence (including within one's family of origin), substance abuse, and attempts to end a relationship (separation and divorce) are linked to the likelihood of violence (Catalano 2007; Tjaden and Thoennes 2000; Kantor and Jasinksi 1998).

A common pattern within violent relationships is the isolation that battered partners experience. When a pattern of violence emerges in a relationship, the batterer may work to isolate the partner from friends, families, and other support networks. Violence by intimates is often accompanied by emotionally abusive and controlling behavior. Thus, women whose partners are jealous, controlling, or verbally abusive are much more likely to report being raped, physically assaulted, or stalked by their partners (Tjaden and Thoennes 2000).

Being battered not only puts one at risk of injury and perhaps death, but it also produces psychological problems, including depression and anxiety. These problems then further isolate someone from potential support networks with the isolation then feeding on a cycle of violence, leaving victims feeling that they have no options other than continuing the relationship.

The cycle of violence explains a common reaction to domestic violence: Why doesn't the victim leave? Studies of wives show that at some points in the relationship, most do in fact leave, but often only temporarily. Once a pattern of violence is established in a relationship, women may believe they have no options. Their feeling that they have no place to go is often a realistic assessment of their economic situation and their powerlessness to effect changes within the relationship; women are much more likely to leave if they have some economic independence (Anderson 2007). When women do stay in abusive relationships, they tend to rationalize the violence to themselves—perhaps thinking the violence will stop, the man will change, or they will find some way to change the relationship. Research finds that women who stay within violent relationships use these different types of rationalizations, including believing that the man can be "saved" or explaining the battering as the result of external forces that the batterer cannot control, thereby excusing the behavior and putting themselves in the traditional role of "helper" trying to save someone else rather than themselves.

When women do decide to prosecute their batterers, they are faced with the problem of having to prosecute a man who is both their partner and, possibly, the father of their children. Even if the wife brings charges, when the husband is released, he returns to the home—probably angrier than when the violence began. If the husband was employed but jailed, she will also experience a decline in family income. Thus, despite good intentions, policies that remove violent men from the home may actually impose different forms of hardship on women who depend on their earnings (S. Miller 2005).

Shelters for battered women have proliferated in communities throughout the country, largely as the result of the women's movement which early called attention to this huge problem. Shelters are an important part of the support network for women and their children, although they are usually strained to meet the demands of those who need them.

Violence is not confined to marriage or to heterosexual couples. Unmarried, cohabiting couples actually have a higher risk of partner violence than married couples (Tjaden and Thoennes 2000). Studies of violence within same-sex relationships indicate that lesbian women (living with other women) are the most likely women to be victims of violence, *but their assailants are men*. Intimate relationships between women are the least likely form of relationship to actually produce violence. That does not mean that violence does not occur in lesbian relationships—only that the rate is lower than that involving male–female intimates and male–male intimates (Tjaden and Thoennes 2000; West 1998; Renzetti 1997). Within same-sex relationships, homophobia plays a role in the perpetration of violence. Homophobia can be used as a psychological weapon if a partner threatens to expose the relationship to parents or employers. Internalized homophobia can also lead to patterns of violence (West 1998; Renzetti 1997).

The consequences of violence are many, ranging from psychological harm to death. Women's risk of homicide from family violence is much greater than men's, and women are far more likely to be injured through violence. Even when men are the victims of family violence—a phenomenon that has been exaggerated in the media but does occur—men are less likely to be seriously injured than are women in violent relationships (Catalano 2007). For children, witnessing family violence also has a strong effect, including emotional and physical distress, personality and adjustment problems, disciplinary problems, and educational underachievement, as well as being in physical danger (Wolak and Finkelhor 1998).

Feminist scholars argue that violence is a weapon men use to control women. Although women sometimes do commit violence against men, domestic violence emerges from the power dynamics between men and women in the family. Men abuse women typically as an expression of power. Violence is one way that men maintain their power over women.

Marital Rape

Marital rape is defined as "forced sexual activity demanded of a wife by her husband" (Frieze 1983). Legal definitions of marital rape vary from state to state, and in many states forced sex is still not considered a crime in marriage. Historically, the "right" to sex was fundamental to the legal definition of marriage (Ryan 1995). Many still view rape as something that cannot happen in marriage; studies find that rape myths (such as "the woman asked for it") are more likely to be believed when the rape occurred within marriage (Ferro et al. 2008).

Forced sexual activity occurs in about 10 percent of all married couples (Basile 2002)—more common than rape by a stranger. Most wives experiencing marital rape have experienced it multiple times in the marriage (Basile 2008; Mahoney and Williams 1998; Tjaden and Thoennes 2000).

Marital rape is associated with other forms of violence—both in the relationship and in prior relationships. Studies find a strong association between having been abused as a child and the likelihood of rape within marriage. An earlier history of abuse also makes women more vulnerable to repeated rape within marriage. Studies also show some increase in marital rape during pregnancy and after a wife has been hospitalized for illness, suggesting that these vulnerabilities influence women's power within marriage. Wives who have experienced sexual assault in marriage also report having been forced to engage in sex with other people, in public or even with their children. Sexual assault occurs when the husband suspects sexual infidelity and/or when the couple is in the process of separating. In other words, power, control, dominance, and humiliation are common patterns in marital rape and, as with other forms of rape, offenders also typically do not understand the harm they have caused as the result of their violence (Basile 2008; Mahoney and Williams 1998; Yllo 1990).

Incest and Sexual Abuse

Accurate estimates of the extent of incest and sexual abuse are very difficult to establish. Russell's (1986) study, the most widely cited, indicates that 16 percent of women have been sexually abused by a relative by the time they are 18 years old; other forms of incest range between 4 and 12 percent of the population. Girls are far more likely to be abused than boys and, when they are, to experience greater harm (Nelson and Oliver 1998).

Mothers may be aware of abuse, but they are typically powerless to stop it. A mother may become a silent bystander because her emotional and/or economic dependence on her husband prevents her from confronting the situation. Studies of different cultures where various forms of sexual abuse are inflicted on daughters (including genital mutilation, infanticide, footbinding, and other practices) explain mothers' participation in such harm in the context of power relations within the family and the culture at large (Candib 1999). Particularly in families where mothers are unusually powerless as a result of battering, disability, or mental illness there is an especially high risk of sexual abuse, especially among daughters who have taken on the household responsibilities. In such families, the daughter is often led to believe that she must comply with the father's demands if she is to hold the family together (Herman and Hirschman 1977). Abused daughters in this situation are still dependent on their fathers for care and, because this may be the only affection they receive, they often report warm feelings for their fathers, who make them feel special (Herman 1981).

This research finds that the father/assailant feels no contrition about his behavior. When mothers are incapacitated, fathers do not take on the nurturing functions, nor do they express nurturing feelings for the child or understand the destructiveness of the incest. Fathers typically blamed their wives or their daughters for the abuse (Herman 1981).

This portrait of sexual abuse underscores that the intersection of power and gender relations in families is a contributing factor. There are multiple consequences of sexual abuse. For example, childhood abuse is linked to a variety of social problems, including delinquency, substance abuse, developmental problems, and later violence in relationships (Milner and Crouch 1993; Hernandez 1995; Conte 1993). These associations suggest that sexual abuse is important for practitioners to consider when developing treatment programs for other social problems concerning women and young girls.

Feminists have pointed to violence as the logical result of both women's powerlessness in the family and a male culture that emphasizes aggression, domination, and violence. The modern form of the family leads women to be economically and emotionally dependent on men, and as a result, the traditional family is a source of social conflict and a haven only for men (Hartmann 1981a). The phenomenon of violence in the family shows clearly the problems that traditional family structures create for women. Feminist criticism of the family rests, in part, on the psychological, physical and economic threats families pose for women, and it is for those reasons that feminists argue for a change in traditional family structures. These changes, intended to empower women, would not necessarily abolish the family, but they would create new values regarding women's work in the family and new rewards for women in the family, regardless of whether they are also working in the public labor force.

Teen Pregnancy

There is much public concern about teen pregnancy, witnessed most recently in programs calling for sexual abstinence among teens. The politics surrounding teen pregnancy often cloud the actual facts—one of which is that the teen birth rate has actually been declining since 1990. The current rate of teen (ages 15 to 19) births is 42.5 births per 1,000 women in that age bracket. Moreover, contrary to popular stereotypes, the rate of teen births among Black teens is decreasing faster than among White teens, although the teen birth rate among African Americans, Native Americans, and Hispanics remains higher than among Whites. Probably the most significant fact is not so much the birth rate per se but the fact that so many teen mothers are not married. But, again, the reality of race in this regard is different from what popular stereotypes suggest: The rate of birth to unmarried White women has increased since 1990, whereas the birth rate for unmarried Black women declined over the same period of time. The birth rate among unmarried Hispanic teens also increased over this time period, but not as much so as for Whites (U.S. Census Bureau 2009).

One of the concerns about teen pregnancy is the fact that teen mothers are so likely to be poor. But the reality is that, for most of those who are poor, they were poor *before* their pregnancy. Thus, the idea that teen pregnancy somehow causes poverty is simply wrong. Teen mothers do face higher medical risks in pregnancy, with a much greater risk of having low–birth-weight babies, which is linked to greater infant mortality. Teen parents face chronic unemployment; when they do work, they face low earnings and low-status jobs. Thus, one-third of teen mothers live in poverty, regardless of race; poverty is especially a problem for those who live on their own..

Compared with teen mothers of the past, present-day teen mothers from all races and classes feel much less pressure to marry, although research finds many teens no longer think that marriage is necessary to legitimate a birth. And, when they discover they are pregnant, teens often conclude that the father is not willing or ready to marry. Low-income teens place the same value on marriage as do middle-class people, but they think the ideal marriage is just not attainable (Edin and Kefalas 2005). Myths about race and teen pregnancy are also pervasive and, as we have seen in the preceding chapter, are linked to public stereotypes about welfare mothers. Contrary to public stereotypes, studies find that African American communities do not condone teen pregnancy. In a detailed study of low-income African American mothers, Elaine Bell Kaplan has found that these young women were embarrassed by their pregnancy and had numerous conflicts with their mothers when they learned they were pregnant. The mothers saw their daughters' pregnancies as disrupting the hopes they had for their daughters' success. Moreover, the teen mothers were ashamed if they had to accept welfare, and they tried to hide that they were struggling to make ends meet. These conclusions are directly counter to the public image of these young mothers (Kaplan 1997).

As we saw in Chapter 4, most people have sexual intercourse for the first time while they are teenagers, most initiating sex in their mid- to late teens. About two-thirds use a contraceptive during their first experience with intercourse—a number that has increased in recent years because of an increase in condom use among teens (largely because of the campaign for safe sex that emanated from the AIDS epidemic).

Recently, promoting abstinence has been suggested as the best way to reduce teen pregnancy. The reduction in teen pregnancy in recent years might lead you to think that abstinence campaigns have been a success, but studies have found that sex education programs focusing exclusively on abstinence have virtually no effect in delaying sexual activity among teens. In a detailed study comparing abstinence pledgers to nonpledgers, researchers have found *no differences* in teen frequency of sex, their age at first sex, or whether they had engaged in oral or anal sex. The main difference found was that, when they had sex, pledgers were less likely to use birth control, meaning they are far less likely to prevent pregnancy—or, for that matter, sexual disease (Rosenbaum 2009). Scholars have concluded that abstinence policies account for a very small portion of the decline in teen pregnancy—probably only about 10 percent of the difference (Santelli et al. 2007; Boonstra et al. 2006).

Among teens using birth control, the most frequent contraceptive is the pill (53 percent), followed by the condom (27 percent). Injectable birth control, withdrawal, and the implant account for the remainder. Still, a large number of young women have sex without birth control (26 percent). A sexually active teen female who does not use contraception has a 90 percent chance of getting pregnant within one year (Guttmacher Institute 2008).

Many have argued that a sociological reason for young women not using birth control is that the regular use of contraceptives requires conscious recognition of oneself as sexually active (Luker 1975). Teenage sex tends to be episodic; for a young woman to make calculated plans for contraceptive protection requires her to see herself as a sexually active person. Cultural and legal proscriptions that encourage the denial of sexuality to young women seem likely to only exacerbate this situation.

Many also argue that sex education does not filter down to adolescents before they start having sex. Girls often have little or no information about their bodies and are often seriously misinformed about sex (for example, believing they cannot get pregnant if they are standing up during intercourse!). The fact that mothers, not fathers, talk to their children about sex also spreads the message that men have no responsibility in this area, discouraging young men from being responsible for birth control and resting the decision to avoid pregnancy only on young girls. Researchers find that pregnant teens romanticize the demands of motherhood, and many believe they can give their babies a better life than they received. Because adolescent pregnancy disproportionately affects poor and minority youth, having children may be their only way of achieving masculinity or femininity in a society that denies them the expression of these traits in adult roles (Ladner 1995; Horowitz 1995). This should lead us to conclude that programs and policies designed to alleviate the problems of teenage pregnancy must recognize the importance of gender relations in understanding and reducing teen pregnancy.

Child Care

Child care in the United States is, by virtue of the character of the family, largely a system of private care. The parent–child unit is allegedly self-sufficient and, given the gender division of labor, the responsibility for child care falls heavily on individual women. The experience of mothers (or other caregivers) is based on the assumption that children are best cared for by their mother. Exceptions to this design do exist, although even then the arrangements for child care are usually managed by the mother and it is other women who do the work. Although it is more and more impractical to do so, mothers usually have the major responsibility for the everyday care of their children.

The privatized and exclusive character of child care seems especially inappropriate when we consider the increased employment of mothers. As already noted, increases in the labor force participation rate are highest among women with children, especially women with children of preschool age.

Women's access to child care can significantly influence their prospects for employment because the cost of child care can be a significant deterrent to women seeking employment (see Figure 6.4). Many must rely on kin or other volunteers for child care. Extended kin networks can facilitate women's access to jobs, but they remind us of how parents must often rely on their own networks and families for child care support (Uttal 2002; Uttal and Tuominen 1999).

Employed women, then, use a variety of arrangements to care for their children. Among children under 5 years of age with employed mothers, most are still cared for by the other parent, a designated parent, a grandparent, or other relatives (including siblings). Among these, grandparents provide the most frequent care. Not quite half are cared for in organized facilities, child-care centers, or preschools—a large increase from the past (U.S. Census Bureau 2006).

The affordability of child care is a serious problem for many families—both low and middle income—and can consume a large portion of a family budget. As Figure 6.5 shows, nearly half of all working families (48 percent) with children incur child-care expenses with an average cost of $286 per month—9 percent of the typical family's earnings. For low-income families, the cost of child care is actually a higher portion of family earnings than for middle-income families; this is because the family budgets are lower and because low-income children spend more time in child care due to their parents' working hours (Giannarelli and Barsimantov 2000). Families with disabled or chronically ill children have an even greater burden in paying for child care (Lukemeyer et al. 2000).

The Family and Medical Leave Act (FMLA) of 1993 provides some help for families because it requires employers to grant 12 weeks of leave to a parent to

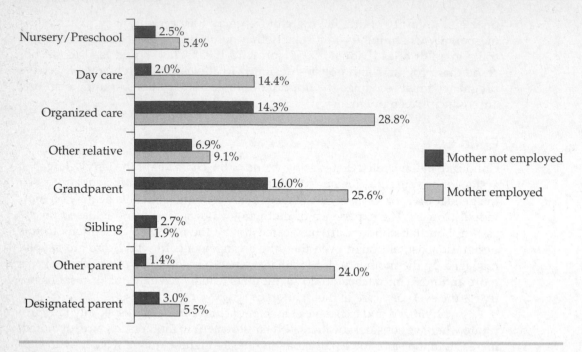

FIGURE 6.4   Child-Care Arrangements

Note: **Percentages do not add to 100 because some have no regular arrangement.** *Organized care* **includes day care, nursery, preschool, federal Head Start programs, and kindergarten programs.**

Source: U.S. Census Bureau. 2006. *Who's Minding the Kids: Child Care Arrangements, Summer 2006.* Washington, DC: U.S. Census Bureau. www.census.gov.

care for newborn or adopted children or to care for a sick child, spouse, or parent. But, the leave is unpaid and only applies to employers in companies with 50 or more workers. In addition, employees are required to first exhaust vacation and sick leave. The law also applies only to married, heterosexual couples, although some companies are more liberal in the implementation of this policy. Although the FMLA has made great improvement in the benefits to working people with family responsibilities, more is needed to help people cope with the strains of balancing work and family. Currently, only 15 percent of companies provide any assistance for child care; 5 percent of these provide on- or off-site child care to employees, and only 3 percent provide some funds to employees for child care. Furthermore, whether employees get such support varies by their status in the organization. Eleven percent of white-collar workers get such support, but only 3 percent of blue-collar employees (Bureau of Labor Statistics 2006).

These facts suggest the need to imagine new models and policies for child care in society (see Table 6.1, earlier in chapter). Historically, depression and war have provided the major impetus for establishing public child-care facilities in the United States. Public child care in the United States first originated in the Works Progress Administration (WPA) of the New Deal. In the 1930s, WPA day-care and nursery schools were designed to provide employment for needy teachers, child-care

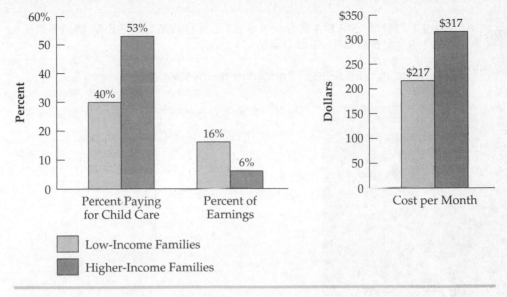

FIGURE 6.5   Child-Care Costs: A Class Comparison

Source: Giannarelli, Linda, and James Barsimantov. 2000. *Child Care Expenses of America's Families.* Washington, DC: The Urban Institute, p. 7. Reprinted with permission.

workers, cooks, janitors, nutritionists, and clerical workers during the Depression. By the end of the Depression and the beginning of World War II, when jobs were no longer in short supply, the WPA nurseries were eliminated. In 1941, the Lanham Act (also known as the Community Facilities Act) was passed by Congress to meet the child-care needs of mothers in wartime employment. The Lanham Act made matching federal funds available to states for the expansion of day-care centers and nursery schools. Following World War II, when women were no longer needed in the labor force, Congress withdrew funds for child care, and most of the Lanham Act nurseries closed (Baxandall 1979).

Since World War II, federally funded day-care programs have been established for the poor. For example, Project Head Start, funded through the Office of Economic Opportunity, was designed primarily for children from families below the poverty line. In the past, public attitudes toward funded child care were stigmatized by the association of federally supported child care with welfare services, but support for increased availability of child care services now runs high.

That women are still socially defined as primarily responsible for children is well illustrated by the now widely recognized phenomenon of *deadbeat dads*—those who, following a custody and support agreement, abandon financial support of their children. What kind of child support do women receive when they have custody of children following a divorce? As we have seen, less than half receive the full amount they are due; 20 percent receive none. In the rare cases where women owe men child support, men are actually less likely to receive it. Yet, women are more economically dependent on receiving support for their children. In these situations, women can feel stuck. They are unlikely to have the

HISTORY SPEAKS: YESTERDAY'S FEMINISTS TALK ABOUT TODAY

Charlotte Perkins Gilman and Sharing Housework

"Until 'mothers' earn their livings, 'women' will not."

—Charlotte Perkins Gilman

Charlotte Perkins Gilman (1860–1935) had a wonderful imagination for thinking about how housework could be organized to free women from what she saw as the constraints on their independence. Gilman's father had abandoned his family when she was young, so she was raised by her mother alone and, as a result, was moved around a lot and struggled to complete an education. She was mostly self-educated, although she attended the Rhode Island School of Design for two years and earned a living through designing greeting cards. She died from suicide, after learning that she had inoperable breast cancer.

Despite her struggles, Gilman was an avid reader and prolific writer. She is perhaps best known for her short story, *The Yellow Wallpaper*, a brilliant essay in which she writes about a woman confined to her home who goes mad. But her novel, *Herland,* is also brilliant—and funny. In it, she creates a feminist utopia—a society of only women who reproduce through artificial means, but are discovered by three men. She also authored *Women and Economics,* a book outlining her sociological and economic analysis of women's status.

Gilman was a feminist who supported suffrage for women, but she thought economic independence was more important than the vote. She argued that the divison of roles by gender was harmful to women and promoted the idea of a more communal life to organize household work so as not to fall on individual women. As an example, she advocated a complete redesign of homes to include "feminist apartment hotels" (Hayden 1981:189) where living spaces would have no kitchens but would be arranged around common facilities and dining areas with roof gardens, day nurseries for children, and kindergartens—all supported through professional teachers, nurses, and other paid workers.

Thinking Further: Gilman was a visionary feminist. If she were to redesign a neighborhood in your community to promote more equitable and shared household work, what might she envision? What obstacles might she face, and how would she (you!) turn these into opportunities to promote equality for women?

Sources: Hayden, Dolores. 1981. *The Grand Domestic Revolution*. Cambridge, MA: MIT Press; books and writers: http://www.kirjasto.sci.fi/gilman.htm; www.biography.com.

resources needed to pursue legally what they are owed. In many cases, particularly those involving young, uneducated men, the father may be unable to pay.

With the number of young people increasing in society and the rate of poverty now being highest among young people, there is a compelling argument for more socially supported programs for child care and child support. Without this, a new generation of people will face economic hardship and the social disadvantage that follows. Simply leaving child-care needs for individual women and men to handle on their own will not serve the overall needs of children and their society well. In general, U.S. society has a poor record of supporting the various forms of care work that sustain human life. Economically, if people and companies actually paid for the now unpaid work of caring for children and kin, the cost would be $196 billion dollars per year (Folbre 2001). Since women now provide most of that unpaid work, the hidden value of care work falls mostly on them. Only in a society where women's work—and women's worth—is systematically devalued, even while being romanticized as part of "family life," could such exploitation of human labor be allowed to continue.

■ Chapter Summary and Themes

The historic evolution of family forms stems from the family's relationship to economic systems and to ideologies of the family that have glorified the home as women's place.

Processes such as the development of capitalism and the growth of industrialization have shaped the forms that families have taken. Ideals such as the cult of domesticity emerged to justify the role of women in families, even though the ideal is race and class specific. Racial–ethnic families also emerge in relationship to the specific forms of labor that different groups have provided in society.

Feminist perspectives on family emphasize a structural diversity that stresses the social construction of family forms in the context of the specific class, race, and gender arrangements in society.

Structural diversity is found in the different ways that families must respond to conditions of inequality. Diversity is also found within families, as women and men have different levels of power in familiar relationships. Despite this diversity, ideology about the family paints it as monolithic and idealized. Even with the social structural influences on families, human beings actively create and adapt to this social institution.

Diversity, not uniformity, characterizes contemporary family forms.

Contemporary U.S. households are characterized by high rates of divorce and a large increase in the number of households headed by women. Households now rarely conform to the family ideal and consist of many types, including married, heterosexual couples, cohabitors, dual-earner families, gay and lesbian families, and singles. Balancing work and family commitments is an increasing challenge for many forms of families.

The race and ethnic relations in society, intertwined with class and gender, organize the social structure of diverse families.

Racial–ethnic families face unique experiences both because of the dominant ideologies that distort the understanding of such families and because racial stratification results in different labor patterns that affect family experiences. Historical realities, such as slavery, immigration, and forced conquest, continue to shape the family experiences of different racial–ethnic groups.

Many of today's social problems directly affect people in families and result from the gender relations that, although seldom recognized in social policy discussions, shape such problems as family violence, teen pregnancy, and the affordability of child care.

Violence against women in families is common and results from the association of gender with power and social control. Teen pregnancy, although decreasing, remains a problem that reproduces poverty and disadvantages young women and their children. The absence of affordable child care reflects the cultural ideal that children are best cared for by women in the home. With more women in the labor force, the lack of affordable child care strains family budgets, especially for the most economically vulnerable families.

■ Key Terms

antimiscegenation	household	nuclear family
cult of domesticity	householder	structural diversity model
Family and Medical Leave Act	human agency	transnational family
family household	marital rape	
gender apartheid	nonfamily household	

■ Discussion Questions/Projects for Thought

1. Identify two families that could be described as having different structural characteristics (i.e., married working couple, commuting marriage, divorced head of household, lesbian couple, single-parent household, etc.) and interview each family member (including any children) about who does what work in the family, including finances, child care, housework, managing social relations, and so on. What does your project tell you about gender and the household division of labor?

2. Identify a group of working mothers and/or fathers and interview them about their child-care practices, including questions such as: Who cares for the child when the parent(s) work? What happens when the child is sick? How much does the child care cost and who pays? When do problems arise and how are they solved? What does your research on this reveal about gender and child care? What new policies would you recommend to provide affordable child care to working parents?

3. Find out if there is a shelter for battered women in your community. If so, interview some of the workers there and ask them about the patterns they see among those who come to the shelter. What do they think would stop violence against women? Do you agree?

Women, Health, and Reproduction

Physical health is one of the most basic of life's privileges. Although we tend to think of our bodies as best cared for through personal hygiene and individual diet and health habits, in fact, physical health is heavily influenced by social factors. Gender plays a significant part in determining physical well-being and in influencing our bodily experience, as do race and class.

For instance, the likelihood that one will encounter stress, become overweight, experience hypertension, or die of certain diseases is significantly affected by one's gender. National health statistics show that hypertension is more common among men than women (at all ages). Women are more likely than men (at every age) to be at a healthy weight, despite the extraordinary fears women seem to feel about being overweight and the enormous resources put into the diet industry. At every age, men are actually more likely to be overweight than women, although women are more likely to be obese, as defined by government standards.

Along with gender and age, race is a complicating factor in predicting health. African Americans are far more likely than Whites to experience disability, to develop hypertension, and to suffer from poor nutrition (see Figure 7.1; National Center for Health Statistics 2009). The likelihood that one will die of cancer, experience an eating disorder, experience the death of a child, or even drink alcohol are all influenced by social patterns of gender along with class and race.

Such data indicate that physical health is mediated by social institutions and cultural beliefs. Gender, along with race and class, also affects access to health care. In the context of national debates about health care, you might want to know that men are actually *less* likely to be covered by medical insurance than are women, for example (National Center for Health Statistics 2009). Gender relations in a society are also reflected in institutional patterns of health-care systems. Who

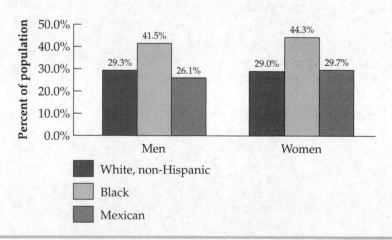

FIGURE 7.1   Hypertension by Race and Gender (percent of population)

Source: Data from National Center for Health Statistics. 2007. *Health United States 2007.* Washington, DC: Department of Health and Human Services, pp. 280–281.

gets care, by whom, and what kind? Even though healing and caring for others have traditionally been defined as the work of women, men still dominate in health-care institutions, even though women are a predominate proportion of workers in such institutions. In addition, because of the structure of health care in this society, women have had little control over their own reproductive lives. Throughout this chapter, you will see the many ways that gender shapes health care in society.

THE SOCIAL STRUCTURE OF HEALTH

Patterns of health change according to the social arrangements of the time. For instance, in the late nineteenth century, illness was quite fashionable for women— at least those of the upper-middle and upper classes. Women in these classes were expected to be idle and delicate; consequently, retiring to bed because of "nerves" was not only acceptable but actually encouraged by medical practitioners (Ehrenreich and English 1973).

Women's health is sometimes compromised by fashion trends. Tightly bound corsets, such as this one, are now known to have caused internal organ damage. What fashion trends today might carry health hazards for women?

Differences in life expectancy for men and women did not emerge in U.S. society until the beginning of the twentieth century. Even now, longer life expectancy for women occurs primarily in highly industrialized Western societies. Japan has the highest life expectancy for women; the highest life expectancy for men is found in Hong Kong. You might be surprised to learn that the United States ranks number 26 in life expectancy for both women and men, compared to number 37 in other industrialized nations, behind, for example, Canada, Australia, France, Sweden, and Norway (National Center for Health Statistics 2007). In most industrialized nations, men lag behind women in life expectancy, largely because of men's greater risk of death by accident, itself a function of men's engagement in risky behavior, violent activity, and alcohol consumption (see Figure 7.2 on page 202).

Women's health, like men's, varies according to the features of their lives. Studies have indicated, for example, that there are higher rates of reported illness among housewives than among women working outside the home; generally speaking, employment has positive effects on women's (and men's) health. This effect, however, is mediated by

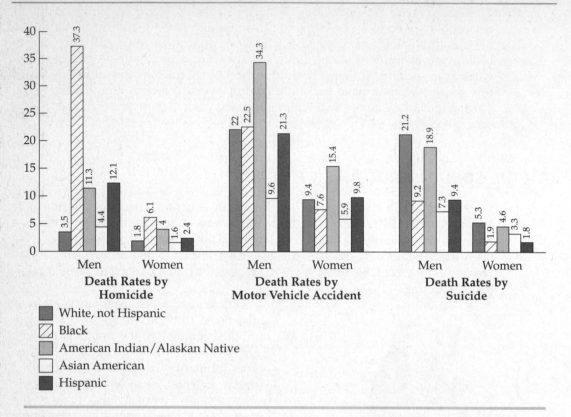

FIGURE 7.2   Death Rates by Homicide, Suicide, and Motor Vehicle Accidents (rate = per 1000 persons)

Source: Data from National Center for Health Statistics. 2007. *Health United States 2007.* Washington, DC: Department of Health and Human Services, pp. 222–230.

other variables. For example, the characteristics of the work site (i.e., job demands, rewards and deprivations, physical environment, and social support) also influence the well-being of workers, as does the division of labor in housework (Loscocco and Spitze 1990; Bird and Fremont 1999). There is little evidence that combining employment and motherhood has harmful health effects (Waldron et al. 1998). Most significant in predicting women's health and mental health are such factors as educational level, income, life satisfaction, and social contact. In other words, it is not employment per se that influences women's health, but rather the overall conditions in women's lives. The stress of balancing work and family, as well as conditions of unmet expectations, poverty, and/or violence in the home, all contribute to women's physical and psychological well-being (Schnittker 2007).

The care work that women do in the home, including caring for ill, disabled, or elderly persons, can significantly increase women's psychological distress (Pavalko and Woodbury 2000). In one study examining mental health differences among married and unmarried mothers, researchers found that mothers who become employed experience little change in their levels of stress, because increases in the stress of managing caregiving activities are offset by a decline in financial stress (Ali and Avison 1997). A recent study has found that even when faced with a life-threatening illness like breast cancer, women often have to provide their own care. Doing so means that women have to juggle the care work they do for others with their own needs—setting boundaries and helping oneself in a way that involves renegotiating the gender roles that expect women to care for others, not necessarily themselves (Sulik 2007).

Women's health, both mental and physical, is also affected by the inequities they routinely face in the labor market. Studies find that, in general, inequality both within and across households is a strong predictor of health problems for different groups; but, more particularly, gender inequality in the workforce produces a range of health consequences for women, including anxiety, depression, and stress—all of which have negative consequences for physical health.

Furthermore, simply being a minority in the workplace—a finding that holds for women and people of color—contributes to higher rates of health problems (Evans and Steptoe 2002; Griffin et al. 2002; O'Campo et al. 2004; Moss 2002). Indeed, minority status in and of itself contributes to health problems. As an example, African American women are not only more likely than White women to experience depression, but cultural norms defining them as "strong" also mean they often maintain a persona that silences Black women's needs (Hill 2009; Beauboef-Lafontant 2007). Together, these studies demonstrate the significance of social factors that shape women's physical and mental health.

Most studies indicate higher rates of mental illness for women than for men, at least as indicated by hospital admissions, clinical treatment, and the duration of treatment. Some explain this finding as a result of women's secondary status in society, which, because it produces stress, results in women becoming mentally ill more frequently than men. Others argue that high rates of mental illness among women reflect the fact that women are more likely to report mental problems, seek help, and think of themselves as emotional and lacking self-control. This explanation interprets women's higher mental illness rate as the consequence of learned gender behavior. Both explanations are probably correct, underscoring the point that mental as well as physical health is connected to one's status in society.

Health is influenced by the social context in which people live. Sociological studies of health look to the environment in which people are located to understand the various health risks that different groups experience. Work environments are an important site for understanding the health risks faced by women and men; moreover, because work organizations are shaped by gender, work may have a different impact on health for women than for men.

The mythology of work in U.S. culture is that it provides an avenue for self-expression and the realization of personal goals. We have increasingly come to see, however, that work can be hazardous to physical and mental health. Toxic chemicals in the workplace produce risks for workers, although, typically, public attention to those risks for women has focused primarily on their reproductive health. Stress is also a significant health problem for workers in different environments; for women, this is more acute because of the "double day" employed women experience at work and at home. Studies of different occupational health hazards also reveal how these health risks are structured by the gender segregation that characterizes the workplace.

Race, Class, and Health

Racial–ethnic and class oppression in U.S. society further complicate patterns of health in men and women. Examination of health statistics by race shows significant differences in the patterns of health for different groups, with death rates by cerebrovascular disease, homicide, and diabetes, for example, significantly higher for Black Americans than for White Americans. As we have seen in Figure 7.1, women and men of color experience higher rates of hypertension than Whites; hypertension also increases with age. Although maternal death from the complications of pregnancy has decreased since 1960, Black women are still three times as likely to die from causes related to pregnancy as are White and Hispanic women. Black, American Indian, and Hispanic women are also less likely to receive prenatal care than White and Asian American women. And, although White women are more likely to get breast cancer than Black women, the rates of death from breast cancer are equal for both groups, suggesting that Black women are less likely to get effective treatment (National Center for Health Statistics 2007; National Cancer Institute 2010).

The effects of racial inequality on health are dramatically shown by data on accidental deaths. Homicide is greater among Black and Hispanic men than among White men, but suicide rates are lower among Black men, although increasing in recent years. Suicide rates for Black women are much lower than the rates for White women. Although violent death is more common for Black Americans, cultural values and the economic dependence of families on Black women's work influence the lesser degree of suicide among them. Native Americans' health is also affected by the degree of oppression they experience. Their mortality rates are especially high among the young, particularly young men; moreover, Native Americans are twice as likely to die by homicide than are others in the general population (National Center for Health Statistics 2007).

Infant mortality, one of the major indices of the health of a population, is still almost twice as high for African Americans and Native Americans as for Whites, Hispanics, and Asian Americans. Although infant mortality rates have been decreasing over recent years, the rate of decline in infant mortality, especially among African Americans, has slowed. Black and Puerto Rican Americans are also more likely to have low–birth-weight babies, a fact that contributes to infant mortality and represents the

Women have mobilized around the nation to support more research on breast cancer and to provide support for women with breast cancer.

health problems faced by these mothers (National Center for Health Statistics 2007).

Both historically and currently, women of color and poor women have been denied control over their reproductive lives. Studies indicate that very high percentages of poor and minority women have been sterilized, often without their consent. African American women are more likely than White and Hispanic women to have been sterilized (National Center for Health Statistics 2007). Although some of this may be voluntary, poor women are often coerced into sterilization. Studies indicate that among samples of welfare mothers, approximately half have been sterilized; the high sterilization rates of Black and poor women mean that feminist calls for "reproductive freedom" have particular meaning and resonance for women of color (Roberts 1997).

Much of the difference in health along lines of race is also attributable to social class. Social class has long been shown to have a strong influence on both physical and mental health, with poverty, in particular, having a strong influence on access to health care and actual physical and mental well-being (Roxburgh 2009). Chronic illness is higher among less prosperous groups, as are disabilities, infectious diseases, and, as we have seen, infant mortality. There is little wonder that the higher one's social class, the better one's chance of a long and healthier life. Racial inequality results in higher rates of poverty for Native Americans, Latinos, and African Americans, making race a major factor in considering the health care of these diverse populations (Smedley et al. 2003; Centers for Disease Control 2005).

Reproduction and Protective Legislation

Historically, concern about women's work and health has almost exclusively focused on women's reproductive health (Novkov 1996; McCammon 1995; Crenshaw 1995). Few researchers considered how reproductive hazards for men are also related to their work. Clearly, occupational toxic agents and carcinogens can equally affect male sperm; yet **protective legislation** against reproductive hazards has historically been aimed at women workers (Daniels et al. 1990).

In the 1920s, the Women's League for Equal Opportunity staunchly opposed the protective legislation proposed by groups such as the Women's Trade Union League and the Consumer League of New York. They argued that consumer restrictions on the conditions of labor should be based on the nature of the industry, not on the sex of the worker (Stellman 1977:3). Yet, history shows that protective laws generally apply only to women workers. The Supreme Court decision in *Muller* v. *Oregon*, for example, held in 1908 that it was constitutional to restrict a woman's workday to 10 hours, but the law did not restrict men's working hours because of health risks. Protecting workers from long workdays and unhealthy environments is a reasonable action, but when applied only to women, these laws can exclude women from jobs under the benign guise of protection (Chavkin 1979).

Protective legislation has also been used to exclude women from work in fields typically populated by men. For instance, Title VII of the 1964 Civil Rights Act prohibited employment discrimination on the basis of sex, race, color, religion, and national origin. It also provided for bona fide occupational qualification (BFOQ), which made it lawful to hire on the basis of sex when sex is a reasonable qualification for performance on the job (Hill 1979). For instance, the BFOQ clause allowed women to be excluded from jobs with weight-lifting limitations that women could not meet. Weight restrictions on some jobs are based on gender stereotypes, indicated by the fact that such restrictions do not typically appear for jobs where women predominate and that involve strenuous physical effort (such as waitressing).

Subsequent court cases made it clear that the BFOQ clause could be applied only in a very restricted way. In both *Weeks* v. *Southern Bell Telephone and Telegraph Company* and *Rosenfeld* v. *Southern Pacific Company,* the courts ruled that individual women, like individual men, have to be given the opportunity to show that they are physically qualified for a job (Hill 1979). In 1991, the Supreme Court ruled (in *Automobile Workers v. Johnson Controls*) that it was discriminatory to bar women from high-risk jobs in which there was potential harm to a fetus or reproductive system. Prior arguments for protective legislation assumed that pregnant women and fetuses are especially susceptible to toxic chemicals, radiation, and other risks.

Although there is little doubt that these hazards affect pregnant women and fetuses, they affect the reproductive health of men as well. Legislation or company practices that apply only to women rest on the faulty assumption that only women reproduce. There is evidence of the damaging effects of lead poisoning on male sperm, the excess of chromosomal aberrations among male vinyl chloride workers, and of a causal relationship between the pesticide dibromochloropropane (DBCP) and male sterility (Wright 1979). Removing only women from jobs in which they are exposed to these substances clearly does not protect the reproductive health of the population.

Gender-biased assumptions in protective regulations are intricately bound to the gender-segregated character of the labor force. Concern for women's health has not caused companies to remove workers from jobs traditionally considered women's work—despite known risks from toxic substances that are found in occupations employing mostly women. For example, women who work in health care are exposed to numerous chemical and toxic hazards, as well as infectious diseases, but no one has argued that women should be excluded from jobs as nurses, scrub personnel, and the like (Kemp and Jenkins 1992). Protective policies that restrict women from hazardous jobs seem to emerge only in higher-paying and traditionally male occupations into which women are moving. Other occupations that pose equally serious hazards, yet are poorly paid and are filled by women, have been excluded from protective legislation. Similarly, risks to the male reproductive system seldom are used to restrict their employment opportunities.

Discussion of women's health and work also cannot ignore the fact that despite real risks to health posed by contemporary jobs, employed women, as far as we can tell, are healthier, on average, than women who are unemployed. Only the future will reveal the long-range effect of carcinogens, toxic substances, and radiation on human life, but current data indicate that employment has positive effects on women's health. Although the specific hazards that workers face will vary depending on the type of work and the specific work conditions they face, there is a serious need for careful study of work-related health hazards.

GENDER, HEALTH, AND SOCIAL PROBLEMS

Gender and the Body: Weight, Food, and Body Image

Do you like your body? If you are like most American women and men, your answer will likely be "No." Women and men obsess about their bodies, their weight, their appearance—at least if the size of the industries supporting diet products, food, and exercise is any indication. How many times have you gone on a diet? Lifted weight to bulk up? Looked at a beautiful person and thought, "I wish I looked like that"? How much money and time do you spend trying to look different from the way you do?

These questions cut to the heart of the cultural obsession with beauty, weight, and appearance—an obsession that is particularly strong among women and young girls, but from which men are not exempt. The obsession varies depending on one's race or class, but in the United States, although not everyone experiences angst over their body in the same way, we nonetheless live in a culture where we are bombarded with body and beauty ideals—ideals that few, if any, can actually achieve. Although physically real, bodies are also socially constructed. That is, our concepts of bodies, how we define them, and what we do to them are deeply social, and therefore reflect the gender, race, and class relations that characterize society.

You can see this by observing popular culture, by noticing the dieting and eating patterns of those around you, or simply by asking people how they feel about their bodies. Popular culture is full of images that encourage us to associate food with desire at the same time that we are constantly sold various diet products. Advertisements also encourage women to associate beauty with thinness, so much so that eating disorders are strikingly common.

Women, and men as well, are taught to dislike their bodies. No matter what their shape, size, or form, women's bodies seem never to meet the ideal promulgated by the advertising and modeling industries. Thus, research finds that, regardless of race or ethnicity, women are more dissatisfied with their bodies than are men. Furthermore, both women and men misjudge the body shapes that they think the other sex will find attractive, with women thinking that men like thinner bodies than men say they like (Demarest and Allen 2000). Such findings indicate the extent to which women's images of themselves—and their subsequent behaviors—can be driven by what they believe men will think of them.

One consequence of the cultural obsession with weight and thinness is the high rate of anorexia nervosa, bulimia, and compulsive eating among women and, increasingly, men. Although anorexia nervosa generally occurs among White, adolescent females, men and minorities are increasingly being affected. Black and Hispanic women, however, are more likely than White women to be overweight, especially those near poverty (National Center for Health Statistics 2007; see Figure 7.3).

Anorexia nervosa is characterized by severe weight loss; anorexics also have delusions about their body images, thinking of themselves as fat when, in actuality, they are dangerously thin. They typically do not recognize signs of nutritional need and may, literally, starve themselves to death. Seen in the context of a whole array of practices designed to reduce women's body size—such as stomach

FOCUS ON RESEARCH

Race, Gender, and Eating Disorders

Although much attention has been given to eating disorders among White, middle-class women, only now are people beginning to see the extent of eating disorders among other groups of women. And whereas the context of a "culture of thinness" has been the prevailing explanation for eating disorders (especially anorexia and bulimia), other explanations emerge when you think about the eating disorders of Black women and Latinas.

Some of the first work done in this regard was by sociologist Becky Thompson (1994). Thompson based her work on a sample of African American, Latina, and lesbian women and found that among them, compulsive overeating was as much a problem as anorexia and bulimia. She interpreted their problematic eating, not with an obsession with appearance, but with attempts to soothe over the rage, fear, and disappointments in their lives. A large proportion (two-thirds) of the women she interviewed who were overeaters had also been molested during childhood.

New research is finding that anorexia and bulimia are becoming more common among African American women and Latinas. Although there has historically been more value placed on large women among African Americans, thinness is becoming more highly valued. As a result, anorexia seems to be increasing especially among

African American middle-class women. Cultural factors play a role, too. Cultures that have a strong tradition of elaborate food rituals can encourage overeating, as can living in the context of conflicting cultural demands. Narratives of young Latinas also show that cultural images of Latinas, as with all women, represent an unattainable standard, but Latinas can find themselves caught in the contradictions of navigating both popular ideals, racial–ethnic stereotypes, and, possibly, traditional familial expectations. This can be particularly complicated for Latinas who are also immigrants, as they may be faced with different cultural norms from home and host societies (Molinary 2007).

Sources: Thompson, Becky. 1994. *A Hunger So Wide and So Deep: American Women Speak Out on Eating Problems.* Minneapolis, MN: University of Minnesota Press; Molinary, Rose. 2007. *Hijas Americanas: Beauty, Body Image, and Growing Up Latina.* Emeryville, CA: Seal Press; Kuba, Sue A., and Diane Harris. 2001. "Eating Disturbances in Women of Color: An Exploratory Study of Contextual Factors in the Development of Disordered Eating in Mexican-American Women." *Health Care for Women International* 22 (April–May): 281–298; Striegel-Moore, Ruth, and Linda Smolak. 2000. "The Influence of Ethnicity on Eating Disorders in Women." Pp. 227–253 in *Handbook of Gender, Culture, and Health,* edited by Richard M. Eisler and Michel Hersen. Mahwah, NJ: Lawrence Erlbaum.

stapling, diet fads, breast reduction surgery, and other extreme procedures—anorexia is even to be expected in a culture so obsessed with thinness (Gimlin 2002; Chernin 1981, 1985; Hesse-Biber 2006).

Other eating problems, such as bulimia and compulsive overeating, also stem from the culture's definition of idealized womanhood. **Bulimia** is the syndrome in which women (typically) binge on huge amounts of food and then purge themselves by vomiting, using laxatives, or engaging in extreme fasting. Both anorexia and bulimia are strongly linked to gender roles, with those who most internalize cultural definitions of femininity being most likely to become anorexic or bulimic. Eating disorders and the associated dissatisfaction with one's body are also most common among heterosexual women and least common among heterosexual men, with lesbian women and gay men falling in between. Eating disorders have

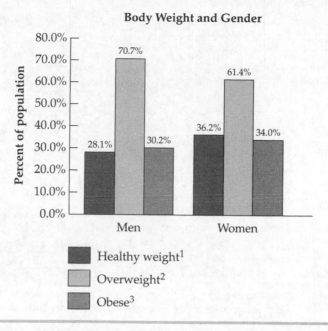

FIGURE 7.3 Body Weight by Gender

[1]Body mass index of 18.5 to less than 25
[2]Body mass index of 25 to less than 30
[3]Body mass index greater than or equal to 30

Source: Data from National Center for Health Statistics 2007. *Health United States 2007.* Washington, DC: Department of Health and Human Services, pp. 288–291.

additionally been linked to a sense among women of hypercompetition with regard to appearance—that is, women who "overvalue" beauty are most likely to develop eating disorders (Strong et al. 2000; Burckle et al. 1999; Lakkis et al. 1999).

Women's concerns with weight and body image can affect self-esteem and academic performance. Research finds that the less attractive a woman perceives herself to be and the more weight she wants to lose, the greater is her sense of academic, social, and psychological impairment (Hesse-Biber 2006). Ironically, eating disorders, although contributing to poor academic performance and low self-esteem, are most common among women who value physical appearance, strive for success in multiple roles, and come from families where their daughters have insecure attachments to their parents (Hart and Kenny 1997).

Most studies of eating disorders have been based on the experiences of White women, and the conclusions should be judged accordingly. Latino, Native American, and African American women have never been portrayed as the "ideal woman." For all groups, body image is conditioned by the specific intersections of race, class, and gender in their experience, as well as specific identities, such as one's ethnic or religious identity (Craig 2002; Molinary 2007). Studies of African American Sunni Muslim women find, for example, that although their perceptions about their bodies are similar to those of other African American women,

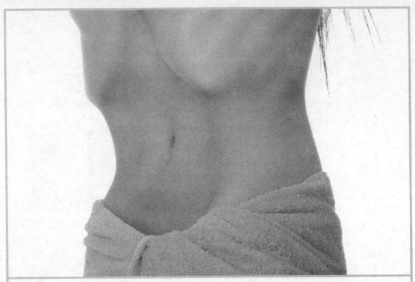

Eating disorders, such as seen in this image of an anorexic woman, are especially common among young, white, middle-class women, although they are by no means exclusive to this group.

their spirituality, along with cultural norms and family expectations, influence their perceptions of their bodies (Odoms-Young 2008).

Beginning in the twentieth century, U.S. culture began to regard fleshiness as not sexy. Sexy bodies are now depicted as thin ones; in fact, cultural images of weight have projected an increasingly thin image, resulting in a very high rate of anorexia among models and actresses who portray these ideals. Being thin is also increasingly associated with wealth and class, because idealized sex objects also portray class images. In an odd sense, only rich women can "afford" to be thin, since poor women are much more likely to be overweight. Fat on women and men also violates gender roles, as we tend to think of overweight women as having improperly indulged themselves, and overweight men are derided for seeming passive, vulnerable, and soft (Millman 1980). Cultural constructions of the body thus create an increasingly narrow—and even dangerous—image of womanhood.

Even without developing the most serious forms of eating disorders, vast numbers of women struggle with issues about beauty, appearance, and weight. Even women who fall within the recommended ranges of weight and body fat typically consider themselves overweight, and estimates are that more than half of women between ages 10 and 30 are dieting. The weight-loss industry is at least a $346 billion industry, with new products (many of them harmful) appearing regularly and promising to make weight loss easy (often in the absence of a good diet and regular exercise). As the beauty ideal has increasingly promoted a "well-toned, but skinny robustness" (Zones 1997:264), the exercise industry—and, for some, compulsive exercise—has also soared. The average person now uses more than 25 pounds of cosmetics, soaps, and toiletries each year, and plastic surgery has become a multibillion-dollar industry as women, the majority of plastic surgery clients, pay to shrink, expand, remove, and otherwise alter various parts of their bodies (Gimlin 2002; Dworkin and Wachs 2009; Bordo 1995; Zones 1997). Think of how different your behavior and that of others around you might change if people were to embrace a more diverse ideal of women's beauty—one that would encompass a full array of how women actually look.

Substance Abuse: Alcohol, Drugs, and Smoking

The problems associated with substance abuse are often understood as originating in personal problems that lead people to engage in behavior damaging to their health. An alternative way to understand these behaviors is to see them in light of gender relations in society. Patterns of substance abuse are clearly marked by gender differences. Thus, men are more likely to abuse drugs and alcohol, although women, especially young women, are more likely to smoke. But beyond noting differences is usage, how does gender shape the patterns of substance abuse—behavior that is known to be a hazard to health?

Alcohol

Men drink more frequently than women and drink more on any given occasion; men are more likely than women to be classified as problem drinkers (National Center for Health Statistics 2007; Wilsnack et al. 2000). Race also matters. African American and Hispanic women are more likely to abstain from drinking and are less likely to be heavy drinkers than White women; Asian American women have low rates of alcohol use, but Native American women have high rates of use, as reflected in high alcohol-related mortality among American Indian and Alaskan Native women (Horton 1995). Among women, drinking is heaviest among singles, those with high incomes, and employed women. Some have argued that women's employment makes them more likely to drink because it gives them greater independence and exposes them to cultural norms and expectations that men experience.

When women do drink, compared with men, they are more likely to drink alone, in private, or with a spouse. Women also tend to be introduced to alcohol by men and are encouraged by men to drink. The greatest amount of problem drinking occurs among women aged 18 to 20; moreover, drinking among young women has dramatically increased in recent years, nearly closing the gender gap between male and female drinkers.

Heavy alcohol use is especially common on college campuses where binge drinking has become a focal point for national concern. *Binge drinking* is defined as drinking enough to raise your blood alcohol content to .08 gram, occurring typically when a man drinks five or more drinks within a two-hour period and a woman consumes four drinks in two hours (National Institute of Alcohol and Alcohol Abuse 2010). Campus binge drinking is also tied to various forms of risk for women as well as men. Alcohol is a known factor in the incidence of sexual assault on campus. Also, those who drink are less likely to have safe sex, especially if they are too drunk to know if they are consenting to sex. Excessive drinking is also related to lower academic performance and to the risk of violence, vandalism, and potential death.

A CLOSER LOOK AT MEN

"This Beer's for You, Loser!"

For decades, men's sporting events have been associated with the consumption and promotion of alcohol. The alcohol industry spends billions of dollars both in the sponsorship of sporting events and in television and print advertising prior to and during these events. What images of masculinity does the alcohol industry portray in sporting event advertisements and how might these images of masculinity affect men's health?

Michael Messner and Jeffrey Montez de Oca examined beer and liquor advertisements in two "mega" sports media events that large numbers of boys and men watch and consume: the 2002 and 2003 Super Bowls and the 2002 and 2003 *Sports Illustrated* swimsuit issues. Messner and Montez de Oca argue that alcohol advertisements construct a "desirable lifestyle" of which their products are essential components. They connect the construction of this "desirable lifestyle" to a cluster of social changes (such as deindustrialization, declining wages, cultural advancements of women and sexual minorities, and challenges to white male dominance by people of color) that have undermined traditional masculinity.

During the 2003 Super Bowl, 15 of the 55 commercials that ran were beer or liquor advertisements (a slight increase from 13 commercials in 2002). The 2003 *Sports Illustrated* swimsuit issue included 29 pages of alcohol advertisements (an increase of 15 pages compared to the 2002 issue). Messner and Montez de Oca found that men's work worlds were mostly absent from these advertisements. Consuming alcohol was not portrayed as a reward for a hard day's work as it had been in past decades, but was now being associated with leisure as a lifestyle in and of itself.

According to Messner and Montez de Oca, the image of masculinity predominantly associated with this "leisure lifestyle" is one of a "loser" status. Men were repeatedly portrayed as losers (i.e., subject to humiliation by their own stupidity, by other men, or by beautiful women) in the alcohol advertisements that were examined. The advertisements suggested to men that they should embrace their loser status. Men should recognize that beautiful women are unavailable to them and appreciate what is within their reach—the company and security of their male friends and an ice-cold, refreshing beer.

Contemporary alcohol advertisements may heighten men's insecurities about the cultural shifts that are occurring within the United States. In doing so, these advertisements portray men as "losers" and encourage alcohol consumption as an effective strategy to deal with this inferior status. The alcohol industry's emphasis on alcohol consumption as part of a "leisure lifestyle" may have a detrimental effect on men's health.

Source: Based on Messner, Michael A., and Jeffrey Montez de Oca. 2005. "The Male Consumer as Loser: Beer and Liquor Ads in Mega Sports Media Events." *Signs: Journal of Women in Culture and Society* 30: 1879–1906.

National surveys of college students find that although men are more likely to drink heavily than women, a large percentage of both women and men college students are binge drinkers (49 percent of men, 41 percent of women). Levels of binge drinking vary tremendously from campus to campus, however, influenced by various conditions on the campus, including such things as presence of sororities and fraternities, the level of supervision, the availability of cheap drinks, and the demographic composition of the campus. Interestingly, the greater the racial–ethnic diversity on campus, the less White students drink, not only because Black and Hispanic students drink less, but White students seem to drink less in more diverse environments (Wechsler and Nelson 2008; Wechsler et al. 2002).

The drinking culture is also strongly influenced by gender norms on campus. Gender plays a clear role in the drinking patterns of college men and women. For men, norms of masculinity permeate the drinking culture on campus. Studies find that men associate heavy drinking with "being a man." Furthermore, the men "perform" masculinity through drinking in that they use drinking to display competition, aggression, and, sometimes, violence. At the same time, drinking lets men excuse behaviors that would otherwise be associated with femininity, such as crying, being overly emotional, and being physically dependent. For women, gender norms also have a significant role in drinking behavior. Women perceive that drinking allows them to loosen the restrictions typically imposed on them because of gender. Unless programs designed to lessen the risks of alcohol abuse address the issue of gender, they are likely to fail, because some of the underlying dimensions of abuse stem as much from gender relations as they do alcohol per se (Peralta 2007, 2002; Bachman and Peralta 2002).

Drugs

Although women are less likely than men to be drug abusers, there are significant health risks for women with substance abuse problems. Legal and illegal drugs, alcohol, tobacco, and caffeine are among the most prominent causes of health problems for premature death among both women and men. Substance abuse significantly increases the risks of pregnancy—both for women and infants (Blumenthal 1998).

Patterns of substance abuse are consistent with images of masculinity and femininity in the culture. According to traditional gender roles, women are not expected to drink and use drugs to the same extent as men. Indeed, women who become alcoholics tend to be perceived as more masculine and "harder" than other women, indicating that this behavior violates expected roles for women. Women heroin addicts are also seen as more deviant, more reprehensible, and less treatable than male addicts.

Research on drug abuse finds that the women most likely to abuse drugs are those whose other life options are significantly narrowed. Thus, women who are intravenous (IV) drugs users are likely to have experienced child sexual abuse, to have few options in the conventional world, and to become inundated with the drug culture (Durr 2005; Ross-Durow and Boyd 2000; Mullings et al. 2001). Women are also likely to begin using illegal drugs in the context of heterosexual relationships where men introduce them into the drug subculture. Men, on the other hand, are more likely to enter this subculture through other male friends and associates (Henderson et al. 1994). Illegal drug use among women has also been connected to trying to cope with violence within relationships (Rosenfield et al. 2006; Sales and Murphy 2000).

The problem of drug abuse, however, is not just a problem with illegal drugs. Women are more likely than men to be prescribed tranquilizers, sedatives, and amphetamines. (Blumenthal 1998). In part, women are more often prescribed tranquilizing drugs because they are more likely to seek help for their problems than are men. Others say that because of structured inequality, women's roles are more stressful and, as a result, women have more real complaints. Women are also about one-third of those admitted to treatment for substance abuse. Also,

MEDIA MATTERS

Gender and the Prozac Nation

In the 1960s, Valium was hailed as "mother's little helper." Mainly prescribed to women, the drug produced sedative, "ambition-thwarting" feelings that reflected the norms for femininity at the time. Now, the antidepressant Prozac has achieved similar celebrity status. Introduced in 1986, Prozac is portrayed as a wonder drug that can help people deal with the "battle" against depression (www. prozac.com). Beginning in 1997, the Eli Lilly Corporation began a $15 to 20 million ad campaign to sell the drug to consumers, including ads in the widely read *Cosmopolitan* magazine, whose audience is almost entirely women Do drug companies sell only drugs—or are they also selling gender narratives about women and depression?

To answer this question, Linda Blum and Nena Stracuzzi analyzed articles in the popular press over a 15-year period—articles about Prozac. At first glance, they found that magazine articles on Prozac usage tended to be gender-neutral. Most articles made no claims that Prozac was used more or less by women or men. The causes of mood disorders (namely, depression) were also described in gender-neutral terms. Blum and Stracuzzi found that within these articles, explanations for mood disorders were mainly biological; 80 percent of the articles they analyzed cited brain/chemical dysfunction as the primary cause of mood disorders. Rarely were families and relationships mentioned.

On closer examination, however, Blum and Stracuzzi argue that the gender-neutral promotion of Prozac is not as neutral as it appears. For example, in the women's magazines in their sample, 9 of 14 articles (64 percent) stated that Prozac (and other similar drugs) usage was escalating among women; three-quarters of these articles depicted women's experiences, not men's. These narratives were riddled with gender stereotypes about women's caregiving and household responsibilities.

Blum and Stracuzzi's analysis also revealed a demand for a new type of "female fitness" to coincide with economic changes. One of Prozac's features is that it "masculinizes femininity." This is a desired "side effect" of the drug because it produces ambitious, assertive, hardworking individuals, especially among those who are most likely to be users (i.e., women).

Gender messages within popular magazine articles on Prozac may be subtle, but Blum and Stracuzzi's research highlights the impact these messages have on women's health. As drug companies are now able to market prescription drugs directly to consumers, they sell not only drugs but also specifically gendered images of women and their health.

Thinking Further: Spend some time analyzing drug advertisements in popular women's magazines. What images of women do they portray? Are particular health problems more likely to be depicted than others (depression, fatigue, anxiety)? What images do these ads convey about women and mental health—or other health experiences? Do these match up with the realities of women's lives? If so, in what ways? If not, why?

Source: Based on Blum, Linda M., and Nena F. Stracuzzi. 2004. "Gender in the Prozac Nation: Popular Discourse and Productive Femininity." *Gender & Society* 18 (June): 269–286.

women are more likely to be admitted for drug abuse than alcohol abuse, whereas the reverse is true for men (Brady and Ashley 2005).

Smoking

Although tobacco has not been considered an addictive drug and therefore has not been regulated to the same extent as other substances, it has come under increasing public attention as an addictive health hazard. Ironically, although tobacco is significantly linked to multiple negative health consequences for all users, it has been manipulated by advertisers as a sign of women's independence.

Historically, men have been more likely to smoke than women. Although the rate of smoking for both women and men in the United States has declined in recent years, one in four men and one in five women smoke. When women start to smoke, they become more likely than men to continue, making the initiation of smoking especially significant for women. Although smoking among young people has declined, the number who do so is still significant: 22 percent of high school seniors (see Figure 7.4).

Smoking patterns among women and men seem significantly affected by gender roles. Researchers studying smoking behavior among adolescents have found, for example, that although peer pressure is significant for both boys and girls in the initiation of smoking, it is more significant for girls. Young men, on the other hand, are more influenced by "sensation seeking" (Martin and Robbins 1995). At the same time, girls (and later, women) are more likely to say that they smoke to control their weight (Logio 1998; Crisp et al. 1999). For both groups, appearance before others—whether it is to appear adultlike, to be slim, to be "tough," or to go along with the crowd—is a significant risk to health. Clearly, despite knowledge about the effects of smoking, gender and social status override rational decisions about health risks.

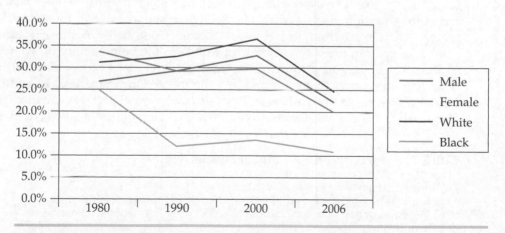

FIGURE 7.4   Cigarette Smoking among High School Seniors (by gender and race, 1980–2006)

Source: Data from National Center for Health Statistics. 2007. *Health United States 2007.* Washington, DC: Department of Health and Human Services, p. 273.

Women and AIDS

Originally identified as a disease affecting primarily gay men, AIDS (acquired immune deficiency syndrome) has taken on new dimensions. Although the majority of AIDS cases involve transmission between men having sex with other men, intravenous drug use is the second-most common form of transmission. Among women, heterosexual contact and intravenous drug use are the most frequent forms of transmission (see Table 7.1).

AIDS is no longer a disease only among men; now, one-third of new AIDS cases are women. Globally, AIDS is the leading cause of death for women of reproductive age. By 2007, of the 30.8 million adults with HIV/AIDS in the world, 15.5 million were women, meaning women are now equally likely to have the HIV virus as are men. AIDS is especially problematic in southern Africa, but in any nation, women are at risk because of gender inequality. Having unprotected sex with an infected partner is the common cause for contracting HIV/AIDS. If women are unable to negotiate safe sex, are not educated about the risk of unsafe sex, or are threatened by violence and other forms of abuse, they are at the greatest risk of contracting AIDS. This means that sex workers and younger women are particularly vulnerable.

In the United States, HIV/AIDS falls especially hard on women of color; 82 percent of all AIDS cases among women are among African American and Hispanic women. As in other parts of the world, in the United States, AIDS is the leading cause of death for Black women aged 25 to 34 and the fourth-leading cause of death for Hispanic women aged 35 to 44 (Centers for Disease Control and Prevention 2010).

Although most people think of HIV/AIDS in medical terms, it is equally clear that HIV/AIDS is a social and political issue—especially when you think about women. Women's social, sexual, and economic standing clearly influences their susceptibility to AIDS. Especially when seen in a global context, women's lack of access to education, medical care, and economic support makes them unable to protect themselves from this serious disease. Conditions of poverty among women of color in the United States contribute to the vulnerability of women to AIDS, because they turn to drugs for relief or have poor access to health and reproductive services that can provide some protection from AIDS. In addition, women's position as sex workers and as vulnerable sexual partners enhances their risk of AIDS. As a consequence, women who have mobilized against AIDS have

TABLE 7.1 Facts on AIDS: A Global Perspective

- Women are half of the newly affected adults.
- Two million people died of AIDS in 2008; 280,000 of these were children.
- In 2008, almost half a million children (430,000) were infected, which has been transmitted from mother to child.
- Sex workers are especially at risk for HIV/AIDS.
- The majority of women contracting HIV/AIDS do so through heterosexual contact.

Source: World Health Organization. 2010. Website: www.who.int.

linked the prevention of AIDS to the necessity of improving women's status worldwide (Schneider and Stoller 1995; World Health Organization 2007).

Disability

Seeing disability through a gender lens reveals things about disability that one might not ordinarily see. The term *disability*, of course, carries multiple meanings—and, in fact, has been challenged by those who think that the term connotes inadequacies rather than the successes and achievements of those so labeled. In addition, the term has a broad range, including those who may be severely paralyzed as well as those with some limiting condition—perhaps even including the decreased abilities that come with aging. In reality, most of us will experience some form of disability at some point in our lives, a reality that advocates for the disabled (or differently abled or physically challenged) have used to invoke empathy for people who are otherwise treated as invisible and stigmatized.

Thinking about the meaning of disability shows how, like gender, it is as much a social construction as a physical reality (Zola 1989, 1993). Thus, physically limiting conditions need not be as "disabling" as society makes them. Note, for example, that in social interaction, people may look away from someone who is physically disabled or may treat them in a childlike fashion, thus diminishing their social presence and identifying them, even if unintentionally, as someone less of a social being. And, as with other "minority" groups in society, issues of access and rights of the disabled have been the basis for a strong and effective disability rights movement.

With regard to gender, you can see the connection between disability and social assumptions about gender simply by thinking about how manhood is associated with physical prowess and womanhood with sexuality. We read onto people's bodies gendered expectations that associate masculinity with strength and independence, not weakness or dependence. A man who is physically disabled is less likely to be seen as "masculine" (Gerschick and Miller 1994). Both men and women who are disabled are also perceived as asexual. These realities show the linkage that feminists have argued exists between social expectations about the conjunction of disability, gender, and sexuality (Smith and Hutchison 2004). It also reveals the extent to which our social expectations about bodies are framed by gender in society.

Gender also is reflected in the likelihood that one will become disabled. Aggregate data show that women are more likely to become disabled so that they need the help of others in handling routine needs; however, this is most likely because of women's longer life expectancy. But, regardless of life expectancy, African Americans are more likely to be disabled than are Whites and Latinos (National Center for Health Statistics 2006).

Some of the societal needs of the disabled have been supported through the passage of the **Americans with Disabilities Act** of 1990. This law protects people who are disabled from discrimination and requires employers and other institutional providers (such as schools) to provide "reasonable accommodation" so that people with disabilities will have access to education, employment, and public facilities (such as transportation, bathrooms, hotel rooms, and so forth). It has been enormously important in extending basic rights to the disabled population, as well as in transforming public awareness about disability.

Health Insurance

With so many known health risks for women, one would hope that national health-care policy and health-care systems would be able to meet the challenges of keeping women and men healthy. Especially in a nation known for its advanced health-care system and in a nation that is affluent relative to other nations in the world, one would expect a health-care system that works for the total population. Prior to the passage of health care reform in 2010, 17 percent of all men and 14 percent of women were not covered by health insurance (U.S. Census Bureau 2009). Women of color and poor were especially at risk of having no coverage. Women's health-care coverage is largely determined by their employment and marital status (Montez et al. 2009). Employed women, prior to health care reform, were are less likely to be covered by health insurance than employed men, because of the structural patterns of gender segregation that place them in occupations with fewer health care benefits (Dewar 2000). Coupled with racial segregation in the workplace, gender segregation makes Black and Hispanic women especially vulnerable to lack of coverage (National Center for Health Statistics 2007). The lack of health insurance can be especially hard for young women, many of whom earn lower wages and are the group least likely to have health insurance. Older women, as well, are disadvantaged by the health-care system. Studies show that older women are more likely than men to pay for a larger share of their health-care costs (Salganicoff et al. 2009).

The passage of health care reform under the Obama administration will change some of these patterns, but not likely all. The Affordable Care Act of 2010, passed by a narrow margin and with great national controversy, does not provide universal health care coverage, but it does protect women and men from losing coverage if they are unemployed and it will, in the future, protect people from being denied insurance coverage because of pre-existing conditions. The bill also protects women against discrimination by private insurers. But some of women's interests were also compromised with the passage of this legislation. The bill maintains a ban on federal funding for abortion and, at this point, it is not clear if expenses of birth control will be covered through health care insurance.

Even with health care reform, numerous issues remain. As only one example, as the population ages—and the aged are predominantly women—long-term care is an increasing need. As people live longer, they run the risk of spending down all their assets (if they have any to start with), especially if they acquire a long-term illness and disability.

With national attention increasingly on the problems that people face because of health care, keeping a focus on the gender, class, and race dimensions of access to health care is an important priority (Ruzek et al. 1997). Although the national discussion of health care is typically cast in a gender-neutral discourse, it is clear that health-care reform is—or certainly should be—a woman's issue.

THE POLITICS OF REPRODUCTION

The issues of abortion, birth control, and pregnancy are at the heart of feminist politics and are core issues around which feminist analysis has been built. Contemporary feminists see women's right to control their own bodies as essential to the realization of other rights and opportunities in society. As the Boston Women's Health Book Collective has written, "Unless we ourselves can decide whether and when to have children, it is difficult for us to control our lives or participate fully in society" (1984: 291).

Whether individual women experience pregnancy, abortion, or birth control as stressful or traumatic is at least partially because of how they are socially organized. Women do not simply get pregnant and give birth in the physical sense alone; they do so within a definite set of social relations (Petchesky 1980). These social arrangements vary not only historically but also cross-culturally. Feminist arguments about the social control of reproduction clearly take this fact into account. Following her early study of seven Pacific Island cultures, Margaret Mead wrote:

> *Whether childbirth is seen as a situation in which one risks death, or out of which one acquires a baby, or social status, or a right to Heaven, is not a matter of the actual statistics of maternal mortality, but of the view that a society takes of childbearing. Any argument about women's instinctively maternal behavior which insists that in this respect a biological substratum is stronger than every other learning experience that a female child faces, from birth on, must reckon with this great variety in the handling of childbirth. (Mead 1962: 221)*

Female control of reproduction is cross-culturally and historically the dominant social arrangement (Oakley 1974); yet, in modern Western societies, reproduction is controlled by men. Traditional social theories have also largely ignored the question of reproduction, as if assuming that it is irrelevant in analyses of human experience and social organization.

Feminist perspectives on reproductive issues assert women's right to control their own bodies. Too often, the medical profession is unresponsive to women's needs. Even after years of reform, it is still typically men—either in medicine or in politics—who make decisions about reproductive issues (Ruzek et al. 1997). Reproduction is embedded in systems of social power and social control (Petchesky 1980). Without the right to choose their own reproductive status, women do not have control over their own bodies.

Reproduction is also entangled with class and race relations, as the history of reproductive issues shows. The politics of birth control and abortion, a recurring history of sterilization abuse, and the manipulation of powerless women for medical experiments are all evidence of how reproductive policies have been formulated at the expense of women. This section reviews the politics of reproduction, focusing on three contemporary issues: birth control, abortion, and racism and reproduction.

Birth Control

Birth control, on the one hand, is a personal matter; on the other hand, it is controlled by decisions of the state, the social organization of scientific and medical institutions, and public values and attitudes. Because birth control regulates sexual activity and population size, its significance extends beyond the individual relationships in which it is actually practiced. The availability, form, and cultural significance of birth control bear directly on the role of women in society (Gordon 1977; Roberts 1997).

Today, most people probably take birth control for granted, but it was not that long ago when the right to practice birth control was first established in law, especially for the unmarried. A 1965 Supreme Court decision (*Griswold* v. *Connecticut*) established the first constitutional precedent that the use of birth control was a right, not a crime. However, this decision extended only to married persons. Not until 1972 (in *Eisenstadt* v. *Baird*) were laws prohibiting the dispensing of contraceptives to any unmarried person, or by anyone other than a physician or pharmacist, declared unconstitutional. This decision by the U.S. Supreme Court followed an incident in which Bill Baird, a long-time birth control activist, handed a package of vaginal foam to an unmarried young woman during a lecture on contraception at Boston University. Baird, in violation of a Massachusetts law that prohibited the distribution of nonprescribed contraceptives, was arrested and convicted of a felony before the case reached the Supreme Court.

Before the establishment of the constitutional right to birth control, laws varied from state to state, and, even in those states where the distribution of birth control devices was legal, dispensing birth control depended on the discretion of individual doctors. The effect was to shift the decision regarding birth control from women to men in the medical and judicial professions. Current policies on birth control are shaped by a political context that puts control in the hands of men and the government. As an example, during the debate over national health-care policy in 2010, a proviso was written into the bill that denied any public funding for abortion. In other words, women's reproductive freedom was sacrificed in the interest of political deal-making.

Gender and sexual politics continue to influence public policy and public funding for reproductive health. If you doubt this, consider the attention given to Viagra, the drug that treats male impotency. The scientists who did the basic research underlying Viagra's functioning were given the Nobel Prize. Has any such celebration been linked to women's reproductive freedom? This bias in favor of men is not unique to the United States. In Japan, women's use of the birth control pill was not even approved until 1999—and only then after a ten-year approval process. In contrast, in Japan, Viagra for men was approved the Ministry of Health and Welfare in a record six months.

Even in a context where birth control and sex education are politically contested, the use of birth control has increased substantially, including among young people. Estimates are that nine in ten sexually active women who do not want to become pregnant are practicing contraception; women who use no contraceptives account for nearly half of unintended pregnancies each year. The pill, sterilization, and the condom are the most widely used forms of contraception (Guttmacher Institute 2008).

Among teens, most (74 percent of women and 82 percent of men) now use contraceptives the first time they have sex, the condom being the most common form of contraceptive at the first sexual experience (see also Figure 7.5). But, among teens, of those who use contraceptives, a little more than half use the pill, but many use both the pill and male condoms. The most striking statistic about teen contraceptive use is that teens are so much more likely to use birth control than in the past. This has helped reduce the rate of teen pregnancy (see Chapter 6), particularly given that it is known that a sexually active teenager who does not use birth control has a 90 percent chance of getting pregnant within one year. Many states now allow teens to have access to birth control even without parental consent. Among teenagers who use clinics for access to birth control, two-thirds say their parents know they are there, but among those whose parents do not know, a large majority (70 percent) say they would not come if their parents had to be notified (Guttmacher Institute 2008)—a fact to consider in public debates about parental notification for teen use of birth control.

Abortion

Women's right to choose abortion was established by the 1973 Supreme Court decision in *Roe* v. *Wade*. This decision held that laws that prohibited abortion were unconstitutional, except where such laws are restricted to the last three months of pregnancy or to the stage of fetal viability. The Court's decision

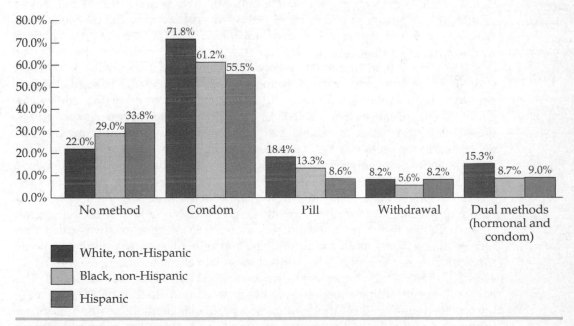

FIGURE 7.5   Contraceptive Use among American Teen Women

Sources: Centers for Disease Control 2009. U.S. *Health United States 2008.* Hyattsville, MD: National Center for Health Statistics. www.cdc.gov/nchs.

acknowledged that on the issue of abortion, separately legitimate social concerns collided: (1) the constitutional right to privacy, (2) the right of the state to protect maternal health, and (3) the right of the state to protect developing life. The Court thus divided the gestation period into thirds and argued that in the first trimester the woman's right to decide her future privately, without interference from the state, took precedence over the other two rights. In the second trimester, the state cannot deny an abortion, but it can insist on reasonable standards of medical procedure. In the third trimester, abortion may be performed to preserve the life or health of the mother.

In 1989, the Supreme Court (in *Webster* v. *Reproductive Health Services*) gave states the right to impose substantial restrictions on abortion (such as requiring fetus viability tests, restricting use of public funding for abortion, and refusing to allow public employees to perform abortions in public hospitals). Continued political pressure from antiabortion groups makes the future of abortion rights uncertain. Already analyses show that the various antiabortion activities have resulted in more scarce abortion services (Kahane 2000). Eighty-seven percent of all U.S. counties have no abortion provider and the majority of abortion providers report that they experience some kind of harassment, ranging from picketing of clinics and staff members' homes to vandalism, bomb threats, physical interference with patients, and even murder of physicians who provide this service to women (Boonstra et al. 2006).

Despite the antiabortion movement, public support for abortion has remained steady, with 46 percent of the public identifying as prochoice and 47 percent as prolife. Although the public is evenly divided on how they define themselves with regard to abortion rights, support for the current law remains strong. Two-thirds of the U.S. public is opposed to any law that would make abortion illegal or any law stricter than under *Roe* v. *Wade*. One-fifth (21 percent) think abortion should be legal under any circumstances; more than half (57 percent) think it should be legal under most or a few circumstances; 18 percent say it should be illegal in all circumstances (Saad 2009). As Baby Boomers age, most who are still in their childbearing years are unlikely to recall what fears unwanted pregnancies generated in the pre-*Roe v. Wade* decades (see Figure 7.6). Thus, while attitudinal surveys show an evenly divided public, changed conditions could also change people's minds on this controversial subject.

In the United States, abortion was not viewed as morally wrong (if performed before quickening at four or five months) until the second half of the nineteenth century. Before that time, abortion was a common practice and was often performed using drugs, potions, techniques, and remedies made popular in home medical guides. Abortion was viewed as relatively safe and was commonly assisted by midwives, "irregular" physicians, and physicians of the period. The earliest laws governing abortion were not enacted until 1821 and 1841, but these laws placed guilt only on those who used particular methods feared unsafe for inducing abortion. None of these laws punished women for having abortions; they were intended as regulations to ensure safe methods (Mohr 1978).

In the mid-nineteenth century, abortion became a widespread phenomenon, especially among White, married, Protestant women. During this period, abortion

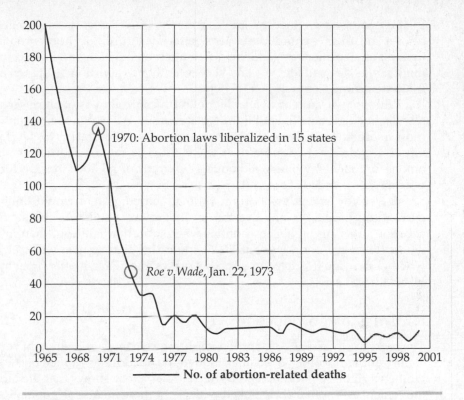

FIGURE 7.6   **Death Rate from Abortion**

Sources: Boonstra, Heather, et al. *Abortion in Women's Lives,* New York: Guttmacher Institute, 2006. Reprinted with permission.

also became increasingly commercialized. One noted woman entrepreneur, Madame Restell, earned an enormous income from her abortion products and spent as much as $60,000 per year on advertising alone (Mohr 1978). As both the drug industry and the medical profession grew in the second half of the nineteenth century, more profits could be made by companies seizing control of the abortion market. In addition to eliminating midwives from the practice of abortion, the medical profession created laws and spread propaganda that altered the perception and practice of abortion.

These changes were additionally fueled by shifts in the class, racial, and ethnic structure of U.S. life. The emerging new class of physicians was not only incensed by the flagrant commercialization of abortion but they also expressed the fear that the growing rate of abortion among the middle and upper classes would cause immigrants, Black Americans, and the poor to outbreed them. Spurred by the growth of social Darwinism and an increasing nativist movement, the antiabortion crusade appealed to racist fears and portrayed abortion as the work of criminals, backward medical practitioners, and immoral social agents (Mohr 1978). Beginning in the period between 1860 and 1880 and continuing through the first two-thirds of the twentieth century, antiabortion policies included strict criminal laws about abortion and put absolute control of abortion in the hands of the medical profession. By these laws, women seeking abortions—and their accomplices—were defined as guilty of murder, abortion was defined as a criminal act, and the distribution of abortion and birth control information was deemed illegal. Only very recently has abortion been seen as a moral issue stemming from religious beliefs.

With the widespread availability of birth control, rates of abortion have actually declined, despite the public outcries about it. Women in their twenties are the most likely group to have an abortion and the abortion rate is higher for women who have already had more than one child. The rate of abortion is also higher among unmarried women, although 17 percent of all abortions performed in a year are for married women (U.S. Census Bureau 2009). The most frequent reasons given for having an abortion are that being a parent would limit women's current responsibilities and that they cannot afford a child. A sobering fact is that abortion rates are higher in counties where abortion is illegal than in countries where it is legal (Boonstra et al. 2006), indicating that women will seek abortions whether they are restricted or not. This makes abortion a matter of women's public health and safety.

Racism and Reproduction

The reproductive issues of abortion, birth control, and sterilization have particular significance for women of color. Although the majority of women of color support women's rights to abortion and birth control, history shows that the birth control movement has been closely linked with racist movements for population control. For women of color, reproductive freedom thus means not just freedom of choice but the freedom to dismantle social arrangements that limit the choices women of color have (Roberts 1997).

In the early twentieth century, when Margaret Sanger was organizing the birth control movement, White birth control reformers were campaigning to prevent so-called racial suicide for themselves through their allowing the overpopulation of Black Americans, immigrants, the poor, and social misfits (Davis 1981; Gordon 1977). The campaign for birth control was interwoven with genocidal movements to eliminate racial groups, and appeals for birth control were clearly intended to limit what was perceived as overbreeding among the poor. Sanger herself made this appeal part of her campaign, and thus seemed to support the racist goals of the eugenics movement.

In the contemporary record, information on the sterilization of women of color and poor women confirms that birth control and population control are often linked. Sterilization rates are highest among African American, Native American, and Puerto Rican women and female welfare recipients. These data raise the issue of the blurred distinction between forced and voluntary sterilization. Although forced sterilization is illegal, reports indicate that doctors and clinics do give misleading information to minority and poor clients. Although clients may technically agree to the procedure, they have frequently been misled or misinformed.

HISTORY SPEAKS: YESTERDAY'S FEMINISTS TALK ABOUT TODAY

Margaret Sanger and the Right to Birth Control and Abortion

"No woman can call herself free who does not own and control her body. No woman can call herself free until she can choose consciously whether she will or will not be a mother."

—Margaret Sanger

Margaret Sanger (1879–1966) is known for being a pioneer feminist because of her advocacy for birth control—at a time, perhaps hard to imagine now—when women would have had very little freedom to manage their own reproductive health. Trained as a nurse, Sanger set up the first birth control clinic in the United States (in New York City) and traveled and published extensively, advocating birth control as a means of freedom for women. She was arrested in 1916 for conducting a birth control clinic in Brooklyn.

Sanger is, however, in retrospect, a controversial figure because of her ties to the racist eugenics movement of the time. Sanger argued that birth control was especially needed among the poor and she is quoted as having promoted "racial health" through birth control. She made a controversial appearance in 1926 before the Ku Klux Klan and has been accused of having Nazi sympathies because of her association with Hitler and his support of her work. Despite her contributions to the modern availability of birth control, in these ways, she remained mired in some of the attitudes of many White people at the time.

If Sanger were to return now and observe today's debates about birth control and abortion, what might she say? She would likely support federal funding for abortion, especially for women on Medicaid. She would no doubt be a strong advocate for sex education in the schools and would have applauded the 1973 *Roe* v. *Wade* Supreme Court decision.

Thinking Further: Do you think Margaret Sander would support the abstinence-only movement? Parental consent laws for minors seeking birth control and/or abortion? Would she have relinquished her eugenicist views or would they still influence her positions on social policies about reproduction? Do eugenicist views, even if more subtle, still influence public opinion on matters of birth control, sex education, and abortion?

Sources: Chesler, Ellen. 2007. *Woman of Valor: Margaret Sanger and the Birth Control Movement in America.* New York: Simon and Schuster; Kennedy, David M. 1970. *Birth Control in America: The Career of Margaret Sanger.* New Haven. CT: Yale University Press; www.womenshistory.about.com.

Federal investigations have revealed a high incidence of sterilization of minors in other government-sponsored clinics. High rates of sterilization, experimentation on Third World women and U.S. women of color for the development of contraceptives, and the inadequacy of health care for women of color all indicate the extent to which racism and sexism are institutionalized in the health care system. White feminists have framed much of their discussion of reproductive health care in the context of individual choice, but for women of color and poor women, choice is restricted by the conditions of oppression they face in health-care institutions. In fact, women of color have been sometimes reluctant to become involved in White feminists' movements for reproductive freedom. People of color have been wary about movements promoting abortion and birth control because historically these movements have been used as racist methods of population control.

Women of color, however, are the most frequent victims of restrictive reproductive policies because poor women and women of color are most dependent on public funding of reproductive services; they are also disproportionately most likely to suffer death and injury if abortion becomes illegal. This suggests that feminist analyses of reproductive freedom should be framed by a political perspective deeper than individual choice; reproductive freedom should be anchored in an understanding of the need for social justice for all women, not just those with the privilege to make free choices. Rights to privacy alone probably cannot achieve such freedom, because privacy itself is largely conditioned through the structured inequalities of race, class, and gender oppression (Petchesky 1990; Roberts 1997).

The Politics of Birth: Pregnancy and Childbirth

The emergence of modern medicine is usually seen as a conquest of ignorance and a triumph over superstition. There was a time when healing was almost solely the province of women. Particularly in matters of birth and child rearing, women were perceived as the experts and birth was a female-centered, home affair (Dye 1980). Until the nineteenth century in this country, women presided over most births, in the presence of female friends and kin who provided comfort and aid to the childbearing woman (Wertz and Wertz 1977).

Because childbirth was originally placed in the hands of women as midwives, developments in the history of childbirth provide a case study in which what was once a female-oriented process has come to be dominated and controlled by men. Although this section focuses primarily on childbirth, it also reveals more general patterns in the emergence of modern medicine. In the end, you will see how particular characteristics of medicine as an institution still take control of reproduction away from women.

Childbirth has a distinctive social history and one that is tied to the emergence of medicine as a profession, as well as to changes in the ideology and structure of women's roles in society. In the colonial United States, childbirth occurred in the home and in the presence of female family members and friends (Dye 1980; Scholten 1977). During this period, six to eight pregnancies were typical for women, as were a fear of pain and the possibility of death in childbirth. Midwives who attended births generally practiced noninterventionist methods of delivery and, along with the other women present, provided comfort and emotional support for the laboring mother. Records of the midwives' practices, successes, and failures are hard to find in this period, so it is difficult to know exactly how skilled or knowledgeable the midwives were. Information and experiences about childbirth were shared by women, and there is little indication in the historical record that midwives posed dangers for childbearing women. There are no recorded epidemics of puerperal fever, such as those that killed thousands of women when childbirth was moved to hospitals, and there are few recorded instances of midwives' incompetence in the colonial period. Without romanticizing midwives and the process of birth, it appears that, unlike images of midwives that appeared later with the advent of scientific medicine, "the stereotype of the midwife as a curse upon women seems unfitting for colonial midwives" (Wertz and Wertz 1977:13).

Certainly, the pain associated with childbirth was a significant factor in women's desire for alternative practices. New interventionist techniques promised by the male founders of medical science appealed to women who sought relief from long and difficult labors. Beginning in the mid-eighteenth century, a slow transition occurred in which birth was shifted from female to male control. Medical men in the United States took their lead from French and English physicians, who described the body as being like a machine and developed instruments or tools to intervene in natural bodily processes. Tools (such as forceps) promised to shorten labor and to make difficult labors more manageable, although such techniques were generally resisted by U.S. and English women midwives, who believed that these techniques introduced new dangers and unsafe procedures to the natural process of birth.

In the mid-eighteenth and early nineteenth centuries, there was an open market for both female midwives and the medical men who were developing new birth techniques. Advances in knowledge about the physiology of labor, as well as various birth techniques, were taught in medical colleges—most of which were located in England and France. Men from the United States learned from these colleges, but, because the government provided no financial support for medical education, women, with fewer financial resources than men, did not attend. Medical education during this period, however, was notoriously poor (Dye 1980), and many have argued that female midwives continued to have greater skills in birth, based on their practical experience, than did medically trained men (Ehrenreich and English 1978, 1973).

By the mid-nineteenth century, medical men had adopted an increasingly interventionist approach toward birth, whereas female midwives relied more on the normal course of delivery. Mary Wollstonecraft (1759–1797), an outspoken English feminist whom you will study in Chapter 12, deplored the takeover of childbirth by men and insisted that her daughter, Mary Shelley (author of *Frankenstein*), be born with a woman attendant. When the placenta was not delivered, a male attendant was called in who, upon inserting his hand to withdraw it, caused Wollstonecraft to hemorrhage and later to die of puerperal fever (Flexner 1972; Wertz and Wertz 1977). Studies indicate that although physicians gained greater control of childbirth during this period, as late as the early twentieth century, midwives had high status in their communities (Litoff 1978), maintained their own apprenticeship systems (Mongeau et al. 1961), and had better mortality records than medical men (Dye 1980).

Transformations in childbirth that ultimately resulted in the medical model of contemporary birth were accelerated in the mid-nineteenth century, when obstetrics was first developed as a medical specialty and when Victorian cultural attitudes transformed bourgeois notions of female sexuality. During the Victorian period, pregnancy was treated with shame and concealment in the middle and upper classes. Because the Victorian period severely restricted women's sexuality and because pregnancy directly acknowledged their sexual activity, it became an event to be hidden and concealed. For example, it is reported that Susan B. Anthony's mother was embarrassed by her own pregnancy (Wertz and Wertz 1977). Like other bourgeois Victorian women, she disappeared from public view when she was pregnant.

At the same time, the emergence of the medical profession provided status to those who could afford new medical treatments. Families that could pay for it, especially in urban areas, began to go to medical specialists. Obstetrics was one of the first of these specialties, although most women continued to employ women midwives because they were more trusting of midwives' noninterventionist techniques and more comfortable in their modesty with other women (Bogdan 1978). Physicians themselves stated that medical midwifery was the key to a successful practice because, if they could eliminate midwives, physicians would have a dependable market; also, the uncharted knowledge of obstetrics provided a chance for the expansion of physicians' careers (Barker-Benfield 1976; Scholten 1977). In keeping with the Victorian sensibilities of the time, the typical obstetrician (so renamed from *male midwives* to symbolize their alleged professionalism) draped his client in cloth and avoided looking at her body; consequently, obstetrics with middle- and upper-class clients was commonly practiced by touch alone. Obstetricians thus gained little knowledge of their female patients and relied on experiments on poor and Black women to advance their field.

Following the Civil War, maternity hospitals were established as charitable asylums for poor and unmarried pregnant women. Stating that such places would provide a more moral and sanitary environment than the patients' own homes, doctors provided free medical treatment for poor women (often servants of the upper classes) in return for using these patients as research subjects (Wertz and Wertz 1977). One of the most outrageous cases of experimentation is found in the practice of J. Marion Sims, originator of gynecology and an early president of the American Medical Association. One of his early claims to fame was the discovery of ways to suture tears that occurred between the vagina and anus. He developed these techniques by purchasing Black female slaves, whom he kept in hospital quarters built in his own yard (Axelson 1985). Seeing Black slaves as enduring, passive, and helpless, he performed countless experimental operations on them without anesthesia. The pain he inflicted on them had to create unimaginable agony, yet this seemed not to faze him in his obsessive search for techniques to build his own career (Barker-Benfield 1976). Nor did it seem to bother upper-class women, who later erected a statue to him in Central Park because of their gratitude for his surgical method! They, of course, experienced it only after the development of anesthesia.

Sims, like other medical men of his day, believed that women's psychology stemmed from their sex organs, and he was anxious to perform clitoridectomies and oophorectomies (removal of the clitoris and ovaries). His drastic use of the knife seemed intended not for the betterment of women but for the enhancement of his own career; an aspiring specialist, then as now, made his name through the invention and publication of new techniques. Indeed, as one historian has noted, the operating rooms where female surgery was performed in the nineteenth century were essentially "an arena for an exchange between men" (Barker-Benfield 1976:101). Sims, in fact, developed gynecological procedures as if he were an explorer charting new frontiers; his own writings clearly show this to be his own metaphor about his work. He was the first to develop the speculum and says of it, "Introducing the bent handle of a spoon, I saw everything as no man had ever seen before. . . . I felt like an explorer in medicine who first views a new and important territory" (Barker-Benfield 1976:95). Other medical men, too, declared his "speculum to be to diseases of the womb . . . what the compass is to the mariner" (Barker-Benfield 1976:95).

The removal of childbirth from the home and the control of women contradicted the Victorian point of view that birth was a private matter, to be conducted in secrecy and within the domestic world. Initially, delivery by men was seen as a breakdown of moral standards and an offense to female delicacy (Donegan 1978). Over time, however, as doctors promised safer and less painful births, women began to desire the new techniques they were offered. Most women wanted less painful childbirth, although in the late nineteenth century, the absence of pain in childbirth was associated with supposedly pre-civilized women—especially Indians and Blacks. Racism in the middle and upper classes defined more "primitive" peoples as closer to nature and therefore unlikely to experience childbirth pain. From the racist perspective of the bourgeois class, to experience pain, and therefore to need relief from it, became a sign of one's civilized nature. Needing relief from childbirth pain was also an indication of the social distance of the upper and middle classes from other strata of the society. Pain, then, became a mark of the "truly feminine"—a fact with its own paradoxical truth because childbirth pain and complications were greatly increased by the "civilized" practices of tight corsets, lack of exercise, fashionable illness, and airless rooms (Wertz and Wertz 1977).

Rather than change their cultural habits, middle- and upper-class women sought relief from childbirth pain and thus became more interested in the promises of modern medicine. Promises were all many of these techniques gave, however, for although they might have alleviated extreme pain, there is little evidence that childbirth was made any safer by medical men of the early twentieth century. Puerperal fever, later found to be caused by infections generated by unsanitary hospital procedures and interventionist techniques, became a major cause of maternal death (Wertz and Wertz 1977). Epidemics of puerperal fever killed thousands of women who sought painless deliveries through hospital births.

The number of births occurring in hospitals increased rapidly after the 1930s. Before this time, hospital birth had been primarily an urban phenomenon and, even there, had occurred on a large scale beginning only in the twentieth century. In 1930, only about 25 percent of all births took place in hospitals; today, 99 percent of all births occur in hospitals. Hospital births represent the ultimate transformation of birth from a female-centered, home activity to one that is medically defined by a profession dominated by men. The prevalence of hospital births followed a direct assault on women midwives in the second half of the nineteenth century, when propaganda to make women fear pregnancy and legislation to eliminate midwives combined to generate new definitions of women's place in childbirth and, more generally, in medicine (Barker-Benfield 1976). Legislation between 1900 and 1930 made licensing for midwives a necessity. To obtain a license, midwives were required to get vouchers of their moral character from a member of the medical profession, to have their homes and outfits inspected by a physician's nurse, and to have attended births under the supervision of a physician. Because few physicians would provide these credentials, the number of practicing midwives radically declined. In New York City, for example, the number of practicing midwives declined from 3,000 in 1908 to 270 in 1939, two in 1957, and one in 1963 (Barker-Benfield 1976). In most cases, women were excluded from medical schools and, if they wanted to enter the health-care system, they were relegated to secondary status as nurses (Ehrenreich and English 1978). Childbirth and, more generally, women's health had effectively been placed in the hands of men as physicians.

The movement of childbirth to hospitals and medical men was further increased by popular racist fears of contagion and germs that were associated with poor, immigrant, and Black people. The fads of genetic science and social Darwinism of the 1920s and 1930s increased middle-class fears of associating with those from the lower strata of society. Coupled with the home economics movement of the 1920s that defined home environments as sources of germs and disease (see Chapter 6), popular opinions laced with racist and class ideologies further generated a social definition of childbirth as a scientific event to be placed under the authority of medical men.

Physicians now routinely define pregnancy and birth as medical events and, because of this model, they are more likely to prescribe drugs during pregnancy and birth, set strict limits on what is considered a "normal" pregnancy, and define medical intervention as essential during birth. Midwives, on the other hand, define pregnancy as a healthy and normal condition—one that is optimized not by intervention and technological management but by providing the best possible environment for the pregnant woman (Rothman 1982). Conflict between the medical and midwifery models of childbirth lies at the struggles over the control of childbirth, including political conflicts regarding the licensing of midwives and the establishment of nonmedical birth settings (Sullivan and Weitz 1988).

The dominance of the medical model in controlling pregnancy and childbirth can be seen in how pregnancy and childbirth are routinely handled by the medical profession. Birth is most likely located in hospitals, where doctors and the staff, not the mother, have control and authority over the delivery procedures. Even in the birthing rooms, which many hospitals have established, ultimate authority lies with the physician, who may (and does) intervene in the birth process at any point.

Interventionist practices characterizing the rise of male control over childbirth continue to dominate women's childbirth experiences. This fact is especially evident in the dramatic increase in the number of cesarean sections being per-formed in hospitals throughout the country. In an age when childbirth is sup-posed to be safer and less threatening than it was in previous years, how do we explain the high proportion of births using a process that can increase the risks to both mother and child? Currently, 32 percent of all births are done by cesarean section—an increase of 50 percent over ten years (from 1997 to 2007; Hamilton et al. 2009).

Researchers cite the routine practices of technological monitoring of birth as contributing significantly to the increase in cesarean births. Although some also mention physicians' greed for higher compensation and their desire for predictable schedules as contributing to the incentives to perform cesarean, it seems most likely that the social organization of childbirth around technological intervention is responsible for the increase. Typically, the process of labor is now observed by an electronic fetal-monitoring device that not only replaces the monitoring originally performed by nurses but can keep the laboring woman passively strapped to the device and immobile throughout the course of labor. Even though changes in the baby's breathing and heartbeat are routine features of the birth process, the close detection of these changes by the electronic fetal monitor results in a high number of false indications of fetal distress (Corea 1980). As a result of this situation, which is complicated by doctors' fears of malpractice if an actually distressed fetus is missed, doctors seem to react quickly to the slightest indication of change in the fetal condition by performing a vast number of unnecessary cesarean sections.

As women, inspired by the feminist health movement, have become more critical of the medical management of childbirth, many changes have taken place in how birth is handled, even in hospitals. Mothers and newborn infants are no longer necessarily separated following the birth; fathers, friends, and family mem-bers are often welcome in the delivery room and actively participate in the process; birth centers are common in hospitals; and midwives often practice in conjunction with obstetricians. These changes, now common, can be directly attributed to the influence of the feminist health movement—one of the many ways that the feminist movement has transformed even some of life's most inti-mate and special moments.

New Reproductive Technologies

New reproductive technologies—including artificial insemination, in vitro fertil-ization, embryo transfer, cloning, and genetic engineering—raise new concerns and questions about women's control of their bodies. Feminists point out that although some of these technologies seem to offer liberating possibilities, at the same time they make women new targets for the manipulation of reproductive engineers (Roberts 1997).

Donor insemination, for example, means that lesbian women or women who merely want children without men can become pregnant. In vitro fertilization makes it possible for those who are infertile to have children. Amniocentesis and an array of other tests now allow for prenatal evaluation of the embryo, meaning that characteristics such as sex, disability, and disease can be determined before birth. Although these may appear to be laudable developments, they also raise disturbing questions. Why, for example, is biological parenthood so important that we would go to such lengths and costs to bear children rather than considering adoption? What are the implications of determining sex before birth, especially in cultures where female infants are less valued than males? What does it say about the oppression of people with disabilities and our prejudices against them if we screen for disabilities before birth?

The eugenics movement in the United States in the earlier part of the twentieth century, like that of Nazi Germany, sought to apply the principles of genetic selection to improve the offspring of the human race. In both Nazi Germany and the United States, the process was explicitly racist, including, for example, compulsory sterilization of those defined as "unfit" or "defective." Many feminists equate the contemporary development of reproductive technology with the possibility of a new eugenics movement—one that, although it may not appear blatantly racist, is still embedded in a racist, sexist, and homophobic culture. Would reproductive technology be used, for example, to control the fertility of those deemed unworthy? To whom are reproductive technology and choice over reproduction most likely made available?

Although new reproductive technologies appear to give women choices over how and when they will have children, these technologies do not affect all women equally. Some women may have "rights to choose," but the choices women have are structured by race, class, and gender inequality (Roberts 1997). Reproductive control can, in fact, become a façade for population control and, in the context of racism, population control is often a mechanism for more social and political control (Rothman 1982).

At the same time, new technologies also hold the promise of helping women to have children when they otherwise could not—such as to have children when they (or their partners) are infertile or when a woman wants to have a child outside of a heterosexual relationship. It is not that new technologies are in and of themselves harmful, but that they are developed and consumed within a social structure that is entrenched in gender, race, and class inequality. Thus, for example, even though low-income women are more likely to be infertile than are better-off women, the infertility industry embeds certain class and race stereotypes that disadvantage low-income, infertile women who may want to have children (Bell 2009). Such class stereotypes play out in the public imagination: Think of how reviled the woman labeled as "Octomom" was when she gave birth to eight babies, compared to how celebrated the middle-class heroine of *Jon and Kate Plus Eight* (now *Kate Plus Eight*) has been—with the exact same number of children! Had Nadya Suleman—the so-called Octomom—not been on welfare and of an Iraqi background, but had been White and wealthy, do you think she would have been the recipient of many gifts instead of the object of collective hatred?

The point is that an analysis of inequality and power relations is central to any discussion of reproductive technology. Feminists do not necessarily believe that reproductive technology should be eliminated altogether, but they argue that as long as it is embedded in a system of gender, race, and class inequality—as well as sexual inequality—women will still be denied the right to control their bodies. Only organized resistance to the control of women's bodies by men will ensure that these technologies do not become a new means for the oppression of women.

GENDER AND THE HEALTH-CARE SYSTEM

Like other social institutions, health care is a *gendered* institution (see Chapter 2). That is, its structure, organization, and ideology reflect gendered relationships and meanings. This is also an institution in transition with more women physicians than ever before and women as a growing proportion of medical school students. Within the health-care system, women are more likely to be clients, since women exceed men in most measures of health-care utilization, including number of physician visits, hospital admissions, and the prescription of drugs (National Center for Health Statistics 2009). Women's health care is intricately interwoven with gender, race, and class relations, all of which affect the quality of care received and the status of women workers within the health-care system. Feminist criticism of medical institutions is a response to this gendered institution.

Women as Health-Care Workers

Women constitute 75 percent of all health-care workers, yet they are heavily segregated within the health-care field—often found in the least prestigious and most poorly paid positions in this field. There has been huge growth in the number of female physicians—now up to 31 percent of all physicians. Women have also dramatically increased their representation in medical schools, now constituting close to half of medical school students (U.S. Department of Labor 2009). Because of the long period of training, internship, and residence in medical professions, the impact of women's increased enrollment on the composition of practicing physicians is only beginning to be felt.

These are major breakthroughs for women in medicine, but this generation is not the first to witness such changes. At the turn of the twentieth century, women were a significant proportion of all physicians, with some cities reporting almost 20 percent of all physicians to be women (Walsh 1977). The entry of women into medicine is historically closely aligned with feminism and the new opportunities it encourages for women. Although the feminist movement at the turn of the century was quite different from contemporary feminism, it did encourage women, at least of the upper and middle classes, to use their skills, especially in areas perceived as helping professions. Since the turn of the century, women were excluded from medicine through overt discrimination (denied entrance to medical schools) and through informal practices whereby they received little encouragement or support. They were channeled into nursing schools, encountered hostility from peers, and were excluded from the "old boy" network that placed persons in their careers.

Even now, the lack of sponsorship, tracking systems, nonsupportive peer environments, and overt ridicule can restrict opportunities for women in medicine, although women within medicine have created a number of organizations to counter such tendencies. The women's movement has helped create a climate of mutual support among women students and professionals, leading to the creation of an environment more conducive to women's success. But the historical record of women's decline in medical careers indicates that none of these gains can be taken for granted. Continual lobbying, network building among women, and federal support for women's medical education are all necessary for stabilizing the role of women in this profession.

Most women workers in the health-care system are there as nurses, dietitians, health technicians, and aides. Ninety-two percent of registered nurses are women (U.S. Department of Labor 2009). African American and Hispanic women in health care are concentrated in the lowest paying of these occupations. Women who are nurses do not face the problem of existing in a male-dominated occupation, as women physicians do, but their position relative to that of male professionals creates its own set of problems. Women of color in these fields also face the problems of racism and discrimination, which hamper their career development. Nurses and other health-care workers are put in the position in which male professionals hold authority over them, in addition to receiving greater material benefits. Moreover, men who enter nursing tend to progress to higher echelons than do women within the profession (compounding the problem of sexism that women in this field face).

Despite recent increases in their salaries, nurses face sexist attitudes that define their work as less valuable than that of men. On the job, nurses are subordinate to the doctors in authority; innumerable accounts have described the sexist put-downs, innuendoes, and insults that some doctors have directed toward the nursing staff. More generally, physicians maintain a monopoly over medical knowledge and medical practice, even though nurses have more actual contact with hospitalized patients (Ehrenreich and English 1973). Such working conditions lead to a high sense of dissatisfaction among nurses and, as a result, high job turnover.

The subordination of the nursing profession to the authority of doctors has resulted in a split between the activities of curing and caring. Stereotypically, nurses are alleged to provide nurturing, whereas doctors maintain the expertise in healing. Such a myth not only belittles the professional knowledge of nurses but also creates an atmosphere that may not work in the best interest of patients. As alternative medical practices have shown, a patient's health involves a complex configuration of physiological, emotional, and social systems. It appears that a more useful system of medicine is one that integrates the process of healing with the complexities emerging from the interaction of these systems.

The Women's Health Movement

Many of the now-routine things that you can observe in the health-care system have their origins in the women's health movement. Hospitals and physicians' practices have established women's health centers; birthing rooms have been transformed in many hospitals; even the pink ribbons that one routinely sees as part of breast cancer awareness can be attributed to the mobilization of feminists on issues of women's health. Critical of the sexist practices of medical institutions and practitioners, feminists organized a grassroots women's health movement in the early

1970s that has had a dramatic impact on the health-care system and its treatment of women (Thomas and Zimmerman 2007; Ruzek et al. 1997; Morgen 2002).

The thrust of the women's health movement has been to help women have more control over their own health and reproductive lives. This includes providing women with more information about their own bodies, organizing on behalf of women's health issues (such as promoting more support for breast cancer research), and establishing self-help clinics. Other feminist organizations also lobby to create changes in the health-care system and its policies.

Altogether, the women's health movement has the goals of reducing differences in knowledge between patient and practitioner, challenging the mandate of physicians as the sole providers of health care and thus supporting a more holistic form of care, reducing the professional monopoly over goods and services, increasing the number of women practitioners, and organizing clients around health issues (Ruzek 1978). The emergence of the women's health movement is indicative of the dissatisfaction women have shown in health-care institutions and over issues involving reproduction and health. As this chapter has shown, feminist perspectives on health and reproduction insist on women's right to control their own bodies. As long as the power to control women's bodies remains predominantly in the hands of men, feminists are likely to continue organizing on these issues.

Chapter Summary and Themes

Physical and mental health is fundamentally shaped by social factors, most especially gender, race, and class.

Evidence shows that women's health, like men's, is shaped by their gender status, although this is compounded by race and class status. On measures such as life expectancy, likelihood of disease, and rates of mental health, significant gender differences emerge.

Because health is influenced by social context, the work that women (and men) do has an impact on their health.

Women's employment status affects their health, with women working solely in the home generally having higher rates of illness and depression than women in the labor force. Protective legislation has historically excluded women from jobs deemed risky to their reproductive health, even when the same risks have not excluded men from such work.

Social problems involving health are shaped by the gender expectations in society.

Cultural obsessions with thinness means that women are especially likely to suffer from various eating disorders, although the form they take varies by race, class, and sexual orientation. Women are now the group most likely to be new AIDS cases, although they typically acquire AIDS from heterosexual men. Public issues regarding health insurance coverage also have a gender component; thus, analyzing gender is important for fully understanding the need for effective social policies.

Feminist perspectives on reproduction see this as an area where men have accumulated the power to control women's bodies, even though in earlier periods women have controlled reproduction.

Rights to birth control, abortion, and other forms of reproductive freedom have been achieved through feminist activism. Practices such as childbirth and reproduction are now largely managed through a medical model that places power in the hands of male-dominated professions. Race and class are also integrally linked to reproductive politics, with women of color having the least freedom to control their own bodies.

Health care is a gendered institution, meaning that it has taken on the characteristics that are associated with masculinity in this culture.

In the health-care system, women and people of color are typically in the lowest-status positions, and men have the power to control medical decisions and medical knowledge. The women's health-care movement has resulted in many reforms in this system and continues to press for changes that give women more control over their own bodies.

▨ Key Terms

Americans with Disabilities Act
anorexia nervosa
Automobile Workers v. *Johnson
    Controls*

bulimia
Eisenstadt v. *Baird*
Griswold v. *Connecticut*
infant mortality

Muller v. *Oregon*
protective legislation
Roe v. *Wade*

▨ Discussion Questions/Projects for Thought

1. Identify a group of women workers in the health-care field (nurses, women physicians, medical technologists, radiologists, physicians' assistants, etc.) and interview them about their work. What opportunities are available to them? Are their jobs segregated by gender and race/ethnicity? How do they see themselves relative to men they work with? What happens to those who try to move up? Are they satisfied with their jobs? If not, why not; if so, why? What do your interviews tell you about the social structure of gender in the health-care field?

2. Using a recent sampling of the magazines read most frequently by your peers, describe what the magazine conveys as the ideal image for women's bodies. How does this influence the eating behavior of those who read it? How extensive are eating disorders among women and men on your campus? What do you think are the origins of these problems?

3. Identify a group of women and men on your campus who smoke. Interview them about when they started smoking, why they do so, and what they perceive it as doing for them. Are they aware of the risks of smoking to their health? When you analyze the answers to your questions, ask yourself how gender influences the smoking patterns of people on your campus.

In 1895, Elizabeth Cady Stanton, a passionate feminist, close friend of Susan B. Anthony, and founder of equal rights and suffrage associations during the first wave of feminism in the nineteenth century, wrote:

> From the inauguration of the movement for women's emancipation the Bible has been used to hold her in the "divinely ordained sphere," prescribed in the Old and New Testaments. The canon and civil law; church and state; priests and legislators; all political parties and religious denominations have alike taught that woman was made after man, of man, and for man, an inferior being, subject to man. Creeds, codes, Scriptures and statutes, are all based on this idea. The fashions, forms, ceremonies and customs of society, church ordinances and discipline all grow out of this idea. (Stanton 1895/1974:7)

More than 100 years later, Stanton's words still ring true. Religious beliefs have aroused conservative political movements that threaten many of the rights that women have won as the result of feminism, and in many religions, women continue to be excluded from positions of leadership. In those where they are permitted to hold positions of leadership, they are still a small minority. Both in the United States and worldwide, some religious beliefs are the core of sexist ideologies that promote women's exclusion from the public world and maintain women's subordination in the home.

Religion is a powerful source for the subordination of women in society; yet, across the years, religion has also been an important source for the feminist movement and other movements for human liberation. This is evident particularly, but not exclusively, in the African American community, where religion has been a powerful instrument for social change and where women's roles in the church have provided African American women with opportunities for leadership, education, and the development of organizational skills. In addition, religious belief in the Black community rests on a strong faith in justice, fairness, and equality. The liberating effects of religion are also evident in Judaism—one of the most conservative religions in its doctrine about women—yet, its religious faith has spawned feminism and liberalism. There are many feminists who are also devout Christians, and there is a feminist movement among Islamic women (Fernea 2000; Mernissi and Lakeland 1992; Mir-Hosseini 1999).

Thus, although religion has been a repressive force in women's lives, it has also been a source of liberation. Bernice Johnson Reagon, Black feminist and performer, reflects on her religious experience in childhood, writing in her autobiography:

> Everybody in church talked about/Miss Nana's relationship with God/People thought she had a sort of audacity/Everybody else would say/"Now, Lord, here comes me your meek and undone servant and you know me and you know my condition"/This was a way of saying/"Now Lord, I don't even need to go over my situation/Let us start now with where I am and what I need today"/ . . . /Miss Nana was grateful for what she got but she didn't let up on God for what she wanted/God had already given her a soul, right?/But then she'd say,/"That ain't all I need, Lord/You are not off the hook/I expect you to be here on time tomorrow night." (1982: 90–91)

Understanding these dual tendencies of repression and liberation is best developed through exploring sociological and feminist perspectives on religion. The sections that follow explore several themes in the feminist analysis of religion, including the historical relationship of women, religion, and feminism; women's religious beliefs and status within churches; the role of the church in minority communities; and new perspectives inspired by feminist spirituality and theology.

SOCIOLOGICAL PERSPECTIVES ON RELIGION

For most people, religion is something they hold dear, sometimes so much so that they see it as the only possible view of the world. Paul Tillich (1957), a liberal theologian, defines *religion* as the expression of humanity's ultimate concerns, the articulation of longing for a center of meaning and value and for connection with the power of being. Sociologists who study religion take another approach. They are not so much interested in the truth or falsity of a religious belief system but in how belief systems and religious institutions shape social behavior and reflect the collective experience of society's members.

Religion provides a culture with powerful symbols and concepts that are deeply felt and that shape a group of people's view of the world around them. Religious belief is often the basis for cultural and societal conflict and is frequently so strongly felt that people will fight and die for it. Religion is also the basis for in-group membership, sometimes strongly protected by sanctions against interfaith or same-sex marriages.

Sociological perspectives on religion also take the institutional structure of religion as significant in a variety of ways. Like other institutions in society, religious institutions socialize their members through enforcing group norms that dictate many aspects of everyday life, including what men and women wear; how life events (such as birth, puberty, marriage, and death) are defined and ritualized; and how men and women are defined in terms of home, work, child care, politics, and the law. Religious institutions also include power structures and, like other social institutions, are characterized by a system of stratification, which is clearly demarcated by gender, race, and class. Religious belief is a particularly important part of many aspects of our experience. Religion, for example, influences how tolerant one is on sexual matters, with those who are most religious generally being less tolerant of premarital sex, same-sex marriage, and marital infidelity (Scott 1998; Hager 1996; Saguy 1999). However, this relationship is not as strong as one might think because secular (i.e., nonreligious) forces also influence people's beliefs. Thus, among evangelicals—those generally seen as sexual conservatives—there is diversity in opinions about sexual morality (Park 1999). Evangelicals have generally been portrayed as antifeminist and conservative in views about women's roles. However, research finds that support for egalitarian gender roles (i.e., shared housework and child care, leadership for women in the church, and women's employment) has changed among evangelical, conservative Protestants as they attempt to reconcile traditional beliefs about women's roles with the reality of a changing

HISTORY SPEAKS: YESTERDAY'S FEMINISTS TALK ABOUT TODAY

Sor Juana Ines de la Cruz: Religion as Oppression or Freedom?

Sor Juana Inez de la Cruz (1651–1695) was a seventeenth-century Mexican nun—perhaps one of the least likely places for feminism to emerge. But she is now known as one of the outstanding writers of the Latin colonial period and one of the earliest feminists—someone who felt she had no need to marry and wanted to pursue an occupation that would not interfere with her desire to study and read. She entered a convent in 1669 and spent the remainder of her life cloistered there. Amassing one of the largest libraries in the New World, she was an intellectual, a philosopher, a poet, and a feminist.

Her feminism stemmed in part from her interpretation of religious saints, whose thoughts she would bend to support her ardent belief in the rights of women to be educated. She also maintained an intimate friendship with Maria Luisa—the Countess de Pareda—a friendship that contemporary writers say likely crossed the boundaries of the time for women's intimacy.

Sor Juana Ines de la Cruz's writings indicate her intense feelings of solidarity with women and her passionate belief in women's rights. Her life story is one of transgression—that is, transgression against dominant beliefs, including those of the Church, even while, at the same time, she took one of the few paths that enabled her to pursue her intellectual passions.

Thinking Further: In what ways does knowing about Sor Juana's life make you think differently about the life of contemporary nuns? Often derided as harsh, stolid, and mean, nuns play an important role both within the church and in the community—indeed, providing global social services. How might nuns view the tension between religion as a source of freedom and religion as a source of oppression for women?

Sources: Based on Kirk, Pamela. 1998. *Sor Juana Ines de la Cruz: Religion, Art and Feminism*. New York: Continuum Press; Mirrim, Stephanie. 1999. *Feminist Perspectives on Sor Juana Ines de la Cruz*. Detroit, MI: Wayne State University Press; www.biography.com.

world (Gallagher 2003; Hoffman 1997; Petersen and Donnenwerth 1998; Gallagher and Smith 1999). Nonetheless, fundamentalist religious groups have politically taken the position that the family should be morally autonomous. Therefore, the dominant political agenda of the religious right is one opposed to abortion and sex education and supportive of school prayer (Bendroth 1999). In sum, religion has a strong influence on the political climate within which gender relations are being negotiated.

For feminist scholars, one of the beginning points of the analysis of religion is the fact that, as measured by a variety of indicators, women are more religious than men in U.S. society. Women are more likely to attend church than men and to attend on a regular basis. Women express higher degrees of religiosity, but, as feminists have pointed out, despite the fact that women outnumber men in religious faith and in attendance at worship services, it is men, regardless of religious denomination, who usually maintain religious authority. In Christian churches, men, for the most part, are the priests and clergy, and they are typically backed up in the institution by men as deacons, elders, and vestry of the church. Orthodox Jews and Roman Catholics still deny ordination to women, and, although their numbers are growing, women are a numerical minority in seminaries of all faiths.

These patterns of gender inequality in religious institutions have raised the question of the extent to which religious traditions contribute to the subjugation of women. Religion is clearly one of the foremost forces in society to preserve traditions, conserve established social order, stabilize worldviews, and transmit values through generations, but religion is equally important in social transformation. Religious beliefs can and do frame new sources of human potential and possibility, and organized religious groups can release enormous bursts of political energy. This is well demonstrated in the history of the civil rights movement, with its organizational center in African American churches. The civil rights movement demonstrates that religious institutions can provide liberation movements with the leadership, organizational structure, and values that provide both the support network for social movements and the visions for new futures that such movements need.

RELIGION AND SOCIAL CONTROL

Religion is one of the forces that hold society together. Although it is also a source of conflict, both within and between different groups and societies, religion is an integrative force in that it shapes collective belief and therefore collective identity. Religious rituals—such as weddings, christenings, and bar and bat mitzvahs—promote group solidarity and symbolize group cohesion. Promoting identification with a religious group gives members a feeling of belonging; at the same time, it promotes feelings of exclusionary or outsider status to those outside of the group. Jewish or Muslim people living in a predominantly Christian society therefore feel estranged from the dominant culture; yet, their religious faith creates their own collective sense of group identity.

Because religion is such a powerful source of collective identity, it also is a form of social control. Religious sanctions, whether formal or informal, chastise those who violate religious norms. Religious beliefs, if internalized (i.e., learned and developed as part of one's self-concept and moral development), direct individual and group beliefs and behaviors. In this way, religion controls the development of self and group identity. At the societal level, religion also can be a form of social control. In the extreme, groups who deviate from religious proscriptions may be tortured, executed, or excommunicated; in more subtle ways, religious deviants may be ridiculed, shunned, or ostracized.

In the history of Western religion, the persecution of witches is a good illustration of the connections between religion, social control, and gender. During the Middle Ages in western Europe, it is estimated that between 30,000 and 9,000,000 women were killed or tortured as witches (Daly 1978). The breadth of this estimate indicates how difficult it is to pinpoint the number of witch persecutions. Toward the end of the seventeenth century in the United States, another 20 persons (7 of whom were men) were tried and executed as witches. Although the scope of this experience hardly matches that of the witch craze that swept Europe during the period of the Inquisition, the sociological impetus was the same. In both places, witches were believed to be women influenced by the devil, and they were perceived to be threats to social purity.

In western Europe, the *Malleus Maleficarum,* issued by the Catholic Church in 1484, defined the church's position on witches. This document defined witchcraft, described the alleged practices of witches, and standardized trial procedures and sentencing for those persecuted as witches throughout Europe. The *Malleus Maleficarum* defined witchcraft as stemming from women's carnal lust; women were seen as instruments of Satan because of their insatiable desire. According to the *Malleus Maleficarum,* "All witchcraft comes from carnal lust, which is in women insatiable." Quoting Proverbs XXX: "There are three things that are never satisfied, yea, a fourth thing which says not, it is enough; that is, the mouth of the womb" (*Malleus Maleficarum,* cited in Dworkin 1974: 133). People believed that witches collected male organs for use in satanic rituals and stole semen from sleeping men. They were also believed to cast spells over male organs so that the organs disappeared entirely!

Who were these women, and what was happening in history that there was such organized madness to eradicate them? Historians explain the witch hunts as stemming from the historical movement of the Catholic and Protestant Churches to establish themselves as supreme authorities over sacred and secular matters. The period of the witch hunts in western Europe was a period of the solidification of church authority. Women who were singled out as witches were women who deviated from the religious norms of the time; they were healers, wise women, and midwives. Those who formed witch cults were women who had a strong sense of people as a part of nature and who, because of this belief, gave animals a prime place in some of their rituals. Such a belief system, with its integrated view of human life and nature, was anathema to the patriarchal and hierarchical structure of the church. As feminists have argued, because the church was the ultimate representation of male power, witchcraft also symbolized men's fears of female sexuality, its assumed relationship to nature, and its unbounded expression. Feminists describe the witch hunts as a means of men's desire to control women's sexuality (Daly 1978; Dworkin 1974). Women defined as witches also were often widows and spinsters—in other words, single women who were living independently of men (Anderson and Gordon 1978; Szasz 1970). In sum, the witch hunts were a mechanism for ensuring the social control of women (and those who supported them), as represented in the emerging hegemony of organized patriarchal religion.

The persecution of women as witches is a historical case of the imposition of serious sanctions against women who lived outside the developing control of patriarchal religious bodies and outside the control of men. Their persecution was the persecution of sexual and religious deviants (Szasz 1970). Although, in retrospect, the treatment of women as witches may seem like an extreme case of religious persecution, there are contemporary equivalents. The treatment of women under Taliban rule in Afghanistan from 1996 to 2001 also illustrates the extreme to which some fundamentalist interpretations of religious belief can be taken. Under Taliban rule, women were banished from schools and workplaces, forbidden to leave their homes without a male relative escorting them, and could be beaten or stoned for the slightest infraction of Taliban rules. Sociologists who have analyzed the political, social, and economic subordination of Muslim women often see this as stemming from interpretations of Islamic theology to require the restriction of female sexuality (Mernissi 1987). But one can also interpret Islamic theology to support more liberal views about women, as well. Muslim men are more conservative in their views about women than are women themselves, and how the text of the Koran is interpreted has varied both over time in different contexts (Khalid and Frieze 2004; Sechzer 2004). The point is that in all religions, religious texts are interpreted. More fundamentalist interpretations tend to subordinate women, while different readings can support greater freedom for women.

RELIGION AND THE EMERGENCE OF FEMINISM IN THE UNITED STATES

Discussion of religion as a form of social control may create an impression that religion is a negative force only in women's lives. Religion, however, is also a source of resistance to oppression. This duality is well illustrated by the history of feminism in the United States.

In the United States, the power of the Protestant and Catholic faiths was well established during the colonial period, and, although women outnumbered men in the churches, the church hierarchy was exclusively male (Cott 1977). Not until the nineteenth century in the United States do historians typically see the beginnings of significant social change in women's religious roles and the seeds of developing feminism. Two particular developments in the nineteenth century in the United States have major significance for the role of women in religion and the development of the feminist movement: the evangelical spirit of the

Second Great Awakening and the widespread belief in the cult of womanhood that defined and restricted women's world to the world of domesticity (Hargrove et al. 1985).

The **Second Great Awakening** was a social movement in the early nineteenth century that emphasized a revivalist and egalitarian spirit in religion. During this period, ministers and laypersons began to see religion as a route to salvation on earth, and they used this belief to teach the restraints they believed were necessary for an orderly society. Occurring in the aftermath of the French Revolution and in the midst of worries about the destructive influence of growing urban populations and Catholic immigration, the Second Great Awakening had a democratic impulse—reaching out to the urban poor and western frontier residents. The Second Great Awakening created a lay missionary spirit in which conversion and religious benevolence were seen as the solution to the social ills generated by widespread social transformations affecting the fabric of American society (Cott 1977).

During this period, Christianity was softened (or "feminized"); rather than stressing dogma, it instead exalted meekness. Christians also began to reinterpret Christ as embodying these more gender-typed images of love, forgiveness, and humility. The "feminization" of American culture and religion meant that, among other things, by the middle of the nineteenth century, women were the majority in American religion (Douglas 1977; Welter 1976). During this time, women were defined as the keepers of the private refuge of the home—the place where piety and religious spirit were to prosper. In this domestic refuge, women's purity and piety were regarded as vehicles for redemption; women were seen in opposition to the aggressiveness and competition of the public sphere that was identified with men. Although these images exalted the traditional status of women, many have suggested that they also provided women with positive roles and images—at least ones that did not degrade and denigrate women's culture. The exaltation of women's culture encouraged women to speak in prayer meetings and congregations and to participate in voluntary religious associations.

Women's religious societies were especially successful at fundraising, and these societies became the basis for a developing sense of sisterhood among women. Local missionary activities trained women for what was defined as a life of social usefulness, teaching them hygiene, citizenship, family values, and social relationships, and engaging them in fieldwork in the cities. As a consequence, women's religious activities engaged women in other social reform movements.

During the nineteenth century, women—White women, at least—were considered to be more spiritual and more naturally prone to religious observance and piety than were men. The belief that women were naturally good also influenced the development of the feminist movement in this period. Women's alleged moral superiority was perceived to have a potentially benevolent impact on the more callous and harsh realities of the public world. Some feminists argued that extending the values of the domestic or private sphere to the public would create a more compassionate public world—a theme now resounded among some contemporary feminists, as well (Miller 1977). Throughout the nineteenth-century women's movement, religious faith played an important part in articulating feminist concerns. Women in the Women's Christian Temperance Union, one of the first feminist organizations, extolled the virtues of women and blamed the impersonal and competitive culture of the male public world for a variety of social ills.

Belief in the virtues of women's culture led early feminists to use the values of the home as the basis for crusading in the public world and for demanding women's rights. At the same time, as the suffrage movement developed, men (and some women) also used arguments from the Bible against women's suffrage and other changes in women's status. They maintained that scripture ordered a different and higher sphere of life apart from public life and that this "higher" sphere was the responsibility and, in fact, nature of women. As a result, many feminists eventually gave up on the traditional churches and turned to experimental religious societies, such as the Quakers, for more inner-directed spiritual experiences.

For most early feminists in the United States, religious faith was a significant part of their feminist ideology. Elizabeth Cady Stanton was herself relatively alone in seeing the domination of women as having religious roots. By the late nineteenth century, when Stanton first published *The Woman's Bible,* the influence of Darwin's thought was also paramount in U.S. culture. Stanton had likely been influenced by the more relativistic view of culture that Darwin's work inspired. His work encouraged the development of anthropological relativism—a system of thought that saw ideas in society as emerging from culture. Such a belief made it possible to doubt that the Bible had been divinely inspired. Although Stanton seemed to be influenced by this developing social consciousness, other feminists of the period did not share her perspective.

The first publication of *The Woman's Bible* in 1895 (reprinted in 1898) reflected Stanton's belief that domination of women had deep ideological and religious roots. Other feminists, however, did not share her sense of its importance. Members of the National American Women Suffrage Association, with the exception of Susan B. Anthony and a few others repudiated any connection with this view (Hole and Levine 1971). Afterwards, *The Woman's Bible* went into obscurity, not to be rediscovered until the 1970s during the second wave of feminism in the United States.

Historians of religion have since asked why Christianity was a basis for women's progressive movements in the nineteenth century when, in the twentieth century, Christianity is more often perceived as an enemy to feminists than a friend (Reuther and Keller 1986). The answer lies in observing the social transformations occurring in the nineteenth century. Throughout the nineteenth century, the process of industrialization meant that men had entered a new secular world. Even when women worked in the industrial sector, the cultural ideology of the time defined women's world as being in the home. Religion was defined as a part of women's culture, although, for women, religion was one of the few dimensions of public culture in which they were allowed to participate.

By the early twentieth century, White women's winning of the vote coincided with shifts in the boundaries between religious and secular domains. White women in the twentieth century entered the public world with men. Feminist social reformers of the 1920s and 1930s were more likely to use the language and philosophy of social science than they were to use theology to articulate their concerns. In the twentieth century, religion for women, if they believed it at all, had become more a private culture. At the same time, secularization resulted in the increasing conservatism of churches on women's issues. Churches, particularly Evangelical and Catholic churches, perceived secularism as having a pernicious influence on society. As a result, the churches politicized religious culture by using religious doctrine as a platform against women's equality—including their social, legal, and reproductive rights.

By the time of the emergence of the second wave of feminism in the 1970s, women's religious roles had changed dramatically. Although many feminists were still active in religious life, their critical distance from religious institutions and their understanding of religion's sexist roots created a new basis for feminist criticism of religion and a new basis for feminist transformation of religious thought.

WOMEN AND RELIGIOSITY

Images of Women in Religion

Feminists have contended that the traditional view of women in most religious faiths idealizes and humiliates women (Daly 1978). Images of women in religious texts reflect and create stereotypical gender roles and legitimate social inequality between men and women. The New Testament of the Bible, for example, urges women to be subordinate to husbands, thereby fulfilling the assumed proper hierarchy of women as subordinate to men as men are subordinate to God. Jewish feminists have also repudiated the traditional Jewish morning prayer in which a man blesses God for not creating him as a woman, while a woman blesses God for creating her in accordance with His will.

The humiliation of women through religious texts is especially clear in religious depictions of female sexuality, defined by both Christianity and Judaism as a dangerous force to be feared, purified, and controlled by men. In Orthodox Judaism, the myth that women are unclean during menstruation and seven days thereafter also reflects a negative view of female sexuality. Feminists see **misogyny**, meaning the hatred of women, depicted in the creation stories in male-dominated cultures that assign women responsibility for evil. In most of these legends women are seen as sexually alluring, curious, gullible, and insatiable. The biblical story of Adam and Eve is, of course, the classic example. Eve is depicted as cajoling Adam into eating the apple, thereby dooming them to live in a world of trouble and evil. Hebrew myth depicts Lilith, the first woman, as equal to Adam in all ways, but she refused to do what he wanted her to do. As this myth goes, in response to Adam's demands, the Lord created Eve from Adam's rib and made her inferior and dependent. One version of this legend in Hebrew tradition is that it was Lilith who persuaded Eve to eat the apple from the Tree of Knowledge. Feminists suggest that this creates dual stereotypes of woman—one as evil, the other as gullible. Either way, women are defined through these myths as bad (McGuire 2008).

Religious Texts as Interpretive Documents

Whether a group of religious believers accepts their religious tradition as literally true and divinely ordained by God or whether the group sees their religious text as subject to interpretation influences the group's acceptance of transformed religious roles for women. All religious texts, including the Bible, the Koran, and the Torah, are cultural and historical documents. That is to say, these texts are cultural artifacts—records of particular cultural beliefs, historical practices, and societal legends. The legends and beliefs that the texts communicate are the basis for what Durkheim called the **collective consciousness** of a society—the system of beliefs in a society that create a sense of belonging to the community and the moral obligation to live up to the society's demands. Thus, these texts are neither true nor false, but symbols, powerful as they may be, of group belief and collective consciousness. Consequently, they are subject to interpretation and symbolic use by religious groups and adherents.

Seeing the Bible as a document to be interpreted, not just the literal word of God, is probably the most contentious point between analysts of religion and those with strong and traditional commitments to religious worldviews. The use of Christianity to justify slavery shows, however, how Christianity and the Bible have been interpreted to support human oppression. European explorers who traveled to African cultures in the sixteenth century encountered societies having religious practices and beliefs quite unlike the Christian traditions of western Europe. Their response to such practices was to define African people as heathens and savages who worshipped pagan gods (Jordan 1968). Europeans' identification of Africans as heathens led them to believe that Black women and men were lustful, passionate, and sexually aggressive; this became the basis for racial and sexual stereotypes of Black men and women. White beliefs in Black men's sexual prowess created fears among White men that were the basis for extreme measures of social control—including lynching—throughout U.S. history. The identification of Black women as lustful also established White men's belief in their rights to sexual relations with Black women.

Christian beliefs played a central role in legitimating the exploitative treatment of African people. Slave traders and owners believed that Africans needed Christian salvation. Slaveowners saw their exploitation of slaves as the justifiable and necessary conversion of heathens, even going so far as to think that the slaves could not take care of themselves. Slaveowners reasoned it was their Christian duty, although a burden, to care for the slaves (Genovese 1972).

Although Christianity was a tool of the oppressing class, used to justify and legitimate the economic and cultural exploitation of millions of African American slaves, it also reinforced slaves' own belief in their rights as human beings. As a result, Christianity provided the basis for slaves' political resistance to exploitation. The slaves came to believe in the Christian values that slaveowners taught them, and therefore continued to believe in their own humanity and their rights to social justice. So, while Christianity was interpreted by slaveowners to justify slavery, Christianity was a source of salvation for the slaves. Understanding the relationship between Christianity, slavery, and emancipation also helps us understand why feminists who reject the misogynist traditions of religious beliefs and institutions sometimes see Christianity as providing the theological and philosophical basis for advocating women's liberation.

In other contexts as well, including in religiously devout communities, religion can support the liberation of women. As one example, in a study of Muslim women in the United States, Jamillah Karim shows how African American Muslim women and Southeast Asian Muslim immigrant women create a common sense of sisterhood via their shared religious identities. Even though they are typically pitted against each other because Southeast Asians are stereotypically upheld as the "model minority," the women in Karim's study created bonds of sisterhood based in their common religious experience (Karim 2008). This example shows how women can transform traditional theologies to promote liberation.

Gender and Religious Beliefs

As we have already seen, studies show that women are more religious than men, both in expressed religious faith and in women's participation in worship services (see Figures 8.1 and 8.2). This difference has persisted over time, despite the fact that church attendance has declined in U.S. society. Women are more likely than men to say they are religious (Carroll 2004; see Figure 8.3).

In the United States, 63 percent of the population report that they are members of a church or synagogue, although considerably fewer (40 percent) say they attend church weekly (Gallup Poll 2007). Because in polls more people report church membership than the churches themselves report to data-gathering agencies, poll data are not totally reliable. Nonetheless, the poll data indicate the public importance people attribute to religious affiliation, and polls are a sound measure of where people place their religious identification.

Despite the historical decline in religious faith and attendance at worship services, religion still plays a significant role in U.S. society. Religious belief influences a

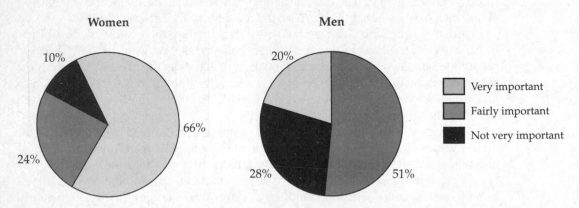

Question: How important would you say religion is in your life?

FIGURE 8.1   The Significance of Religion

Source: Data from Newport Frank and Lydia Saad. 2006. "Religion Most Important to Blacks, Women and Older Americans." *The Gallup Poll.* Princeton, NJ: Gallup Organization.

Question: How often do you attend church or synagogue — at least once a week, almost every week, about once a month, seldom, or never?

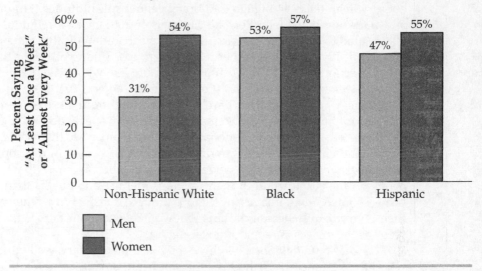

FIGURE 8.2 **Frequent Church Attendance: Men vs. Women**

Source: Data from Albert L. Winseman. 2004. "U.S. Churches Looking for a Few White Men." Princeton, NJ: The Gallup Organization. www.gallup.com.

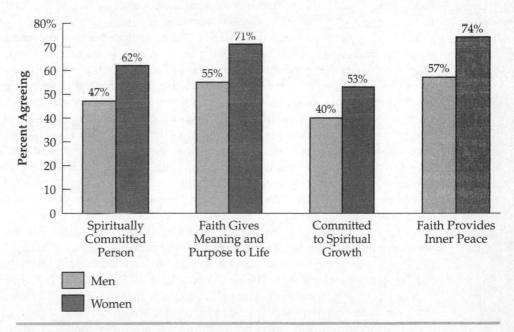

FIGURE 8.3 **Religion and Spirituality: Does Gender Matter?**

Source: Data from Albert L. Winseman. 2004.. "U.S. Churches Looking for a Few White Men." Princeton, NJ: The Gallup Organization. www.gallup.com

wide array of other social attitudes and behaviors. As previously discussed, this is especially evident on matters involving sexual attitudes and behaviors. Religious conservatism tends to engage traditional gender role attitudes (Hunt 2001; Ellison and Bartkowski 2002; Becker and Hofmeister 2001). One's religious affiliation is also related to one's politics, with those of Jewish faith typically being more socially and politically liberal than other religious groups. Studies also find that, at least in recent elections, American Muslims were more likely than the public in general to support Democratic candidates (Pew Research Center 2007).

Women's understandings of religion may differ from those of men, and women may adopt those aspects of religious belief that speak best to their situations (McGuire 2008). It is also questionable whether women see themselves as their religion sees them. Although the traditional image of women in religious texts is one that views women as more passive, docile, and pious, women may be more active agents in the construction of their religious identity and beliefs than has typically been assumed. Sexist images in religious thought remain, but women adapt them to their own circumstances, indicating that women's religious faith is not as passive or meek as the images in religious texts suggest.

This has been demonstrated in a study of contemporary, well-educated women who have returned to Orthodox Judaism. Lynn Davidman, a feminist sociologist, wondered how women who have the modern options of a career would turn to a traditional religious faith, one that professes very traditional roles for women. Such a conversion seems contrary to societal movement toward women's greater independence and new gender roles—transformations one would especially expect to see among well-educated women. Davidman found, however, that joining an orthodox religious community where women retreated from the public world was one way her respondents avoided the difficulties faced by other women who have to balance the competing definitions of womanhood generated by dual and competing roles for women in the family and at work. For the women she studied, religious orthodoxy provided meaning and a sense of self that was less fragmented than more modern and evolving definitions for career women. Davidman (1991) is careful to point out that the construction of women's identities, including their religious identities, is an active and conscious decision the women make. This perspective sees women not as mere victims of religious and gender roles but as active agents in the construction of their own identities and religious worldviews.

In recent years, there has been a dramatic resurgence of traditional evangelical Christianity. Evangelicals, popularly known as "born-again Christians," are those who claim to have been born again through conversion, who accept Jesus as a personal savior, who believe the scriptures are the authority for all doctrine, who feel urgency in spreading their faith, and who claim to have had a dramatic witnessing of the presence of a divine spirit (Flowers 1984; Pohli 1983). They also hold highly traditional views of womanhood. Forty-three percent of the U.S. population identifies themselves as "born again." The resurgence of this movement has created a consequent rise in the political power of this group. More women than men identify themselves as evangelical Christians (Gallup Poll 2007; Winseman 2004). Studies also find that among both young men and women a positive attitude toward Christianity is associated with belief in more traditional gender roles (Francis and Wilcox 1998).

MEDIA MATTERS

Muslim Women after September 11

It has been estimated that three to five million Muslims currently live in the United States. After the September 11, 2001, terrorist attacks, it became increasingly dangerous to be Muslim in America. This was particularly true for Muslim women who wear *hijab* or headscarves (also referred to as "covering"). Wearing hijab easily identifies women as Muslim and thus makes them easy targets for religiously motivated hate violence. What does covering mean to Muslim women and how did the media affect their decisions to cover in the aftermath of September 11?

Two months following the September 11 attacks, Hoda Badr interviewed 67 Muslim women who resided in or near Houston, Texas. Badr's sample was relatively well educated, ranging in age from 18 to 63 years. Thirty-five percent worked either full or part time; 74 percent were married with an average of two children. The sample was recruited from a well-established mosque in the Houston area. Immigrant Muslims made up 45 percent of the sample, and the remaining 55 percent were American Muslims. Some 50 percent of immigrant Muslims and 70 percent of American Muslims wore hijab.

Badr found that an overwhelming majority of her sample (92 percent) admitted to being afraid of a backlash as an immediate response to the September 11 attacks. Sixty percent of the immigrant Muslim women were hesitant to go to the mosque for weeks or months following September 11. In contrast, 57 percent of American Muslim women reported that they attended mosque services more frequently after September 11. American Muslim respondents explained that going to mosque meant more to them than just having a place to pray. The mosque was essential to their identity as Muslims.

When asked about their perceptions of Muslims in the media, 69 percent mentioned the negative portrayal of Muslim women—particularly the wearing of hijab. Badr found that 85 percent of the women who wore hijab were fearful to go out in public after September 11; however, only four women (all of whom were Muslim immigrants) reported removing their hijab. The majority of Muslim immigrant women reported wearing hijab for either cultural purposes or because they believed it was a commandment from God. Interestingly, three American Muslim women reported that they had decided to start wearing hijab after September 11. In addition to believing that covering was a commandment from God, for American Muslim women, wearing hijab was a way for them to assert their Islamic identity in mainstream American society.

Badr recognizes that because a mosque served as her recruiting site, her sample may be biased toward more religiously minded, practicing Muslim women. Nonetheless, she concludes that the negative images of hijab in the media following September 11 may have strengthened its symbolic power—particularly for some American Muslim women.

Thinking Further: In France there has been a controversy over policies that do not allow Islamic school girls to wear their the hijab (head scarf) in school. This debate is a clash between different groups: those who think the head scarf is a symbol of the oppression of women, those who see it as a symbol of their religious identity, those who say it is a matter of religious freedom, and others who wear the veil because of their beliefs in what makes women respectable. If you were asked to implement a policy to ban or allow the hijab in your school, what would you do? Why?

Source: Based on Badr, Hoda. 2004. "Islamic Identity Re-Covered: Muslim Women After September 11th." *Culture and Religion* 5: 321–338; see also: Ahmed, Leila.1993. *Women and Gender in Islam: Historical Roots of a Modern Debate*. New Haven, CT: Yale University Press; Mernissi, Fatima, and Mary Jo Lakeland. 1992. *The Veil and the Male Elite: A Feminist Interpretation of Women's Rights in Islam*. New York: Perseus.

WOMEN'S STATUS IN RELIGIOUS INSTITUTIONS

Gender and Religious Participation

Measures of church attendance and identification alone do not fully reveal the extent of women's religious participation. Although women have been excluded from positions of religious leadership, nonetheless it is women who constitute the vast bulk of religious activity (Heyer-Gray 2000). Many of these activities are difficult to measure numerically, but observations of women's activities in religious organizations show that women run the church bake sales, dinners, and bazaars. Women also teach Sunday schools, babysit during religious services, visit the sick, join prayer circles, and arrange and staff religious social events. In fact, women have historically been those who raise funds for churches, temples, and mosques. Although Orthodox Judaism defines women's religious role as centered in the home, women in Reform temples participate fully in the life of the temple, and they engage in a wide array of volunteer religious, educational, and philanthropic activities (Hargrove et al. 1985).

These activities in different religious organizations make important social ties for women, but they also reflect a gender division of labor within religious institutions. In Protestant churches, women rarely preach, serve as trustees, control funds, or make decisions about the pastor, church, or church programs. In Roman Catholic churches, men have held all the positions of religious authority. This means that despite the greater participation and faith of Roman Catholic women, the organizational structure, beliefs, ritual expressions, and prescribed norms of the Catholic Church are patriarchal (McGuire 2008; Fisher 2006; Wallace 1992).

Within the African American community, as in other communities, it is the work of African American women that holds the church together. It is estimated that Black churches are 75 percent female. In the **sanctified church**—the term used to refer to Holiness and Pentecostal churches—women are 90 percent of the congregation. Women's activities are crucial to African American churches, and Gilkes (2000) contends that all African American churches have been influenced by the militancy of women in the sanctified church. Gilkes also points out that historically men have rarely matched the financial contributions of women in the sanctified church.

Gender segregation in religious institutions is also evident in various religious cults. These cults tend to be based on patriarchal authority systems in which women serve the men in exchange for the rewards of emotional gratification. The very intense nature of commitment in these nontraditional groups can lead to extremely repressive aspects.

Women provide much of the volunteer work in religious organizations, such as these women supporting the work of a Jewish community center.

Women usually have domestic obligations required as demonstration of their religious commitment, and they are often expected to engage in sexual relations with male cult leaders. Whereas male devotees have access to positions of power as a means of bonding and sustaining their group affiliation, love and devotion are seen as leading to spiritual fulfillment for women in these movements. Women in these cults are also often subjected to psychological, physical, and sexual abuse, as they are expected to be devoted to the religious leaders. Those who have studied women who leave such movements have found that after leaving, women tend to be depressed, spiritually confused, and alienated (Boeri 2002).

Despite the patriarchal structure of religious institutions, women develop organizational and leadership skills through their work in these institutions (Gilkes 2000). Although their contribution is often trivialized, there is a heavy dependence on women's labor in religious organizations; however, in most churches and temples, it seems that women are in the background. They play the support roles, but not the leadership roles. The Catholic Church, for example, relies heavily on the work of nuns in the church, the schools, and the community, but, until the mid-1960s when Vatican II modernized the role of nuns by allowing them to discard their habits and take on a more public role, nuns were cloistered and kept silent. Now they are among the active women within the church and are urging that women be ordained and given access to real power in the Catholic Church.

Women as Clergy

The restriction of women to support positions in the church and their exclusion from making policies has led women to organize for the ordination of women in all the major denominations. Women now constitute 15 percent of all clergy, an increase from the past, but still a small proportion, especially considering that women are 66 percent of all religious workers. Even in the Catholic Church, where women cannot be ordained, women serve as parish leaders in many places where there is no priest present (Wallace 1992; U.S. Department of Labor 2009).

The entry of women into the clergy is not entirely new, although its magnitude is certainly unprecedented. Throughout the nineteenth century, women were licensed as evangelists, and, beginning in the 1880s, African American women began to press for ordination in the mainline Protestant denominations. The African Methodist Episcopal Zion Church ordained women as early as 1884, and the African Methodist Episcopal Church began ordaining women in 1948, but Harvard Divinity School did not even open its doors to women until 1955.

Although African American women have played a central role in the church, they too have been excluded from many positions of authority and leadership, except in smaller congregations. Holiness and Pentecostal denominations account for the largest share of all clergywomen, where women are seen as spiritual and professional role models. Gilkes (2000) argues that there is a feminist infrastructure in the sanctified church that has its origins in women's racial uplift movements of the late nineteenth and early twentieth centuries. She shows that the collectivist orientation of these churches has emerged from the relationship of African American culture and its churches to the dominant culture. Rejecting the patriarchal organization of

Women clergy are becoming more common in many denominations. African American women have tended to hold more leadership roles in churches than is the case for other women.

major denominational churches, has, in turn, encouraged a cooperative model of gender relations and pluralistic political practices within the church. In this sense, these churches can provide a feminist model of institutional organization and practice for the larger society, but as other churches evolve into more traditional and bureaucratic organizations and away from more spiritual symbolic roles, the proportion of women in positions of clerical leadership decreases (Barfoot and Sheppard 1980).

More people now support having women in positions of religious leadership, with 75 percent of Lutherans, Methodists, Episcopalians, and Presbyterians supporting equality in church leadership. Half of Catholics now endorse this idea, but members of more conservative Christian denominations (e.g., Southern Baptists and Assemblies of God) are unlikely to support women's roles as leaders. Religious faiths that assign a more priestly role to leadership and define women as supporters, rather than as leaders, are least likely to support women as clergy (Hoffman 1997; Nason-Clark 1987; Jelen 1989). People are also more likely to endorse the idea of women's leadership in the church once they have experienced having a woman in this role. Women, young people, and those with more formal education are also most likely to support women's ordination (Dudley 1996). Generally, as the women's movement has changed the public perception of women's roles, resistance to women as clergy has declined over time (Chaves and Cavendish 1997). Because women are more liberal on critical issues facing religious organizations, such as abortion and the acceptance of gays and lesbians, an increase in women's leadership may well influence church positions on social issues (Finlay 1997).

Those who advocate women's greater leadership in religious institutions often do so by asserting that women will bring a more woman-centered approach to these leadership roles (Lummis and Nesbitt 2000). Studies of women ministers and rabbis find that women in these roles do tend to have a more collaborative style than men and that there are gender-specific approaches to women's leadership roles. Women ministers also tend to be more open to a wide variety of service-oriented roles, whereas male clergy are more likely to want a high-status clientele (Finlay 1996). How women specifically define their roles depends somewhat on their faith. Women rabbis, for example, are more likely to emphasize the secular aspects of their leadership (as teacher, counselor, and community leader), whereas women ministers emphasize the more spiritual components of their role (saying they are a "moral voice" and emphasizing that they have been "called" to the ministry). In either case, women believe they carry out their role differently from male colleagues, saying they are more engaging, less formal, more people oriented, and less concerned about power struggles (Lehman 1994; Wallace 1992; Simon et al. 1994).

FOCUS ON RESEARCH

Is There a (Stained) Glass Ceiling for Women Ministers?

Women are more involved in church, but greatly underrepresented in positions of church leadership. Why? In some cases, this is an official policy of church bodies, but other organizational characteristics, even in denominations that do not formally bar women from leadership, also operate.

Jimi Adams has addressed this question by utilizing a national survey of church congregations known as the National Congregations Study (NCS). In her research, she asked five major questions:

1. Do mainline denominations have more women in positions of leadership than conservative/evangelical congregations?
2. Do resource-poor congregations have more women in positions of leadership than those that are resource-rich?
3. Are there fewer women in positions of leadership in congregations that believe in the inerrancy (i.e., literal truth) of the Bible?
4. Do Black Protestant congregations have more women in leadership roles?
5. Are higher levels of conservatism associated with the likelihood of women in positions of leadership?

Adams found that mainline denominations do have more women in leadership positions than conservative/evangelical congregations; Black Protestant congregations are the most likely to have women in leadership. Resource-poor congregations also have more women in leadership positions. But the strongest predictor of women's leadership is the congregation's belief in the literal word of the Bible. One of Adams's unpredicted results is that rural and urban congregations are equally likely to have women in leadership—both more so than suburban congregations.

Adams interprets her results to argue that the organizational characteristics of the church create a glass ceiling for women in positions of church leadership. When church organizations actively promote beliefs that create barriers to women's leadership, the result is not surprising: Fewer women are in leadership roles. The implication is also clear: Promoting more women into such roles requires a strong commitment in belief and action on the part of religious organizations.

Source: Based on Adams, Jimi. 2007. "Stained Glass Makes the Ceiling Visible: Organizational Opposition to Women in Congregational Leadership." *Gender & Society* 21 (February): 80–105.

RELIGION AND SOCIAL JUSTICE

The role of religion in social change movements is a complex one. Many see religion as a force against progressive social change, but religion plays an important role in promoting, not just resisting, change. Especially now, with religion taking center stage in some of the world's most pressing conflicts, understanding the role of religion in promoting social justice is compelling and timely.

Race, Religion, and Civil Rights

For numerous racial and ethnic minority groups, religion is a strong basis for one's political identity. For Jewish women and men, religious and ethnic identities are fused as a public and political culture. For Native Americans, Latinos, and African Americans, religion is one way to affirm one's ethnic subculture while simultaneously creating a basis for political and social organizing. For African Americans, strong religious faith has buttressed and inspired activities for social justice. Muslim Americans are divided on questions of the role religion should play in political matters. Overall, they are less likely than Christians to believe that religious groups should express their views on politics and social issues; half (49 percent) say that mosques should stay out of political matters, compared to 54 percent of Christians who think churches should become politically involved (Pew Research Center 2007). These facts reveal the complex relationship between religion, race and ethnic identity, and politics.

Among Latinas, although the Catholic Church has been seen as an oppressive social force, it also plays a positive role in relationships with friends, family, and community. Religion sustains ties to family and friends in the face of more industrialized and bureaucratic public life, although among both Catholic and Protestant Latinas, the influence of religion varies by social class, with the working class more committed to religious beliefs than the professional class (Williams 1990). The influence of religion is not monolithic, however—as is popularly imagined. Urbanization, education, and other social influences shape how Latinos interpret the meaning of religion in the context of their lives. Seen in this way, the influence of religion is not always one of resistance to social change; indeed, in **liberation theology** throughout Latin America, religious belief has provided the foundation for movements for social change.

The role of religion among African Americans reveals a similarly complex relationship between religion, conservatism, and social justice movements. The role of African American churches is multidimensional and includes religious, as well as social and political, work. Because the central theme of Black theology is liberation (Flowers 1984), African American churches have been meeting places for political organizing and have been highly significant in the historical development of Black protest. The liberating function of the African American church is evidenced by the fact that African Americans define the education of both oppressed people and oppressors as central tasks of Christian missions. Black spirituals and sermons are full of protest symbolism. The musical ministries of African American women have advanced and institutionalized their forms of creative expression (Dodson and Gilkes 1986). There is, in fact, enormous cultural significance to African American church music; almost every popularly recognized indigenous musical style in the United States has antecedents in the oral tradition of African American worship services.

Despite the librating functions of the African American church, religion can serve as an "opiate" for social protest. In other words, sociologists use the term **religion as opiate** to describe the fact that religion can also suppress social protest by encouraging people to accept their social position (Marx 1967).

Within African American and other minority communities the church has historically provided a buffer against segregation, discrimination, and bigotry. African American churches provide for the release of emotion that cannot be expressed in the dominant White racist society (Blackwell 1991). Most recognize that the church is, along with the family, the most important institution in African American society. It is the one institution over which African Americans have their own control (Frazier 1964), and it is an important source of social cohesion. African American churches are often described as the organizational and expressive core of African American culture and community, where the church performs a variety of social and community functions (Gilkes 2000).

Religion and Antifeminism

As within racial justice movements, the feminist movement has a complex relationship to religion. Many people simply associate religion with antifeminism, but doing so overlooks not only the feminist movement that has emerged within various religious faiths but it also ignores the way some feminists interpret religious values as providing the basis for their feminism. Thus, a vast body of literature has emerged wherein feminists examine the relationship between their beliefs as feminists and the beliefs that emerge from their religious views.

A CLOSER LOOK AT MEN

Gender, Religion, and the "Ex-Gay" Movement

The "ex-gay" movement began in the 1970s and has subsequently sprouted into a large, worldwide movement, promoting the conversion of gay men to both straight and Christian identities. Now a vast network of organizations—both religious and political—the ex-gay movement promotes an active, antigay agenda based on the idea that gay men can "convert" and "heal" themselves. Having joined forces with the Christian Right, this movement claims that gay men can—and should—change. The movement argues that being gay results from "sin," not biology, and thus, gay men, should resist this "temptation."

In a study of the documents produced by this movement, researchers Christine Robinson and Sue Spivey find that gender ideologies are the primary way that movement adherents articulate the need for men to change. Movement leaders see faulty socialization and a "deficit of masculinity" as lying at the heart of gay men's behaviors. Mothers, in particular, get the blame for most of this problem, according to the ex-gay movement, supposedly because they are too close to their sons or too dominant in the family. Fathers, on the other hand, are said to be too passive, not controlling enough. To "cure" gay men, movement advocates have men "practice" masculinity by mimicking stereotypical masculine qualities, encouraging marriage and fatherhood and repressing any behaviors and attitudes that might be construed as feminine. As a consequence, the ex-gay movement attempts to reinstate a patriarchal gender order, assisted by the organization of the religious, Christian right.

The ex-gay movement is an example of a religious organization that mobilizes gender ideologies to consolidate and enforce men's power and the power of heterosexuality. Other religious movements and organizations support a more progressive agenda—one that embraces gays and lesbians and resists that notion that being gay is a sin. Within such organizations, gay members do not have to struggle to reconcile their religious, gender, and sexual identities.

Sources: Robinson, Christine M., and Sue E. Spivey. 2007. "The Politics of Masculinity and the Ex-Gay Movement." *Gender & Society* 21 (October): 650–675; Erzen, Tanya. 2006. *Straight to Jesus: Sexual and Christian Conversions in the Ex-Gay Movement*. Berkeley, CA: University of California Press; Wolkomir, Michelle. 2006. *Be Not Deceived: The Sacred and Sexual Struggles of Gay and Ex-Gay Christian Men*. New Brunswick, NJ: Rutgers University Press; Moon, Dawne. 2009. "Conservative Theology and Same-Sex Desire." *Contemporary Sociology* 38 (July): 305–308.

One compelling example comes from examining the beliefs of the Islamic faith—an issue particularly compelling in the context of the U.S. war in Afghanistan following terrorist attacks on the United States on September 11, 2001. The subsequent interest in Islamic traditions—including the treatment of women—though it had long been on feminists' agenda, has captured more public attention. Under the rule of the Taliban regime in Afghanistan—a regime that had taken control of the nation in 1996 following the Afghani war with the Soviet Union—women were forcibly excluded from all public participation, including schools, health-care facilities, work, and even public baths. Women were forced to stay inside their homes and, if seen in public, had to be accompanied by a male relative and fully covered in the now widely recognized *burqa*—a covering that completely concealed women except for a narrow mesh slit over their eyes. When the Taliban were overthrown by other Afghani groups, with the support of the United States, many women jubilantly removed the burqa and returned to public life. Others remained veiled, although not always so fully covered as by the burqa. Is the Islamic faith inherently antifeminist or can it support movements for women's liberation?

This is a complex question, not easily answered without careful study of Islamic theology. But, like other religions, Islam is subject to interpretation and can be compatible with both antifeminist and feminist values. For some, the veiling of women in Islam stems from beliefs about women's sexuality—that women's sexuality is so compelling that they must be covered or men will lose control. But this is interpreted differently among different Islamic groups. Indeed, the whole subject of feminism and Islamic belief is much debated within Islam, with many arguing that Islamic beliefs are fully consistent with the liberation of women and others taking a more fundamentalist view that Islam requires the subordination of women (Mernissi 1987; Mernissi and Lakeland 1992; Fernea 1998). In this regard, Islam is no different from other faiths, although its practice has been dominated by extremist and patriarchal groups in many contemporary nations. But Islam is not the only religion that has been used to justify the oppression of various groups, as a review of the role of Christianity in supporting slavery clearly shows. Extremism emerges within every religious tradition, just as feminism has grown within the diverse religions of the world (Ahmed 1993).

Feminism and the Religious Right in the United States

Within the United States, the rise of the **religious right**—the term used to refer to fundamentalist Christian groups that have politically mobilized on behalf of conservative causes—has generated a new period of religious activism. Conservative Christian groups have been strongly opposed to abortion rights, gay marriage, sex education in the schools, and other social changes. Many in the religious right see the church as the defender of public morality and perceive contemporary social changes associated with feminism and liberalism as threatening the values of family life and as violating the hierarchy of God to man to woman. Whether one believes in such an antifeminist doctrine, however, depends on the extent to which one sees the Bible as a literal document or as one subject to interpretation. The most conservative and antifeminist evangelicals are those who take a more literalist position—that is the Bible is not subject to interpretation. Evangelicals with a more interpretive perspective tend to give women a stronger voice in church leadership and are more willing to challenge patriarchal structures of authority (Riesebrodt and Chong 1999).

In one of the most comprehensive studies of evangelical beliefs about feminism, sociologist Sally Gallagher found that religiously conservative Protestants are not as antifeminist as their image suggests. She found that 10 percent actually identify as feminists and 10 percent identify as distinctly antifeminist, but most find feminism to be a mixed blessing. In her sample, evangelical women were appreciative of the greater opportunities for women that feminism has generated, although they also believed that other aspects of feminism were opposed to their values, especially around the issue of abortion. She also found that evangelical Christians were critical of feminism for what they perceived as excessive individualism—a charge that, though false, they perceive as antithetical to their more family-centered values. One of Gallagher's major conclusions is that there is diversity among evangelical Christians with regard to their beliefs about feminism (Gallagher 2003, 2004).

Regardless of the diverse beliefs found among those of deep religious faith, the religious right has been a politically effective force because of the strong organizational infrastructure it has established within Protestant and Catholic churches. Evangelical churches provide a massive communication network that has contributed to the mobilization of voters and has thus become a powerful source for conservative social changes. Although membership in Catholic or fundamentalist Protestant churches does not necessarily predict support for right-wing attitudes, there is a strong relationship between church attendance in these groups and conservative political attitudes.

One of the puzzling features of the religious and political right is that many of its activists are women. How can women be so numerous in a movement that seems opposed to women's interests? Studies show that women in the antifeminist movement tend to be White, middle-aged housewives (married or widowed), relatively new to politics, and focused usually on a single issue. But they are not monolithic in their beliefs. Some define their political activism in terms of gender roles, defending traditional roles in the family, which they see under siege by social changes that erode women's position. Others take the approach that individual lives should be free from government intrusion; their politics are not a defense of traditional gender arrangements per se, although many find themselves in coalition with socially conservative women (Klatch 1988).

The Abortion Debate: A Conflict of Worldviews

One of the most active programs of the religious right has been its organized opposition to abortion rights for women. Spurred by the 1973 Supreme Court case *Roe* v. *Wade* (see Chapter 7), many women who previously had not been politically active were prompted into antiabortion activism. Studies of women active in the prolife movement have found that they tend to be women who are married, with children, generally not employed, and with high school and sometimes some college education. The most thorough study of the abortion movement has come from sociologist Kristin Luker (1984), who analyzed the debate over abortion as a matter of conflicting worldviews—not just views on abortion, but fundamental differences in the gender location of different groups of women.

Luker based her study on two groups: those identified as prochoice and those identified as prolife. The prolife women were antiabortion activists who tended to believe that giving women control over their fertility (through abortion or birth control) breaks up the traditional relationships in families that have women caring for the home and children and men being responsible for the family's income. Prochoice women, on the other hand, saw women's control over reproduction as essential for them to have control over their lives. Prochoice women do not see reproduction as the primary purpose of sex; instead, they think of sex as a means of communication between partners and, if they think of it as sacred at all, it is because they see sex as a mystical experience that breaks down the boundaries between self and other. Women in the antiabortion movement, on the other hand, tended to see sex in more sacred terms, and they believed that the widespread availability of contraception encourages teens to have sex.

In Luker's research, prochoice and antiabortion activists also differed in their social characteristics. Generally speaking, prochoice activists are better educated and more likely to be single than are those organized against abortion. Prochoice activists are likely to be employed with incomes of their own; if married, their husbands also usually have above-average incomes. Those active in the prolife movement were less likely to be employed and generally had lower family incomes than prochoice women. Luker found that the most dramatic difference between these two groups is in the role religion played in their lives, a fact supported by other research (Himmelstein 1986). Three-quarters of the prochoice people in Luker's study said that formal religion is either unimportant or completely irrelevant to them. In contrast, over two-thirds (69 percent) of those opposed to abortion stated that religion is important in their lives.

Luker interprets what she found as a struggle over very basic values—not just about abortion, but about religion, motherhood, and the direction of contemporary social changes. Those active in the antiabortion movement, she argued, tend to be concerned about a broad decline in religious commitment and a sense of common community. The struggle over abortion, in Luker's thinking, is also a struggle over the meaning of motherhood itself. She sees antiabortion activism as stemming from the status anxiety some women experience when social and economic changes in the society threaten their social and cultural status (Ehrenreich 1983; Luker 1984). Thus, antifeminism is not seen as just a function of socioeconomic variables like age, education, and class, but is explained by the fact that some groups see themselves as vulnerable to the very social, cultural, and economic changes that have also spawned feminism. Antifeminism, seen in this light, is then interpreted as the result of status anxieties that are produced for women who may interpret social changes as generating weakened commitments to family.

The majority of Americans support abortion rights, although some say only under some circumstances. Still, the political effort of antiabortion groups has led to more restrictions on and less availability of abortions.

Faith, Feminism, and Spirituality

The connection between feminism and religion is not always one of opposition. Many feminists have developed their feminist politics through their religious faith. Although critical of patriarchal religion and its subordination of women, feminists have also developed a feminist view within diverse religious traditions. This concluding section examines the work of feminist theologians and activists who are working to construct new forms of faith and spirituality that will also support the liberation of women.

At the heart of the feminist critique of religion is a deep-felt sense of injustice (Christ and Plaskow 1992). This is particularly evident in the personal accounts some feminist scholars have written of their experiences in divinity school. Judith Plaskow, a noted feminist theologian, describes the reaction of her thesis advisor at Yale Divinity School when she said she wanted to do her thesis on theology and women's experience. " 'Fine,' he told her—it was a good subject as long as she dropped all the references to women" (Christ and Plaskow 1992: i–ii). Both she and Carol Christ, another feminist theologian and scholar, were told by divinity faculty that the history of Christian attitudes toward women was not an important area for study (Christ and Plaskow 1992).

Theologians such as Christ and Plaskow nonetheless persisted in their studies of women and religion. The first feminist analyses of religion during feminism's second wave in the 1970s criticized the explicit statements of female inferiority found in religious texts, the subordination of women in the church, and the exclusion of women from ministry. Christian women, for example, rejected the biblical teaching that women must be subordinate to their husbands as indicated in, among other things, the passage in wedding ceremonies that women must obey their husbands. They also criticized the image of God as male and have developed new images for feminist worship. Feminists came to believe that the church and theology will transcend sexist ideologies only when women are granted full spiritual, theological, and ecclesiastical equality. They are not hesitant to acknowledge the interest-laden character of feminist theology, since they have openly declared the commitments out of which it emerges.

Beyond this reform position, however, is a deepening analysis of the **androcentrism,** or male-centered view, of traditional theological views. This developing analysis is one that is critical of the theological worldview of biblical faith and that sees sexism in religion as integrally tied to the dualistic and hierarchical mentality of traditional Christian theology (Reuther 1979). From this analytical perspective, feminist transformation of patriarchal religion will take more than eliminating or changing sexist images in religious thought and admitting women to positions of religious leadership. The more radical feminist critique suggests that the patriarchal models of patriarchal religions cannot be simply rehabilitated to include women. Instead, the radical perspective understands the exclusion and domination of women to be fundamental to the very nature of patriarchal systems of religious thinking. The radical view sees sexism as so deeply embedded in the theology of patriarchal religion that reforms alone could never create the postpatriarchal future that feminist theologians seek (Christ and Plaskow 1992).

Radical feminist theology sees the need for revolutionary changes in religious thought, practices, and organizations and refuses even to accept the possibility of the male messiahs of Christian tradition. Whereas many feminists believe that traditional religions can be reformed by identifying sexist language and symbols and giving women full status in places of worship, more radical feminist theologians say that women should simply discard patriarchal religious traditions and forge new visions of women's spirituality—ones that are distinctively based on women's experiences.

Several themes emerge from this radical theological stance: (1) patriarchal religions rest on and re-create the domination of women by men; (2) women, like nature, are degraded and seen as needing control; (3) patriarchal religion forms the basis for other patriarchal institutions; (4) patriarchal religion has emerged historically through the suppression of female power; and (5) spirituality based on women's experience is the only way of reclaiming a fully human faith and librating vision of the future.

Reuther (1979) early articulated the feminist view that Christian theology is centered on a domination model. She argues that traditional Christian theologies depict the soul and spirit as opposed to the human body—flesh, matter, and nature. This worldview sees human beings as standing between God and nature and teaches human beings that they must subdue the irrational desires of the flesh to spiritual life. This creates a model for domination—one that sees human life as dominated by God, just as some human lives are dominated by others; furthermore, because Christianity depicts the desires of the flesh as needing suppression, the domination model of Christianity has justified the historical domination of those seen by Christians as more carnal (including Jews, African Americans, and

Native Americans). Reuther contends that Christianity encourages a worldview characterized by dualisms—such as the ethnocentric "we/they" view of the world that sees one group as superior and all others as inferior and in need of salvation and civilization. As a result, the missionary spirit of Christianity feeds the historical development of racism and the development of imperialistic power by seeking to create a monolithic empire.

Similarly, Daly argues that the "widespread conception of the 'Supreme Being' as an entity distinct from this world, but controlling it according to plan and keeping human beings in a state of infantile subjection, has been a not too subtle mask of the divine patriarch" (1979: 56–57). Unmasking the patriarchal character of religious traditions causes us to see the powerful alliance between religion and oppressive social structures. Patriarchal theologies have in this way directly contributed to the oppression of women.

This more radical feminist critique of patriarchal religion leads to more fundamental changes in feminist visions of faith and spirituality—ones that are stimulated by asking what it would mean if women's experience were the basis for theological and religious worldviews. Experience is the key term in this developing feminist analysis. Feminist religious scholars take experience to mean the fabric of life as it is lived. In keeping with the feminist practice of consciousness raising and defining the personal as political, they believe there is something unique about women's experience and that women's faith and spirituality should be centered on those experiences (Saiving 1979).

This has also led such thinkers to distinguish between religion and spirituality. They claim that religion is that which is historically associated with established and institutionalized structures and ideologies, whereas spirituality suggests a vital, active, and energizing interior perception of the power of being (Yates 1983). This vision of spirituality is exemplified in Ntozake Shange's play, *for colored girls who have considered suicide/when the rainbow is enuf:* "i found god in myself/& i loved her/i loved her fiercely" (1975:63).

Because religion has such a deep hold on the human psyche, radical feminist theologians believe one cannot afford to leave religion in the hands of men. They see that men's control of religion emerged only with the suppression of female power and symbolism through the historical demise of goddess worship. They argue that there is nothing natural about patriarchal religion, pointing out that the introduction of male gods and messiahs occurs at specific historical points in the development of human experience and that before the introduction of male messiahs, goddess worship was a nearly universal phenomenon. The earliest artifacts of human culture, they suggest, are female statues and symbols, indicating the awe our ancestors felt for women and their bodily mysteries (Spretnak 1994).

The creation of new symbols, legends, myths, and rituals centered on women's experiences is central to new forms of feminist worship. Often, these rituals are explicitly linked to attempts by women to release anger and fear and to increase a sense of power and community. One study found that participation in such rituals helped women recover from sexual victimization and improved their mental health (Jacobs 1994). For contemporary women spiritualists, reclaiming the goddess has become symbolic of the affirmation of female power and the female body, the celebration of female will, and the recognition of women's bonds and heritage (Christ 1979). Positive attitudes about women's bodies are an essential dimension to this new feminist spirituality.

The positive value of female will is also expressed by newly celebrated practices such as women's spell-casting and witchcraft—forms of spirituality that have now come full circle from the persecution of women as witches to woman-centered forms of "new age" spirituality. The Wicca movement is a good example of some of new age and countercultural feminist movements. Founded in the 1950s by Englishman Gerald Gardner, a central concept in this movement is an ecological approach that links the health of the person to the health of the earth (Di Santo 2004). Based on ancient pagan rituals and other practices of witchcraft, those in the movement stress ancient belief systems and rituals. In such movements, spirituality and feminism often become merged as participants define spiritual healing as part of transforming their traditionally gendered identities (Foltz 2000). Some Wicca groups focus specifically on sexuality, blending pagan traditions with queer theory (Neitz 2000).

New religious movements, such as Wicca, often reclaim goddess imagery as a way of acknowledging female power as beneficent and independent. This is, of course, in radical contrast to the patriarchal perception of women's power as inferior and dangerous. The significance of the goddess for reevaluating women's bonds and heritage is that "as women struggle to create a new culture in which women's power, bodies, will, and bonds are celebrated, it seems natural that the Goddess would reemerge as symbol of the newfound beauty, strength, and power of women" (Christ 1979: 285).

In sum, the emphasis in radical **feminist theology** is not just to point out the androcentric bias of traditional religious worldviews, but to fundamentally change theology and religion to represent women's experiences in all its forms. The many attempts to re-create systems of faith to acknowledge the presence and power of women are indicative of the far-reaching attempts of feminist thinkers to create new visions and worldviews that will provide the foundations for building a feminist society.

▪ Chapter Summary and Themes

Religion can be interpreted as both a powerful source of subordination for women and a powerful instrument for feminist social change.

Although many think of religion as repressive to women, there are numerous historical and current examples of religious faith inspiring feminist movements. From a sociological perspective, religion provides powerful symbols and beliefs that shape people's worldviews.

Historically, the advent of patriarchal religion identified spiritual women as sexual and religious deviants.

Religion can be a system of social control, especially under conditions of intolerance and strongly patriarchal religious tenets. There are many historic examples of women resisting this form of religious oppression.

Images of women in religious texts tend to rely on stereotypical gender roles that subordinate women to men.

Women tend to be more religious than men, in both belief and practice, despite the fact that interpretations of most traditional religious texts relegate women to subordinate positions relative to men. On various measures of religiosity and religious participation, women are seen to be more religious than men. Religion is a gendered institution in that women, although providing the majority of religious work, have been denied equal access to positions of religious leadership.

Religious beliefs are linked both to antifeminist values and movements for social justice.

Religion can be a source of liberating social change, such as in how religion inspired the civil rights movement. At the same time, religion has also been a source of the antifeminist movement in the contemporary United States. This is despite the fact that many women within evangelical Christianity see themselves as having benefited from the feminist movement.

New feminist forms of religion and spirituality are trying to create new theologies based on more woman-centered worldviews.

Feminist theologians and laypeople have been interpreting religion in new ways that link spirituality and feminism. Some of these new theologies occur within mainstream churches, others in movements such as New Age spirituality, Wicca, and the like.

■ Key Terms

androcentrism	liberation theology	religious right
collective consciousness	misogyny	sanctified church
feminist theology	religion as opiate	Second Great Awakening

■ Discussion Questions/Projects for Thought

1. Talk with a group of people from different religious backgrounds (this could be a discussion group in class) and ask the men and women in the group what their religion taught them about women's roles. How did these ideas influence each person's self-concept?

2. Select a group of students who are opposed to abortion and another group who are prochoice. Interview people within each group; ask them about their religious beliefs and their attitudes toward women's roles. Do you find support for Luker's idea that those who are prochoice have less religious commitment and that those who are opposed to abortion are more traditional in their attitudes about women's roles?

3. Attend the religious services of a group with which you are unfamiliar. While there, observe who is in attendance and what they are doing and also observe the teachings of this religious group. What do your observations tell you about the role of women and men in this particular faith?

9

Women, Crime, and Deviance

When you think of women and crime, what comes to mind? Chances are you imagine a widely publicized trial where a husband is being tried for the murder of his wife. You might think of a high-profile case of rape or sexual assault, where the woman was vilified for her sexual past. Or perhaps you imagine a serial killer, such as those frequently depicted on crime shows, where numerous women are brutally murdered, their bodies discarded, but the crime is ultimately solved by clever and beautiful women scientists. You might have noticed that women are now highly visible as crime solvers or legal professionals on popular shows such as *CSI: Miami*, *Bones*, *Castle*, and even *Judge Judy*.

Media depictions provide one way of looking at the world of women, crime, and deviance, though seldom are the actual crimes against women given such a high profile. When women are victims of crime, it is usually not by a celebrity or serial killer, but by someone they are close to—a boyfriend, husband, or other known acquaintance. And, when women commit crime, it is usually an economic crime—selling drugs, passing bad checks, or petty theft.

This chapter examines the subject of women, crime, and deviance, using a perspective on gender and its relationship to race and class to understand not only the crime and deviance that women commit but also patterns of victimization. We begin with a basic review of the sociological framework that informs the analysis of gender and crime.

SOCIOLOGICAL PERSPECTIVES ON CRIME AND DEVIANCE

Do women commit less crime than men and, if so, why? Are there distinctive characteristics of women as deviants and criminals? How can we explain the high rates of violence against women in society? Why are men the vast majority of those who commit violent acts? These and other questions form the basis for the study of gender, crime, and deviance—a field that has been transformed through the development of feminist scholarship.

Individual men or women may commit crimes or engage in deviant behavior, but these behaviors are related to the status of women in society—and more broadly, to how the social structure of gender is related to patterns of crime and deviance in society.

The earliest studies of women's deviance reflected highly sexist assumptions about women and, for a long time, distorted what was known about women either as victims or perpetrators of crime. A brief review of this history shows how the assumptions made about gender at any given time in history can influence what is known, even within the social sciences.

Early Studies of Crime and Deviance

Early studies of women and deviance mostly depicted women's deviance as rooted in their biological and psychological predispositions. Cesare Lombroso's work in the 1920s, although now discredited, was one of the earliest studies of female crime. Lombroso believed that crime represented the survival of primitive traits. His theory was explicitly linked to popular racist and sexist notions of the time, and depicted crime as based on biological differences between women and men, White and Black Americans, and the "fit" and the "unfit" (Higham 1965). He explained female crime by arguing that women are less highly evolved than White men and thus are more susceptible to primitive urges. He also depicted women as substandard in their mental capacities and, in general, more passive and sedentary than men (Klein 1980). As he said, "Even the female criminal is monotonous and uniform compared with her male companion, just as in general woman is inferior to man" (Lombroso 1920: 122, cited in Klein 1980: 78).

In his early work, W. I. Thomas, like Lombroso, traced women's crime to biological differences between the sexes and to deep-seated psychological "wishes" of maternalism that he defined as unique to young girls. Thomas claimed that females are biologically "anabolic"—motionless and conservative—whereas males are "katabolic"—destructive of energy, yet creative because of the outward flow of this drive. Thomas's later work (*The Unadjusted Girl* 1923) contained an important sociological insight—that female delinquency is a normal response to certain social conditions. He still emphasized, however, that social behavior is a result of "primary wishes" that are derived from biological instincts. In Thomas's view, delinquents are driven to crime because they long for new experiences. Girls, in particular, he says, engage in deviance in order to manipulate others, and their maternal instincts lead them to crimes such as prostitution, in which he claims they are seeking love and tenderness (Klein 1980).

Although seemingly crude now, Thomas's work has left an important message for more recent sociological work. He attempted to find a behavioral basis for sex differences in delinquency, and he tried, even if unsuccessfully, to relate those differences to attitudes that we now see as reflecting gender socialization. Whether patterns of women's crime can be properly attributed to gender socialization is an important question that is explored further in this chapter.

Like Lombroso and Thomas, Otto Pollak (1950) traced women's deviance to their biological and psychological being. He claimed that the basis for female crime is women's passive role in sexual intercourse. According to Pollak, women are able to conceal their sexual arousal from men and, because of this physiological manipulation, women become socially deceitful. His major concern with women's crime was the "masked" character of female criminality. He argued that the real extent of female crime is hidden from the public's view. Women, according to Pollak, are the masterminds behind crime, manipulating men into committing offenses while they themselves remain immune from prosecution. In Pollak's view, men have been so duped by women that they protect women through chivalry and thus fear to charge and convict them for their crimes (Smart 1977).

Although the views of Lombroso, Thomas, and Pollak are quite outlandish now, some of the issues they raised continue to be addressed in current research and theory. Many continue to assert that biological differences between women and men explain differences in their criminal behavior. More contemporary analysts Wilson and Herrnstein (1985) have argued that sex differences in crime among men and women must be understood as a function of aggression, which they see as rooted in the hormonal constitution of the sexes. Although Wilson and Herrnstein admit that social and cultural arrangements may have some influence on the gender gap in crime, they believe that the biological differences between women and men explain more of the gap than social structure.

Wilson and Herrnstein's work has been soundly criticized by other scholars for its simplistic view of biology and culture as opposing systems, its misuse of scientific research, and its confusion of correlates (such as gender, race, and crime) with genetic cause (Kamin 1986). But the popularity of recurring arguments about the biological basis for criminal behavior cannot be ignored. Even feminists have been known to make such arguments. Consider the case of Andrea Yates, the woman who confessed to murdering her five children in Texas in 2001. Many attributed her crime to the postpartum depression she developed following the births of her fourth and fifth children. Although few excused her behavior, following her arrest and conviction, a public debate ensued that centered on the role depression played in her behavior. The debate was further sparked when NOW (National Organization for Women) attributed her crime to postpartum depression and established a legal defense fund for her. Although feminists did not argue that her depression was the result of innate sex differences, the association of postpartum depression with her crime conjures up biologically based arguments. Such reductionist arguments ignore the complex origins of various forms of behavior, including criminal and deviant behavior. The social context is critical in explaining human behavior.

Understanding deviance (of which crime is a part) is based on three primary points: (1) deviance is social behavior that departs from conventional social norms, (2) deviance involves a process of social labeling, and (3) deviance becomes recognized within the context of social institutions that reflect the power structure and gender, racial–ethnic, and class relations of society.

Defining Deviance

From a commonsense point of view, deviance is behavior that is bizarre, unconventional, and perhaps hard to understand. However, this definition is inadequate and misleading. First of all, what is unusual in one situation may be quite ordinary in another; second, even the most extraordinary behavior can often be understood if we know the context in which it occurs. **Deviance** is behavior that departs from conventional norms, noting that norms vary from one situation to another; consequently, deviance is located in a social context. Knowing and understanding this context is essential to understanding deviant behavior.

Although deviance is defined as behavior that departs from conventional norms, deviant behavior, like conventional behavior, is often guided by norms and rules, both formal and informal. In fact, the social norms of peer groups may encourage members to engage in deviant acts. One example comes from the research on "hogging"—the practice in which men prey on overweight or unattractive women to satisfy their competitive and sexual urges (Gailey and Prohaska 2006). For many of the men who engaged in "hogging," fitting into their peer group and impressing their friends were more important than conforming to the rules of society. According to Kimmel (1996), homosocial interaction plays a role in the achievement of masculinity. In peer groups, humiliating

Research finds that some situations, such as binge drinking, put women at greater risk of sexual violence. Scholars have identified "rape prone" environments as those characterized by strong masculinist norms and a definition of women as sexual prey.

or degrading women is a strategy men use to prove their manhood, and doing so often bonded them with other group members (Gailey and Prohaska 2006; Kimmel 1996).

Another commonsense definition of deviance is that it is behavior of which people disapprove. This idea, too, is inaccurate because deviance is subject to social definition, and whether it is approved or disapproved depends on who is doing the defining. Because deviance is situationally specific, it is sometimes difficult to distinguish deviant behavior from conventional behavior. In fact, there is probably more overlap between deviant and conventional behavior than one might think. Most people engage in deviant behavior, sometimes on a regular basis. Whether they become identified as deviant may be a function of their social standing (including their gender, race, and class), the context of their deviant acts, and their ability to maintain a conventional identity.

For example, many would consider that the enjoyment of pornography is deviant behavior. It offends many people's moral sensibilities (including that of some feminists, who see it as portraying women in a degrading and dehumanizing way). The easy availability of pornography, its widespread consumption, and its appearance in even the most respectable settings, however, make it seem that pornography is a normal feature of everyday life. Whether one is perceived as deviant for reading or watching pornography depends on one's social standing and the social context in which pornography is viewed. This fact is evident when we consider the deviant label attached to a frequenter of peep shows or pornography houses, in contrast to the socially legitimate label afforded to the young man who rents pornographic videos for his fraternity house. When we analyze pornography as an economic industry, we see that its social organization is very similar to (although perhaps more coercive than) that of other industries in which workers are exploited for profit and products are marketed by the use of women as sex objects.

Labeling and Social Deviance

This discussion brings us to the second major point about deviant behavior: Deviance involves a social labeling process (Becker 1963). One cannot be called deviant without being recognized as deviant, and sometimes people become labeled as deviant regardless of whether they have actually engaged in deviant behavior. Becoming deviant involves societal reactions to one's behavior—or alleged behavior. **Labeling theory** emphasizes that some groups with the power to label deviance exercise control over what and who is considered deviant. Police, courts, school authorities, and other agents of the state thus wield a great amount of power through their control of institutions. For example, social workers, psychiatrists, and other agents of the state who define a woman as mentally ill can have a drastic effect on her behavior, identity, and life options.

Labeling theory points out that in the absence of a deviant label, actual deviant behavior may have no consequences at all, but the process of being labeled as deviant may involve real changes in a person's self-image as well as one's public identity. Once people are labeled deviant, they are likely to become deviant. This new identity, however, usually does not emerge suddenly or as the result of a single act. Instead, it involves a process of transformation wherein people adapt their self-images and behavior to the new identity being acquired (Lemert 1972). You can see the influence of the labeling process in thinking about how gender constructs different definitions for women and men who engage in the same behavior. The sexual double standard is an example: Women who visibly have multiple sex partners are judged as deviants and "sluts"; men who do the same are praised for being "studs."

Deviance, Power, and Social Conflict

Labeling theory helps us see that deviance occurs in the context of social institutions. People in these institutions have the power to label some as deviant and others as not. This fact is especially true to the degree that the official agents of these institutions carry gender, race, and class stereotypes or biases that make them more likely to discover deviance in some groups than in others. These agents include the police, judges, lawyers, prison guards, and others who may enter the official process of labeling deviant behavior (e.g., psychologists, psychiatrists, counselors, social workers, and teachers). Because these official agents of social institutions have the power to label some groups and persons as deviant and others as not, and because these institutions reflect the power structure and the systems of race, class, and gender relations in the society, deviance tends to be a label that falls most frequently on less powerful people in the society. The labeling of deviant behavior can thus be seen as a form of social control.

Were deviance seen from the point of view of the deviant person, not those who label, a different view might emerge. Consider prostitution as an example.

HISTORY SPEAKS: YESTERDAY'S FEMINISTS TALK ABOUT TODAY

Ida B. Wells-Barnett and Lynching and The Myth of the Black Rapist

"One had better die fighting against injustice than die like a dog or a rat in a trap."

—Ida Wells Barnett

Ida B. Wells-Barnett (1862–1931) was born a slave and dedicated her life to the struggle for racial justice and women's rights. She learned to read and write at Shaw University (now Rust College), a school established for freed slaves. She later earned her teaching credentials at Fisk University in Nashville, Tennessee.

She was an early crusader for racial justice. Long before Rosa Parks refused to give up her seat on the segregated bus in Montgomery, Alabama, Ida B. Wells refused to move from her seat in the first-class "ladies" car on a train in Memphis, Tennessee, in 1883. At the time, Reconstruction laws that were passed after the Civil War forbade discrimination in public accommodations based on race. (Such laws were later rescinded by the *Plessy v. Ferguson* U.S. Supreme Court decision in 1896). Dressed in fine clothes and having paid for a first-class ticket, Ida B. Wells took her seat in the "whites only" ladies section, only to be removed by the conductor who insisted that she had to sit in the smoky, dirty "colored only" car. Wells filed suit against the railroad company. Not only did she win her case, but she wrote about the incident, thus establishing her career as a journalist.

This was only one of many confrontations that Ida Wells Barnett had with a system of gross racial injustice. After three of her friends were lynched for a crime that they did not commit, she began her long and vigorous campaign against lynching. She vehemently argued that lynching was a mechanism designed to keep free Black people in a subordinated place. The late nineteenth and early twentieth centuries were a time when racial tensions were extremely high, marked by periodic race riots and frequent lynchings—a period described as a "reign of terror."

In this context, Wells traveled throughout the United States, capturing the attention of the public with her passionate appeals for racial justice. She was often met with the very violence that she so abhorred and was frequently threatened, both in writing and in actual threats. Because of this, she often wrote under an assumed name.

Thinking Further: Ida Wells Barnett was one of the first to identify what Alice Walker later called "the myth of the Black rapist" (Davis 1981)—that is, the perception that Black men are a threat to white supremacy and are thus dangerously stereotyped and met with suspicion that turns into attempts to "contain" them. In Ida B. Wells's time, this took the form of lynching. What form would you say this perception takes in our times? Does it help explain the mass incarceration of Black and Hispanic men? If Ida Wells Barnett were with us today, how would she theorize about the connection between gender, race, class, and sexuality?

Sources: Giddings, Paula J. 2009. *Ida: A Sword among Lions.* New York: Amistad; Ida B. Wells Memorial Foundation; 2010. www.idabwells.org.

Prostitution has traditionally been described in terms of men's demands for sexuality and women's supply of this "service." Although this is an apt description of the economic nature of prostitution, it also makes ideological assumptions about both men's and women's sexuality. Women are depicted as merely providing an outlet for male sexual needs, and men are defined as having greater sexual urges than women. Casting prostitution instead in the context of work raises new questions and new insights, including that prostitution is part of a gender division of labor in a global network of work, colonization, and the commodification of women's bodies (Pyle and Ward 2003; West and Austin 2002; Min 2003). People estimate that the global economy of human trafficking, most of which involves sex workers, is a $5 billion to $7 billion industry—one that builds on the economic needs of women, especially in poor countries. Sex tourism, a central part of this trafficking, draws men from the wealthier nations to places such as Thailand, Amsterdam, and other locations where women, often very young girls, work to support themselves and, frequently, their families (Wonders and Michalowski 2001). Reframing prostitution in this way focuses less on treating individual deviance and more on seeing prostitution in terms of women's rights to a safe life (West 2000).

Feminist Perspectives on Deviance

Feminist perspectives have added new dimensions to the understanding of deviant behavior. Early studies of women's deviance typically rested on stereotypes about women's sexual behavior, and often used a double standard of morality, marking some behaviors as deviant in women that were not considered deviant when done by men, such as teenage promiscuity. Teen boys are expected, if not encouraged, to be aggressive in their sexual encounters and accumulate as many sexual "conquests" as possible; girls who do the same thing are labeled as "sluts," "whores," or "skanks."

Women's deviance is often attributed to individual maladjustment or a poor family background. It is true that some deviance (including sexual deviance) involves psychosexual adjustment, and traumatic experiences in one's life (such as childhood sexual abuse), may interfere with this adjustment. Such experiences may provoke a woman to engage in deviant behavior, but events in her biography (which are by no means true for all women deviants) are not always the sole or the primary cause of deviant behavior. Feminist scholars argue that women's deviance, including that of girls and young women, is the result of the social context in which they live (Cepeda and Valdez 2003). The social context of gender, race, and class relations—as well as age—shapes both the causes and consequences of women's deviant behavior. Increasingly, scholars are also showing how social norms of masculinity also shape the deviant behavior of men (Messerschmidt 2000). Whether studying violence against women, violence that women and men commit, or the treatment of women and men in the criminal justice system, gender has emerged as a significant factor.

As an example, we can look at a recent ethnographic study that examines how gender shapes African American girls' uses of inner-city violence. Nikki

Jones (2008) argues that "being a girl" does not protect inner-city girls from much of the violence previously believed to affect mostly inner-city boys and men. Inner-city environments are often governed by "the code of the street" (Anderson 1999)—a system of accountability that organizes social life in urban areas, particularly interpersonal violence. At the heart of this "code" is the battle for respect. For inner-city boys and men, respect and manhood are one in the same—young men are often willing to risk their lives to attain respect and be respected by others *as a man*. In contrast, the inner-city girls in Jones's study considered the use of physical violence as a means to an end—not as a defining characteristic of being a woman. For example, when asked about her fighting history, one of the girls, 13-year-old Takeya, explains to Jones that she is "a good girl," and that she'll also be "a pretty girl" when she turns 18 years old. Although Takeya is "committed" to "being a good girl," she confirms to Jones that she knows how to fight, and that she is aware that others recognize her as a more than capable fighter. From her interviews with Takeya and other inner-city girls, Jones concludes that girls' use of "physical aggression and violence is tempered—though not extinguished—by seemingly typical 'female' concerns: being a 'good' and 'pretty' girl" (2008: 76).

Studies of juvenile delinquency also reveal the importance of gender in shaping girls' behavior and the response of the justice system to their behavior (Heimer and DeCoster 1999). Girls are still more likely to be held in the juvenile justice system for relatively minor offenses, although boys are more likely to be arrested for juvenile crimes (Chesney-Lind 1999). Much of the literature on juvenile justice has situated girls' delinquent behavior in the context of the sexism and racism that they experience in their lives (Holsinger 2000).

Many studies of girls' and women's deviance have also shown the great extent of sexual abuse in the life histories of women who engage in various forms of deviance, including gang activity, prostitution, drugs, and other forms of deviant behavior. Numerous studies document a strong association between deviant and criminal behavior and patterns of sexual abuse (Chesney-Lind 1999; Walker-Barnes and Mason 2001; Dembo et al. 1998)—so much so that one cannot help but wonder if preventing sexual abuse by changing the social attitudes and structures that perpetuate abuse would be the most effective deterrent to deviant behavior (Goodkind et al. 2006).

Another major point of revision by feminist scholars of deviance has been in reconsidering what is considered deviant behavior. The deviant label often attached to lesbianism makes it appear that there is something perverted about loving persons of one's own sex. Instead of assuming that sexual preference is the result of individual maladjustment, being a lesbian can involve conscious resistance to conventional heterosexuality whereby women are defined as the adjuncts of men, and female sexuality is seen as passive acquiescence to male demands. Feminist scholarship has thus rejected the deviance framework as a way of understanding gay and lesbian experience. It is the heterosexist structure of institutions that defines lesbians as deviant. Challenging such assumptions has created new knowledge about how gays and lesbians negotiate the worlds in which they live (Nardi and Schneider 1997).

Feminist research has produced new insights for understanding how gender shapes deviance and how the institutions that manage deviance are themselves gendered. The remainder of this chapter reviews the knowledge we have now accrued about crime and the victimization of women.

WOMEN AS VICTIMS OF CRIME

Statistics indicate that, overall, women are less likely to be victimized by crime than are men, although rates of violent crime victimization for men and women are getting closer (Bureau of Justice Statistics 2010). The **National Crime Victimization Survey** (NCVS) is the primary source for national data on crime victimization rates. The NCVS collects information on nonfatal crimes, reported and *not reported* to the police, against persons age 12 years or older from a nationally representative sample of U.S. households. Data reported by the NCVS are not without flaws. One of the main methodological issues in measuring crime victimization is recall. The NCVS asks respondents to report crime victimization experiences occurring within the past six months. The length of the reference period may create the potential for respondents to underestimate or overestimate the number of crime victimizations they experienced. Additionally, some respondents may be unwilling to disclose their victimization experiences to researchers. Particularly in the case of rape, it is quite possible that, if a woman never reported it to the police, she is also unlikely to report it to a researcher.

Despite these methodological issues, we can characterize the victimization of women by crime. As you can see from Figure 9.1, White women, in general, are less likely to be victimized by robbery, purse snatching/pocket picking,

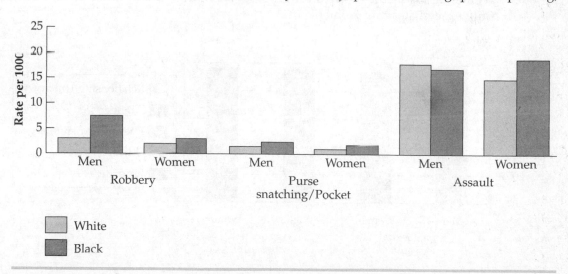

FIGURE 9.1   Crime Victimization (by gender and race)

Source: Bureau of Justice Statistics. 2010. *Criminal Victimization in the United States, 2007 – Statistical Tables.* Washington, DC: U.S. Department of Justice.

and assault; they have the lowest rates of victimization for these crimes compared to Black women and men overall. Black women are as likely to be victimized by robbery as White men, but are more likely to be victimized by assault than White and Black men.

Data from the NCVS show that almost two-thirds of all rapes and sexual assaults perpetrated against women are committed by someone they know—an intimate partner, a relative, or a friend or acquaintance (see Figure 9.2). The same data show that when men are raped or sexually assaulted, they too, are more likely to be victimized by a known assailant (a friend or acquaintance); however, men are much more likely to be raped or sexually assaulted by a stranger than women are. The same is true for aggravated assault: Almost 62 percent of women are victimized by known assailants compared to 41 percent of men (Bureau of Justice Statistics 2010). Additionally, when women are murdered, the odds are that they will be murdered by someone they know. In 2007, 10 percent of female murder victims were killed by a stranger compared to 29 percent of male murder victims. Most female murder victims (64 percent) are killed by a family member or intimate partner (Catalano, Smith, Snyder, Rand 2009).

Studies have shown that women's fear of sexual victimization spills over into a more generalized fear of crime (Ferraro 1996; May 2001). Women's fear of crime also increases with age, even though older women are less likely to be crime victims. Sociologist Esther Madriz (1997) argues that fear of rape is used as a mechanism to socially control women because it restricts their freedom to move about freely and without trepidation. Her studies show how fear of crime perpetuates stereotypes of women as powerless and vulnerable, limiting their public behavior, not men's. The frequent depiction of women in the media as victims of rapists, serial killers, and other violent men only exacerbates this problem.

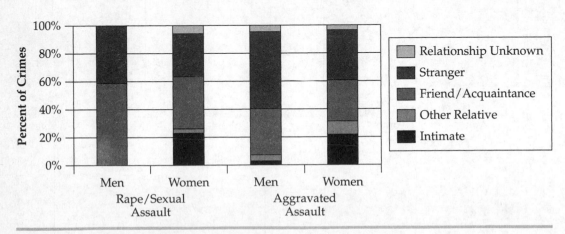

FIGURE 9.2 Victim–Offender Relationship for Violent Crimes

Source: Bureau of Justice Statistics. 2010. *Criminal Victimization in the United States, 2007 – Statistical Tables.* Washington, DC: U.S. Department of Justice.

Rape

The case of rape illustrates how isolation and powerlessness make women vulnerable to crime. Women *report* 89,000 rapes per year (a rate of 29 per 100,000 women in 2008), but this figure is the subject of debate. Through the media, we often hear about celebrity rape cases being reported to police. For example, two-time Super Bowl winning quarterback, Ben Roethlisberger, was accused of sexually assaulting a Nevada casino waitress in 2008 and a female college student in Georgia in 2010. Despite the visibility of these "celebrity" cases, rape is a seriously underreported crime. The FBI estimates that only one in four rapes actually shows up in the official statistics that are published in the *Uniform Crime Reports;* moreover, the *Uniform Crime Reports* do not include rapes that end in death, because those are reported as homicides (Federal Bureau of Investigation 2009). Perhaps it is more important to understand how the official data on rape can be distorted by the different factors that result in underreporting than it is to know exactly how many rapes there are.

Specific data show the connection of rape to women's status in society; women of the lowest status are the most vulnerable to rape. Victimization surveys show that young women (between the ages of 16 and 24) have the highest rates of rape victimization. African American women are twice as likely to be raped as White women are (Catalano et al. 2009). Divorced, separated, and never married women are much more likely to be raped than women who are married or widowed. For all women, the rape rate is higher for those with incomes under $7,500 per year (Bureau of Justice Statistics 2010).

Stereotypical images of rape associate it with strangers in public places. Yet, increasing attention has been given to **acquaintance rape,** also called *date rape*—defined as sexual assault by an individual known to the victim, including forced, coerced, or unwanted sexual contact. Acquaintance rape is the most underreported form of rape and thus is much more prevalent than official crime statistics show. Young women are the most likely victims of this form of rape.

Whereas all forms of rape are traumatic, some argue that rape by someone you know is particularly traumatic because it erodes a trusting relationship. Victims may also be part of a friendship circle that includes the assailant, making it even more difficult to talk about it with friends. As with other forms of rape, victims of acquaintance rape may fear being alone, become depressed, have sexual problems, or feel guilt and anxiety.

National surveys find that, among college women, 1.7 percent are raped each year and 1.1 percent experience attempted rate. Adjusting for the short length of the academic year, this translates to a rate of 35 rapes or attempted rapes for every 1,000 women students. Most of the victims knew the person who victimized them, as shown in Figure 9.3, and most incidents occurred in the student's living quarters. In more than three-quarters of the cases, the victim used some form of resistance against her assailant. Only 5 percent of the cases identified in this national survey had been reported to the police (Fisher et al. 2000).

Stalking on college campuses is also a common problem for women. Thirteen percent of women college students report having been stalked in the previous

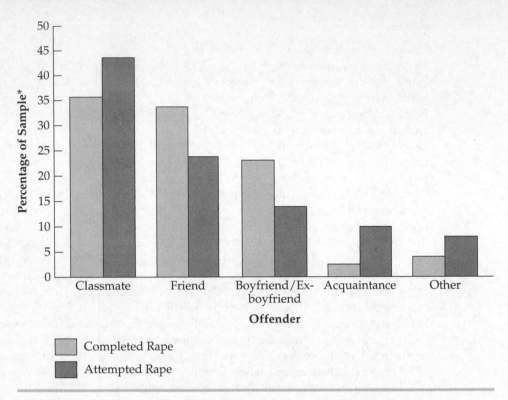

FIGURE 9.3   Victim–Offender Relationship for Rape Victimization among College Women

*Sample includes only victims, not all college women.

Source: Data from Bonnie S. Fisher, Francis T. Cullen, and Michael G. Turner. 2000. *The Sexual Victimization of College Women.* Washington, DC: U.S. Bureau of Justice Statistics, p. 19.

year (before the survey). Comparing by racial–ethnic identity, studies find that American Indian/Alaskan Native women have the highest likelihood of any racial–ethnic group of being stalked (Tjaden and Thoennes 2000; Fisher et al. 2000). Women who have been stalked typically report psychological intimidation as the result of stalking, although some also experience physical injury. Stalking is also more likely to be reported to the police than is rape or attempted rape (Fisher et al. 2000; Davis et al. 2002).

Stalking frequently occurs after the end of an intimate relationship. Studies have found that as many as 20 percent of women who have broken off relationships with men are stalked to the point where they fear for their safety (Haugaard and Seri 2003). Although fewer than half of stalking victims report being physically assaulted, they do report intense psychological intimidation, and many also report financially controlling behaviors (such as having to change one's locks, change telephone numbers, or perhaps even lose control over one's finances). Stalking involves men's use of power and social control to attempt to dominate—or even possess—women. And in many cases, such power and control was also a problem in the relationship prior to the breakup (Brewster 2003).

Sexual violence—on campus and elsewhere—has been shown to be more likely to occur in some organizational contexts than others. Military academies (Army, Air Force, and Navy), for example, often have an organizational culture that is ripe for sexual harassment and sexual assault. A survey conducted by the Office of the Inspector General of the Department of Defense (2005) found that over 50 percent of female respondents and approximately 11 percent of male respondents experienced some type of sexual harassment since entering their respective military academies. The survey also found that a total of 262 (of 1,906) female respondents indicated that they had experienced 302 incidents of sexual assault between 1999 and 2004. A total of 54 (of 3,107) male respondents

A CLOSER LOOK AT MEN

Is Participation in Aggressive Male Sports Related to Dating Aggression and Sexual Coercion in College?

Although there are many positive benefits to sports participation, feminist scholars have concerns about the relationship between sports participation and violence against women. Is there empirical evidence to support such a claim?

Gordon R. Forbes and associates report that participation in aggressive high school sports (i.e., football, basketball, wrestling, and soccer) is associated with self-reported psychological and physical aggression and sexual coercion by college men. Participants for their study were 147 college-aged men (18 to 22 years old) who were in enrolled in freshmen composition classes at a small, private, midwestern university. The university is classified as an NCAA Division III school. No athletic scholarships are offered by the university, and unlike major NCAA Division I schools, neither athletics nor athletes were very visible on campus.

The researchers divided the sample for this study into an aggressive sports group (N = 101) and a comparison group of men who had not participated in aggressive high school sports (N = 46). Men who participated in aggressive high school sports scored higher on measures of sexism, rape myth acceptance, acceptance of violence and hostility (especially toward women), and negative attitudes about homosexuality than did men in the comparison group.

Forbes and associates examined if participation in aggressive high school sports was related to aggressive and sexual coercive behaviors in college. Men who participated in aggressive high school sports self-reported on anonymous questionnaires that they had used more psychological and physical aggression and more sexual coercion in their college dating relationships than did men in the comparison group. Additionally, the men participating in aggressive sports were more likely than others to use threats or physical force to obtain sexual activity.

Of course, it would be wrong to conclude that participation in aggressive sports causes violence against women. The study by Forbes and colleagues shows only a greater likelihood of violence by men who also participate in violent sports. Not all men who do so commit violent acts. Yet, this study suggests that educating male athletes about violence against women might reduce *some* of the violence against women on campus.

Source: Based on Forbes, Gordon B., et al. 2006. "Dating Aggression, Sexual Coercion, and Aggression-Supporting Attitudes among College Men as a Function of Participation in Aggressive High School Sports." *Violence against Women* 12: 441–455.

experienced 55 sexual assaults during the same time period. Offenders were primarily fellow cadets/midshipmen.

Not surprisingly, most of these incidents were not reported to military authorities. As social groups, military academies are defined by long-standing traditions and core values, and are responsible for educating and training future military personnel who will serve and protect our nation. To achieve these goals "requires an intensely disciplined education and training environment that addresses intellectual, emotional, moral, spiritual, and physical development over the course of four years" (U.S. Department of Defense Task Force 2005: 8). The cultural system within the military academies places a high value on "masculine" qualities such as competitiveness, dominance, and aggressiveness (Malamuth et al. 1991, Rosen and Martin 1998). The U.S. Department of Defense Task Force (2005: 8) identifies the service academy culture as the "real challenge" because of its "significant impact on sexual harassment and assault."

One additional factor that influences the culture at the military academies is students' attitudes on gender disparities. Women are not as highly valued as men: They remain a statistical minority in the military academies, they continue to be excluded from some combat specialties, and they are held to different physical standards as men. The task force contends that when women are devalued, the likelihood of sexual harassment and sexual assault increases. Other factors that influence military culture that were identified by the task force include peer loyalties, power and authority, and reporting backlash. These (and other factors) should be addressed by the service academies because of their particular relevance to sexual harassment and sexual assault.

Causes of Rape

This information gives a compelling picture of women's experience and its relationship to violence as a system of social control. Explanations of violence against women have usually suggested that its cause lies within the personalities and social backgrounds of individuals who commit violence, but the empirical data on women as victims indicate that the causes of violence lie not in the characteristics of offenders but in the social status of their victims. This is *not* to say that women are responsible for the violence committed against them. Quite the opposite; it locates the causes of violence within the political and economic status of women in society. How one understands the causes of rape is significant—not just for understanding rape, but because different causal explanations have different implications for change. Rape crisis centers, for example, may see the causes of rape in individualistic or social structural terms; this is significant in what they advocate and how they assist victims (Schmitt and Martin 1999; Martin 2005).

One theoretical explanation of rape that has been extensively challenged is the **subculture of violence** theory. This theory sees the social environment as the origin of violent behavior, but it is extremely biased by its differential emphasis on the behavior of African American, Hispanic, and working-class men. Although, as we have seen, some organizational contexts may be more conducive to violence, the subculture of violence theory tends to associate violence with working-class

The feminist movement is responsible for generating greater public awareness and support for victims of rape and other forms of sexual violence.

and minority communities. In this perspective, men's violence and aggression are explained as adaptations to poverty, but the emphasis is placed on the collective psychological maladjustment of minority and working-class populations (Wolfgang and Feracuti 1967; Amir 1971). The problem with the subculture of violence thesis is not that violence in these communities is not a problem, but that this theory blames the culture of these communities for violent behavior.

Such a perspective begs the question of whether violence is more widespread in poor and working-class communities or whether it is just less hidden. It is important to note that the most violent crimes (rape and homicide) show smaller race differences than the less violent crime of robbery (Bureau of Justice Statistics 2010). This fact seemingly discredits the subculture of violence theory. Critics of this perspective also point out that violence is equally extensive in the dominant culture; it is just more easily hidden or legitimized as appropriately masculine behavior. In the end, the subculture of violence theory gives us an inadequate explanation of violence against women because, in its focus on society's under-classes, it does not explain why violence is also widespread in the dominant culture. Theoretical explanations of rape that have endured over time can be broadly categorized into two categories: gender socialization theory and political-economic theory (Andersen and Renzetti 1980).

Gender Socialization as a Cause of Rape

Feminists have suggested that the causes of rape can be traced to the dominant culture and its emphasis on masculinity as a learned pattern of aggression and domination. Unlike psychological and subcultural theories that emphasize deviations from the mainstream culture, feminist explanations show rape as an exaggeration of traditional gender roles. Gender socialization theory provides a perspective on rape that is sensitive to the variety of contexts in which it occurs. For example, as you have learned, a large proportion of rapes are committed by persons who are known to the victim. Many of these violent events occur in the context of an intimate relationship or some other close relationship between the person being raped and the rapist.

There is support in the research literature for this explanation. Men who rape are more likely to endorse traditional definitions of masculinity that include being competitive, taking risks, and having power over women. Such attitudes normalize and legitimize sexual aggressiveness (Locke and Mahalik 2005). This perspective also helps us understand the commonly reported finding that men who rape typically do not define their activities as rape or think they have done anything wrong. A study conducted on a sample of college men found that although 8.5 percent admitted to engaging in an act that met the legal definition of rape, only 16 percent of those men actually labeled the experience as rape (Koss et al., 1988). Additionally, research that supports the gender socialization perspective suggests that the presence of sexually aggressive friends is also a good predictor of whether a man will act sexually aggressive, indicating that a man's image among other men is an important context for understanding his willingness to rape. According to Thompson and Cracco, engaging in sexual aggressiveness (particularly in bar/party settings) serves as a way for men to earn their manhood and have their masculinity performances approved by others. The researchers argue that sexually aggressive behavior is "context-fixed, rather than an essential characteristic of the men doing masculinity" (2008: p. 91).

From the perspective of gender socialization theory, rape occurs because men have learned that forcing women to have sex is legitimate and normal behavior. Understanding rape from this perspective helps us see how traditional gender reactions encourage the high incidence of rape in this culture, but we cannot limit our understanding of rape only to socialization and interpersonal relations. Although it is correct to see rape as connected to learned patterns in the culture, this perspective is inadequate without an understanding of how the cultural concepts of masculinity and femininity emerge from the status of women and men in the society.

Rape and the Political-Economic Status of Women

Feminists suggest a second perspective on rape that explains violence against women as founded on the political and economic status of women in patriarchal and capitalist societies. This political-economic theory states that women have historically been defined as the property of men in these societies. For example, the rape of African American women by White slaveowners is evidence of the relationship between rape and the property status of women. Although women in contemporary society are no longer explicitly defined as the property of men, their use as sexual objects in advertising reduces their sexuality to a commodity. Images of violence against women in advertising and the popular media legitimate violent behavior against women and reiterate their status as sexual objects. This status, according to feminists, dehumanizes women and makes them an object for male violence (Kilbourne 1999).

The fact that most rapists do not believe they have done anything wrong shows that violence against women carries some degree of legitimacy within society. Those women who are perceived as the least valuable in society are apparently

MEDIA MATTERS

Rape Is Just a Click Away—Analyzing Internet Rape Sites

Much of the existing research on pornography has been limited to pornographic adult films and magazines. Until now, pornography on the Internet has not been adequately addressed in social science research.

To fill this gap, Jennifer Lynn Gossett and Sarah Byrne conducted a content analysis of violent pornography on the Internet. Their research focused exclusively on images of rape, so only Internet sites with the words *rape* or *forced sex* in their title, text, or address were included in their sample. Thirty-one Internet sites met their criteria. In addition to analyzing the textual material on these sites, Gossett and Byrne analyzed the 113 images contained within these sites. They were able to access all the sites without paying for any of the initial images (anything beyond these initial images required a credit card) and without verifying their ages (a simple click of "yes, I am 18 years of age or older" sufficed).

According to Gossett and Byrne, a "typical" pornography site provides viewers with descriptions or images of the kinds of scenes that are available. Words with violent connotations (i.e., abuse, torture, brutal, pain) regularly appear on these sites. Whether alluded to in the text or depicted in the images on the sites, a weapon is frequently used by the perpetrator to accomplish the rape. Most commonly, the images show the victim being tied with a rope. Almost all of the sites and images analyzed by

Gossett and Byrne show the rape of one victim by one perpetrator. Only four sites contained more than one perpetrator—two of which depicted a "gang rape" with four or five perpetrators.

Identifying the race of the perpetrator was particularly difficult for Gossett and Byrne because, in many of the sites, the perpetrator is an "invisible man": he is neither shown nor described in the text of the rape. In contrast, race and ethnicity were particularly important in constructing the image of the victim. Gossett and Byrne found that Asian women were overrepresented on Internet sites that advertised and sold rape pornography. Thirty-four of the fifty-six clear (i.e., with race/ethnicity easily identifiable) images on Internet sites depicted Asian women, and nearly half of the Internet sites contained a text reference or an image of an Asian woman.

Gossett and Byrne's research highlights how gender and racial inequalities are portrayed in the construction of violent pornographic images on the Internet. Because other research has demonstrated that violent pornographic images increase the risk of violence and because of the increased use of the Internet by so many people, these findings reveal a potentially increased threat for additional sexual assault.

Source: Based on Gossett, Jennifer Lynn, and Sarah Byrne. 2002. "'Click Here' A Content Analysis of Internet Rape Sites." *Gender & Society* 16 (October): 689–709.

most likely to be raped. This fact explains why African American, Hispanic, poor, unemployed, and unmarried women are those most frequently raped. The evidence is that high rates of poverty and divorce have the strongest relationship to the likelihood of rape. This is a suggestive finding, since we have already seen the increasing linkage between divorce and poverty.

Cross-cultural evidence discloses that the level of violence against women is lowest in those societies where women have the most social, political, and economic autonomy (Friedl 1975; Sanday 2007). In patriarchal societies, where men rule women, women lose their autonomy and are encouraged to be dependent on men. Research on women who are raped shows that women who are not identified as belonging to a man (i.e., women who are alone in public, single, divorced, separated, or living with nonfamily members) are raped most often. At the same time, increasing social isolation seems to be a pattern in the phenomenon of wife beating (Dobash and Dobash 1979), and in the case of incest, the isolation of women in the privacy of family life keeps that act a closely guarded secret.

Feminist research on rape has shattered the myths surrounding the crime. Still, women are told that they should not resist, that giving in is safer than fighting to avoid rape. Research refutes this. Women who confront rapists both physically and verbally and who use a variety of resistance strategies are most likely to avoid rape. Research has confirmed that those who resist are much less likely to have rape completed; furthermore, most forms of resistance are not associated with higher rates of injury to women. Ullman stresses that "[d]espite the fact that resistance can help women to avoid rape, this should not be taken to mean that they must resist rape or that it is their fault if they are unable to stop it" (2007: 415). Violence against women is based on the economic and political powerlessness of women living in patriarchal societies. Understanding violence against women requires an analysis that shows the relationship of violence to the structure of major social institutions. In this sense, stopping violence against women is intricately connected to the liberation of women from oppressive social and economic relations. In sum, violence against women is supported through the institutions of society. Cultural institutions ideologically promote violence against women; patriarchal social institutions encourage violence against women; criminal justice institutions minimize or cover up violence against women; and legal institutions resist radical change in policies to protect women from violence.

WOMEN AS CRIMINALS

In general, women commit much less crime than do men—in terms of both violent crimes and property crimes. Men are 75.5 percent of all persons arrested (Federal Bureau of Investigation 2009), thus comprising the majority of criminal offenders. However, women's participation in some crimes has increased in recent years. Central questions asked in the research on women and crime are: Has women's crime increased and, if so, for what types of crime? Is the amount of crime by women beginning to approximate the amount of male crime? How are women's crimes linked to gender relations, and have changes in gender roles created more opportunities for women to commit crimes?

The Extent of Criminality among Women

Available information on female crime comes primarily from official statistics (the FBI's *Uniform Crime Reports*), from self-report surveys, and from national victimization and crime surveys (see Table 9.1). Although each data source reveals different kinds of information, taken together they give a consistent picture of women's crime. Overall, crime (as measured by arrests) has decreased since the mid-1990s. Examining 10-year arrest trends (1999–2008), we can see that although arrests of men have decreased (by 3.1 percent), for women they have increased (by 11.6 percent). Why?

TABLE 9.1   Arrests by Gender (2008)

	Percent of Persons Arrested	
	Male	Female
Murder	89.2%	10.8%
Forcible Rape	98.8	1.2
Robbery	88.4	11.6
Aggravated Assault	78.5	21.5
Burglary	85.4	14.6
Larceny-Theft	58.7	41.3
Arson	84.1	15.9
Forgery	62.1	37.9
Fraud	56.5	43.5
Prostitution/Commercial Vice	30.6	69.4
Drug Abuse Violations	81.6	18.4
Driving under the Influence	78.6	21.4

Source: Federal Bureau of Investigation. 2009. *Uniform Crime Reports.* Washington, DC: Federal Bureau of Investigation.

First, arrest data must be interpreted with caution because arrest rates measure police activity as well as the actual commission of crime. Apparent increases and decreases in crime among different groups can reflect as much about police activity as they do the actual behavior of various groups. Nonetheless, it is likely that women's crime has actually increased, reflecting not only changes in the likelihood that police will arrest women but also changes in women's criminal activities.

Second, of the crimes considered part of the FBI's **crime index**—a measure of the overall volume and rate of crime, as indicated by offenses reported to the police (including murder and non-negligent manslaughter, rape, robbery, aggravated assault, burglary, larceny-theft, motor vehicle theft, and arson)—larceny-theft is the single greatest category of women's crime. These are crimes that include any form of theft without threat of force (which defines robbery) or breaking and entering (which defines burglary). In other words, larceny usually includes less serious theft, where there is no threat of violence to another person, or fraud; it includes shoplifting, pick-pocketing, bicycle theft, and the like. In other words, the highest arrest rates for women are for crimes that, although part of the FBI crime index, are relatively minor.

Causes of Women's Crime

Some criminologists suggest that patterns of crime among women represent extensions of their gender roles. Activities such as shoplifting, credit card fraud, and the passing of bad checks result from the opportunities women have as consumers.

Likewise, the crimes that are less frequent for women (e.g., armed robbery, aggravated assault, forgery, and counterfeiting) involve either physical strength or economic opportunities more usually associated with men's gender roles.

These associations have led some to conclude that women's involvement in criminal behavior changes when there are changes in their social roles (Adler 1975). Some have, in fact, attributed increases in women's crime in recent years to the development of the women's movement. Adler argues that shifts in gender roles make women more willing to participate in crime and that this explains recent increases in crime among women. Others say that objective changes in women's situations, particularly their greater labor force participation, make more criminal opportunities available to women. Is either of these a valid explanation of increases in women's crime?

Even with increased economic opportunity for women in the labor force, the vast majority of women remain in low-paid, low-status jobs; thus, it is an exaggeration to say that women's opportunities for crime are related to women's rapid advancement in the labor force. Additionally, increases in women's crime that show up in the arrest statistics do not necessarily reflect an increase in the actual extent of crime; rather, these statistics may reflect an increase in the detection of women's crimes. This increased detection can occur in several ways.

Although the amount of crime may remain the same, the police may now be more likely to arrest women for offenses they commit, given a change in attitudes about women. A second possibility is that changes in the rate of women's crime do not result from changes in gender roles per se, but instead from broad structural changes in the economy, technology, legal systems, and law enforcement procedures. Greater reliance on electronic transactions, credit cards, and self-service markets has increased the opportunities for crime for all consumers. At the same time, detection systems (including national information systems, technological surveillance, and an expansion of private security forces) have increased the amount of social control and law enforcement.

Miller (1986) reminds us that increases in crime among women have been almost entirely in property crimes. Rather than attributing the causes of women's crime to the women's movement and the changes it engenders, Miller argues that the women's movement coincides with (and, in fact, stems from) other structural changes that best explain women's criminal behavior as well. Those who have associated increases in women's crime with the rise of the women's movement do so because the women's movement and increases in women's crime can be marked in the same period of time; however, according to Miller, those who argue the association overlook important facts about women's employment status and high rates of poverty.

According to Miller (1986), the increased labor force participation of women beginning in the mid-1960s was especially marked among better-educated women with children who had never worked. Occupational segregation also depresses the wages of all women workers. At the same time minority, poor, and younger women face a labor market in which, when they find work, they are in jobs that are low paying and with little opportunity for advancement. The effect is to create an underclass of women, for whom criminal activity may be the only means of supporting themselves and their children. This argument is also supported by historical evidence that there are significant increases in property crimes by women in periods of economic depression.

Women's crime, Miller (1986) argues, cannot be understood separately from the crime of the men for whom they often work. Her research on women hustlers shows that women's crime often benefits men—directly and indirectly. The street hustlers in Miller's study worked in the context of street networks controlled by men who have lengthy criminal records. Further encounters with the criminal justice system will likely lead to long prison sentences for these men, so their major source of income is derived from the street-hustling work of women. The men create street networks in which women do the crime and the men take the money, maintaining their criminal activity without as great a risk of prosecution.

Miller's (1986) explanation of women's crime places the causes in the context of women's social class status, thereby also supporting the long-standing association sociologists have seen between poverty, unemployment, and crime. This explanation

FOCUS ON RESEARCH

Working the Streets—Violence and Victimization among Prostitutes

Although women are victimized by violence in many contexts, street-level prostitutes are especially vulnerable. Moreover, violence against street prostitutes has increased in recent years, largely attributed to the rise in crack cocaine use. In general, the sex work industry is marked by violence and victimization, but the risk of violence against women who work on the streets is even greater. Studies also show that the majority of those working in the sex industry (women and men) have been subjected to sexual abuse during childhood.

Rochelle Dalla, Yan Xia, and Heather Kennedy studied violence against street prostitutes by interviewing a sample of prostitutes who were participants in an intervention program designed to help women leave the streets; a smaller number of those in their study were incarcerated. The mean age of the women in the study was 19 years old; their mean time in the sex industry was 11.5 years (with a range of 6 months to 44 years). All of the women in their sample reported experiencing sexual molestation as young women. Most of the women in the sample reported severe abuse from partners, clients, and/or pimps. None of them reported the violence to authorities, saying that it just "goes along with the lifestyle" (2003: 1361).

Given the level of violence and dehumanization that prostitution entails, you might wonder what drew the women into this form of sex work. About half worked for pimps who kept a "stable" of women who worked for them simultaneously. Violence was often used by pimps to maintain power and control over their workers. In many cases, the women had entered relationships with pimps as runaways; the pimp offered them shelter and clothing, only later expecting them to return favors by engaging in sex work. In some cases, the women's relationship with the pimp also involved drug addictions. Thus, not only were the women vulnerable to begin with, but their vulnerabilities were manipulated by pimps who then exercised tremendous power over them.

Dalla and colleagues concluded their study by suggesting various intervention strategies to help prostitutes leave the streets. They argue that forming healthier social support systems and providing safe shelter are key to making these women safer.

Source: Based on Dalla, Rochelle L., Yan Xia, and Heather Kennedy. 2003. "You Just Give Them What They Want and Pray They Don't Kill You." *Violence against Women* 9 (November): 1367–1394.

of crime is particularly compelling because it explains women's and men's crime in the context of structural characteristics that involve class, race, and gender relations. Although the majority of the poor are certainly not criminals, poverty and blocked opportunity—and the economic need they create—are major underlying causes of crime.

Feminist scholars studying women's crime have also pointed to the strong connections between women's involvement in crime and women's victimization. What Daly (1994) calls the **reproduction of harm** means that women who have been emotionally and sexually abused, raised in families that are marginalized by poverty, and subjected to violence in relationships with men are more likely to become deviant or engage in criminal behavior. Engagement in deviant and criminal activity for some women and young girls may also be a strategy for coping with oppression—an argument that has been used to understand the deviance of young Black women. Arnold's (1994) research on African American women in prison, for example, found that most of these women who are habitual criminals were abused as children, had few social networks to assist them in overcoming abuse, and grew up with a profound sense of powerlessness and isolation, feeling alienated both at home and school. Without what Arnold calls "structural supports" and with few skills, little education, and no occupational training, they turn to alcohol abuse, drug addiction, and criminal involvement as a form of rebellion against their marginal status.

Likewise, research by Richie (1996) suggests that many women are coerced into crime by their male partners. Her study of African American women in jail focuses on women who were battered by their male partners. Richie argues that women who are marginalized in the culture because of their race, ethnicity, class, and gender are vulnerable to abusive relationships. Although the women she studied aspired to "normal" family relationships, they were unable to establish these relationships and instead became subjected to escalating violence—ultimately coerced into the patterns of crime resulting in their incarceration. Richie's analysis, like that of Arnold and Miller, locates the causes of women's crime in the societal factors that shape women's conduct, not simply in flawed character types or individual maladjustment.

WOMEN IN THE CRIMINAL JUSTICE SYSTEM

What happens to women when they enter the criminal justice system—either as victims or as defendants? Women in the criminal justice system are treated differently from men both as offenders and as victims. Is the symbol of justice—a blindfolded woman—representative of what happens to women in the criminal justice system?

Gender and the Courts

Even with much legal reform, research, particularly in the area of rape, shows that women victims are not equally credible before the law. In many rape trials, the victim's past sexual history may be introduced to discredit her testimony against her assailant. Many states have reformed their legal statutes to make a woman's past sexual history inadmissible as evidence in a rape trial, but, despite legal reforms, trial evidence indicates that lawyers' allegations about a woman's character are still used to discredit her testimony or to make her appear to have an illegitimate claim. Even before trial, police and prosecutors make judgments about the victim's credibility and the prosecutable merit of her case. Page found that although police officers view the crime of rape as a significant and awful crime, they often discounted the experiences of specific victims. Her research suggests that it does in fact matter what "'kind' of woman claims she was raped" (2008: 406). While 94 percent of the police officers in her study agreed that any woman can be raped, when asked about victim credibility, 19 percent were unlikely to believe a married woman who claimed that she was raped by her husband and 44 percent were unlikely to believe a prostitute who claimed that she had been raped. In comparison, only 5 percent of police officers were unlikely to believe a virgin and just 2 percent of police officers were unlikely to believe a professional woman who claimed she was raped. Additional factors that may influence police and prosecutors' judgments about a rape victim's credibility include (1) if she delayed reporting the crime; (2) if she was under the influence of drugs or alcohol when the rape occurred; or (3) if she is a woman of color, a welfare recipient, or a hitchhiker. How well a particular case fits prosecutors' preexisting ideas of what constitutes rape determines whether a case even goes to trial. Prosecutors' judgments about whether a case will hold up and result in conviction are an important predictor of whether a case goes to trial (Frohmann 1991; Spohn et al. 2001).

Women's perceptions of the criminal justice system clearly influence their willingness to report and prosecute rape. They are much more likely to report rape when they see a high probability of conviction and when the rape fits prevailing definitions of a "classic" rape—that is, rape involving the use of a weapon, rape by a stranger, rape that results in serious injury, rape in a public place, or rape through unlawful entry into the victim's home (Pino and Meier 1999; Clay-Warner and McMahon-Howard 2009).

Further research finds gender bias for women in the courts, in roles as both adjudicators and as defendants. The eighteenth-century legal scholar Blackstone, whose work provides the cornerstone for English and American law, thought women were rightfully prohibited from jury service because of the "defect" of sex. Although women are now being fairly represented on juries, until very recently they were severely underrepresented and were often permitted exemptions from jury service simply because of their sex.

Gender bias in the courtroom also affects the disposition of jury cases, although not directly because of the gender of jurors. In cases of rape, jurors' beliefs about rape influence their willingness to convict or acquit. Men are more likely than women to believe in rape myths (Reilly et al. 1992). As a result, the greater representation of women on juries has resulted in a higher rape conviction rate in recent years. Women and men do however recommend similar punishments for defendants found guilty of rape (Hans and Vidmar 1986).

For women offenders brought before the criminal justice system, a number of factors influence the disposition of cases. Specifically, Daly (1989) found that a defendant's work and family situation influenced sentencing of both men and women.

Judges perceive men on a continuum, ranging from "good" men, who work and support dependents, to "irresponsible" men, who may or may not have a job and dependents but who do not contribute support. Men perceived as irresponsible, along with those who do not have jobs or dependents, are more likely to be sentenced. Similarly, women are judged along a similar continuum—the "good" woman being one who has dependents for whom she cares regularly (regardless of whether she holds a job) and the "irresponsible" woman being one who has dependents but does not care for them regularly. As with men, women judged to be irresponsible are more likely to be sentenced. This research concludes that judges seek to protect children and families, not women per se, as prior arguments about judicial paternalism and chivalry have implied.

This conclusion is further elaborated by subsequent research finding that women's family situations, such as whether there is someone who can care for her children, influence judges' sentencing of women. For men, this does not come into play as much as factors such as their prior record and the seriousness of the offense (Flavin 2001; Koons-Witt 2002).

Women and Prison

The number of women in prison is a small percentage (7 percent) of all state and federal prisoners. Although both the rate of male and female imprisonment has increased over recent years, the female prison population has increased at a faster rate. The number of women serving sentences of more than one year grew by 757 percent between 1977 and 2004. This is nearly twice the 388 percent increase in the male prison population (Frost, Greene, and Pranis 2006). A disproportionate number of people in prison are members of racial minority groups. More than half of women prisoners are African American and Latinas, and almost two-thirds of men in prison are Black or Hispanic. The highest rates of imprisonment of women are for those between 30 and 39 years of age—years when they are also likely to be mothers (Bureau of Justice Statistics 2010).

Two-thirds of women in prison have at least one child under age 18; about half of these children live with grandparents, and about one-fourth live with their fathers (Sharp and Marcus-Mendoza 2001; Enos 2001). Consistent with patterns of crime, a greater percentage of women are imprisoned for property and drug offenses than is the case for men (Mullings et al. 2002).

Once women are in prison, little attention is paid to their special needs. Some have argued that this is because, until recently, there have been so few women in prison that it is costly to develop special programs for them. Prisons are "gendered institutions," where organizational policies and practices are modeled on men's needs and interests, even while such practices (such as job training) are assumed to be gender neutral (Britton 1997). Gender stereotypes also shape the vocational training women get in prison; the prison experience typically leaves women marginalized upon their exit (Morash et al. 1994). Although men in prison may be trained in relatively well-paying trades (e.g., mechanics, carpentry, etc.), job training for women, to the extent that it exists, is for poorly paid, gender-segregated jobs that offer little hope for advancement (e.g., laundress, assembly line worker, homemaker, or beautician).

The job training that women prisoners receive typically reflects gender-segregated skills.

Women's prisons are smaller than men's prisons but have also become increasingly overcrowded. More and more, however, women in prison are being treated no differently than men—a mixed message, since this means that women are now subject to much of the same degradation as male prisoners (Chesney-Lind 1997).

Health care in women's prisons is also limited, particularly in meeting needs specific to women's medical and reproductive care. Many women enter prison with existing medical problems, including drug addiction, psychiatric illness, hypertension, and respiratory disease. One in four is pregnant or has recently given birth. If women become pregnant while in prison, they may have a long wait for medical care, making abortion a potentially high risk. Some facilities do not allow abortions at all. Should a woman prisoner carry through her pregnancy, she may not receive adequate prenatal care and, when she gives birth, is likely to be separated from her child (Ingram-Fogel 1991, 1993; McQuiade and Ehrenreich 1998; Young and Reviere 2001; Stoller 2003).

Women in prison say that separation from their children is the most difficult part of their sentence, and they see few alternatives for their children's care. They typically give them up for adoption, release them to foster care, or leave them with relatives (the choice most often selected). Studies find that women in prison are greatly concerned for their children and that this strain can be reduced by engaging them in mothering activities (Enos 2001; Forsyth 2003; Berry and Ergenberg 2003).

The conditions in women's prisons often lead them to fend for themselves. In the face of these conditions, research indicates that women's own social networks in prison are more supportive and affectionate than those formed in male prisons. This suggests that women actively construct a supportive subculture within prison, the characteristics of which vary in different institutional settings (Kruttschnitt et al. 2000). Although women in prison do not all come from similar cultural backgrounds, the subcultures they form in prison often exhibit resource-fulness, flexibility, and creativity in the social relations they develop. They are not merely passive victims of their situation; instead, they develop adaptive strategies to cope with the conditions they face.

Part of women's prison subculture is reflected in the lesbian relationships that emerge between some women prisoners. Women prisoners often have economic motivations, such as the exchange of favors or commercial goods, for forming sexual relationships with other women in prison. Compared to men, women are also more likely to form interracial relationships in prison, and women's relationships are generally less violent and involve less gang activity (Greer 2000). Still, coerced sex in women's prisons involves about 4 percent of prisoners (Hensley et al. 2003). Little research has been done on the sexual abuse of women prisoners by prison staff, although women prisoners report that this abuse is common. The women clearly see sexual abuse as part of the power dynamics that exist between prison staff and the inmates (Calhoun and Coleman 2002).

Somewhat ironically, studies show that the number of women in prison is highest in those countries where women have advanced the most with regard to education, employment, and their overall social status (Heitfield and Simon 2002). Perhaps this reflects the diminution of protective attitudes toward women, as well as more opportunities for women to engage in crime. But it also shows the need for women's advancement to continue so that they will not experience the abusive relationships that can land them in prison, and women need better opportunities in the "outside" world to reduce the need to commit property crimes. Clearly, the increase in the number of women in prison calls for new social policies to deal with this growing population, including programs to help women readjust to a productive life once they are released (Kruttschnitt and Gartner 2003).

■ Chapter Summary and Themes

Sociological perspectives on gender, crime, and deviance locate the origins of such behavior in the social structural conditions in which different groups live.
Early explanations of women's deviance were riddled with assumptions about women's maladjusted social-sexual identity. Such thinking was also bounded by the racism of the time. As people began to think about the social origins of women's deviance, attention turned to such things as the labeling process and the role of social inequality in producing crime and deviance. Feminist perspectives have added the significance of women's location in power relationships and their economic status as causal factors in deviance and crime.

Men are more likely to be victims of crime than women, but women's sexual victimization is a form of social control that can restrict women's freedom of movement.
Men are far more likely to be victims of crime than are women, except for rape. Among women, women of color and younger women are the most likely crime victims, although older women are more fearful of crime. Sociological studies of

rape and other forms of sexual assault find that power dynamics between men and women are the best explanation of sexual victimization, even when people continue to blame victims for rape. Some organizational contexts—those based on highly masculine characteristics—are the most rape-prone environments.

Although women are less likely to commit crime than men, you can trace the sources of women's crime to the status of women in society.

The kinds of crime that women commit are primarily property crimes—indicative of the poor economic status of women. Often, women's engagement in crime stems from a history of sexual abuse and/or their relationships with men.

Women have an increasing presence in the criminal justice system.

Although the rate of men's imprisonment has begun to decline, the rate for women is increasing, although women remain a small proportion of prisoners overall. But a prison system that was designed primarily for men needs revision if it is to meet the health, labor, and family needs of women in prison.

■ Key Terms

acquaintance rape	labeling theory	reproduction of harm
crime index	*National Crime Victimization*	subculture of violence
deviance	*Survey*	*Uniform Crime Reports*

■ Discussion Questions/Projects for Thought

1. Think of a time when you engaged in some activity that was considered deviant for someone of your gender. Alternatively, without putting yourself at risk, do something that violates the routine expectations associated with your gender. How do people react to you? How does this make you feel? What does your experiment tell you about the concepts of deviance, gender, and social control?

2. What services does your campus or community offer to assist women who are victims of violence? Contact some of those who work (or volunteer) in one such organization and ask them what they have learned about violence against women. Based on these discussions, what links do you see between violence and women's status?

3. Follow the daily newspaper for one week, noting the stories involving criminal activity. What evidence of men's and women's crime do you see and how do your anecdotal observations support (or not) the data on gender and crime reported in this chapter?

10

Gender, Education, and Science

Think back to when you were a young school child. Were girls and boys engaged in the same things in school? Did teachers treat them differently? Or, for that matter, look around your campus now and see if there are differences in the subjects women and men are pursuing—or if there are even fairly equal numbers of women and men in your classroom. Your observations—both of elementary/secondary education and college education—will tell you a lot about the kinds of questions that those who study gender and education are asking. And, they will also show you the kinds of changes in educational institutions that are essential if the society wants to achieve more gender equity, not just in education but also in the outcomes for which education is critical.

Education is one of the most important factors influencing people's life chances. Without a good education, you are likely to be vulnerable to a lifetime of low-wage work. And, even with a good education, the field of study you pursue can also shape your life options. This is not just a matter of individual success; it is also a question of how well positioned our society is to maintain its global edge in science and technology. Because the U.S. national population is becoming more diverse, there is widespread concern that if we do not educate women and minorities for scientific careers, the United States will fall behind as a world leader. Thus, the study of gender—and its connections with race and class inequality—is critical for shaping educational policy and practice.

But education is not only about skill development. The experiences we have in school are also a significant part of our identity development, as we saw in Chapter 2. Interactions with peers and teachers are a major context for the development of gender identity. Our self-esteem, aspirations, and self-concept are formed in large part through our experiences in educational institutions. If the schools value the attributes and accomplishments of our gender (and race and class) group, we are far more likely to grow up with identities that lead to achievement, not failure.

In some societies, studying gender and education may be as basic as working to extend literacy to women. In contemporary Afghanistan, for example, like other poor nations, only 13 percent of women can read, compared with 43 percent of men (United Nations 2007). But even in the United States, where 99 percent of the adult population is literate, there are significant gaps in educational achievement—gaps that stem from gender, race, and class inequalities in the schools. In a society so technologically advanced, not having a good education can leave you behind in access to good jobs and other benefits of democratic citizenship. People increasingly need the skills that scientific and technological literacy bring. Anyone who lags behind in such skills is at a disadvantage. Thus, closing the gender gap that persists in science and technology is an important part of achieving gender equity.

This chapter reviews gender and education. As we will see, much progress has been made in educating girls and women beyond the narrowly prescribed gender roles that characterized education in the past. But significant gender differences remain in the skills, identities, and opportunities that schools create.

WOMEN AND THE HISTORY OF EDUCATION

The pursuit of knowledge has historically been considered the work of men. Either excluded by formal admissions policies or tracked into gender-typed fields and specialties, women were historically viewed as outsiders in education. And change has been fairly recent. Even someone as distinguished as Supreme Court Justice Ruth Bader Ginsburg can recall in her own career as a Harvard law student not being allowed into the Harvard Law Library simply because she was a woman. This may seem like something from the nineteenth century, but Justice Ginsburg completed her Harvard law degree in 1959, having to ask her husband to get books from the library for her! Furthermore, it was not that long ago when prestigious universities admitted women at all. Princeton University, for example, did not admit women until 1969. Interestingly, women now occupy the two top administrative posts at Princeton. Change does occur!

In the public schools, mass public education is a phenomenon of the twentieth century. In the earliest part of the twentieth century, only a small proportion of the population completed even a high school education, and college was reserved for only the privileged few. As recently as 1950, only one-third of the population over age 25 had graduated from high school; that number now is about 87 percent. And, in 1950, only 6 percent of the population held a college degree; that figure is now 30 percent (National Center for Education Statistics 2008).

In the early part of U.S. history, education was largely seen as a privilege for a few. Slaves, for example, were forbidden to read, although many learned to do so secretly by studying the Bible or the books of owners' children. Poor and working-class people seldom got much education because young people, including children, were needed as laborers. Among the advantaged classes, women's education was judged as important mostly because it was believed to make women better mothers. Not until 1918 was public education made compulsory—and then only because schools were thought to "Americanize" the many immigrants who were entering the country. Many historians of education have argued that public education expanded as a way of keeping young immigrant men and women off the streets. Fears of crime, juvenile delinquency, and other troubles that came with urbanization and immigration resulted in people believing that schools inculcated the values of discipline and hard work in the nation's youth (Greene 1978; McMannon 1997).

From the start, then, schools reflected needs of society that were not simply those of educating people. You can see this even today: The school calendar reflects the original needs of an agricultural-based society where young people were out of school during time periods when their labor was needed to bring in crops. With industrialization, schools became places where literacy was extended to masses who would occupy positions in a more bureaucratized society, where many would be employed in white-collar work. Today, with the growth of an information-based, highly scientific, and technological society, schools are needed to prepare students for the jobs that characterize the twenty-first century.

As public education developed, women were actually somewhat more likely than men to complete high school. Thus, until as late as 1980, more women than men completed a high school education (although men were much more likely to attend college). The predominance of women in the public schools reflects the fact that men could find decent employment without completing high school. For women, through the 1940s and 1950s, the curriculum taught them typing, short-hand, and other skills associated with women's presumed proper role. At the same time, women were the majority of high school teachers, although many states prohibited women from teaching once they were married.

With regard to college education, one of the most notable trends in recent years has been the vast expansion of college enrollment (see Figure 10.1) and, most recently, the fact that women now outnumber men as college students. College enrollment for both men and women expanded dramatically beginning in the 1970s and continued until the present. Now, the majority of college graduates are women, though, as we saw in Chapter 5, women college graduates still earn less than men. Moreover, women are more likely to graduate in certain fields—namely, education, the arts, humanities, social sciences, and law—whereas men more likely graduate in sciences, mathematics, and engineering (Bradley 2000). This pattern of gender segregation in the curriculum significantly affects the outcomes of education for both groups.

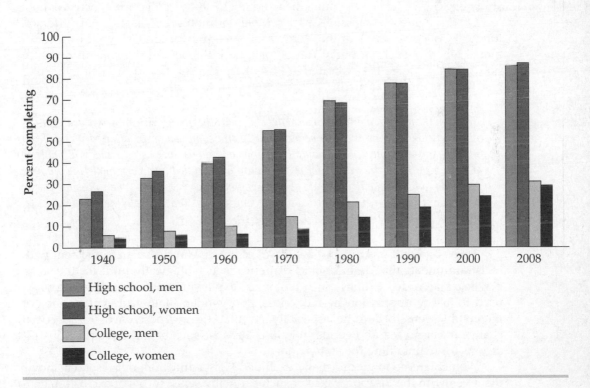

FIGURE 10.1   Men's and Women's Educational Attainment

Source: Data from National Center for Educational Statistics. 2008. *Digest of Education Statistics 2008.* Washington, DC: U.S. Department of Education. Website: http://nces.ed.gov.

Because of its importance in shaping life chances, education has long been an area of feminist activism. In the nineteenth century, campaigns for women's educational rights were central to the growth of feminism. Early feminists, such as Emma Willard, who founded the Troy Female Seminary in 1821, understood the need for women to have an education that taught skills other than those associated with good mothering. Thus, Willard included algebra, geometry, and physiology in the curriculum of the seminary.

In most schools, however, women's education was restricted by ideologies that depicted their minds as directed and limited by their bodies. Especially in the post-Civil War period, when major transformations were occurring in the gender roles, leading educational reformers claimed that women's wombs dominated their mental life and thus they should not study or work vigorously! One such reformer, Dr. Edward Clarke, was a member of the Harvard Board of Overseers and a member of its medical faculty. He published several popular books in the late nineteenth century warning of the dangers that education and study posed for women. Clarke wrote, "A girl upon whom Nature, for a limited period and for a definite purpose, imposes so great a physiological task, will not have as much power left for the tasks of school, as the boy of whom Nature requires less at the corresponding epoch" (Clarke 1873:54, cited in Rosenberg 1982:10). Accordingly, Clarke advised young women to study one-third as much as young men and not to study at all during menstruation!

Others agreed. Professor Charles Meigs admonished his class at Jefferson Medical College to think of the womb as a "great power and ask your own judgments whether such an organ can be of little influence on the constitution and how much!" (Meigs 1847:18, cited in Rosenberg 1982:6). The prominent gynecologist Thomas Emmet argued:

> To reach the highest point of physical development the young girl in the between classes of society should pass the year before puberty and some two years afterwards free from all exciting influences. She should be kept as a child as long as possible, and made to associate with children . . . . Her mind should be occupied by a very moderate amount of study, with frequent intervals of a few moments each, passed when possible in the recumbent position, until her system becomes accustomed to the new order of life. (Emmet 1879:21, cited in Rosenberg 1982:10)

These admonitions reflect class biases of the time and also are consistent with racist arguments that defined Black Americans as biologically unfit for the same privileges accorded Whites. Such biological explanations of inequality are often used to justify oppression by race, class, and gender. Biological explanations of inequality seem to become especially popular during periods of rapid social change in class, race, and gender relations, because such beliefs develop as justifications for maintaining the status quo.

Women are no longer formally excluded from education, but research shows that even with the disappearance of such explicitly sexist forms of exclusion, gender bias in education persists. Beginning with preschool and extending through higher education, girls and women encounter perceptions and practices that can have long-term consequences for their life chances.

HISTORY SPEAKS: YESTERDAY'S FEMINISTS TALK ABOUT TODAY

Mary McLeod Bethune: Education for a Change

"From the first, I made my learning, what little it was, useful every way I could."
—Mary McLeod Bethune

Mary McLeod Bethune (1875–1955) was born in Mayesville, South Carolina, the daughter of slaves and the fifteenth of seventeen children. At age 11, she entered a school that had been established by religious missionaries—a common pattern in the aftermath of slavery where education had been denied to slaves. Walking five miles to and from school every day, Bethune used what she learned to educate her own family in the evening. Perhaps this was the beginning of her lifelong commitment to education for Black people.

Initially, Bethune wanted to become an African missionary, a dream that proved unattainable because she was told African Americans could not do so. Thwarted in this career, she remained undaunted. After graduating from the Presbyterian Mission School in South Carolina and, later, the Haines Institute in Augusta, Georgia, Bethune established a school (in 1904) for African American girls in Daytona Beach, Florida: the Daytona Literary and Industrial School for Training Negro Girls, which opened with six pupils—five girls and her own son.

Mary McLeod Bethune did everything at the school—educating the children, cleaning the school, even crushing berries to use for ink. As the school grew, so did her determination, and she began seeking donations to keep the school going. She was successful and in 1923 the school merged with a boys' school, becoming Bethune-Cookman College, where she served as President until 1942. Bethune-Cookman University now enrolls over 3,500 students with over 35 degree programs.

In addition to her work as an educator, Mary McLeod Bethune was a major force in the Black women's club movement, founding the National Council of Negro Women, still active today with over four million members nationwide. She was an advisor to four presidents, including Franklin Delano Roosevelt, for whom she served as a major "race advisor."

Thinking Further: Mary McLeod Bethune believed that education was not just about skills, but also about developing the Black community. Were she with us today, she would likely be horrified by the condition of public education, especially for poor and working-class minority students. Imagine that she were serving as an advisor to yet a fifth president: What might she see as the role of education in uplifting Black women and men—and others in similar plights? How can education do this and what is needed to make it so?

Sources: Collins, Patricia Hill. 2000. *Black Feminist Thought: Knowledge, Consciousness, and the Politics of Empowerment.* New York: Routledge; Encyclopedia of World Biography, www.notablebiographies.com; www.bethune.cookman.edu.

GENDER AND EDUCATIONAL SUCCESS

When girls and boys begin school, they encounter a new world of gender expectations. Gender influences numerous facets of the experience boys and girls have in school, including their interactions with each other, relationships with teachers, and concepts of self. As a result, the outcomes of education reveal strong evidence of the influence of gender—in such things as achievement tests, course-taking patterns, curriculum content, and student interests. We have seen how schools work as agents of gender socialization (see Chapter 2), but what happens in schools that affects girls' and boys' opportunities?

Gender and Schooling

Remember your first day of school? Perhaps you were excited, maybe scared, and possibly feeling shy. Maybe you wondered what it would be like to meet new girls and boys, be away from home, and have a new teacher. But it is unlikely that you thought that your experience would be shaped by the simple fact of whether you were a girl or a boy. Yet, that fact does have significant consequences for your education—beginning from your first day and continuing through your last year of school—whether that is a year you drop out of high school, the year you complete a bachelor's degree, or when you go on to graduate or professional school.

Moreover, the gender gap in education exists despite many years of reform and policies that legally bind the nation to provide equal educational opportunities to women and men. **Title IX of the Educational Amendments** of 1972 is a federal law prohibiting sex discrimination in federally funded education programs and activities. This law has been critical in establishing equal educational opportunity for women, not just in schools, but also in state-sponsored athletics. Before Title IX, women in schools could be denied admission to various programs, often sat in sex-segregated classrooms, and had little access to the resources that supported school-sponsored athletics. Title IX mandated schools to open the doors of education to women on equal terms with men, and its implementation has been responsible for many of the successes and gains that women have seen in education in the years since its passage. Title IX has also been interpreted by the courts as prohibiting *sexual harassment* in schools, an issue discussed later in this chapter (see also Chapter 5).

Despite the gains that have come from the implementation of Title IX, gender inequities in education remain, and they are reflected in what students learn, how teachers interact with them, what teachers expect, and how students perceive themselves in school. As Myra and David Sadker write, "Sitting in the same classroom, reading the same textbook, listening to the same teacher, girls and boys get very different educations" (Sadker and Sadker 1994:2).

How does this happen? Girls and boys enter schools as equals, but over the years, the gender gap in education actually increases. Moreover, much of what happens is not consciously intended to discriminate against girls; rather, there is a hidden bias throughout education that may not even be visible to those who engage in it. Consequently, creating gender equity in education requires a conscious effort to overcome the gender bias that persists in education and that narrows the options that young women—and young men—will have later in life.

Observations of children in elementary school settings show how gender is given meaning through the ordinary interactions students have in school. Something as subtle as teachers always referring to boys first when referring to both girls and boys (e.g., "Boys and girls, open your books to page 56") defines boys as more important, as the dominant group (Thorne 1993). Likewise, calling on boys more often, even if they are being singled out because of disruptive behavior, makes boys more noticeable, thereby communicating their greater sense of place. Gendered patterns in who talks more, who gets recognized, and who is rewarded for what kind of behavior all operate to produce a definition of gender that differentiates boys and girls (Sadker and Sadker 1994).

Teacher expectations also influence how girls and boys see themselves and are seen by others. The term **self-fulfilling prophecy** has been used to refer to the outcomes that occur as the result of teachers' and counselors' expectations. Thus, the counselor who thinks that girls are unlikely to become scientists is unlikely to encourage girls to pursue advanced science and math coursework. Consequently, fewer girls take such courses, possibly reinforcing the counselor's belief and producing a self-fulfilling prophecy. Research has clearly shown that what teachers expect of students has a strong effect on how students perform. Thus, the student labeled a high achiever is quite likely to live up to that expectation, just as the student labeled as deficient is likely to perform poorly.

Tracking systems in the schools, also known as *streaming* (where students are sorted into groups based on their presumed abilities), contribute to the self-fulfilling prophecy. Students placed in the higher academic tracks routinely get the better teachers, a more innovative curriculum, and greater access to educational advantages than do students placed in the lower tracks (Lucas 1999). Tracking has been shown to be strongly related to social class and race, but it is also related to gender, especially with regard to math placement (Ansalone 2001; Kubitschek and Hallinan 1996). Tracking also strongly affects women's and men's self-esteem and thus their educational performance. Studies also show that women placed in high tracks actually get more positive outcomes than men in high tracks, although the reverse is true for women and men placed in low tracks, where women are more negatively affected than men (Catsambis et al. 1999).

Research on the self-fulfilling prophecy indicates that the stereotypes teachers (and others) hold of students have a huge impact on student outcomes. Teachers who have high expectations for certain students will call on them more, praise them frequently, and give them more opportunities to demonstrate success. These stereotypes typically are based on gender, as well as on race and social class. Latinas and African American students risk being thought of as stupid; Asian Americans who are stereotyped as the "model minority" feel pressure to excel (Olsen 1997).

The influence of gender, race, and class stereotypes has been aptly demonstrated by the concept of **stereotype threat** (Steele and Aronson 1995). Steele and his associates have shown that negative stereotypes suppress academic performance. Developed first to explain differences in Black and White scores on standardized tests, stereotype threat means that when students (or others) perceive that they risk being judged by a negative stereotype, they do not perform as well as they otherwise might. Faced, for example, with the stereotype that women are worse at math than men are, women's apprehension about the stereotype actually lowers their performance on math exams. Interestingly, this research has also shown that the higher the perceived threat, the lower the performance and, conversely, when the threat of the stereotype is eliminated, women and men actually perform similarly on math tests. The strong implication is that the presence of stereotypes, not an actual difference in women's and men's abilities, is what produces differences in such things as math testing (Spencer et al. 1999).

You can see that the power of stereotypes is enormous. But stereotypes do not come only from teachers. Studies find that girls are actually more likely to blame their peers than teachers for discouraging school achievement (Haag 1999). Thus, girls who are smart report feeling tension between peer approval and academic performance. Thus, teachers and students construct the meanings of gender—and race and class—that permeate educational institutions. These patterns strongly mark girls' and boys' experiences in school. Seating patterns at lunchroom tables, lines where students stand, and playground activities all become constructed as gendered spaces. Although not strictly segregated by gender, such interactions reinforce gender as a primary social category—one that, as sociologist Barrie Thorne has analyzed it, "provides a continuously available line of difference that can be drawn on at any time in the ongoing life of schools" (1993:35). Moreover, although gender segregation is present as early as the preschool and elementary levels, it becomes heightened over time, as students get older and move into higher grade levels.

Such gendered patterns have consequences, not only for how boys and girls define each other, but also for how they define themselves. **Self-esteem**—that is, how well one thinks of oneself—is critical, not just because positive self-esteem is related to one's mental health, but because self-esteem is also linked to the aspirations one has for one's future. Studies show that by the middle years of school, girls generally have lower self-esteem than boys (Phillips 1998; Haag 1999). Students who develop poor self-concepts are likely to lower their aspirations, thereby paying less attention to doing well and limiting their educational performance. Once they do so, teachers come to expect less and label them as underachievers, thereby reinforcing their negative self-image and establishing a cycle of poor educational performance.

Athletic opportunities have opened up for girls and women as the result of Title IX legislation, passed in 1972.

Schools are the places where many young people make the transition from childhood to adulthood. By the time young girls and boys enter middle school, gender has already taken a strong hold on their self-concepts and interactions with each other. But the transition into the middle-school years magnifies the significance of gender. All of the studies, as well as casual observations, that examine young girls in their teens note the extraordinary concern with appearance, popularity, and image that emerges during these years. As one 13-year-old puts it, "Girls struggle the most to fit in out of everything else in their lives. We try to wear the right clothes, be slim, and not say the wrong thing. Most girls would do anything to get a boyfriend. Girls also don't stay true to themselves. While trying to fit in, they become clones of each other. They need help finding themselves" (Haag 1999:10). Girls in these years may spend more time worrying about their clothes, makeup, and other features of their attractiveness than they do focusing on their schoolwork. Furthermore, the preoccupation with appearance is supported not just by the fashion and cosmetic industries and the media that support them, it is bolstered by numerous institutional supports in the schools: Note the large number of school contests and activities that emphasize attractiveness for girls, including pompom teams, baton twirling, cheerleading, prom queen, homecoming queen, and so forth (Eder et al. 1995).

The enormous pressure to conform in school is one of the hallmarks of adolescent culture. Social cliques are a major feature of the landscape of schools. Ask any student to describe the different groups in schools. Although the names change over time, students are highly aware of the status rankings of different groups: "Preppies," "jocks," "geeks," "druggies" describe some of the various groups that fall into the status hierarchy in schools. The insecurities brought on by status hierarchies in the schools generate anxiety and insecurity, reactions that then accentuate the need to conform to group standards. The social cliques that emerge in schools also have a clear hierarchy—a social ranking system that is structured along lines of class, gender, and race. For example, cheerleading usually has high social status, but it is linked to a particular gender performance. Most students in this status hierarchy are generally unwilling to associate with groups perceived as lower status. Students in such low-status groups are usually ridiculed, teased, and generally looked down upon. Studies show that these patterns of the status rankings of different social groups are related to extracurricular activities, but are particularly marked by the social-class background of students. Within the hierarchical structure of schools, the routine practices of interaction—talk, gossip, routines, and rituals—all reinforce gender beliefs (Eder et al. 1995).

It is not just girls in this context who become disadvantaged. In what has been called the "miseducation of boys" (Sadker and Sadker 1994; Ferguson 2000; Mead 2006), educational researchers point out that schools are places where boys become labeled as problematic troublemakers (Ferguson 2000). Moreover, the informal expectations that are communicated about gender track boys into certain areas, for example, putting pressure on them to be strong athletes. Boys and young men are also encouraged by gender norms to repress emotions, be tough, and display masculinity at all costs (Pascoe 2008). Most important, boys and young men learn, above all, not to cross gender lines. For boys, being "tough" is an important part of the construction and display of masculinity in schools. The importance of toughness is constantly communicated through the insults boys give to each other: "weenie," "wimp," "fag," "queer"—all are derogatory labels routinely directed against boys who show any sign of weakness that is associated with femininity or homosexuality. Such ritualized insulting has been shown to be especially common among male athletes. Thus homophobia reinforces the gender norms that force boys and girls into narrowly conscripted social roles (Eder et al. 1995).

With increased attention to the education of girls in recent years, some now worry that boys are now at a disadvantage in schools. Is this true? In fact, boys are achieving more than ever in schools, and girls have closed some of the gaps in educational achievement that have been a problem in the past. As shown in the box "A Closer Look at Men," the public hype about boys failing is overblown. Gaps in educational achievement by race, however, are highly evident, leading scholars to conclude that boys would benefit more from focusing on closing economic and racial achievement gaps (Mead 2006).

Schools, then, are the stage where society's roles—roles defined by gender, class, race, sexuality, and age—are played out. The entire context of school is one where educational achievement is strongly influenced by the personal issues that young girls and boys face. Issues about identity, sexuality, relationships, and family are all part of the context for student learning and development. Focusing solely on educational performance without an understanding of how gender, race, class, and other factors influence students' lives may leave teachers and school officials unable to fully understand the context in which students learn or don't learn. In a national climate where school reform is on the national agenda, it is important that the underlying conditions in young people's lives be addressed if we are to understand what makes students succeed or fail.

Title IX prohibits sex discrimination in any school receiving federal funding. It has been a key law opening educational opportunities to women—including school-sponsored athletics, although some are in favor of limiting the impact of Title IX.

A CLOSER LOOK AT MEN

(Some) Boys Are Falling Behind in School

Recently, there has been much discussion about the "boy crisis" in the American educational system. Researchers and popular media have touted that school policies and requirements for graduation discriminate against boys. The claim is that schools are now guilty of "shortchanging boys" as they once shortchanged girls. What does the evidence suggest?

Sara Mead, a senior policy analyst at Education Sector, argues that the truth is much different from what the popular media suggest. She analyzed data from the National Assessment of Educational Progress (NAEP) test conducted by the U.S. Department of Education. This test has tracked student performance since the early 1990s and is administered to a large, representative sample of American students in grades 4, 8, and 12.

Overall, Mead found that fourth-grade boys' scores have improved in reading, math, and other subjects such as history, writing, and science. Eighth-grade boys have improved in reading, math, history, and writing, but have not significantly changed in science. Twelfth-grade boys' achievement, however, appears to be declining in most subjects with the exception of math. Mead contends that this decline may not be an issue for just older *boys*, but for older *students*. She found that achievement for older students has remained the same or declined for both boys and girls.

Although most American boys are scoring higher on achievement tests, Mead found that there are some groups of boys for whom the term *crisis* accurately captures their educational standing. When race and social class are taken into account along with gender, achievement scores in reading are disturbingly low for poor, Black, and Hispanic boys. Overall, the gaps between students of different races and social classes are much larger—two to five times larger—than gaps by gender. Mead concludes that in schools, poor and minority boys would benefit more if racial and social class achievement gaps were closed than they would if gender gaps were closed.

Mead's study highlights the complex interaction among race, class, and gender and educational achievement among students. Her findings suggest that the popular discussion on gender gaps in achievement may be distracting attention away from larger issues faced by poor and minority boys.

Source: Mead, Sara. 2006. "The Truth about Boys and Girls." Washington, DC: Education Sector. http://www.educationsector.org.

Academic Achievement: Is There a Gender Gap?

Comparing the academic achievement of young women and men, girls and boys, is a complex topic of research. Moreover, whether or not researchers find gender differences depends on what they measure and how they measure different forms of ability and learning. For example, girls earn higher grades than boys in all subjects throughout schooling. And, on national tests of reading and writing, girls perform equally to boys. But on other standardized tests, differences emerge, although only depending on the subject matter. The most dramatic gender differences appear on the tests with the highest stakes, tests like the Preliminary Scholastic Aptitude Test (PSAT), Scholastic Aptitude Test (SAT), and Advanced Placement (AP) tests.

Because educational testing has such influence on decisions about student placement and educational opportunities, it has been the subject of much research. This research is highly detailed and therefore difficult to summarize. In general, it shows the following:

- Girls and boys show similar levels of achievement in many areas, but gaps exist in others. On closer examination, there are areas where girls exceed boys in academic achievement, whereas boys exceed girls in other areas.
- In some subject areas, although overall scores of girls and boys are similar, boys tend to outperform at the more advanced levels, such as in mathematics.
- Even when boys' and girls' overall performance is comparable, performance in particular skill areas can substantially diverge (such as in object rotation where boys exceed girls or writing where girls exceed boys).
- Gender differences in performance (at least as measured by standardized tests) are usually similar at lower grade levels, but diverge in later grades (Phillips 1998; Mead 2006).

It is often thought that girls and boys differ significantly in their verbal and mathematical abilities. Girls, the standard argument goes, excel in verbal skills, boys, in math. This is not entirely supported by research. Although earlier researchers could document differences in girls' and boys' scores on verbal ability tests, these differences have decreased over time. Girls' do tend to outperform boys on writing skills, although these results are inconsistent. In math and science skills, whether or not differences between boys and girls appear in standardized tests depends on the age of the sample, how academically selective the test is, and what cognitive level the test is measuring. The gender gaps that exist in math testing, however, tend to increase in the later grades (American Association of University Women, 1992, 1998). At earlier levels—namely, fourth and eighth grades—gender differences on standardized math tests are minimal.

High-stakes tests, such as the PSAT, the SAT, and AP tests, show larger gender gaps than do standardized tests. This is important to understand because these tests have such a tremendous influence on entrance to college and, thus, students' futures. What does the gender gap mean?

Researchers have found that the construction of the test itself can advantage one group over another. Thus, boys tend to outperform girls on multiple-choice sections of standardized tests, whereas free-response sections tend to favor girls. Also, sections that involve mechanical drawing or object rotation tend to favor boys. These conclusions indicate that the design of the test itself can generate a gender bias—one that has significant implications for students' educational outcomes (American Association of University Women 1998).

Understanding the gender bias that occurs in standardized testing is even more important since national educational policy has moved toward more required testing at various grade levels. The massive effort in recent years to enhance the science and math skills of the nation's young women has resulted in a decline of gender differences in math and science testing. But, failure to pay attention to the sources of these differences, including in test design, could erode the progress that has been made.

Gender and the Curriculum

Educational reforms to enhance the status of women and girls in education have focused not just on academic achievement but also on the content of what is learned in schools. This is reflected both in the content of the curriculum and in the course-taking patterns of students.

Before the emergence of the second wave of feminism in the last quarter of the twentieth century, women were rarely present at all in the educational curriculum at all levels. The growth of women's studies has changed this, although women and girls are still frequently stereotyped or missing altogether in what students learn. Events such as Women's History Month in March and Black History Month in February have highlighted the accomplishments of people long overlooked in school curricula, though many point out that segregating this material into one part of the academic calendar can reproduce the marginalization of excluded groups.

Publishers of educational material have become more attentive to including diverse groups, including women, in teaching materials. But as this has happened, new technologies have emerged that have brought new forms of gender inequality. Studies of technologically based course materials find that women are depicted far less often than men, and, when women are found, they are typically in stereotypical roles, such as mother or princess. Although computing technology has the potential to eliminate gender bias, it may only play on existing stereotypes, especially because fewer women than men have entered this field as software designers and computer engineers (American Association of University Women 1998).

In addition to gender stereotyping in curriculum materials, studies find that there are significant gender differences in what curriculum students are exposed to. This is especially apparent in science education. Numerous studies have shown that there are significant differences in the science curriculum that girls and boys take in school. In high school—a pattern then reflected later in college—girls are more likely to participate in biological sciences, boys in the physical sciences. Course-taking patterns are also reflected in the stereotypes that students hold: that "biology is for girls" and the other sciences are for boys. Girls also end up having less experience in manipulating laboratory equipment, even though studies find that girls tend to benefit from this kind of "hands-on" learning in science (Brotman and Moore 2008). In math, too, although boys and girls tend to take the same number of math courses, there are differences in what courses they take. Young women are more likely than boys to end their math studies after a second algebra course; in fact, girls now outnumber boys in taking algebra and geometry. But young men are more likely to take trigonometry and calculus, thereby giving them an advantage on higher-level math skills (American Association of University Women 1998).

In computer science courses, too, boys and young men outnumber girls. Although girls learn computer skills in courses such as data entry and word processing, these are skills that limit them to less stimulating and less lucrative jobs. Courses like graphic arts and computer-aided design, which can lead to better jobs, attract significantly fewer girls (American Association of University Women 1998). This contributes to the **digital divide**, referring to the gap that has opened between groups with strong computing skills and those without.

MEDIA MATTERS

Only Macho Boys Allowed

Since the passage of Title IX, which prohibits sex discrimination against students (and employees) in federally funded programs, numerous institutional changes that challenge gender bias in education have occurred. For example, in the 1980s and 1990s, researchers found that the number of female characters increased in educational textbooks, and these characters were often portrayed as possessing both masculine and feminine traits. Although this finding is important, it tells us only half the story. Are male characters in educational textbooks being portrayed in less stereotypical ways?

To answer this question, Lorraine Evans and Kimberly Davies analyzed the personality traits of 132 characters portrayed in first-, third-, and fifth-grade literature textbooks (*N* = 13 books). Based on a widely used psychological measure of masculinity and femininity, they developed an instrument that included 16 personality traits. The 8 masculine traits included aggressive, competitive, argumentative, decisive, assertive, risk-taker, self-reliant, and adventurous. The 8 feminine traits included nurturing, affectionate, tender, understanding, passive, impetuous, emotionally expressive, and panicky.

Evans and Davies found that the number of male and female characters in the stories they analyzed was relatively equal: 54 percent of characters were male and 46 percent of characters were female. However, when the number of characters was broken down by personality traits, they found that male characters were portrayed as significantly more aggressive, argumentative, and competitive and significantly less affectionate, emotionally expressive, passive, and tender than female characters. Female characters were shown more often as possessing many of the stereotypical feminine traits than male characters; however, they were also likely to possess some of the "less extreme" masculine traits such as self-reliance and assertiveness.

When the researchers compared the personality traits of characters by grade level, either no or very few significant differences were found between the male and female characters in the first- and fifth-grade readers. In third-grade readers; however, male and female characters were more likely to be portrayed on opposite ends of the gender spectrum. For example, male characters were significantly more likely to be depicted as aggressive, competitive, and argumentative than female characters. Female characters were significantly more likely than male characters to be portrayed as affectionate and passive.

Evans and Davies concluded that appropriate gender behavior for boys is as narrowly defined today as it was 30 years ago. Female characters have been given the opportunity to develop and express several masculine traits within textbooks, but male characters have been confined to displaying only the traits deemed socially appropriate for masculine behavior.

Source: Evans, Lorraine, and Kimberly Davies. 2000. "No Sissy Boys Here: A Content Analysis of the Representation of Masculinity in Elementary School Reading Textbooks." *Sex Roles* 42: 255–270.

Taken together, gender differences in science education result in problematic patterns—namely, that girls' attitudes toward science decline with age, as do girls' perceptions of their competence in science (Brotman and Moore 2008). But the problem is not attitudes alone. Teachers who are more attuned to issues of gender equity in science tend to generate more equitable classroom experiences (Bailey et al. 1999), thus creating more gender-inclusive practices can transform the participation of women in science-based fields.

TABLE 10.1   High School Graduates Taking "New Basics"* Curriculum

	Less than $25,000		$25,000–$75,000		More than $75,000	
	Men	Women	Men	Women	Men	Women
Asian American	24%	21%	29%	23%	32%	24%
Hispanic	12	13	22	19	N/A	N/A
African American	7	17	18	20	N/A	N/A
White	11	14	18	20	29	29

*Includes: 4 years English; 3 years social science; 2 years math and science; foreign language; and one semester computer science.

Source: Data from Jacqueline E. King. 2000. *Gender Equity in Higher Education: Are Male Students at a Disadvantage?* Washington, DC: American Council on Education, p. 5.

Beyond the formal curriculum, extracurricular activities also reproduce gender inequities in the curriculum. Even with the presence of Title IX, boys in school are more likely to participate in team sports, especially in the upper years of school. Girls are more likely to participate in the performing arts, school government and clubs, and literary activities. Each type of activity develops definite skills, but these choices tend to reinforce traditional areas of "gender competency" (American Association of University Women 1998).

Furthermore, sports receive the most attention of all of the extracurricular activities. Although girls and women have become much more active in sports (largely as the result of the Title IX legislation), boys' high-profile teams—football and basketball—receive the most attention and, typically, the highest school budgets. You can see this simply by checking the newspaper coverage of different athletic activities. Research on the connection between students' athletic involvement and their academic work also reveals fascinating gender patterns. The graduation rates of male college athletes, particularly in those schools with the most prestigious football and sports programs, are notoriously low. Graduation rates for women athletes, on the other hand, are typically at or above the graduation rates for women who are not athletes. Different from boys, girls who participate in sports are consistently shown in the research literature to have stronger self-esteem, good physical and mental health, and strong academic performance (American Association of University Women 1998). However, an interesting caveat comes from studies of cheerleaders: Participation in cheerleading is negatively associated with success in science (Hanson and Kraus 1998).

In sum, research on gender and academic achievement shows that efforts to reduce the gender gap have been successful in many ways, although much remains to be done. Developing educational programs—including educational assessment—that take the diversity of students into account seems to be the path most likely to produce favorable outcomes for both young women and young men.

Class and Race Inequality

The gender gap in education is further exacerbated by race and class inequalities that permeate educational institutions. Education is one area where much progress has been made in recent years. African Americans and Hispanics have improved their high school completion rates, although they still lag behind Whites. And the gender gap within racial ethnic groups is telling, as Figure 10.2 shows. Nationally, the high school dropout rate for Hispanics (men and women) is higher than for any other group—four times that for Whites and nearly three times that for African Americans (National Center for Educational Statistics 2009).

In looking at educational attainment data, it is important to look at diversity within groups—not only gender but also class. Class and immigration patterns matter in predicting educational attainment. For example, by the year 2000, 75 percent of Asian school-age children were either foreign born or children of recent immigrants and, thus, more likely than other groups to be poor. Despite stereotypes of Asian Americans as high achievers, many live in poverty and are poorly educated. And there is a tendency to overlook Asian Americans, given the Black–White model that dominates the study of U.S. race relations (Olsen 1997). The diverse backgrounds of African American, Hispanic, Asian American, and Native American children make it important to examine race, class, and gender when studying educational achievement.

Even with the disadvantages that accrue to different groups by virtue of race, class, and gender, the majority do succeed! Understanding how they do so is as important to building equitable educational policy as understanding the obstacles to success. A study of Latinas who have been successful in school (Barajas and Pierce 2001), reveals some of the factors that can encourage success: Latinos and Latinas who have successfully navigated the path from high school to college

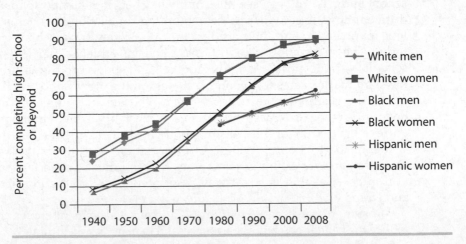

FIGURE 10.2   High School Completion by Gender and Race

Source: Data from: National Center for Educational Statistics. 2009. *Digest of Education Statistics 2008*. Washington, DC: U.S. Department of Education. Website: http://nces.ed.gov.

are shown to have maintained positive definitions of themselves, definitions that are often developed in the context of "safe spaces" where they develop positive relationships with other Latinas and where they have been carefully mentored by sponsors who look out for their well-being.

Research on student success has led researchers to move away from the *deficit model of education* in which women and people of color are seen as lacking and the focus becomes on changing them rather than changing the system. Different groups have their own educational needs. The point is not just to provide the same thing to everyone—or to postulate women and people of color as needing to catch up—but instead to shape education around the varying needs of diverse groups of students. Those who have reviewed patterns of gender, race, and class in educational achievement and opportunity thus conclude that "the gender gap is dwarfed by the educational chasms related to race/ethnicity and social class" (King 2000). This is not a reason to abandon efforts to build more gender equity, but it emphasizes the need to consider educational reforms in the full context of gender, race, and class inequality.

WOMEN IN HIGHER EDUCATION

In higher education, women are no longer formally excluded as they were previously. In fact, women are now a majority of college students; however, as the educational pyramid represented in Figure 10.3 (page 312) shows, the percentage of women in higher education declines as one moves up the educational hierarchy. Women and men are equally likely to complete a high school education; then women are the majority of entering college students and recipients of associate's, bachelor's, and master's degrees. They have gained as the percentage of those receiving doctorates and professional degrees and are expected to continue receiving the same percentage of such degrees into the foreseeable future.

As faculty, however, women are concentrated in the lower ranks, clustered in colleges at the lowest-status and lowest-paid faculty positions, as instructors and lecturers. And, to this day, the more elite and prestigious the institution, the smaller the likelihood that women will be found in the highest ranks of the faculty.

Race further complicates this picture. As students, African Americans, Hispanics, and Native Americans are less likely to attend college than Whites, although all three groups have increased their college attendance quite substantially in recent years. Among both African Americans and Hispanics, women are more likely to attend college than are men. Women of color, then, earn more college degrees (at every level: associate's, bachelor's, master's, and doctoral) than men of color. Oddly, this does not translate into women of color being more likely to be on the faculty, since among all minority groups—African American, Hispanic, Asian American, and Native American—men outnumber women as full-time faculty members, even though the percentage of both is quite small relative to White men and women. And, just as with the pattern by gender, the higher the academic rank, the smaller the proportion of men and women faculty of color (Harvey 2003).

The status of women and people of color in higher education is important not only because of the opportunity structure that gender, race, and class are

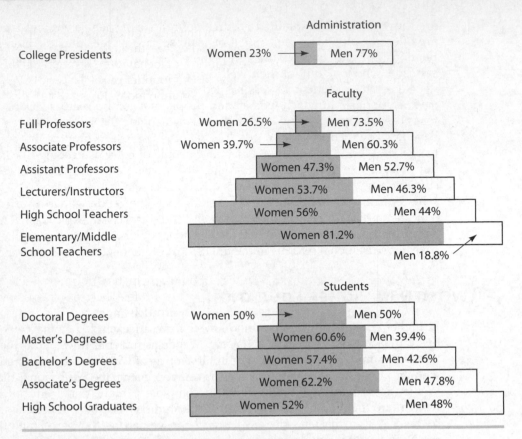

FIGURE 10.3 The Educational Pyramid

Sources: U.S. Department of Labor. 2009. *Employment and Earnings.* Washington, DC: U.S. Department of Labor, p. 210; American Council on Education. 2007. *American College President.* Washington, DC: American Council on Education; National Center for Educational Statistics. 2008. *Digest of Education Statistics 2008.* Washington, DC: U.S. Department of Education. Website: http://nces.ed.gov.

embedded within but also because the status of women and people of color in educational institutions has important ramifications for how academic knowledge is constructed. In Chapter 3, we studied how ideas are constructed within institutional contexts. Academic knowledge is no exception. Like popular culture, the creation of academic knowledge is shaped by the context in which it is developed. Because what is generated as knowledge is the basis of our understanding of the world and the source of new discoveries, understanding the setting in which research and scholarship is produced can teach you much about the assumptions built into what we know.

Because of the status of women in higher education—a status that is marked both by exclusion, invisibility, and segregation—women have often been either overlooked or distorted in the research that forms our society's body of knowledge. This inaccuracy has several consequences both for the personal experiences of women faculty and for the state of knowledge in general. At the personal level, women may find that their personalities (formed as they are through cultural expectations of femininity) are at odds with the values and behaviors surrounding them. This dilemma was expressed by sociologist (and a founder of the National Organization of Women) Alice Rossi in 1970 and is still common today. Rossi wrote:

> *Women who are intellectually or politically brilliant are more readily accepted by men if they are also properly feminine in their style and deportment with men. This helps to assure that there will be few women of achievement for men to "exempt" from the general category of women, since the traits associated with traditional femininity—softness, compliance, sweetness—are rarely found together with the contradictory qualities of a vigorous and questioning intellect, and a willingness to persist on a problem against conventional assumptions. (1970:36)*

For students, the gender bias in education can also seriously affect their learning. Women may be discouraged from classroom participation or may even steer them away from particular courses and departments. Professors who make sexist, racist, or homophobic comments can fill students with such anger that it is impossible for them to learn in that environment. Men, too, are affected by such an environment because it prevents men from regarding women as full peers and it hampers men's ability to relate to women as equals in the worlds of work and families. Or, simply ignoring women can make men feel marginalized, even if it is not explicitly intended by the teacher or professor.

Of special concern is women's and young girls' risk of **sexual harassment** in schools. Large numbers of both girls and boys report being sexually harassed by their peers, including as early as grade school. In surveys, 87 percent of girls and 79 percent of boys report being sexually harassed by peers, although girls experience overt forms of sexual harassment more than boys and boys are more likely to perpetrate it (Fineran and Bennett 1999; Murinen and Smolak 2000). Much, but not all, of the harassment that occurs is between students. And, although students may interpret harassment by peers as "just fun between friends," studies find that it nonetheless harms students' sense of self-worth (Hysock 2006). Studies also indicate that sexual harassment is most often directed against gay and lesbian students, who also feel more upset and threatened by harassment by peers than their heterosexual counterparts (Fineran 2001). Although subject to change, current constitutional law makes schools liable for sexual harassment by a teacher against a student when a district official knows about it and does nothing.

The consequences of gender bias in education are that women seem to feel that they are outsiders in a predominantly man's world. Men's unequal power in academic institutions also influences the social production of knowledge because the existing schemes of understanding have been created within a particular setting, one in which men have been the primary subjects and are seen as holding authority. The status of being an outsider does, however, influence how people see the world, an insight gained from sociological theory. Georg Simmel (1858–1918) described a stranger as someone who is "fixed within a particular spatial group whose boundaries are similar to spatial boundaries. But his [or her] position in this group is determined, essentially, by the fact that he [or she] has not belonged to it from the beginning, that he [or she] imports qualities into it which do not and cannot stem from the group itself" (cited in Wolff 1950: 402). The stranger, like an outsider, is both close to and distant from the group and its beliefs. The outsider is both involved with and indifferent to the shared perspectives of the group as a whole. This detachment creates critical distance, so that what is taken for granted by group members may be held in doubt by outsiders. As feminists have put it, "The outsider is denied the filtered vision that allows men to live without too troubling an insight" (Gornick 1971:126).

In women's studies, then, many have argued that women's status as outsiders in academic disciplines has given them a unique form of knowledge. Thus, Marcia Westkott writes:

> When women realize that we are simultaneously immersed in and estranged from both our own particular discipline and the Western intellectual tradition generally, a personal tension develops that informs the critical dialogue. This tension, rooted in the contradiction of women's belonging and not belonging, provides the basis for knowing deeply and personally that which we criticize. A personally experienced, culturally-based contradiction means that in some fundamental way we as critics also oppose ourselves, or, at least, that part of us continues to sustain the very basis of our own estrangement. Hence, the personal struggle of being both an insider and outsider is not only a source of knowledge and insight, but also a source of self-criticism. (1979: 422)

In the history of sociological thought, marginality and alienation, especially during periods of rapid social change, have produced many valuable insights. Scientific thinking, including sociological thinking, has flourished in periods of uncertainty because doubt and transformation foster the development of personal and collective creative thought. Recall that in Chapter 1, we noted C. Wright Mills's assertion that personal and societal troubles that destroy the facades of conventional wisdom also form the scientific basis of the sociological imagination.

For outsiders, their paradoxical closeness to and remoteness from social groups may result in new perspectives on knowledge. It is the outsider who suspends belief in the taken-for-granted attitudes of institutions. As a result, the status of women as outsiders in intellectual life results in new methodologies and new perspectives in social and political thought. Women of color within the academy also stand as outsiders, or as what Patricia Hill Collins (1986, 1998) calls "outsiders within." Marginalized by both their race and gender, women of color have a unique standpoint in the academy and can therefore provide distinct and revealing analyses of race, class, and gender. Insiders to any group develop similar worldviews; as a result, it often takes the perspective of outsiders to challenge these taken-for-granted views. As outsiders within the academy, women of color are in a unique position to generate new knowledge. They are trained in the methods and theories of their disciplines but do not necessarily share the privileges, patterns of belief, or historical experiences of insiders. Because they are outsiders within, women of color can generate new forms of insight and make visible those structures of oppression that are less apparent to members of more privileged groups.

GENDER, SCIENCE, AND SOCIETY

Women's status as outsiders in education has been especially important in studying women in science. As one of the areas where women have been most excluded, science has been a strongly *gendered institution*. In the remainder of this chapter, we look at the status of women in science with a particular eye to what this means for the social construction of knowledge in a society so strongly rooted in scientific thought and discovery.

The Status of Women in Science

Even a cursory look at the position of women in science shows the gender segregation and gender hierarchy of science as an institution. As we have seen, beginning early in students' learning, boys and girls begin to depart in their expressed interest in math and science. Furthermore, the gap is reflected in course-taking patterns. By the college years, gender segregation in the math and science curriculum is especially high, with women being a significant minority of majors in math and science (except biology). And, except for the social sciences, women are then a relatively small proportion of the scientific workforce. On the positive side, the number of women receiving science and math degrees, and therefore being more likely to move into scientific careers, has increased substantially. But science continues to bear the imprint of the fact that most scientists have been men. Increasing the numbers of women in science is one thing, but scholars have also shown that the culture of scientific workplaces (including in industry, research, and academia) is marked by an organizational culture that values the attributes most often associated with men. Thus, women report that they are not often taken

Research finds that young girls do just as well, if not better, in math and science in the early years, but as they begin to think that these are fields mostly for men, their interest often declines.

seriously and that scientific careers follow a male life course trajectory (such as in the fact that one is expected to do one's best work while still quite young—a time when many will be establishing families). For this reason, feminist scholars have argued that bringing more women into science is not just about numbers; it's also about transforming the culture that marks science as an institution (Fox 2001).

Women are not, of course, absent from science; they constitute a large proportion of the technical, clerical, domestic, teaching, and plant maintenance staffs required to do scientific work. Still, women, and especially women of color, appear as objects and "others" in science; they are exploited as research subjects, and their labor in the production of science remains invisible to the scientific elite. The decision makers in science—those who define scientific problems, set scientific agendas, fund scientific projects, and relate science to public policy—are overwhelmingly men (See Figure 10.4).

Some feminists argue that science is produced and applied within a distinctively masculine framework, one that values objective separation from the objects of research and yet is nonetheless gendered in the descriptions and explanations it offers of the natural and social worlds. Evelyn Fox Keller calls this a "science/gender"

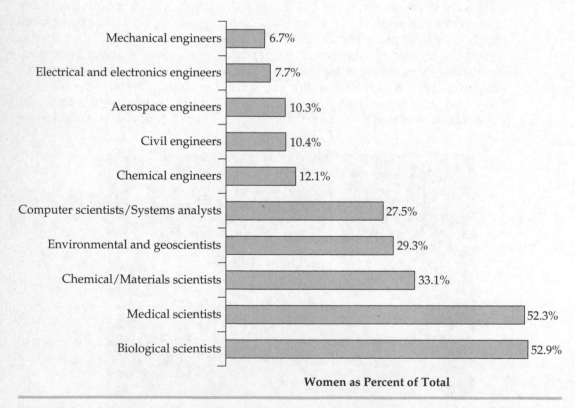

FIGURE 10.4 Women in Science and Engineering Professions

Source: Bureau of Labor Statistics. 2009. *Employment and Earnings.* Washington, DC: U.S. Department of Labor, pp. 209–210. www.bls.gov.

system, a network of associations between our concepts of masculinity and femininity and the construction of science. She argues that to examine the roots, dynamics, and consequences of the science/gender system, it is necessary to understand how ideologies of gender and science inform each other and how this affects social arrangements between men and women, science and nature (Keller 1985).

Asking how and why women have been excluded from the practice of science is one way to reveal deeply embedded gender, race, and class patterns in the structure of scientific professions and consequently in the character of scientific thought. Rossiter's (1982) work on the history of women in science shows that the concept of a woman scientist is perceived as a contradiction in terms, since scientists are supposed to be tough, rigorous, rational, impersonal, unemotional, and competitive, which women are presumed not to be. Often, when women make major contributions to science, their work is ignored, belittled, or claimed by men. A classic example is the discovery of DNA. James Watson, one of the scientists who discovered DNA, tells the story of his and Francis Crick's (a man) discovery in a famous book, *The Double Helix* (1968). The book reveals a woman colleague, Rosalind Franklin, who, it is clear from other accounts, should have shared Watson's and Crick's credit (Sayre 1975).

Sometimes women's exclusion from science is not only as scientists but also as subjects of scientific research. In the early 1990s, for example, several reports published in medical journals and reported in the national press documented the exclusion of women from major national health studies of heart disease, lung cancer, and kidney disease. As a result, a federal law was passed requiring researchers using federal funds to analyze the effects of new drugs and treatments on women. But a report issued in 2000 indicated that researchers often skirt the law, thereby producing conclusions that cannot be generalized to the whole population (Pear 2001). Extrapolating from studies of men to the treatment of women leads to potentially faulty treatment. Men and women sometimes report different symptoms of the same disease, and some treatments may be more effective for one group than another. For example, although women suffer from depression more than do men, much of the research on antidepressant drugs has involved only male research subjects. Treating women based on the results of research from all male samples can be risky.

Science, Feminism, and the Social Construction of Knowledge

Understanding the relationship between the gendered structure of institutions (such as education) and how knowledge is constructed within these institutions is key to understanding the critique of science that has emerged from feminist studies. Scientific knowledge in our society is seen as a source of great authority. Scientific careers carry much prestige, and scientists have a great deal of power to influence the everyday experiences of our lives. Scientific explanations are generally thought to be objective accounts that are uninfluenced by the values and interests of scientific thinkers. Science thus has the image of being value neutral and true to the facts. Objectivity in science is depicted as stemming from the calculated distance between the observer and the observed. In the scientific framework, personal characteristics of scientific observers are not expected to influence their results.

Despite the strong claims of neutrality and objectivity by scientists, the fact is that science is closely tied to the centers of power in this society and interwoven with capitalist and patriarchal institutions. This has many implications for understanding the social structure of science as well as for understanding how the social structure of science influences the production of scientific knowledge. As you have already seen, allegedly scientific claims are often used to support sexist and racist beliefs. One could argue that such claims are simply a case of bad science, but feminist critiques of scientific knowledge go deeper, asking how the

FOCUS ON RESEARCH

Genes, Gender, and the Market in Eggs and Sperm

New advances in reproductive medicine now allow reproduction to occur through various scientific means. This had led to the development of new markets in egg donation and sperm banks where men and women can be paid through donation of bodily material and others can purchase a fertilized embryo. In this process, eggs are removed from the donor woman through outpatient surgery and then mixed with sperm from a sperm bank. If fertilization occurs, the embryo is implanted in the recipient's uterus with, presumably, a resulting birth. Although biological differences between women and men affect how the donation takes places (surgery for the donating woman and ejaculation for the donating man), the products sold—eggs and sperm—have equal value in that both are necessary for reproduction to occur.

So, where does gender enter the picture? This is what Rene Labeling studied in her analysis of the medical market in eggs and sperm. She interviewed staff at two egg agencies and two sperm banks and observed for several days in the offices of each. In addition, she analyzed the blank donor applications from each agency and studied their medical releases, legal consent forms, and marketing materials. What she found was a highly gendered process.

Beginning with the recruitment of potential donors, gender differences emerge. Sperm banks highlight the financial interests of potential donors in their advertising, often employing humor, such as depicting cartoon-like images of sperm and telling potential donors they can "get paid for what they are already doing" (p. 325). Sperm banks also tend to locate their business near prestigious university campuses where the financial needs of students also provide some economic incentive for donation. In contrast, at the egg agencies, the appeal is made to potential donors in terms of an altruistic appeal—that they will be helping others. Their marketing strategy is seldom framed by economic incentive, even though there is a financial benefit to the donor. Instead, the marketing shows images of plump, happy babies where donors have helped others achieve parenthood.

Egg agencies look for highly educated women who are physically attractive and who have caring and motherly personalities. By comparison, the primary characteristics sought of sperm donors are being highly educated and tall. The egg agencies require donors to be psychologically assessed, but neither of the sperm banks have such a requirement. Both egg and sperm banks recruit from a diverse racial, ethnic, and religious pool, but organize their donor files by race.

Labeling concludes that the medical marketplace is indeed a highly gendered place, where the economic value of human body parts intertwines with cultural norms about gender. Her research shows how presumably scientifically neutral bodily practices are transformed by the social relations of gender.

Source: Based on Almeling, Rene. 2007. "Selling Genes, Selling Gender: Egg Agencies, Sperm Banks, and the Medical Market in Genetic Material." *American Sociological Review* 72 (June): 319–348.

social structure of scientific professions is related to the scientific views and conclusions scientists make.

Many argue (Fee 1983; Harding 1986, 1991, 1993, 1998) that gender identity is at the very heart of the definition of science because scientific norms of detachment, distance, and rationality match those of masculine culture. Feminist critiques of science also reveal that scientific thought often reflects the patriarchal ideology of the culture. One way this happens is through the projection of patriarchal values onto scientific descriptions of the physical world. For example, kingdoms and orders are not intrinsic to the nature of organisms but have evolved in a patriarchal world that values hierarchy and patrilineage (Hubbard 1984). Note, also, the description of the experimental **scientific method** offered by Francis Bacon, one of the sixteenth-century founders of modern scientific thought:

> *For you have but to follow and as it were hound nature in her wanderings, and you will be able when you like to lead and drive her afterward to the same place again . . . . Neither ought a man to make scruple of entering and penetrating into those holes and corners, when the inquisition of truth is his whole object. (cited in Harding 1986:116)*

The emergence of modern science is founded on an image of rational man as conquering the passions of nature, which is depicted as female. Consider Machiavelli's famed quotation from *The Prince* regarding fortune:

> *Fortune is a woman and it is necessary if you wish to master her to conquer her by force; and it can be seen that she lets herself be overcome by the bold rather than by those who proceed coldly, and therefore like a woman, she is always a friend to the young because they are less cautious, fiercer, and master her with greater audacity. (cited in Harding 1986:115)*

Such depictions of science and nature might be dismissed as old-fashioned ramblings of patriarchal days gone by, except for the fact that gendered descriptions of biological phenomena still influence the way we imagine physical events. Think, for example, of sperm, popularly depicted as lively and aggressive swimmers, rigorously pursuing the waiting egg. Alice Rossi describes this as a fantasy of male sexual power. She writes:

> *Ever since Leewenhoek first saw sperm under the microscope, great significance has been attached to the fact that sperm are equipped with motile flagella, and it was assumed that the locomotive ability of the sperm fully explained their journey from the vagina through the cervix and uterus to the oviduct for the encounter with the ovum . . . . Rorvik (1971) describes the seven-inch journey through the birth canal and womb to the waiting egg as equivalent to a 500-mile upstream swim for a salmon and comments with admiration that they often make the hazardous journey in under an hour, "more than earning their title as the most powerful and rapid living creatures on earth." The image is clear: powerful active sperm and a passive ovum awaiting its arrival and penetration, male sexual imagery structuring the very act of conception. (1977:16–17)*

In fact, as Rossi points out, uterine contractions, stimulated by the release of the hormone oxytocin, propel the sperm through the female system so that "completely inert substances such as dead sperm and even particles of India ink reach the oviducts as rapidly as live sperm do" (Rossi 1977:17).

In her study analyzing the images of reproduction in contemporary biology textbooks, Emily Martin, an anthropologist, found that sperm are still described as active, aggressive agents, while eggs are portrayed in passive terms. According to Martin, the texts stress that sperm are actively produced, while female ova "merely sit on the shelf, slowly degenerating and aging like an overstocked inventory" (1991:487). Citing text authors, Martin writes that texts liken the egg's role to that of Sleeping Beauty: "a dormant bride awaiting her mate's magic kiss, which instills the spirit that brings her to life." Sperm, by contrast, have a "mission," which is to "move through the female genital tract in quest of the ovum." One popular account has it that the sperm carry out a "perilous journey" into the "warm darkness," where some fall away "exhausted." "Survivors" "assault" the egg, the successful candidates "surrounding the prize" (1991:490).

The fact is, sperm do not merely penetrate a passive egg; rather, the sperm and egg stick together because of adhesive molecules on the surface of each. Nor are sperm as mobile as their descriptions suggest. Despite knowledge to the contrary, metaphorical descriptions of the biological reproductive process make the event seem like a contemporary soap opera or moral fable. As Martin illustrates, the descriptions used by scientists have prevented them from seeing how eggs and sperm actually interact. Thus, cultural values influence the discovery of scientific facts (Bordo 1995).

The point is not to abandon science, but to understand that within scientific studies, bias can enter the scientist's choice of topic, choice of research subjects, definitions of concepts, method of observation, analysis and interpretation of data, and manner of reporting (Longino and Doell 1983). Gendered assumptions infiltrate the scientific record; many of the "truths" alleged by scientific studies merely reflect the interests of a male-dominated society. Feminist revisions of science call for a more inclusive and reflective perspective by recognizing the interplay between scientific knowledge and the social systems in which science is produced. Feminist revisions of science also seek a more humanistic science, one in which science is used for human liberation from race, class, and gender oppression.

Social experience and consciousness are conditioned by the location of our existence. Because men and women have quite different life situations, their consciousness, culture, and ideas are also different. As Dorothy Smith (1987, 1990) argues, the activity of women (and, by implication, men) forms the basis for their ideas. Because sex-gender systems organize social relations and because intellectual thought is shaped by social relations, the sex-gender system shapes our perspectives as social thinkers and researchers.

Epistemology refers to the ways of knowing that form systems of social thought. This idea emphasizes that knowledge is socially constructed and that ways of thinking are embedded in a variety of assumptions, implicit and explicit, that guide their shape and form. Feminist epistemology, a relatively recent development in feminist theory, is the examination of how gender relations shape the production of thought, including feminist theory itself. Feminist epistemology raises new questions, both about the systems of thinking that have been derived from androcentric (i.e., male-centered) ways of knowing and about new ways of constructing knowledge to be more inclusive of and centered in women's experiences.

One major area of discussion in feminist epistemology is the social construction of science, a particularly important subject because of the deep and central ways that scientific knowledge shapes Western ways of knowing. In the seventeenth century, as modern science began, scientific inquiry was justified for its specific social value; moreover, the legitimacy of scientific inquiry rested on the same principles of reform that today sound like feminist social practices—antiauthoritarianism, progressiveness, anti-elitism, educational reform, humanitarianism, and the unity of experience and knowing (Van Den Daele 1977). Contemporary debates about the social and political application of scientific knowledge, for example, in genetic engineering of food, indicate that scientific application is not separate from the practice of scientific inquiry.

Historically, science emerged in specific opposition to the canons of traditional belief, especially as a challenge to the state and the political authority of the church. As historians of science write, "The breakdown of older patterns of authority and traditionally-held dogmas or consensus positions allows much broader boundaries for exploration and the staking out of positions previously proscribed—either tacitly or implicitly" (Mendelssohn et al. 1977:10). By removing the blinders of earlier commitments, scientists have argued that more objective inquiry would provide the new facts and new perspectives needed to meet the emerging needs of society.

Feminists argue that new perspectives on women's lives—specifically ones that challenge sexist assumptions—will result in more accurate explanations of women's experiences. Feminists thus still use scientific methods in their studies, but claim that their work is more objective because it is more inclusive of all persons' experiences.

A central question in feminist scholarship is the issue of objectivity and its relationship to the process of knowing (Harding 1986, 1991, 1998). According to standard arguments about sociological research, rigorous observation and the use of the scientific method eliminate observer bias, but many feminists argue that the observer is not a neutral party. Because knowledge is socially produced, the particular experiences and attitudes that observers bring to their work influence what they study, how they study it, and what they conclude about it. Untangling the relationship between the knower and the known is essential, according to feminist scientists. Thus, all research is done from a particular standpoint or location in the social system (Smith 1990; Harding 1986; Collins 1990). The world is known from the perspective of the researcher. In any given research project, we must know both the subjects' and the researcher's points of entry to the project. Most often, sociologists enter research projects through official institutions (e.g., schools, police, social welfare agencies, etc.); consequently, the work they do may support the status quo and be distorted by the view of official agencies. The most objective inquiries can be produced only by those with the least interest in preserving the status quo (Smith 1990).

Dorothy Smith, a Canadian feminist sociologist, explains this idea by using an example from the German philosopher Hegel. Suppose we want to comprehend the world of a master and a slave. Both of them live in the same world, but their experience within that world is quite different. The master takes the slave's labor (in fact, the slave's very existence) for granted; thus, the master's needs are immediately satisfied through slave labor. The slave, on the other hand, conforms to the master's will; his or her labor is an object of the master's consciousness. The organization of this relationship is invisible to the master. If the master were describing the world they both inhabit, the master's account would be less objective because the structures of that world are invisible to him or her. The slave's description of the world, on the other hand, would include the master, plus the fact of his or her own labor and its transformation to the status of an object. As a result, the slave is more objective because his or her account is both more complete and more directly related to the empirical events within the relationship and the world in which it is located.

When we begin describing the world by examining women's experiences, the knowledge we create does not merely add to the already established constructs of sociological thought. The experience of women, like that of the slave, has been invisible. Women inhabit the same world as men; in fact, women's labor shapes men's experience in the world (through housework and the maintenance of social and bodily relations). Women's labor makes men's mode of operation, detached and rational, possible; yet, it remains invisible to men as the dominant class. An objective sociological account of reality must make sense of both women's and men's experiences and must therefore be constructed from the vantage point of both.

Smith (1987) also argues that sociological research and theory must situate social actors within their everyday worlds. In other words, unless research begins with the ordinary facts of lives, then the knowledge that sociologists construct will be both alienating and apart from the actual experiences of human actors. Sociological analysis begins with the immediate experience of social actors, but goes beyond that experience by discovering the social-institutional context of their lives. Although the institutional context of everyday experience is not immediately visible to those who live it, the sociological perspective makes this context available and thus is a powerful agent of social change. Like that of C. Wright Mills, Smith's objective is to establish the relationship between social structure and everyday life. This relationship is especially important in comprehending women's experiences because the affairs of everyday life are the specific area of women's expertise. Given the gender division of labor, women are charged with maintaining everyday life. To overlook that fact or to treat it as insignificant is to deny women's reality (Rineharz 1983; Smith 1987).

Feminist **standpoint theory** suggests that the specific social location of the knower shapes what is known and that not all perspectives are equally valid or complete. Again, think of the master and the slave. Because the master takes the slave's existence for granted, the master cannot see the world as the slave sees it—including the world that constructs the relationship of the master and the slave. The slave's view is not as partial, or as incomplete, as that of the master, and it is likely to produce a less distorted account of the world in which both the slave and the master live.

Likewise, feminist standpoint theory argues that women's specific location in patriarchal societies is actually a resource in the construction of new knowledge (Harding 1991, 1998; Collins 1998). This does not result from the biological fact of being a woman but from the unique experience of women as an oppressed group confronting a patriarchal society. Standpoint theory assumes that systems of privilege are least visible to those who benefit the most from them and who, at the same time, control the resources that define dominant belief systems. Whites, for example, are more likely to deny that racism exists; people of color both see the assaults racism produce and understand the nuances of racism in everyday life. Similarly, men can more easily deny the presence of patriarchy than can women, even when women do not fully grasp the workings of sexist oppression. It takes the standpoint of oppressed groups to see and recognize systems of race, class, and gender privilege. Dominant groups can, of course, learn to see how race, gender, and class privilege structure social relations, but they do so through analysis and observation, not simply from the conditions of their own experience.

Standpoint theory does not mean that we have to take the word of oppressed groups at face value to know how society is structured. Systems of oppression also shape the consciousness of the oppressed. Theory constructed from the observed experiences of dominant and subordinate groups yields the insights that produce liberating knowledge.

Chapter Summary and Themes

Historically, education has been defined as the privilege of a few, but the growth of public education has, over time, been extended to diverse groups.

Initially, public education was intended to inculcate dominant group values among immigrant groups. Denying women's education was justified by ideologies that promoted biologically determinist arguments about women's abilities to learn.

Although women are now the majority of students at virtually every level of public education, a gender gap persists in various dimensions of the schooling experiences.

A hidden curriculum in schools is part of the gender socialization that produces different educational outcomes for women and men. Women become segregated into particular fields of education and still fall behind in education that leads to careers in math and science.

Women in higher education are the majority of students, but they are segregated into particular fields and, as faculty, have not achieved equity with men.

An educational pyramid shows that the higher one goes in education, the less likely one will find women—as students or as faculty. Although women are making many gains, they are still marginalized within higher education. These patterns are exacerbated for women of color.

Scientific fields are still largely perceived as the world of men, although women have been making inroads into these professions.

Patterns of gender exclusion in the sciences begin early in schooling and are reflected in the lower percentages of women, compared to men, who enter scientific careers.

Feminist scholars have identified scientific knowledge as socially constructed through masculine imagery, thus distorting what is scientifically known.

Feminist standpoint theory suggests that the social location of "knower" shapes what is known, including in the sciences. This perspective suggests that only with the greater inclusion of those who have been excluded can objective scientific knowledge be created.

■ Key Terms

digital divide	self-fulfilling prophecy	Title IX of the Educational
epistemology	sexual harassment	Amendments
scientific method	standpoint theory	tracking
self-esteem	stereotype threat	

■ Discussion Questions/Projects for Thought

1. Find out what the proportion of women is compared with men in your school, as well as the areas of study that each group pursues. Do you see evidence of gender segregation in education? If so, what explains it, and do you think this is changing over time?

2. Interview a group of young girls in elementary school, junior high school, and high school and ask about their interests in science and math. Do you see evidence of change in scientific interests over time? What do you think explains this?

3. Identify one of the other courses you are taking and examine the textbook to see where women are included and/or excluded. What does this tell you about the construction of knowledge in that field?

Women, Power, and Politics

For the first time in our nation's history, we are witnessing an extraordinary transformation of the place of women in the political system. Hillary Rodham Clinton, now Secretary of State and former First Lady, was a serious contender for the highest office in the land: the presidency. Sarah Palin, former governor of Alaska and vice presidential candidate in the 2008 election, has become a major political spokesperson for the Republican Party—and the conservative movement in the United States—a place once inhabited mostly by White men. Record numbers of women are serving in national office and in presidential appointments. More women serve in the U.S. Senate than at any time in history—17 of 100 (enough that as recently as 1992 the Senate had to be remodeled because there was no bathroom for women near the Senate floor!).

Yet, although women are reaching new heights of political power, old attitudes and stereotypes still remain. Think of how First Ladies are considered—the very role presuming a certain gender order. What if a woman were elected to the presidency? Would there be a First Man? What would his role be? And doesn't this presuppose that the highest position in the nation—indeed the world—must be a married, heterosexual man? First Ladies themselves are also subjected to particular gender expectations. They are widely adored when they adopt a traditional helpmate role—supporting their husband, staying in the background, and focusing on concerns traditionally thought of as in women's realm, such as children, health, and education.

This became even more complicated by race when First Lady Michelle Obama stepped into this role. She was completely dissected in the press—mostly for her well-toned arms. Media pundits raged on about whether it was "appropriate" for her to wear sleeveless dresses; her arms were scrutinized every which way—as if she were simply a body specimen, not an intelligent, well-educated, highly accomplished person. Would this have ever happened to someone of a different race or gender?

Contradictions abound and opposing movements define the contemporary place of women in politics. The juxtaposition of Hillary Clinton and Sarah Palin in the 2008 election and its aftermath could not make this clearer. Although both hold power and influence, what they support and what they represent could not be more divergent. Even the public reaction to each of them is moored in gendered beliefs that, whatever you think of Clinton's or Palin's political position, reflect a deep discomfort with outspoken women. Like all women in the political realm, they exist within a system of power and politics that is a deeply gendered institution.

Feminist scholars have shown how deeply gender influences political behavior, political attitudes, and the structure of political institutions. Gender shapes power and politics, although the dominant construction of gender in politics has been resisted and fought by the many women who have organized politically to create social change. The feminist movement has been one of the most powerful forces of social change in our times, and women have also been critical in the mobilization of other movements—the civil rights movement, the environmental movement, and antiwar movements. As you read about women, gender, and political behavior, you should keep this resistance in mind. It is evidence of the capacity of women—and men—to make change even in the face of what seems to be intractable.

DEFINING POWER

Power has traditionally been believed to be the province of men. Indeed, judging by some indicators, this has changed very little—just notice how few women are heads of state, particularly in the major world powers. Women, instead, are seen as exercising power primarily at home (a myth exposed by considering men's power in the family; see Chapter 6). Women have also been stereotyped as holding the "power behind the throne," as if women's power comes primarily from their presumed manipulation of men and as if women's primary political role is to remain invisible and out of public view.

Power is the ability to influence others. Power comes in many forms. It can be exercised by individuals or groups and within and outside of formal social institutions. Power can come through persuasion, charisma, law, political activism, and coercion. It is not just an individual attribute, even though some individuals may be more powerful than others. Power in society comes as the result of a social process and social relationships; the use of power cannot be understood without reference to this social context. To explain further, although an individual may have characteristics that make him or her more powerful (i.e., the person's race, gender, age, religion, social class, education, etc.), it is the value that society has placed on these characteristics that gives the person power. Moreover, exercising power means people have to be situated such that they can mobilize the resources needed to influence others.

Consider men's power. Feminists describe men's power as a system of **patriarchy**, meaning an organized social structure whereby men as a group hold more power than women. Patriarchal societies give men power and authority over women; this can be institutional and/or individual. Societies will differ in exactly how patriarchal power is structured. For example, in a monarchy, an individual man (e.g., as a king or an emperor) may have ultimate power and authority. In a democratic society, power is determined through law and the various regulatory institutions that uphold and enforce the law. If men control the law-making process and the institutions that implement the law, however, they hold institutional power. In this sense, patriarchy becomes part of the structure of the society, even if power is not held by a single or particular man. In such a system, patriarchy structures the many social institutions that regulate and determine the nature of women's lives. In this sense, the United States is a patriarchal society.

Men's power does not stem from the mere fact of their being biologically male, nor does having institutions that are patriarchal mean that every individual man is powerful. Patriarchy in an institutional sense means that social institutions have been organized over time to give men more advantage than women (recognizing that this advantage is also influenced by other factors, such as one's social class, religion, race, etc.). It is the structural supports given to men's power that constitute the institutional basis of patriarchy.

To understand this, think about the subject of marital violence. Feminists explain men's violence against women as an expression of men's power, a power manifested in the actual marital relationship where violence occurs. Beyond the relationship between these two people, other institutions are organized to support men's power. Women who turn to these institutions for help often find that the system does not work on their behalf. Understanding violence against women, then, is a matter of understanding both individual power relationships and institutional power relationships.

Power is not all one-sided, however. People can mobilize to challenge existing power arrangements in society, and individuals can work to create more egalitarian relationships. Power does not come only from within existing institutions. People can mobilize to alter the structural supports that give power to some groups and not others; thus, social movements and other forms of political action are means of challenging and transforming the status quo. Although the existing system may give certain power resources to certain groups, people can develop the resources to alter social institutions. Power can come through mobilization of vast numbers of people (such as in mass movements); through effective use of strategies such as boycotts, civil disobedience, and media campaigns; and through the exercise of law, including, if needed, legal reforms. These forms of political action can change the circumstances even of those considered to be the most powerless.

The women's movement, as an example, has mobilized women and men to make a number of changes that have altered the power that women hold both as a group and as individuals. Likewise, the civil rights movement involved the mass mobilization of African American people who were otherwise quite powerless—unable to vote, unable to use public accommodations, and without access to the best educational institutions. And the mobilization of gay/lesbian/bisexual/transgender people has brought a new consciousness to the need for changes in social policy to extend full civil rights to people regardless of their sexual orientation. These political movements have altered the power base of gender, race, and sexuality in the United States.

We can also distinguish the concepts of power and authority. **Authority** is power that is perceived by others as legitimate and that is structured into specific social institutions. Authority comes not just because a person or group exercises power, but because their constituents believe their power is legitimate and because there are institutional supports in place that make this authority legitimate. The recognition of authority varies across societies, depending on the structure of that society. In a monarchy, for example, the king or queen has authority over all matters; in a totalitarian society, the dictator or emperor has total authority over all affairs. In a democratic society based on the rule of law, the law serves as the system of authority, with those who interpret and execute it as the primary agents of authority. One of the further consequences of patriarchy is the tendency to see men and men's activities as more authoritative in the areas deemed to be most important.

 ## WOMEN AND THE STATE

The institution that embodies the official power system is the *state*. The term **state** refers to the organized system of power and authority in society. This is different from the ordinary meaning of the term as a geographic area (e.g., California, Missouri, or Georgia). As a concept, the *state* refers to all of the institutions that represent official power and authority in society. The state regulates many societal relations, ranging from individual behavior and interpersonal conflicts to international affairs. Different institutions make up the state, including formal systems of government, the military, the courts, and the law.

Feminist thinking about the state begins from the premise that an analysis of gender is critical to understanding the state. Feminists see the state as a *gendered institution*—that is, an institution that embeds within it the characteristics associated with a particular gender. Feminists conceive of the state as embodying the masculine characteristics of presumed rationality, detachment, power, forcefulness, and impersonality. As one of the most bureaucratic of all institutions, the state operates as if it were neutral, when, in fact, according to feminists, it is organized on quite gender-specific grounds. Not surprisingly, then, some of the specific institutions composing the state (e.g., the military and the police) are the most masculine (in the cultural sense) and male-dominated of all social institutions.

Because the state represents the imposition of power and authority in society, it is characterized by feminists as representing men's interests more than women's. Furthermore, it is an imposing force in many women's lives. Poor women who receive public assistance, for example, have the state intruding in their affairs more than happens for women with more class privilege. The state may regulate how one lives, whether one is forced to work, how one cares for children, and what kind of health care is available. For all women, the state is also a source for laws that govern many features of everyday life, ranging from reproductive rights to rights to work and rights for equal protection.

Two primary theoretical models have been used by social scientists to explain how the state operates. The first, the **pluralism** model, sees the state as representing the plural interests of different groups in society. According to this model, the state tries to balance the different interest groups in society. *Interest groups* are those that are organized around a specific cause or purpose, such as the National Gay and Lesbian Task Force, Planned Parenthood, and the National Organization for Women (NOW). This model interprets the state as representing the diverse interest groups in society. These groups mobilize to achieve political results and use their influence to achieve their political ends.

The other model of the state is known as the **power elite**. According to this perspective, a powerful ruling class controls the actions of the state. The power elite consists of those who hold power in the economy, the executive branch of the government, and the military. Elites in these institutions share common interests and shape the political agendas in the society. Because this powerful group is primarily men, the power elite model represents men's interests as shaping the major decisions in society. This model also sees a strong alliance between government and corporate business, since the power elite, through their role in government, shape decisions that protect the interests of big business. The power elite model sees the state as part of the structure of domination in society, including gender domination, racial domination, and class domination.

Feminists have supplemented these models of state theory with the argument that the state essentially reflects men's interests, not only because men are those most likely to be in the power elite but also because men control most of the major interest groups that influence the workings of the state. Feminist theory sees the state as fundamentally patriarchal—that is, representing the power of men over women. Some have concluded that despite the presence of some women in positions of authority in the state, on the whole, the state promotes men's interests. As Catharine MacKinnon, a noted feminist legal scholar, puts it, "the state is male" (1983:644). The argument that "the state is male" can be vividly seen if you just visualize the nation's leadership. Although women are increasingly present in highly visible positions, men are hardly represented in proportion to their presence in the population.

Ironically, although some feminists analyze the state as essentially oppressive to women because the state represents men's interests, feminists also see the state as the only institution to which disadvantaged groups can turn for redress. Both the women's movement and the civil rights movement have used state power to enforce existing laws or to work to change the law. While the state can (and does) support gender inequality—for example, by denying women the right to vote or, as was the case in the early history of this country, denying women the right to speak in public—the state is also the institution that guarantees women equal protection under the law. Legislation that has brought women civil rights, defined sexual harassment as illegal, and provided some degree of reproductive freedom has been developed through the state. It is important to point out, however, that this state action has come only as the result of political mobilization by feminist groups.

WOMEN AND THE LAW

Law is the written system through which state authority is defined; thus, the study of law is extremely significant in feminist analysis. Like the state, the law is both a source for the denial of women's rights and one of the avenues to which feminists have turned to address the problems of women's inequality. Significant scholarship in women's studies has developed both to describe the changes in law that have stemmed from the women's movement and to understand the process by which the law has encoded men's interests. Feminist legal scholars have also developed the analysis of feminist jurisprudence—that is, they have developed studies of law that interpret the law as reflecting men's power but that try to revise legal doctrine to be consistent with feminist theory and practice. These studies have shown that although the law is a significant source of change for women, it is also limited in its ability to transform women's lives (Baer 1998; Crenshaw et al. 1996).

Since the 1960s, women's position relative to the law has changed dramatically. Whereas historically the law officially excluded women from full citizenship, now the law has taken a neutral position on gender. Early on, there was no protection for those women who departed from traditional roles in family. Laws overtly prohibited women from entering certain professions and treated men and women differently at every level. The **Equal Pay Act of 1963**, which required equal pay for equal work, was the first law to begin breaking this discriminatory framework. Strengthened by the **Civil Rights Bill of 1964** and subsequent pieces of legislation, the law now, at least in theory, gives women equal civil rights to men.

As they are written, laws provide some basis for the equal treatment of men and women before the law. How the law is interpreted and implemented, however, may be another matter. Even with an equal rights framework in place, executing the law is a function of many sociological factors, including how police, lawyers, and judges interpret and execute the law and how the legal system is structured to give legal advantage to some groups and not others.

On the first point, feminists have pointed out that women are underrepresented among those who are responsible for interpreting and exercising the law. As lawyers, women have dramatically increased their representation in recent years, now comprising 34 percent of lawyers. Women lawyers are more likely to practice some areas of law than others, and although they are more widely distributed across legal specialties than in the past, the largest percentage of women lawyers are found in family and public service law (Commission of Women in the Profession 2010). Women are 44 percent of judges, magistrates, and other judicial workers—a seemingly large percent, but most of these are in small jurisdictions. Women are 26 percent of state court judges (National Association of Women Judges 2010).

Do women judges matter? Some think that women would bring a unique perspective to the bench as a result of their presumably different gender perspective (Coontz 2000). The evidence is mixed. While some studies actually find that women impose harsher sentences on criminal defendants and are generally more liberal (Steffensmeier and Hebert 1999; Songer and Crews-Meyer 2000), other research finds that gender of the judge is less important than such things as severity of the offense, the victim's gender and age, and the defendant's prior record (Bogoch 1999b; Neilson 2002). Women judges are less likely to support death penalty verdicts, and their presence on the bench also seems to influence male judges not to support death penalty verdicts (Songer and Crews-Meyer 2000). Where women judges seem to make a great difference is in cases involving gender equality and battering and abuse (Martin et al. 2002). Studies find that judges now, regardless of their gender, are less likely to blame battered women for their own abuse, indicative of some of the progress made by the women's movement in the realm of judicial reasoning (Cassidy and Trafimow 2002). The rationale that women should serve on the bench because they bring a different perspective to the administration of justice may not hold up, but it is certainly the case that a judiciary that does not itself represent gender equality is suspect in a democratic society (Malleson 2003).

Feminist critiques of the law have asked whether the law is really neutral as it is intended to be—or does it only encode the power of men, at least in how it is practiced and interpreted. This is a complex question, particularly for a society where the rule of law is a primary social value. Under the U.S. Constitution, citizens have "equal protection" of the law and this concept has been the basis for many of the nation's most progressive changes with regard to extending civil rights to diverse groups. But there is also tension within the execution of law because legal institutions, like other social institutions, continue to reflect systemic structures of gender, race, and class inequality.

Given these institutional realities, another question is: Are equal rights enough? As you will see in Chapter 12 on liberal feminism, many feminists take the position that creating equal rights for women is the best strategy for social change. Others argue that this strategy does not recognize the unique life experiences of women. For example, should women be given special treatment before the law for pregnancy and maternity? This is a source of debate. Some feminists, for instance, have been opposed to protective legislation that has excluded pregnant women from certain occupations (see Chapter 7). Under current law, maternity has no special place; it is defined as a disability. Is this an adequate framework for the legal protection of pregnant women? More radical feminists have argued that the presumed neutrality of the law is problematic for women, because the law protects men's power under the guise of legal neutrality.

As an example, consider rape law. Most state laws define rape as occurring only when penetration has taken place—a definition that feminists would argue takes a phallocentric position, as if sexual intercourse has only taken place when a man inserts himself (or an object) into a woman. Despite changes in the law that make it illegal to bring up a woman's past sexual history in a rape trial ("rape shield laws"), in reality, women are still sexualized during rape trials; men are not. In rape cases, the law also makes consent the crux of whether the assailant is guilty, thereby making most rape trials as much a trial for the victim as for the rapist. In a society where women are defined as sexual objects, any number of factors can influence whether consent is perceived by the police, the defense attorney, the judge, or the jury. A woman is easily discredited on the issue of consent, particularly if she had been drinking or was under the influence of drugs at the time of the assault or if she had any prior relationship (including marriage) with the assailant. What the woman was wearing, where she was walking, how she earns her income, and any number of other factors influence people's judgments about consent.

What if a different standard existed in the law and a woman's consent was not the most significant issue? For example, how would rape laws and trials be different if men's dominance was the major point to prove? This is the kind of thinking that feminist scholars consider when they argue that the law, presumably neutral, is masculinist in its very framework.

Finally, feminists also argue that the legal method reflects masculinist culture. Legal interrogation is adversarial, based on rational argument, outdoing one's opponent, and arguing minute details. Think again of a rape trial; the method of interrogation is so masculine that rape victims report that the trial feels like a repetition of the rape. Some feminists have concluded that the legal method—debate and argument—is a masculine mode of thinking and acting. The reliance on former precedent and case law also replicates gender inequities, because this reliance gives weight to tradition without looking at the gendered context in which that tradition was constructed.

In sum, feminist studies of the law have both analyzed the legal reforms that have produced more equity for women and, as well, have criticized the gendered basis of the law. As you will see in the chapters to come, different theoretical and political positions underlie feminist arguments and form a substantive debate around the use of the law as a framework for liberating social change for women.

 ## WOMEN IN GOVERNMENT

One way to change women's standing before the law is to increase the number of women who are lawmakers; thus, one of the major feminist political strategies in recent years has been to expand the number of women serving in public political office. In the past, women were explicitly barred from political office. In the early history of the nation, political rights were based on birth, property, race, age, and religion. Basic political rights that have defined this nation as democratic were not originally extended to women; women were denied rights to free speech and property and the right to assemble. They were effectively excluded from participating—not just as political officials, but in sharing the same political rights as White men. When the American Revolution gave universal suffrage to White men, women were officially denied the right to vote (Darcy et al. 1994).

With this history behind us, feminists now ask why there are still so few women elected to political office in the United States. Compared with most other democratic, industrialized nations, women in the United States are an amazingly small number of elected officials (see Figure 11.1), although women's representation in government has been increasing (see Figure 11.2, page 334). The number of women in the U.S. House of Representatives reached an all-time high in 2009

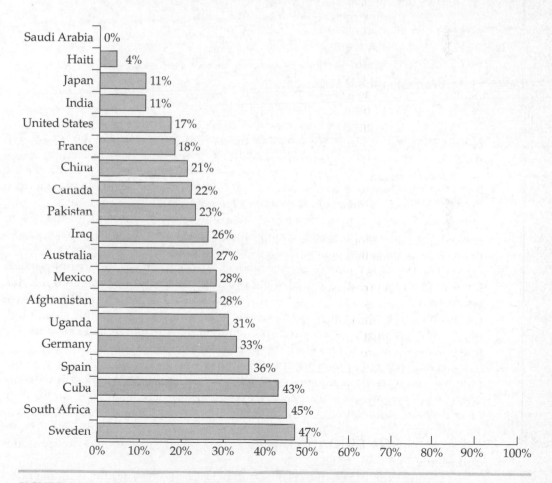

FIGURE 11.1   Women's Representation in Selected National Legislatures

Source: United Nations. 2009. Statistics and Indicators on Women and Men. http://unstats.un.org.

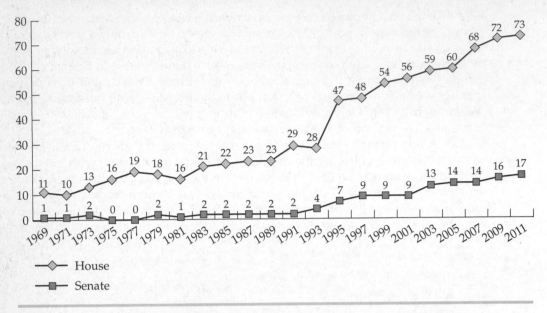

FIGURE 11.2   Women in the U.S. Congress

Sources: Congressional Research Service. 2010. www.opencrs.com

(73 women of 435 members); 17 women (the historic high) serve in the Senate. Yet, women are still a small portion of the total.

Women fare somewhat better in statewide offices; in 2010, 23 percent of state legislators and six governors were women (Center for the Women and American Politics 2010). This means that matters of greatest national importance are still determined mostly by men. Since holding a state office is also typically a route to mobility in the political system, being underrepresented there has consequences for women's likelihood of being elected to higher office.

Why are so few women elected officials? Research offers a number of possible answers. One explanation is that sheer prejudice has taught people to think that women are not well suited to politics. This is reflected in the attitude that women do not have the personality characteristics that suit them for politics. Although only a small minority of people in the United States explicitly believes this, the attitude persists in some people's minds.

Some 20 percent of men and 14 percent of women say that the country would be governed worse if women were in charge (see Figure 11.3). Still, attitudes are changing. Young people are especially likely to think there would be benefits from electing more women to office. And 86 percent of Americans say they would vote for a woman if she were nominated—an increase from 66 percent in 1971 and only 33 percent in 1937 when the question was first asked in a national survey (Jones and Moore 2003; Jones 2005).

A second explanation of the small number of women in politics is that gender-stereotyped socialization does not encourage women to see themselves as potential political candidates. A large number of people think that women do not enter

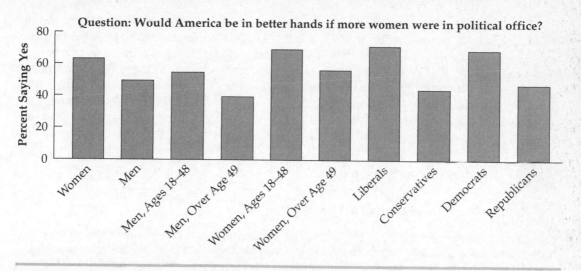

FIGURE 11.3   Women in Politics: Public Attitudes

Source: Data from Wendy Simmons. 2001. "Majority of Americans Say More Women in Political Office Would Be Positive for the Country." Princeton, NJ: The Gallup Organization. www.gallup.com. Reprinted with permission.

politics because, as girls growing up, they are not encouraged to do so. One-third of the public still think that men are emotionally better suited for politics than most women (General Social Survey 2004).

Explaining women's underrepresentation in politics as a matter of prejudice and socialization, however, does not expose the institutional forces that discourage women's greater political participation. Being successful in politics requires, among other things, having the support of party leaders. If those leaders do not encourage women to run for office, there is little likelihood of women's success as politicians. Other institutional factors also influence women's likelihood of winning political office. Being an incumbent, regardless of one's gender, carries a huge advantage in political elections. As new entrants to politics, women are at a disadvantage in challenging those who already hold office.

One of the ways that people succeed in politics, as in other high-level careers, is through the use of social and political networks. These networks are important resources for people in positions of influence because they provide systems of support for information, communication, and acquaintances where associates can be counted on for help. In any high-level job, networks are critical. Women, however, tend to have less extensive networks than do men and to be isolated from the male-centered networks where the most power lies. Because of this, many political women have organized their own networks, such as the Congressional Women's Caucus, as a way of providing support and networking to women in office.

Campaign financing is another area where women are at a structural disadvantage relative to men. Political campaigns are notoriously expensive. Women, who as a group have lower incomes than men and fewer economic resources, are not likely to have the financial resources necessary to mount expensive political campaigns. One way that women have organized to counter this disadvantage is through groups such as Emily's List. Emily is an acronym for "Early Money Is Like Yeast." Begun in 1985, Emily's List is a national organization whose purpose is to raise funds that are used to support women's election campaigns. Emily's List is the largest fundraiser for Democratic candidates. Other groups are now engaging in similar fundraising efforts on women's behalf, including Sisters United, a New Jersey organization that supports Black Democratic women.

Finally, women's dual roles in work and the family may put them at a disadvantage in running for political office. As long as women hold the primary responsibility

MEDIA MATTERS

Media Coverage of First Ladies

Historically, the traditional roles of the First Lady have consisted primarily of host or escort, but in recent years, several First Ladies have taken more active roles in leadership and decision making. Has media coverage of First Ladies changed with their increased visibility?

Erica Scharrer and Kim Bissell examined media coverage of three First Ladies: Nancy Reagan, Barbara Bush, and Hillary Clinton. In study 1, Scharrer and Bissell conducted a content analysis of newspaper stories in *The New York Times* and the *Washington Post*. They analyzed a total of 371 stories that were collected from both newspapers during the first two years in which each woman was First Lady. In study 2, Scharrer and Bissell analyzed the photographic content of *Time* magazine's coverage of Nancy Reagan, Barbara Bush, and Hillary Clinton. They limited their examination of each First Lady to the first term of her husband's presidency. In total, they analyzed 176 photographs from 312 issues of *Time*.

Results from study 1 indicated there was a more "negative tone" in news stories about First Ladies when they were more active in political activity. Also, the news coverage of Hillary Clinton was notably different from the news coverage of both Nancy Reagan and Barbara Bush because, Scharrer and Bissell contend, Hillary Clinton, a vocal proponent for health-care reform, was the most politically active.

In study 2, Scharrer and Bissell found that, in general, the First Lady is most often photographed in nonpolitical activities. Barbara Bush and Nancy Reagan were rarely photographed in politically active scenarios (5 percent and 3 percent of the

photographs, respectively), whereas Hillary Clinton was photographed in a politically active setting in 31 percent of her total coverage. Photographs that Scharrer and Bissell coded as nonpolitically active ($N = 145$) portrayed the First Lady in more stereotypical ways compared to photographs coded as politically active ($N = 31$). For example, in nonpolitically active photographs, First Ladies were engaged in "traditional" activities for First Ladies—they were shown entertaining guests: spending time with children, the elderly, or the ill: and greeting other politicians. As Scharrer and Bissell anticipated, because of her greater involvement in political activities, Hillary Clinton was photographed far less stereotypically than either Barbara Bush or Nancy Reagan.

Scharrer and Bissell's findings suggest that First Ladies must walk a fine line in their pursuit of political endeavors. They have the double task of conforming not only to their roles as women but also to their roles as spouses to the president as well.

Thinking Further: Scharrer and Bissell's research was done before Michelle Obama became First Lady of the United States. If you were replicating their study, but adding Michelle Obama to the research design, what questions would you ask? What do you see when you systematically examine media coverage of Michelle Obama, compared with these three White women?

Source: Based on Scharrer, Erica, and Kim Bissell. 2000. "Overcoming Traditional Boundaries: The Role of Political Activity in Media Coverage of First Ladies." *Women & Politics* 21: 55–83.

for family care, it is difficult for them to meet the time and energy requirements of political office. Numerous studies have shown that women's family obligations, including the availability of child care, interfere with their ability to take on political jobs. Despite the structural barriers to women's increased role in politics, women are making numerous inroads to political power. Their increased representation in formal government is partially the result of a concerted effort by many groups to increase women's political power in formal political systems. Without such political activism on behalf of more women in politics, one wonders if there would have been much change at all.

The Gender Gap

Studying women and politics is not just a matter of studying women as elected officials. Gender is also a major social factor influencing political attitudes and behavior. The term **gender gap** refers to the differences in women's and men's political behavior and political attitudes. One indication of the gender gap is that women are more likely than men to hold and support liberal views—and to identify and vote as Democrats. The development of the gender gap is a recent phenomenon, however. For many decades, men were more likely to vote than women, and, when asked, women reported voting the same as their husbands or fathers. Now, this trend is reversing. Women are also more likely than men to vote for Democratic candidates. Black men and women voters overwhelmingly vote for Democratic candidates.

Women are now equally likely to vote as men do, but there are significant differences between their political outlooks. The gender gap is widest on issues involving violence and the use of force. Women, for example, are more likely than men to be peace-seeking and to support gun control. The gender gap is also evident on so-called compassion issues. Women are more likely to support government spending for social service programs, and they are more liberal on issues such as abortion, gay and lesbian rights, and women's rights.

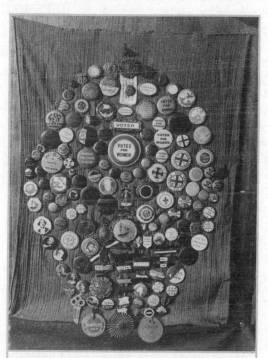

Women are more likely to vote for Democratic candidates than are men and tend to be more liberal on social issues.

Do Women Make a Difference?

Some argue that women's increased representation in government will bring a more compassionate view to politics. Gender differences between women and men suggest that women might bring different interests and different values to their work as elected officials. Do women have a different view? Does their participation in politics differ from that of men?

Research on women politicians indicates that they tend to be most active in areas traditionally associated with women, including education, health, and welfare. In general, women are also more liberal and more feminist than their male counterparts, even controlling for political party and age. On a variety of issues, women differ from men—for example, in being less likely to support the death penalty, not trusting the private sector to solve economic problems, and opposing laws requiring parental consent for minors to have an abortion. Women are also more likely than before to make women's issues a priority. In public opinion polls, women are more pacifist than men, and they hold less militaristic values. Some feminists argue that women's traditional roles as mothers and caregivers produce these different value systems. Carol Gilligan's work on women's moral values, for example, suggests that women have different moral values than men and make value judgments by different sets of criteria—using an ethic of caring rather than absolute judgments about moral right and wrong, which is more characteristic of men (Gilligan 1982).

These contrasts suggest that women will make a difference as they move further into the political area. Some feminists caution us about such an expectation, however, claiming that arguments about women's different ways of being are based in **essentialism**—in other words, there are basic differences between women and men. Although those who argue that women are different recognize the socially constructed nature of these differences, their critics argue that some too easily base women's differences from men in their reproductive roles and their psychosexual makeup. This ignores how women's distinctive consciousness is shaped by history and the specific politics of race, class, and gender that create diverse experiences for different groups of women.

Those who claim that there are basic differences between women and men tend to ignore or understate differences among women. Critics of the essentialist position suggest that the gender gap in women's attitudes and behaviors may be explained by other factors. For example, some of the largest differences in political opinion are those between middle-class and working-class women; because middle-class women are more likely to get elected to political office, this may confound some of the research results purporting to find a gender gap.

The fact is that having such a small number of women in elected office makes it difficult to tell if their presence makes a difference in political outcomes, because they are typically a numerical minority and can be treated like tokens. If the number of women in office truly represented women's proportion in the population, perhaps there would be a big difference in political agendas, but we also have to be cautious about using gender stereotypes to assume that women will inevitably be different from men once they enter dominant social institutions.

WOMEN AND THE MILITARY

Women now serve in all branches of the military, and some have made it to the very top ranks of military service. Still, it was only as recently as 1996 when the U.S. Supreme Court (in *United States* v. *Virginia*) ruled that women could not be excluded from state-supported military academies. This case involved The Citadel and the Virginia Military Institute (VMI), which had excluded women from admissions based on arguments that women were unfit for the required and rigorous physical training that the institutions required. The Supreme Court disagreed, saying that women were protected under the equal protection clause of the Fourteenth Amendment (Kimmel 2000).

There are now over 200,000 women in active military duty, including serving as soldiers in Afghanistan and Iraq as well as other parts of the world. A substantial number of U.S. troops killed in Iraq are also women, in part because the front line in this war could be anywhere (Wertheimer 2005). It was only in 1976 that women were first allowed into any of the military academies. Since then, there have been profound changes in the presence of women in the military. The percentage of women has increased from a mere 1.6 percent in 1973 to 14 percent in 2009. There are an additional 191,000 women in the reserves. Women, however, are underrepresented as military officers; 15 percent of officers are women, even though, in general, women in the military are better educated than their male counterparts. Nearly all women (99.8 percent) in the military are high school graduates (not much different from men, 98 percent of whom are high school graduates), but women are more likely than men to have attended college—27 percent of women versus 21 percent of men (Women's Education and Research Institute 2007).

In the past, the exclusion of women from full participation in the military, especially combat, has been justified by the belief that women need protection by men and that they can best carry out their womanly duties as mothers and wives. The fear among many that women might have to serve in combat was one of the major ideological reasons for defeat of the Equal Rights Amendment. Despite these public reservations, women are actively serving in combat-related roles in the military. The Defense Authorization Act of 1992 also allows women to fly combat aircraft, traditionally an option only for men. Sixty-seven percent of the public now think women should be allowed into combat jobs (Gallup Poll 2009).Currently, women are technically barred by law from direct combat in the military, but as the nature of

Women are an increasing presence in the military.

"combat" has changed, this is becoming less meaningful. Many other nations have rescinded their laws and now restrict women from combat, though. Israeli women, like Israeli men, are subject to military conscription and are assigned to combat units; however, if the unit is deployed on a combat mission, the women are evacuated. The only NATO countries to exclude women from the military are Italy and Spain.

Gender relations in the military extend beyond looking at women who serve in the military. The experience of military wives, for example, is greatly affected by their husbands' employment as soldiers. Frequent moving means that military wives are less competitive in the labor market. And the presence of a military base in a given area seems to depress women's wages in the area (Booth 2003; Booth et al. 2000). At the same time, wives of military officers are expected not to pursue their own careers or risk their husbands' promotion (Harrell 2001).

A CLOSER LOOK AT MEN

Physical Training and "Equality" in the Military

Public debates for and against women in the military are ongoing and numerous. One area of contention that is often used as evidence that "women can't cut it in the military" is the physical training involved. Public opinion centers on fairness: If women want to enjoy full equality in the military, then they should have to meet the same training requirements as men in the military. Unfortunately, public opinion tells us very little about how men in the military frame their feelings about the issue.

Carol Cohn conducted over 80 interviews with male and female military personnel. Her sample was diverse in terms of race as well as military rank. Most of her sample was drawn from the Army and Air Force, with a few representatives from the Marines and Navy.

The men that Cohn interviewed differed in their level of enthusiasm regarding women in the military: Some of the men were quite supportive of the inclusion of women, and other men were quite opposed. Cohn found that men's negative feelings about women in the military were framed most frequently in terms of the unfairness of having different standards for physical training (PT) for men and women. Cohn calls this the "PT protest."

According to Cohn, some men used the PT protest as a way of reasserting gender differences and implying that women are inferior to men. For example, when female military personnel shared stories of excelling at their PT tests with male peers, the men often responded by saying that the military's physical standards were not set very high for women.

Additionally, some men used the PT protest as a socially acceptable way of expressing resentment about women's expanding role in the military. Although a relationship between leadership potential and upper body strength has yet to be discovered, men expressed resentment toward women who were securing leadership roles in the military without necessarily "proving" (i.e., women are not required to do as many push-ups as men) that they belonged there.

It is important to reiterate that not all of the men in Cohn's study were opposed to women's inclusion in the military. Men's opposition to women in the military is complex and multifaceted. Therefore, Cohn concludes that simply requiring equal physical training standards for military men and women will not overcome men's resistance.

Source: Based on Cohn, Carol. 2000. "'How Can She Claim Equal Rights When She Doesn't Have to Do as Many Push-Ups as I Do?' The Framing of Men's Opposition to Women's Equality in the Military." *Men and Masculinities* 3 (October): 131–151.

Lesbians and Gays in the Military

Prejudices against women in the military pale beside the related prejudices that characterize gay and lesbian experiences in the military. There has been a long-standing policy to exclude gays and lesbians from the military, although gays and lesbians have made significant contributions to the nation's armed forces. Until recently, they have had to remain deeply closeted, however, including under the "Don't ask, don't tell" policy, adopted by the Clinton administration, and now being debated. According to this policy, recruiting officers may not ask about sexual preference, and individuals should not reveal their sexual preference; those who reveal that they are gay or lesbian could be excluded from military service, based on their sexual orientation. Although this policy did not allow the explicit discharge of individuals because of being gay, it restricted the civil rights of gays and lesbians. At this time, it remains to be seen if the policy will be overturned.

Those who oppose the inclusion of gay men and lesbians in the military argue, among other things, that their presence affects the morale of the troops, making the military less effective. Opponents seem to assume that gays and lesbians cannot control their sexuality when living so close to members of the same sex. Their assumption is that gays and lesbians are out to convert all others to their lifestyle. Fear and misunderstanding about AIDS has fueled these homophobic ideas (Belkin and Bateman 2003).

Ironically, there seems to be more cause for worry about sexual harassment, in general, in the military—particularly the harassment of heterosexual men toward military women. Various scandals and the exposure of widespread sexual harassment in the military have exposed this issue before the public. Unlike the homophobic arguments that gays should be excluded from the military because they cannot control their sexuality and might affect military morale, no one has argued that heterosexual men should be excluded. Indeed, a culture of masculinity permeates the military, making sexual harassment a systemic problem (Firestone and Harris 2003).

Ideas like those being used to exclude gays and lesbians from the military were also used earlier in history to exclude African Americans from military service. Opponents of desegregating the armed services argued that it would lower military morale and that it would be difficult for Whites and Blacks to live together in close quarters. In fact, when President Truman ordered the racial desegregation of the military by executive order in 1948, he showed that these arguments were not true. Although racial integration in the military has not been fully achieved, the military is one of the most desegregated institutions in the nation.

Feminism and Militarism

Feminists have criticized the military not just for its discriminatory treatment against women and gays and lesbians, but also for the masculine character of the institution as a whole. Earlier, the concept of a *gendered institution* was discussed—a gendered institution being one that embodies the characteristics of a specific gender. The military is a perfect example of a gendered institution in that it is characterized as a most masculine institution, one emphasizing hierarchy, force, violence, and aggression (Connell 1992). This can be seen in a variety of ways.

First, national involvement in war and military aggression is often justified in terms of a nation being "tough," "supreme," and "heroic"—all characteristics associated with men's gender role. Numerous examples throughout history also show how military propaganda uses images of threatened manhood to rationalize a nation's engagement in war. Aggression and the capacity for violence are seen as indicating national strength, just as they are seen as indicating the strength of individual men. Although men's violence occurs in day-to-day interactions, in its most escalated form it results in war and terrorism.

Second, militaristic values also legitimate much violence and sexual aggression against women, especially that which accompanies war and military occupation. The large-scale rape of women by invading armies in the war-torn Sudan is an example of how military conquerors tend to see sexual violation of women as their right following a military victory. Rape is common in war, as is the widespread use of women sex workers in brothels and as prostitutes in occupied territories and war zones (Enloe 1989).

But you do not have to look abroad to see the extent of violence against women within military institutions. A study released in 2008 by the military itself found that fully one-third of women in the military (and 6 percent of men) say they have been sexually harassed while serving. In addition, the same report found over 2,600 cases of sexual assault against women in the military in the same year, an average of 1.8 per 1,000 military members. In addition, studies of sexual assault and harassment have also focused on the military academies, where 15 percent of women in the academies report that they have been sexually harassed. Although the military academies have rates of sexual assault that are comparable (or even slightly lower) to those on other college campuses, sexual harassment is a serious and ongoing problem on military campuses. The military has responded to these problems by establishing reporting procedures as well as services for victims of sexual assault and harassment. It has also established a task force for ongoing accountability and has developed policies and procedures to combat sexual violence (National Women's Law Center 2008; U.S. Department of Defense 2008). But the very presence of this problem within military institutions indicates the harm done to women through the link between militarism and exaggerated forms of masculine control. The strong association between militarism and masculinity is also evident in military training practices where homophobic socialization forces military recruits to be tough, aggressive, and strong as a way of proving their masculine heterosexuality. Those who are perceived as weak are labeled as "faggots" is one way that military recruits are initiated into military roles.

RETHINKING THE POLITICAL

Reviewing the workings of state institutions—including courts and the law, government, and the military—raises many new questions for feminist analysis. One of the primary questions to have emerged from feminist studies in this area is a rethinking of what *political* means. When most people think of something political, they likely think in terms of election politics and the workings of official government. In this sense, political behavior is only that which occurs within public political institutions. Feminist scholars, on the other hand, have defined the term *political* more broadly and have argued that traditional concepts of the political have been marked by an incorrect conceptual dichotomy between the public and private spheres of life. Assuming that political behavior only occurs in the formal, public sphere overlooks significant political activity by women in other spheres, such as volunteer work in communities. A narrow understanding of what is political that includes only what occurs in the formal, public sphere limits our understanding of political behavior and restricts our understanding of political behavior to places where men have predominated. In addition, feminist scholars argue that the conceptual separation of the public and private spheres leads to oversight of how the public and private spheres intersect, as, for example, in understanding how women's work in the private sphere supports public institutions, even when that work is devalued and ignored.

Redefining the political to include a broader spectrum of behavior encourages thinking of political behavior in new ways. Women's community activism is one such area that has long been overlooked by those studying politics, but which, on closer look, reveals the many ways that women engage in political behavior. As examples, Gilkes (1980) has shown how African American women who have careers as community workers use their work both to help their communities in everyday survival and to transform social institutions. Although these women are seldom recognized as "political women," their work in social service organizations, on the boards of local organizations, and as directors of agencies has important political ramifications for the African American community. Their political work stems not from their activity in dominant institutions but from their commitments to change and their mobilization of resources in service to the Black community. In a similar vein, Naples (1992) has studied low-income Latina and African American mothers, finding that they see their community work as stemming from their desire to improve the lives of their families and neighbors, the specific problems around which they organize include health care, housing, crime and safety, and sanitation. As activist mothers, their political action is part of the continuum of their care work.

These are but two examples of how women engage in political action, but from the grassroots (that is, the local level). This gives political activism a different meaning from that which is associated with mainstream politics. In both cases, the distinction between women's private work in their families and communities is blurred with their public work as political actors.

Although women's grassroots activism is rarely the substance of evening news headlines, as is the formal political work of men, it is nonetheless significant in women's contributions to political life. Feminists argue that the media have obscured much of women's political activism, thereby lending the impression that women are not interested in politics or are ineffective in mobilizing on behalf of their interests. Furthermore, redefining the political to include the work that women do sheds more light on the political activism of working-class women and women of color—groups whose political contributions are largely ignored in the dominant culture, despite the fact that working-class women and women of color have a rich history of political organizing. Women work politically in the contexts in which they are found—local communities, workplaces, churches, and social service organizations, to name a few.

Because women's political action has been understudied and misunderstood, theories of political behavior typically fail to deal with gender as a central concept (Bookman and Morgen 1988); moreover, political theory has only in rare cases made women major subjects for analysis. As a consequence, much political analysis has made women invisible as political actors and made politics appear to be gender neutral. As two feminist scholars note, "Politics is conventionally understood as the activities of elected officials and the workings of government, both out of the reach of ordinary people" (Bookman and Morgen 1988:4). Such portrayals also create, among many women, a sense of disenfranchisement and alienation from mainstream politics, especially the working-class and poor women who are most disaffected by dominant institutions. This means that working-class and poor women have to make gains outside of traditional electoral politics—in factory organizing, in churches, on the streets, and through other grassroots activities—areas of political life that have been largely ignored by academic scholars.

Within grassroots politics, women are much more likely to contend with the intersecting politics of race, class, and gender. Through such political behavior, women challenge the dominant power relations of society and recognize the systematic forces that oppress women. Often through grassroots politics, women also change their ideas about the sources of their powerlessness and act to change conditions of their lives.

In sum, women are not as peripheral to politics as they might appear in an analysis of women and politics in the electoral world alone. Understanding the full range of women's political behavior means also seeing how working-class women and women of color have a long history of political activism, despite their invisibility in recorded history. These groups have also had a very feminist analysis, supporting women's independence and activism, even when this kind of feminism differs from—and is sometimes in conflict with—the feminism of White, middle-class women. For all women engaged in the feminist work, however, phrases such as *the personal is political* and *sexual politics* show how women have linked their everyday lives to their political action and beliefs.

 ## THE WOMEN'S MOVEMENT

Women's political activism can be found on any number of issues, particularly if you look beyond the formal political system. Women have been important in the work of many political groups that are organized on social and political issues, including environmental-action groups, groups uniting to fight racism, gay and lesbian movements, abortion rights groups, and many others too numerous to mention.

The women's movement, or the feminist movement, is one of the most significant and influential movements of our times. Imagine life where women cannot choose their career, no matter their interests or talent; where becoming pregnant means having to leave your job; where you have no access to birth control; where you cannot attend the best schools in the country; or when you could not wear pants to school or work! Not that long ago (as recently as the 1960s), this would have been the case for most women in the United States. You can thank the women's movement for some of the very basic privileges and rights that you have today. There is probably no woman, or for that matter no man, in this country who has not been touched by some aspect of the women's movement, even though there is work still to be done, as the content of this book is showing you. Moreover, although many are reluctant to call themselves feminists, opinion polls show that the majority of people in the United States support the values and programs that the women's movement has encouraged and supported (Robison 2002; Saad 2003).

Social movements are groups that promote or resist changes in society. Movements often emerge because of a perceived sense of injustice and people's wishes to make change that will redress such injustices (Turner and Killian 1972). Social movements involve the sustained activity of organized groups, and they often include a network of organizations that, although they may have different goals and members, have a shared sense of belonging to the movement. Those who study social movements also try to identify the societal conditions that foster the development of the movements. To understand fully the contemporary women's movement, it is then necessary to look at the earlier development of feminism, thus we turn to the nineteenth century and the emergence of feminism therein.

American Feminism in the Nineteenth Century

In the United States, many of the early feminists were women who advocated the equal rights of women to acquire an education. You have seen this in some of the "History Speaks" features in this book. Women such as Mary McLeod Bethune, Anna Julia Cooper, and others were activists for women's education, understanding that this was essential for women to live freely in a democratic society.

Another early advocate of education for women was Emma Willard, who campaigned actively for the establishment of colleges for women in the 1920s. Frances Wright also was an active spokeswoman for the establishment of equal educational training for women. Education for women, these women argued, would extend the "rights of man" to all persons and therefore make for general and human improvement. As the result of their efforts, Oberlin College was the first college to admit women in 1833. Mount Holyoke College opened in 1837, Vassar in 1865, both Smith and Wellesley in 1875, Radcliffe in 1879, and Bryn Mawr in 1885 (Flexner 1975). Although extending education primarily to women of the upper class, these institutions nonetheless created an educated class of women, many of whom worked on behalf of women's rights.

Feminism did not, however, have its origins only in the activism of educated White women. Its political origins also lie in the abolitionist movement of the 1830s and the efforts of African American and White women and men to struggle for the abolition of slavery and women's rights. Charlotte Forten (1784–1884), an African American woman reformer and abolitionist, was a founder of the Philadelphia Female Anti-Slavery Society. She tutored her three daughters, Margaretta, Harriet, and Sarah Louise, each of whom was also active in the abolitionist and feminist movements. The Grimke sisters, Sarah (1792–1873) and Angelina (1805–1879), were daughters of a slaveholding family who traveled and spoke out vigorously against slavery in the 1830s. Both the Grimke sisters and Sarah Forten were delegates to the first Anti-Slavery Convention of American Women held in 1837. The correspondence between Sarah Forten and Angelina Grimke records their friendship and their strong sentiments about both **abolitionism** and feminism (Sterling 1984).

Frederick Douglass, a former slave and ardent abolitionist, supported women's rights for many years and was a strong supporter of women's suffrage. He and other male abolitionists believed that women's suffrage was necessary for the full enfranchisement of all citizens, although racism among White women and men in the women's rights movement forced Douglass and other abolitionists to subordinate the issue of women's suffrage to that of Black suffrage (DuBois 1978). The abolitionists saw clear links between freedom for slaves and freedom for women, although as the women's rights movement developed, White women discriminated against Black women in the movement and used racist appeals to argue for the extension of voting rights to White women.

From their work in the abolitionist movement, women learned how to organize a political movement. They challenged the assumption of the natural superiority of men and understood that suffrage was an important source for self-respect and social power. Historian Ellen Carol DuBois concluded that

> abolitionism provided [American women] with a way to escape clerical authority, an egalitarian ideology, and a theory of social change, all of which permitted the leaders to transform the insights into the oppression of women which they shared with many of their contemporaries into the beginnings of the women's rights movement. (1978:32)

In 1840, a World Anti-Slavery Convention was held in London. The mere presence of women delegates at this convention generated excitement about the potential power of women, although women were relegated to the galleries and were prohibited from participating in the proceedings. But their exclusion ironically produced an increased awareness among women of the need for a women's movement. Upon returning to the United States, two of the women attending the convention, Lucretia Mott and Elizabeth Cady Stanton, continued to meet and discussed strategies for establishing women's rights. On July 14, 1848, they called for a Woman's Rights Convention to be held in Seneca Falls, New York, five days later. Despite such short notice, 300 men and women came to Seneca Falls and there approved a Declaration of Sentiments, modeled on the Declaration of Independence. The Declaration of Sentiments declared that "all men and women are created equal; that they are endowed by their Creator with certain inalienable rights; that among these are life, liberty, and the pursuit of happiness" (Hole and Levine 1971:6). Those attending the Seneca Falls Convention also passed 12 resolutions, one of which resolved to grant women the right to vote.

The Seneca Falls Convention has since been heralded as the official beginning of the women's suffrage movement in the United States. Other women's rights conventions were then held throughout the United States, including one in 1851 in Akron, Ohio, where Sojourner Truth, a former slave, challenged the popular doctrine of women's delicacy and physical inferiority. She exhorted:

> Nobody ever helps me into carriages or over puddles, or gives me the best place—and ain't I a woman? . . . Look at my arm! I have ploughed and planted and gathered into

barns, and no man could head me—and ain't I a woman? I could work as much and eat as much as a man—when I could get it—and bear the lash as well! And ain't I a woman? I have born thirteen children, and seen most of 'em sold into slavery, and when I cried out with my mother's grief, none but Jesus heard me—and ain't I a woman? (Hole and Levine 1971:191)

In the beginning, the women's movement was not just a single-issue movement. Feminists saw the issue of suffrage as one aspect of women's rights and advocated full equality for women. The momentum of the women's movement was stalled somewhat by the Civil War, but after the war, feminists worked hard to get the word *sex* added to the Fifteenth Amendment. The **Fifteenth Amendment** declares that the right to vote cannot be denied or abridged by race, color, or previous condition of servitude, but it did not extend to women—either White or African American. Although feminists' efforts to get the term *sex* added did not succeed, this setback furthered their resolve for suffrage; in 1869, Susan B. Anthony and Elizabeth Cady Stanton organized the National Woman Suffrage Association (NWSA), which embraced the broad cause of women's rights. A few months later, Lucy Stone and others organized the American Woman Suffrage Association. This organization restricted itself more narrowly to the suffrage issue, trying to avoid more controversial issues such as marriage and the church.

Suffrage, however, was not the only issue for which early feminists fought. The **temperance movement** in the late nineteenth century was organized by women with a strong feminist consciousness. The motto of the Women's Christian Temperance Union (WCTU), under one of its early presidents, Frances Willard, was "Do everything!" Willard organized departments in the WCTU, each with its own programs of activity, including work in prisons, in kindergartens, and with the shut-in sick; other departments were concerned with physical culture and hygiene, prostitution, and motherhood. One department, the most effective, worked for suffrage. The temperance movement pressed for laws restricting the sale and consumption of alcohol; women were encouraged to join because their status as married women gave them no legal protection against abuse or abandonment by a drunken husband (Flexner 1975).

In 1890, the American and National Woman's Suffrage associations merged to become the National American Woman Suffrage Association (NAWSA). By this time, the women's movement had become focused on the right to vote—a right they believed would open other opportunities and give women full rights as citizens. Shortly after the turn of the century, a second generation of U.S. feminists appeared, including women such as Carrie Chapman Catt, president of NAWSA. Also, Alice Paul, a young militant woman, became active in the suffrage movement. She formed a small radical group, the Congressional Union, to work on federal suffrage for women. The Congressional Union used tactics such as parades, mass demonstrations, and hunger strikes to further their cause. The combined efforts of the Congressional Union, NAWSA, and local suffrage groups and activists were eventually successful. On August 26, 1920, the **Nineteenth Amendment**, guaranteeing women the right to vote, was adopted.

With the success of the suffrage movement, the women's movement lost much of its public momentum and, many say, lay dormant for the years between passage of the Nineteenth Amendment and the rebirth of feminism in the United States in the 1960s. Others have shown, though, that feminist activities through this period did not totally disappear. Many women continued to pursue feminist goals in a variety of organizations and contexts; their work provided continuity between the early women's movement and contemporary feminism. Although only a few organizations from the 1920s to the 1960s embraced explicitly feminist goals, the birth control and family planning movement, the settlement house movement, the establishment of organizations working to improve working conditions for employed women, and the founding of professional women's groups (including the National Federation of Business and Professional Women's Clubs, the League of Women Voters, and the American Association of University Women) set the stage for feminist developments in later years (Ferree and Hess 1997).

Even in the post–World War II period, when cultural ideology strongly defended the idea that a woman's proper place was in the home, the National Women's Party, organized by Alice Paul, continued to fight for improving the status of women. The National Women's Party had one major plank in its platform—passage of the **Equal Rights Amendment (ERA)**. Since 1923, when the ERA was first introduced in Congress, Paul and other members of this organization worked to garner support from other women's organizations, lobbied Congress, and sought publicity for the amendment. Most other women's organizations opposed passage of the ERA, believing it would legitimate protective legislation for women. Despite their differing goals and philosophies, all of these organizations provided strong support networks for women in the particularly hostile environment of post–World War II sexist ideology (Rupp and Taylor 1987). And, although parts of the women's movement were less active, Black women in the United States during this period, were laying some of the groundwork for what became perhaps the most significant movement of the twentieth century—the civil rights movement, itself a huge influence on the emergence of the second wave of feminism.

The Emergence of the Contemporary Women's Movement

Several transformations in women's roles occurred during the 1950s and 1960s that influenced the development of contemporary feminism, including changes in women's labor force participation, a change in women's fertility patterns, increases in women's educational levels, and ideological patterns that glamorized women's domestic life. In the 1950s, White women were idealized as happy housewives whose primary purpose was to care for their husbands and children. In that decade, women were marrying younger, but they were also having fewer children because widespread use of contraception gave women control over their fertility. At the same time, White, middle-class women were better educated. Although their education was intended to make them better wives and mothers, they were acquiring many of the same skills as men. For women in the home, technological changes in housework simplified physical tasks, but the increased consumption and new patterns of family life in automobile-based suburbs complicated the role of housewives. Although there was less physical labor associated with housework, housewives were supposed to be constantly available to their children. Whatever

HISTORY SPEAKS: YESTERDAY'S FEMINISTS TALK ABOUT TODAY

Alice Paul and the Equal Rights Amendment

"I never doubted that equal rights was the right direction. Most reforms, most problems are complicated. But to me there is nothing complicated about ordinary equality."

—Alice Paul (interview, 1972; www.alicepaul.org)

Born in Mt. Laurel, New Jersey, Alice Paul (1885–1977) was the daughter of Quaker parents who firmly believed in gender equality. Some have said that Alice Paul was one of the most influential women in America, although she is now often forgotten and rarely taught as one of the nation's pioneering feminists.

Alice Paul was educated at Swarthmore College, where she received a B.A. in Biology (1905), followed by an M.A. in Sociology (1907) and a Ph.D. in Economics (1912) from the University of Pennsylvania. Highly educated, she also received three law degrees (an LL.B. from Washington University and an LL.M. and D.C.L. from American University). Paul worked tirelessly to bring equal rights to women, beginning her political activism while a student at Swarthmore. She became a militant suffragist while studying in England after her college graduation, returning home and committing herself to the struggle for women's suffrage in the United States.

Paul joined the National American Women's Suffrage Association and planned dramatic actions to capture the public's attention and garner support for women's suffrage. This included organizing a massive parade in Washington, DC, on the day of President Woodrow Wilson's inauguration. The march down Pennsylvania Avenue became a violent confrontation when male onlookers shouted obscenities and then physically attacked the suffragists. This event and other militant actions brought the topic of suffrage to public awareness.

But, even once women earned the right to vote, Alice Paul was convinced that this was not enough. She believed that women still needed full and equal rights before the law. In 1923, she announced that she would be working for an amendment to the U.S. Constitution that would guarantee equal rights for women.

"Equality of rights shall not be denied or abridged by the United States or by any state on account of sex." Simple words, complex politics. These are the words of the Equal Rights Amendment that Alice Paul advocated. The Equal Rights Amendment (ERA) was first introduced to the U.S. Congress in 1923, but never passed until 1972. Even then, it failed because an insufficient number of states ratified it. To this day, the ERA has not been adopted as a constitutional guarantee of women's rights.

Thinking Further: If Alice Paul were alive today, she would likely still be advocating for constitutional protections for women. Why do you think the amendment has not passed? What would it take to get it passed?

Source: Based on information provided by the Alice Paul Institute. 2010. www.alicepaul.org.

time was saved by labor-saving appliances was more than replaced by increased shopping, transporting of children, and nurturing of family members. The dominant ideology of housework and motherhood told middle-class women that their work in the home would bring them fulfillment and gratification, but, in fact, many found the experience to be depressing, isolating, and boring.

This situation created a crisis for White, middle-class White women that was brought to the attention of the public by the appearance of Betty Friedan's best-seller, *The Feminine Mystique*. Friedan's book, published in 1963, identified what she called "the problem that has no name"—in other words, the isolation of women in the family was a source for women's discontent. In her book, Friedan critically assailed the establishment (including mass advertising, women's magazines, and Freudian psychology) as contributing to women's problems. The chord she struck was soon repeated by a number of critical assessments of women's roles that appeared in academic and popular literature (Evans 1979).

In addition to experiencing a crisis in domestic life, women were, at the same time, appearing in the labor force in greater numbers. Throughout the 1950s, women from White, middle-class families entered the labor force at a faster rate than any other group. They were working not just in the years before marriage but later, in addition to their marriage and family roles. Although married women's work experience was defined in terms of helping their families, it broadened their horizons at the same time that it made them conscious of discrimination in the workplace. The decade of the 1950s and the early 1960s created a self-conscious cohort of women who lived in the contradictions of a society that idealized their role and promised them opportunity and gratification while it devalued their labor and denied them self-expression.

Professional women working within established institutions began pressuring politicians to recognize the problems facing women in the United States. In 1961, although it was likely done for political reasons, President John F. Kennedy appointed a Presidential Commission on the Status of Women, chaired by Eleanor Roosevelt. The Commission was charged with documenting "prejudices and outmoded customs that act as barriers to the full realization of women's basic rights" (Hole and Levine 1971:18) and with making recommendations designed to alleviate the problem. The Commission report, *American Women*, was released in 1963, the same year that Friedan's *The Feminine Mystique* appeared.

The Commission's report made a number of recommendations involving employment and labor discrimination. It was the basis for the Equal Pay Act of 1963, requiring that men and women receive equal pay for equal work performed under equal conditions (Hole and Levine 1971:28ff). Problems in enforcing this law and exemptions that were later attached to it prohibited the act from making the radical changes it implied; thus, the commission's work had only a moderate effect. The commission also held steadfastly to the idea that the nuclear family was the foundation of U.S. history and that women's role in the family was an invaluable and necessary resource. Although recognizing the contribution that women made to the home, the commission ignored the effects of home life on women that Friedan's book so strikingly portrayed.

These developments within both the government and the society provided the context for women to begin to question their traditional roles, but it remained for major social movements of the period to crystallize the vague discontent that women felt. The birth of contemporary feminism must be seen as also stemming from the civil rights movement and, later, the anti–Vietnam War and student movements.

Feminism and Civil Rights

The civil rights movement was initiated within African American communities of the South during the 1950s as a challenge to public racial segregation and White racial prejudice. Although there had been a longer history within Black communities of organizing for civil rights, the 1950s provided the spark that mobilized this mass social movement. Like the nineteenth-century U.S. feminists who had developed their feminist politics through participation in the abolitionist movement, women working in the civil rights movement soon saw their own oppression as similar to the racial injustices against which they were organizing. Women worked in the civil rights movement out of their felt need to remedy the inequities of racial injustice, which they saw as a moral issue calling for their humanitarian participation. For White women and men, joining the civil rights movement required a radical departure from the dominant beliefs and practices of White society. Their challenge to the status quo on racial issues was soon to influence the way they also interpreted other social issues (Evans 1979).

Between 1963 and 1965, White liberals from the North (especially male and female college students) went to the South in great numbers to assist in the civil rights struggle. The nonviolent direct-action projects in which they engaged (voter registration drives, protest marches, and sit-ins) forced them to encounter institutional racism and generated a new consciousness not only of racial issues but of the institutional structure of society in the United States (Rothschild 1979). Most important, the civil rights movement's emphasis on examining the roots of oppression caused many White people to look into their own experience so as to comprehend their relationship to dominant institutions. In so doing, White women in the movement began to see the origins of their own oppression—both as they had learned sexism in their own lives and as it was reflected in the public institutions of society.

Both White and Black women believed that the movement had failed to address the issue of sexual inequality. Black women in the Student Non-Violent Coordinating Committee (SNCC) wrote position papers protesting the fact that women in the movement were relegated to clerical work, were not given leadership and decision-making positions, and were belittlingly referred to as "girls." White women, supporting the idea that the movement should be led by Black activists, were reluctant to present their own analysis of sexism. At the same time, distrust between Black and White women made the alliance between Black and White women uneasy (Breines 2006; Evans 1979). Yet, the consciousness of both Black and White women around gender inequality was strongly influenced by their activism within the Black protest movement.

For African American women, however, the concept of sisterhood was developed in a different context than is the case for White women. African American women's political identity has more likely been formed around racial consciousness, and as a result, Black women tend to see feminist issues in a different context than do White women (Dill 1983). Especially in the early days of second wave feminism, White women tended to see themselves oppressed as a sexual group. It has been the awareness of African American women that has generated an understanding within feminism that gender inequality is intricately linked to race and class inequality (Collins 1990).

The Second Wave of Feminism

By the late 1960s, feminism had developed as a full-fledged movement, with a variety of organizations, local consciousness-raising groups, and political strategies intended to advocate transformations in women's status in society. Referred to as "the second wave of feminism" (in contrast to the nineteenth-century "first wave"), the women's movement in the 1960s and 1970s had diverse origins, philosophies, and strategies for change.

Two major branches of the feminist movement evolved: the *women's rights* branch and the *women's liberation* branch. The women's rights branch took an "equal rights" strategy—working to extend equal rights to women, particularly through legal reform and antidiscrimination policies. Important in this part of the feminist movement was the **Equal Rights Amendment** (ERA), the proposed amendment to the U.S. Constitution that states: "Equality of rights under the law shall not be denied or abridged by the United States or by any state on the basis of sex." Advocates of the ERA saw it as essential for providing a constitutional foundation to protect women from gender inequality; opponents feared it would force women into military combat. Trivial as it seems, much of the opposition voiced their opposition by worrying about it eliminating separate public bathrooms for men and women! To date, the Equal Rights Amendment—a simple statement of gender equality—has not been approved, although there is a persistent effort to make this historic amendment to the U.S. Constitution.

The women's rights branch of the women's movement was centered in a philosophy of antidiscrimination; thus, the best remedies would be the creation of gender-blind policies and institutions in which all persons, regardless of sex (or race, religious preference, sexual preference, or physical disability), have equal rights. The women's liberation branch of the feminist movement, on the other hand, took a more far-reaching analysis, seeing that transformation in women's status requires not just legal and political reform but radical transformation of basic social institutions, including, to name a few, the family, sexuality, religion, and education. Women's rights and women's liberation are not separate movements, but the analytical distinction between the two shows the different political and social theories on which feminism is built. As you will see, the women's rights approach is more centered in the context of liberal political theory, while women's liberation has its roots in more radical political theory.

Each wing of the feminist movement developed different strategies for change. The women's rights wing mobilized for equal rights and tends to work within existing political institutions. The organizations that have evolved from this branch of feminism are typically more formal, with hierarchical leadership and authority structures, and with more formal procedures and rules for membership (Freeman 1973).

The style and organization of women's liberation groups, on the other hand, reflected their more radical and grassroots base. The organization of feminist groups within this branch of the women's movement was deliberately nonhierarchical and with informal procedures and networks (Freeman 1973). This encouraged analyses that were more critical of established institutions, but it also engaged individual women in examining their own experience and its relationship to institutionalized inequality and sexism. This branch of feminism also recognized that personal life was tied to the structure of public institutions and would be altered only as these institutions changed.

The more radical feminist groups often emerged from the New Left and drew their participants from women who were critical of the often sexist and patronizing behavior of radical men (Evans 1979). Their early political analysis was forged from the appeals to justice that the civil rights and leftist movements had articulated and that women felt were being denied to them. Women in the antiwar and student movements of the 1960s were radicalized not only by the philosophies of these movements but also by the sexist behavior of men within the movements. African American women whose leadership had been central in the civil rights movement were often relegated to secondary status in the Black power movement, as the movement became more influenced by advocates of Black nationalism. Women's participation in all of these movements had the effect of further radicalizing White and African American women's feminist perspectives.

Feminism for the Twenty-First Century: A Third Wave?

With the evolution of the feminist movement over time, early distinctions between the equal rights and women's liberation branches of feminism have blurred, although diverse political beliefs and strategies among feminists remain. Some of those who were radical feminists in the 1960s and 1970s—then younger women, students, and movement activists—now work in positions of some power and influence. At the same time, liberal feminist organizations, although they work within the existing political system, are also influenced by more radical feminist thought. Race, class, *and* gender have also become more central to feminist politics and feminist analyses. Although tensions continue to exist between White women and women of color, the feminism of women of color has become more elaborated, and more White women have worked to challenge their own racism and to build analyses that are inclusive of race, class, and gender.

Starting in the 1990s, feminists faced two new challenges: the identification of a so-called postfeminist generation and a backlash against feminism, both from the mainstream media and from the rise of the new religious and political right. The dominant media generated a strong image of feminism as no longer necessary and a thing of the past (Faludi 1991). In addition, the media created a stereotype of feminism that stigmatized it in the eyes of many, especially younger women. This image of feminists as anti-male, lesbian, humorless, and politically correct ideologues made feminism seem unapproachable to many, including those who otherwise supported its values and goals (Whittier 1995).

The rise of the religious right has also promoted values specifically opposed to the feminist agenda. The right's advocacy of "traditional family values" endorses

FOCUS ON RESEARCH

I'm Not a Feminist, But . . .

What does it mean to call oneself a feminist? Not surprisingly, many women and men support feminist policies, but do not call themselves "feminists." Perhaps this is not surprising because of the derogatory terms often used to describe feminists ("man-haters," "feminazis," "politically correct"). The rise of conservatism and a backlash against the feminist movement all contribute to a reluctance on the part of many to call themselves feminists.

Curious about this phenomena, especially given the widespread support for feminist goals (such as equal employment, family leave policies, anti-rape action, and so forth), Janice McCabe studied the relationship between feminist identity and support for other social and political issues. In her study, and drawing from others, she notes that women with feminist identities generally are better educated, urban, and with smaller families. She also notes the studies that show more support for feminist policies than for actually calling oneself a feminist. But in her research, she extends these results to examine more fully the relationships between feminist identity and support for gender-related attitudes.

Using data from the National Opinion Research Center, a nationally based survey based on a random sample of respondents, McCabe finds that 29 percent of women and 12 percent of men identify as feminists. Consistent with earlier research, she also finds that education is related to feminist identity. But race, family status, and work status is not. She finds that rural residents are less likely than others to identify as feminists, but residence in the South is not related to whether one identifies as feminist or not. In other words, feminists are not just White, middle-class, northern women.

The most detailed parts of McCabe's work examine the relationship between feminist self-identity and support for other issues. She finds that feminist identity among women is not related to attitudes about ideal gender arrangements. And she finds that those with feminist identities are more likely to explain women's status as the result of broad societal arrangements, even when, among feminists, the particulars of this explanation vary.

McCabe's work shows that feminism is a more complex identity and set of beliefs than is commonly assumed in public stereotypes about feminism. Her work cautions us against assuming a simplistic understanding of the label *feminist*.

Source: Based on McCabe, Janice. 2005. "The Relationship between Feminist Self-Identification and 'Feminist' Attitudes among U.S. Women and Men." *Gender & Society* 19 (August): 480–505.

an antifeminist stance, one promoting a strong connection of women to the home, little tolerance of diverse family forms, and many extremely homophobic platforms directed against gays and lesbians, such as some of the ballot initiatives in different states to deny same-sex marriage. The influence of the conservative right wing in politics has meant lost ground on important issues such as abortion rights, gay and lesbian rights, and state or federal support for any number of social programs that support women and their children. And, the right-wing attack on being "politically correct" has thus also generated a climate that is less tolerant of—indeed, hostile to—feminist perspectives.

In this context, there is little wonder that younger women in the new century may find themselves confused by feminism. Although the media has portrayed this generation as a "postfeminist" one, a more careful look finds that young women and men are those most likely to support feminist values, even though they may be reluctant to call themselves feminists. When asked if they support the specific goals of feminism, the majority of young people say yes, with widespread support for such feminist issues as equal employment opportunities for women, more equality in family roles, support of reproductive freedom, agreement with affirmative action, and support for more women in public office (Schnittker et al. 2003; Hall and Rodriguez 2003). The most likely age groups to support feminism are younger women and women who are now middle-aged who became adults during the second wave of feminism in the 1960s and 1970s (Peltola et al. 2004; Aronson 2003).

Ironically, the image of young women and men as uninterested in feminism has been most prevalent at the same time that enrollments in women's studies courses have soared on most college campuses. It is probably more accurate to say that young women are not so much antifeminist as they are cautious about being identified with a movement so reviled in the media and that they see as stemming from the concerns of a different generation.

Young women growing up today have had very different experiences from those of their mothers' generation, many of whom were part of the second wave of feminism. Younger women have grown up in a period dominated by conservative, not progressive, values. They have also benefited from the gains made by the second wave of feminism, so they do not have to worry so much about access to birth control, rights to education and employment, or exclusion from formerly men-only occupations and organizations—some of the issues that activated the second wave of feminism.

Still, issues about women's safety from violence, men's and women's sexual identities, work and family roles, and other opportunities are by no means resolved. Young people have also grown up in a context where the politics of personal identity—gender identity, racial–ethnic identity, and sexual identity—have been a vocal topic in the political world. The generational differences between young women and their feminist foremothers thus shape the reactions of many young women to feminist politics (Whittier 1995). At the same time, however, the shape of the third wave of feminism will be determined by the political action taken by younger women and men who define feminism in the context of their own life experiences and needs (Baumgardner and Richards 2000; Moraga et al. 2002; Labaton and Martin 2004; Walker 1995; Hernández and Rehman 2002).

In sum, there has been no demise of the women's movement. Quite the contrary, the women's movement remains one of the most influential sources of social change, even though there is not a single national organization that is identified as representing feminism. Some of the most radical feminist activities occur at the grassroots level, where women struggle against poverty, violence, harassment, and exploitation. At the same time, more mainstream feminist organizations continue to work on behalf of women's health and welfare, safety and security, and educational and employment rights. Just as the feminist movement has ebbed and flowed with different emphases and different agendas over the past 100 years or more, so will its future be influenced by the needs of diverse women in their own times.

■ Chapter Summary and Themes

Power is the ability to influence others; as an organized system of power, the state has operated as a gendered institution, excluding women from positions of leadership and operating within a masculinist framework.

One of the ironies of considering the state from a feminist perspective is that it has operated as a patriarchal institution—against women's interests—at the same time that the state has been an avenue by which feminists have sought to eliminate formal discrimination and others forms of gender inequity.

As women have moved into more professional roles within the legal system, many have wondered whether women will administer justice differently from men, based on presumed gender differences in women's values.

Evidence of gender differences in the administration of justice is mixed. Some studies show that women use a unique standpoint in judgments about sentencing and in their perspective on issues before the law, but one must be careful not to overstate such differences, given the empirical evidence.

Women continue to be underrepresented in all aspects of formal political institutions, even though their numbers are increasing in this arena.

Explanations of the underrepresentation of women as elected officials include such factors as gender socialization, persistent gender bias in attitudes about political skills, exclusion from political networks, women's lesser resources for financing campaigns, and the dual roles that women have in the family and at work.

A gender gap in men's and women's attitudes about political and social issues persists, with women generally being more liberal than men.

Although women are generally more likely to support values such as peace, government support for social services, feminist issues, and so forth, one has to be careful not to attribute this to *essential* differences between women and men. People's opinions vary by other factors, such as generational differences, race, social class, and other social factors. Also, changes in the society at large can result in changed public attitudes.

Although still a minority of those serving in active military duty, women have increased their representation within the military, even though the military is still well-described as a gendered institution.

Women's historic exclusion from the military was justified based on their need for men's protection. As that attitude has eroded, women have moved into diverse military roles, although they are still underrepresented as officers. Public support for women serving in combat has grown. The extent of sexual harassment in the military and the suspicion directed against gays and lesbians shows how the military is structured around a culture of masculinity.

Although women have historically been excluded from many roles in the major political institutions, they have nonetheless been politically active, often in grassroots movements organized to meet community needs.

Although women have not always been visible in public political roles, when you think about political behavior more broadly, you see that women have a long history of political activism—activism that shows women to be strong, independently minded, and attentive to the needs of diverse groups, including their own communities.

The feminist movement, which dates to the nineteenth century, appeared in a "second wave" beginning in the late 1960s. It has been one of the most influential social movements of recent history.

Studies find that a substantial majority of the U.S. public supports feminist issues, although many are reluctant to call themselves feminist because of how the dominant culture stigmatizes that label. Still, younger generations, now constituting a third wave of feminism, support feminist issues and have actively engaged in actions intended to reduce violence against women, protect women's rights in education and employment, and to promote women's health and security.

■ Key Terms

abolitionism	Fifteenth Amendment	power
authority	gender gap	power elite
Civil Rights Bill of 1964	Nineteenth Amendment	social movement
Equal Pay Act of 1963	patriarchy	state
Equal Rights Amendment	pluralism	temperance movement
essentialism		

■ Discussion Questions/Projects for Thought

1. Watch the national evening news for one week, keeping notes on which stories are reported and when women are mentioned. How frequently do women appear in the news? When they do, what is being reported? Are women depicted as active political news makers or are they "on the sidelines" of the news? What does this tell you about gender and politics?

2. Contact the military base nearest to you and inquire about services for military wives. What services are provided? What does this teach you about the experiences of women associated with the military? In what ways is the military a gendered institution?

3. Take a current piece of legislation being debated by your state legislature or the federal government, and ask yourself: What are the implications of this law for women? Are the implications being considered as part of this political debate? If so, in what terms? If not, why not?

12

Women and Social Reform: Liberal Feminism

As a social movement, feminism has brought many changes to society—not the least of which is change in intellectual life. Perhaps to many in the public, intellectual life seems like a rarified thing—distant, aloof, disconnected, but intellectual thought guides many of the changes in the world around us. As policymakers debate reforms in jobs, family policy, health care, or any other arena of life, they often draw on the knowledge of experts to guide their work as agents of change. These experts come from a variety of intellectual and political perspectives—thus, we have the great debates that characterize some of the more difficult and pressing issues of our times. In the absence of feminist thinking, few of these changes are likely to be informed by an analysis that understands the implications of such change for women.

In addition, sometimes people advocate changes with an implicit, and perhaps even unconscious, set of assumptions built into their ideals for change. Words like *liberal, conservative,* and *progressive* are tossed about in political discussion, but often without an understanding of their actual meaning in political theory. For example, liberalism has been much reviled by conservatives in recent years. But the basic premise of liberal political theory is that all people should be treated alike, with no formal barriers to opportunity and equal rights before the law—ironically, a philosophy that many conservatives now use to actually thwart progressive social changes.

You will notice that the term *liberal* is being used differently here than the way it is bandied about in the press. In current political discourse, *liberal* has come to mean the opposite of conservative, but this is not the true meaning of liberalism in political and social theory.

Liberalism has a very particular meaning in philosophical and social thought. Understanding the philosophical origins and framework of liberalism is critical if you are to be fully informed about contemporary debates regarding social policy—especially as those policies affect women and people of color.

Should we create gender-blind social policies? Can such policies address the persistent inequities that women face? Where do men fit in such a picture? Should we just treat women and men the same, or must we somehow account for gender differences in social policies for gender justice? These questions lie at the heart of feminist theory and are vitally important to the formulation of social policy. Although not everyone engaged in such discussions is consciously guided by a theoretical perspective, understanding theory helps you dissect the assumptions that undergird various perspectives on the possibilities for social change.

Feminist theory is the social and political thought that lies behind much of feminist politics. It forms the basis for social policies and social actions that have driven change in recent years. The development of feminist theory is not separate from the women's movement; indeed, the two are inextricably linked. Behind feminist politics lie modes of analysis (i.e., feminist theory) that guide and inform social and political action. These modes of thought are as diverse as the feminist movement itself, but they can be roughly grouped into broad categories, including liberal feminism and more radical forms of feminist thought.

As you will see in this chapter, throughout history feminist theory has been tied to broad intellectual and social changes in society. The social thought of influential European thinkers in the eighteenth and nineteenth centuries (Mary Wollstonecraft, John Stuart Mill, and Harriet Taylor Mill) laid the groundwork for contemporary liberal feminism. During the nineteenth century, Karl Marx, whose writings changed the course of world history, also influenced the development of feminist thought. Within the United States, social movements—including abolition, temperance, and the women's suffrage movement—have also influenced the development of feminist theory. At the same time, contemporary social changes taking place in society—including globalization, increased diversity in the population, and the expansion of educational opportunities for women, have all influenced the development of feminist thought over time. In the chapters that follow, you will examine this thought with the goal of understanding the underlying assumptions in diverse theoretical perspectives, since these same assumptions shape the imaginations people have for envisioning social change.

FRAMEWORKS OF FEMINIST THEORY

To many people, the idea of theory implies a way of thinking that is highly abstract and perhaps void of any connection to the "real" world. Many tend to think of theories as ideas that hold a certain degree of fascination for intellectuals but that are not particularly relevant for the ordinary person's understanding of life or the world. Most of us, however, do have ideas about how society is organized. Although we may not think of ourselves as theorists, we hold many assumptions, unexamined as they may be, about the organization of society and the possibilities for social change.

Feminist theory attempts to situate the everyday events of women's and men's lives in an analysis that links our personal and collective experience to an understanding of the structure of gender relationships in society and culture. Feminists also claim that what we know, both intellectually and practically, is thoroughly infused with gendered assumptions about the character of the social world, its problems, its inhabitants, and its meaning.

The purpose of feminist theory is to help us understand conditions in society and to envision the possibilities for liberating social changes. Feminist theory is not written about and discussed just for its own sake but also for what it suggests about political change. Although theoretical analyses may seem complex and sometimes abstract, their purpose is to help understand the character of social structure and therefore the possibilities for social change. Different political frameworks in the feminist movement rest on different theoretical assumptions. Although these assumptions are not always evident in political discourse, understanding them can sharpen political analyses and inform strategies for social change.

For example, since feminism has moved into the mainstream of life in the United States, many people identify themselves as feminists with little understanding of the liberal framework they assume (Eisenstein 1981; see Figure 12.1). Whether one assumes a liberal or a radical feminist stance, examining the intellectual roots of different feminist perspectives provides a more complete understanding of the assumptions of a given perspective, as well as the different programs for social change that given perspectives imply. Careful study of particular feminist frameworks enables us to more accurately answer questions about women's status in society and therefore allows for a better assessment of possible directions for social change.

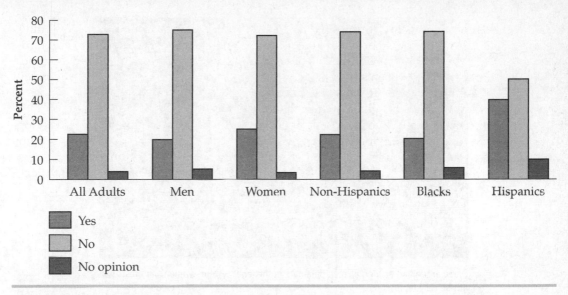

FIGURE 12.1   Do You Consider Yourself a Feminist?

Source: Data from Lydia Saad. 2001. "Women See Room for Improvement in Job Equity." *Gallup Poll* (June). Princeton, NJ: The Gallup Organization. Reprinted by permission.

The theoretical and political frameworks of feminist thought emerge from some of the classical traditions of social and political theory. Feminists have revised some of these classical perspectives to better explain the position of women in society. Like the intellectual traditions from which feminist thought stems, feminist theory is organized around varying assumptions about social organization and social change. These assumptions also guide how we interpret the empirical observations of social research. Depending on the theoretical position used to understand data, the data may take on a different meaning. Facts do not usually speak for themselves; they are interpreted within the context of assumptions made about their meaning and their relationship to other facts. Theories guide this interpretation and are therefore an integral part of the process of knowledge construction.

This chapter focuses on the framework of liberal feminism, a long-standing and far-reaching framework for feminist social change. Liberal feminism is rooted in the history of liberalism as a mode of political theory—one that developed particularly over the course of the nineteenth century—and it is centered on the premise of equality and the capacity for existing democratic social institutions to create equal rights and equal opportunity for all. Liberalism is the foundation for democracy; it promotes the removal of particularistic barriers—that is, practices that discriminate based on particular characteristics such as gender, race, and religion. Although to many this seems like an ideal solution for promoting gender equality, you will see that there are some fundamental limitations to this approach.

Liberal feminism emphasizes social and legal reform through policies designed to create equal opportunities for women. In addition, it emphasizes

Many argue that as long as men dominate in the legal system, women's interests will not be fully represented.

gender socialization as the origin of gender differences, thereby assuming that changes in socialization practices will result in more egalitarian gender relations.

Liberal feminism differs from other feminist theoretical perspectives in accepting the basic structure of democratic social institutions as conducive to social change. As you will see in the subsequent chapter, socialist feminism is a more radical perspective—one that interprets the origins of women's oppression in the systems of capitalism and patriarchy. Radical feminism analyzes patriarchy as the primary cause of women's oppression. Socialist feminism and radical feminism are examined in Chapter 13, along with other contemporary modes of feminist thought, including postmodernist feminist theory, multiracial feminism, and queer theory. No single perspective provides the singularly most correct analysis of women's place in society. As these two chapters will show, each perspective has its own conceptual strengths and weaknesses and thus is able to answer some questions better than others. Together, these feminist theoretical perspectives provide a rich and engaging analysis of women and men in society.

The adequacy of each perspective should be assessed, in part, in terms of its ability to address several fundamental issues in feminist thought. Most important, because feminism purports to liberate *all* women, a sound feminist analysis must be able to address the interrelationship of race, class, and gender. And, feminist theory must explain some of the central questions that emerge from thinking about women.

THE LIBERAL BASIS OF MODERN FEMINISM

In political and sociological theory, *liberal* has a particular meaning quite different from its common usage to mean open-minded, tolerant, or socially nontraditional. The specific philosophical meaning of **liberalism** is characterized by an emphasis on individual rights and equal opportunity.

Liberalism is the dominant political philosophy in the United States. Those who might never consider themselves liberal—in the sense the label has come to imply—nonetheless are likely to believe that the best society is one in which no group receives special treatment based on its race, color, religion, national origin, or gender. Indeed, this philosophy is the very foundation for modern civil rights legislation. It is a position that advocates a color-blind and gender-neutral society. Many take this position to the extreme, thinking that even to acknowledge another's gender or race is to be sexist or racist.

As a political and social theory, liberalism has generated quite specific programs for social change—notably, eliminating any practices or laws that either discriminate against particular groups and, as with the movement among current conservatives, trying to eliminate any programs that have race- or gender-specific components (such as affirmative action). Ironically, this has now become the agenda of conservatives—though they would never think of themselves as operating within the framework of classic liberalism.

The origins of liberal philosophy lie in western Europe and the societal transitions of the eighteenth and nineteenth centuries. By examining this context and the social thought produced within it, you will see the theoretical tenets of the liberal perspective, as well as its connection to the evolution of feminist thought. Although you have already reviewed the growth of feminism in the United States in the nineteenth and twentieth centuries, this historical analysis of liberal thought will give a more detailed and analytical vision of the liberal basis of some feminist beliefs and politics.

🔥 LIBERALISM AS A MODE OF SOCIAL THOUGHT

The origins of contemporary liberal feminism reach back to the seventeenth- and eighteenth-century **Age of Enlightenment** in western Europe (also known as the *Age of Reason*). This period fostered an array of political, social, and intellectual movements, most of them characterized by an explicit faith in the capacity of human reason to generate social reform. As the setting for the early philosophies of feminism, the Age of Enlightenment is noted for its libertarian ideals, its pleas for humanitarian reform, and its conviction that "reason shall set us free" (Rossi 1973).

The Origins of Liberal Thought

The philosophy of the period provided the theme for major changes in Western social organization (including the French and American Revolutions), and it set the stage for the eventual development of social-scientific thought and the emergence of sociology as an academic field. The historical context of early feminist thought is found in conditions that inspired more general appeals to social reform through the application of human reason. This period provides the historical arena for the emergence of contemporary liberal feminism.

Two notable developments influenced broad-scale change in the West: the consolidation and expansion of a world system of capital (Wallerstein 1976) and a decline in the traditional sacred authority of religion (Nisbet 1970). The development of Western capitalism created new systems of inequality marked by the displacement of the poor from rural land and the concentration of wealth in the hands of the new capitalist class. The related developments of urbanization and industrialization also planted the seeds of the social problems that continue to confront us today: urban crowding and the development of slums, pollution and waste, poverty, crime, and new tensions in family life. In the Age of Enlightenment, political thinkers who observed these changes also delighted in the decline of the influence of the sacred authority of the church and the secular feudal state. Enlightenment thinkers fostered the hope that the human ability to reason would provide societies with reasonable solutions to the new problems they encountered.

One of the central tenets of Enlightenment philosophy and the political-social thought it inspired was that free, critical inquiry was to be the cornerstone for the future. At heart, the Enlightenment thinkers were optimists, and they seemed undaunted by the vast problems surrounding them. Although, in retrospect, they can be criticized for their naive faith in human rationality, their work emphasized open inquiry (Hughes 1958).

The Enlightenment libertarian ideals challenged the power of feudal elites and assumed that the future was in the hands of the masses. As they considered the development of history, they envisioned a decline in the brutal and "uncivilized" physical abuses of the past (de Tocqueville 1945). They believed that the church, identified by most Enlightenment thinkers as the villain of past repression, would continue to decline in its authoritarian influence; modern society would instead be regulated by the rational construction of democratic government.

The influence of the Enlightenment extends beyond the eighteenth century, laying the foundation for the development of social science in the nineteenth and twentieth centuries and influencing later thinkers such as John Stuart Mill (1806–1873) in the nineteenth century. Sociology, in particular, is indebted to the Enlightenment for its emphasis on the application of reason and the scientific method to the solution of social problems. Early sociological thinkers such as **Auguste Comte** (1798–1857) and **Henry Saint-Simon** (1760–1825) believed that social knowledge would take the form of social laws, telling us how the social world operated and how we could therefore engineer positive changes. The simplicity of their faith in sociology as the ultimate science is now apparent, but their influence on the positivist methods of sociology is immeasurable. The positivism they inspired and that others have developed since assumes that the techniques of scientific observation in the physical sciences can be used in the discovery of social behavior. Their insistence on the application of sociological knowledge for engineering social change continues to influence the activities of modern social planners.

We are not sure what the Enlightenment was like for women, because its recorded history has been largely that of men's accomplishments. We do know that women's historical experience differs significantly from men's (Kelly-Gadol 1976), and feminist historians have suggested that the Enlightenment is no exception. They would argue that the Age of Reason is a reference only to the reason of certain men. During this same era, women's work was idealized as belonging in the emotional world of the home; nevertheless, women's labor (both in the home and outside of it) constituted a major part of the society's economic productivity. Most women still produced marketable goods in the home, and as factories became the sites for production, women and children were employed for long hours at low wages.

Seen in the context of women's lives, the period of Enlightenment takes on a somewhat different meaning. Both women and the working class seem to have been left out of the Age of Reason, because the intellectual movement of the Enlightenment was largely based on the thought of bourgeois White men. During this same period in the United States, most African American women and men were still enslaved, and, although slavery was one of the concerns of the men of the Enlightenment, histories of feminist thought rarely look to the thoughts of African American women, slave or free, as an origin for early feminist work. The development of feminist thought cannot be placed exclusively, though, in the Enlightenment. African American women such as Charlotte Forten, Maria Stewart, Sojourner Truth, and Ida Bell Wells articulated some of the early principles of feminist thought (Lerner 1973; Sterling 1984; Collins 1990). Maria Stewart, a former servant to a clergy family in New England, was the first woman in the United States to deliver a public lecture (in Boston on September 21, 1832). Although rarely recognized in the histories of feminism, her exhortations to women domestic workers and day laborers to improve their minds and talents, which she saw as thwarted by women's servitude, are clear and passionate feminist ideals. When she left Boston because of hostile public response to her work, she delivered a parting speech ardently defending the right of women to speak in public (Sterling 1984). To exclude women such as Stewart and the many other African American thinkers and activists of this early period from the history of feminist thought is to take White European and American philosophers as creating the history of feminism and to see African American women's feminist ideas only as secondary or as a reaction to White thought (Gilkes 1985).

This interpretation does not mean we should disregard the influence of Enlightenment thought on the history of feminism, but it does cast this history in a different light. The legacy of the Enlightenment as the triumph of man's reason is a celebration of the growing preeminence at this time of men's rational power. Women during this period were identified with the irrational and emotional side of life. The ascent of rationality, which the Enlightenment celebrates, can then be seen as the ascent of male rational power over the presumed emotionality and inferiority of women. This revision puts the thinkers of the Enlightenment period into a different context and also reveals different aspects of their work. Feminist historians who have studied the major Enlightenment philosophers (Rousseau, Diderot, and Condorcet, for example) conclude that although the Enlightenment philosophers had the potential to decry the sexist ideas of sacred traditions, most of the Enlightenment thinkers ignored the revolutionary potential of their ideas for change in women's lives (Kleinbaum 1977). Still, the thinkers of the Enlightenment did have a strong influence on the development of modern feminism.

The Continuing Influence of Liberal Thought

Even with the caveat that most women did not experience the Enlightenment in the way men did, this period left a philosophical tradition in the dominant culture that lives on. The two central principles of this framework of thinking are the concept of individual liberty and the emphasis on human reason as the basis for humanitarian social change. In liberal feminism, these philosophical ideals are the basis for the principle of equal opportunity and social reform. Much of the focus of social change among liberal feminist groups lies in the construction of legislation and in the regulation of employment practices. According to the liberal perspective, the obstacles to equal rights for women (as well as other groups) lie in traditional laws and practices that deny the same individual rights to women that men already have.

The liberal perspective assumes that persons can create humanitarian change through the use of human rationality. Injustice is viewed as the result of irrationality and ignorance. Reason and the pursuit of knowledge are believed to be the source of social change; consequently, liberal policies for change rely on a faith in the process of social reform. Liberal feminists' practical solutions to inequality include programs that prohibit **discrimination** (e.g., differential treatment). Given women's reports of continuing discrimination (see Figure 12.2), this is clearly an important goal. Liberal feminism also seeks the reform of individuals through, for example, the resocialization of children and the relearning of appropriate social roles for adults. A central emphasis of the liberal perspective is that all persons' abilities are culturally learned; therefore, egalitarian gender relations will follow from relearning traditional gender-role attitudes and behaviors.

The popularity of the liberal perspective makes it difficult to identify as a specific social and political philosophy. It is the philosophical backdrop to many contemporary programs for change, and it has been widely adopted by diverse groups working for legal and economic reform. Liberalism also encourages the acceptance of diverse lifestyles, because it sees lifestyle as a matter of individual choice. Within the liberal perspective, persons and the societies they create should be tolerant and respectful of the choices persons make. Because persons have civil rights to exercise their freedom, societies should not erect barriers to individual liberties.

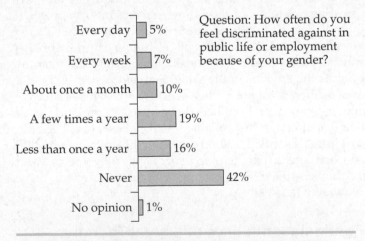

FIGURE 12.2   Women's Perception of Discrimination

Source: Saad, Lydia. 2003. "Women Skeptical of Societal Fairness to Their Gender." *The Gallup Poll.* Princeton, NJ: The Gallup Organization. Reprinted by permission.

FOCUS ON RESEARCH

Implementing the Law—Title IX and the Making of Feminists

Title IX (passed in 1972) is the federal law requiring schools to provide equal opportunities to women in all aspects of education. Once a law is passed, how is it implemented? In the case of Title IX, the common practice is for schools to have a Title IX coordinator—a staff member whose job it is to monitor the implementation of Title IX, such as assuring that women are given equal opportunities in admissions, athletics, counseling, course offerings, and so forth. Would you expect that those appointed to such positions would be feminists from the start—women (or men) who embraced feminist values and wanted a job where they could work on behalf of women and gender equity?

In her study of Title IX coordinators, Judith Taylor found that this was not so much the case. She studied Title IX coordinators working in a large, urban school district. Her research method includes participant observation in the school district for one year, interviews with Title IX coordinators and other school administrators, analysis of school records and local newspapers, and follow-up e-mails.

Taylor points out that within large bureaucracies, compliance officers have fairly wide latitude in defining compliance with the law they are charged to implement. If you have ever encountered a bureaucratic worker, you know how this works: Some bureaucratic workers refuse to budge from narrowly defined bureaucratic rules; others use whatever discretion they can muster to bend the bureaucratic apparatus.

Taylor found that, among the Title IX coordinators she studied, most were not feminists before taking these jobs. Instead, they initially took the jobs to join administrative ranks, earn more money, have more authority, and do something new. But, in the context of their work, they became feminists; only one was self-identified as a feminist before doing this work. Three factors influenced them to become a feminist: One, in doing their job, they directly observed the mistreatment of women. Two, they became frustrated with the intransigence of the bureaucratic organization in being able to address women's concerns. And, three, they experienced themselves feelings of isolation and belittlement by virtue of being associated with a gender cause. As a consequence, the coordinators became feminists and thus used their position within the schools to try to generate more equity for women.

Taylor's work suggests that you do not become a feminist just because you are a woman, as some assume, but that more complex factors generate feminist work and self-identity. Witnessing discrimination, being stereotyped as a woman, and being denied respect in the workplace can result in people's using their positions, even in large bureaucracies, to work on behalf of gender equity.

Source: Based on Taylor, Judith. 2005. "Who Manages Feminist-Inspired Reform? An In-Depth Look at Title IX Coordinators in the United States." *Gender & Society* 19 (June): 358–375.

In sum, liberal feminism assumes that the inequality of women stems both from the denial of equal rights and from women's learned reluctance to exercise their rights. The goal of liberal feminism is equality—the construction of a social world where all persons can exercise individual freedom. At its heart, the liberal perspective is a philosophy based on the principle of individual liberty. In the liberal framework, every person should be allowed to exercise freedom of choice, unfettered by either public opinion or law. In effect, all persons should be given equal opportunities, and civil rights should be extended to all. Liberal feminist philosophy lies behind the call for reforms such as the Equal Rights Amendment, which, if it had been enacted, would amend the Constitution to state: "Equality of rights under the law shall not be denied or abridged by the United States or by any state on the basis of sex" (see also previous chapter). One indication of the nation's unwillingness to fully embrace liberal feminist ideals is the fact that such an amendment has never been ratified so as to make it the law of the land.

EARLY LIBERAL FEMINISTS

Who were the early thinkers who developed the framework of liberal feminism? Mary Wollstonecraft is one of the first to provide the philosophical foundations of modern feminism. Harriet Martineau is another of the early women to analyze women's condition in society. And most political philosophers recognize John Stuart Mill as one of the founders of liberal political philosophy; feminists have added his life partner, Harriet Taylor Mill, to the history of liberal thought. Because of their importance in articulating the framework of liberal feminism, their works are detailed next.

Mary Wollstonecraft

Mary Wollstonecraft's (1759–1797) essay, *A Vindication of the Rights of Women,* first published in London in 1792, was so provocative that editions of it quickly appeared in Dublin, Paris, and New York (Poston 1975). So astutely did she outline the position of women that her essay was equally provocative to White, middle-class women who discussed it in consciousness-raising groups in the 1960s and 1970s. Her words continue to inspire women more than 200 years after the original edition was published—a testimony to the influence Wollstonecraft has had.

Wollstonecraft left her home as a teenager in 1778. Distressed by her father's excessive demands for obedience and her family's continued poverty, she wandered from town to town in the countryside of Wales and England (Rossi 1973). Her independence and self-sufficiency established a lifetime pattern of refusing to submit to authority—both in her life and in her writings. She later wrote:

I will venture to affirm, that a girl, whose spirits have not been damped by inactivity, or innocence tainted by false name, will always be a romp, and the doll will never excite attention unless confinement allows her no alternative. Girls and boys, in short, would play harmlessly

Mary Wollstonecraft was an 18th century founder of feminist thought.

together, if the distinction of sex was not inculcated long before nature makes any difference. I will go further and affirm, as an indisputable fact, that most of the women, in the circle of my observation, who have acted like rational creatures, or shown any vigour of intellect, have accidentally been allowed to run wild. (Wollstonecraft 1792/1975:43)

Her concern with subservience to authority recurs as a central theme in her work, and it is tied to her argument that learning and socialization are responsible for the formation of mind. Foretelling generations of feminists to come, Wollstonecraft argued that gender role characteristics were the result of education (used broadly in her work to mean all social learning). What appeared to be the natural weakness of women was the result of their lack of liberty and their dependence on men. She wrote, "All the differences that I can discern, arise from the superior advantage of

---

MEDIA MATTERS

Mean Girls

Over the past several years, aggression in girls has received sensationalized attention in popular culture. Mean girls have been the focus of several Hollywood movies, the most popular being *Mean Girls*, which depicts girls as living in chaotic worlds of manipulation, jealousy, ridicule, and harassment. Additionally, authors who have written books about the subject have appeared on *The Oprah Winfrey Show*. For example, Rachel Simmons, author of *Odd Girl Out*, talked with Oprah about the "epidemic of relational aggression" among girls. Why is girls' aggression being given so much attention in popular media?

To answer this question, Jessica Ringrose examined recent sensationalist media attention to mean girls. Ringrose does not discuss how she conducted her analysis or the methodology she employed to collect her sample. However, most of her discussion criticizes journal articles, books, and newspaper stories that were written on the subject of female aggression.

Ringrose found that early research conducted on female aggression sought to challenge the male bias in studying aggression. In the mid-1990s, the term *relational aggression* was introduced by developmental child psychologists. Research conducted at this time focused on illustrating how girls aggressed differently than boys. Psychologists claimed that, whereas boys used direct, physical aggression to hurt one another, girls used indirect forms of aggression to hurt other girls. Girls engage in much higher levels of relational aggression than boys because their friendships are characterized by greater degrees of emotional closeness and intimacy, which girls use against other girls. Examples of relationally aggressive behaviors include retaliating against a peer by excluding her from the group, withdrawing friendship in order to hurt or control a peer, spreading rumors about a peer so that other peers will reject her, and so on.

According to Ringrose, although developmental research started out as a feminist challenge to male-biased research on aggression, this literature has used the differences in female aggression to define girls in pathological terms (that is, as if they were "sick" or "deranged"). Direct aggression (the type used by boys) is maintained as the neutral and normative standard. In contrast, indirect aggression (the type used by girls) is viewed as different from and inferior to this standard. Ringrose concludes that the explosion of mean girls in popular culture reinforces gender differences between boys and girls and buttresses the boundaries of femininity.

Source: Based on Ringrose, Jessica. 2006. "A New Universal Mean Girl: Examining the Discursive Construction and Social Regulation of a New Feminine Pathology." *Feminism & Psychology* 16: 405–424.

liberty, which enables the former to see more of life" (Wollstonecraft 1792/1975:23). She went on to say:

> It is vain to expect virtue from women till they are in some degree independent of men; nay, it is vain to expect that strength of natural affection which would make them good wives and mothers. Whilst they are absolutely dependent on their husbands they will be cunning, mean and selfish, and the men who can be gratified by the fawning fondness of spaniel-like affection have not much delicacy, for love is not to be bought; its silken wings are instantly shriveled up when anything besides a return in kind is sought. (1792/1975:144)

Throughout her essay, Wollstonecraft emphasized that blind submission to authority not only limits social and political freedom but also inhibits the development of mental reasoning. Like others in the Enlightenment, she imagined that the downfall of tyranny would occur as society became organized around the principle of rational thought. She wrote, "Tyrants would have cause to tremble if reason were to become the rule of duty in any of the relations of life, for the light might spread till perfect day appeared" (1792/1975:150).

Wollstonecraft equated the life of a dutiful soldier to that of a well-socialized woman:

> They both acquire manners before morals, and a knowledge of life before they have, from reflection, any acquaintance with the grand ideal outline of human nature. The consequence is natural; satisfied with common nature, they become a prey to prejudices, and taking all their opinions on credit, they submit blindly to authority. So that, if they have any sense, it is a kind of instinctive glance, that catches propositions, and decides with respect to manners but fails when arguments are to be pursued below the surface, or opinions analyzed. (1792/1975:24)

More than other early White feminists, Wollstonecraft was sensitive to the issue of social class and the artificial distinctions among persons that she believed social class created. She directed her arguments especially to leisure-class women, for, she said, it is in that class that women are most dependent on men. She held in contempt the idleness of mind and attention to gentility that she believed wealth produced: "The education of the rich tends to render them vain and helpless, and the unfolding mind is not strengthened by the practice of those duties which dignify the human character" (1792/1975:9). "The preposterous distinctions of rank, which render civilization a curse by dividing the world between voluptuous tyrants and cunning envious dependents, corrupt, almost equally, every class of people, because respectability is not attached to the discharge of the relative duties of life, but to the station" (1792/1975:144). Although she recognized that her observations were of a particular social class, she gave little, if any, attention to women of other classes and cultures.

Wollstonecraft's outspoken portrayals of femininity, authority, and property relations earned her a lifetime of insults and insinuations about her bad character. Her contemporaries indexed articles written about her under the topic "prostitution" (Rossi 1973; Wardle 1951); more recently, her feminist beliefs have raised charges that she was "pitifully weak," "consumed with penis envy," and an "extreme neurotic" (Lundberg and Farnham 1947). These same critics wrote, "Out of her illness arose the ideology of feminism, which was to express the feelings of so many women in years to come" (Lundberg and Farnham 1947:145–159).

Wollstonecraft's work is a powerful criticism of women's role and its connection to power and social control. Her writing typifies the passion with which the Enlightenment thinkers pursued their condemnations of traditional authority, and it stands as one of the most persuasive accounts of the effects of women's subservience on their powers of thought, behavior, and self-concept. Her statement that more egalitarian education was needed to liberate women sounds as if it could have been written yesterday. It is a tribute to Wollstonecraft's own capacities for reason and her unchecked passion for justice that her words continue to inspire people more than two centuries after they were written.

Harriet Martineau

Not long after Wollstonecraft's death in 1797, another woman was born who could appropriately be called the mother of sociology. Little recognized in contemporary histories of sociological thought, English woman **Harriet Martineau** (1802–1876) was one of the first to use field observation as a method for the development of social knowledge. She was the translator of Auguste Comte's (the father of sociology) *Positive Philosophy*; and, like her counterpart, Alexis de Tocqueville, she traveled widely in the United States, producing a descriptive and analytic account of her observations in her book *Society in America* (1837). Her other book, *How to Observe Manners and Morals* (1838), was the first methodology book in sociology, for in it she detailed the method of participant observation as she developed it in her own work (Lipset 1962; Rossi 1973; Hill and Hoecker-Drysdale 2002).

Like many of the early feminists, Martineau matched her concern for women's emancipation with her support for the U.S. abolition movement. Her outspokenness on the slavery issue, coupled with her daring to travel as a single woman in the nineteenth century, generated threats against her life. She was eventually forced to restrict her travels to the northern section of the country, but in her analysis she insisted on the right of women to speak their conscience. She wrote:

The whole apparatus of opinion is brought to bear offensively upon individuals among women who exercise freedom of mind in deciding upon what duty is, and the methods by which it is to be pursued. . . . The

Harriet Martineau was a keen observer of society and women's roles within society. She can also be considered as one of the founders of sociology.

reproach in all the many similar cases I know is, not that the ladies hold anti-slavery opinions, but that they act upon them. The incessant outcry about the retiring modesty of the sex proves the opinion of the censors to be that fidelity to conscience is inconsistent with retiring modesty. If it be so, let the modesty succumb. (1837:158–159)

As Marx and Engels were also later to proclaim, she also wrote, "If a test of civilization be sought, none can be so sure as the condition of that half of society over which the other half has power" (1837:156).

The connection Martineau made between the abolition and feminist movements is indicative of the association that early feminists had with their antislavery movement in the United States. White women's dissatisfaction with their position likely led to their involvement in and appreciation for the abolitionist cause (DuBois 1978). Their involvement in the antislavery movement taught White feminists how to understand and change their situation.

African American women in the antislavery movement were more likely to put racial prejudice at the center of their feminist analyses. Sarah Forten, for example, writing in 1837, discussed the influence of prejudice on her life. She said:

It has often embittered my feelings, particularly when I recollect that we are innocent victims of it . . . and [I] consequently seek to avoid as much as possible mingling with those who exist under its influence. I must also own that it has often engendered feelings of discontent and mortification in my breast when I see that many were preferred before me, who by education—birth—or worldly circumstance were not better than myself—their sole claim to notice depending on the superior advantage of being white. (Sterling 1984:124)

White women who worked in the abolition movement gained an understanding from African American women of the concept of institutional power and adopted the political conviction of natural rights for all individuals, regardless of race or sex. Their analysis of racial and sexual oppression, however, remained at the level of analogy. Early White feminists did not develop an understanding that took account of the historical specificity of the African American experience in the United States, nor did they ever make the kind of analysis that could adequately account for class and other cultural differences among women (DuBois 1978). As a result, the liberal tradition of feminism that was established by leaders such as **Elizabeth Cady Stanton** (1815–1902) and **Susan B. Anthony** (1820–1906) began and continued with an inadequate comprehension of race and class issues in women's experience.

Martineau's own analysis of race and class is filled with contradictions. She appealed to justice and freedom, yet maintained the ethnic stereotypes typical of her period. She wrote:

The English, soon find it impossible to get American domestic help at all, and they are consigned to the tender mercies of the low Irish; and everyone knows what kind of servants they commonly are. Some few of them are the best domestics in America; those who know how to value a respectable home, a steady sufficient income, the honour of being trusted, and the security of valuable friends for life; but too many of them are unsettled, reckless, slovenly; some dishonest, and some intemperate. (1837:171–172)

HISTORY SPEAKS: YESTERDAY'S FEMINISTS TALK ABOUT TODAY

Abigail Adams and Women's Rights

"I long to hear that you have declared an independancy— and by the way in the new Code of Laws which I suppose it will be necessary for you to make I desire you would Remember the Ladies, and be more generous and favourable to them than your ancestors. Do not put such unlimited power into the hands of the Husbands. Remember all Men would be tyrants if they could. If particuliar care and attention is not paid to the Ladies we are determined to foment a Rebellion, and will not hold ourselves bound by any Laws in which we have no voice, or Representation."

—Abigail Adams (1776, letter to John Adams)

Abigail Adams (1744–1818) is known widely as the wife of President John Adams (the second president of the United States). But more than her role as a presidential wife, she was an early feminist whose letters to her husband (now housed in the Massachusetts Historical Society) document her feminist thinking and her strong opposition to slavery—even 100 years prior to the Civil War.

During the first few years of her marriage to John, she lived apart from him, taking full responsibility for the management and business affairs of their farm in Braintree, Massachusetts, while John Adams pursued his political work in Boston. At the time, women were forbidden by law in most places from owning property. She believed that boys and girls should receive equal educations and thought that educated mothers would produce educated daughters—a radical idea at a time when the formal education of women was so limited.

While John Adams was serving as the Massachusetts representative to the Continental Congress in Philadelphia where the Declaration of Independence was produced, Abigail Adams wrote to him, beseeching him to "remember the ladies" as he developed the nation's new laws.

During the time John Adams was president, Abigail Adams's opponents complained that she had too much influence on her husband and that she should have taken a more backstage role—a criticism one still hears today when powerful women occupy the role of First Lady.

Thinking Further: *It is doubtful that Abigail Adams would have ever imagined herself as becoming President of the United States, but if she were alive today, what office might she hold? She says that without "care and attention paid to [women]," they might rebel. Why did they not? How might our nation's history of women's rights be different had women's rights been explicitly included in the Declaration of Independence? Where would Abigail Adams stand on the Equal Rights Amendment?*

Sources: Based on Rossi, Alice. 1973. *The Feminist Papers.* New York: Columbia University Press; Public Broadcasting System. 2005. *American Experience: John and Abigail Adams* (film). www.pbs.org.

Martineau's work stands as an example of early White feminist thought, complete with its class and race contradictions. More generally, despite appeals to reason, free will, humanitarianism, and liberty, liberal feminism has never adequately addressed the issues of race and class inequality. In stating that racism and sexism are analogous forms of oppression, liberal feminism suggests an analysis that would take race, class, and gender into account, but, as the concluding section of this chapter shows, this analysis is not provided by liberal White feminists, leaving the theoretical and political task of comprehending race, class, and gender oppression to other thinkers.

John Stuart Mill and Harriet Taylor Mill

No thinkers have been more influential in the development of liberal feminism than **John Stuart Mill** (1806–1873) and **Harriet Taylor Mill** (1807–1858). *The Subjection of Women*, first published in 1851, was the philosophical inspiration for the British suffrage movement and, like Wollstonecraft's *A Vindication of the Rights of Women*, continues to be studied. Their essays relate women's oppression to a systematic critique of liberty and the relations between women and men.

From an early age, John Stuart Mill was steeped in the rigors of intellectual thought and disciplined study. Under his father's stern supervision, he began a course of study at age 3 that created his intellectual genius at the same time that it apparently robbed him of emotional gratification (Rossi 1970). His life was one of continuous intellectual production mixed with political activism and long struggles with emotional depression. His father's intense emphasis on rational thought left Mill with a long struggle to "cultivate the feelings," an accomplishment perhaps best made through his strong relationship with Harriet Taylor (later to become Harriet Taylor Mill).

Although she is often overlooked, Harriet Taylor Mill was a lifelong companion and intellectual peer of John Stuart Mill.

The relationship between John Stuart Mill and Harriet Taylor is one that matches romantic commitment and intellectual collaboration with a fervor for individual liberty; so passionate and unusual was their life together that it is still the subject of discussion. Through their correspondence and conversation with each other, their published ideas were formed. Mill himself wrote that the ideas in *The Subjection of Women* (published after Harriet's death) belonged to his wife and had emerged from their vast discussions on a topic dear to them both. Over the years, scholars have seldom given Harriet Mill the recognition she deserves for her contribution to these works or, for that matter, to her own writing. The fact that Harriet Taylor Mill has so seldom been cited in the many detailed reviews of the Mills' work underscores the sexist character of philosophical criticism and points out how little credit has been given to women thinkers of the past. Alice Rossi has made a convincing case that the Mills' work was a joint effort, even though it was published under his name. She also argues that *Enfranchisement of Women* (published in 1851) was actually written by Harriet Mill (Rossi 1970).

Taken together, the Mills' essays provide the most comprehensive statement of the liberal perspective of feminist thought. The issues they raise can be grouped into several key areas—the logic of inquiry, gender differences, work and the family, and the process of modernization and social change.

The Logic of Inquiry

The logic of the Mills' arguments is typical of that inspired by the rational perspective of the Enlightenment thinkers. Convictions, the Mills claimed, fare poorly in argumentative debate, for the resistance of conviction to reason makes rational argument impossible. Strong feelings, they maintained, are impenetrable by rational debate; consequently, those who argue against almost universally held opinions will, most certainly, have a hard time being heard. In discussing the subordination of women, the Mills clearly argued that open inquiry—especially listening to women's voices—is a prerequisite to establishing knowledge of women's lives. They wrote:

> We may safely assert that the knowledge which men can acquire of women, even as they have been and are, without reference to what they might be, is wretchedly imperfect and superficial and always will be so, until women themselves have told all they have to tell. . . . Let us remember in what manner, up to a recent time, the expression, even by a male author, of uncustomary opinions, or what are deemed eccentric feelings, usually was, and in some degree still is, received; and we may form some faint conception under what impediments a woman, who is brought up to think custom and opinion her sovereign rule, attempts to express in books anything drawn from the depths of her own nature. (cited in Rossi 1970:152–153)

The starting point of their argument, as well as the central concept in the liberal perspective, is that all persons have equal liberty, and therefore human institutions should treat all alike. Their words provide the philosophy behind the modern practice of equal employment opportunity and equality before the law. They wrote, "The law should be no respecter of persons, but should treat all alike, save where dissimilarity of treatment is required by positive reasons, either justice or of policy" (Mill 1970:4). They defined human liberty as a natural right and one that should not be denied on the basis of any individual or group characteristics. As their writing shows, the rational style of their argument is coupled with a passionate emphasis on the necessity for liberating social changes.

The Social Construction of Gender

The Mills showed how social conditions create gender-specific attitudes and behaviors. By imagining new alternatives, the Mills showed how a change in the relationship between men and women would likely alter the characteristics usually thought to be natural differences. They argued that there is no reasonable defense for the current state of affairs and that the creation of liberty for women would benefit not just women but society as a whole. The social benefits of liberation would include "doubling the mass of mental faculties available for the higher service of humanity" (Mill 1970:153), overcoming the selfish attitudes and self-worshipping characteristics of humanity (1970:148), and enhancing the "softening influence" (1970:156) of women's moral tendencies.

What is considered to be natural is only what is taken for granted, they argued. Foretelling the thoughts of contemporary feminists, they wrote:

> *Was there ever any domination which did not appear natural to those who possessed it? There was a time when the division of mankind into two classes, a small one of masters and a numerous one of slaves, appeared, even to the most cultivated minds, to be a natural, and the only natural, condition of the human race. . . . Did not the slave owners of the Southern United States maintain the same doctrine, with all the fanaticism with which men cling to the theories that justify their passions and legitimate their personal interests? (Mill 1970: 20–21)*

Like contemporary social scientists, the Mills saw that what appears natural is primarily the result of social learning. Because women had been held in such an unnatural state of submission and domination, the Mills believed it was impossible to make claims about natural gender differences. All that we see as masculinity or femininity, they contended, is the result of learned, not actual, differences. They wrote, "Women have always hitherto been kept, as far as regards spontaneous development, in so unnatural a state, that their nature cannot but have been greatly distorted and disguised" (1970:104–105). They went on, "I deny that any one knows, or can know, the nature of the sexes, as long as they have only been seen in their present relation to one another" (1970:38), and said, "One thing we may be certain of—that what is contrary to women's nature to do, they will never be made to do by simply giving their nature free play" (1970:48).

The Mills made the case for liberty by identifying the detrimental effects of social learning or, in their words, education and custom, under a state of subjection. They assumed that persons construct their social arrangements and social identities, although some may have more power than others to do so. Human beings, they argued, are rational and creative. Only by removing constraints and obstacles to liberty can the free expression of rational choice and humane social development be encouraged. According to the Mills, human beings have a natural right to self-expression that unnatural systems of authority and rule take away.

The Mills' concept of liberty rests on the idea of voluntary contracts among human actors. Accordingly, they argued that marriage ties should be based on free and voluntary choice and that law, in marriage and other areas, should treat all alike—giving no unnatural advantage to one group or another. The purpose of *The Subjection of Women* is, in fact, to show the following:

> *The principle which regulates the existing social relations between the two sexes—and legal subordination of one sex to the other—is wrong in itself, and now one of the chief hindrances to human improvements; and that it ought to be replaced by a principle of perfect equality, admitting no power or privilege on the one side, nor disability on the other. (Mill 1970:1)*

Harriet Taylor Mill, in her own essay, "Enfranchisement of Women," argued, in addition, that "we deny the right of any portion of the species to decide for another portion, or any individual for another individual, what is and what is not their proper sphere" (Rossi 1970:100). Although the Mills differed on their opinions about women's place in marriage, their attitude toward self-determination was clearly one that denies the right of any one group to restrain another: "The law which is to be observed by both should surely be made by both; yet, as hitherto, by the stronger only" (Rossi 1970:68). This premise in their work is also the foundation for their ideas on women's position in the workplace and the family.

Work and the Family

The Mills' belief in individual liberty is also seen in their arguments on women's occupations. They believed in the *laissez-faire* operation of the economic market, meaning that they favored a noninterventionist approach to economic processes. Their assumption was that if persons are free to choose their occupations, then the best qualified will fill the positions most appropriate to their talents.

These assumptions are grounded in the earlier work of the British economist *Adam Smith*. Smith maintained that the economic market should be based on open competition and a lack of regulation or interference. According to Smith, this laissez-faire policy best suits the laws of the market. He identified the laws of the market as stemming from the self-interest of individuals and reasoned that open competition between individuals will establish a harmony of interests as individuals mutually compete to establish reasonable prices for the sale of goods. Because Smith believed this process to be the natural law of the market, he concluded that the most effective policy is a hands-off, or laissez-faire, approach.

Although the Mills did not speak so directly about the laws of the economy, they similarly assumed that free competition is the key to economic equity—at least in terms of occupational choice. In *The Subjection of Women*, they wrote:

> *It is not that all processes are supposed to be equally good, or all persons to be equally qualified for everything; but that freedom of individual choice is now known to be the only thing which procures the adoption of the best processes, and draws each operation into the hands of those who are best qualified for it. . . . In consonance with this doctrine, it is felt to be an overstepping of the proper bounds of authority to fix beforehand on some general presumption, that certain persons are not fit to do certain things. (Mill 1970:32)*

The Mills' arguments about an open choice of occupation have one important qualifier, however. Despite their general position on the emancipation of women, John Stuart Mill and Harriet Taylor Mill disagreed about women's preferred occupation. John Stuart Mill believed that the occupation women should (and would) choose is marriage. He argued that in marriage, women's work is to be the moral educators of children and to make life beautiful; thus, regardless of his advocacy of an open marketplace, in his correspondence with Harriet Taylor, he wrote:

> *It does not follow that a woman should actually support herself because she should be capable of doing so: in the natural course of events she will not. It is not desirable to burden the labour market with a double number of competitors. In a healthy state of things, the husband would be able by his single exertions to earn all that is necessary for both: and there would be no need that the wife should take part in the mere providing of what is required to support life: it will be for the happiness of both that her occupation should rather be to adorn and beautify it* (John Stuart Mill and Harriet Taylor Mill, Early Essays on Marriage and Divorce, *in Rossi 1970:74–75*)

Later, in *The Subjection of Women*, Mill wrote:

> *In an otherwise just state of things, it is not, therefore, I think, a desirable custom that the wife should contribute by her labour to the income of the family. . . . Like a man when he chooses a profession, so, when a woman marries, it may in general be understood that she makes choice of the management of a household, and the bringing up of a family, as the first call upon her exertions, during as many years of her life as may be required for the purpose; and that she renounces, not all other objects and occupations, but all which are not consistent with the requirement of this. (Mill 1970:88–89)*

Despite his general arguments to the contrary, John Stuart Mill thought that women were more self-sacrificing than men and that they would by nature want marriage. Only a free market, however, will sort out which individuals have this nature and which do not. Still, he would prefer not to change the traditional activities of women in the family. He wrote, "The education which does belong to mothers to give . . . is the training of the affections. . . . The great occupation of women should be to beautify life" (Rossi 1970:76).

Harriet Taylor Mill disagreed with Mill on this subject, and her arguments show her to be the more radical of the two. In *The Enfranchisement of Women*, she argued, "To say that women must be excluded from active life because maternity disqualifies them for it, is in fact to say, that every other career should be forbidden them in order that maternity may be their only resource" (Rossi 1970:105). In the same essay, she said, "Let every occupation be open to all, without favour or discouragement to any, and employments will fall into the hands of those men or women who are found by experience to be most capable of worthily exercising them" (Rossi 1970:100–101).

The disagreement between John Stuart Mill and Harriet Taylor Mill indicates one of the shortcomings in liberal feminist philosophy. He stops short of advocating full equality for women, because he does not support major changes in family relations. Harriet Taylor Mill's analysis is more far-reaching because she argues for the unqualified equality of women with men. Both of them, however, fail to make a radical analysis of women's status because their assumptions ignore the limits to individual free choice that are created by structured inequality.

The Mills' analysis of occupation is characterized by meritocratic assumptions. A **meritocracy** is a system in which persons hold their positions allegedly on the

A CLOSER LOOK AT MEN

Men with Feminist Partners: Is Feminism Good for Romance?

People—men and women alike—often think that being a feminist conflicts with romance. Is this true?

Such a belief is tangled up with men's and women's perceptions of feminism, which—especially among younger adults—tends to be based in stereotypes of feminists as unattractive, gruff, and likely to be lesbians—all stereotypes that are completely untrue and, yet, which shape people's attitudes about feminism. In their research on attitudes toward feminism, psychologists Laurie Rudman and Julie Phelan examined whether or not feminist beliefs and identities among both men and women actually were in conflict with romantic relationships.

Their research involved a controlled experiment with 242 research subjects (all college students; 156 women and 86 men, all of whom were involved in heterosexual relationships). The researchers measured the extent to which men and women identified themselves as feminists and how "healthy" they thought their

relationships were. Their results found no support for the idea that feminism is harmful to romantic relationships. Quite the contrary, the researchers reported that "feminist men are important for women's relationship health" (2007:797). Women who identified as feminists reported more conflict in relationships when the male partner was not feminist. The women in relationships with feminist-identified men reported greater quality, equality, and stability in their relationships. They also reported more sexual satisfaction.

Although this study focused on women's satisfaction with romantic relationships, it suggests that feminism is also good for men, especially if men want to be paired with women with strong careers and feminist ideals.

Source: Rudman, Laurie, and Julie E. Phelan. 2007. "The Interpersonal Power of Feminism: Is Feminism Good for Romantic Relationships." Sex Roles 57 (December): 787–799.

basis of their individual talents and achievement. Although meritocracies supposedly allow anyone to succeed, regardless of their class, race, or gender, we know that these factors matter—and matter a lot—in shaping opportunities. The Mills' analysis ignores how social systems are marked by unequal power, privilege, and rewards. In short, their analysis does not overcome inequality.

Because the Mills do not develop a theory of social class or a perspective on racism, their view of the emancipation of women is also based primarily on the optimistic belief that social progress is marked by the increased liberty of the individual. As a central tenet in liberal philosophy, this concept of individual liberty leaves unanswered the question of how institutions are structured around inequality. At the same time, the liberal perspective implies that individual liberty will result in the social transformation of the whole society.

Modernization and Social Change

The picture of the future that liberalism portrays tends to be an optimistic one. The Mills' view of history assumes that modern Western civilization is more progressive than past civilizations because, in the Mills' language, the modern, advanced state leaves behind the tyrannies and repressions of the past. The Mills conceptualized history in terms of progressive improvement, and they imagined the future as lacking the subjugation and repression of the past.

In keeping with the Enlightenment perspective, the Mills assumed that the historical rule of force would end with the development of modern rationalized institutions. History, they argued, replaces the use of force with the use of reason. Accordingly, social organization is—at least in principle—not based on birth origins, roles, but rather on individual merit. The Mills wrote:

> *For what is the peculiar character of the modern world—the difference which chiefly distinguishes modern institutions, modern social ideas, modern life itself, from those of times long past? It is, that human beings are no longer born to their place in life, and chained down by an inexorable bond to the place they are born to, but are free to employ their faculties, and such favourable chances as offer, to achieve the lot which may appear to them most desirable. (Mill 1970:29–30)*

The Mills' attitude toward this alleged change is consistent with their desire for equality of choice. Their plea for the enfranchisement of women was based on the argument that women are the only exception to an otherwise emancipated world. They wrote:

> *At present, in the more improved countries, the disabilities of women are the only case, save one, in which laws and institutions take persons at their birth, and ordain that they shall never in their lives be allowed to compete for certain things. The one exception is that of royalty. . . . The disabilities, therefore, to which women are subject from the mere fact of their birth, are the solitary examples of the kind in modern legislation. (Mill 1970:35).*

Although this essay was published following the emancipation of the slaves in the United States, the Mills' arguments reveal naive optimism about the actual disenfranchisement of many social groups. Although broad-scale legislation had struck down many barriers in the law, in practice a large majority of society remained oppressed. The Mills' naiveté in considering that inequality of rights was a "relic of the past" (1970:30) rests solely on their belief that rationality provides a new moral base for society. The Mills envisioned the Western world as the most advanced of all forms of civilization; yet this view is both **ethnocentric** (meaning that it regards one's own group as superior to all others) and is founded on class- and race-based assumptions about the desirability of present social arrangements. The Mills' commitment to rationality as a moral basis for society blinded them to the facts of continuing inequality and oppression of underprivileged peoples in the contemporary Western world.

The Mills' optimism about social change also led them to assume that women's status had necessarily improved over time. They wrote:

> *Experience does say, that every step in improvement has been so invariably accompanied by a step in raising the social position of women, that historians and philosophers have been led to adopt their elevation or disbasement as on the whole the surest test and most correct measure of the civilization of a people or an age. Through all the progressive period of human history, the condition of women has been approaching nearer to equality with men. (Mill 1970:37)*

Feminist studies have shown that women's status has not necessarily improved with time (Kelly-Gadol 1976). In Western culture, women's status has fluctuated, depending on developments in industrialization, capitalism, the advent of technology, and transformations in patriarchal relations. The Mills' assumption that the position of women was necessarily improving is a reflection of their sincere commitment to bringing about that change. Because they did not study specific historical developments in women's roles created by capitalism and patriarchy, however, their analysis of social change has a hollow ring.

These criticisms aside, the Mills' arguments for the emancipation of women still stand as provocative, replete with insightful ideas on the relationship of gender inequality to other systems of unjust authority and to the repression of individual freedom. Their failures result from what they did not explain, not from the errors of their inquiry. It is uncanny how truthful the Mills' ideas seem today. Apart from the particular eloquence of their style, their words could be those of a contemporary feminist. This discovery is, in fact, rather disheartening, for it indicates how unchanged are many of the structures resulting in women's inequality, despite the many changes that have occurred.

THE CRITIQUE OF LIBERAL FEMINISM

The strengths of the liberal feminist position are its insistence on individual freedom, its toleration for diverse lifestyles, and its support of economic, social, and political reform. These ideas reflect the bourgeois origins of liberal thought, which emphasize the importance and autonomy of the individual. Liberal philosophy reflects Western cultural values of individualism and personal achievement (Eisenstein 1981). But, liberalism's strengths are also its weaknesses, because each of these ideas has serious limitations that the liberal framework does not address.

Consider, for example, the theme of individual liberty and tolerance. Many probably agree that it is important to tolerate the individual's right to choose his or her lifestyle. The liberal perspective encourages us to say, for example, that gays and lesbians are entitled to live as they please. What liberalism does *not* do is to recognize that heterosexuality is institutionalized in this society and, thus, is made compulsory, with penalties for those who do not conform.

Similarly, the liberal perspective fails to explain the institutionalized basis for race and class oppression. By claiming that all persons—regardless of race, class, or gender—should have equal opportunities, liberals accept the existing system as valid, often without analyzing the structured inequality on which it is based. From a liberal feminist perspective, experiences of women of color are some among many. Explaining how White women's and White men's experience is also conditioned by racism is not part of the liberal program. Liberal feminism sees race as a barrier to individual freedom, but it does not see that the position of White women is structurally tied to that of women of color. This connection remains for other theoretical perspectives to make. The goal of liberal feminism is equality, but in saying that women should be equal to men, liberal feminism does not specify which men women want to be equal to. Thus, it glosses over the class and race structure of societal relations (Eisenstein 1981).

As a result, liberal feminism leaves much unanswered. It does not explain the emergence of gender inequality, nor can it account, other than by analogy, for effects of race and class stratification in women's lives. Its analysis for change tends to be limited to issues of equal opportunity and individual choice. As a political philosophy, it insists on individual liberty and challenges any social, political, and economic practice that discriminates against persons on the basis of group or individual characteristics. The major change advocated by liberal feminists is that more women should be admitted to the existing political and economic systems; consequently, discrimination is a key concept within the liberal framework, as is the conceptualization of women's oppression as the result of learned gender roles. The liberal perspective emphasizes gradual reform and assumes that progress can be accomplished within the structure of existing political, social, and economic institutions.

Some of the problems of liberal thinking are found in contemporary debates about whether social policies should be gender and race-blind. Conservatives have said yes. And, many of the recent decisions of an increasingly conservative Supreme Court have moved constitutional law toward a more gender and race-blind approach to jurisprudence. But can such gender and race-blind approaches actually achieve social justice for disadvantaged groups?

Take the subject of **affirmative action.** Affirmative action was a policy for addressing racial inequity, first adopted under the Republican presidency of Richard Nixon. Nixon required federal contractors to set goals and timetables for hiring minority employers—or face the risk of losing federal contracts.

The idea was that people had to act affirmatively to root out the effects of historic discrimination. Since the vestiges of discrimination from the past become rooted in the opportunity structure that people face in the present, affirmative action was developed to eliminate the favoritism accruing to those (i.e., White men) who, by virtue of gender and race discrimination, were in an advantaged position in the labor market relative to women and racial minorities. Affirmative action policies mean that employers have to take special note of the available pool of qualified women and minority applicants for a given job, thereby developing goals for employment that match the available pool of potential applicants.

Now, opponents of affirmative action argue that race-specific and gender-specific policies should not be allowed. But, ask yourself: If you do not acknowledge race or gender, what is the result? Affirmative action plans do recognize the race and gender characteristics of job applicants and student applicants as a factor to be considered, but not because the intent is to discriminate. Rather, the intent is to eliminate the influence of past discrimination (such as favoritism toward those with prior connections to the employer or, in the case of college admissions, so-called "legacy admissions"—meaning the favoritism given to children of alumni).

Affirmative action was upheld as a legal principle in a Supreme Court decision in 2004. Although opponents had filed two lawsuits based on an argument that affirmative action constituted "reverse discrimination," the Court ruled that race (thus, presumably gender as well) could be taken into account in affirmative action policies so long as they were narrowly tailored—that is, did not explicitly exclude people based on race. At the same time, however, the Court concluded that such policies would not be needed 25 years subsequent to their decision, leaving an optimistic footprint in the decision that race and gender discrimination would have disappeared by then. Time will tell.

The debates around affirmative action reveal some of the contradictions brought up by a liberal perspective: A gender-neutral, race-blind society may be ideal, but achieving true equality may mean having to acknowledge factors like gender and race (and perhaps other characteristics as well, such as disability or sexual orientation) in order to produce social policies and social practices that treat people equally while also overtly acknowledging their different life experiences. As Supreme Court Justice Harry Blackmun once wrote (in his decision on a major case on affirmative action, *Bakke* v. *Regents of the University of California*), "In order to get beyond racism, we must first take account of race. There is no other way, and in order to treat some persons equally, we must treat them differently" (Blackmun 1978). The issue is how to change the cumulative and continuing privilege that accrues to some groups by virtue of their gender, race, and class while also creating a liberal, democratic society where—at least in the ideal—gender, race, and class no longer matter. Grappling with this question and with the fundamental injustices that are built into social institutions is the starting point for more radical feminist perspectives—examined in the following chapter.

Chapter Summary and Themes

Feminist theory provides various frameworks for organizing the analysis of gender in society; each framework also underlies strategies for social change.

Liberal feminism is based on a reform framework, one that takes individual rights and neutrality in the law as the model for social change. Socialist feminism centers its analysis on the operation of the class system—and its relationship to the exploitation of women's work. Radical feminism analyzes patriarchy as the central cause of women's subordination. Each framework provides unique ways of analyzing women in society, and they can be used together for a comprehensive theoretical and political analysis.

Liberal feminism has its origins in the work of Enlightenment thinkers who valued human reason over traditional authority as the means to liberty and freedom for women.

Thinkers such as Mary Wollstonecraft, John Stuart Mill, and Harriet Taylor Mill have left a legacy of analysis of the status of women that still informs us about women's role in society. Their work is founded on liberalism as a philosophical tradition that sees social tradition, not nature, as generating differences between men and women. They also argued passionately for women's rights, based on the liberal philosophy of equality before the law.

Even with its strengths, liberal feminism can be criticized for its focus on individual autonomy and the absence of an analysis of structured inequality. Liberal feminism, like the liberal philosophy on which it is based, does not include an analysis of race or class differences. It assumes that the basis for inequality lies mostly in past tradition, not in the continuing operation of systems of power and privilege.

■ Key Terms

affirmative action	ethnocentric	liberalism
Age of Enlightenment	feminist theory	meritocracy
discrimination	liberal feminism	

■ Discussion Questions/Projects for Thought

1. Identify a nineteenth-century African American woman whose works have been published. (See the collections by Anne Sterling, *We Are Your Sisters*, New York: Norton 1984, or Gerda Lerner, *Black Women in White America*, New York: Vintage 1973.) How would you describe the political theory of this thinker? How does her thinking compare to the feminism of White women during this period?

2. Identify one of the feminist organizations in your local community or state. Ask the organization for any material it has describing its goals and orientation. How would you describe the political orientation of this group? Is it based in liberal, socialist, or radical feminism? Identify the specific political ideals and actions that explain your answer.

3. Suppose that Mary Wollstonecraft were to return today and observe gender relations. How might she revise her feminist theory? What would she retain in her thinking?

13

Contemporary Frameworks in Feminist Theory

The women's movement emerged from multiple locations in society and embraces diverse perspectives and politics, as we have seen in previous chapters. Feminist theory is a mosaic of ideas, yet it is anchored in continuing questions about the structure of gender in society and the connection of gender to other forms of oppression. As feminism has developed and changed, so have the questions for feminist theory.

We have already seen how liberal feminism grew from the movement to establish equal rights for women. During the growth of the second wave of feminism throughout the 1970s and 1980s, the major paradigms of feminist theory were liberal feminism, socialist feminism, and radical feminism. Now, feminist theory is not so easily characterized within the bounds of these particular paradigms. Feminist theory has also evolved into new paradigms that reflect the transformation and growth of feminist thinking and the women's movement. Multiracial feminism, postmodernist feminism, and questions about sexuality now frame much of the scholarship feminists are producing. These new frameworks of thought stem from important contemporary questions about diversity among women, globalization and the international status of women, men's place in feminism, sexuality and gender, and the ongoing structure of power, as reflected in relations of gender, race, class, and power.

In this chapter, we review the emergence of more radical forms of feminism—namely, socialist feminism and radical feminism—as frameworks that have guided the development of feminist theory. Following that review, we turn to contemporary perspectives in feminist theory and the new questions that such theorizing evokes.

THE RADICAL ORIGINS OF FEMINIST THEORY: THE CRITIQUE OF LIBERAL FEMINISM

We have already seen that liberal feminism is grounded in some of the central principles of Western, democratic societies—particularly the focus on individual rights, freedom from discrimination, and equal access to social and political institutions. Liberal feminism is, to a large extent, compatible with dominant social institutions, even though women's rights are routinely compromised by these same institutions. Because liberal feminism is based on the concept of equal rights, a principle around which institutions have at least in theory been built, it has been the work of more radical perspectives to provide a deeper challenge to these institutional structures.

In the early years of the second wave of the women's movement (beginning in the 1960s), socialist and radical feminism emerged as the major alternatives to liberal feminism. With their roots in more radical wings of the women's movement, these perspectives—along with the ongoing critique of feminism developed by women of color—provided alternative frameworks for the development of feminist theory.

Socialist feminism locates women's oppression in the structure of capitalism and its interrelationship with patriarchal gender relations. **Radical feminism** identifies patriarchal social relations as the primary cause of women's oppression. Since the origins of feminism, women of color have criticized the "whiteness" of the women's movement, seeing race and gender all along as intricately linked in women's experiences. This criticism from within feminism has produced the rich body of theorizing known as **multiracial feminism**. Feminist studies have also been enriched by the development of **postmodernist feminism**—a perspective that emphasizes the socially constituted basis of gender in society. And, as feminists have sought to include sexuality in their analyses of gender, postmodernism and feminist theory have spawned **queer theory**—an analysis of sexualities that sees sexuality as highly fluid and subject to social definition. All of these forms of feminist theory are examined in this chapter, but first we examine socialist and radical feminism.

Whereas the liberal framework emphasizes learned gender roles and discrimination as the primary causes of women's oppression, more radical feminists argue that dominant institutions are organized through gender, race, and class oppression. Radical feminists criticize liberal feminists for assuming that sexism is largely a remnant of traditional beliefs and practices—in other words, located in the past. As shown in the previous chapter, the liberal feminist perspective takes women's equality with men as its major political goal, and liberal feminists have documented the effects of discrimination and have identified the institutional practices and policies that foster continuing discrimination. In distinct contrast to this perspective, other feminists argue that the success of liberal feminism puts only some women on a par with men without transforming the conditions of oppression that produce gender as well as class and race inequality.

HISTORICAL ROOTS OF RADICAL FEMINISM

Just as liberal feminism has its roots in the historical frameworks of liberal thought, so do more radical feminist perspectives have earlier intellectual and political roots. In the nineteenth century, the same political and economic changes that fostered the development of liberal political philosophy also stimulated the emergence of more radical perspectives, most notably the work of **Karl Marx** (1818–1883) and his collaborator, **Friedrich Engels** (1820–1895). Although working in the same period of time, the differences between the radical perspective of Marx and Engels and the liberal perspective of Mill point to the profound controversies over the analysis of social structure and social change that historical changes in the structure of Western society were generating at this time.

The middle and second half of the nineteenth century in western Europe and the United States were marked by the vast growth of capitalism and the rapid expansion of industrialization. These changes were accompanied by the widespread social and political changes inspired by the French Revolution and, in the United States, by the elimination of slavery, the expansion of western territories, and urbanization The climate of social reform that began in this period set the stage for the British suffrage movement and the American feminist movement of the late nineteenth and early twentieth centuries. The political discourse that this period fostered created a diversity of political and social thought that fostered the growth of sociological theory (Bramson 1961; Zeitlin 1968).

Nineteenth-century feminism is characterized typically as a reform movement whose ideas are rooted in the liberal thought of persons such as John Stuart Mill and Harriet Taylor Mill, but the politics of this movement also emerged through debate and action between radical and reform leaders. Some groups in the nineteenth- and early twentieth-century feminist movement were as much influenced by class and union politics as they were by the spirit of moral reform characterizing the women's rights approach of nineteenth-century feminism. Case studies of both the suffrage movement (DuBois 1978) and the women's trade union movement (Dye 1975) in the United States reveal the complexities of the movements' attempts to grapple with the complexities of class, race, and gender politics. In the end, however, most nineteenth-century feminists were unable to transcend the class biases of their middle-class leadership. Some feminist leaders, such as Susan B. Anthony, also used prevailing racist and anti-immigrant sentiments to attract members and to articulate movement ideologies (DuBois 1978; Dye 1975). These failures to unite women across class and race limited the effectiveness of nineteenth-century feminism, but some feminists in this period established a radical tradition for alliances with working-class women and articulated the beginnings of an analysis linking gender, race, and class oppression.

Many of the feminists of this period and the early twentieth century were also socialists who worked for radical causes, in addition to their feminist politics. Charlotte Perkins Gilman (1860–1935) developed a socialist feminist analysis in *Women and Economics* (published in 1898; see the "History Speaks" feature on Charlotte Perkins Gilman in Chapter 6). She proposed that housework should be communally organized, particularly for working mothers, who were entering the paid labor force at this time. She suggested that apartment houses have one common kitchen where all families could be served and that cleaning, child care, nursing, and teaching should be paid professional work. The responsibility for this work should not fall on individual families, she thought, but instead on apartment house managers (Rossi 1973). Other radical thinkers of the time, such as Emma Goldman (1869–1940; see "History Speaks" box in Chapter 5) and Agnes Smedley (1892–1950), did not define feminism as their primary cause, but they clearly linked the oppression of women to other forms of economic and political oppression.

SOCIALIST FEMINISM: THE IMPORTANCE OF CLASS AND CAPITALISM

The stage for nineteenth-century feminism was one where capitalist society was developing rapidly, bringing with it new forms of poverty, wage labor, and other changes that continue to mark our time. Slavery had just ended in the United States (following the end of the Civil War in 1865). Immigration from Europe to the United States was becoming more common. Women, although in many regards confined to families, were also moving into factory labor, as well as continuing their roles working in fields and in homes. Feminism was just emerging as a social and political force. This is the context for one of the most radical thinkers whose work continues to inspire both intellectual and political movements: Karl Marx.

Karl Marx and Historical Materialism

Marxist thought is one of the most influential and insightful analyses in modern intellectual history. Some argue that most sociological theory developed as a dialogue with the ideas that Karl Marx inspired (Zeitlin 1968). Certainly, for modern feminism,

Marx's ideas are pivotal. Marx (1818–1883) began writing as a student; he was involved in some of the most politically and intellectually controversial movements of his time. He was active in a group known as the Young Hegelians, who based their studies and activities on the work of the German philosopher Georg Wilhelm Friedrich Hegel (1770–1832). Hegel's philosophy is based on the idea that persons create their world through reason; thus, rational ideas form the objective reality through which human beings construct their world. Hegel's philosophy, furthermore, sees the "real" as emanating from the "divine" (Giddens 1971:3), and Christian theology is an important foundation for his work. The Young Hegelians followed Hegel's concern with theology and adopted his philosophical perspective, until their outlook was radically transformed by the appearance of Ludwig Feuerbach's work *The Essence of Christianity* in 1841. Feuerbach (1804–1872) reversed the philosophy of ideas in Hegel's work by arguing that ideas follow the existence of human action. Feuerbach wrote, "Thought proceeds from being, not being from thought" (Giddens 1971:3). From Feuerbach's thesis, the divine is a construction of human thought; human activity, not ideas, provides the basis for social reality.

This philosophy led Marx's teacher and sponsor, Bruno Bauer (1809–1882), to assert that the Bible was a historical document and that Christian theology was a social and historical myth. Bauer was consequently dismissed from the university because he was declared to be dangerous to the state. In a university system where one's future was dependent on academic sponsorship, Bauer's dismissal meant the end of Marx's academic career. Although Marx received his doctorate of philosophy from the University of Jena in 1841, he, who had once been predicted to be the most outstanding professor of his time, was never to hold a university post. The remainder of his life was spent in political exile and poverty. He continued to write, working occasionally as a journalist, but he was forced to move from Germany to Paris and later to London because he was expelled by various governments.

In 1849, Marx moved to London, where he was to spend the last 34 years of his life. His family was extremely poor; several of his children died of malnutrition and disease. When his sixth child was born, he saw the birth as a catastrophe, because two of his children had already died and a third was gravely ill. He was scarcely consoled when the child was born a girl, Jenny Julia Eleanor, as he announced to his friend and collaborator Friedrich Engels that the child was "unfortunately of the sex par excellence" and "had it been a male the matter would be more acceptable" (Kapp 1972:21). Loans from Engels supported the family, along with Marx's occasional journalism jobs. Throughout this difficult time, Marx continued writing and studying, and he produced several works that would change the course of world history and the history of social thought.

The ideas Marx developed always reflected the early influences of Hegel and Feuerbach and resulted in a theoretical perspective often called **historical materialism** (also referred to as **dialectical materialism**). The central thesis of historical materialism is that the material conditions of people's lives shape their behavior and their beliefs. Human consciousness and behavior are formed by the interplay between persons as subjects and as objects in the world in which they live. Because human beings have the capacity to reflect on their actions, their ideas (and ideals) are reflections of their material world. People's relationships to their environment and what they think of it are mediated by the particular historical and social milieu of which they are a part. The possibilities for human existence are shaped by the choices and constraints imposed by material organization. Specifically, for Marx, the materialist thesis saw human production—what men and women actually do—as the basis for social structure. The cause of social change, for Marx, lay not in ideas and values that are abstracted from human experience. Instead, he saw societal change as emerging from the social relations and activities that emerge through human labor (Giddens 1971).

The method of dialectical materialism, unlike that of many other sociological theories, is not deterministic. In other words, Marx did not see human history and experience as determined by particular features of social structure; rather, he believed that social structure and social change are always emerging and reemerging according to the choices human beings make. In addition, Marx said there will always be contradictions within society and in the experience of human beings in society. That is to say, because social life is not simply determined, it will always involve inconsistencies and the tendency for conflict. Social change, according to Marx, arises from these contradictions and the action of human groups in trying to solve them.

According to Marx, human beings do more than merely exist; they reach their full human potential for creative living through social consciousness and their struggle against oppression. Capitalist social relations, he argued, distort human potential because, if human work is oppressive, then all social life is distorted. This must be changed—through a revolution against capitalism.

Marx saw systems of human production and reproduction as creating the conditions for everyday life. Marx and Engels defined *production* as the labor humans perform to satisfy their immediate needs and *reproduction* as the physical re-creation of both the species and the social systems in which human beings reproduce. In Engels's words, production and reproduction are the central features of human society:

> *According to the materialistic conception, the determining factor in history is, in the final instance, the production and reproduction of immediate life. This, again, is of a two-fold character: on the one side, the production of the means of existence, of food, clothing and shelter and the tools necessary for that production; on the other side, the production of human beings themselves, the propagation of the species. The social organization under which the people of a particular historical epoch and a particular country live is determined by both kinds of production: by the stage of development of labor on the one hand and of the family on the other. (Engels 1884/1972:71–72)*

Class and Capitalism

The materialist perspective of Marx and Engels sees human activity (as it is engaged in productive relations) as the mainspring of social change and as the determining feature of social organization. In Marx's analysis, the economic mode of production forms the **infrastructure** of social organization; other institutions form the **superstructure,** meaning that they reflect the essential character of the economic system.

In the Western capitalist societies that Marx observed, the economic infrastructure was marked primarily by class struggle—the division of society into

A CLOSER LOOK AT MEN

Latino Feminist Masculinities: A Lesson in Intersectionality

The dominant conception of Latino working-class men is mired in stereotypes about machismo, and beliefs about working-class men that see them as dominating, antifeminist, and oppressive to women. But research on Latino, working-class men shows a different picture of their identities and connections to feminism.

Aída Hurtaso and Mrinal Sinha studied a sample of working-class, Latino men who identify as feminists and probed, through a qualitative research study, the men's identities as constructed via their gender, race, class, ethnic, and sexual identity. What they found was a far more complex view of manhood, as understood by Latino working-class men, than is typically assumed.

The men in their research sample were keenly aware of the negative associations with their racial and ethnic identities. Although the men did not have a uniform understanding of their identities as men, they saw their racial–ethnic identities as shaping their conceptions of themselves *as men*. Their understandings of "manhood" ranged from seeing a man as deeply connected to family and community, as well as involving an ethical dimension of standing by one's word, honoring people, and respecting others. They tended to reject concepts of manhood that define it as sexually aggressive or necessarily heterosexual.

This study suggests the need to challenge dominant understandings of manhood as it is connected to class, race, and sexual identities. Hurtado and Sinha find a much more nuanced and complex relationship between feminist identities and the race, class, and gender identities of Latinos.

Source: Based on Hurtado, Aída, and Mrinal Sinha. 2008. "More than Men: Latino Feminist Masculinities and Intersectionality." *Sex Roles* 59 (September): 337–349.

groups characterized by their relationship to the means of production. Under capitalism, two new major classes emerge: *capitalists*, who own the means of production, and the *proletariat* (or working class), who sell their labor to capitalist owners in exchange for wages. Two minor classes also exist: the *bourgeoisie* (merchants, managers, and artisans, for example), who become functionally dependent on capitalism, although they do not own the means of production; and the *lumpenproletariat*, who have no stable social location because they are individuals from a variety of classes and social locations. In Marx and Engels's words, they form "the 'dangerous class,' the social scum, that passive rotting mass thrown off by the lowest layers of old society" (Tucker 1972:25).

The Marxist concept of class differs significantly from that of non-Marxist social scientists who use it to refer to stratified status or income hierarchies (see Chapter 5). **Class**, in the Marxist sense, refers specifically to the relationship of a group to the societal means of production; thus, it indicates a system of relationships, not a unit of like persons. Similarly, the concept of "ownership" refers not primarily to the accumulation of goods (which in Marxist theory may occur in any class), but to the actual ownership of a society's productive enterprises. To illustrate, a person in the proletariat class (working class) may own his or her shoes, but it is the capitalist class that owns the system of production that manufactures the shoes and profits from them.

Society emerges, according to Marxist thought, through class struggle. According to Marx and Engels, "The history of all hitherto society is the history of class struggles" (1970:16). Classes emerge as a society produces a surplus; as a division of

FOCUS ON RESEARCH

Organizing Immigrant Women—A Case Study of Unions

Labor unions have historically been a way that working-class groups have mobilized for workers' rights. Unions have been dominated by men, even explicitly excluding people of color and women in the early course of union history. But in recent years unions have become more diverse. Indeed, people of color and women, though less likely in the workforce to be represented by unions, are now a large percentage of union members. Men, however, remain in most of the key leadership positions.

As labor unions have declined in their number and influence, many have seen women, immigrants, and people of color as essential for renewing the historic strength of labor unions. Cynthia Cranford has studied the mobilization of women in the union Justice for Janitors (also referred to as J4J), a union affiliated with the Service Employees International Union. Justice for Janitors (J4J) is an example of tremendous union renewal, and it has led some of the most successful union campaigns in recent years. The J4J represents a low-wage sector of workers where women and people of color are many of the employees. Cranford's Los Angeles-based study was a case study involving Latina immigrants, many of them undocumented workers. These women mobilized to challenge gender inequality within their union.

Cranford did her research with extensive interviews with union members/janitors, most of whom were undocumented immigrant women. She also interviewed many of the union staff women. Doing so over a period of three years and observing the union's activity during this time gave her rich data from which to see how Latina immigrants were able to change their union.

Cranford found that in the beginning, women were well represented in union committees but were not in positions of formal leadership. Staff women and women in the union engaged in a number of activities intended to increase women's leadership. Among other things, the women noted that traditional indicators of leadership were excluding women from being seen as leaders. Traditionally, leaders were seen as those who would speak out in front of a group, have charisma, and were respected by others. Instead, women in the union began identifying as leaders women who listened to others, were patient, and engaged people one-on-one. Union women developed training sessions to promote leadership among women, and they intervened when women were interrupted or otherwise pushed aside during meetings. Within committees, where women did much of the work, they developed additional tiers of leadership, giving women more opportunity to demonstrate their organizational skills and providing a venue where their leadership would be identified. In addition, union women began to see that other women were neither being nominated for positions of leadership nor thinking of themselves as leaders. Thus, they began noting other women with leadership potential.

The women in Justice for Janitors engaged in a number of other feminist practices and goals that resulted in women taking on more formal leadership roles. Cranford's work shows not only how Latina immigrants transformed their union, but demonstrates the practices that can transform other organizations where business as usual continues to exclude women from positions of formal leadership.

Source: Based on Cranford, Cynthia. 2007. "'It's Time to Leave Machismo Behind': Challenging Gender Inequality in an Immigrant Union." *Gender & Society* 21 (June): 409–438.

labor emerges, thereby allowing for surplus production, the accumulation of a surplus can be appropriated by one group. As a result, this group stands in an exploitative relationship to the mass of producers, and class conflict is established (Giddens 1971). Marx and Engels point out that the first division of labor is the division of labor by sex for the purpose of propagating children and controlling women's labor in the household; gender thus provides the first class antagonism. They (and most subsequent Marxist thinkers), however, leave this point without further development.

As capitalism develops, the capitalist class appropriates the wealth produced by the subordinate classes because the capitalists have the power to control the conditions under which other classes work. The working class owns only its labor, which it must sell for wages; the capitalists, in turn, exercise the power to determine what wages they will pay and the conditions under which people work. As capitalists try to increase their profits, they do so at the increasing expense of laborers. Profit comes from the fact that workers produce more value than the wages they receive. The craft of distinctive workers becomes less important than the value of mass-produced commodities. Material objects, then, take on greater value than the workers who produce them. In effect, in Marxist analysis, the value of individual human activity decreases as the material value of the created products increases. You can see this process working today if you look at the use of labor in poor countries where workers (typically women and children) earn very low wages to make the goods that are consumed in wealthier nations. The capitalist class profits both at the expense of poor workers abroad and displaced workers in the United States.

Human beings, then, become alienated from the process in the sense that they do not control or own the products of their labor; they choose neither the form nor the use of the products they make. Additionally, workers are alienated from each other, and they become alienated from themselves because they do not exercise the human ability to transform nature to their own design. Politically, according to Marx, workers must end the tyranny of private ownership of the means of production by reorganizing the means of production (and, feminists would add, reproduction); the accumulation of profit in the hands of a few must be eliminated. Marxists see that social changes that do not strike at the material basis of social life—capital accumulation by the owning class—will be insufficient because they will not change the underlying causes of social organization.

Ideology and Consciousness

The materialist thesis of Marx is also central to the perspective on consciousness and ideas that are developed throughout Marxist theory. Systems of knowledge take their historical form in response to the mode of production. Marx argued that the ideas of a period are a reflection of the interests of the ruling class (see also Chapter 3). Marx wrote:

> *The production of ideas, of conceptions, of consciousness, is at first directly interwoven with the material activity and the material intercourse of men, the language of real life. . . . We do not set out from what men say, imagine, conceive nor from men as narrated, thought of, imagined, conceived, in order to arrive at men in the flesh. We set out from real, active men, and on the basis of their real life-process we demonstrate the development of the ideological reflexes and echoes of this life process. (Marx,* The German Ideology, *in Tucker 1972:118–119)*

Basic to this perspective on the sociology of knowledge is the proposition that "it is not the consciousness of men that determines their being, but, on the contrary,

HISTORY SPEAKS: YESTERDAY'S FEMINISTS TALK ABOUT TODAY

Mary Harris "Mother" Jones and Workers' Rights

"If they want to hang me, let them. And on the scaffold, I will shout 'Freedom for the working class!'"

— Mother Jones

Mother Jones (1830/1837–1930) claimed her birth date as May 1, 1830, the date that is on her gravestone. Recent scholarship, however, suggests that she may have "invented" this birth date to correspond with the Haymarket demonstration for the 8-hour work day. It is more likely that she was born on August 1, 1837.

What has not been invented about Mother Jones's life is the conviction and courage she demonstrated on behalf of workers' rights. From the 1870s through the 1920s, she was a social and political "hell-raiser," dedicating herself to inspiring speeches given to mining, railroad, steel, and textile workers who were fighting to organize a labor union. She was denounced by the U.S. Senate as the "grandmother of all agitators." During a 1913 mine strike in West Virginia, she was charged with conspiracy to commit murder and was sentenced to 20 years in prison. Hailed as the "Miners' Angel," national protest led the governor to repeal her sentence. After her release, she went back to her work as an protest organizer; by her estimates, she was then 83 years old.

In 1902, Mother Jones organized one of her best-known demonstrations. She armed Pennsylvania coal miners' wives with brooms and mops in a collective effort to block strikebreakers from entering the mines. Surprisingly, although much of her work involved women, Mother Jones did not support women's suffrage, fearing that a focus on suffrage would distract working-class women from economic issues. Mother Jones thought you did not need a vote to produce social change: "I never had a vote, and I have raised hell all over this country. You don't need a vote to raise hell! You need convictions and a voice!"

Thinking Further: Was Mother Jones a feminist? How were her politics on workers' rights similar to the feminist politics of other radical thinkers during her time—namely, Charlotte Perkins Gilman, Emma Goldman, and Agnes Smedley? If Mother Jones were alive today, what political and social issues would she tackle and how do you think women's issues would be part of this agenda?

Sources: Gorn, Elliot J. 2001. *Mother Jones: The Most Dangerous Woman in America.* New York: Hill and Wang; Mother Jones, retrieved from www.aflcio.org (3/24/2010); Mary Harris Jones, retrieved from www. fembio.org (3/24/ 2010).

their social being that determines their consciousness" (Marx, *A Contribution to the Critique of Political Economy*, in Tucker 1972:4). Those who own the means of production also determine the ruling ideas of the period.

Consciousness is determined by class relations, for even though persons will normally try to identify what is in their best interest, under capitalism the ruling class controls the production of ideas. Also, even though humans create practical ideas from experience, most of their experience is determined by capitalist relations of production. The ideas that are disseminated through communication systems, including language, serve to authorize a reality that the ruling class creates. In this sense, ideas become **ideology**—understood to mean a system of beliefs that legitimate and maintain the status quo (see also Chapter 3).

For feminists, Marx's work on ideology is fundamental to understanding sexism. Sexism, as an ideology that justifies the power of men over women, emerges not in the best interest of women but as a defense of male domination. Like other ideologies, sexist ideology is a means by which one class rules a society and sanctions the society's social relations.

False consciousness emerges as the subordinate group accepts the worldview of the dominant class. Because consciousness changes with historical change, at the time that workers see the nature of their exploitation, false consciousness is transformed into **class consciousness**—the understanding that groups get when they comprehend their material relationship to the capitalist system of production. At this point workers take the revolutionary struggle into their own hands.

Marx's theory is more than an academic analysis, because the idea that theory must be connected to social and political practice (*praxis*, in his words) is central to his work. Revolutionary theory is to be created by intellectuals who emerge from and are associated with the working class. Marx saw human beings as potentially revolutionary because their capabilities for creative work and social consciousness far exceed those allowed them under capitalist organization (Eisenstein 1979). This fact provides the basis for optimism in Marx's work; it lays the foundation for radical change and the transformation from human oppression to human liberation.

The Woman Question

Marx and Engels's analysis of women's oppression is drawn mostly from their writing on the family, especially Engels's essay *The Origin of the Family, Private Property, and the State*, published in 1884 after Marx's death. Feminists who, in the beginning of the contemporary women's movement, were looking for alternative analyses to the liberal perspective began with this classical Marxist perspective.

Although Engels stated in the preface to *The Origin of the Family, Private Property, and the State* that production and reproduction together are the determining factors of history, he saw family relations as derived from the economic mode of production. From a Marxist perspective, in capitalist societies forms of the family change as class relations change, thus making family relations secondary to economic and class relations. In keeping with their perspective on the social origins of ideas, Marx and Engels would say, however, that the social image of the family is an idealized one that disguises the real economic structure of family relations.

They described the family under capitalism as a microcosm of the society's larger class relations; thus, particularly in bourgeois families, the wife is the proletariat. Engels wrote:

In the great majority of cases today, at least in the possessing classes, the husband is obliged to earn a living and support his family and that in itself gives him a position of supremacy, without any need for special legal ties and privileges. Within the family he is the bourgeois and the wife represents the proletariat. (1884/1972:137)

Monogamous marriage, Marx and Engels argued, develops as part of the formation of private property. Particularly in the bourgeois family, the development of private property creates the need to determine lineage for the purpose of inheritance. Engels wrote:

Monogamy arose from the concentration of considerable wealth in the hands of a single individual—a man—and from the need to bequeath this wealth to the children of that man and of no other. For this purpose, the monogamy of the woman did not in any way interfere with open or concealed polygamy on the part of the man. (1884/1972:138)

Engels did not explain how men and not women came to control property; therefore, feminists have criticized the Marxist perspective for not explaining the origins of patriarchy.

Marx and Engels discussed marriage as being a form of prostitution for women. Engels wrote:

Marriage is conditioned by the class position of the parties and is to that extent always a marriage of convenience. . . . This marriage of convenience turns often enough into crassest prostitution—sometimes of both partners, but far more commonly of the woman, who only differs from the ordinary courtesan in that she does not let out her body on piece-work as a wage-worker, but sells it once and for all into slavery. (1884/1972:134)

Marx and Engels defined marriage as based on economic relations, although they clearly would have preferred to see it based on individual sex-love. In marriage and the family, Marx and Engels recognized the woman's role is to be responsible for household management and child care. They argued that household work becomes a private service under advanced capitalism, because it loses the public character it has in earlier forms of economic life. In advanced capitalism, the work of the housewife is both a private service to the male head of the household and an unpaid economic service to the society as a whole. Marx and Engels concluded that "the modern individual family is founded on the open or concealed domestic slavery of the wife, and modern society is a mass composed of these individual families as its molecules." (Engels 1884/1972:137)

Based on their analysis of the family, Marx and Engels saw emancipatory social change in family relations as occurring only with the abolition of private property. Although they maintained a wish for monogamous relationships, they wanted monogamy to be the expression of a sexual commitment based on love, not property.

Because Marx and Engels saw male supremacy in the family as originating with the accumulation of property and the development of class relations, they suggested that the liberation of women will occur as the result of class struggle. Women's status is derived from the economic organization of society; therefore, the liberation of women will follow with the revolution of the workers and the abolition of private property. Although Marx and Engels noted that the gender division of labor is the first class oppression, their analysis assumes that women's oppression is secondary to oppression by class and that women will be liberated when class oppression is ended. It is on this point that socialist feminists begin their critique of Marx.

The Feminist Critique of Marx

When socialist feminism emerged in the 1970s, feminists argued that Marx and Engels had not considered seriously enough their own point that sexual division of labor is the first form of class antagonism. Socialist feminists concluded that women's oppression could not be reduced to capitalism alone, even though capitalism remains a highly significant source of women's oppression. Socialist feminists saw class relations as important in determining women's status, but also saw gender per se as equally important. Class and gender relations intersect in advanced capitalist societies (Hartmann 1976); class relations alone do not account for the location of women and men in social life. Therefore, eradicating social-class inequality alone will not necessarily eliminate sexism as well. Socialist feminists thus agree in many ways with Marx, but disagree that the oppression of women is secondary to class oppression.

Family and Economy in Capitalist Society: Juliet Mitchell

One of the first socialist feminists to expand Marx's theory was the British scholar, Juliet Mitchell. Mitchell (1971), who analyzed the interrelationship between the economy and the family, placed the origins of the family in the dynamics established by the economics of capitalism.

Mitchell began with the classical Marxist premise that the economic mode of production is the defining factor of social organization, but she argued that for Marx and Engels the liberation of women remains an abstract ideal, not a problem to be explained. Marx and Engels too easily assumed that the liberation of women would occur with the transition from capitalism to socialism, she argues. But a specific theory of women's oppression is needed if the liberation of women is to occur. Mitchell linked the subordination of women to the interplay of reproduction, sexuality, and gender socialization with the economic mode of production. She saw the economy as embracing the structure of the family, which, in turn, includes the structures of sexuality, reproduction, and socialization.

Mitchell argued that women were excluded from production in the past because of their presumed physical weakness and the involuntary character of childbearing. Now, however, technological developments have lessened the necessity for physical strength in labor, and the development of contraception makes childbearing a voluntary act. As a result, the ideological basis of family life as the unit of sexual and reproductive activity is destroyed. According to Mitchell, because women's exclusion of public work and their restriction to the private world of the family is the basis for their subordination, the right of women to earn a living wage must be a central goal of feminism.

Mitchell raised a number of issues that remain central to feminist theory. She opened the feminist discussion of the relationship of the family to the economy and noted that the family has changed from a unit of production to a unit of consumption. This has important material as well as ideological consequences. As she saw it, sexuality becomes intermixed with a consumption ethic. Although this can mean more sexual freedom for women, it also increases their use as sexual objects—a point that resonates in contemporary discussions of gender, sexuality, and postmodern culture, as we will see later in this chapter. Mitchell also saw that the family had both an economic and ideological role under capitalism. Its economic role lies not just in the work that is done within families, but it is in the family that workers are created and sustained—a point now being explored by feminists studying the "care work" that women, and especially women of color, do (see Chapter 6).

Ideologically, it is in families where personalities are shaped with characteristics suitable for a capitalist labor force. Mitchell argued that the family promotes individualism and personal freedom at the same time that it encourages the accumulation of property: "The family is a stronghold of what capitalism needs to preserve but actually destroys: private property and individualism. The housewife-mother is the guardian and representative of these. She is a backward, conservative force—and this is what her oppression means" (1971:161). According to Mitchell, the one area of women's power—the socialization of children—becomes a mystique for their own oppression.

The Question of Separate Spheres

Mitchell's argument shows that women have traditionally been associated with the *private sphere* (the domestic world of home, children, reproduction, and sexuality) and men with the *public sphere* (paid work, institutionalized religion, political authority, and so forth). One of the accomplishments of feminist theory has been to make the activities of both men and women in the private sphere more visible. Because the private sphere has been identified with women, it has been perceived as inferior; the public sphere is seen as superior.

The relationship of the public and private spheres is an important theme in the development of feminist theory. Women's relegation to the private, domestic sphere excludes them from public life and thus from equal access to social and economic resources, although the increasing entry of middle-aged, married women and mothers into the labor force makes it less true that women are confined to the home. Still, women's work in public labor is often said to mirror and extend the private services they provide in the home. Others have also argued that women's confinement to the private sphere is largely a White, middle-class phenomenon; the assumption of a public/private split is therefore a race- and class-bound argument. Without arguing that women's exclusion from the public sphere is the primary basis for their subordination, feminists point out that a theory of women's position must account for the relationship of the private, domestic realm to the public realm of social and economic life (Sacks 1975).

The question of separate spheres is one about both social structure and ideology. Structurally, the separation of public and private spheres is one that emerges with the rise of industrial capitalism in the nineteenth century. At that time, women's work was ideologically defined as taking place in the home, even though most working-class, poor, and minority women continued to work in factories, domestic service, agriculture, and other forms of public labor. Ideologically, the values associated with the public and private sphere become attached to assumptions about masculinity and femininity.

Some Marxist-feminists argue that the alleged split between the public and private spheres obscures the economic role of the family (Zaretsky 1976). Moreover, the idea of separate spheres creates a new split: one between our "personal" life and our "public" life. This further obscures the forces of capitalism from political view, as people become more concerned with their own presumed uniqueness or style and are less conscious of the capitalist, material forces that shape their life conditions. As Zaretsky argues, personal life, emerging under capitalism, appears to be an autonomous process, and human relations become seen as an end in themselves, as if they are detached from the material world of economic fact. Individuals appear unique, and the subjective sphere of self and lifestyle take preeminence over the economic relations that define social organization. One consequence is that some men, for example, can pursue their own fulfillment through men's groups, but in the absence of a profeminist stance that is critical of patriarchal power (Messner 1997).

In sum, socialist feminism sees women's status as coming through the transformation of capitalist relations, along with efforts to transform gender as well. Socialist feminism shares with classical Marxism the idea that the oppression of women is primarily an economic fact, buttressed by ideological delusions. But socialist feminism adds to Marxism that women's oppression must be related to their position in the private world of reproduction and the family. Extending this critique, radical feminists argued that patriarchy also had to be considered a historical force of its own. It is to the radical feminist perspective that we now turn.

RADICAL FEMINISM: THE POWER OF PATRIARCHY

Whereas socialist feminists argue that class and capitalism are the basis of women's oppression, radical feminists argue that male domination per se is the basis for women's oppression. Radical feminists define **patriarchy** as a "sexual system of power in which the male possesses superior power and economic privilege" (Eisenstein 1979:17). Radical feminism views patriarchy as being its own social, historical, and political force. Whereas socialist feminism emphasizes the economic basis of gender relations, radical feminism emphasizes male power and privilege as the bases of social relations. Radical feminism sees patriarchal relations as more fundamental than class relations in determining women's experiences. In fact, many radical feminists see class and racial–ethnic oppression as extensions of patriarchal inequality. Accordingly, radical feminists see the abolition of male supremacy as their primary political goal.

Since its inception, the radical feminist position has taken several different directions, some of them more explicitly tied to Marxism than others. Some radical feminist thought is totally apart from the materialist thesis in Marxist work, locating the causes of oppression solely within patriarchal culture and its control of women (Daly 1978). Much of radical feminism, however, has developed specifically because of the

Women supporting women is one of the principles of a strong feminist movement.

failure of Marxist perspectives to explain adequately the emergence and persistence of patriarchy. Some early radical feminists attempted to explain the origins of patriarchy by claiming that women controlled many of the early hunting and gathering societies, but men organized themselves to conquer women by force, thereby also gaining control of originally woman-centered forms of social organization.

Anthropological evidence would caution against such a sweeping claim since the arrangements between women and men vary so widely across different cultures and in different time periods. But the important questions radical feminists raise are, How did men gain and maintain control of the systems of production and reproduction? What is the relationship of men's power to the structure of social institutions and how does it continue to oppress women?

Radical feminists argue that men's control of women cannot be explained simply based on class oppression. As the feminist anthropologist Gayle Rubin has written, "No analysis of the reproduction of labor can explain foot-binding, chastity belts, or any of the incredible array of Byzantine, fetishized indignities, let alone the more ordinary ones, which have been inflicted upon women in various times and places" (1975:163). One strength of the radical feminist perspective is its focus on men's violence against women and its emphasis on the many cultural practices designed to control female sexuality and reproduction. Indeed, the control of women's sexuality is central to many radical feminist analyses.

The Sex–Gender System

Gayle Rubin identified the **sex–gender system** as the "set of arrangements by which a society transforms biological sexuality into products of human activity and in which these transformed sexual needs are satisfied" (1975:159). Rubin argues that the oppression of women lies in social systems that create male solidarity, not simply in systems of economic production. She writes that "the subordination of women can

MEDIA MATTERS

Television's "New" Feminism

Media portrayals of feminism have consistently been found to be problematic. Beyond providing examples of strong, assertive, and independent women, the media have rarely challenged existing race, class, gender, and sexual hierarchies. In the wake of feminism, have the media since overcome these shortcomings and incorporated feminist insights?

Lisa M. Cuklanz and Sujata Moorti analyzed the first five seasons of a popular television series that, because of its subject matter, they characterize as "feminist television." As part of the Law & Order franchise, NBC debuted the *Law & Order: Special Victims Unit (SVU)* series in the fall of 1999. *SVU* is located within the traditionally masculine genre of detective show. However, the series is unique in that it is devoted to crimes of sexual assault and rape. Sexual violence overwhelmingly affects women, and violence against women has been one of the main issues at the forefront of the feminist agenda for decades.

In their analysis, Cuklanz and Moorti found that the storylines on *SVU* feature fundamental elements of feminist understandings of sexual violence. For example, *SVU* did not objectify victims of rape and sexual assault because the storylines typically focused on events after an incident of sexual violence had occurred. Additionally, *SVU* dramatized women who survived their sexual assaults, thus reinforcing the feminist principle that "there is life after rape." Finally, several episodes of *SVU* challenged the black male rapist myth. Men of color were rarely portrayed as the perpetrators of sexual violence against women.

Although these findings seem promising, Cuklanz and Moorti argue that many *SVU* storylines demonize women, specifically mothers. For example, poor mothering was much more frequently depicted as the cause of criminal behavior in adult children than was bad fathering. Similarly, Cuklanz and Moorti analyzed over 20 *SVU* episodes that featured violent and dangerous mothers. These "monstrous maternal figures" poisoned their children's food, psychologically abused their children, abandoned sick children, and so on.

Cuklanz and Moorti conclude that *SVU* has been (mostly) successful in representing feminist perspectives of sexual violence against women. However, the demonization of mothers and the maternal role on *SVU* contradicts these feminist ideas and results in what Cuklanz and Moorti refer to as "misogynist feminism."

Thinking Further: Select a crime drama that is currently airing and systematically observe, as did Cuklanz and Moorti, how storylines depict sexual violence. Are women portrayed as victims or survivors? Who narrates the story and, thus, whose perspective is portrayed as driving the experience of sexual violence? Has television changed as the result of the feminist movement?

Source: Based on Cuklanz, Lisa M., and Sujata Moorti. 2006. "Television's 'New' Feminism: Prime-Time Representations of Women and Victimization." *Critical Studies in Media Communication* 23 (October): 302–321.

be seen as a product of the relationships by which sex and gender are organized and produced" (1975:177). According to Rubin, men "exchange" women through the marketplace. In fact, she was one of the first to introduce the idea of "the traffic in women," now commonly understood to refer to international marketing of women's sexuality. Rubin suggested that we find the location of women's oppression in men's control of women's sexuality.

In the radical feminist analysis, the production of gender also sets the preconditions for other forms of domination (Harding 1986). Men first learn to dominate women, setting a pattern for the domination of others. Economic systems may determine who these others are, but sex and gender systems establish the precon- ditions for domination to emerge. In the end, radical feminism sees systems of domination based on class, race, or nationality as extensions of the underlying politics of male supremacy (Bunch 1975).

Radical feminists also see patriarchal institutions as creating myths and forms of social organization that constrain women to exist in male-centered worlds (Daly 1978). One radical feminist solution to women's subordination is the establishment of women-centered beliefs and systems. For some, this movement has produced the separatist philosophy of radical lesbian feminism, whereby a woman-identified world is created through the attachments women have to each other, not to men.

Sexuality and the State

Catherine MacKinnon has extended the radical feminist analysis to argue that men's control of women's sexuality is the central fact of the domination of women. She writes, "Sexuality is to feminism what work is to Marxism" (1982:515). Mac- Kinnon describes sexuality as a social process that creates, organizes, and directs desire; the process of directing the expression of desire creates the social beings we know as women and men, and their relations create society. She reminds us that through gender socialization, women and men come to identify themselves not just as social beings but also as sexual beings.

Sexuality is the primary sphere of men's power. Through rape, sexual harass- ment, incest, and violence against lesbians, men exercise their sexual power over women. Heterosexuality is the institution through which men's power is expressed; gender relations and the family are the specific forms of compulsory heterosexuality. Because this analysis sees heterosexuality as institutionalizing male dominance, radical feminism has also been critical to the development of new studies in sexuality, as we will see later in this chapter.

MacKinnon also interprets the **state** as embodying masculine authority. Liberals define the state as a form of disembodied reason; Marxists see the state primarily as a reflection of material interests. As a result, according to MacKinnon, liberal analyses of the state see women as simply another interest group and treat women as abstract persons with rights, but they do not see women as a specifically gendered group. In Marxist analyses, the state is a tool of dominance and a force that legitimates ideol- ogy; women in this analysis are relegated to just another subordinated group.

MacKinnon argues that the state—through the rule of law—defines and treats women in the same way that men see and treat women. Thus, the state is coercive and ensures men's control over women's sexuality. The implication of MacKin- non's analysis is that as long as the "state is male"—meaning that its meaning sys- tems, its mode of operations, and its underlying assumptions are based on men's power—women cannot, as liberals would argue, overcome their subordination through actions of the state.

Intersections of Capitalism and Patriarchy

The assumption in radical feminist analyses that gender relations are more funda- mental than class relations has posed important questions for feminist theory. The dialogue between radical feminists and socialist feminists thus raises new questions about the intersections between capitalism and patriarchy. Heidi Hartmann's (1981) analysis of the interaction of patriarchal structures and the development of capitalism is one such work to make this synthesis. Hartmann, a socialist feminist theorist, argues that feminists must identify patriarchy as a social and historical structure if we are to understand Western capitalist societies. She says that Marxist analyses take the relationship of women to the economic system as their central question, but that feminist analyses must take their central question as the relationship of women to men. Understanding capitalism alone will not illuminate women's situation unless we recognize that capitalism is also a patriarchal system of social organization. Hartmann sees the partnership of patriarchy and capitalism as the critical starting point for feminist theory.

In precapitalist societies, Hartmann argues, men controlled the labor of women and children in the family: "In so doing men learned the techniques of hierarchical organization and control" (Hartmann 1976:138). As larger systems of exchange formed beyond local communities, men were faced with the problem of maintaining their control over women. Through patriarchy, men learned techniques of social control that, when capitalism emerged in Western societies, could be transformed from direct and personal systems of control to indirect and impersonal systems of social control. Thus, Hartmann sees capitalism as emerging in interaction with—and reinforcing—patriarchy, but she does not see patriarchy as the sole cause of gender inequality.

Hartmann continues by arguing that "job segregation by sex . . . is the primary mechanism in capitalist society that maintains the superiority of men over women" (1976:139), pointing out that the development of capitalism has had a more severe impact on women than on men. Not only was women's productive role in the family altered, but capitalism made women more economically dependent on men. The crux of Hartmann's research lies in her analysis of men's control of the wage-labor market, where she says the reason men excluded, rather than organized, women workers "is explained, not by capitalism, but by patriarchal relations between men and women: Men wanted to assure that women would continue to perform the appropriate tasks at home" (1976:155). Men both benefit from the higher wages they receive and from the household division of labor in which they receive women's services.

The synthesis of radical and socialist feminism shows how the gender division of labor is related to women's position in society as a whole, leading many to conclude that women's power in society is directly related to their contribution to production and the extent to which they control the resources they produce.

Comparing Liberal, Socialist, and Radical Feminism

Liberal, socialist, and radical feminism each make unique contributions to our understanding of the situation of women. Together, they suggest that we ground discussion of women's position in the dynamics of the gender division of labor, the emergence of class systems, the formation of patriarchal relations, and the social organization of the family. The point is that social change is informed by different premises about the social organization of society. Different feminist perspectives suggest different kinds of social change; therefore, for feminists to realize their goals for an egalitarian society requires careful examination of the underlying assumptions of given theoretical and political perspectives.

Of course, each of these perspectives is an *ideal type*—that is, they are not perfectly distinct from one another. In actuality, feminist organizations (and individual feminists) may use aspects of each framework to organize their thinking about women and gender in society. Moreover, organizations that are generally identified as working within the system and using the framework of liberalism might, on some issues or for some members, also embrace a more radical perspective. The point is that distinguishing different theoretical frameworks sharpens your thinking by helping you identify the underlying assumptions of each and, therefore, the implications of each one for social change.

In comparing them, we can see that liberal feminism emphasizes that social change should establish individual civil rights so that no one is denied access to the existing socioeconomic system based on sex, race, or class. Liberal feminism also tells us that sexism is the result of past traditions and learned identities. Consequently, it suggests reform in gender socialization practices. The political tactics of liberal feminism are primarily those of interest-group politics in which liberal feminists attempt to increase the political influence and power of women. Their political strategy involves building coalitions that align the issues of feminism with other political causes, thereby increasing the strength of the women's movement. This strategy also has its costs, however, because political compromises mean that only the most moderate feminist demands can gain the support necessary for a solid coalition.

Socialist and radical feminism, on the other hand, root the cause of sexism in the fundamental character of political and economic institutions. These perspectives challenge the very basis of social institutions, suggesting that revolutionary changes need to transform both capitalism and patriarchy. Socialist feminists make social class central to their analysis, arguing that classical Marxist theory has obscured the economic and social roles of women. Socialist feminism forces us to remember the significance of class.

Radical feminism locates sexism in the independent existence of patriarchy and the social relations that patriarchy generates. Radical feminism suggests that only the elimination of patriarchy will result in the liberation of women in society. Much of the strategy of radical feminist programs for change has been to redefine social relations by creating a women-centered culture. Radical feminists emphasize the positive capacities of women by focusing on the creative dimensions of women's experience. Radical feminists celebrate the creative dimension of women's lives, specifically because they see women's culture and experience as resisting patriarchal social relations.

The distinctions drawn here between these three feminist perspectives are in no way a perfect description of any of them. In theory and in practice, there are as many shared ideas and politics among feminists as there are differences. Discussion of the different feminist perspectives demonstrates that the questions that feminists raise have different answers and that they are as complex as the systems they seek to change. As you will see in the remainder of this chapter, the analyses of liberal, socialist, and radical feminism are themselves incomplete. It has remained for new feminist perspectives to raise and analyze questions that remain unaddressed in these historic modes of feminist theory.

MULTIRACIAL FEMINISM

As the women's movement has developed, women of color have consistently stated the need for feminism to be inclusive of all women in its vision of change. Early on, Sojourner Truth, in her now well-known speech at the women's rights convention in Akron, Ohio in 1851, "Aint' I a Woman," articulated the need for feminist thinking to embrace the experiences of African American women in its actions and analysis (Collins 1998). With some of its roots in the activism of Black women in the civil rights movement, the women's movement could have from the start built feminist theory to include the experiences of women of color. However, much of the women's movement remained anchored primarily in the experience of White women. It has taken the work of women of color and some White women to build more inclusive feminist theory.

Just as theories that are exclusively centered in the lives of White men are distorted, so is feminist theory inadequate and incomplete, and sometimes just plain wrong, when it is not grounded in the experiences of women in different racial–ethnic and class contexts. Many of the earlier theories we have reviewed tried to build a "grand" theory of women to encompass women as a whole. But, in doing so, they sometimes falsely assumed that "woman" was a unitary category (Andersen 2003; Baca Zinn and Dill 1996). For example, socialist feminism tends to see all women's experience as emerging from their class standing because socialist feminism sees the development of class relations under capitalism as the basis for the exploitation of both women and racial–ethnic groups. Socialist feminism

Women of color have been at the forefront of fighting for women's rights, even when they have also been critical of the women's movement for too often overlooking the specific experiences of women of color.

reminds us of the importance of class in different women's experience. It also points to such facts as the success of many middle-class and professional women resting on the labor of women of color who provide the domestic work (housework and child care) that many successful women no longer do (Dill 1980; Hondagneu-Sotelo 2001). But because of its focus on class, socialist feminism tends to see both gender and race as secondary to class. As a result, socialist feminism understates the independent operation of race and gender relations.

Radical feminism assumes that gender is the primary form of oppression and that class and race are extensions of patriarchal domination (Daly 1978). In assuming that patriarchy is the central cause of all women's oppression, radical feminism provides little explanation of the powerlessness that people of color experience together. Radical feminism's insistence that eliminating sexism is the key to eliminating racism has a hollow ring to women of color, who face oppression on both counts and who experience racism as a more fundamental (or at least equally fundamental) fact of their lives. Radical women of color clearly recognize that sexism exists in their communities, but attributing the primary cause of their experience to patriarchy ignores the racism they encounter not only from men but also from White feminists (Moraga and Anzaldúa 1981).

Now, those working to incorporate race, class, and gender into feminist theory see that there can be no unitary analysis of "woman" as a category. Rather, the inclusion of women of color in feminist theory requires understanding multiple and overlapping forms of oppression. This insight, coming largely through the activism and scholarship of women of color, has now generated a new paradigm in feminist theory, labeled by some as multiracial feminism (Baca Zinn and Dill 1996). Grounded in the experiences of women of color, multiracial feminism provides a new starting point for feminist thought and action.

Multiracial feminism is not itself a unitary framework. Instead, it is a perspective that incorporates the multiple systems of domination that shape the experiences of Latinas/Latinos, African Americans, Native Americans, Asian Americans, and White women and men. Thus, it is grounded in understanding the *intersections* of race, class, and gender in the shaping of people's experiences. A good way to think about this has been articulated by the concept of a "prism of difference." Maxine Baca Zinn, Pierrette Hondagneu-Sotelo, and Michael Messner (2008)—all feminist sociologists—argue that like a prism that shows a structure of relationships between colors, so is the social structure of race, sexuality, class, gender, and other inequalities arrayed in a complex social structure.

Multiracial feminism can be described as organized around several themes. First, multiracial feminism interprets gender as socially constructed through interlocking systems of race, class, and other inequalities. Thus, women are not just gendered subjects, but are situated within an array of social factors, including class, race, sexual orientation, and other facets of their lived experience. Making any one of these dimensions of life visible—within an analysis that recognizes their interlocking character—is likely to make the others visible as well (Andersen and Collins 2010). Furthermore, people—both women and men—experience these interlocking systems simultaneously. Thus, women of color experience their race and their gender, not as separate categories, but as intricately linked in their experience. Although one factor may be more salient at a given moment than another, it is their linkage that shapes the experiences of women of color, not just one or the other added together (Moraga and Anzaldúa 1981; Combahee River Collective 1982; Collins 1990, 1998; Baca Zinn and Dill 1996; Andersen and Collins 2010).

Second, multiracial feminism sees the intersections of race, class, and gender operating at multiple levels of social life. Race, class, and gender are embedded in social institutions (what you might think of as the *macrostructural* level), but they are also part of our immediate social interactions, social identities, and social consciousness (the *microlevel*). This means that they are complex systems of social relationships in which different women and men are embedded. Thus, there are not simple divisions between those with privilege and those without, since the social factors of race, class, and gender cut in many directions. Thus, a Latino (man) may have some privileges associated with his gender, but may be disadvantaged by virtue of his racial–ethnic status and, perhaps, his social class. Multiracial feminism recognizes the complexity of these intersecting hierarchies—at all levels of experience (Baca Zinn and Dill 1996; Andersen and Collins 2010).

Third, multiracial feminism recognizes the socially constructed nature of both gender and race. Just as gender is a social construction, so is race socially constructed. Although many think of race as a biological category, its significance comes from its development as a socially created category of oppression and domination. Thus, the actual meaning of race changes over time, both as it is contested by oppressed racial groups and as the society changes regarding how race operates in social institutions and social relationships. Race is both a fluid category and one that has a concrete location in social institutions, such as in laws that define people in racial categories or in the income brackets that differentiate the class status of different racial–ethnic groups. Saying that race is socially constructed does not mean that it is not real, only that *it is the social reality of race that makes it meaningful in society.*

Fourth, multiracial feminism grows from, but is not limited to, the experiences of women of color. As feminist scholars have thought more inclusively about race, class, and gender as intersecting systems, they have interpreted the experiences of all groups, not just those of women of color, in new ways. Race, class, and gender affect the experience of all groups, not just those who are their victims. Thus, in studying race, Whites and people of color are included, just as studying gender brings new insights about men as well as women (Andersen and Collins 2010; Andersen 2003).

Fifth, multiracial feminism understands that there is an "interplay of social structure and women's agency" (Baca Zinn and Dill 1996:328). This means that women (or other social groups) are not merely passive recipients of abstract forces of social structure. **Agency** refers to the active and creative way that human beings give meaning to their experience and act on their own behalf. People are not just empty vessels into whom social forces are poured. Even under oppressive conditions, people have a consciousness that they use to define their experience; they act in ways that construct a meaningful social existence. This may take the form of accommodating oneself to oppressive social forces, but it also takes the form of resisting oppression—or at the very least, adapting to the conditions one faces. The focus on human agency in multiracial feminism has highlighted the active

The future of women's lives now rests on the actions and beliefs of third wave feminists.

and creative ways that groups resist oppression even at times when oppression seems overwhelming.

Scholarship that stems from a multiracial perspective has used a wide array of methodological techniques to examine the multiple facets of race, class, and gender in women's and men's lives (Baca Zinn and Dill 1996). But, fundamentally, this perspective requires shifting the starting point for the development of feminist thinking. As a result of centering knowledge in the experiences of those who have traditionally been excluded, multiracial feminism questions the assumptions of other, more singular and exclusionary modes of thinking.

As an example, Collins writes that if we want to know the thoughts and lives of African American women as intellectuals, we have to revise our way of thinking about who is an intellectual. African American women have historically been denied access to formal education; they have not had the privilege of finding publishers and public platforms for their ideas. To recover the work of African American women intellectuals, we must look to new sources and find intellectual thought in the everyday activities of Black women. Collins writes, "Reclaiming the Black female intellectual tradition also involves searching for its expression in alternative institutional locations and among women who are not commonly perceived as intellectuals" (1990:14).

Integrating race, class, and gender into feminist thinking requires a process of transformation in which we move from simply adding women of color into existing analyses to seeing race, class, and gender in relational ways. There are many rich empirical studies being produced within multiracial feminism, as well as historical and political analyses that shed new light on social and historical processes. The challenge for feminist theorists in the coming years is to continue developing such work. Without it, feminists cannot hope to generate programs for social change designed for the liberation of *all* women and men.

POSTMODERNIST FEMINISM

Postmodernism is a form of contemporary social theory that explains all knowledge as stemming from the specific historical period and the conditions in which it is produced. But it goes beyond this to claim that communication in all its forms *is* reality. This theoretical framework interprets society not as an objective thing, but as a fluid and illusive construction of alternative meaning systems —although one external to our own consciousness. Thus, to postmodernists, society is only a series of stories that emerge from a variety of points of view and experiences; we can therefore only "know" something by deconstructing these stories or "texts." Linked to a theory known as *poststructuralism*, postmodernists think of social structure as a reified category that is real only because people believe it is and construct ideas to support that belief. To postmodernists, reality is simulated. Therefore, this perspective is particularly attractive in a world marked by highly technological forms of communication that increasingly penetrate everyday life.

Postmodernism recognizes that socially constructed assumptions are built into the knowledge frames that are characteristic of any given historical period or cultural context (Nicholson 1990). Postmodernist theory goes beyond simply understanding the influence of culture (a view common to all social sciences) by arguing that there is not a singular, monolithic social order (i.e., society); rather, society is a series of images and meaning systems over which people struggle (Fraser 1989). Postmodernists see reality as constituted through a broad range of **discourses**—that is, all that is written, spoken, or otherwise represented through language and communication systems. Whether it is science, the media, or other cultural artifacts, postmodernists see these discourses as framing knowledge and reality; in addition, these discourses are systems of social control. Gender ideology, as an example, is a form of social control represented in the discourses (science, language, cultural images) that embed specific representations of what it means to be male and female.

Postmodernism has arisen largely from the field of literary criticism and also from the critiques of science symbolized by feminist standpoint theory (see Chapter 10), but it has influenced many areas of feminist scholarship. Within literary criticism, the basic idea of postmodernism is that texts do not stand alone as objective entities apart from either the author's construction of the text or the reader's response to it. Because the focus of postmodernism is on alternative discourses and meaning systems, it emphasizes this idea of "texts." Texts may be actual literary texts, such as books, but the concept of a text in postmodernist theory is more than the literal text. It refers to the contested and constructed meaning systems that appear in all of social reality, whether that is books, media representations, or other cultural forms. A commercial, a conversation, or the nightly news is considered a text; indeed, from the postmodernist perspective, society itself is only a text in that it is constructed out of the interpretive processes that constitute it. The major method used in postmodernism is to examine texts as socially constructed objects. Because of this focus on texts, postmodernists are fascinated with the various artifacts of popular culture, as seen in the emergence of a new field of study, known as *cultural studies*.

In the social sciences, postmodernism emerges from criticisms of positivist science—that is, the idea that society can be known through systematic observation and generalization. Postmodernist theorists debunk this idea because they assume it is impossible to reflect on something and see the world without presuppositions (Agger 1991). Postmodernists reject the scientific point of view that through detached measurement one can observe a world that is "out there." As we saw in Chapter 10, the scientific perspective is a specific worldview, with its own assumptions about the world. Postmodernists see science, like everything else, as constructed; they do not see it as providing knowledge that is any more real or objective than literature. Instead, postmodernists see science, like literature, as needing to be "deconstructed"—in other words, analyzing the assumptions and meanings embedded in scientific works. Unlike other social scientists, postmodernists are wary about generalization, thinking instead that the world consists of diverse, multiple, and unique experiences.

There are serious challenges posed by postmodernist thought for feminists and social scientists who work within the scientific method—that is, thinking that one can use controlled observation and rigorous study to reveal the workings of something "real" known as social structure. Instead, postmodernism is founded on a distrust of some of the ways of thinking that are basic to the social scientific approach to understanding society and social life.

For feminists, postmodernism has had much appeal because of some commonly shared assumptions in both feminist and postmodernist theory. One of the basic premises of feminist thought is that gender is socially constructed; furthermore, one of the fundamental goals of feminist theory is to examine gender relations, see how they are constituted, and study how they are thought of or not thought of (Flax 1990). This critical attitude makes postmodernism appealing to feminists because feminism and postmodernism are fundamentally skeptical about existing knowledge. Each also recognizes the embedding of social assumptions in such things as language, cultural images, and the ideas of a given period. Because feminists see how ideas and images have been used to oppress women, they want to criticize these discourses, not take them for granted, and, like postmodernist theorists, they see gender and society as socially constituted (Fraser and Naples 2004).

Another basic insight of postmodernist feminism is the idea that there is nothing essentially male or female—an idea referred to as **essentialism**. Rather, there are socially constructed categories that emerge from specific cultural and historical contexts, not from anything fundamental about male or female biology. Postmodernists even challenge the idea that there are real biological categories to begin with, since they understand "male" and "female" only as constructed through human definition. In other words, postmodernists take the social construction of gender to its logical conclusion, arguing that our notion of biological differences between the sexes is itself a social construction. Thus, the body itself, from a postmodernist perspective, is something that is understood only through social interpretation (Bordo 1995; Fausto-Sterling 2000; Nicholson 1994). Some feminist postmodernists argue that the distinction other feminists make between sex and gender (see Chapter 2) is a false one because it still accepts biological differences as real. Instead, postmodernist feminists argue that biological sex differences are only a function of our knowledge, not necessarily objectively "real" categories of difference.

A good way to explain this point is to use the metaphor of a coat rack, suggested by Linda Nicholson, a postmodernist feminist. The coat rack metaphor assumes that the body is a rack upon which differing cultural artifacts are hung. In other words, the idea is that there is some constancy to nature but that culture elaborates this basic difference into different societal forms (Nicholson 1994). Postmodernists question whether the coat rack itself is anything other than a cultural construction. In other words, they deny that there is any essential difference in men and women other than those we construct as significant. As a result, postmodernist feminists challenge the very categories of "man" and "woman," seeing these instead as fluid, artificial, and malleable. Like other postmodernists, feminist postmodernists are skeptical about any categories, because they see all categories and definitions as humanly imposed (Bordo 1995).

Postmodern feminists have also focused on the social construction of language and understand language as not just a technical device for describing something "out there." Rather, they see language itself as actually constituting the thing it allegedly describes (Agger 1991). Postmodernist analyses of language rest on the idea that language, like other forms of knowledge, is not pure. Instead, language reflects the social categories and practices that characterize a given time and cultural period. For example, calling someone a man or a woman, just like calling someone White or Black, has a specific socially constituted meaning that makes no sense outside of its cultural time and place. Because this insight has been central to feminist thought (in that feminists have long deconstructed and exposed the sexist basis of language), many feminists find postmodernist arguments attractive.

In sum, postmodernist feminists see indeterminacy and construction, not determinism and fixedness, as characteristic of society. They emphasize diversity, not unity, in experience, and the unique, not the general. This perspective makes social science more subjective and tentative, since postmodernism is a more relativistic way of viewing the world. Some have argued that one of the reasons postmodernism is so appealing to contemporary intellectuals is that it reflects the disillusionment of the current generation (Rosenau 1992). Postmodernism causes people, including scholars, to examine their assumptions in constructing knowledge and formulating a worldview. Its theorists also deny that a singular voice defines all experience, as has been the case in androcentric and ethnocentric scholarship. Through their recognition that various disciplines encode value positions, such as standpoint theory, postmodernists help us deconstruct the gendered basis of knowledge.

One of the criticisms of postmodernist theory is its very high level of abstraction—what one sociologist has called work that is "incredibly, extravagantly convoluted" (Agger 1991). Almost as a way of emphasizing the contextual nature of all that is known, postmodernists have often purposefully produced work that is obtuse and difficult to understand. As a consequence, the essence of postmodernism is typically inaccessible to those without a high degree of schooling in its interpretation. This fact has led some to charge that postmodernist theory is elitist, since it disallows one of the objectives of feminist theory—accessibility to wide audiences, particularly women who may not have access to the elite educational institutions in which postmodernism is produced.

Postmodernism makes it difficult ever to generalize about any characteristic or experience, as if all the world were merely individual discourses or voices. This is strikingly at odds with the basic principles of social sciences—that one can generalize through careful observation and analysis. Postmodernist thinkers are opposed to the concept of social structure as something that is "there." By criticizing an overly determinist view of gender, race, and class, they actually can "deconstruct gender right out of operation" (Bordo 1992:160), as if it hardly existed at all. Postmodernist theory has the advantage of emphasizing diversity and thus has added to new work on race, class, and gender, but it does so in a way that denies the reality of structurally based oppression. This makes it limited in its ability to explain structured inequality, whether by gender, race, class, or by all three (Collins 1998). It is as if studying race, class, and gender is just a matter of different voices, since it reduces the experience of oppression to cultural analysis texts and discourses alone. By denying the concept of social structure, postmodernism limits the framework through which one can understand oppression by gender, race, and class; furthermore, it makes social science only a matter of accounting for diverse social experiences (Agger 1991) instead of being committed to studying general principles of social structure and organization.

QUEER THEORY AND SEXUALITIES

The influence of postmodernist theory has been especially strong in new feminist scholarship on sexuality. In part because feminists have wanted to break down taken-for-granted categories of sexual differentiation, postmodernist thought is consistent with the value placed on the fluidity of sexual categories. Postmodernist feminist theorists have thus found subjects like cross-dressing, transvestitism, and the crossing of sexual categories represented in some new forms of gay and lesbian studies to be fascinating and to provide new theoretical constructs for all feminist thought.

Queer theory is a new perspective emerging from studies of sexuality and from postmodernism. Queer theory understands sex and the body as purely social concepts. That is, the discourses and practices of popular and scientific thought construct sex and the body in particular ways. Therefore, interpreting sex and the body is a matter of challenging how sexual categories and understandings of the body are socially developed. As one sociologist writes, "Sex is viewed as fundamentally social: the categories of sex—especially heterosexuality and homosexuality, but also the whole regime of modern sexual types, classifications, and norms—are understood as social and historical facts" (Seidman 1994:171).

One of the arguments, from a postmodernist perspective, is that categories such as homosexual and heterosexual have emerged as particular social types only in modern Western societies. We have seen this in the studies of earlier work on sexual categories in other cultures (see Chapter 4). Beyond the recognition of cross-cultural differences in the social construction of sexuality, however, queer theorists make a more fundamental point: The categories of homosexual and heterosexual themselves have been constructed through particular scientific discourses—namely, the work of sexologists and others who have labeled sexual behaviors in dichotomous categories. Furthermore, these "discourses" have assumed an authoritative stance, with systems of power enforcing these labels. To postmodernists, sexual power is embodied in various aspects of social life (popular culture, scientific writings, literary texts, and daily conversations, to name a few). These discourses establish sexual boundaries that regulate sexual behavior and identities.

One of the major contributions of queer theory is its deconstruction of sexual categories. That is, it questions the presumed natural basis of sexual categories altogether, arguing instead, that all sexual identities are composites of socially defined distinctions (Stein and Plummer 1994; Seidman 2003). It is not that sexual categories and differences are not "there," only that the differences we think matter are the result of social constructions. Thus, the construction of a category such as *homosexual* imposes a particular construction of sex on its subjects and presumes the existence of some other normal and taken-for-granted category—that is, *heterosexual.*

Queer theory, like postmodernist feminism, criticizes traditional empirical studies of sexuality for being unreflective about the categories on which such research is based. According to queer theory, studies of sexuality that compare men and women—or gays, bisexuals, transsexuals, and straights—presume that these different types have some fixed meaning. Instead, queer theory interprets these as highly fluid categories (Seidman 2003, 1994). This mode of thinking shifts the analysis of sexuality away from dualistic categories to a more fluid understanding of difference. At the same time, it challenges the assumption (one even made within the gay and lesbian community) that there is some natural basis to homosexuality. From this point of view, no one sexual identity is privileged over another; rather, sexual identity is all performance and meaning (Butler 1990).

There are important implications of queer theory for political action by groups who want to challenge the oppression of gays and lesbians. Queer theorists are less inclined to support the civil rights strategy that has characterized the gay and lesbian political movement. The civil rights strategy is one that recognizes gays and lesbians as a minority group and contests that this group has rights, just as do other minority groups in society. Instead, the politics of a more postmodernist approach are to transgress and challenge sexual categories (Stein and Plummer 1994; Taylor and Rupp 2003), thus subverting the dominant sexual order to resist and rebel against taken-for-granted sexual categories (Butler 1990). This political strategy challenges sexual categories, even when behavior may be outrageous to others (e.g., by cross-dressing and having "kiss-ins"). The shock and outrage that such acts produce are deliberate ways of making people face the socially constructed assumptions about sex that they would normally take for granted. Often, such political behavior takes a playful and risqué attitude, again reflecting the postmodernist appeal to seeing sexual identities as scripts or performances.

Not all new feminist studies of sexuality use a queer theory framework. Indeed, as you have seen throughout this book, much of the new scholarship on sexuality has used both existing frameworks of sociological and feminist research and new theories to explore various questions about sexuality and its relationship to gender. Many feminists are, indeed, critical of the queer and postmodernist approaches to sexuality, arguing that they do not provide a political perspective that challenges the real structural basis of sexual oppression (Kitzinger and Wilkinson 1994). In their criticisms, feminists are arguing that structural systems of heterosexual privilege and power are real and cannot be reduced to texts, discourses, and performance. As in other areas of feminist thought, there are multiple frameworks for understanding sexuality; queer theory is only one such approach.

CONTINUING QUESTIONS FOR FEMINIST THEORY

The discussion of different modes of feminist theory reveals the richness that the women's movement has brought to intellectual life. But remember that one of the central tenets of feminist theory is that theory is not just for theory's sake. Rich as the intellectual discussions of feminist theorists are in intellectual life, their purpose is to improve the actual conditions in which women live.

Feminist theory, like the movements from which it stems, is also an evolving body of knowledge—one that, as we have seen, incorporates multiple questions and multiple ways of interpreting and thinking. Still, at different moments in time certain questions guide the development of feminist theory. Some of the questions currently being considered in feminist theory have been present from the beginning. For example, debates about essentialism have long characterized feminist scholarship and continue to do so as they are elaborated in postmodernist feminist thinking. Are men and women fundamentally different? Of course, many feminists reject an essentialist position that men and women are different, arguing instead that to the extent that differences exist, they are wholly socially constructed. But other feminists celebrate differences between women and men, seeing such differences as strengths, not weaknesses. Questions about essentialism and difference will likely continue to foster debate within feminist studies.

Other questions have newly emerged, particularly as feminist theory has become more attentive to the diverse experiences among women. Thus, an important question now guiding feminist thought is how to explain the relations of power that exist between women and men when we know, based on multiracial feminism, that not all men are equally powerful. Indeed, many men exercise less power over others—even over their own lives—than some women exercise (Andersen et al. 2004). And, although socialist feminist theory has waned given the absence of a viable socialist movement in the United States, it is important to continue analyzing the significance of class, as well as race and gender, in feminist scholarship. New studies of feminism are also grappling with questions about the dialectical relationship between agency and social structure. That is, how will social structures that are organized around race, class, and gender emerge as the result of women's and men's actions and consciousness in the years ahead?

As feminist theory develops in the future, new generations of feminist thinkers will generate new discussions and raise new questions, although they will likely also elaborate some of the persistent issues that feminism addresses. But the gains made in feminist thinking—gains that reflect the diverse origins of feminist thought—will continue to emphasize the fundamental idea that knowledge about gender is socially constructed and must therefore be seen in the context of the social relations in which knowledge is produced. As you have seen throughout this book, knowledge is incomplete without considering the multiple experiences of diverse groups in society and how their experiences are intertwined. This recognition has brought increased attention within feminist thought to race, class, and gender and the interrelationships between these different axes of social experience. Future feminist studies will build on this and the insights of earlier thinkers to guide feminist research and action in the years ahead.

◼ Chapter Summary and Themes

While liberal feminism emphasizes equal rights, more radical feminist theories center their analysis on social class and its relationship to gender inequality and on men's power in patriarchal social systems.

More radical forms of feminist theory are critical of existing dominant institutions, criticizing liberal feminism for working within a system that holds gender, race, and class inequality at its core.

Socialist feminism, based on the work of Karl Marx, locates the cause of women's oppression in the workings of the system of capitalism and the interconnection between productive and reproductive labor.

Marx and Engels's analysis of how capitalism worked emphasizes the ownership of systems of production and the exploitation of wage labor. Their work includes women only insofar as they are wage laborers, although socialist feminists added women's unpaid labor in the home to classical Marxist theory, thus analyzing women's role in production (as well as in reproductive labor) to socialist feminist theory.

Radical feminism locates the primary cause of women's oppression in the system of patriarchy in which men hold power over women.

Radical feminists see the power of men, as manifested in men's sexual violence toward women, as a primary factor in the oppression of women. Some combine the insights of radical feminism and its emphasis on patriarchy to socialist feminism, thus theorizing the connections between capitalism and patriarchy.

Multiracial feminism studies gender by analyzing the interlocking relationships between race, class, and gender.

Multiracial feminism understands that race, class, and gender together influence all aspects of people's lives and together construct dominant social institutions. Thus, different from other forms of feminist theory, multiracial feminism sees gender as part of the systemic character of inequality, locating the oppression of different groups of women—and men—in the connections between race, class, and gender as structured forms of inequality.

Postmodernism interprets all forms of knowledge as constructed through discourses that are culturally and socially created.

Postmodernist feminist theory has thus emphasized the influence of cultural images and texts in the creation of meaning systems about gender that, although illusory, have real consequences for how people experience their social worlds.

Queer theory interprets sexualities as socially constructed forms, thus subject to transgression and challenge as people come to deconstruct—or challenge—presumed categories of sexual difference.

Although dominant cultural beliefs identify sexual categories in dichotomous terms (that is, either "gay" or "straight"), queer theory sees such categories as socially created and thus subject to change. In this sense, sexual identity is fluid and can be challenged through political activism and active transgression against fixed categories of presumed sexual difference.

Feminist theory hinges on actively thinking about social structures and their relationship to gender, as well as the understanding that human beings can think their way of out oppressive social relations.

Feminist theory emerges in relationship to the feminist movement and thus engages new questions over time, especially as feminist thinkers identify new questions for new generations. Nonetheless, the classic questions of feminist theory include understanding the relationship of gender to other forms of inequality and the ability of human beings—through human agency—to challenge existing social systems.

■ Key Terms

agency
class
class consciousness
dialectical materialism
discourse
essentialism
false consciousness

historical materialism
ideology
infrastructure
multiracial feminism
patriarchy
postmodernist feminism
queer theory

radical feminism
sex–gender system
socialist feminism
state
superstructure

■ Discussion Questions/Projects for Thought

1. Imagine that Karl Marx has returned to the world as a woman. How might he revise his theory if he were analyzing capitalism and gender relations today?

2. Radical feminism has been vital to the growing awareness of violence against women and the role that men's power plays in generating such violence. Do you think that patriarchy is a continuing feature of contemporary society? If so, what influence does it have on violence against women? If you think it is not as relevant as radical feminists believe, what other framework might you use to explain the high rates of violence against women?

3. Using any one of the topics discussed in this book, identify the new questions that would be asked if you were to use an analysis emphasizing the intersections of race, class, and gender versus one that only looked at gender.

Glossary

abolitionism nineteenth-century movement organized to oppose slavery

acquaintance rape (also known as *date rape*) sexual assault where the assailant is an acquaintance of the victim

affirmative action policy by which women and minorities are given extra consideration as a remedy against past discrimination

Age of Enlightenment period in seventeenth- and eighteenth-century Europe marked by a belief in the ability of human reason to be used for humanitarian social change

agency active and creative way that human groups give meaning to their experience and act on their own behalf

Americans with Disabilities Act (ADA) federal law requiring protecting disabled people from discrimination and requiring employers, schools, and other institutions to provide reasonable accommodations

androcentrism thought that is centered in men's experiences only

anorexia nervosa condition characterized by severe weight loss and delusions about one's body size

antimiscegenation prohibition of marriage between different racial groups

authority power that is perceived by others to be legitimate and that is structured into specific social institutions

Automobile Workers **v.** *Johnson Controls* Supreme Court decision in 1991 holding that it is discriminatory to bar women from high-risk jobs in which there is potential harm to a fetus or reproductive system

biological determinism faulty reasoning assuming that a single condition inevitably determines a given outcome

biological reductionism faulty argument that reduces a complex phenomenon to a singular cause

bisexual term used to describe those who have sexual attraction to members of both sexes

bulimia eating disorder in which people, typically women, binge on huge amounts of food, followed by their purging through vomiting, laxatives, or extreme fasting

care work forms of labor (often unpaid) needed to nurture, reproduce, and sustain people

Civil Rights Bill (1964) federal law prohibiting discrimination based on race, color, religion, sex, or national origin

class social position of group or individuals within the system of class stratification whereby some groups and individuals within these groups have greater access to resources and power than others

class consciousness in Marxist theory, understanding that develops as class groups comprehend their relationship to the system of production

cognitive-developmental theory theory, based on the work of Jean Piaget, that explains children's development of the mental categories formed through interaction with others

collective consciousness system of beliefs within a society that create a sense of belonging to the community and convey the moral obligation to live up to the society's demands

comparable worth principle of paying women and men equivalent wages for performing jobs involving comparable levels of skill

compulsory heterosexuality institutionalized practices that presume women are innately sexually oriented toward men and that support privileges associated with heterosexuality

content analysis research method by which researchers analyze the content of documents or other artifacts

contingent workers temporary employees, contract workers, and part-time workers

controlling images concept referring to the power of media ideals to direct our concepts of ourselves and others

crime index measure of the overall volume and rate of crime, as indicated by offenses reported to the police (including murder, non negligent manslaughter, rape, robbery, aggravated assault, larceny-theft, motor vehicle theft, and arson)

cult of domesticity Victorian ideal that made women responsible for the moral and everyday affairs of the home

culture patterns of expectations, beliefs, values, ideas, and material objects that define the taken-for-granted way of life for a society or group

deviance behavior that departs from conventional norms and is labeled and so recognized by groups with the power to do so

dialectical materialism *see* **historical materialism**

digital divide gap that has opened between groups with strong computing skills and those without

discourse used by postmodernist theorists to refer to all that is written or spoken and that requires analysis by social theorists

discrimination act or practice of systematically disadvantaging one or more groups

"doing gender" sociological perspective that sees gender as an activity accomplished through routine social interaction

dual labor market theory explanation of gender inequality as the result of a labor market organized into two segments: the primary and secondary market—where jobs in the primary labor market are more valued and more valuable than those in the secondary labor market

economic restructuring multidimensional process of change in the nation's economy, including the transition from a manufacturing-based economy to a service-based economy, increasing globalization, technological change, and the increasing concentration of capital in the hands of a few

Eisenstadt **v.** *Baird* Supreme Court decision (1972) extending unmarried persons the right to use birth control

emotional labor work people do to manage the emotions of others and that is part of one's work evaluation

empirical facts (or data) that are based on careful observation

epistemology derived from the philosophy of science, a theoretical way of knowing

Equal Pay Act first federal legislation requiring equal pay for equal work

Equal Rights Amendment proposed amendment to the U.S. constitution that would prohibit the denial of rights based on sex (i.e., gender)

essentialism the idea that there are fundamental differences between women and men

ethnocentric seeing one's group as superior to all others; taking one's own group experience as the starting point for understanding all other experiences

false consciousness beliefs that emerge when a subordinate group accepts and internalizes the worldview of the dominant group

Family and Medical Leave Act federal law enacted in 1993 that requires employers to grant 12 weeks of unpaid leave to a parent to care for newborn or adopted children or to care for a sick child, spouse, or parent

family household U.S. Census Bureau term for a household maintained with a family or unrelated persons residing together

family-based economy form of economic production wherein the household is the basic unit of the economy and the site for most economic production and distribution

family-consumer economy form of economic production in which mass production of goods leads to increased consumerism in families and households

family-wage economy form of economic production in which production moves out of the household into a factory system, where a wage-based system of labor is created

faulty generalization mistakenly assuming that something is true for an entire group when it is not

feminism belief and action supporting social justice for women

feminist theology new models of religious belief founded in feminist ethics

feminist theory analyses explaining the position of women in society, intended also to provoke the possibilities for liberating social changes

feminization of poverty trend by which a growing proportion of the poor are women and their children

Fifteenth Amendment amendment to the U.S. Constitution (passed in 1865) guaranteeing that the right to vote cannot be abridged because of race, color, or prior servitude

gender socially learned behaviors and expectations associated with men and women

gender apartheid extreme segregation and exclusion of women from public life

gender display demonstrations of behavior that communicates gendered identity

gender gap differing political opinions and voting patterns between women and men

gender identity an individual's specific definition of self, based on that person's understanding of what it means to be a man or a woman

gender roles patterns of behavior in which women and men behave, based on the cultural expectations associated with their gender

gender segregation pattern whereby women and men are located in different categories of jobs throughout the labor force

gender stratification the hierarchical distribution of economic and social resources along lines of gender

gendered institution total pattern of gender relations embedded in societal institutions

glass ceiling popular phrase referring to the invisible mechanism that discourages women's advancement in organizations

Griswold **v.** *Connecticut* first Supreme Court decision (1965) allowing married couples to use birth control

heteronormativity norms and institutional structures that presume and enforce heterosexuality as the only acceptable form of sexual expression and identity; *see also* **heterosexism**

heterosexism institutionalized set of behaviors and beliefs that presume heterosexuality to be the only acceptable form of sexual expression

historical materialism theoretical position postulating that the material organization of the world (i.e., economic systems) shapes people's behavior and beliefs; the basis for Marxist social theory

homophobia fear and hatred of homosexuals

household economic unit of those residing together, with a common economic base

householder term used by U.S. Census Bureau to refer to the person in whose name a household unit is owned or rented

human agency intentional actions that people take in adapting to and sometimes changing the conditions they face in life

human capital theory explanation of wage differentials as the result of different characteristics of workers

identification theory perspective that young children feel an affinity for the parent of their same sex

ideology system of beliefs that distorts reality at the same time that it provides justification for the status quo

infant mortality rate of infant death within a population

infrastructure derived from Marxist theory, refers to the system of economic production as the determining feature of social organization

institutions *see* **social institution**

intersexed persons persons born with mixed sex characteristics

labeling theory theoretical perspective in sociology, emphasizing that some groups with the power to label deviant behavior exercise control over who and what is considered deviant

liberal feminism feminist theoretical position that interprets the origins of women's oppression as in blocked opportunities and legal obstacles to equal participation in society

liberalism political philosophy characterized by an emphasis on individual rights and equal opportunity; the basis for liberal feminism

liberation theology interpretations of religious belief that promote resistance to oppression; common in Latin American societies, but also significant in U.S. social movements against racial and ethnic oppression

marital rape forced sexual activity demanded of a wife by her husband

matrix of domination complex system of inequality involving the intersection of race, class, and gender

men's studies field of study that examines men's lives from a feminist perspective

meritocracy social systems in which persons hold their particular positions on the basis of individual talents and achievements

misogyny hatred of women

Muller v. Oregon Supreme Court decision in 1908 holding it constitutional to restrict the working day to 10 hours only for women

multiracial feminism a perspective incorporating the multiple systems of domination that shape the experiences of Latinas and Latinos, and African American, Native American, Asian American and White women and men and that is grounded in understanding the intersections of race, class, and gender differences—and similarities—in the shaping of people's experiences

Nineteenth Amendment amendment to the U.S. Constitution that gives women the right to vote, passed in 1920

nonfamily household a person living alone or one where a householder shares the unit with nonrelatives

nuclear family family structure in which husband and wife reside together with their children

object relations theory theory of psychological development that sees children as identifying with their same-sex parent but forming their own identities through detaching from the parents

patriarchy institutionalized power relationships that give men power over women

Personal Responsibility and Work Reconciliation Act federal law that eliminated former welfare programs (AFDC) and placed lifetime limits on the receipt of welfare while also imposing work requirements

personal troubles problematic events in the immediate experience of an individual

pluralism model of the state that interprets political action as the result of balancing the needs and actions of diverse interest groups

popular culture beliefs, practices, and objects that are part of everyday traditions

postmodernism form of contemporary social theory positing that society is not an objective entity and that all knowledge is situated in specific assumptions stemming from the historical period in which they develop; a theoretical perspective that sees society as not unitary, but instead as composed of socially constituted and highly unstable images and selves

postmodernist feminism theoretical framework that interprets society and social action as a series of illusions and discourses

poverty line index developed by the U.S. Social Security Administration that defines the official rate of poverty

power individual or group ability to influence others

power elite model of the state that sees power as stemming from the influence of a powerful ruling class

protective legislation laws and policies prohibiting women from participating in certain jobs because of perceived risks to their reproductive health—generally thought to be discriminatory, since such protections have not been directed toward men as workers

public issues social phenomena that produce personal troubles but have their origins in social structures of society

queer theory an argument that interprets sexuality as socially constructed through institutional practices

radical feminism feminist theoretical position positing that male power is the source of women's oppression

reflection hypothesis explanation of the depiction of women in the mass media that assumes the mass media reflect the values of the population

religion as opiate idea that religion is a form of social control that discourages social protest by oppressed groups

religious right fundamentalist Christian groups that have politically mobilized on behalf of conservative causes

reproduction of harm   the idea that women who have been victims of sexual and emotional abuse, raised in poverty, and subjected to violent relationships are more likely to engage in deviant and/or criminal behavior

Roe v. Wade   1973 Supreme Court decision upholding women's right to abortion

role-learning theory   explanation of media images of women and men that assumes that these images encourage role modeling by men and women observing the images

sanctified church   Holiness and Pentecostal churches within the African American community

scientific method   series of rigorous steps that test theories based on empirical research and systematic observation

Second Great Awakening   social movement in the early nineteenth century, emphasizing a revivalist and egalitarian spirit in religion

second shift   work women do at home, in addition to paid labor

self-esteem   the regard with which someone holds themself

self-fulfilling prophecy   outcomes that occur as the result of others' expectations

sex   biological identity of a person

sex chromosomes   chromosomal pairs that determine the biological sex of an offspring

sex–gender system   set of arrangements by which a society transforms biological sexuality into products of human activity

sex trafficking   transporting (often involuntary) of women and girls for purposes of commercial sex

sex work   employment within the sex industry; can include work done by either women or men

sexism   beliefs that see women as inferior and that defend their traditionally subordinated place in the world

sexual harassment   unwanted imposition of sexual requirements in the context of a relationship of unequal power

sexual politics   link between sexuality and power

sexually dimorphic traits   differences appearing between males and females

social construction of gender   different processes by which expectations associated with being male or female are passed on through society

social construction theory   perspective viewing people as constructing gender through their ongoing interaction with others

social institutions   established patterns of behavior with a particular and recognized purpose; institutions include specific participants who share expectations and act in specific roles, with rights and duties attached to them

social learning theory   theory of socialization emphasizing the significance of environment in explaining the socialization process

social movement   work of groups organized to promote or resist change in society

social roles   culturally prescribed expectations, duties, and rights that define the relationship between a person in a particular position and the other people with whom she or he interacts

social structure   term used to describe the abstract, yet still real, social forces that shape society and social situations

socialist feminism   feminist theoretical position that interprets the origins of women's oppression in the system of capitalism; some socialist feminists also analyze the intersections of capitalism and patriarchy

socialization   process by which social roles are learned

sociological imagination   ability to conceptualize the relationship between individuals and the society in which they live

sociology of knowledge   the study of how what we know is shaped by society

standpoint theory   feminist theoretical argument postulating that the specific social location of the "knower" shapes what is known and that not all perspectives on social life are valid or complete because of the different positions of "knowers" within systems of power and privilege

state   organized and institutionalized system of power and authority in society, including the government, the police, law, and the military

stereotype threat   concept that explains the pattern whereby students (or others) perceive that they risk being judged by a negative stereotype and thus do not perform as well as they otherwise might

stratification   process by which groups or individuals in a society are located in a hierarchical arrangement on the basis of their differential access to social and economic resources

structural diversity model   framework for understanding families that focuses on the changing dynamics of race, class, and gender as they influence family forms

subculture of violence   idea that violence stems from the cultural attributes of particular groups

superstructure   in Marxist theory, institutions of society as they reflect the economic system (law, family, and the like)

sweatshop   workplace where an employer violates more than one law regarding safety and health, workers' compensation, or industry regulation

symbolic interaction theory   theoretical perspective in sociology that interprets social behavior as stemming from the meanings people attribute to things, including how they act

temperance movement   nineteenth-century social movement with feminist values, organized to oppose alcohol abuse

Temporary Assistance for Needy Families (TANF)   state-based program providing limited economic support to poor families

Title VII of the Civil Rights Bill   federal law prohibiting discrimination on the basis of race, color, national origin, religion, or sex, in any terms, conditions, or privileges of employment

Title IX of the Educational Amendments   federal law prohibiting sex discrimination in federally funded education programs and activities; part of the Educational Amendments of 1972

tracking   groups of students are sorted into groups in school based on their presumed abilities

transgender   people living in a gender that is not the gender they were assigned at birth; people who deviate from the binary system of gender as either male or female

transnational families   families whose members live in different countries, usually at a considerable distance from one another, but with a pattern of moving back and forth across national boundaries

Uniform Crime Reports   official reports produced by the Federal Bureau of Investigation detailing the amount of reported crime and arrests

victimization surveys   studies based on large, national samples that estimate the extent of crime victimization among particular groups

women's studies   field of study that examines women's lives from a feminist perspective

Bibliography

Acker, Joan. 1992. "Gendered Institutions: From Sex Roles to Gendered Institutions." *Contemporary Sociology* 21 (September): 565–569.

Acker, Joan. 2005. *Class Questions, Feminist Answers*. Lanham, MD: Rowman and Littlefield.

Adler, Freda. 1975. *Sisters in Crime*. New York: McGraw-Hill.

Agger, Ben. 1991. "Critical Theory, Poststructuralism, Postmodernism: Their Sociological Relevance." Pp. 105–131 in *Annual Review of Sociology* 17, edited by W. Richard Scott and Judith Blake. Palo Alto, CA: Annual Reviews, Inc.

Ahmed, Leila.1993. *Women and Gender in Islam: Historical Roots of a Modern Debate*. New Haven, CT: Yale University Press.

Alden, Helena L. 2001. "Gender Role Ideology and Homophobia." Paper presented at the Annual Meetings of the Southern Sociological Society.

Ali, J., and W. R. Avison. 1997. "Employment Transitions and Psychological Distress: The Contrasting Experiences of Single and Married Mothers." *Journal of Health and Social Behavior* 38 (December): 345–362.

Alicea, Marixsa. 1997. "'A Chambered Nautilus': The Contradictory Nature of Puerto Rican Women's Role in the Social Construction of a Transnational Community." *Gender & Society* 11 (October): 597–626.

Almeling, Rene. 2007. "Selling Genes, Selling Gender: Egg Agencies, Sperm Banks, and the Medical Market in Genetic Material." *American Sociological Review* 72 (June): 319–348.

Amadiume, Ifi. 1987. *Male Daughters, Female Husbands: Gender and Sex in an African Society*. London: Zed Books.

American Association of University Women. 1992. *How Schools Shortchange Girls*. Washington, DC: American Association of University Women.

American Association of University Women. 1998. *Gender Gaps: Where Schools Still Fail Our Children*. Washington, DC: American Association of University Women.

American Medical Association. 2004. "Women Physicians by Specialty." www.ama-assn.org.

American Psychological Association. 2007. *Report of the APA Task Force on the Sexualization of Girls*. Washington, DC: American Psychological Association.

American Sociological Association. 2005. "Statement of the American Sociological Association on the Causes of Gender Differences in Science and Math Career Advancement." Washington, D.C.: American Sociological Association. www.asanet.org.

Amir, M. 1971. *Patterns of Forcible Rape*. Chicago: University of Chicago Press.

Amott, Teresa L., and Julie A. Matthaei. 1996. *Race, Gender, and Work: A Multicultural History of Women in the United States*, rev. ed. Boston: South End Press.

Anderson, Elijah. 1999. *Code of the Street: Decency, Violence, and the Moral Life of the Inner City*. New York: W.W. Norton Press.

Andersen, Margaret L. 2003. "Whitewashing Race: A Critical Review." Pp. 21–34 in *Whiteout: The Continuing Significance of Racism*, edited by Woody W, Doana and Eduardo Bonilla-Silva. New York: Routledge.

Andersen, Margaret L., Anne Bowler, and Michael Kimmel. 2004. "Do We Still Need Feminist Theory?" in *The Gender Kaleidoscope: Prisms, Patterns, and Possibilities*, edited by Catherine Valentine and Joan Spade. Belmont, CA: Wadsworth.

Andersen, Margaret L., and Patricia Hill Collins. 2010. *Race, Class, and Gender: An Anthology*, 7th ed. Belmont, CA: Wadsworth.

Andersen, Margaret L., and Claire Renzetti. 1980. "Rape Crisis Counseling and the Culture of Individualism." *Contemporary Crises* 4: 323–339.

Anderson, A., and R. Gordon. 1978. "Witchcraft and the Status of Women—The Case of England." *British Journal of Sociology* 29: 171–184.

Anderson, Kristin J., and Campbell Leaper. 1998. "Meta-Analyses of Gender Effects on Conversational Interruption: Who, What, When, Where, and How." *Sex Roles* 38 (August): 225–252.

Anderson, Kristin L. 2007. "Who Gets Out?" *Gender & Society* 21 (June): 173–201.

Andrews, W., and D. C. Andrews. 1974. "Technology and the Housewife in Nineteenth Century America." *Women's Studies* 2: 309–328.

Ansalone, George. 2001. "Schooling, Tracking, and Inequality." *Journal of Children and Poverty* 7 (March): 33–47.

Applebaum, Richard, and Peter Dreier. 1998. "The Campus Anti-Sweatshop Movement." *The American Prospect* 46 (September–October): 71.

Arendell, Terry. 1992. "After Divorce: Investigations into Father Absence." *Gender & Society* 6 (December): 562–586.

Aries, Philip. 1962. *Centuries of Childhood*. New York: Vintage.

Armstrong, Elizabeth A., Laura Hamilton, and Brian Sweeney. 2006. "Sexual Assault on Campus: A Multilevel, Integrative Approach to Party Rape." *Social Problems* 53 (4): 483–499.

Arnold, Regina. 1994. "Black Women in Prison: The Price of Resistance." Pp. 171–184 in *Women of Color in U.S. Society*, edited by Maxine Baca Zinn and Bonnie Thornton Dill. Philadelphia: Temple University Press.

Aronson, Pamela. 2003. "Feminists or 'Postfeminists?' Young Women's Attitudes toward Feminism and Gender Relations." *Gender & Society* 17 (December): 903–922.

Arrighi, Barbara A., and David J. Maume Jr. 2000. "Workplace Subordination and Men's Avoidance of Housework." *Journal of Family Issues* 21 (May): 464–486.

Atchley, Robert C. 2000. *Continuity and Adaptation in Aging: Creating Positive Experiences*. Baltimore, MD: The John Hopkins University Press.

Avalos, Manual. 1996. "Gender Inequality: Sorting out the Effects of Race/Ethnicity and Gender in the Anglo Male-Latino Female Earnings Gap." *Sociological Perspectives* 39 (Winter): 497–515.

Avila-Saavedra, Guillermo. 2009. "Nothing Queer about Queer Television: Televised Construction of Gay Masculinities." *Media, Culture & Society* 31 (1): 5–21.

Axelson, D. E. 1985. "Women as Victims of Medical Experimentation: J. Marion Sims' Surgery on Slave Women, 1845–1850." *Sage* 2 (Fall): 10–13.

Axtell, J. 1981. *The Indian Peoples of Eastern America: A Documentary History of the Sexes*. New York: Oxford University Press.

Baca Zinn, Maxine, and Bonnie Thornton Dill. 1996. "Theorizing Difference from Multiracial Feminism." *Feminist Studies* 22 (Summer): 321–331.

Baca Zinn, Maxine, and D. Stanley Eitzen. 2010. *Diversity in Families*, 9th ed. Boston: Allyn and Bacon.

Baca Zinn, Maxine, Pierrette Hondagneu-Sotelo, and Michael A. Messner, eds., 2005. *Gender Through the Prism of Difference*, 3rd ed. New York: Oxford University Press.

Bachman, Ronet, and Robert Peralta. 2002. "The Relationship between Drinking and Violence in an Adolescent Population: Does Gender Matter?" *Deviant Behavior* 23: 1–19.

Badgett, M. V., and Mary C. King. 1997. Pp. 73–86 in *Homo Economics: Capitalism, Community, and Lesbian and Gay Life*, edited by Amy Gluckman and Betsy Reed. New York: Routledge.

Badgett, M. V. Lee. 1995. "The Wage Effects of Sexual Orientation on Discrimination." *Industrial and Labor Relations Review* 48 (July): 726–739.

Baer, Judith A. 1998. *Our Lives Before the Law: Constructing a Feminist Jurisprudence*. Princeton, NJ: Princeton University Press.

Bailey, B. L., K. C. Scantlebury, and E. M. Johnson. 1999. "Encouraging the Beginning of Equitable Science Teaching Practice: Collaboration is the Key." *Journal of Science Teacher Education* 19: 159–171.

Baldwin, Mark W., and John Patrick Richard Keelan. 1999. "Interpersonal Expectations as a Function of Self-Esteem and Sex." *Journal of Social and Personal Relationships* 16 (December): 822–835.

Barajas, Heidi Lasley, and Jennifer Pierce. 2001. "The Significance of Race and Gender in School Success among Latinas and Latinos in College." *Gender & Society* 15 (December): 859–878.

Barber, Jennifer S., and William G. Axinn. 1998. "Gender RoleAttitudes and Marriage among Young Women." *Sociological Quarterly* 39 (Winter): 11–31

Barfoot, C. H., and G. T. Sheppard. 1980. "Prophetic vs. Priestly Religion: The Changing Role of Women Clergy in Classical Pentecostal Churches." *Review of Religious Research* 22 (September): 2–17.

Barker-Benfield, G. J. 1976. *Horrors of the Half-Known Life*. New York: Harper & Row.

Barriga, Claudia A., Michael A. Shapiro, and Rayna Jhaveri. 2009. "Media Context, Female Body Size and Perceived Realism." *Sex Roles: A Journal of Research* 60 (1–2): 128–141.

Barron, Martin, and Michael Kimmel. 2000. "Sexual Violence in Three Pornographic Media: Towards a Sociological Explanation." *Journal of Sex Research* 37: 161–168.

Bartling, Carl, and Brenda Broussard. 1999. "Effects of Experimenter Gender, Testing Context and Marital Status upon Marital Role Expectations." *International Journal of Adolescence and Youth* 7: 317–325.

Barton, Bernadette. 2006. *Stripped: Inside the Lives of Exotic Dancers*. New York: New York University Press.

Basile, Kathleen C. 2002. "Prevalence of Wife Rape and Other Intimate Partner Sexual Coercion in a Nationally Representative Sample of Women." *Violence and Victims* 17 (5): 511–524.

Basile, Kathleen C. 2008. "Histories of Violent Victimization among Women Who Reported Unwanted Sex in Marriages and Intimate Relationships: Findings from a Qualitative Study." *Violence Against Women* 14 (1): 29–52.

Basow, Susan A. 2003. "'Troubles Talk': Effects of Gender and Gender-Typing." *Sex Roles* 48 (February): 183–187.

Battle, Juan, and Anthony J. Lemelle Jr. 2002. "Gender Differences in African American Attitudes toward Gay Males." *The Western Journal of Black Studies* 26: 134–139.

Baumgardner, Jennifer, and Amy Richards. 2000. *Manifesta: Young Women, Feminism, and the Future*. New York: Farrar, Straus, and Giroux.

Baxandall, R. F. 1979. "Who Shall Care for Our Children? The History and Development of Day Care in the United States." Pp. 134–149 in *Women: A Feminist Perspective*, edited by Jo Freeman. Palo Alto, CA: Mayfield.

Baxter, Janeen, and Eric Olin Wright. 2000. "The Glass Ceiling Hypothesis: A Comparative Study of the United States, Sweden, and Australia." *Gender & Society* 14 (April): 275–294.

Beauboeuf-Lafontant, Tamara. 2007. "'You Have to Show Strength': An Exploration of Gender, Race, and Depression." *Gender & Society* 21 (February): 28–51.

Becker, Howard. 1963. *The Out-siders*. New York: Free Press.

Becker, Penny Edgell, and Heather Hofmeister. 2001. "Work, Family, and Religious Involvement for Men and Women." *Journal for the Scientific Study of Religion* 40: 707–722.

Becker, Penny Edgell, and Phyllis Moen. 1999. "'Scaling Back' Dual-Earner Couples' Work-Family Strategies." *Journal of Marriage and the Family* 61 (November): 995–1007.

Beins, Agatha. 2009. "Comparative Perspectives Symposium: Feminist Zines." *Signs* 35: 1–276.

Belkin, Aaron, and Geoffrey Bateman. 2003. *Don't Ask, Don't Tell: Debating the Gay Ban in the Military*. Boulder, CO: Lynne Reinner Publishers.

Bell, Ann V. 2009. "'It's Way Out of My League': Low-income Women's Experiences of Medicalized Infertility." *Gender & Society* 23 (October): 688–709.

Belsky, Jay, and John Kelly. 1994. *The Transition to Parenthood*. New York: Delacorte Press.

Bendroth, Margaret Lamberts. 1999. "Fundamentalism and the Family: Gender, Culture, and the American Pro-Family Movement." *Journal of Women's History* 10 (Winter): 35–54.

Benet, M. K. 1972. *The Secretarial Ghetto*. New York: McGraw-Hill.

Berger, Peter. 1963. *Invitation to Sociology*. Garden City, NY: Doubleday-Anchor.

Berger, Peter, and Thomas Luckmann. 1966. *The Social Construction of Reality*. Garden City, NY: Doubleday-Anchor.

Berheide, Catherine. 1992. "Women Still 'Stuck' in Low-Level Jobs." *Women in Public Services: A Bulletin for the Center for Women in Government* 3 (Fall). Albany, NY: Center for Women in Government, State University of New York.

Bernard, Jessie. 1972. "Marriage: His and Hers." *Ms.* 1: 46ff.

Bernard, Jessie. 1975. *Women, Wives, Mothers: Values and Options*. Chicago: Aldine.

Berry, Phyllis E., and Helen M. Eigenberg. 2003. "Role Strain and Incarcerated Mothers: Understanding the Process of

Mothering." *Women & Criminal Justice* 15: 101–119.

Bettie, Julie. 1995. "Class Dismissed? Roxanne and the Changing Face of Working-Class Iconography." *Social Text* 45 (Winter): 125–149.

Bianchi, Suzanne M. 2000. "Maternal Employment and Time with Children: Dramatic Change or Surprising Continuity?" *Demography* 37 (4): 401–414.

Bianchi, Suzanne M., and Marybeth J. Mattingly. 2004. "Time, Work, and Family in the United States." *Advances in Life Course Research* 8: 95–118.

Bigner, Jerry J., and Frederick W. Bozett. 1989. "Parenting by Gay Fathers." *Marriage and Family Review* 14: 155–175.

Billingsley, Andrew. 1966. *Black Families in White America*. Upper Saddle River, NJ: Prentice-Hall.

Bird, Chloe E., and Allen M. Fremont. 1999. "Are Socio-logical Models of the Effects of Gender, Paid Work, and Unpaid Work on Depression and Self-Rated Health Generalizable to Mental and Physical Health?" Paper presented at the Annual Meetings of the American Sociological Association, Washington, DC.

Blackmun, Justice Harry. 1978. *Regents of the University of California vs. Bakke*, U.S. Supreme Court, No. 76–811.

Blackwell, James. 1991. *The Black Community: Diversity and Unity*. New York: HarperCollins.

Blackwood, Evelyn. 1984. "Sexuality and Gender in Certain Native American Tribes: The Case of Cross-Gender Females." *Signs* 10 (Autumn): 27–42.

Blakemore, J. E. O. 1998. "The Influence of Gender and Parental Attitudes on Preschool Children's Interest in Babies: Observations in Natural Settings." *Sex Roles* 38 (January): 73–94.

Blood, Robert, and Donald Wolfe. 1960. *Husbands and Wives: The Dynamics of Married Living*. New York: Free Press.

Blum, Linda. 1986. "Women and Advancement: Possibilities and Limits of the Comparable Worth Movement." Paper presented at the Annual Meetings of the

American Sociological Associa-tion, New York City, September.

Blumenthal, Susan J. 1998. "Women and Substance Abuse: A New National Focus." Pp. 13–32 in *Drug Addiction Research and the Health of Women*, edited by Cora Lee Wetherington and Adele B. Roman. Washington, DC: National Institute on Drug Abuse.

Blumstein, Philip, and Pepper Schwartz. 1983. *American Couples*. New York: William Morrow.

Boeri, Miriam Williams. 2002. "Women After the Utopia: The Gendered Lives of Former Cult Members." *Journal of Contempo-rary Ethnography* 31: 323–360.

Bogdan, Bryna. 1999b. "Judging in a 'Different Voice': Gender and the Sentencing of Violent Offences in Israel." *International Journal of the Sociology of Law* 27: 51–78.

Bogdan, J. 1978. "Care or Cure? Childbirth Practices in Nineteenth-Century America." *Feminist Studies* 4: 92–99.

Bogle, Kathleen. 2008. *Hooking Up: Sex, Dating and Relationships on Campus*. New York: New York University Press.

Bogoch, Bryna. 1999. "Judging in a 'Different Voice': Gender and the Sentencing of Violent Offences in Israel." *International Journal of the Sociology of Law* 27(1):51–78.

Bonacich, Edna, and Richard P. Applebaum. 2000. *Behind the Label: Inequality in the Los Angeles Apparel Industry*. Berkeley: University of California Press.

Bonilla-Silva, Eduardo, and Mary Hovespan. 2000. "If Two People Are in Love: Deconstructing Whites' Views on Interracial Marriage with Blacks." Paper pre-sented at the Annual Meetings of the Southern Sociological Society.

Bookman, Ann, and Sandra Morgen. 1988. *Women and the Politics of Empowerment*. Philadelphia: Temple University Press.

Boonstra, Heather D., Rachel Benson Gold, Cory L. Richards, and Lawrence B. Finer. 2006. *Abortion in Women's Lives*. New York: Guttmacher Institute.

Booth, Bradford. 2003. "Contextual Effects of Military Presence on

Women's Earnings." *Armed Forces and Society* 30 (Fall): 25–51.

Booth, Bradford, William W. Falk, David R. Segal and Mady W. Segal. 2000. "The Impact of Military Presence in Local Labor Markets on the Employment of Women." *Gender & Society* 14(2):318–332.

Bordo, Susan. 1992. "Feminist Skepticism and the 'Maleness' of Philosophy." Pp. 143–162 in *Women and Reason,* edited by Elizabeth D. Harvey and Kathleen Okruhlik. Ann Arbor: University of Michigan Press.

Bordo, Susan. 1995. *Unbearable Weight: Feminism, Western Culture, and the Body.* Berkeley: University of California Press.

Boston Women's Health Book Collective. 1984. *The New Our Bodies, Ourselves.* New York: Simon and Schuster.

Bradford, J., Ryan, C., and E. D. Rothblum. 1994. "National Lesbian Health Care Survey: Implications for Mental Health Care." *Journal of Counseling and Clinical Psychology* 62: 228–242.

Bradley, Karen. 2000. "The Incorporation of Women in Higher Education: Paradoxical Outcomes?" *Sociology of Education* 73 (January): 1–18.

Brady, Thomas M., and Olivia Sibler Ashley. 2005. Women in Substance Abuse Treatment. Results from the Alcohol and Drug Services Survey. U.S. Department of Health and Human Services. www.oas.samhsa.gov.

Bramson, Leon. 1961. *The Political Context of Sociology.* Princeton, NJ: Princeton University Press.

Breines, Winifred. 2006. *The Trouble Between Us: An Uneasy History of White and Black Women in the Feminist Movement.* New York: Oxford University Press.

Brewster, Mary. 2003. "Power and Control Dynamics in Prestalking and Stalking Situations." *Journal of Family Violence* 18: 207–217.

Brines, Julie, and Kara Joyner. 1999. "The Ties That Bind: Principles of Cohesion in Cohabitation and Marriage." *American Sociological Review* 64 (June): 333–355.

Britton, Dana M. 1997. "Gendered Organizational Logic: Policy and Practice in Men's and Women's Prisons." *Gender & Society* 11 (December): 796–818.

Brotman, Jennie S., and Felicia M. Moore. 2008. "Girls and Science: A Review of Four Themes in the Science Education Literature." *Journal of Research in Science Teaching* 45: 971–1002.

Brown, Brett V. 2000. "The Single-Father Family: Demographic, Economic, and Public Transfer Use Characteristics." *Marriage and Family Review* 29: 203–220.

Brown, C. 1981. "Mothers, Fathers, and Children: From Private to Public Patriarchy." Pp. 239–267 in *Women and Revolution,* edited by Lydia Sargent. New York: South End Press.

Brown, Susan L. 1996. "Relationship Quality and the Transition to Marriage among Cohabitors." Paper presented at the Annual Meetings of the American Sociological Association.

Browne, Irene, ed. 1999. *Latinas and African American Women at Work: Race, Gender, and Economic Inequality.* New York: Russell Sage Foundation.

Browne, Malcolm W. 1998. "Can't Decide if That Centerfold Is Really a Perfect 10? Just Do the Math." *The New York Times,* October 20, p. D5.

Brubaker, Sarah J. and Jennifer A. Johnson. 2008. "'Pack a More Powerful Punch' and 'Lay the Pipe': Erectile Enhancement Discourse as a Body Project for Masculinity." *Journal of Gender Studies* 17 (2): 131–146.

Bunch, Charlotte. 1975. "Lesbians in Revolt." Pp. 29–38 in *Lesbianism and the Women's Movement,* edited by N. Myron and C. Bunch. Oakland, CA: Diana Press.

Burckle, Michelle A., Richard M. Ryckman, Joel A. Gold, Bill Thornton, and Roberta J. Audesse. 1999. "Forms of Competitive Attitude and Achievement Orientation in Relation to Disordered Eating." *Sex Roles* 40 (June): 853–870.

Bureau of Justice Statistics. 2005. *Sourcebook of Criminal Justice Statistics.* Washington, DC: U.S. Department of Justice.

Bureau of Justice Statistics. 2006a. *Prisoners in 2005.* Washington, DC: U.S. Department of Justice.

Bureau of Labor Statistics. 2006b. *National Compensation Survey.* Washington, DC: U.S. Department of Labor. www.bls.gov.

Bureau of Justice Statistics. 2010. *Criminal Victimization in the United States, 2007 – Statistical Tables.* Washington, DC: U.S. Department of Justice.

Bureau of Justice Statistics. 2008. *Criminal Victimization in the United States.* Washington, DC: Office of Justice Statistics.

Bureau of Labor Statistics. 2009 (March). www.bls.gov.

Burgess, Melinda C. R., Steven P. Stermer, and Stephen R. Burgess. 2007. "Sex, Lies, and Video Games: The Portrayal of Male and Female Characters on Video Game Covers." *Sex Roles: A Journal of Research* 57 (5–6): 419–433.

Burgess, Samuel H. 2001. "Gender Ideology and Anti-Gay Opinion in the United States." Paper presented at the Annual Meetings of the Southern Sociological Society.

Burris, Beverly H. 1991. "Employed Mothers: The Impact of Class and Marital Status on the Prioritizing of Family and Work." *Social Science Quarterly* 72 (March): 50–66.

Butler, Judith. 1996. *Gender Trouble: Feminism and the Subversion of Identity.* New York: Routledge.

Buysse, Joann M., and Melissa Sherman Embser-Herbert. 2004. "Constructions of Gender in Sport: An Analysis of Intercollegiate Media Guide Cover Photographs." *Gender & Society* 18 (February): 66–81.

Calasanti, Toni. 2007. "Bodacious Berry, Potency Wood and the Aging Monster: Gender and Age Relations in Anti-Aging Ads." *Social Forces* 86(1): 335–355.

Calasanti, Toni M., and Kathleen F. Slevin. 2001. *Gender, Social Inequalities, and Aging.* Walnut Creek, CA: AltaMira Press.

Calasanti, Toni M., and Kathleen F. Slevin. 2006. *Age Matters: Realigning Feminist Thinking.* New York: Routledge.

Caldera, Yvonne, and Mary A. Sciaraffa. 1998. "Parent-Toddler Play with Feminine Toys: Are All Dolls the Same?" *Sex Roles* 38 (November): 657–658.

Calhoun, Avery J., and Heather D. Coleman. 2002. "Female Inmates' Perspectives on Sexual Abuse by Correctional Personnel: An Exploratory Study." *Women and Criminal Justice* 13: 101–124.

Califia, Pat. 1997. *Sex Changes: The Politics of Transgenderism.* San Francisco: Cleis Books.

Cameron, Deborah. 1998. "Gender, Language, and Discourse: A Review Essay." *Signs* 23 (Summer): 945–974.

Campbell, Jacquelyn C., et al. 2003. "Risk Factors for Femicide in Abusive Relationships: Results from a Multisite Case Control Study." *American Journal of Public Health* 93: 1089–1097.

Campenni, C. Estelle. 1999. "Gender Stereotyping of Children's Toys: A Comparison of Parents and Nonparents." *Sex Roles* 40 (January): 121–138.

Cancian, Francesca. 1987. *Love in America: Gender and Self-Development.* New York: Cambridge University Press.

Cancian, Maria, and Daniel R. Meyer. 2000. "Work after Welfare: Women's Work Effort, Occupation, and Economic Well-Being." *Social Work Research* 24 (June): 69–86.

Candib, Lucy M. 1999. "Incest and Other Harms to Daughters across Cultures: Maternal Complicity and Patriarchal Power." *Women's Studies International Forum* 22 (March–April): 185–201.

Carr, C. Lynn. 1999. "Tomboy Resistance and Conformity: Agency in Social Psychological Gender Theory." *Gender & Society* 12 (October): 643–664.

Carroll, Joseph. 2004. "Religion is 'Very Important' to 6 in 10 Americans." *The Gallup Poll.* Princeton, NJ: Gallup Organization.

Carroll, Joseph. 2007. "Most Americans Approve of Interracial Marriages." *Gallup Poll*, April 16. www.gallup.com.

Cassidy, Margery A., and David Trafimow. 2002. "The Influence of Patriarchal Ideology on Outcomes of Legal Decisions Involving Woman Battering

Cases: An Analysis of Five Historical Eras." *The Social Science Journal* 39: 235–245.

Catalano, Shannon. 2007. *Intimate Partner Violence in the United States.* Washington, DC: U.S. Department of Justice, Bureau of Justice Statistics.

Catalano, Shannan, Erica Smith, Howard Snyder, and Michael Rand. 2009. *Bureau of Justice Statistics Selected Findings: Female Victims of Violence.* Washington, DC: U.S. Department of Justice.

Catsambis, Sophia, Lynn M. Mulkey, and Robert L. Crain. 1999. "To Track or Not to Track? The Social Effects of Gender and Middle School Tracking." *Research in Sociology of Education and Socialization* 12: 135–163.

Caulfield, Mina Davis. 1985. "Sexuality in Human Evolution: What Is 'Natural' in Sex?" *Feminist Studies* 11 (Summer): 343–364.

Center for Women and American Politics. 2010. *Fast Facts.* New Brunswick, NJ: Rutgers University. www.cawp.rutgers.edu.

Centers for Disease Control and Prevention. 2005. "Health Disparities Experienced by Black or African Americans—United States." *Morbidity and Mortality Weekly Report*, January 15.

Centers for Disease Control and Prevention. 2010. "HIV/AIDS among Women." www.cdc.gov.

Cepeda, Alice, and Avelardo Valdez. 2003. "Risk Behaviors among Young Mexican American Gang-Associated Females: Sexual Relations, Partying, Substance Use, and Crime." *Journal of Adolescent Research* 18: 90–106.

Chang, Mariko L. 2004. "Growing Pains: Cross-National Variation in Sex Segregation in Sixteen Developing Countries." *American Sociological Review* 69 (1): 114–137.

Charles, Maria, and David M.Grusky. 2004. *Occupational Ghettoes: The Worldwide Segregation of Women and Men.* Palo Alto, CA: Stanford University Press.

Chaves, Mark, and James Cavendish. 1997. "Recent Changes in Women's Ordination Conflicts: The Effect of a Social Movement on Intraorganizational Controversy." *Journal for*

the Scientific Study of Religion 36 (December): 574–584.

Chavkin, W. 1979. "Occupational Hazards to Reproduction: A Review Essay and Annotated Bibliography." *Feminist Studies* 5 (Summer): 310–325.

Chen, Anthony S. 1999. "Lives at the Center of the Periphery, Lives at the Periphery of the Center: Chinese American Masculinities and Bargaining with Hegemony." *Gender & Society* 13 (October): 584–607.

Cherney, Isabelle D., and Kamala London. 2006. "Gender-Linked Differences in the Toys, Television Shows, Computer Games, and Outdoor Activities of 5- to 13-Year-Old Children." *Sex Roles: A Journal of Research* 54 (9–10): 717–726.

Chernin, Kim. 1981. *The Obsession.* New York: Harper Colophon.

Chernin, Kim. 1985. *The Hungry Self: Women, Eating, and Identity.* New York: Times Books.

Chesney-Lind, Meda. 1997. "Equity with a Vengeance." *The Women's Review of Books* 14 (July): 5.

Chesney-Lind, Meda. 1999. "Challenging Girls' Invisibility in Juvenile Court." *Annals of the American Academy of Political and Social Science* 564 (July): 185–202.

Childs, Erica Chito. 2005. *Navigating Interracial Borders: Black-White Couples and Their Social Worlds.* New Brunswick, NJ: Rutgers University Press.

Chodorow, Nancy. 1978. *The Reproduction of Mothering.* Berkeley: University of California Press.

Chow, Esther. 1987. "The Development of Feminist Consciousness among Asian American Women." *Gender & Society* 1 (September): 284–299.

Christ, Carol, and Judith Plaskow, eds. 1992. *Womanspirit Rising,* 2nd ed. New York: Harper and Row.

Chrobot-Mason, Donna, Scott B. Button, and Jeannie D. DiClementi. 2001. "Sexual Identity Management Strategies: An Exploration of Antecedents and Consequences." *Sex Roles* 45 (September): 321–336.

Clark, Roger. 2007. "From Margin to Margin? Females and Minorities in Newbery and Caldecott

Medal-Winning and Honor Books for Children." *International Journal of Sociology of the Family* 33(2): 263–283.

Clark, Roger, Rachel Lennon, and Leanna Morris. 1993. "Of Caldecotts and Kings: Gendered Images in Recent American Children's Books by Black and Non-Black Illustrators." *Gender & Society* 7 (June): 227–245.

Clarke, E. 1873. *Sex in Education; Or, A Fair Chance for the Girls.* Boston: Osgood and Company.

Clark-Ibanez, and Marisol Karina. 1999. "Gender, Race, and Friendships: Structural and Social Factors Leading to the Likelihood of Inter-Ethnic Dating." Paper presented at the Annual Meetings of the American Sociological Association, Washington, DC.

Clay-Warner, Jody, and Jennifer McMahon-Howard. 2009. "Rape Reporting: 'Classic Rape' and the Behavior of Law." *Violence and Victims* 24, 6: 723–743.

Clearfield, Melissa W., and Naree M. Nelson. 2006. "Sex Differences in Mothers' Speech and Play Behavior with 6-, 9-, and 14-Month-Old Infants." *Sex Roles: A Journal of Research* 54 (1–2): 127–137.

Collins, Patricia Hill. 1986. "Learning From the Outsider Within: The Sociological Significance of Black Feminist Thought." *Social Problems* 33 (December): 514–532.

Collins, Patricia Hill. 1987. "The Meaning of Motherhood in Black Culture and Black Mother-Daughter Relationships." *Sage* 4 (Fall): 3–10.

Collins, Patricia Hill. 1990. *Black Feminist Theory: Knowledge, Consciousness and the Politics of Empowerment.* Boston: Unwin Hyman.

Collins, Patricia Hill. 1998. *Fighting Words: Black Women and the Search for Social Justice.* Minneapolis: University of Minnesota Press.

Collins, Patricia Hill. 2000. *Black Feminist Thought: Knowledge, Consciousness and the Politics of Empowerment.* New York: Routledge.

Collins, Patricia Hill. 2004. *Black Sexual Politics: African Americans, Gender, and the New Racism.* New York: Routledge.

Coltrane, Scott, and Michele Adams. 1997. "Work-Family Imagery and Gender Stereotypes: Television and the Reproduction of Difference." *Journal of Vocational Behavior* 50 (April): 323–347.

Combahee River Collective. 1982. "A Black Feminist Statement." Pp. 13–22 in *But Some of Us Are Brave*, edited by Gloria T. Hull, Patricia Bell Scott, and Barbara Smith. Old Westbury, NY: The Feminist Press.

Commission of Women in the Profession. 2010. *Goal III Report Card.* Chicago, IL: American Bar Association. www.abanet.org

Connell, Bob. 1992. "Masculinity, Violence, and War." Pp. 176–183 in *Men's Lives*, 2nd ed., edited by Michael S. Kimmel and Michael A. Messner. New York: Macmillan.

Conrad, Peter. 1998. Constructing the "Gay Gene" in the News: Optimism and Skepticism in the American, British, and Gay Press. Paper presented at the International Sociological Association.

Conte, Jon R. 1993. "Sexual Abuse of Children." Pp. 56–85 in *Family Violence: Prevention and Treatment*, edited by Robert L. Hampton, Thomas P. Gullotta, Gerald R. Adams, Earl H. Potter III., and Roger P. Weissberg. Newbury Park, CA: Sage.

Cook, D. T., and S. B. Kaiser. 2004. "Betwixt and Between: Age Ambiguity and the Sexualization of the Female Consuming Subject." *Journal of Consumer Culture* 4: 203–227.

Coontz, Phyllis. 2000. "Gender and Judicial Decisions: Do Female Judges Decide Cases Differently than Male Judges?" *Gender Issues* 18: 59–73.

Corea, Gena. 1980. "The Caesarian Epidemic." *Mother Jones* 5: 28ff.

Corra, Mamadi K., and Sitawa R. Kimuna. 2009. "Double Jeopardy? Female African and Caribbean Immigrants in the United States." *Journal of Ethnic and Migration Studies* 35 (6): 1015–1035.

Cott, Nancy. 1977. *The Bonds of Womanhood.* New Haven, CT: Yale University Press.

Cotter, David A., Joan M. Hermson, Seth Ovadia, and Reeve Vanneman. 2001. "The Glass Ceiling Effect." *Social Forces* 80 (December): 655–682.

Cowan, R. S. 1976. "Two Washes in the Morning and a Bridge Party at Night: The American Housewife between Wars." *Women's Studies* 3: 147–171.

Crabb, Peter B., and Dawn Bielawski. 1994. "The Social Representation of Material Culture and Gender in Children's Books." *Sex Roles* 30 (January): 69–80.

Craig, Maxine Leeds. 2002. *Ain't I a Beauty Queen? Black Women, Beauty, and the Politics of Race.* New York: Oxford University Press.

Cranford, Cynthia J. 2007. "'It's Time to Leave Machismo Behind!': Challenging Gender Inequality in an Immigrant Union." *Gender & Society* 21 (3): 409–438.

Crawford, Mary. 1995. *Talking Difference: On Gender and Language.* Thousand Oaks, CA: Sage.

Crawford, Mary, and M. MacLeod. 1990. "Gender in the College Classroom: An Assessment of the 'Chilly Climate' for Women." *Sex Roles* 23: 101–122.

Crenshaw, Carrie. 1995. "The 'Protection' of 'Woman': A History of Legal Attitudes toward Women's Workplace Freedom." *Quarterly Journal of Speech* 81 (February): 63–82.

Crenshaw, Kimberle, Neil Gotanda, Garry Peller, Kendall Thomas, and Cornel West. 1996. *Critical Race Theory: The Key Writings That Formed the Movement.* New York: New Press.

Crenshaw, Kimberle Williams. 1991. "Mapping the Margins: Intersectionality, Identity Politics, and Violence against Women of Color." *Stanford Law Review* 43 (6): 1241–1299.

Crisp, Arthur, Philip Sedgwick, Christine Halek, Neil Joughin, and Heather Humphrey. 1999. "Why May Teenage Girls Persist in Smoking?" *Journal of Adolescence* 22 (October): 657–672.

Croteau, James M. 1996. "Research on the Work Experiences of Lesbian, Gay, and Bisexual People: An Integrative Review of Methodology and Findings."

Journal of Vocational Behavior 48 (April): 195–209.

Currie, Dawn. 1997. "Decoding Femininity: Advertisements and Their Teenage Readers." *Gender & Society* 11 (August): 453–477.

D'Emilio, John. 1998. *Sexual Politics, Sexual Communities: The Making of a Homosexual Minority in the United States, 1940–1970.* Chicago: University of Chicago Press.

Dailard, Cynthia. 2003. "'Understanding' Abstinence: Implications for Individuals, Programs, Policies." *The Guttmacher Report* 6. www.agi-usa.org.

Dalla, Rochelle L., Yan Xia, and Heather Kennedy. 2003 "You Just Give Them What They Want and Pray They Don't Kill You." *Violence against Women* 9 (November): 1367–1394.

Dalton, Susan E., and Denise D. Bielby. 2000. "'That's Our Kind of Constellation': Lesbian Mothers Negotiate Institutionalized Understandings of Gender within the Family." *Gender & Society* 14 (February): 36–61.

Daly, Kathleen. 1989. "Rethinking Judicial Paternalism: Gender, Work-Family Relations, and Sentencing," *Gender & Society* 3 (March): 9–36.

Daly, Kathleen. 1994. *Gender, Crime and Punishment.* New Haven, CT: Yale University Press.

Daly, Kathleen, and Michael Tonry. 1977. "Gender, Race, and Sentencing." *Crime and Justice* 22: 201–252.

Daly, Mary. 1978. *Gyn/Ecology: The Meta-Ethics of Radical Feminism.* Boston: Beacon Press.

Daly, Mary. 1979. "After the Death of God the Father: Women's Liberation and the Transformation of Christian Consciousness." Pp. 53–62 in *Womanspirit Rising,* edited by C. P. Christ and J. Plaskow. New York: Harper and Row.

Daniels, Cynthia R., Maureen Paul, and Robert Rosofsky. 1990. "Health, Equity, and Reproductive Risks in the Workplace." *Journal of Public Health Policy* 11 (Winter): 449–462.

Darcy, R., Susan Welch, and Janet Clark. 1994. *Women, Elections, and Representation.* Lincoln: University of Nebraska Press.

Das Gupta, Monica. 1995. "Life Course Perspectives on Women's Autonomy and Health Outcomes." *American Anthropologist* 97 (3): 481–491.

Davidman, Lynn. 1991. *Tradition in a Rootless World: Women Turn to Orthodox Judaism.* Berkeley: University of California Press.

Davis, Angela. 1971. "Reflections on Black Women's Role in the Community of Slaves." *The Black Scholar* 3: 2–15.

Davis, Angela. 1981. *Women, Race and Class.* New York: Random House.

Davis, Keith E., Ann L. Coker, and Maureen Sanderson. 2002. "Physical and Mental Health Effects of Being Stalked for Men and Women." *Violence and Victims* 17 (August): 429–433.

Davis, Shannon N. 2003. "Sex Stereotypes in TV Programs Aimed at the Preschool Audience: An Analysis of Teletubbies and Barney & Friends." *Sociological Spectrum* 23 (October–December): 407–424.

de Tocqueville, Alexis. 1945. *Democracy in America.* New York: Knopf.

Defey, Denise, Eduardo Storch, Silvia Cardozo, Olga Diaz, and Graciela Fernandez. 1996. "The Menopause: Women's Psychology and Health Care." *Social Science and Medicine* 42: 1147–1156.

Delaney, J., M. J. Lupton, and E. Toth. 1988. *The Curse: A Cultural History of Menstruation.* Urbana: University of Illinois Press.

Dellinger, Kirsten, and Christine L. Williams. 1997. "Makeup at Work: Negotiating Appearance Rules in the Workplace." *Gender & Society* 11 (April): 151–177.

Demarest, Jack, and Rita Allen. 2000. "Body Image: Gender, Ethnic, and Age Differences." *Journal of Social Psychology* 140 (August): 465–472.

Dembo, Richard, Kimberly Pacheco, James Schmeidler, Gabrella Ramiresx-Garmica, Julie Guide, and Atiq Rahman. 1998. "A Further Study of Gender Differences in Service Needs among Youths Entering a Juvenile Assessment Center." *Journal of Child and Adolescent Substance Abuse* 7: 49–77.

DeNavas-Walt, Carmen, Bernadette D. Proctor, and Jessica C. Smith. 2009. *Income, Poverty, and Health Insurance Coverage in the United States: 2008.* Washington, DC: U.S. Census Bureau.

Dentinger, Emma, and Marin Clarkberg. 2002. "Informal Caregiving and Retirement Timing among Men and Women: Gender and Caregiving Relationships in Late Midlife." *Journal of Family Issues* 23 (October): 857–879.

DeVault, Marjorie L. 1991. *Feeding the Family: The Social Organization of Caring as Gender Work.* Chicago: University of Chicago Press.

Dewar, Diane M. 2000. "Gender Impacts on Health Insurance Coverage: Findings for Unmarried Full-Time Employees." *Women's Health Issues* 10: 268–277.

Di Santo, Annamaria. 2004. "Witch Healing. The Neo-Pagan Wicca Movement." *Religioni e Societa* 19: 106–110.

Diamond, Milton, and H. K. Sigmundson. 1997. "Sex Reassignment at Birth: Long-Term Review and Clinical Implications." *Archives of Pediatric and Adolescent Medicine* 151 (March): 298–304.

Dickens, W. J., and D. Perlman. 1981. "Friendship over the Life Cycle." Pp. 91–122 in *Personal Relationships, Vol. 2, Developing Personal Relationships,* edited by S. Duck and R. Gilmour. New York: Academic Press.

Dickerman, Charles, Jeff Christensen, and Stella B. Kerl-McClain. 2008. "Big Breasts and Bad Guys: Depictions of Gender and Race in Video Games." *Journal of Creativity in Mental Health* 3 (1): 20–29.

Dickerson-Putnam, Jeannette. 1996. "From Pollution to Empowerment: Women, Age, and Power among the Bena Bena of the Eastern Highlands." *Pacific Studies* 19: 41–70.

Dietz, T. L. 1998. "An Examination of Violence and Gender Role Portrayals in Video Games: Implications for Gender Socialization and Aggressive Behavior." *Sex Roles* 38 (March): 425–442.

Dill, Bonnie Thornton. 1980. "'The Means to Put My Children Through': Childrearing Goals and Strategies among Black Female Domestic Servants." Pp. 107–123 in *The Black Woman*, edited by L. F. Rodgers-Rose. Beverly Hills, CA: Sage.

Dill, Bonnie Thornton. 1983. "Race, Class, and Gender: Prospects for an All Inclusive Sisterhood." *Feminist Studies* 9 (Spring): 131–150.

Dill, Bonnie Thornton. 1988. "Our Mothers' Grief: Racial Ethnic Women and the Maintenance of Families." *Journal of Family History* 13: 415–431.

Dill, Bonnie Thornton. 1994. "Fictive Kin, Paper Sons, and *Compadrazgo.*" Pp. 149–170 in *Women of Color in U.S. Society*, edited by Maxine Baca Zinn and Bonnie Thornton Dill. Philadelphia: Temple University Press.

Dill, Karen E., and Kathryn P. Thill. 2007. "Video Game Characters and the Socialization of Gender Roles: Young People's Perceptions Mirror Sexist Media Depictions." *Sex Roles: A Journal of Research* 57 (11–12): 851–864.

Dines, Gail, and Jean M. Humez. 2002. *Race, Class, and Gender in the Media*, 2nd ed. Thousand Oaks, CA: Sage.

Dobash, R. E., and R. Dobash. 1977. "Love, Honor, and Obey: Institutional Ideologies and the Struggle for Battered Women." *Contemporary Crises* 1: 403–415.

Dobash, R. E., and R. Dobash. 1979. *Violence against Wives*. New York: Free Press.

Dodson, J. E., and C. T. Gilkes. 1986. "Something Within: Social Change and Collective Endurance in the Sacred World of Black Christian Women." Pp. 80–130 in *Women and Religion in America, Volume 3: 1900–1968*, edited by R. Reuther and R. Keller. New York: Harper and Row.

Donegan, J. 1978. *Women and Men Midwives: Medicine, Morality and Misogyny in Early America*. Westport, CT: Greenwood Press.

Donnerstein, Edward, and Daniel Linz. 1986. "Mass Media, Sexual Violence, and Male Viewers: Current Theory and Research." *American Behavioral Scientist* 29: 601–618.

Douglas, A. 1977. *The Feminization of American Culture*. New York: Knopf.

DuBois, Ellen Carol. 1978. *Feminism and Suffrage*. Ithaca, NY: Cornell University Press.

Dudley, Roger L. 1996. "How Seventh-Day Adventists Lay Members View Women Pastors." *Review of Religious Research* 38 (December): 133–141.

Duffy, Mignon. 2007. "Doing the Dirty Work: Gender, Race, and Reproductive Labor in Historical Perspective." *Gender & Society* 21 (3): 313–336.

Dugger, Karen. 1988. "The Social Location of Black and White Women's Attitudes." *Gender & Society* 2 (December): 425–448.

Durbin, Susan. 2002. "Women, Power, and the Glass Ceiling: Current Research Perspectives." *Work, Employment, and Society* 16 (December): 755–759.

Durose, Matthew, Caroline Wolf Harlow, Patrick Langan, Mark Motivans, Ramona R. Rantala, and Erica L. Smith. 2005. *Family Violence Statistics: Including Statistics on Strangers and Acquaintances*. Washington, DC: U.S. Department of Justice Bureau of Justice Statistics.

Durr, Marlese. 2005. "Sex, Drugs, and HIV: Sisters of Laundromat." *Gender & Society* 19 (6): 721–728.

Dworkin, Andrea. 1974. *Woman Hating*. New York: E. P. Dutton.

Dworkin, Shari, and Faye Wachs. 2009. *Body Panic: Gender, Health, and the Selling of Fitness*. New York: New York University Press.

Dye, Nancy Schrom. 1975. "Creating a Feminist Alliance: Sisterhood and Class Conflict in the New York Women's Trade Union League, 1903–1914." *Feminist Studies* 2: 24–38.

Dye, Nancy Schrom. 1980. "History of Childbirth in America." *Signs* 6: 97–108.

Eder, Donna, Catherine Colleen Evans, and Stephen Parker. 1995. *School Talk: Gender and Adolescent Culture*. New Brunswick, NJ: Rutgers University Press.

Edin, Kathryn, and Maria Kefalas. 2005. *Promises I Can Keep: Why Poor Women Put Motherhood*

Before Marriage. Berkeley, CA: University of California Press.

Edin, Kathryn, and Laura Lein. 1997. *Making Ends Meet: How Single Mothers Survive Welfare and Low-Wage Work*. New York: Russell Sage Foundation.

Ehrenreich, Barbara. 1983. *Hearts of Men*. Garden City, NY: Anchor.

Ehrenreich, Barbara. 1987. *Re-Making Love: The Feminization of Sex*. New York: Anchor.

Ehrenreich, Barbara, and Deidre English. 1973. *Complaints and Disorders*. Old Westbury, NY: Feminist Press.

Ehrenreich, Barbara, and Deirdre English.1978. *For Her Own Good*. Garden City, NY: Anchor-Doubleday.

Eisenstein, Zillah, ed. 1979. *Socialist Feminism and the Case for Capitalist Patriarchy*. New York: Monthly Review Press.

Eisenstein, Zillah. 1981. *The Radical Future of Liberal Feminism*. New York: Longmans.

Ellison, Christopher G., and John P. Bartkowski. 2002. "Conservative Protestantism and the Division of Household Labor among Married Couples." *Journal of Family Issues* 23 (November): 950–985.

Emerson, Rana A. 2002. "'Where My Girls At': Negotiating Black Womanhood in Music Videos." *Gender & Society* 16 (February): 115–135.

Emmet, T. 1879. *Principles and Practices of Gynaecology*. Philadelphia: Lea.

Engels, Friedrich. 1884 [1972]. *The Origins of the Family, Private Property and the State*, edited by Eleanor Leacock. New York: International.

Enloe, Cynthia. 1989. *Bananas, Beaches, and Bases: Making Feminist Sense of International Politics*. Berkeley: University of California Press.

Enos, Sandra. 2001. *Mothering from the Inside: Parenting in a Women's Prison*. Albany, NY: State University of New York Press.

Epstein, C. 1993. *Women in Law*. Chicago: University of Chicago Press.

Erzen, Tanya. 2006. *Straight to Jesus: Sexual and Christian Conversions in the Ex-Gay Movement.* Berkeley, CA: University of California Press.

Espiritu, Yen Le. 1997. *Asian American Women and Men.* Thousand Oaks, CA: Sage.

Evans, Lorraine, and Kimberly Davies. 2000. "No Sissy Boys Here: A Content Analysis of the Representation of Masculinity in Elementary School Reading Textbooks." *Sex Roles* 42 (February): 255–270.

Evans, Olga, and Andrew Steptoe. 2002. "The Contribution of Gender-Role Orientation, Work Factors and Home Stressors to Psychological Well-Being and Sickness Absence in Male- and Female-Dominated Occupational Groups." *Social Science and Medicine* 54: 481–492.

Evans, S. 1979. *Personal Politics: The Roots of Women's Liberation in the Civil Rights Movement and the New Left.* New York: Knopf.

Ex, Carine T. G. M., and Jan M. A. M. Janssens. 1998. "Maternal Influences on Daughters' Gender Roles Attitudes." *Sex Roles* 38 (February): 171–186.

Falk, William, David R. Segal, and Mady Wechsler Segal. 2000. "The Impact of Military Presence in Local Labor Markets on the Employment of Women." *Gender & Society* 14 (April): 318–332.

Faludi, Susan. 1991. *Backlash: The Undeclared War on American Women.* New York: Crown.

Fausto-Sterling, Anne. 1992. *Myths of Gender,* 2nd ed. New York: Basic Books.

Fausto-Sterling, Anne. 2000. *Sexing the Body: Gender Politics and the Construction of Sexuality.* New York: Basic Books.

Federal Bureau of Investigation. 2009. *Uniform Crime Reports.* Washington, DC: Federal Bureau of Investigation.

Fee, Elizabeth. 1983. "Woman's Nature and Scientific Objectivity." Pp. 9–28 in *Woman's Nature,* edited by Marion Lowe and Ruth Hubbard. New York: Pergamon Press.

Ferber, Abby L. 2000. *Hate Crime in America: What Do We Know?* Washington, DC: American Sociological Association.

Ferguson, Ann Arnett. 2000. *Bad Boys: Public Schools in the Making*

of Black Masculinity. Ann Arbor: University of Michigan Press.

Fernea, Elizabeth. 2000. "The Challenges for Middle Eastern Women in the 21st Century." *The Middle East Journal* 54 (Spring): 185–189.

Ferraro, Kenneth F. 1996. "Women's Fear of Victimization: Shadow of Sexual Assault?" *Social Forces* 75: 667–690.

Ferree, Myra Marx, and Beth Hess. 1997. *Controversy and Coalition: The New Feminist Movement,* rev. ed. Boston: Twayne Publishers.

Ferro, Christine, Jill Cermele, and Ann Saltzman. 2008. "Current Perceptions of Marital Rape: Some Good and Not-so-Good News." *Journal of Interpersonal Violence* 23 (6): 764–779.

Fetner, Tina. 2001. "Working Anita Bryant: The Impact of Christian Anti-Gay Activism on Lesbian and Gay Movement Claims." *Social Problems* 48 (August): 411–428.

Field, Dorothy. 1999. "Continuity and Change in Friendships in Advanced Old-Age: Findings from the Berkeley Older Generation Study." *International Journal of Aging and Human Development* 48: 325–346.

Fineran, Susan. 2001. "Sexual Minority Students and Peer Sexual Harassment in High School." *Journal of School Social Work* 11 (Spring): 50–69.

Fineran, Susan, and Larry Bennett. 1999. "Gender and Power Issues of Peer Sexual Harassment among Teenagers." *Journal of Interpersonal Violence* 14 (June): 626–641.

Finlay, Barbara. 1996. "Do Men and Women Have Different Goals for Ministry? Evidence from Seminarians." *Sociology of Religion* 57 (Fall): 311–318.

Finlay, Barbara. 1997. "Future Ministers and Legal Abortion: Gender Comparisons among Protestant Seminary Students." *Women and Politics* 17: 1–15.

Finlay, Barbara, and Carol S. Walther. 2003. "The Relation of Religious Affiliation, Service Attendance, and Other Factors to Homophobic Attitudes among University Students." *Review of Religious Research* 44: 370–393.

Firestein, Beth, ed. 1996. *Bisexuality: The Psychology and Politics of an Invisible Minority.* Thousand Oaks, CA: Sage.

Firestone, Juanita M., and Richard J. Harris. 2003. "Perceptions of Effectiveness of Responses to Sexual Harassment in the US Military, 1988 and 1995." *Gender, Work and Organization* 10: 42–64.

Firestone, Juanita M., Richard J. Harris, and Linda C. Lambert. 1998. "Gender Role Ideology and the Gender Based Differences in Earnings" Paper presented at the Annual Meetings of the American Sociological Association, San Francisco.

Fishbein, Allan J., and Patrick Woodall. 2006. *Women are More Likely to Receive Subprime Home Loans: Disparity Highest for Women with Highest Incomes.* Washington, DC: Consumer Federation of America.

Fisher, Bonnie S., Francis T. Cullen, and Michael G. Turner. 2000. *The Sexual Victimization of College Women.* Washington, DC: U.S. Bureau of Justice Statistics.

Fisher, Mary Pat. 2006. *Women in Religion.* New York: Longman.

Flack, William F., et al. 2007. "Risk Factors and Consequences of Unwanted Sex among University Students: Hooking Up, Alcohol, and Stress Response." *Journal of Interpersonal Violence* 22 (February): 139–157.

Flavin, Jeanne. 2001. "Of Punishment and Parenthood: Family-Based Social Control and the Sentencing of Black Drug Offenders." *Gender & Society* 15 (August): 611–633.

Flax, Jane. 1990. "Postmodernism and Gender Relations in Feminist Theory." Pp. 39–62 in *Feminism and Postmodernism,* edited by Linda J. Nicholson. New York: Routledge.

Flexner, Eleanor. 1972. *Mary Wollstonecraft: A Biography.* New York: Coward, McCann, and Geoghegan.

Flexner, Eleanor. 1975. *Century of Struggle: The Woman's Rights Movement in the United States.* Cambridge, MA: Harvard University Press.

Flowers, R. B. 1984. *Religion in Strange Times: The 1960s and*

1970s. Macon, GA: Mercer University Press.

Folbre, Nancy. 2001. *The Invisible Heart: Economics and Family Values*. New York: Free Press.

Foltz, Tanice G. 2000. "Women's Spirituality Research: Doing Feminism." *Sociology of Religion* 61 (Winter): 409–418.

Foner, Nancy. 2005. *In a New Land: A Comparative View of Immigration*. New York: New York University Press.

Forbes, Gordon B., et al. 2006. "Dating Aggression, Sexual Coercion, and Aggression-Supporting Attitudes among College Men as a Function of Participation in Aggressive High School Sports." *Violence against Women* 12: 441–455.

Forsyth, Craig J. 2003. "Pondering the Discourse of Prison Mamas: A Research Note." *Deviant Behavior* 24: 269–280.

Foucault, M. 1965. *Madness and Civilization: A History of Insanity in the Age of Reason*. New York: Vintage.

Fouts, Gregory, and Rebecca Inch. 2005. "Homosexuality in TV Situation Comedies: Characters and Verbal Comments." *Journal of Homosexuality* 49 (1): 35–45.

Fox, Bonnie, and Pamela Sugiman. 1999. "Flexible Work, Flexible Workers: The Restructuring of Clerical Work in a Large Telecommunications Company." *Studies in Political Economy* 60 (Autumn): 39–84.

Fox, Jesse, and Jeremy N. Bailenson. 2009. "Virtual Virgins and Vamps: The Effects of Exposure to Female Characters' Sexualized Appearance and Gaze in an Immersive Virtual Environment." *Sex Roles: A Journal of Research* 61 (3–4): 147–157.

Fox, Mary Frank. 2001. "Women, Science, and Academia: Graduate Education and Careers." *Gender & Society* 15 (October): 654–666.

Fraser, Nancy. 1989. *Unruly Practices: Power, Discourse, and Gender in Contemporary Social Theory*. Minneapolis: University of Minnesota Press.

Fraser, Nancy, and Nancy A. Naples. 2004. "To Interpret the World and to Change It: An Interview with Nancy Fraser." *Signs* 29 (Summer): 1103–1124.

Frazier, E. Franklin. 1948. *The Negro Family in the United States*. New York: Citadel Press.

Frazier, E. Franklin. 1964. *The Negro Church in America*. New York: Schocken.

Freedman, Estelle B., and John D'Emilio. 1988. *Intimate Matters: A History of Sexuality in America*. New York: Harper and Row.

Freedman, Estelle B., and Barrie Thorne. 1984. "Introduction to 'The Feminist Sexuality Debates.'" *Signs* 10 (Autumn): 102–105.

Freeman, Jo. 1973. "The Origins of the Women's Liberation Movement." *American Journal of Sociology* 78: 792–811.

Freund, Kurt, and Robin J. Watson. 1992. "The Proportions of Heterosexual and Homosexual Pedophiles among Sex Offenders against Children: An Exploratory Study." *Journal of Sex and Marital Therapy* 18 (Spring): 34–43.

Friedl, E. 1975. *Women and Men*. New York: Holt, Rinehart and Winston.

Frieze, I. H. 1983. "Investigating the Causes and Consequences of Marital Rape." *Signs* 8 (Spring): 532–553.

Frohmann, Lisa. 1991. "Discrediting Victims' Allegations of Sexual Assault: Prosecutorial Accounts of Case Rejections." *Social Problems* 38 (May): 213–226.

Frost, Natasha A., Judith Greene, and Kevin Pranis. 2006. *Hard Hit: The Growth in the Imprisonment of Women, 1977–2004*. New York: Women's Prison Association.

Frye, Marilyn. 1983. *The Politics of Reality*. Trumansburg, NY: Crossing Press.

Fullerton, Jami A., and Alice Kendrick. 2000. "Portrayals of Men and Women in U.S. Spanish-Language Television." *Journalism and Mass Communication Quarterly* 77 (Spring): 128–142.

Furnham, A., and L. Gasson. 1998. "Sex Differences in Parental Estimates of Their Children's Intelligence." *Sex Roles* 38 (January): 151–162.

Furnham, Adrian, and Twiggy Mak. 1999. "Sex Role Stereotyping in Television Commercials: A Review and Comparison of Fourteen Studies Done on Five Continents over 25 Years." *Sex Roles* 41 (September): 413–437.

Gager, Constance T., Teresa M. Cooney, and Kathleen T. Call. 1999. "The Effects of Family Characteristics and Time Use on Teenagers' Household Labor." *Journal of Marriage and the Family* 61 (4): 982–994.

Gagne, Patricia, and Richard Tewksbury. 1998. "Conformity Pressures and Gender Resistance among Transgendered Individuals." *Social Problems* 45 (February): 81–101.

Gagnon, John. 1995. *Conceiving Sexuality: Approaches to Sex Research in a Postmodern World*. New York: Routledge.

Gailey, Jeannine A., and Ariane Prohaska. 2006. "'Knocking off a Fat Girl:' An Exploration of Hogging, Male Sexuality, and Neutralizations." *Deviant Behavior* 27: 31–49.

Gallagher, Sally. 2003. *Evangelical Identity and Family Life*. Piscataway, NJ: Rutgers University Press.

Gallagher, Sally. 2004. "Where Are the Antifeminist Evangelicals? Evangelical Identity, Subcultural Location, and Attitudes toward Feminism." *Gender & Society* 18 (August): 451–472.

Gallagher, Sally, and Christian Smith. 1999. "Symbolic Traditionalism and Pragmatic Egalitarianism: Contemporary Evangelicals, Families, and Gender." *Gender & Society* 13 (April): 211–233.

Gallup, George H., Jr. 2003, June 24. "Current Views on Premarital, Extramarital Sex." *The Gallup Poll*. www.gallup.com.

Gallup Poll. 2004, October. "Abortion." *The Gallup Poll*. Princeton, NJ: Gallup Organization.

Gallup Poll. 2005, June. "Military and National Defense." *The Gallup Poll*. Princeton, NJ: Gallup Organization.

Gallup Poll. 2007. "Religion." Princeton, NJ: Gallup Organization. www.gallup.com.

Gallup Poll. 2009. "Military and National Defense." www.gallup.com.

Gamson, Joshua. 1995. "Must Identity Movements Self-Destruct? A Queer Dilemma." *Social Problems* 42 (August): 390–407.

Gamson, Joshua. 1998. "Publicity Traps: Television Talk Shows and Lesbian, Gay, Bisexual, and Transgender Visibility." *Sexualities* 1 (February): 11–42.

Garcia-López, Gladys. 2008. "'Nunca Te Toman En Cuenta: They Never Take You into Account': The Challenges of Inclusion and Strategies for Success of Chicana Attorneys." *Gender & Society* 22 (5): 590–612.

General Social Survey. 2004. Chicago: National Opinion Research Center.

Genovese, Eugene. 1972. *Roll, Jordan, Roll.* New York: Pantheon.

Gerbner, George. 1978. "The Dynamics of Cultural Resistance." Pp. 46–50 in *Hearth and Home: Images of Women in the Media,* edited by Gaye Tuchman, Arlene Kaplan Daniels, and James Benét. New York: Oxford University Press.

Gerschick, Thomas J., and Adam Stephen Miller. 1994. "Gender Identities at the Crossroads of Masculinity and Physical Disability." *Masculinities* 2 (Spring): 34–55.

Gerson, Kathleen. 2002. "Moral Dilemmas, Moral Strategies and the Transformation of Gender: Lessons from Two Generations of Work and Family Change." *Gender & Society* 16 (February): 8–28.

Gerstel, Naomi, and Dan Clawson. 2001. "Unions' Responses to Family Concerns." *Social Problems* 48 (May): 277–297.

Gerstel, Naomi, and Sally K. Gallagher. 2001. "Men's Caregiving: Gender and the Contingent Character of Care." *Gender & Society* 15 (April): 197–217.

Giannarelli, Linda, and James Barsomantov. 2000. *Child Care Expenses of America's Families.* Washington, DC: The Urban Institute.

Gibson, Diane. 1996. "Broken Down by Age and Gender: 'The Problem of Old Women' Revisited." *Gender & Society* 10 (August): 443–448.

Giddens, Anthony. 1971. *Capitalism and Modern Social Theory: An Analysis of the Writings of Marx, Durkheim, and Max Weber.* Cambridge: Cambridge University Press.

Gilkes, Cheryl Townsend. 1980. "'Holding Back the Ocean with a Broom:' Black Women and Community Work." Pp. 217–232 in *The Black Woman,* edited by L. F. Rodgers-Rose. Beverly Hills: Sage.

Gilkes, Cheryl Townsend. 1985. "Together and in Harness: Women's Traditions in the Sanctified Church." *Signs* 10 (Summer): 678–699.

Gilkes, Cheryl Townsend. 2000. *"If It Wasn't for the Women . . .":* *Black Women's Experience and Womanist Culture in Church and Community.* Mary Knoll, NY: Orbis Books.

Gilligan, Carol. 1982. *In a Different Voice.* Cambridge, MA: Harvard University Press.

Gimlin, Debra. 2002. *Body Work: Beauty and Self-Image in American Culture.* Berkeley: University of California Press.

Gitlin, Todd. 2001. *Media Unlimited: How the Torrent of Images and Sounds Overwhelms Our Lives.* New York: Metropolitan Books.

Glass, Jennifer, and Tetushi Fujimoto. 1994. "Housework, Paid Work, and Depression among Husbands and Wives." *Journal of Health and Social Behavior* 35 (June): 179–191.

Glass Ceiling Commission. 1995. *Good for Business: Making Full Use of the Nation's Capital.* Washington, DC: U.S. Government Printing Office.

Glenn, Evelyn Nakano. 1986. *Issei, Nisei, War Bride: Three Generations of Japanese-American Women in Domestic Service.* Philadelphia: Temple University Press.

Glenn, Evelyn Nakano. 2009. *Shades of Difference: Why Skin Color Matters.* Palo Alto, CA: Stanford University Press.

Glenn, Evelyn Nakano, Grace Chang, and Linda Rennie Forcey, eds. 1993. *Mothering: Ideology, Experience, and Agency.* New York: Routledge.

Gluckman, Amy, and Betsy Reed. 1997. *Homo Economics: Capitalism, Community, and Lesbian and Gay Life.* New York: Routledge.

Goodkind, Sara, Irene Ng, and Rosemary C. Sarri. 2006. "The Impact of Sexual Abuse in the Lives of Young Women Involved or At-risk of Involvement with the Juvenile Justice System." *Violence Against Women* 12, 5: 456–477.

Gordon, L. 1977. *Woman's Body/Woman's Right.* New York: Penguin.

Gordy, Laurie K. 2002. "Distorted Progress: Images of Women in Sports Magazines." Paper presented at the annual meetings of the Southern Sociological Society.

Gorman, Elizabeth H., and Julie A. Kmec. 2007. "We (Have to) Try Harder: Gender and Required Work Effort in Britain and the United States." *Gender & Society* 21 (December): 828–856.

Gornick, V. 1971. "Woman as Outsider." Pp. 126–144 in *Woman in Sexist Society,* edited by V. Gornick and B. Moran. New York: Basic Books.

Gossett, Jennifer Lynn, and Sarah Byrne. 2002. "'Click Here': A Content Analysis of Internet Rape Sites." *Gender & Society* 16 (October): 689–709.

Gough, Kathleen. 1975. "The Origin of the Family." Pp. 51–76 in *Toward an Anthropology of Women,* edited by Rayna Reiter. New York: Monthly Review Press.

Grauerholz, Elizabeth. and A. King. 1997. "Primetime Sexual Harassment." *Violence against Women* 3: 129–148.

Gray, John. 1994. *Men Are from Mars, Women Are from Venus.* New York: HarperCollins.

Green, Gary P., and Christopher Mayhew. 2003. "Hiring Welfare Recipients: Employer Practices and Experiences." *Journal of Poverty* 7 (4): 37–51.

Greene, B. 1994. "Ethnic-Minority Lesbians and Gay Men: Mental Health and Treatment Issues." *Journal of Counseling and Clinical Psychology* 62: 243–251.

Greene, Maxine. 1978. *Landscapes of Learning.* New York: Teachers College Press.

Greer, Kimberly R. 2000. "The Changing Nature of Interpersonal Relationships in a Women's Prison." *Prison Journal* 80: 442–468.

Gregoire, Thomas K., Keith Kilty, and Virginia Richardson. 2002. "Gender and Racial Inequities in

Retirement Resources." *Journal of Women & Aging* 14: 25–39.

Greif, Geoffrey L. 1985. "Children and Housework in the Single Father Family." *Family Relations* 34 (July): 353–357.

Grella, Christine E. 1990. "Irreconcilable Differences: Women Defining Class After Divorce and Downward Mobility." *Gender & Society* 4 (March): 41–55.

Griffin, Joan M., et al. 2002. "The Importance of Low Control at Work and Home on Depression and Anxiety: Do these Effects Vary by Gender and Social Class?" *Social Science and Medicine* 54 (March): 783–798.

Grindstaff, Laura. 2002. *The Money Shot: Trash, Class, and the Making of TV Talk Shows.* Chicago: University of Chicago Press.

Groves, Melissa M., and Diane M. Horm-Wingerd. 1991. "Commuter Marriages: Personal, Family, and Career Issues." *Sociology and Social Research* 75 (July): 212–217.

Gupta, Sanjiv. 1999. "The Effects of Transitions in Marital Status on Men's Performance of Housework." *Journal of Marriage and the Family* 61 (3): 700–711.

Gutman, Herbert. 1976. *The Black Family in Slavery and Freedom.* New York: Vintage.

Guttmacher Institute. 2008. *Facts on Contraceptive Use.* www. guttmacher.org.

Haag, Pamela. 1999. *Voices of a Generation: Teenage Girls on Sex, School, and Self.* Washington, DC: American Association of Women Educational Foundation.

Hager, Mark A. 1996. "Education Level, Liberal Attitudes, and Sexual Behavior: A Reinterpretation." *Alberta Journal of Educational Research* 42 (December): 400–405.

Hall, Elaine J., and Marnie Salupo Rodriguez. 2003. "The Myth of Postfeminism." *Gender & Society* 17 (December): 878–902.

Hall, J A. 1998. "How Big Are Nonverbal Sex Differences? The Case of Smiling and Sensitivity to Nonverbal Cues." Pp. 155–177 in *Sex Differences and Similarities in Communication: Critical Essays and Empirical Investigations of Sex and Gender in Interaction,* edited

by D. J. Canary & K. Dindia LaFrance. Mahwah, NJ: Erlbaum.

Hamer, Dean H., Stella Hu, Victoria L. Magnuson, Nan Hu, and Angela M. L. Pattatucci. 1993. "A Linkage between DNA Markers on the X Chromosome and Male Sexual Identification." *Science* 261 (July): 321–327.

Hamer, Jennifer. 2001. *What It Means to Be Daddy.* New York: Columbia University Press.

Hamilton, Brady E., Joyce A. Martin, and Stephanie Ventura. 2009, March 18. "Births: Preliminary Data for 2007." *National Vital Statistics Report* 57. Hyattsville, MD.

Hamilton, Mykol C. 1988. "Using Masculine Generics: Does Using He Increase Male Bias in the User's Imagery?" *Sex Roles* 19 (December): 785–799.

Haninger, K., and K. M. Thompson. 2004. "Content and Ratings of Teen Rated Video Games." *Journal of the American Medical Association* 291: 856–865.

Hans, Valerie P., and Neil Vidmar. 1986. *Judging the Jury.* New York: Plenum Press.

Hanson, Sandra L., and Rebecca S. Kraus. 1998. "Women, Sports, and Science: Do Female Athletes Have an Advantage?" *Sociology of Education* 71 (April): 93–110.

Harding, Sandra. 1986. *The Science Question in Feminism.* Ithaca, NY: Cornell University Press.

Harding, Sandra. 1991. *Whose Science? Whose Knowledge?: Thinking from Women's Lives.* Ithaca, NY: Cornell University Press.

Harding, Sandra. 1993. *The Racial Economy of Science.* Bloomington: Indiana University Press.

Harding, Sandra. 1998. *Is Science Multicultural? Postcolonialisms, Feminisms, and Epistemologies.* Bloomington, IN: Indiana University Press.

Hargrove, B., J. M. Schmidt, and S. G. Davaney. 1985. "Religion and the Changing Role of Women." *Annals of the American Academy of Political and Social Science* 480 (July): 117–131.

Harland, M. 1889. *House and Home: The Complete Housewives' Guide.* Philadelphia: Clawson.

Harrell, Margaret C. 2001. "Army Officers' Spouses: Have the

White Gloves Been Mothballed?" *Armed Forces & Society* 28: 55–75.

Harris, R. J., and J. M. Firestone. 1998. "Changes in Predictors of Gender Role Ideologies among Women: A Multivariate Analysis." *Sex Roles* 38 (February): 239–252.

Harrison, J. 1978. "Men's Roles and Men's Lives." *Signs* 4 (Winter): 324–336.

Hart, K., and M. E. Kenny. 1997. "Adherence to the Super Woman Ideal and Eating Disorder Symptoms among College Women." *Sex Roles* 36 (April): 461–478.

Hartmann, Heidi. 1976. "Capitalism, Patriarchy, and Job Segregation by Sex." *Signs* 1: (Spring): 137–169.

Hartmann, Heidi. 1981. "The Family as the Locus of Gender, Class, and Political Struggle: The Example of Housework." *Signs* 6 (Spring): 366–394.

Hartmann, Heidi, and Ashley English. 2009. "Older Women's Retirement Security: A Primer." *Journal of Women, Politics, and Policy* 30 (2) (April–September):109–140.

Hartmann, Heidi, and Sunhwa Lee. 2003 (April). *Social Security: The Largest Source of Income for Both Women and Men in Retirement.* Washington, DC: Institute for Women's Policy Research. www. iwpr.org

Harvey, William B. 2003. *Minorities in Higher Education, 2002–2003.* Washington, DC: American Council on Education.

Hashemi, Mahasti. 2007. "Immigrants and Exiles: Iranian Women in the United States." *Dissertation Abstracts International, A: The Humanities and Social Sciences* 67 (11): 43–47.

Hatch, Laurie R. 2005. "Gender and Ageism." *Generations* 29 (3): 19–24.

Haugaard, Jeffrey J., and Lisa G. Seri. 2003. "Stalking and Other Forms of Intrusive Contact after the Dissolution of Adolescent Dating or Romantic Relationships." *Violence and Victims* 18: 279–297.

Hawkins, R. A., and R. E. Oakey. 1974. "Estimation of Oestrone Sulphate, Oestradiol-17B and Oestrone in Peripheral Plasma: Concentrations during the Menstrual Cycle and in Men." *Journal of Endocrinology* 60: 3–17.

Hays, Sharon. 2003. *Flat Broke with Children: Women in the Age of Welfare Reform.* New York: Oxford University Press.

Hecht, Marvin A., and Marianne LaFrance. 1998. "License or Obligation to Smile: The Effect of Power and Sex on Amount and Type of Smiling." *Personality and Social Psychology Bulletin* 24 (12): 1332–1342.

Heimer, Karen, and Stacey DeCoster. 1999. "The Gendering of Violent Delinquency." *Criminology* 37 (May): 277–318.

Heitfield, Heather, and Rita J. Simon. 2002. "Women in Prison: A Comparative Assessment." *Gender Issues* 20: 53–75.

Helwig, A. A. 1998. "Gender-Role Stereotyping: Testing Theory with a Longitudinal Sample." *Sex Roles* 38 (March): 403–423.

Henderson, Dorothy J., Carol Boyd, and Thomas Mieczkowski. 1994. "Gender, Relationships and Crack Cocaine: A Content Analysis." *Research in Nursing and Health* 17 (August): 265–272.

Hensley, Christopher, Tammy Castle, and Richard Tewksbury. 2003. "Inmate-to-Inmate Sexual Coercion in a Prison for Women." *Journal of Offender Rehabilitation* 37: 77–87.

Hequembourg, Amy L., and Michael P. Farrell. 1999. "Lesbian Motherhood: Negotiating Marginal-Mainstream Identities." *Gender & Society* 13: 540–557.

Herd, Pamela. 2009. "Women, Public Pensions, and Poverty: What Can the United States Learn from Other Countries?" *Journal of Women, Politics & Policy* 30 (2–3): 301–334.

Herek, Gregory M., and Milagritos Gonzalez-Rivera. 2006. "Attitudes toward Homosexuality among U.S. Residents of Mexican Descent." *Journal of Sex Research* 43 (May): 122–135.

Herman, Judith. 1981. *Father-Daughter Incest.* Cambridge, MA: Harvard University Press.

Herman, Judith, and Hirschman, L. 1977. "Father-Daughter Incest." *Signs* 2 (Summer): 735–756.

Hernández, Daisy, S. Bushra Rehman, and Cherrie Moraga. 2002. *Colonize This! Young Women of Color on Today's Feminism.* New York: Seal Press.

Hernández, Jeanne. 1995. "The Concurrence of Eating Disorders with Histories of Child Abuse among Adolescents." *Journal of Child Sexual Abuse* 4: 73–85.

Herring, Cedric, Verna Keith, and Heyward Derrick Horton. 2003. *Skin Deep: How Race and Complexion Matter in the "Color-Blind" Era.* Champaign-Urbana: University of Illinois Press.

Hertz, Rosanna. 2006. *Single by Chance, Mothers by Choice: How Women are Choosing Parenthood without Marriage and Creating the New American Family.* New York: Oxford University Press.

Hesse-Biber, Sharlene. 2006. *The Cult of Thinness.* New York: Oxford University Press.

Heyer-Gray, Zoey A. 2000. "Gender and Religious Work." *Sociology of Religion* 61 (Winter): 467–471.

Higginbotham, Elizabeth. 2001. *Too Much to Ask: Black Women in the Era of Integration.* Chapel Hill, NC: University of North Carolina Press.

Higginbotham, Elizabeth. 2009. "Entering a Profession: Race, Gender and Class in the Work Lives of Black Women Attorneys." Pp. 22–49 in *Emerging Intersections: Race, Class, and Gender in Theory, Policy and Practice,* edited by Bonnie Thornton Dill and Ruth Zambrana. New Brunswick, NJ: Rutgers University Press.

Higham, J. 1965. *Strangers in the Land.* New York: Atheneum.

Hill, A. C. 1979. "Protection of Women Workers and the Courts: A Legal Case History." *Feminist Studies* 5 (Summer): 247–273.

Hill, Michael, and Susan Hoecker-Drysdale. 2002. *Harriet Martineau: Theoretical and Methodological Perspectives.* New York: Routledge.

Hill, Shirley A. 2009. "Cultural Images and the Health of African American Women." *Gender & Society* 23 (December): 733–746.

Hill, Shirley A., and Joey Sprague. 1999. "Parenting in Black and White Families: The Interaction of Gender with Race and Class." *Gender & Society* 13 (August): 480–502.

Hipple, Jay. 2001. "Contingent Work in the Late-1990s."

Monthly Labor Review 124 (March): 3–27.

Hochschild, Arlie Russell. 1983. *The Managed Heart: Commercialization of Human Feeling.* Berkeley: University of California Press.

Hochschild, Arlie Russell. 1989. *The Second Shift: Working Parents and the Revolution at Home.* New York: Viking.

Hochschild, Arlie Russell. 1997. *The Time Bind: When Home Becomes Work and Work Becomes Home.* New York: Metropolitan Books.

Hoffman, Thomas. 1997. "Women in Church Leadership: An Analysis of Religious Beliefs." *Free Inquiry in Creative Sociology* 25 (November): 137–143.

Hoffnung, Michele. 2004. "Wanting It All: Career, Marriage, and Motherhood among College-Educated Women's 20s." *Sex Roles* 50 (May): 711–723.

Holden, Karen C., and Angela Fontes. 2009. "Economic Security in Retirement: How Changes in Employment and Marriage have Altered Retirement-Related Economic Risks for Women." *Journal of Women, Politics & Policy* 30 (2–3): 173–197.

Hole, J., and Levine, E., eds. 1971. *Rebirth of Feminism.* New York: Quadrangle Books.

Holsinger, Kristi. 2000. "Feminist Perspectives on Female Offending: Examining Real Girls' Lives." *Women and Criminal Justice* 12: 23–51.

Hondagneu-Sotelo, Pierrette. 1992. "Overcoming Patriarchal Constraints: The Reconstruction of Gender Relations among Mexican Immigrant Women and Men." *Gender & Society* 6 (September): 393–415.

Hondagneu-Sotelo, Pierrette. 1994. *Gendered Transitions: The Mexican Experience of Immigration.* Berkeley: University of California Press.

Hondagneu-Sotelo, Pierrette. 1997. "'I'm Here, but I'm There': The Meanings of Latina Transnational Motherhood." *Gender & Society* 11 (October): 548–571.

Hondagneu-Sotelo, Pierrette. 2001. *Doméstica: Immigrant Workers Cleaning and Caring in the Shadows of Affluence.* Berkeley: University of California Press.

Horowitz, Ruth. 1995. *Teen Mothers: Citizens or Dependents?* Chicago: University of Chicago Press.

Horton, Richard. 1995. "Is Homosexuality Inherited?" *New York Review of Books* 42 (July 13): 36–41.

Hosken, F. P. 1979. *The Hosken Report: Genital and Sexual Mutilation of Females.* Lexington, MA: Women's International Network News.

Hoyenga, K. B., and K. Hoyenga. 1979. *The Question of Sex Differences: Psychological, Cultural, and Biological Issues.* Boston: Little, Brown.

Hubbard, Ruth. 1984. "Feminist Science: A Meaningful Concept?" Paper presented at the Annual Meetings of the National Women's Studies Association, New Brunswick, NJ.

Hughes, H. S. 1958. *Consciousness and Society.* New York: Knopf.

Hull, Kathleen E. 1999. "The Paradox of the Contented Female Lawyer." *Law and Society Review* 33 (October): 687–702.

Hunt, Larry L. 2001. "Religion, Gender, and the Hispanic Experience in the United States: Catholic/Protestant Differences in Religious Involvement, Social Status, and Gender-Role Attitudes." *Review of Religious Research* 43: 139–160.

Hvas, Lotte. 2006. "Menopausal Women's Positive Experiences of Growing Older." *Maturitas* 54 (June): 245–251.

Hysock, Dana Ann. 2006. "Fun between Friends? How Peer Culture Influences Adolescents' Interpretations of and Responses to Peer Sexual Harassment in High School." *Dissertation Abstracts International, A: The Humanities and Social Sciences,* 67 (6): 259.

Illich, I. 1977. *Disabling Professions.* Salem, NH: Boyars.

Ingram-Fogel, Catherine. 1991. "Health Problems and Needs of Incarcerated Women." *Journal of Prison and Jail Health* 10 (Summer): 43–57.

Ingram-Fogel, Catherine. 1993. "Hard Time: The Stressful Nature of Incarceration for Women." *Issues in Mental Health Nursing* 14 (October–December): 367–377.

Institute for Women's Policy Research. 2001. *Working First but Working Poor: The Need for Education and Training Following Welfare Reform.* Washington, DC: Institute for Women's Policy Research.

Irvine, Janice M. 2002. *Talk about Sex: The Battles over Sex Education in the U.S.* Berkeley, CA: University of California Press.

Irvine, Janice M. 2006. "Selling Viagra." *Contexts* 5 (2): 39–44.

Jackson, Nicky-Ali. 1996. "Observational Experiences of Intrapersonal Conflict and Teenage Victimization: A Comparative Study among Spouses and Cohabitors." *Journal of Family Violence* 11 (September): 191–203.

Jacobs, Janet L. 1994. "The Effects of Ritual Healing on Female Victims of Abuse: A Study of Empowerment and Transformation." Pp. 127–142 in *Gender and Religion,* edited by William H. Swatos Jr. New Brunswick, NJ: Transaction Publishers.

Janus, Samuel S., and Cynthia L. Janus. 1993. *The Janus Report on Sexual Behavior.* New York: Wiley and Sons.

Jefferson, Therese. 2009. "Women and Retirement Pensions: A Research Review." *Feminist Economics* 15 (4): 115–145.

Jelen, Ted G. 1989. "Gender Role Stereotypes and Attitudes toward Female Ordination." *Social Science Quarterly* 7 (September): 579–585.

Jenness, Valerie, and Kendal Broad. 1997. *Hate Crimes: New Social Movements and the Politics of Violence.* New York: Aldine.

Jenness, Valerie, and Ryken Grattet. 2001. *Making Hate a Crime: From Social Movement to Law Enforcement.* New York: Russell Sage.

Jones, Jacqueline. 1985. *Labor of Love, Labor of Sorrow: Black Women, Work, and the Family from Slavery to the Present.* New York: Basic Books.

Jones, Jeffrey M. 2005, October. "Nearly Half of Americans Think U.S. Will Soon Have a Woman President." *The Gallup Poll.* Princeton, NJ: Gallup Organization.

Jones, Jeffrey M., and David W. Moore. 2003. "Generational Differences in Support for a Woman President." *The Gallup Poll.* Princeton, NJ: Gallup Organization.

Jones, Nikki. 2008. "Working 'the Code': On Girls, Gender, and Inner-city Violence." Special Issue: Current Approaches to Understanding Female Offending. *The Australian and New Zealand Journal of Criminology* 41, 1: 63–83.

Jones-DeWeever, Avis. 2008. "Losing Ground: Women and the Foreclosure Crisis." *Journal of the National Council of Jewish Women.* www.ncjw.org.

Jordan, Winthrop. 1968. *White over Black.* Baltimore: Penguin.

Jurik, Nancy C., and Cynthia Siemsen. 2009. "'Doing Gender' as Canon or Agenda: A Symposium on West and Zimmerman." *Gender & Society* 23: 72–75.

Kahane, Leo H. 2000. "Anti-Abortion Activities and the Market for Abortion Services." *American Journal of Economics and Sociology* 59 (July): 463–485.

Kalmijn, Matthijs. 1999. "Father Involvement in Childrearing and the Perceived Stability of Marriage." *Journal of Marriage and the Family* 61 (May): 409–421.

Kalof, Linda. 1999. "The Effects of Gender and Music Video Imagery on Sexual Attitudes." *Journal of Social Psychology* 139 (June): 378–385.

Kamin, L. J. 1986. "Is Crime in the Genes?" *Scientific American* 254 (February): 22–27.

Kamo, Yoshinori. 2000. "'He Said, She Said': Assessing Discrepancies in Husbands' and Wives' Reports on the Division of Household Labor." *Social Science Research* 29 (4): 459–476.

Kane, Emily W. 2000. "Racial and Ethnic Variations in Gender-Related Attitudes." *Annual Review of Sociology* 26: 419–439.

Kanter, Rosabeth Moss. 1977. *Men and Women of the Corporation.* New York: Basic Books.

Kantor, Glenda Kaufman, and Jana L. Jasinksi. 1998. "Dynamics and Risk Factors in Partner Violence." Pp. 1–43 in *Partner Violence: A Comprehensive Review of 20 Years of Research,* edited by Jana L. Jasinkski and Linda M. Williams. Thousand Oaks, CA: Sage.

Kaplan, Elaine Bell. 1997. *Not Our Kind of Girl: Unraveling the Myths of Black Teenage Motherhood.* Berkeley: University of California Press.

Kapp, Yvonne. 1972. *Eleanor Marx, Volume One.* New York: Pantheon.

Karim, Jamillah. 2008. *American Muslim Women: Negotiating Race, Class, and Gender within the Ummah.* New York: New York University Press.

Katzman, David. 1978. *Seven Days a Week: Women and Domestic Service in Industrializing America.* New York: Oxford University Press.

Kaufman, Gayle. 1999. "The Portrayal of Men's Family Roles in Television Commercials." *Sex Roles* 41 (September): 439–458.

Kearney, Margaret H., Sheigla Murphy, and Marsha Rosenbaum. 1994. "Mothering on Crack Cocaine: A Grounded Theory Analysis." *Social Science and Medicine* 38 (January): 351–361.

Keller, Evelyn Fox. 1985. *Reflections on Gender and Science.* New Haven, CT: Yale University Press.

Kelly, J., and J. L. Smith. 2006. "Where the Girls Aren't: Gender Disparity Saturates G-Rated Films." Research Brief: www.thriveoncreative.com.

Kelly-Gadol, J. 1976. "The Social Relations of the Sexes: Methodological Implications of Women's History." *Signs* 1 (Summer): 809–824.

Kemp, Alice Abel, and Pamela Jenkins. 1992. "Gender and Technological Hazards: Women at Risk in Hospital Settings." *Industrial Crisis Quarterly* 6: 137–152.

Kennedy, Edward M. 2008, April. *Taking a Toll: The Effects of the Economic Recession on Women.* Washington, DC: U.S. Senate Committee on Health, Education, Labor, and Pensions.

Kennelly, Ivy. 1999. "'That Single-Mother Element': How White Employers Typify Black Women." *Gender & Society* 13 (April): 168–192.

Kessler-Harris, Alice. 1982. *Out to Work: A History of Wage-Earning Women in the U.S.* New York: Oxford University Press.

Khalid, Ruhi, and Irene H. Frieze. 2004. "Measuring Perceptions of Gender Roles: The IAWS for Pakistanis and U.S. Immigrant Populations." *Sex Roles* 51 (5–6): 293–300.

Khanna, Nikki D., Cherise Harris, and Rana Cullers. 1999. "Attitudes toward Interracial Dating." Paper presented at the Annual Meetings of the Society for the Study of Social Problems, Washington, DC.

Kibria, Nazli. 1994. "Household Structure and Family Ideologies: The Dynamics of Immigrant Economic Adaptation among Vietnamese Refugees." *Social Problems* 41 (February): 81–96.

Kiefer, Heather Mason. 2004. "Empty Seats: Fewer Families Eat Together." Princeton, NJ: The Gallup Poll.

Kilbourne, Jean. 1999. *Can't Buy My Love: How Advertising Changes the Way We Think and Feel.* New York: Touchstone.

Kimmel, Michael S. 2000. "Saving the Males: The Sociological Implications of the Virginia Military Institute and the Citadel." *Gender & Society* 14 (August): 494–516.

Kimmel, Michael S. 2001. "Masculinity as Homophobia: Fear, Shame, and Silence in the Construction of Gender Identity." Pp. 226–287 in *The Masculinities Reader,* edited by Stephen M. Whitehead and Frank J. Barrett. Cambridge: Polity.

Kimmel, Michael S. 1996. *Manhood in America: A Cultural History.* New York: Free Press.

Kimmel, Michael, and Annulla Landers. 1996. "Does Censorship Make a Difference? An Aggregate Empirical Analysis of Pornography and Rape." *Journal of Psychology and Human Sexuality* 8: 1–20.

Kimmel, Michael S., and Michael A. Messner, eds. 2009. *Men's Lives,* 8th ed. Boston: Allyn and Bacon.

King, Jacqueline E. 2000. *Gender Equity in Higher Education: Are Male Students at a Disadvantage?* Washington, DC: American Council on Education.

Kirschenman, Joleen, and Kathryn M. Neckerman. 1999. "'We'd Love to Hire Them, But . . . ' The Meaning of Race for Employers." Pp. 152–161 in *Race and Ethnic Conflict: Contending Views on Prejudice, Discrimination, and Ethnoviolence,* edited by Fred L. Pincus and Howard J. Ehrlich. Boulder, CO: Westview.

Kirton, Gill. 1999. "Sustaining and Developing Women's Trade Union Activism: A Gendered Project." *Gender, Work, and Organization* 6 (October): 213–223.

Kitzinger, Celia A., and Sue Wilkinson. 1994. "Virgins and Queers: Rehabilitating Heterosexuality?" *Gender & Society* 8 (September): 444–462.

Klatch, Rebecca. 1988. "Coalition and Conflict among Women of the New Right." *Signs* 13 (Summer): 671–694.

Klein, D. 1980. "The Etiology of Female Crime: A Review of the Literature." Pp. 70–105 in *Women, Crime, and Justice,* edited by Susan K. Datesman and Frank R. Scarpitti. New York: Oxford University Press.

Kleinbaum, A. R. 1977. "Women in the Age of Light." Pp. 217–235 in *Becoming Visible: Women in European History,* edited by R. Bridenthal and C. Koonz. Boston: Houghton-Mifflin.

Klinger, Lori J., James A. Hamilton, and Peggy J. Cantrell. 2001. "Children's Perceptions of Aggression and Gender-Specific Content in Toy Commercials." *Social Behavior and Personality* 29: 11–20.

Kluckhohn, C. 1962. *Culture and Behavior.* New York: Free Press.

Kohlberg, Lawrence. 1966. "A Cognitive Developmental Analysis of Children's Sex Role Concepts and Attitudes." Pp. 82–166 in *The Development of Sex Differences,* edited by Eleanor Maccoby. Stanford, CA: Stanford University Press.

Koons-Witt, Barbara A. 2002. "The Effect of Gender on the Decision to Incarcerate before and after the Introduction of Sentencing Guidelines." *Criminology* 40: 297–327.

Korenman, Sanders. 2002. "The Low-Wage Labor Market and Welfare Reform." Pp. 204–210 in *Laboring Below the Line,* edited by Frank Munger. New York: Russell Sage Foundation.

Kornblum, J. 2005. "Adults Question MySpace's Safety." *USA Today,* January 12, www.usatoday.com.

Koss, Mary P., Rosemary Gartner, and Amy Miller. 2000. "Doing Her Own Time? Women's Responses to Prison in the

Context of the Old and the New Penology." *Criminology* 28 (August): 681–718.

Koss, Mary P., Thomas E. Dinero, Cynthia A. Seibel, and Susan L. Cox. 1988. "Stranger and Acquaintance Rape: Are There Differences in the Victim's Experience?" *Psychology of Women Quarterly* 12, 1: 1–24.

Krieder, Rose M., and Diana B. Elliott. 2009. *America's Families and Living Arrangements: 2007.* Washington, DC: U.S. Census Bureau. www.census.gov.

Kruttschnitt, Candace, and Rosemary Gartner. 2003. "Women's Imprisonment." *Crime and Justice* 30: 1–81.

Kruttschnitt, Candace, Rosemary Gartner, and Amy Miller. 2000. "Doing Her Own Time? Women's Responses to Prison in the Context of the Old and the New Penology." *Criminology* 28 (August): 681–718.

Kubitschek, Warren N., and Maureen T. Hallinan. 1996. "Race, Gender, and Inequity in Track Assignments." *Research in Sociology of Education and Socialization* 11: 121–146.

Kurz, Demie. 1995. *For Richer for Poorer: Mothers Confront Divorce.* New York: Routledge.

Labaton, Vivien, and Dawn Lundy Martin. 2004. *The Fire Next Time: Young Activists and the New Feminism.* New York: Anchor.

Ladner, Joyce. 1995. *Tomorrow's Tomorrow: The Black Woman.* Lincoln: University of Nebraska Press.

LaFrance, M., & Hecht, M. A. 2000. "Gender and Smiling: A Meta-Analysis." Pp. 118–142 in *Gender and Emotion: Social Psychological Perspectives,* edited by H. Fischer. Cambridge, UK: Cambridge University Press.

LaFrance, Marianne. 2002. "Smile Boycotts and Other Body Politics." *Feminism and Psychology* 12 (August): 319–323.

Lai, Tracy. 1992. "Asian American Women: Not for Sale." Pp. 163–171 in *Race, Class, and Gender: An Anthology,* edited by Margaret L. Andersen and Patricia Hill Collins. Belmont CA: Wadsworth.

Lakkis, Jacqueline, Lina A. Ricciardelli, and Robert J. Williams. 1999. "Role of Sexual Orientation and Gender-Related Traits in Disordered Eating." *Sex Roles* 41 (July): 1–16.

Lamb, Michael E., and Lori D. Bougher. 2009. "How Does Migration Affect Mothers' and Fathers' Roles within Their Families? Reflections on Some Recent Research." *Sex Roles: A Journal of Research* 60 (7–8): 611–614.

Lampman, C., et al. 2002. "Messages about Sex in the Workplace: A Content Analysis of Prime-Time Television." *Sexuality & Culture* 6: 3–21.

Larson, Mary Strom. 2003. "Gender, Race, and Aggression in Television Commercials That Feature Children." *Sex Roles* 48 (January): 67–75.

Laumann, Edward O., John H. Gagnon, Robert T. Michael, and Stuart Michaels. 1994. *The Social Organization of Sexuality: Sexual Practices in the United States.* Chicago: University of Chicago Press.

Lee, Byoungkwan, Bong-Chul Kim, and Sangpil Han. 2006. "The Portrayal of Older People in Television Advertisements: A Cross-Cultural Content Analysis of the United States and South Korea." *International Journal of Aging and Human Development* 63 (4): 279–297.

Lee, Janet. 1994. "Menarche and the (Hetero)sexualization of the Female Body." *Gender & Society* 8 (September): 343–362.

Lee, Janet. 1996. *Blood Stories: Menarche and the Politics of the Female Body in the United States.* New York: Routledge.

Lee, Sunhwa. 2009. "Racial and Ethnic Differences in Women's Retirement Security." *Journal of Women, Politics & Policy* 30 (2–3): 141–172.

Lehman, E. C., Jr. 1994. "Gender and Ministry Style: Things Not What They Seem." Pp. 3–14 in *Gender and Religion,* edited by William H. Swatos Jr. New Brunswick, NJ: Transaction Publishers.

Leistyna, Pepi. 2005. *Class Dismissed: How TV Frames the Working Class.*

Northampton, MA: Media Education Foundation.

Lemert, E. 1972. *Human Deviance, Social Problems, and Social Control.* Upper Saddle River, NJ: Prentice-Hall.

Leong, Russell, ed. 1996. *Asian American Sexualities: Dimensions of the Gay and Lesbian Experience.* New York: Routledge.

Lerman, Robert, and Theodora J. Ooms. 1993. *Young Unwed Fathers: Changing Roles and Emerging Policies.* Philadelphia: Temple University Press.

Lerman, Robert, and Elaine Sorenson. 2000. "Father Involvement with Their Nonmarital Children: Patterns, Determinants, and Effects on Their Earnings." *Marriage and Family Review* 29: 137–158.

Lerner, Gerda. 1973. *Black Women in White America: A Documentary History.* New York: Vintage.

Lerner, Gerda. 1976. "Placing Women in History: A 1975 Perspective." Pp. 357–367 in *Liberating Women's History,* edited by Berniece Carroll. Champaign–Urbana: University of Illinois Press.

Levy, Ariel. 2005. *Female Chauvinist Pigs: Women and the Rise of Raunch Culture.* New York: Free Press.

Levy, Donald. 2005. "Hegemonic Masculinity, Complicity and Comradeship: Validation and Causal Processes among White, Middle-Class, Middle-Aged Men." *The Journal of Men's Studies* 13 (Winter): 199–224.

Lewis, Gregory B. 2003. "Black-White Differences in Attitudes toward Homosexuality and Gay Rights." *The Public Opinion Quarterly* 67: 59–78.

Limbaugh, H. Rush, III. 1992. *The Way Things Ought to Be.* New York: Pocket.

Lindsey, Eric W., and Jacquelyn Mize. 2001. "Contextual Differences in Parent-Child Play: Implications for Children's Gender Role Development." *Sex Roles* 44 (February): 155–176.

Lindsey, Eric W., J. Mize, and G. S. Pettit. 1997. "Differential Play Patterns of Mothers and Fathers of Sons and Daughters: Implications for Children's

Gender Role Development." *Sex Roles* 37 (November): 643–661.

Lipset, S. M., ed. 1962. *Harriet Martineau: Society in America.* New York: Doubleday.

Lipton, Eric S., and David Barboza. 2007. "As More Toys Are Recalled, Trail Ends in China." *The New York Times* (June 19). www.nytimes.com.

Litoff, J. B. 1978. *American Midwives: 1860 to the Present.* Westport, CT: Greenwood Press.

Liu, Meizhu, Barbara Robles, and Betsy Leondar-Wright. 2006. *The Color of Wealth: The Story Behind the U.S. Racial Wealth Divide.* New York: New Press.

Lock, Margaret. 1993. *Encounters with Aging: Mythologies of Menopause in Japan and North America.* Berkeley: University of California Press.

Lock, Margaret. 1998. "Anomalous Aging: Managing the Post-menopausal Body." *Body and Society* 4 (March): 35–61.

Locke, Benjamin D., and Mahalik, James R. 2005. "Examining Masculinity Norms, Problem Drinking, and Athletic Involvement as Predictors of Sexual Aggression in College Men." *Journal of Counseling Psychology* 52, 3: 279–283.

Logio, Kim. 1998. *Here's Looking at You, Kid: Gender, Race, Body Image and Adolescent Health.* Ph.D. Dissertation, University of Delaware.

Lombardo, William K., Gary A. Cretser, and Scott C. Roesch. 2001. "For Crying Out Loud— The Differences Persist into the '90s." *Sex Roles* 45 (December): 529–547.

Lombroso, N. 1920. *The Female Offender.* New York: Appleton.

Longino, Helene, and R. Doell. 1983. "Body, Bias, and Behavior: Comparative Analysis of Reasoning in Two Areas of Biological Science." *Signs* 9 (Winter): 206–227.

Lopata, Helene Z., and Barrie Thorne. 1978. "On the Term 'Sex Roles.'" *Signs* 3 (Spring): 718–721.

Lorber, Judith. 1994. *Paradoxes of Gender.* New Haven, CT: Yale University Press.

Loscocco, Karyn A., and Glenna Spitze. 1990. "Working Conditions, Social Support and the Well-Being of Female and Male Factory Workers." *Journal of Health and Social Behavior* 31 (December): 313–327.

Lucas, Samuel R. 1999. *Tracking Inequality: Stratification and Mobility in American High Schools.* New York: Teachers College Press.

Lukemeyer, Anna, Marcia K. Meyers, and Timothy Smeeding. 2000. "Expensive Children in Poor Families: Out-of-Pocket Expenditures for the Care of Disabled and Chronically Ill Children in Welfare Families." *Journal of Marriage and the Family* 62 (May): 399–415.

Luker, Kristen. 1975. *Taking Chances.* Berkeley: University of California Press.

Luker, Kristen. 1984. *Abortion and the Politics of Motherhood.* Berkeley: University of California Press.

Lummis, Adair T., and Paula D. Nesbitt. 2000. "Women Clergy Research and the Sociology of Religion." *Sociology of Religion* 61 (Winter): 443–453.

Lundberg, F., and M. Farnham. 1947. *Modern Woman: The Lost Sex.* New York: Harper.

Lye, Diane N., and Ingrid Waldron. 1997. "Attitudes toward Cohabitation, Family, and Gender Roles: Relationships to Values and Political Ideology." *Sociological Perspectives* 40 (Summer): 199–225.

MacCorquodale, P. L. 1984. "Gender Roles and Premarital Contraception." *Journal of Marriage and the Family* 46 (February): 57–62.

MacKinnon, Catharine. 1982. "Feminism, Marxism, Method, and the State: An Agenda for Theory." *Signs* 7 (Spring): 515–544.

MacKinnon, Catherine. 1983. "Feminism, Marxism, Method, and the State: Toward Feminist Jurisprudence." *Signs* 8 (Summer): 635–658.

Madriz, Esther. 1997. *Nothing Bad Happens to Good Girls: Fear of Crime in Women's Lives.* Berkeley: University of California Press.

Mahoney, Patricia, and Linda M. Williams. 1998. "Sexual Assault in Marriage: Prevalence, Consequences, and Treatment of Wife Rape." Pp. 113–162 in *Partner Violence: A Comprehensive Review of 20 Years of Research,* edited by Jana L. Jasinkski and Linda M. Williams. Thousand Oaks, CA: Sage.

Majete, Clayton A. 1999. "Family Relationships and the Interracial Marriage." Paper presented at the Annual Meetings of the American Sociological Association, Washington, DC.

Malamuth, Neil M., Robert J. Sockloskie, Mary P. Koss, and J.S. Tanaka. 1991. "Characteristics of Aggressors against Women: Testing a Model Using a National Sample of College Students." *Journal of Consulting and Clinical Psychology* 59 (5): 670–681.

Malleson, Kate. 2003. "Justifying Gender Equality on the Bench: Why Difference Won't Do." *Feminist Legal Studies* 11: 1–24.

Mannheim, K. 1936. *Ideology and Utopia.* New York: Harcourt, Brace, and World.

Mansfield, Phyllis Kernoff, Patricia Bartalow Koch, Julie Henderson, Judith R. Vicary, Margaret Cohn, and Elaine W. Young. 1991. "The Job Climate for Women in Traditionally Male Blue-Collar Occupations." *Sex Roles* 25 (July): 63–79.

Marchevsky, Alejandra, and Jeanne Theoharis. 2008. "Dropped from the Rolls: Mexican Immigrants, Race, and Rights in the Era of Welfare Reform." *Journal of Sociology and Social Welfare* 35 (3): 71–96.

Markens, Susan. 1996. "The Problematic of 'Experience': A Political and Cultural Critique of PMS." *Gender & Society* 10 (February): 42–58.

Marshall, Nancy L., and Rosalind C. Barnett. 1995. "Child Care, Division of Labor, and Parental Emotional Well-Being among Two-Earner Couples." Paper presented at the Annual Meetings of the American Sociological Association.

Marsiglio, William. 1995. "Young Nonresident Biological Fathers." *Marriage and Family Review* 20: 325–348.

Martin, Emily. 1991. "The Egg and the Sperm: How Science Has Constructed a Romance Based on Stereotypical Male-Female Roles." *Signs* 16 (Spring): 485–501.

Martin, Patricia Yancey. 2004. "Gender as Social Institution." *Social Forces* 82 (June): 1249–1273.

Martin, Patricia Yancey. 2005. *Rape Work: Victims, Gender, and Emotion in Organization and Community*. New York: Routledge.

Martin, Patricia Yancey, John R. Reynolds, and Shelley Keith. 2002. "Gender Bias and Feminist Consciousness among Judges and Attorneys: A Standpoint Theory Analysis." *Signs* 27: 665–701.

Martin, Steven S., and Cynthia Robbins. 1995. "Personality, Social Control and Drug Use in Early Adolescence." Pp. 145–161 in *Drugs, Crime and Other Deviant Adaptations*, edited by Howard B. Kaplan. New York: Plenum Press.

Martineau, Harriet. 1837. *Society in America*. Paris: Baudry's European Library.

Marx, G. 1967. "Religion: Opiate or Inspiration of Civil Rights Militancy among Negroes." *American Sociological Review* 32 (February): 64–72.

Marx, K., and F. Engels. 1970. *The Communist Manifesto*. New York: Pathfinder Press.

Massoni, Kelley. 2004. "Modeling Work: Occupational Messages in *Seventeen* Magazine." *Gender & Society* 18 (February): 47–55.

Mast, Marianne Schmid, and Judith A. Hall. 2001. "Gender Differences and Similarities in Dominance Hierarchies in Same-Gender Groups Based on Speaking Time." *Sex Roles* 44 (May): 537–556.

Mast, Marianne Schmid, and Judith A. Hall. 2004. "When Is Dominance Related to Smiling? Assigned Dominance, Dominance Preference, Trait Dominance, and Gender as Moderators." *Sex Roles* 50 (March): 387–299.

Masters, W. H., and V. E. Johnson. 1966. *Human Sexual Response*. Boston: Little, Brown.

Maume, David J., Jr. 1999. "Glass Ceilings and Glass Escalators: Occupational Segregation and Race and Sex Differences in Managerial Promotions." *Work and Occupations* 26 (November): 483–509.

May, David C. 2001. "The Effect of Fear of Sexual Victimization on Adolescent Fear of Crime." *Sociological Spectrum* 21: 141–174.

Mayer, Vicki. 2005. "Soft-Core in TV Time: The Political Economy of a 'Cultural Trend.'" *Critical Studies in Media Communication* 22 (4): 302–320.

McCabe, Janice. 2005. "What's in a Label? The Relationship between Feminist Self-Identification and 'Feminist' Attitudes among U.S. Women and Men." *Gender & Society* 19 (August): 480–505.

McCammon, Holly J. 1995. "The Politics of Protection: State Minimum Wage and Maximum Hours Laws for Women in the United States, 1870–1930." *Sociological Quarterly* 36 (Spring): 217–249.

McCloskey, Laura Ann. 1996. "Socioeconomic and Coercive Power within the Family." *Gender & Society* 10 (August): 449–463.

McComb, Chris. 2001. "Few Say It's Ideal for Both Parents to Work Full Time Outside of Home." *The Gallup Poll*. Princeton, NJ: Gallup Organization.

McCrate, Elaine, and Joan Smith. 1998. "When Work Doesn't Work: The Failure of Current Welfare Reform." *Gender & Society* 12 (February): 61–80.

McGuffey, C. Shawn, and B. Lindsay Rich. 1999. "Playing in the Gender Transgression Zone: Race, Class, and Hegemonic Masculinity in Middle Childhood." *Gender & Society* 12 (October): 608–627.

McGuire, Meredith. 2008. *Religion: The Social Context*. Long Grove, IL: Waveland Press.

McIntosh, Peggy. 1983. "Interactive Phases of Curricular Re-Vision: A Feminist Perspective." Working Papers Series. Wellesley, MA: Wellesley Center for Research on Women.

McKinney, Kathleen, and Kelly Crittenden. 1992. "Contrapower Sexual Harassment: The Offender's Viewpoint." *Free Inquiry in Creative Sociology* 20 (May): 3–10.

McMannon, Timothy J. 1997. "The Changing Purposes of Education and Schooling." Pp. 1–17 in *The Public Purpose of Education and Schooling*, edited by John I. Goodlad and Timothy J. McMannon. San Francisco: Jossey-Bass.

McNelles, Laurie R., and Jennifer A. Connolly. 1999. "Intimacy between Adolescent Friends: Age and Gender Differences in Intimate Affect and Intimate Behaviors." *Journal of Research on Adolescence* 9: 143–159.

McQuade, Sharon, and John H. Ehrenreich. 1998. "Women in Prison: Approaches to Understanding the Lives of a Forgotten Population." *Affilia: Journal of Women and Social Work* 13 (Summer): 233–247.

McQueeney, Krista B. 2003. "The New Religious Rite: A Symbolic Interactionist Case Study of Lesbian Commitment Rituals." *Journal of Lesbian Studies* 7: 49–70.

McQuiade, Sharon, and John H. Ehrenreich. 1998. "Women in Prison: Approaches to Understanding the Lives of a Forgotten Population." *Affilia: Journal of Women and Social Work* 13 (Summer): 233–247.

McQuillan, Julia, Arthur L. Greil, Karina M. Shreffler, and Veronica Tichenor. 2008. "The Importance of Motherhood among Women in the Contemporary United States." *Gender & Society* 22 (August): 477–496.

Mead, Margaret. 1962. *Male and Female*. London: Penguin.

Mead, Sara. 2006. "The Truth about Boys and Girls." Washington, DC: Education Sector. www .educationsector.org.

Meigs, C. D. 1847. *Lecture on Some of the Distinctive Characteristics of the Female: Delivered before the Class of the Jefferson Medical College*. Philadelphia: Collins.

Mendelsohn, E., P. Weingart, and R. Whitely, eds. 1977. *The Social Production of Scientific Knowledge*. Dordrecht, The Netherlands: Riedel.

Mernissi, Fatima. 1987. *Beyond the Veil: Male-Female Dynamics in Modern Muslim Society*. Bloomington: Indiana University Press.

Mernissi, Fatima, and Mary Jo Lakeland. 1992. *The Veil and the Male Elite: A Feminist Interpretation of Women's Rights in Islam*. New York: Perseus.

Merskin, D. 2004. Reviving Lolita? A Media Literacy Examination of Sexual Portrayals of Girls in Fashion Advertising." *American Behavioral Scientist* 48: 119–129.

Messerschmidt, James. 2000. *Nine Lives: Adolescent Masculinities, the Body, and Violence*. Boulder, CO: Westview.

Messner, Michael A. 1997. *Politics of Masculinities: Men in Movements*. Thousand Oaks: Sage.

Messner, Michael A. 1998. "The Limits of 'The Male Sex Role': An Analysis of the Men's Liberation and Men's Rights Movements' Discourse." *Gender & Society* 12 (June): 255–276.

Messner, Michael A. 2000. "Barbie Girls versus Sea Monsters: Children Constructing Gender." *Gender & Society* 14 (December): 765–784.

Messner, Michael A. 2001. "Friendship, Intimacy, and Sexuality." Pp. 253–265 in *The Masculinities Reader*, edited by Stephen M. Whitehead and Frank J. Barrett. Cambridge: Polity.

Meyer, Jan. 1990. "Guess Who's Coming to Dinner This Time? A Study of Gay Intimate Relationships and the Support for Those Relationships." *Marriage and Family Review* 14: 59–82.

Meyer, M. H., and E. K. Pavalko. 1996. "Family, Work, and Access to Health Insurance among Mature Women." *Journal of Health and Social Behavior* 37 (December): 311–325.

Middlebrook, Diane. 1998. *Suits Me: The Double Life of Billy Tipton*. Boston: Houghton Mifflin.

Milkie, Melissa A., and Pia Peltola. 1999. "Playing All the Roles: Gender and the Work-Family Balancing Act." *Journal of Marriage and the Family* 61 (May): 476–490.

Mill, J. S. 1970. *The Subjection of Women*. New York: Source Book Press.

Miller, D. 1975. *American Indian Socialization to Urban Life*. San Francisco: Institute for Scientific Analysis.

Miller, Eleanor. 1986. *Street Women*. Philadelphia: Temple University Press.

Miller, J. B. 1977. *Toward a New Psychology of Women*. Boston: Beacon Press.

Miller, Monica K., and Alicia Summers. 2007. "Gender Differences in Video Game Characters' Roles, Appearances, and Attire as Portrayed in Video Game Magazines." *Sex Roles: A Journal of Research* 57 (9–10): 733–742.

Miller, Susan L. 2005. *Criminalized Conduct: The Paradox of Women Arrested for Domestic Violence*. New Brunswick, NJ: Rutgers University Press.

Millman, Marcia. 1980. *Such a Pretty Face: Being Fat in America*. New York: Norton.

Mills, C. Wright. 1959. *The Sociological Imagination*. New York: Oxford University Press.

Milner, Joel S., and Julie L. Crouch. 1993. "Physical Child Abuse." Pp. 25–55 in *Family Violence: Prevention and Treatment*, edited by Robert L. Hampton, Thomas P. Gullotta, Gerald R. Adams, Earl H. Potter III, and Roger P. Weissberg. Newbury Park, CA: Sage.

Min, Pyong Gap. 2003. "Korean 'Comfort Women': The Intersection of Colonial Power, Gender, and Class." *Gender & Society* 17: 938–957.

Minnich, Elizabeth Kamarck. 1990. *Transforming Knowledge*. Philadelphia: Temple University Press.

Mirandé, A. 1979. "Machismo: A Reinterpretation of Male Dominance in the Chicano Family." *The Family Coordinator* 28: 447–479.

Mir-Hosseini, Ziba. 1999. *Islam and Gender: The Religious Debate in Contemporary Iran*. Princeton, NJ: Princeton University Press.

Mishel, Lawrence, Jared Bernstein, and Sylvia Allegretto. 2005. *The State of Working America 2004/2005*. Washington, DC: The Economic Policy Institute.

Misra, Joya, Stephanie Moller, and Marina Karides. 2003. "Envisioning Dependency: Changing Media Depictions of Welfare in the 20th Century." *Social Problems* 50 (November): 482–504.

Mitchell, G., Stephanie Obradovich, Fred Herring, Chris Tromborg, and Alyson L. Burns. 1992. "Reproducing Gender in Public Places: Adults' Attention to Toddlers in Three Public Locales." *Sex Roles* 26 (September): 323–330.

Mitchell, Juliet. 1971. *Woman's Estate*. New York: Pantheon.

Modleski, T. 1980. "The Disappearing Act: A Study of Harlequin Romances." *Signs* 5 (Spring): 435–448.

Moen, Phyllis. 2004. *The New "Middle" Work Force*. The Life Course Center, University of Minnesota, Minneapolis, and the Bronfenbrenner Life Course Center (and Cornell Careers Institute) at Cornell University, Ithaca, New York.

Moen, Phyllis, Jungmeen E. Kim, and Heather Hofmeister. 2001. "Couples' Work/Retirement Transitions, Gender, and Marital Quality." *Social Psychology Quarterly* 64 (March): 55–71.

Mohr, J. 1978. *Abortion in America*. New York: Oxford University Press.

Molinary, Rose. 2007. *Hijas Americanas: Beauty, Body Image, and Growing Up Latina*. Emeryville, CA: Seal Press.

Money, John. 1988. *Gay, Straight, and In-Between: The Sexology of Erotic Orientation*. New York: Oxford University Press.

Money, John. 1995. *Gendermaps: Social Constructionism, Feminism and Sexosophical History*. New York: Continuum.

Money, John, and A. A. Ehrhardt. 1972. *Man, Woman, Boy and Girl: The Differentiation and Dimorphism of Gender Identity from Conception to Maturity*. Baltimore: Johns Hopkins University Press.

Mongeau, B., H. L. Smith, and A. C. Maney. 1961. "The 'Granny' Midwife: Changing Roles and Functions of a Folk Practitioner." *American Journal of Sociology* 66: 497–505.

Montez, Jennifer K., Jacqueline L. Angel, and Ronald J. Angel. 2009. "Employment, Marriage, and Inequality in Health Insurance for Mexican-Origin Women." *Journal of Health and Social Behavior* 50 (2): 132–148.

Moon, Dawne. 2009. "Conservative Theology and Same-Sex Desire." *Contemporary Sociology* 38 (July): 305–308.

Moore, David. 2004. "Modest Rebound in Public Acceptance of Homosexuals." *The Gallup Poll*. Princeton, NJ: The Gallup Organization, May 20.

Moore, David. 2005. "Gender Stereotypes Prevail on Working Outside the Home." *The Gallup Poll*. Princeton, NJ: The Gallup Organization, August 17.

Moore, Gwen. 1990. "Structural Determinants of Men's and Women's Personal Networks." *American Sociological Review* 55 (October): 726–735.

Moore, Gwen. 1992. "Gender and Informal Networks in State Government." *Social Science Quarterly* 73 (March): 46–61.

Moorti, Sujata. 2002. *The Color of Rape: Gender and Race in Television's Public Sphere*. Albany: State University of New York Press.

Moraga, Cherríe, and Gloria Anzaldúa. 1981. *This Bridge Called My Back: Radical Writings by Women of Color*. Watertown, MA: Persephone Press.

Morales, Lymari. 2009. "Knowing Someone Gay/Lesbian Affects Views of Gay Issues." *Gallup Poll*, May 29. www.gallup.com.

Morash, Merry, Robin N. Harr, and Lila Rucker. 1994. "Comparison of Programming for Women and Men in U.S. Prisons in the 1980s." *Crime and Delinquency* 40 (April): 197–221.

Moremen, Robin D. 2008. "Best Friends: The Role of Confidantes in Older Women's Health." *Journal of Women & Aging* 20: 149–167.

Morgan, Leslie A. 2000. "The Continuing Gender Gap in Later Life Economic Security." *Journal of Aging and Social Policy* 11: 157–165.

Morgen, Sandra. 2002. *Into Our Own Hands: The Women's Health Movement in the United States, 1969–1990*. Piscataway, NJ: Rutgers University Press.

Morin, S. F., and E. M. Garfinkle. 1978. "Male Homophobia." *The Journal of Social Issues* 34 (Winter): 29–47.

Moss, Nancy E. 2002. "Gender Equity and Socioeconomic Inequality: A Framework for the Patterning of Women's Health." *Social Science and Medicine* 54: 649–661.

Moss, Philip, and Chris Tilly. 2001. *Stories Employers Tell: Race, Skill, and Hiring in America*. New York: Russell Sage Foundation.

Mullings, Janet L., James W. Marquart, and Pamela M. Diamond. 2001. "Cumulative Continuity and Injection Drug Use among Women: A Test of the Downward Spiral Framework." *Deviant Behavior* 22 (May–June): 211–238.

Mullings, Janet L., Joycelyn Pollock, and Ben M. Crouch. 2002. "Drugs and Criminality: Results from the Texas Women Inmates Study." *Women and Criminal Justice* 13: 69–96.

Murinen, Sarah K., and Linda Smolak. 2000. "The Experience of Sexual Harassment among Grade-School Students: Early Socialization of Female Subordination?" *Sex Roles* 43 (July): 1–17.

Nagel, Joanne. 2003. *Race, Ethnicity, and Sexuality. Intimate Intersections, Forbidden Frontiers*. New York: Oxford University Press.

Nanda, Serena. 1998. *Neither Man nor Woman: The Hijras of India*. Belmont, CA: Wadsworth.

Naples, Nancy A. 1992. "Activist Mothering: Cross-Generational Continuity in the Community Work of Women from Low-Income Urban Neighborhoods." *Gender & Society* 6 (September): 441–464.

Nardi, Peter M., and Beth Schneider. 1997. *Social Perspectives on Lesbian and Gay Studies*. New York: Routledge.

Nason-Clark, Nancy. 1987. "Are Women Changing the Image of Ministry? A Comparison of British and American Realities." *Review of Religious Research* 28 (June): 330–340.

National Association of Women Judges. 2010. www.nawj.org.

National Cancer Institute. 2010. "Surveillance Epidemiology and End Results." www.seer.cancer.gov.

National Center for Education Statistics. 2008. *Digest of Educational Statistics*. Washington, DC: U.S. Department of Education.

National Center for Education Statistics. 2009. "Fast Facts." Washington, DC: U.S. Department of Education.

National Center for Health Statistics. 2007. *Health United States 2007*. Washington, DC: Department of Health and Human Services.

National Center for Health Statistics. 2009. *Health United States 2009*. Washington, DC: Department of Health and Human Services.

National Institute of Alcohol and Alcohol Abuse. 2010. "Quick Stats: Binge Drinking."

National Women's Law Center. 2008. "Eliminating Sexual Assault Should Be a Top Priority of the Department of Defense." www.nwlc.org.

Neckerman, Kathryn M., and Joleen Kirschenman. 1991. "Hiring Strategies, Racial Bias, and Inner-City Workers." *Social Problems* 38 (November): 433–447.

Neilson, Linda C. 2002. "Comparative Analysis of Law in Theory and Law in Action in Partner Abuse Cases: What Do the Data Tell Us?" *Studies in Law, Politics, and Society* 26: 141–187.

Neitz, Mary Jo. 2000. "Queering the Dragonfest: Changing Sexuality in a Post-Patriarchal Religion." *Sociology of Religion* 61 (Winter): 369–391.

Nelson, Andrea, and Pamela Oliver. 1998. "Gender and the Construction of Consent in Child-Adult Sexual Contact: Beyond Gender Neutrality and Male Monopoly." *Gender & Society* 12 (October): 554–577.

Nelson, Fiona. 1999. "Lesbian Families: Achieving Motherhood." *Journal of Gay & Lesbian Social Services* 10: 27–46.

Newport, Frank. 2005. "Americans Turn More Negative toward Same Sex Marriage." Princeton, NJ: The Gallup Poll.

Nicholson, Linda E., ed. 1990. *Feminism and Postmodernism*. New York: Routledge.

Nicholson, Linda E. 1994. "Interpreting Gender." *Signs* 20 (Autumn): 79–105.

Nisbet, Robert. 1970. *The Social Bond.* New York: Knopf.

Nock, Steven L. 1995. "A Comparison of Marriages and Cohabiting Relationships." *Journal of Family Issues* 16 (January): 53–76.

Novkov, Julie. 1996. "Liberty, Protection, and Women's Work: Investigating the Boundaries between Public and Private." *Law and Social Inquiry* 21 (Fall): 857–899.

Ntiri, Daphne W. 2000. "The Transition of Female Family Heads of Household from Welfare to Work: Implications for Adult Education. *Western Journal of Black Studies* 24 (Spring): 34–42.

O'Campo, Patricia, William W. Eaton, and Carles Muntaner. 2004. "Labor Market Experiences, Work Organization, Gender Inequalities and Health Status: Results from a Prospective Analysis of U.S. Employed Women." *Social Science and Medicine* 58: 585–594.

O'Connell, Colleen, and Karen Korabik. 2000. "Sexual Harassment: The Relationship of Personal Vulnerability, Work Context, Perpetrator Status, and Type of Harassment to Outcomes." *Journal of Vocational Behavior* 56 (June): 299–329.

O'Kelly, C. G., and L. S. Carney. 1986. *Women and Men in Society,* 2nd ed. Belmont, CA: Wadsworth.

O'Rand, Angela M., and John C. Henretta. 1999. "Labor Markets and Occupational Welfare in the United States." Pp. 131–157 in *Age and Inequality: Diverse Pathways through Later Life,* edited by Angela O'Rand and John C. Henretta. Boulder, CO: Westview.

Oakley, A. 1974. *The Sociology of Housework.* London: Mertin Robertson.

Odoms-Young, Angela. 2008. "Factors That Influence Body Image Representations of Black Muslim Women." *Social Science and Medicine* 66 (June): 2573–2584.

Office of the Inspector General of the Department of Defense. 2005. *Report on the Service Academy Sexual Assault and Leadership Survey, Project No. 2003C004.* Washington, DC: U.S. Department of Defense.

Ogletree, Shirley M., and Ryan Drake. 2007. "College Students' Video Game Participation and Perceptions: Gender Differences and Implications." *Sex Roles: A Journal of Research* 56 (7–8): 537–542.

Olsen, Laurie. 1997. *An Invisible Crisis: The Educational Needs of Asian Pacific American Youth.* New York: Asian Americans/Pacific Islanders in Philanthropy.

Padavic, Irene, and Barbara Reskin. 2002. *Women and Men at Work,* 2nd ed. Thousand Oaks, CA: Pine Forge Press.

Page, Amy Dellinger. 2008. "Judging Women and Defining Crime: Police Officers' Attitudes toward Women and Rape." *Sociological Spectrum* 28: 389–411.

Palmer, Phyllis. 1989. *Domesticity and Dirt: Housewives and Domestic Servants in the United States, 1920–1945.* Philadelphia: Temple University Press.

Papper, Bob. 2007. "Women and Minorities in the Newsroom." *Communicator* (July–August): 20–27.

Parents Television Council. 2009, October. *Women in Peril: A Look at TV's Disturbing New Storyline Trend.*

Park, Jerry Z. 1999. "Empowering Chastity: Sexual Morality among American Evangelicals." Paper presented at the Annual Meetings of the American Sociological Association, Washington, DC.

Pascoe, C. J. 2008. *Dude, You're a Fag: Masculinity and Sexuality in High School.* Berkeley: University of California Press.

Patterson, Charlotte J. 2000. "Family Relationships of Lesbians and Gay Men." *Journal of Marriage and the Family* 62 (November): 1052–1069.

Pavalko, Eliza K. 2001. "Sex Differences Called Key in Medical Studies." *The New York Times* (April 25): A14.

Pavalko, Eliza K., and Shari Woodbury. 2000. "Social Roles as Process: Caregiving Careers and Women's Health." *Journal of Health and Social Behavior* 41 (March): 91–105.

Pear, Robert. 2001. "Sex Differences Called Key in Medical Studies." *The New York Times* (April 25): A14.

Pearson, A. F. 2007. "The New Welfare Trap." *Gender & Society* 21 (5): 723–748.

Peltola, Pia, Melissa Milkie, and Stanley Presser. 2004. "The 'Feminist' Mystique: Feminist Identity in Three Generations of Women." *Gender & Society* 18 (February): 122–144.

Peralta, Robert L. 2002. "Getting Trashed in College: Doing Alcohol, Doing Gender, Doing Violence." *Dissertation Abstracts International, A: The Humanities and Social Sciences* 63 (1): 368-A.

Peralta, Robert L. 2007. "College Alcohol Use and the Embodiment of Hegemonic Masculinity among European American Men." *Sex Roles* 56: 741–756.

Perry, Imani. 2003. "Who(se) Am I? The Identity and Image of Women in Hip-Hop." Pp. 136–148 in *Gender, Race, and Class in Media,* 2nd ed., edited by Gail Dines and Jean M. Humez. Thousand Oaks, CA: Sage.

Petchesky, Rosalind. 1980. "Reproductive Freedom: Beyond a Woman's Right to Choose." *Signs* 5 (Summer): 661–685.

Petchesky, Rosalind. 1990. "Giving Women a Real Choice." *The Nation* (May 28): 732–735.

Petersen, Larry R., and Gregory V. Donnenwerth. 1998. "Religion and Declining Support for Traditional Beliefs about Gender Roles." *Sociology of Religion* 59 (Winter): 353–371.

Pew Research Center. 2007. *Muslim Americans: Middle Class and Mostly Mainstream.* Washington, DC: Pew Research Center for the People and the Press.

Pharr, Suzanne. 1999. *Homophobia: A Weapon of Sexism.* Little Rock, AR: Chardon Press.

Phillips, Lynn. 1998. *The Girls Report: What We Know and Need to Know about Growing Up Female.* New York: National Council for Research on Women.

Pino, Nathan W., and Ronert F. Meier. 1999. "Gender

Differences in Rape Reporting." *Sex Roles* 11–12 (June): 979–990.

Pohli, C. V. 1983. "Church Closets and Back Doors: A Feminist View of Moral Majority Women." *Feminist Studies* 9 (Fall): 529–558.

Pollak, Otto. 1950. *The Criminology of Women.* Philadelphia: University of Pennsylvania Press.

Porter, Jennie Lee. 2003. "An Investigation of the Glass Ceiling in Corporate America: The Perspective of African-American Women." *Dissertation Abstracts International, A: The Humanities and Social Sciences*, 297-A.

Poston, C., ed. 1975. *A Vindication on the Rights of Woman.* New York: Norton.

Powell, Kimberly, and Lori Abels. 2002. *Women and Language* 25 (Spring): 14–22.

Powers, M. 1980. "Menstruation and Reproduction: An Oglala Case." *Signs* 6 (Autumn): 54–65.

Press, Eyal. 1996. "Barbie's Betrayal." *The Nation* (December 30): 11–16.

Presser, Harriet B. 2000. "Nonstandard Work Schedules and Marital Instability." *Journal of Marriage and the Family* 62 (February): 93–100.

Preves, Sharon E. 2003. *Intersex and Identity: The Contested Self.* New Brunswick, NJ: Rutgers University Press.

Pyke, Karen D. 1994. "Women's Employment as a Gift or Burden? Marital Power across Marriage, Divorce, and Remarriage." *Gender & Society* 8 (March): 73–91.

Pyle, Jean L., and Kathryn B. Ward. 2003. "Recasting Our Understanding of Gender and Work during Global Restructuring." *International Sociology* 18: 461–489.

Quillian, Lincoln, and Mary E. Campbell. 2003. "Beyond Black and White: The Present and Future of Multiracial Friendship Segregation." *American Sociological Review* 68 (August): 540–566.

Raag, Tarja. 1999. "Influences of Social Expectations of Gender, Gender Stereotypes, and Situational Constraints on Children's Toy Choices." *Sex Roles* 41 (December): 809–831.

Raag, Tarja, and C. L. Rackliff. 1998. "Preschoolers' Awareness of Social Expectations of Gender:

Relationships to Toy Choices." *Sex Roles* 38 (May): 675–700.

Radway, Janice. 1984. *Reading the Romance: Women, Patriarchy, and Popular Literature.* Chapel Hill: University of North Carolina Press.

Raley, Sara B., Marybeth J. Mattingly, and Suzanne M. Bianchi. 2006. "How Dual Are Dual-Income Couples? Documenting Change from 1970 to 2001." *Journal of Marriage and Family* 68 (1): 11–28.

Rapp, R., E. Ross, and R. Bridenthal. 1979. "Examining Family History." *Feminist Studies* 5 (Spring): 174–200.

Reagon, B. J. 1982. "My Black Mothers and Sisters or On Beginning a Cultural Autobiography." *Feminist Studies* 8 (Spring): 81–96.

Redhorse, J. G., R. Lewis, M. Feit, and J. Decker. 1979. "American Indian Elders: Needs and Aspirations in Institutional and Home Health Care." Manuscript, Arizona State University.

Reeder, Heidi M. 2003. "The Effect of Gender Role Orientation on Same- and Cross-Sex Friendship Formation." *Sex Roles* 49 (August): 143–152.

Reilly, Mary Ellen, Bernice Lott, Donna Caldwell, and Luisa DeLuca. 1992. "Tolerance for Sexual Harassment Related to Self-Reported Sexual Victimization." *Gender & Society* 6 (March): 122–138.

Reinharz, Shulamith. 1983. "Experiential Analysis: A Contribution to Feminist Research." Pp. 162–194 in *Theories of Women's Studies*, edited by G. Duelli-Klein and R. Duelli-Klein. Boston: Routledge and Kegan Paul.

Renzetti, Claire M. 1997. "Violence in Lesbian and Gay Relationships." Pp. 285–293 in *Gender Violence: Interdisciplinary Perspectives*, edited by Laura L. O'Toole and Jessica R. Schiffman. New York: New York University Press.

Repak, Terry A. 1994. "Labor Recruitment and the Lure of the Capital: Central American Migrants in Washington, DC." *Gender & Society* 8 (December): 507–524.

Reskin, Barbara. 1992. "Occupational Desegregation in the

1970s: Integration and Economic Equity?" *Sociological Perspectives* 35 (Spring): 69–91.

Reskin, Barbara. 1999. "Occupational Segregation by Race and Ethnicity among Women Workers." Pp. 183–204 in *Latinas and African American Women at Work: Race, Gender, and Economic Inequality*, edited by Irene Browne. New York: Russell Sage Foundation.

Reskin, Barbara, and Irene Padavic. 1988. "Supervisors as Gatekeepers: Male Supervisors' Response to Women's Integration in Plant Jobs." *Social Problems* 35 (December): 536–550.

Reskin, Barbara, and Patricia Roos. 1990. *Job Queues, Gender Queues: Explaining Women's Inroads into Male Occupations.* Philadelphia: Temple University Press.

Reuther, R. 1979. "Motherearth and the Megamachine: A Theology of Liberation in a Feminine, Somatic, and Ecological Perspective." Pp. 43–51 *Womanspirit Rising*, edited by C. P. Christ and J. Plaskow. New York: Harper and Row.

Reuther, Rosemary, and R. S. Keller, eds. 1986. *Women and Religion in America, Volume 3: 1900–1968.* New York: Harper and Row.

Rich, Adrienne. 1976. *Of Woman Born: Motherhood as Experience and Institution.* New York: Norton.

Rich, Adrienne. 1980. "Compulsory Heterosexuality and Lesbian Existence." *Signs* 5 (Summer): 631–660.

Richardson, Virginia E. 1999. "Women and Retirement." *Journal of Women and Aging* 11: 49–66.

Richie, Beth E. 1996. *Compelled to Crime: The Gender Entrapment of Battered Black Women.* New York: Routledge.

Riday, Jennifer Dawn. 2003. "'First and Foremost, I'm a Mom!': The Experience of Full-Time and Part-Time Stay-at-Home Mothering." *Dissertation Abstracts International, A: The Humanities and Social Sciences* 1095-A.

Ridgeway, Cecilia L. 2001. "Gender, Status, and Leadership." *The Journal of Social Issues* 57 (Winter): 637–655.

Riesebrodt, Martin, and Kelly H. Chong. 1999. "Fundamentalisms and Patriarchal Gender

Politics." *Journal of Women's History* 10 (Winter): 55–77.

Riley, Anna L., and Verna M. Keith. 2003. "Work and Housework Conditions and Depressive Symptoms among Married Women: The Importance of Occupational Status." *Women & Health* 38: 1–17.

Risman, Barbara. 1999. *Gender Vertigo*. New Haven. CT: Yale University Press.

Risman, Barbara. 2004. "Gender as a Social Structure: Theory Wrestling with Activism." *Gender & Society* 18 (August): 429–450.

Rist, Darrell Yates. 1992. "Are Homosexuals Born That Way?" *The Nation* 255 (October 14): 424–429.

Roberts, Dorothy. 1997. *Killing the Black Body: Race, Reproduction and the Meaning of Liberty*. New York: Vintage Books.

Robinson, Christine M., and Sue E. Spivey. 2007. "The Politics of Masculinity and the Ex-Gay Movement." *Gender & Society* 21 (October): 650–675.

Robinson, Dawn T., and Lynn Smith-Lovin. 2001. "Getting a Laugh: Gender, Status, and Humor in Task Discussions." *Social Forces* 80 (September): 123–158.

Robison, Jennifer. 2002. "Feminism—What's in a Name?" *The Gallup Poll*. Princeton, NJ: The Gallup Organization.

Rollins, Judith. 1985. *Between Women: Domestics and Their Employers*. Philadelphia: Temple University Press.

Romero, Mary. 1992. *Maid in the U.S.A*. Philadelphia: Temple University Press.

Roper Organization. 1995. *The 1995 Virginia Slims Opinion Poll*. Storrs, CT: Roper Search Worldwide.

Rosenau, Pauline Marie. 1992. *Postmodernism and the Social Sciences: Insights, Inroads, and Intrusions*. Princeton, NJ: Princeton University Press.

Rosen, Leora N., and Lee Martin. 1998. "Predictors of Tolerance of Sexual Harassment among Male U.S. Army Soldiers." *Violence Against Women* 4, 4: 491–504.

Rosenbaum, Janet Elise. 2009. "Patient Teenagers: A Comparison of the Sexual Behavior of Virginity Pledgers and Matched Nonpledgers." *Pediatrics* 123 (January): 110–120.

Rosenberg, R. 1982. *Beyond Separate Spheres: Intellectual Roots of Modern Feminism*. New Haven, CT: Yale University Press.

Rosenfield, Sarah, Julie Phillips, and Helene White. 2006. "Gender, Race, and the Self in Mental Health and Crime." *Social Problems* 53 (2): 161–185.

Ross, Josephine. 2002. "The Sexualization of Difference: A Comparison of Mixed-Race and Same-Gender Marriage." *Harvard Civil Rights–Civil Liberties Law Review* 37 (Summer): 255–288.

Ross-Durow, Paula L., and Carol J. Boyd. 2000. "Sexual Abuse, Depression, and Eating Disorders in African American Women Who Smoke Cocaine." *Journal of Substance Abuse Treatment* 18 (January): 79–81.

Rossi, Alice. 1970. *Essays on Sex Equality*. Chicago: University of Chicago Press.

Rossi, Alice. 1973. *The Feminist Papers*. New York: Columbia University Press.

Rossi, Alice. 1977. "Toward a Biosocial Perspective on Parenting." *Daedalus* 106 (Spring): 1–31.

Rossiter, M. 1982. *Women Scientists in America*. Baltimore: Johns Hopkins University Press.

Rothman, Barbara Katz. 1982. *In Labor: Women and Power in the Birthplace*. New York: Norton.

Rothschild, M. A. 1979. "White Women Volunteers in the Freedom Summers." *Feminist Studies* 5 (Fall): 466–495.

Rousey, Annmaria, and Erich Longie. 2001. "The Tribal College as Family Support System." *American Behavioral Scientist* 44: 1492–1504.

Roxburgh, Susan. 2009. "Untangling Inequalities: Gender, Race, and Socioeconomic Differences in Depression." *Sociological Forum* 24 (2): 357–381.

Rubin, G. 1975. "The Traffic in Women." Pp. 157–211 in *Toward an Anthropology of Women*, edited by R. Reiter. New York: Monthly Review Press.

Rupp, Leila, and Verta Taylor. 1987. *Survival in the Doldrums: The American Women's Rights Movement, 1945 to the 1960's*. New York: Oxford University Press.

Russell, Diane E. H. 1986. *The Secret Trauma: Incest in the Lives of Girls and Women*. New York: Basic Books.

Rust, Paula. 1995. *Bisexuality and the Challenge to Lesbian Politics: Sex, Loyalty, and Revolution*. New York: New York University Press.

Rust, Paula. 2000. *Bisexuality in the United States: A Social Science Reader*. New York: Columbia University Press.

Ruzek, Sheryl Burt. 1978. *The Women's Health Movement: Feminist Alternatives to Medical Control*. New York: Praeger.

Ruzek, Sheryl Burt, Virginia L. Olesen, and Adele E. Clarke, eds. 1997. *Women's Health: Complexities and Differences*. Columbus: Ohio State University Press.

Ryan, Rebecca. 1995. "The Sex Right: A Legal History of the Marital Rape Exemption." *Law and Social Inquiry* 4 (Fall): 941–1001.

Saad, Lydia. 2001. "Women See Room for Improvement in Job Equity." Princeton, NJ: *The Gallup Poll*. Princeton, NJ: The Gallup Organization. www.gallup.com.

Saad, Lydia. 2003. "Pondering 'Women's Issues,' Part II." *The Gallup Poll*. Princeton, NJ: The Gallup Organization. www .gallup.com.

Saad, Lydia. 2007a. "Tolerance for Gay Rights at High-Water Mark." *The Gallup Poll*. Princeton, NJ: The Gallup Organization. www.gallup.com

Saad, Lydia. 2007b. "Women Slightly More Likely to Prefer Working to Homemaking." *The Gallup Poll*. Princeton, NJ: The Gallup Organization. www.gallup.com.

Saad, Lydia. 2008. "Americans Evenly Divided on Morality of Homosexuality." *The Gallup Poll*. Princeton, NJ: The Gallup Organization. www.gallup.com.

Saad, Lydia. 2009. "U.S. Abortion Attitudes Closely Divided." *The Gallup Poll*. Princeton, NJ: The Gallup Organization. www. gallup.com.

Sacks, Karen. 1975. "Engels Revisited: Women, the Organization of Production, and Private Property." Pp. 211–234 in *Toward* an *Anthropology of Women*, edited by R. Reiter. New York: Monthly Review Press.

Sacks, Karen Brodkin. 1984. "Generations of Working Class Families." Pp. 15–38 in *My Troubles Are Going to Have Trouble with Me*, edited by K. B. Sacks and D. Remy. New Brunswick, NJ: Rutgers University Press.

Sadker, M., and D. Sadker. 1994. *Failing at Fairness: How America's Schools Cheat Girls*. New York: Charles Scribner's Sons.

Saguy, Abigail Cope. 1999. "Puritanism and Promiscuity? Sexual Attitudes in France and the United States." *Comparative Social Research* 18: 227–247.

Saiving, V. 1979. "The Human Situation: A Feminine View." Pp. 25–42 in *Womanspirit Rising*, edited by C. P. Christ and J. Plaskow. New York: Harper and Row.

Sales, Paloma, and Sheigla Murphy. 2000. "Surviving Violence: Pregnancy and Drug Use." *Journal of Drug Issues* 30 (Fall): 695–724.

Salganicoff, Alina, Juliette Cubanski, Usha Ranji, and Tricia Neuman. 2009. "Health Coverage and Expenses: Impact on Older Women's Economic Well-Being." *Journal of Women, Politics & Policy* 30 (2–3): 222–247.

Salmon, Catherine, and Don Symons. 2003. *Warrior Lovers: Erotic Fiction, Evolution, and Female Sexuality*. New Haven, CT: Yale University Press.

Sanchez, Laura, Wendy D. Manning, and Pamela J. Smock. 1998. "Sex-Specialized or Collaborative Mate Selection? Union Transitions among Cohabitors." *Social Science Research* 27 (September): 280–304.

Sanday, Peggy. 2007. *Fraternity Gang Rape: Sex, Brotherhood, and Privilege on Campus*, 2nd ed. New York: New York University Press.

Sanday, Peggy Reeves. 1996. "Rape-Prone versus Rape-Free Campus Cultures." *Violence against Women* 2: 191–208.

Sanders, Teesa. 2005. *Sex Work: A Risky Business*. Devon, UK: Willan Publishing.

Santelli, John et al. 2007. "Explaining Recent Declines in Adolescent Pregnancy in the United States: The Contribution of Abstinence and Increased Contraceptive Use." *American Journal of Public Health* 97: 150–156.

Sassler, Sharon. 2004. "The Process of Entering Cohabiting Unions." *Journal of Marriage and the Family* 66 (May): 491–505.

Sayers, S. L., Baucom, D. H., and A. M. Tierney. 1993. "Sex Roles, Interpersonal Control, and Depression: Who Can Get Their Way." *Journal of Research in Personality* 27: 377–395.

Sayre, Anne. 1975. *Rosalind Franklin and DNA*. New York: Norton.

Schilt, Kristen, and Catherine Connell. 2007. "Do Workplace Gender Transitions Make Gender Trouble?" *Gender, Work, and Organization* 14 (6): 596–618.

Schmidt, Kathyrn J. 2003. "'I Didn't Say Anything, but Everybody Knew': Sexual Orientation Disclosure through Tacit Understandings and Silence." Paper presented at the annual meetings of the Southern Sociological Society.

Schmitt, David P., Anu Realo, Martin Voracek, and Juri Allik. 2008. "Why Can't a Man Be More Like a Woman? Sex Differences in Big Five Personality Traits across 55 Cultures." *Journal of Personality and Social Psychology* 94: 168–182.

Schmitt, Frederika E., and Patricia Yancey Martin. 1999. "Unobtrusive Mobilization by an Institutionalized Rape Crisis Center: 'It Comes from the Victims.'" *Gender & Society* 13: 364–384.

Schneider, Beth. 1984. "Perils and Promise: Lesbians' Workplace Participation." Pp. 211–230 in *Women-Identified Women*, edited by Trudy Darty and Sandee Potter. Palo Alto, CA: Mayfield.

Schneider, Beth, and Nancy E. Stoller. 1995. *Women Resisting AIDS: Feminist Strategies of Empowerment*. Philadelphia: Temple University Press.

Schnittker, Jason. 2007. "Working More and Feeling Better: 1974–2004." *American Sociological Review* 72 (April): 221–238.

Schnittker, Jason, Jeremy Freese, and Brian Powell. 2003. "Who Are Feminists and What Do They Believe? The Role of Generations." *American Sociological Review* 68 (August): 607–622.

Scholten, C. M. 1977. "On the Importance of the Obstetric Art: Changing Customs of Childbirth in America." *The William and Mary Quarterly* 34: 426–445.

Schwartz, Pepper, and Virginia Rutter. 1998. *The Gender of Sexuality*. Thousand Oaks, CA: Pine Forge Press.

Scott, Jacqueline. 1998. "Changing Attitudes to Sexual Morality: A Cross-National Comparison." *Sociology* 32 (November): 815–845.

Secada, Walter G. et al. 1998. *No More Excuses: Final Report of the Hispanic Dropout Project*. Washington, DC: Office of Educational Research and Improvement.

Sechzer, Jeri A. 2004. "'Islam and Woman: Where Tradition Meets Modernity': History and Interpretations of Islamic Women's Status." *Sex Roles: A Journal of Research* 51 (5–6): 263–272.

Segura, Denise. 1998. "Working at Motherhood: Chicana and Mexican Immigrant Mothers and Employment." Pp. 727–744 in *Families in the U.S.: Kinship and Domestic Politics*, edited by Karen V. Hansen and Anita Ilta Garey. Philadelphia: Temple University Press.

Segura, Denise, and Jennifer L. Pierce. 1993. "Chicana/o Family Structure and Gender Personality: Chodorow, Familism, and Psychoanalytic Sociology Revisited." *Signs* 19 (Autumn): 62–91.

Seidman, Steven. 1994. "Symposium: Queer Theory/Sociology: A Dialogue." *Sociological Theory* 12 (July): 166–177.

Seidman, Steven. 2003. *The Social Construction of Sexuality*. New York: Norton.

Seltzer, Judith A. 2000. "Families Formed Outside of Marriage." *Journal of Marriage and the Family* 62 (November): 1247–1268.

Shange, Ntozake. 1975. *for colored girls who have considered suicide / when the rainbow is enuf*. New York: Bantam Books.

Sharman, Arvind, and Katherine K. Young. 1998. *Feminism and World Religions*. New York: State University Press.

Sharp, Susan F., and Susan T. Marcus-Mendoza. 2001. "It's a Family Affair: Incarcerated Women and Their Families." *Women and Criminal Justice* 12: 21–49.

Sherman, Jennifer. 2009. "Bend to Avoid Breaking: Job Loss, Gender Norms, and Family Stability in Rural America." *Social Problems* 56 (November): 599–620.

Shih, Johanna. 2006. "Circumventing Discrimination: Gender and Ethnic Strategies in Silicon Valley." *Gender & Society* 20 (2): 177–206.

Signorielli, Nancy. 1989. "Television and Conceptions about Sex Roles: Maintaining Conventionality and the Status Quo." *Sex Roles* 21: 341–360.

Signorielli, Nancy, and Aaron Bacue. 1999. "Recognition and Respect: A Content Analysis of Prime-Time Television Characters across Three Decades." *Sex Roles* 40 (April): 527–544.

Silverstein, Louise B., and Carl F. Auerbach. 1999. "Deconstructing the Essential Father." *American Psychologist* 54 (June): 397–407.

Simien, Evelyn M., and Rosalee A. Clawson. 2004. "The Intersection of Race and Gender: Black Feminist Consciousness, Race Consciousness, and Policy Attitudes." *Social Science Quarterly* 85 (September): 793–810.

Simon, Rita J., Angela R. Scanlan, and Pamela S. Nadell. 1994. "Rabbis and Ministers: Women of the Book and the Cloth." Pp. 45–52 in *Gender and Religion*, edited by William H. Swatos. New Brunswick, NJ: Transaction Publishers.

Simon, William, and John H. Gagnon. 1998. "Homosexuality: The Formulation of a Sociological Perspective." Pp. 59–67 in *Social Perspectives in Lesbian and Gay Studies*, edited by Peter M. Nardi and Beth E. Schneider. New York: Routledge.

Siwatu, Mxolisi S. 2003. "Platonic Same-Sex Friendship Intimacy: The Effects of Sex and Gender." Paper presented at the Southern Sociological Society meetings, New Orleans.

Skirboll, Esther, and Rhoda Taylor. 1998. "Two Homes, Two Jobs, One Marriage: Commuter Spousal Relationships." Paper presented at the International Sociological Association meetings.

Sklar, Holly. 1994. "Disposable Workers." *Z Magazine* (January): 36–41.

Slevin, Kathryn F., and C. Ray Wingrove. 1998. *From Stumbling Blocks to Stepping Stones: The Life Experiences of Fifty Professional African American Women*. New York: New York University Press.

Smart, C. 1977. *Women, Crime and Criminology: A Feminist Critique*. London: Routledge & Kegan Paul.

Smedley, Brian D., Adrienne Y. Stith, and Alan R. Nelson. 2003. *Unequal Treatment: Confronting Racial and Ethnic Disparities in Health Care*. Washington, DC: National Academies Press.

Smith, Barbara. 1983. "Homophobia: Why Bring It Up." *Interracial Books for Children Bulletin* 12: 112–113.

Smith, Bonnie G., and Beth Hutchison, eds. 2004. *Gendering Disability*. Piscataway, NJ: Rutgers University Press.

Smith, Dinitia. 1998. "One False Note in a Musician's Life." *The New York Times*, June 2, pp. B1, 4.

Smith, Dorothy E. 1974. "Women's Perspective as a Radical Critique of Sociology." *Sociological Inquiry* 44: 7–13.

Smith, Dorothy E. 1987. *The Everyday World as Problematic: A Feminist Sociology*. Boston: Northeastern University Press.

Smith, Dorothy E. 1990. *The Conceptual Practices of Power: A Feminist Sociology of Knowledge*. Boston: Northeastern University Press.

Smock, Pamela J. 2000. "Cohabitation in the United States: An Appraisal of Research Themes, Findings, and Implications." *Annual Review of Sociology* 26: 1–20.

Songer, Donald R., and Kelley A. Crews-Meyer. 2000. "Does Judge Gender Matter? Decision Making in State Supreme Courts." *Social Science Quarterly* 81: 750–762.

Spencer, Steven J., Claude M. Steele, and Diane M. Quinn.

1999. "Stereotype Threat and Women's Math Performance." *Journal of Experimental Social Psychology* 35 (January): 4–28.

Spohn, Cassia, Dawn Beichner, and Erike Davis-Frenzel. 2001. "Prosecutorial Justifications for Sexual Assault Case Rejections: Guarding the 'Gateway to Justice.'" *Social Problems* 48 (May): 206–235.

Spretnak, C., ed. 1994. *The Politics of Women's Spirituality: Essays on the Rise of Spiritual Power within the Feminist Movement*, 2nd ed. Garden City, NY: Anchor Books.

Sprock, June, and Carol Y. Yoder. 1997. "Women and Depression: An Update on the Report of the APA Task Force." *Sex Roles* 36 (March): 269–303.

Stacey, Judith, and Timothy J. Bibliarz. 2001. "(How) Does the Sexual Orientation of Parents Matter?" *American Sociological Review* 66 (April): 159–183.

Stack, Carol, and Linda Burton. 1993. "Kinscripts." Pp. 405–417 in *Families in the U.S.: Kinship and Domestic Politics*, edited by Karen V. Hansen and Anita Ilta Garey. Philadelphia: Temple University Press.

Stanton, Elizabeth Cady. 1974. *The Woman's Bible*. New York: Arno Press.

Staples, R. 1971. *The Black Family*. Belmont, CA: Wadsworth.

Staples, R., and A. Mirandé. 1980. "Racial and Cultural Variations among American Families." *Journal of Marriage and the Family* 42: 887–903.

Steele, Claude M., and Joshua Aronson. 1995. "Stereotype Threat and the Intellectual Performance of African Americans." *Journal of Personality and Social Psychology* 69 (November): 797–811.

Steffensmeier, Darrell, and Chris Hebert. 1999. "Women and Men Policymakers: Does the Judge's Gender Affect the Sentencing of Criminal Defendants?" *Social Forces* 77(3):1163–1196.

Stein, Arlene, and Ken Plummer. 1994. "'I Can't Even Think Straight': Queer Theory and the Missing Sexual Revolution in Sociology." *Sociological Theory* 12 (July): 178–187.

Steinbugler, Amy C., Julie E. Press, and Janice Johnson Dias. 2006. "Gender, Race, and Affirmative Action: Operationalizing Intersectionality in Survey Research." *Gender & Society* 20 (August): 805–825.

Stellman, J. M. 1977. *Women's Work, Women's Health: Myths and Realities.* New York: Pantheon.

Sterling, Anne. 1984. *We Are Your Sisters: Black Women in the Nineteenth Century.* New York: Norton.

Sternheimer, Karen. 2007. "Do Video Games Kill?" *Contexts* 6 (Winter): 13–17.

Stier, Haya, and Noah Lewin-Epstein. 2000. "Women's Part-Time Employment and Gender Inequality in the Family." *Journal of Family Issues* 21 (3): 390–410.

Stohs, Joanne Hoven. 1995. "Predictors of Conflict over the Household Division of Labor among Women Employed Full-Time." *Sex Roles* 33 (August): 257–275.

Stoller, Eleanor Palo, and Rose Campbell Gibson. 2000. *Worlds of Difference: Inequality in the Aging Experience.* Thousand Oaks, CA: Pine Forge Press.

Stoller, Nancy. 2003. "Space, Place and Movement as Aspects of Health Care in Three Women's Prisons." *Social Science & Medicine* 56: 2263–2275.

Stone, Pamela. 2007. *Opting Out: Why Women Really Quit Careers and Head Home.* Berkeley: University of California Press.

Strazdins, Lyndall, and Dorothy H. Broom. 2004. "Acts of Love (and Work): Gender Imbalance in Emotional Work and Women's Psychological Distress." *Journal of Family Issues* 25: 356–378.

Strong, Scott M., Donald A. Williamson, Richard G. Netemeyer, and James H. Geer. 2000. "Eating Disorder Symptoms and Concerns about Body Differ as a Function of Gender and Sexual Orientation." *Journal of Social and Clinical Psychology* 19 (Summer): 240–255.

Sulik, Gayle A. 2007. "The Balancing Act: Care Work for the Self and Coping with Breast Cancer." *Gender & Society* 21 (December): 857–877.

Sullivan, Deborah A., and Rose Weitz. 1988. *Labor Pains: Modern Midwives and Home Birth.* New Haven, CT: Yale University Press.

Sullivan, Maureen. 1996. "Rozzie and Harriet? Gender and Family Patterns of Lesbian Coparents." *Gender & Society* 12 (December): 747–767.

Szasz, T. 1970. *Manufacture of Madness.* New York: Dell.

Takaki, Ronald. 1989. *Strangers from a Different Shore: A History of Asian Americans.* New York: Penguin.

Takaki, Ronald. 1993. *A Different Mirror: A History of Multicultural America.* Boston: Little, Brown.

Tannen, Deborah, ed. 1993. *Gender and Conversational Interaction.* New York: Oxford.

Taylor, Verta, and Nicole C. Raeburn. 1995. "Identity Politics as High-Risk Activism: Career Consequences for Lesbian, Gay, and Bisexual Sociologists." *Social Problems* 42 (May): 252–273.

Taylor, Verta, and Leila J. Rupp. 2003. *Drag Queens at the 801 Cabaret.* Chicago: University of Chicago Press.

Tea, N. T., M. Castanier, M. Roger, and R. Scholler. 1975. "Simultaneous Radioimmunoassay of Plasma Progesterone and 17-Hydroxyprogesterone in Men and Women throughout the Menstrual Cycle and in Early Pregnancy." *Journal of Steroid Biochemistry* 6: 1509–1516.

Teachman, Jay, Lucky M. Tedrow, and Kyle D. Crowder. 2000. "The Changing Demography of America's Families." *Journal of Marriage and the Family* 62 (November): 1234–1246.

Thomas, Jan E., and Mary K. Zimmerman. 2007. "Feminism and Profit in American Hospitals: The Corporate Construction of Women's Health Centers." *Gender & Society* 21 (June): 359383.

Thompson, Becky W. 1994. *A Hunger So Wide and So Deep: American Women Speak Out on Eating Problems.* Minneapolis: University of Minnesota Press.

Thompson, Edward H., and Elizabeth J. Cracco. 2008. "Sexual Aggression in Bars: What College Men Can Normalize." *The Journal of Men's Studies* 16, 1: 82–96.

Thorne, Barrie. 1993. *Gender Play.* New Brunswick, NJ: Rutgers University Press.

Thorne, Barrie, ed., with Marilyn Yalom. 1992. *Re-thinking the Family: Some Feminist Questions,* 2nd ed. Boston: Northeastern University Press.

Thornton, Arland, William G. Axinn, and Jay D. Teachman. 1995. "The Influence of School Enrollment and Accumulation on Cohabitation and Marriage in Early Adulthood." *American Sociological Review* 60 (October): 762–774.

Tichenor, Veronica. 2005. "Maintaining Men's Dominance: Negotiating Identity and Power When She Earns More." *Sex Roles: A Journal of Research* 53 (3–4): 191–205.

Tichenor, Veronica Jaris. 1999. "Status and Income as Gendered Resources: The Case of Marital Power." *Journal of Marriage and the Family* 61 (August): 638–650.

Tillich, P. 1957. *The Dynamics of Faith.* New York: Harper and Row.

Tilly, L. A., and J. W. Scott. 1978. *Women, Work, and Family.* New York: Holt, Rinehart and Winston.

Tjaden, Patricia, and Nancy Thoennes. 2000. *Extent, Nature and Consequences of Intimate Partner Violence: Findings from the National Violence against Women Survey.* Washington, DC: National Institute of Justice.

Tomaskovic-Devey, Donald, Kevin Stainback, Tiffany Taylor, Catherine Zimmer, Corre Robinson, and Tricia McTague. 2006. "Documenting Desegregation: Segregation in American Workplaces by Race, Ethnicity, and Sex, 1966–2003." *American Sociological Review* 71: 565–588.

Tovée, M., J. S. M. Mason, J. L. Emery, S. E. McCluskey, and E. M. Tovée. 1997. "Supermodels: Stick Insects or Hourglasses?" *Lancet* 350 (November 15): 1474–1475.

Tovée, M., J. S. Reinhardt, and J. L. Emery. 1998. "Optimum Body-Mass Index and Maximum Sexual Attractiveness." *Lancet* 352 (August 15): 548.

Tuan, Yi-Fu. 1984. *Dominance and Affection: The Making of Pets.* New Haven, CT: Yale University Press.

Tuchman, Gaye. 1979. "Women's Depiction by the Mass Media." *Signs* 4 (Spring): 528–542.

Tuchman, Gaye, Arlene K. Daniels, and James Benét. 1978. *Hearth and Home: Images of Women in the Mass Media.* New York: Oxford University Press.

Tucker, R., ed. 1972. *The Marx-Engels Reader.* New York: Norton.

Turner, Ralph, and Lewis M. Killian. 1972. *Collective Behavior.* Upper Saddle River, NJ: Prentice-Hall.

Ullman, Sarah E. 2007. "A 10-Year Update of 'Review and Critique of Empirical Studies of Rape Avoidance'." *Criminal Justice and Behavior* 34, 3: 411–429.

United Nations. 2007. *Statistics and Indicators on Women and Men.* New York: United Nations. unstats.un.org.

U.S. Census Bureau. 2006. *Who's Minding the Kids: Child Care Arrangements, Summer 2006.* Washington, DC: U.S. Census Bureau. www.census.gov.

U.S. Census Bureau. 2006a. *America's Families and Living Arrangements, Detailed Tables, Table A1.* Washington, DC: www.census.gov.

U.S. Census Bureau. 2006b. *Detailed Poverty Tables, Table POV 14.* www.census.gov.

U.S. Census Bureau. 2007. *Statistical Abstract of the United States 2007.* Washington, DC: ww.census.gov.

U.S. Census Bureau. 2009. *Statistical Abstract of the United States 2008.* Washington, DC: ww.census.gov.

U.S. Department of Defense. 2003. Website www.defenselink.mil.

U.S. Department of Defense. 2008. *FY08 Report on Sexual Assault in the Military.* Washington, DC: U.S. Department of Defense.

U.S. Department of Defense Task Force. 2005. *Report of the Defense Task Force on Sexual Harassment and Violence at the Military Service Academies.* Washington, DC: U.S. Department of Defense.

U.S. Department of Labor. 2009. *Employment and Earnings.* Washington, DC: U.S. Department of Labor. www.bls.gov..

U.S. Department of Labor Women's Bureau. 2010. *Statistics and Data.* www.dol.gov.

U.S. Department of State. 2009. *Trafficking in Persons Report.* www.state.gov.

Uttal, Lynet. 2000. "Using Kin for Child Care: Embedment in the Socioeconomic Networks of Extended Families." *Journal of Marriage and the Family* 61 (November): 845–857.

Uttal, Lynet. 2002. *Making Care Work: Employed Mothers in the New Childcare Market.* New Brunswick, NJ: Rutgers University Press.

Uttal, Lynet, and Mary Tuominen. 1999. "Tenuous Relationships: Exploitation, Emotion, and Racial Ethnic Significance in Paid Child Care Work." *Gender & Society* 13 (December): 758–780.

Van Den Daele, W. 1977. "The Social Construction of Science: Institutionalization and Definition of Positive Science in the Latter Half of the Seventeenth Century." Pp. 27–54 in *The Social Production of Scientific Knowledge,* edited by E. Mendelsohn, P. Weingart, and R. Whitley. Dordrecht, The Netherlands: Riedel.

Vanek, J. A. 1978. "Housewives as Workers." Pp. 392–414 in *Women Working,* edited by Anne H. Stromberg and Shirley Harkess. Palo Alto, CA: Mayfield.

Vanneman, Reeve, and Lynn Weber Cannon. 1987. *The American Perception of Class.* Philadelphia: Temple University Press.

Vespa, Jonathan. 2009. "Gender Ideology Construction." *Gender & Society* 23 (3): 363–387.

Vigorito, Anthony J., and Timothy J. Curry. 1998. "Marketing Masculinity: Gender, Identity and Popular Magazines." *Sex Roles* 39 (July): 135–152.

Voydanoff, Patricia, and Brenda W. Donnelly. 1999. "The Intersection of Time in Activities and Perceived Unfairness in Relation to Psychological Distress and Marital Quality." *Journal of Marriage and the Family* 61 (August): 739–751.

Waldron, I., C. C. Weiss, and M. E. Hughes. 1998. "Interacting Effects of Multiple Roles on Women's Health." *Journal of Health and Social Behavior* 39 (September): 216–230.

Walker, Karen. 1995. "'Always There for Me': Friendship Patterns and Expectations among Middle- and Working-Class Men and Women." *Sociological Forum* 10 (June): 273–296.

Walker, Rebecca, ed. 1995. *To Be Real: Telling the Truth and Changing the Face of Feminism.* New York: Anchor.

Walker-Barnes, Chanequa J., and Craig A. Mason. 2001. "Perceptions of Risk Factors for Female Gang Involvement among African American and Hispanic Women." *Youth and Society* 32: 303–336.

Wall, Glenda, and Stephanie Arnold. 2007. "How Involved in Involved Fathering?" *Gender & Society* 21: 508–527.

Wallace, Ruth A. 1992. *They Call Her Pastor: A New Role for Catholic Women.* Albany: State University of New York Press.

Wallerstein, I. 1976. *The Modern World System.* New York: Academic Press.

Walsh, Anthony. 1994. "Homosexual and Heterosexual Child Molestation: Case Characteristics and Sentencing Differentials." *International Journal of Offender Therapy and Comparative Criminology* 38 (Winter): 339–353.

Walsh, M. R. 1977. *Doctors Wanted: No Women Need Apply.* New Haven, CT: Yale University Press.

Walters, Suzanna. 1995. *Material Girls: Making Sense of Feminist Cultural Theory.* Berkeley: University of California Press.

Walzer, Susan. 1996. "Thinking about the Baby: Gender and Divisions of Infant Care." *Social Problems* 43 (May): 219–234.

Ward, Jane, and Beth Schneider, eds. 2009. "The Reaches of Heteronormativity" *Gender & Society* 23 (August): 433–439.

Ward, L. M., and R. Rivadeneyra. 2002. "Dancing, Strutting, and Bouncing in Cars: The Women of Music Videos." Paper presented at the Annual Meeting of the American Psychological Association, Chicago, August.

Wardle, R. M. 1951. *Mary Wollstonecraft: A Critical Biography.* Lawrence: University of Kansas Press.

Warren, Tracey, Karen Rowlingson, and Claire Whyley. 2001. "Female Finances: Gender Wage Gaps and Gender Assets Gaps." *Work, Employment, and Society* 15 (September): 465–488.

Watson, James D. 1968. *The Double Helix*. New York: Atheneum.

Weber, Lynn. 2010. *Understanding Race, Class, Gender, and Sexuality*. New York: Oxford.

Wechsler, Henry, Jae Eun Lee, Meichun Kuo, Mark Sebring, Toben F. Nelson, and Hang Lee. 2002. "Trends in College Binge Drinking during a Period of Increased Prevention Efforts: Findings from Four Harvard School of Public Health College Alcohol Surveys, 1993–2001." *Journal of American College Health* 50 (5): 203–217.

Wechsler, Henry, and Toben F. Nelson. 2008. "What We Learned from the Harvard School of Public Health Study: Focusing Attention on College Student Alcohol Consumption and the Environmental Conditions That Promote It." *Journal of Studies on Alcohol and Drugs* 69 (July): 481–490.

Weitzer, Ronald. 2009. "Sociology of Sex Work." *Annual Review of Sociology* 35: 213–234.

Welsh, Sandy. 1999. "Gender and Sexual Harassment." *Annual Review of Sociology* 25: 169–190.

Welter, B., ed. 1976. *Dimity Convictions*. Athens: Ohio University Press.

Wertheimer, Linda. 2005. "Wounded in War: The Women Serving in Iraq." Washington, DC: National Public Radio. www.npr.org.

Wertz, R. W., and D. C. Wertz. 1977. *Lying In: A History of Childbirth in America*. New York: Free Press.

West, Candace. 1998. "Leaving a Second Closet: Outing Partner Violence in Same-Sex Couples." Pp. 163–183 in *Partner Violence: A Comprehensive Review of 20 Years of Research*, edited by Jana L. Jasinski and Linda M. Williams. Thousand Oaks, CA: Sage.

West, Candace, and Sarah Fenstermaker. 1995. "Doing Difference." *Gender & Society* 9 (February): 8–37.

West, Candace, and Don Zimmerman. 1987. "Doing Gender." *Gender & Society* 1 (June): 125–151.

West, Jackie. 2000. "Prostitution: Collectives and the Politics of Regulation." *Gender, Work and Organization* 7: 106–118.

West, Jackie, and Terry Austin. 2002. "From Work as Sex to Sex as Work: Networks, 'Others' and Occupations in the Analysis of Work." *Gender, Work, and Organization* 9: 482–503.

Westkott, Marcia. 1979. "Feminist Criticism of the Social Sciences." *Harvard Educational Review* 49: 422–430.

Whitley, Bernard E. 2001. "Gender-Role Variables and Attitudes toward Homosexuality." *Sex Roles* 45 (December): 691–721.

Whittier, Nancy. 1995. *Feminist Generations: The Persistence of the Radical Women's Movement*. Philadelphia: Temple University Press.

Wilkie, Jane Riblett. 1993. "Changes in U.S. Men's Attitudes toward the Family Provider Role, 1972–1989." *Gender & Society* 7 (June): 261–280.

Willemsen, Tineke M. 2002. "Gender Typing of the Successful Manager: A Stereotype Reconsidered." *Sex Roles* 46 (June): 385–391.

Williams, Christine. 1995. *Still a Man's World: Men Who Do Women's Work*. Berkeley: University of California Press.

Williams, David R. 1990. "Socioeconomic Differentials in Health: A Review and Redirection." *Social Psychology Quarterly* 53: 81–99.

Willie, Charles Vert, and Richard Reddick. 2003. *A New Look at Black Families*. Walnut Creek, CA: AltaMira Press.

Wilsnack, Richard W., Nancy D. Vogeltanz, Sharon C. Wilsnack, and T. Robert Harris. 2000. "Gender Differences in Alcohol Consumption and Adverse Drinking Consequences: Cross-Cultural Patterns." *Addiction* 95 (February): 251–265.

Wilson, J. Q., and R. J. Herrnstein. 1985. *Crime and Human Nature*. New York: Simon and Schuster.

Wilson, William Julius. 1987. *When Work Disappears*. New York: Knopf.

Wingfield, Adia Harvey. 2009. "Racializing the Glass Escalator." *Gender & Society* 23 (February): 5–26.

Winn, Jillian, and Carrie Heeter. 2009. "Gaming, Gender, and Time: Who Makes Time to Play?" *Sex Roles* 61 (1–2): 1–13.

Winseman, Albert L. 2004. "Born Agains Wield Political/Economic Influence." *The Gallup Poll*. Princeton, NJ: The Gallup Organization.

Winterich, Julie A. 2003. "Sex, Menopause, and Culture: Sexual Orientation and the Meaning of Menopause for Women's Sex Lives." *Gender & Society* 17 (August): 627–642.

Wolak, Janis, and David Finkelhor. 1998. "Children Exposed to Partner Violence." Pp. 73–112 in *Partner Violence: A Comprehensive Review of 20 Years of Research*, edited by Jana L. Jasinski and Linda M. Williams. Thousand Oaks, CA: Sage.

Wolf, Margery. 1972. *Women and the Family in Rural Taiwan*. Stanford: Stanford University Press.

Wolff, Kurt H. 1950. *The Sociology of Georg Simmel*. New York: Free Press.

Wolfgang, M., and F. Feracuti. 1967. *The Subculture of Violence: Toward an Integrated Theory in Criminology*. London: Tavistock.

Wolkomir, Michelle. 2006. *Be Not Deceived: The Sacred and Sexual Struggles of Gay and Ex-Gay Christian Men*. New Brunswick, NJ: Rutgers University Press.

Wollstonecraft, Mary. 1792 [1975]. *A Vindication of the Rights of Woman*, edited by C. Poston. New York: Norton.

Women's Education and Research Institute. 2007. "Active Duty and Reserve/Guard Statistics as of September 2006." Washington, DC. www.wrei.org.

Wonders, Nancy A., and Raymond Michalowski. 2001. "Bodies, Borders, and Sex Tourism in a Globalized World: A Tale of Two Cities—Amsterdam and Havana." *Social Problems* 48: 545–571.

Woo, Deborah. 1992. "The Gap between Striving and Achieving: The Case of Asian American Women." Pp. 191–200 in *Race, Class and Gender: An Anthology,* edited by Margaret L. Andersen and Patricia Hill Collins. Belmont, CA: Wadsworth.

World Health Organization. 2007. *Women and HIV/AIDS.* www .who.Int.

World Health Organization. 2009. *Women and Health: Today's Evidence and Tomorrow's Agenda.* Geneva, Switzerland.

Wray, Sharon. 2007. "Women Making Sense of Midlife: Ethnic and Cultural Diversity." *Journal of Aging Studies* 21 (January): 31–42.

Wright, M. J. 1979. "Reproductive Hazards and 'Protective' Discrimination." *Feminist Studies* 5 (Summer): 302–309.

Wrong, D. 1961. "The Oversocialized Conception of Man in Modern Sociology." *American Sociological Review* 26: 183–193.

Yates, G. G. 1983. "Spirituality and the American Feminist Experience." *Signs* 9 (Autumn): 59–72.

Yaughn, Elizabeth, and Stephen Nowicki Jr. 1999. "Close Relationships and Complementary Interpersonal Styles among Men and Women." *Journal of Social Psychology* 139 (August): 473–478.

Yllo, Kersti. 1999. "Wife Rape: A Social Problem for the 21st Century." *Violence against Women* 5 (September): 1059–1063.

Yoder, Janice, and Patricia Aniakudo. 1997. "'Outsider Within' the Firehouse: Subordination and Difference in the Social Interactions of African American Women Firefighters." *Gender & Society* 11 (June): 324–341.

Young, Vernetta D., and Rebecca Reviere. 2001. "Meeting the Health Care Needs of the New Woman Inmate: A National Survey of Prison Practices." *Journal of Offender Rehabilitation* 34: 31–48.

Zaidi, Arishia U., and Muhammad Shuraydi. 2002. "Perception of Arranged Marriages by Young Pakistani Muslim Women Living in Western Society." *Journal of Comparative Family Studies* 33 (Autumn): 495–514.

Zaretsky, E. 1976. *Capitalism, the Family, and Personal Life.* New York: Harper and Row.

Zeitlin, I. 1968. *Ideology and the Development of Sociological Theory.* Upper Saddle River, NJ: Prentice-Hall.

Zhou, Min, and Carl L. Bankston. 1998. *Growing Up American: How Vietnamese Children Adapt to Life in the United States.* New York: Russell Sage Foundation.

Zola, Irving. 1989. "Toward the Necessary Universalizing of a Disability Policy." *The Milbank Quarterly* 67 (Supplement 2): 401–428.

Zola, Irving. 1993. "Self, Identity and the Naming Question: Reflections on the Language of Disability" *Social Science and Medicine* 36 (January): 167–173.

Zones, Jane Sprague. 1997. "Beauty Myths and Realities: Their Impact on Women's Health." Pp. 249–275 in *Women's Health: Complexities and Differences,* edited by Sheryl Burt Ruzek, Virginia L. Olesen, and Adele E. Clarke. Columbus: Ohio State University Press.

Zucker, Alyssa N., and Laura J. Landry. 2007. "Embodied Discrimination: The Relation of Sexism and Distress to Women's Drinking and Smoking Behaviors." *Sex Roles: A Journal of Research* 56 (3–4): 193–203.

Photo Credits

Name Index

Subject Index

Note: page references with "f" indicate figures; those with "t" indicate tables.